"*Sakhalin Island* should be compulsory reading for all those who are anywhere and in any way involved with the so-called penal system."
Heinrich Böll

"*Sakhalin Island* shows off the breadth of Chekhov's reading as well as the depth of his fieldwork… This is a much needed new annotated translation."
The Independent

"As a work of literature, *Sakhalin Island* is a masterpiece of restrained, dignified, unsentimental prose… a work of complete seriousness, full of clear; humane, practical suggestions for reform."
The Observer

"Mr Reeve's work reminds one that Chekhov was as great a master of the documentary genre – and also of the best academic prose – as of drama and narrative fiction… *Sakhalin Island* will never eclipse *The Cherry Orchard*. But it is every bit as impressive a masterpiece, and this new version will surely make its merits more widely known."
Times Literary Supplement

"*Sakhalin Island* is the work of a sensible and sympathetic recorder of the facts, and Mr Reeve has done us a favour in his handsome and useful edition."
Stephen Tumm, Former HM Chief Inspector of Prisons

Sakhalin Island

Anton Chekhov

Translated by

Brian Reeve

ONEWORLD
CLASSICS

ONEWORLD CLASSICS LTD
London House
243-253 Lower Mortlake Road
Richmond
Surrey TW9 2LL
United Kingdom
www.oneworldclassics.com

Sakhalin Island first published in Russian in 1895
This translation first published by Ian Faulkner Publishing Ltd in 1993
Translation and notes © Brian Reeve, 1993
This revised edition first published by Oneworld Classics Limited in 2007
Extra material © Oneworld Classics Ltd, 2007

Printed in Great Britain by TJ International, Padstow, Cornwall

ISBN-13: 978-1-84749-003-2
ISBN-10: 1-84749-003-4

1005156164

The Forest Stewardship Council (FSC) is an international, non-governmental organization dedicated to promoting responsible management of the world's forests. FSC operates a system of forest certification and product labelling that allows consumers to identify wood and wood-based products from well-managed forests. For more information about the FSC, please visit the website at www.fsc-uk.org.

Contents

Anton Chekhov (1860–1904)

Anton Chekhov with his
brother Nikolai

Maria Chekhova,
Anton's sister

Yevgenia and Pavel, Chekhov's parents

The birthplace of Anton Chekhov
in Taganrog

The out-building to Chekhov's residence in Melikhovo,
where he wrote *The Seagull*

Chekhov's dacha near Yalta, where he lived with his
family after 1899

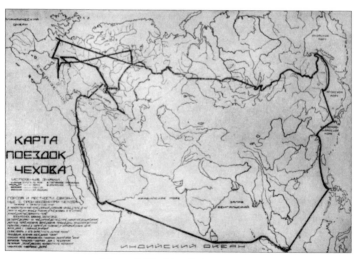

КАРТА
ПОЕЗДОК
ЧЕХОВА

Map of Chekhov's journey to
Sakhalin Island

The main street in Alexandrovsk,
Sakhalin Island

A picture of Sakhalin convicts dating
from the 1890s

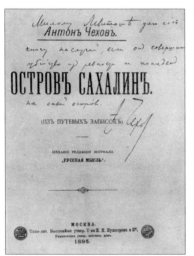

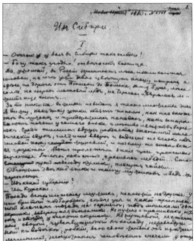

Title page of the first volume edition of *Sakhalin Island*

A manuscript page from Chekhov's 'From Siberia'

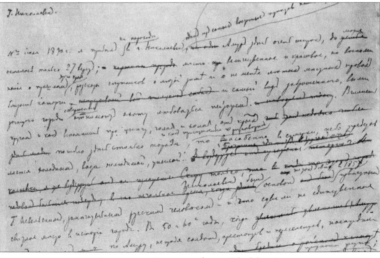

A manuscript page from Chekhov's
Sakhalin Island

Olga Knipper as Mme Ranevskaya
in *The Cherry Orchard*

Olga Knipper as Masha
in *Three Sisters*

The House-Museum in Sadovo-Kudrinskaya Street, Moscow,
where Chekhov lived between 1886 and 1890

Chekhov in front of his Melikhovo residence,
*c.*1897

Sakhalin Island

From Siberia*

1

"WHY IS IT SO COLD in this Siberia of yours?"

"Cos that's the way God wants it!" replies the coach driver.*

Yes, it's May now, and by this time in European Russia, the woods are turning green and the nightingales are pouring out their songs, while in the south the acacia and lilac have been in blossom for ages already, yet here, along the road from Tyumen to Tomsk, the earth is brown, the forests are bare, there is dull ice on the lakes, and snow still lying on the shores and in the gullies.

But to make up for this, never in my life have I seen such a vast number of wildfowl. I catch sight of wild ducks walking on the ground, swimming in the pools and roadside ditches, constantly fluttering almost right up to my carriage, and flying lazily off into the birch woods. Amidst the silence, a familiar melodious sound rings out, you glance up and see high above your head a pair of cranes, and for some reason you're overcome by melancholy. Two wild geese have flown across, a row of beautiful swans, white as snow, sweep over... woodcocks wail all around, seagulls squall...

We overtake two carts covered with hoods, and a crowd of country-men and women. They are migrants.*

"What province are you from?"

"Kursk."

Right at the back trudges a peasant who is unlike the others. He is clean-shaven, has a grey moustache and is carrying some kind of mystifying valve behind him in a piece of coarse woollen cloth; under his armpits are a couple of violins, wrapped up in shawls. There's no need to ask who he is or where he got these violins from. A ne'er-do-well, volatile, sickly, sensitive to the cold, not unattracted to a few drops of vodka, and timid, he has lived his entire life as a superfluous and unnecessary person, first in his father's house, then with his brother.

They have never got him set up on his own, never married him off. A worthless human being! At work he would freeze, he would get tipsy from two wineglasses full of hard drink, would come out with nothing but idle chatter, and knew only how to play the violin and romp about with the kids on the stove.* He would play in dives of pubs, at weddings and out in the fields, and my God! how he could play! But then his brother sold up the cabin,* the cattle and all the household goods, and is now off with his family to remote Siberia... And the bachelor is going too – he has nowhere else to go. He's taking the two violins with him as well. And when they arrive on the spot, he will begin to freeze from the Siberian cold, will wither away, and die gently, silently, so that nobody will notice, and his violins, which once made his native village feel gay and mournful, will go for tuppence to some clerk from their new area, or to an exile; the clerk's children will rip out the strings, snap the bridge, fill the inside with water... Please go back, Uncle!

I saw the migrants again when I took the steamer along the Kama.* I recall one peasant man of about forty with a light-brown beard; he was sitting on a bench on the ship; at his feet were sacks containing his domestic bits and pieces, while on the sacks lay children in bast sandals,* huddling together against the sharp, chill wind which was blowing from the deserted bank of the Kama. His face expressed the thought: "I'm resigned to it all now." There was mockery in his eyes, but this mockery was directed inwards, onto his soul, onto his past life, which had so cruelly cheated him.

"It won't get any worse!" he would say, and smile with his upper lip alone.

In response to this, you would remain silent and put no questions to him about anything, but a minute later he would repeat:

"It won't get any worse!"

"It will get worse!" a nasty ginger lout who was not a migrant would reply from another bench, with a pointed glance.

These people traipsing along the roadway around their carts are doing so in silence. Their faces are earnest, intense... I gaze at them and think: "To cut loose from a life which seems to be going unusually badly, and to sacrifice for this one's own locality, one's beloved domestic nest, can only be done by an exceptional human being, a hero..."

Then, a little later, we overtake a party of convicts walking to Siberia. Shackles jingling, a group of thirty to forty prisoners is going along the road, soldiers with rifles at their sides, and behind, two carts. One prisoner resembles an Armenian priest; another, tall, with an aquiline nose and a large forehead, I seem to have seen in a chemist's shop somewhere serving behind the counter; and a third has a pallid, emaciated and grave face, like a monk on a long fast. There is not time to take all of them in. The prisoners and the soldiers are exhausted; the road is bad, they have no strength to carry on... There are still ten versts* to go to the village where they will spend the night. And when they do arrive there, they will hastily get some food down them, have a drink of brick tea,* and straight away doss down to sleep – and instantly bedbugs will swarm all over them – the most bitter and invincible foe of those who are utterly worn out and who desperately wish to sleep.

In the evening the ground begins to freeze over, and the mud turns to hummocks. My hooded sledge bucks, crashes, and screeches diverse notes from bass to soprano. But it's cold. There is not a dwelling, not a single traveller coming in the other direction... Nothing stirs in the dim air, nothing makes a sound; the only thing that can be heard is my sledge bumping over the frozen earth, and when you try to light up a cigarette, along the roadway two or three ducks flap up, aroused by the flame.

We come to a river. We shall have to cross over by ferry. On the bank there is not a soul.

"They've gone rowing off to the other side, a pox on their souls!" says the sledge driver. "Come on, Yer Honour, let's roar."

To cry out with pain, to weep, to call for help or to call out in general are all known as "roaring" here, and so in Siberia not only beasts roar, but sparrows and mice as well.

"When a cat gets it, it roars," they will say about a mouse.

We begin to roar. The river is broad, and in the darkness the other bank cannot be seen. From the dampness of the river your feet freeze, then your legs, and then your entire body...We carry on roaring for half an hour, and still no ferry. We swiftly grow thoroughly fed up with the water and the stars strewing the sky, and with this sombre, grave-like silence. Out of boredom I strike up a conversation with my elderly driver, and learn that he has been married sixteen years, that he has had eighteen children, of whom only three have died, and that his father and mother are still alive; that his father and mother are *kirzhaks*, that is to say, religious dissenters, that they do not smoke and

5

have never seen a single town in their lives except for Ishim,* but that he, the old driver, as a young man, allowed himself to mess around a bit, and smoked. I discover from him that in this dark and grim river, sterlets, nelmas,* burbots and pike are to be found, but that there is nowhere to fish from and nothing to fish with.

But at last a rhythmical splashing becomes audible, and on the river something dark and clumsy appears. It's the ferry. It has the appearance of a small barge; there are five oarsmen, and the two oars of each of them, with their broad blades, look like crayfish's pincers.

On pulling into the bank, the first thing the oarsmen do is to set about abusing each other. They swear with malevolence, for no reason at all, and obviously in a half-asleep state. Listening to their choice vituperation, you might think that not only my driver, the horses and they themselves, but even the water, the ferry and the oars, have mothers.* The gentlest and most inoffensive piece of abuse with the oarsmen is "A pox on you!" or "Pox pustules in yer gob!" Which particular pox is desired I fail to understand, although I do make enquiries. I am dressed in a sheepskin jacket and high boots, and have a cap on; in the darkness it is not clear that I am a "Your Honour", and one of the oarsmen hollers at me raucously: "Oy you, yer pox-ulcer, whaddya doin' standin' about, gawpin' with yer mouth wide open? Get that side-'orse un'arnessed!"

We drive onto the ferry... The boatmen, swearing away, take to the oars. These are not local country-people, but exiles, sent here under sentence by society for a depraved life. In the village they have been assigned to, they simply cannot exist; it's tedious, they don't know how to till the soil, or have lost the knack of it, and anyway land not in one's home region is not pleasant to work on, and so they have come here to work on the ferry. Their faces are haggard, exhausted and battered.

And what expressions on their faces! It's obvious that these people, while sailing here on the prisoners' barges, were manacled together in chains, and while they were making their way in a chain gang on foot over the main highways, spending the night in cabins where their bodies were intolerably nipped by bugs, they became numbed to the marrow of their bones, and now, hanging around day and night in cold water, and seeing nothing except barren banks, they have lost for ever what warmth they did once have, and only one thing now remains in life for them – vodka, sluts, more sluts, more vodka. In this world, they are no longer human beings but wild beasts, while in the view of the old man, my driver, in the next world it will be even worse for them – for their sins they will go to hell.

2

O N THE NIGHT OF 5TH MAY I am being driven our of the sizeable village of Abatskoye, 375 versts from Tyumen, by an elderly man about sixty years old; shortly before harnessing the horses, he had had a good steaming in the village bathhouse and applied cupping glasses to himself. What were the cupping glasses for? He tells me he had an ache in the small of his back. He is unusually perky for his age, and is spry and voluble, but he walks with difficulty; apparently he has dorsal tabes.*

I am sitting in a *tarantas** pulled by a pair of horses. The old man swings his whip and shouts, although he no longer bellows as he did previously, but simply groans and moans like an Egyptian dove.*

Along the margins of the roads and far off on the horizon, serpent-shaped fires are blazing; this is last year's grass, which they set fire to intentionally here. It is damp and does not easily yield to the flames, and so the fiery serpents crawl along slowly, now splitting off into patches, now dying away, and then flaring up afresh. The fires throw out showers of sparks, and over each of them hangs a white cloud of smoke.

It's a beautiful sight when a fire suddenly seizes some tall grass; a column of flame a *sazhen** high rises above the ground, casting towards the heavens a large puff of smoke, and instantly collapsing, as if wishing the earth would open and swallow it up. It is still more beautiful when the little snakes of flame worm their way through a birch wood; the entire forest is lit up from end to end, the white boles distinctly visible, while the shadows of the birch trees are iridescent with speckles. Illuminations such as these are just a little scary.

Straight towards us, at full tilt, thundering over the hummocks, is heading a mail troika.* The old man hastily swings to the right, and instantly there flashes past us the enormous and weighty mail troika, in which the driver for the return journey is sitting. But suddenly a new din resounds: straight towards us another mail troika is heading, also at top speed. We hurriedly swing right, but, to my huge perplexity and terror, the troika swings, for some reason, not to the right, but to the left, and flies straight at us. And what if we collide? Hardly have I had time to put that question to myself, when a crashing sound rings out, and our pair of horses and the mail troika are mixed together in one dark pile. The *tarantas* is rearing up on end and I am plunging to the ground, with my cases and bundles on top of me... While I am lying, thoroughly shaken up, on the ground, I hear a third troika making towards us... "Well," I think, "this one'll finish me off for sure." But, thank God, I have not broken anything, am not seriously hurt, and can stand up. I leap up, rush aside, and bellow at the top of my voice:

"Stop, stop!"

From the bottom of the empty post-cart a figure arises and grasps the reins, and the third troika comes to a halt almost on top of my belongings.

A couple of minutes pass in silence. There is a kind of dull bewilderment, as if none of us can understand what has happened. The shafts are smashed, the harness snapped, the shaft-bow from which the bells hung is lying on the earth, and the horses are breathing heavily; the old man, sighing and groaning, gets up off the ground; the first two troikas have come back, and a fourth troika is approaching now, and a fifth...

Then commences the most ferocious abuse.

"Pox take you!" screams the coachman who had collided with us. "Pox pustules in yer gob! Where were you keeping yer eyes, you old dog?" "And just whose fault was it?" shouts the old man whiningly. "You're the one to blame, yet you're the one who's coming out with all this bad language!" As far as can be understood through the swearing, the cause of the collision was as follows: five troikas had been heading back to Abatskoye, bringing the mails; by law, returning troikas must go at a walking pace, but the leading coachman, growing bored and wanting to get into the warmth quicker, had driven his horses at full lick, while in the following four the drivers had fallen asleep, and there was nobody to guide the horses; the remaining four had raced off at full pelt after the first one. If I had been sleeping in my *tarantas*, or if the third troika had been tearing along on the very heels of the second, then, of course, things would not have worked out so fortunately for me.

The drivers were abusing each other at the tops of their voices, so that they must have been heard ten versts away. They swore intolerably.

How much wit, malice and mental impurity is expended in concocting these vile words and phrases, which have as their purpose the defiling and profaning of everything that a man holds holy, dear and worthy of love! Only Siberian coachmen and ferrymen know how to curse this way, and it is said they have learnt this from the prisoners being led into exile. The loudest and most vicious abuser of all the coachmen was the one who was to blame.

"Stop this swearing, you blithering idiot!" the old man defends himself. "And what if I don't?" asks the guilty coachman, a youngster of nineteen or so, approaching the old man with a threatening look, and standing eyeball to eyeball with him. "What if I don't?"

"You're not such a clever lad as you think you are!"

"And what if I don't? You just answer me: what'll 'appen then? I'll get hold of a bit of that there smashed-up shaft, and smash you up with it, you pox pustule!"

Judging from the tone of the voices, there is going to be a mêlée. In the night, just before daybreak, in the middle of this wild cursing bunch of savages, in sight of conflagrations near and far devouring the grass, but not warming the chilly night air one iota, beside these restive and agitated horses, which have huddled together in a bunch neighing, I feel the kind of isolation and loneliness it is difficult to describe.

The old man, grumbling and lifting his feet up high – from his illness – paces around the *tarantas* and horses, and unfastens, where he possibly can, cords and thongs, so as to bind the snapped shaft, then, lighting match after match, crawls along the roadway on his belly, searching for the trace. Even my baggage straps are utilized. Dawn is already breaking in the east, the wild geese have been awake and honking for ages already, the coach drivers have gone at last, and we are still standing in the road carrying out repairs. We are on the point of starting off again, but from the fastened shaft – crack! – and we have to stop again... and it's cold!

Somehow we struggle at a walking pace to a village. We halt by a two-storey log cabin.

"Ilya Ivanych, are there any horses here?"

"Yes, there are!" somebody responds hoarsely from behind a window.

In the cabin I encounter a tall fellow in a red shirt, barefoot, sleepy and for some reason smiling drowsily.

9

"We've beaten the bugs, matey!" he says, scratching and smiling still more broadly. "We purposely didn't heat the bedchamber up. When it's cold they don't walk." Here, bugs and cockroaches do not crawl, they "walk"; travellers do not travel, but "run". They ask "Where yer runnin' to, Yer Honour?" This means "Where are you travelling to?"

While they are greasing the sledge and jingling its bells, and while Ilya Ivanych – who will be my driver – is dressing, I seek out a comfortable spot, lay my head on a sack of something or other – grain, probably – and am instantly overcome by a deep sleep; right away I start dreaming of my own bed, my room, and I dream that I am sitting in my own house, at the table, and recounting to my family and friends how my coach-and-pair collided with a mail troika; but two or three minutes pass and I hear Ilya Ivanych tugging at my sleeve, and saying:

"Up, mate, 'orses are ready."

What banter there is over my laziness, over my aversion to the cold, which snakes up and down my spine, and the length and breadth of my body! We're off again... Light already, and the sky glows golden just before sunrise. The road, the grass in the fields and the forlorn young birch trees are covered with hoar frost, as if they have been sprinkled with sugar. Somewhere woodcocks are calling...

8th May

3

A LONG THE SIBERIAN HIGHWAY from Tyumen to Tomsk, there are no small settlements and no farmsteads, but only large villages separated from each other by twenty, twenty-five and even forty versts. One doesn't encounter country estates on the way, since there are no landed gentlemen here; neither will you see factories, mills or coaching inns... The sole reminders of humankind along the way are the telegraph wires moaning in the wind, and the wayside posts at intervals of a verst.

In each village there is a church, and sometimes two; there are also, apparently, schools in all the villages. The cabins are of wood, often two storeys high, with roofs of board.* By each cabin on the fence or on a birch tree stands a starling house, and they are so low that they can be reached by hand. Starlings are loved by everybody here, and even the cats do not touch them.

At 5 a.m., after a frosty night and a fatiguing journey, I was sitting in the cabin of a free driver,* in his "chamber",* drinking tea. A "chamber" is a bright, spacious room, with furnishings of which our countrymen from the Kursk or Moscow Regions can only dream. The cleanliness is marvellous: not a grain of dust or speck of dirt. The walls are white, the floors invariably of wood, painted or spread with linen covers; two tables, a divan, chairs, a dresser with crockery and pots of flowers on the window sills. In the corner stands a bedstead, piled with a whole mountain of feather mattresses and pillows in pretty cases; to clamber up this mountain you have to place a chair beside it, and the instant you lie down you sink. The Siberians love to have a good sleep in a soft bed.

From the icon in the corner,* bast prints extend along both sides; there is a portrait of His Majesty the Tsar – invariably several examples of this – St George the Victorious,* "sovereigns of Europe", among whom for some reason the Shah of Persia has turned up, then depictions of saints with Latin and German inscriptions, a half-length portrait of Battenberg, Skobelyev,* more saints. To decorate the walls they use sweet-papers, labels from vodka bottles and cigarette packets, and this deficiency does not tally at all with the substantial bed and painted floors. But what can be done about it? There is a high demand for artistry here, but God has not supplied the artists. Take a look at the door, on which is painted a tree with red and dark-blue flowers, and with some kinds of birds, which are more similar to fishes; this tree is growing out of a vase, and from this vase it is clear that the picture was painted by a European Russian, that is to say, an exile; an exile has also daubed the circle on the ceiling and the patterns on the stove. It is simple and unpretentious art, but it is beyond the capabilities of the local peasant. He does not take off his gauntlets and flex his fingers for nine months; now there is forty degrees of frost, now the meadows are inundated over a distance of twenty versts, and then comes the short summer – his back aches from the labour and his sinews are overstretched. Just when would he have time to paint? Since he spends the whole year round in a brutal struggle with nature, he is neither an artist, a musician, nor a singer. In the Siberian countryside you will rarely hear a concertina, and you do not expect a coach-driver to strike up a song.

The door is open, and across the entrance hall another room is visible, light and with wooden floors. It's seething with exertion. The lady of the house, a woman of about twenty-five, tall, lean, with a kind and gentle face, is kneading dough on the table; the morning sun beats into her eyes, on to her chest and arms, and it seems as if she is kneading dough out of sunlight; the landlady's younger sister is cooking bliny,* the cook is pouring boiling water over a piglet that has just been slaughtered, while the landlord is pressing wool into felt to make boots. Only the old ones are not doing anything. The grandmother sits on the stove, legs dangling, sighing and moaning; the grandfather is lying on the bed-board above the stove coughing, but, observing me, scrambles down and comes across the hallway into my chamber. He would like to have a chat... He starts off by saying that it's cold this spring, the kind of spring they haven't had for ages. Tomorrow is St Nikolai's Day,* for Heaven's sake, the day after tomorrow is Ascension Day, but snow fell during the night, and along the road to the village some woman froze to death; the cattle are wasting away from lack of fodder, the calves are suffering from the flux due to the frosts... Then he asks me where I'm from, where I'm "running" to and why, whether I'm married, and is it true what the women are saying, that there will soon be a war?

The sound of a child crying can be heard. Only now do I notice that, between the bed and the stove, a tiny cradle is hanging. The landlady drops the dough-making and rushes into the chamber.

"What an extraordinary thing happened to us!" she says to me, rocking the cradle and smiling gently. "A couple of months back a townswoman drove to us from Omsk with her little boy; dressed like a gentlewoman,* she was, though... She'd given birth to the baby at Tyukalinsk and had him christened there; after the confinement she took poorly on the journey and started to live with us, in this here bed-chamber. Married, she said she was, but nobody knew her. It wasn't written all over her face, and she had no identity documents on her... Maybe the kid's illegitimate."

"It's not for us to judge," mutters the grandfather.

"She spent a week with us," continues the landlady, "then she says, 'I'm going to Omsk, to my husband, but please let my Sasha stay with you; I'll come back for him in a week's time.' So I says to her: 'Listen, My Lady, God sends people children; some He sends ten, some as many as twelve, but me and the landlord, He's punishing us by not giving us a single one; leave us your Sasha, we'll take him in as our own son.' She thinks a bit and she says: 'Anyway, just hold on a bit, I'll ask my husband, and in a week's time I'll send you a letter. I don't dare make a decision without my husband.' She left us her Sasha and went. And now two months have gone already, and she's neither come herself nor sent a letter. A punishment from the Lord! We've grown to love Sasha like our own child, and now we ourselves don't know whether he's ours or somebody else's."

"You should write a letter to this townswoman yourself." I advise.

"Yes, you're right, we should!" says the landlord from the entrance hall.

He enters the chamber and gazes at me in silence; am I going to give any further advice of some sort?

"But just how are you going to write to her?" says the landlady. "She never told us her surname – just her first two names – Mariya Petrovna – that's all. And they do say as well that Omsk is a big town – you won't find her there. You might as well hunt for the wind in the fields, or a needle in a haystack!"

"Which all means that she won't be found," agrees the landlord, and looks at me as if wanting to ask: "Please help, for God's sake!"

"We've all got used to Sasha,"says the landlady, giving the child his dummy. "If he starts howling day or night, you feel different deep down inside, and it's as if even our cabin's a different one now as well. But then, in an evil moment, she's going to come back and take him away from us…"

The landlady's eyes redden and fill with tears, and she rapidly leaves the chamber. The landlord inclines his head after her, smiles wryly, and says:

"She's got used to him; it's obvious – it'd be a real shame!" He has grown accustomed to the boy himself, and it would be a shame for him, too, but he is a man, and to acknowledge this is awkward for him.

What fine people! While I drink tea and hear about Sasha, my belongings are lying in the sledge in the courtyard. When I ask whether they won't be stolen, they reply with a smile:

"Who is there to steal them here? They don't even go thieving at night-time."

And indeed, along the whole length of the highway, one will not hear of a wayfarer having anything stolen. In this respect, morality here is wonderful, and the traditions are excellent. I am profoundly convinced that if I were to drop some money in the sledge, then a free, non-exile coachman, on finding it, would return it to me without even glancing into the wallet. I travelled but little on the mail troikas and can say just one thing about the mail drivers: in the complaints books which I read out of boredom at the way stations, only one complaint of theft came to my notice: a traveller's bag containing boots had disappeared, but even upon this complaint, as is evident from the appended notes of the postal authorities, no action was taken, since the bag was discovered shortly afterwards and returned to the traveller. It is not common even to mention highway robbery here, which is unheard of. And the vagabonds* I encountered on the journey – the frequent mention of whom had scared me so much on my way here – are as terrifying as the hares and ducks.

With my tea, I am served bliny made from wheat flour, pies of cottage cheese and eggs, fritters and shortbread. The bliny are thin and rich, while the shortbread in both taste and appearance is reminiscent of those yellow, spongy cracknels which the Ukrainians sell in the markets at Taganrog and Rostov-on-Don. Everywhere along the Siberian Highway the most delicious bread is made; it's baked every day and in great quantities. Wheat flour is cheap here – thirty to forty copecks a pood.*

But man doesn't live by bread alone. If at midday you request something cooked, then you are offered nothing but "duck skilly" – and that is all. And it is impossible to eat this soup: it is a murky liquid in which float pieces of wild duck and their giblets, not totally cleansed of their contents. It's unappetizing and nauseating to look at. In every cabin there is a host of dead game birds. In Siberia they are not aware of any hunting laws, and shoot birds the whole year round. But the wildfowl will hardly soon be wiped out here. Over an expanse of 1,500 versts from Tyumen to Tomsk there is a great deal of wildfowl, but you will not come across a single decent gun, and only one out of every hundred hunters is able to shoot a bird in flight. Usually the huntsman crawls up to the ducks on his stomach through the tussocks and the wet grass, and will only fire from behind a bush at a sitting target from twenty to thirty paces, upon which his rifle misfires half a dozen times, and then, having finally gone off, kicks back sharply into his shoulder and cheek; if he does happen to hit the target, that creates not a little anguish, too;

off come his boots and baggy trousers, and he struggles through the cold water. There are no hunting dogs here.

9th May

4

A CHILL, BITING WIND has sprung up, it has started to rain heavily and has been doing so day and night without interruption. Eighteen versts from Irtysh, the peasant Fyodor Pavlovich – to whom I had been driven by the free coachman – says it is impossible to go any further, since the meadows along the bank of the Irtysh are submerged from the rains; yesterday Kuzma came from Pustynnoye, and, so he said, his horses had almost been drowned; we would have to wait.

"But just how long will we have to wait?" I ask.

"Who the hell knows? Ask the Lord!"

I enter the cabin. There in the chamber sits an old man in a red shirt, breathing heavily and coughing. I give him some Dover's powders;* the symptoms are alleviated, but he doesn't believe in medicine, and says he is better because he has "had a sit-down".

I take a seat and think: "Will we have to stay the night?" But supposing this old man really does keep coughing all night; there are almost certain to be bedbugs; and will anybody really commit themselves to saying that tomorrow the waters will not have spread over an even broader area? No, it's far better to be off!

"Let's go, Fyodor Pavlovich!" I say to the host. "I shan't wait."

"Just as you like," he consents mildly. "As long as we don't wind up spending the night in the water."

Off we set. The rain is not "pouring", but, as they put it here, "thrashing" down with all its might; into the bargain my carriage is not covered. The first eight versts we travel over a muddy road, but still manage a trot.

"Oh, this weather!" says Fyodor Pavlovich. "I must admit I haven't been there for ages, and haven't seen a flood, but it was Kuzma that got scared. Perhaps, God willing, we'll get across."

But suddenly a broad lake sweeps in front of our eyes. It's the inundated water meadows. The wind ripples noisily over its surface, raising a swell. Here and there islets are visible, and strips of land still not submerged. The bearing of the road is indicated by bridges and roadways made from logs which are soft from moisture, loose and almost all displaced from their true positions. Far beyond the lake extends the tall bank of the Irtysh, brown and bleak, while above it hang heavy grey clouds; here and there on the bank there is the white gleam of snow.

We begin to drive across the lake. It is not too deep, the wheels sit in the water only to a depth of a quarter of an arshin.* The going would very likely be pretty tolerable if it were not for the raised causeways. At every causeway we have to clamber out of the carriage and stand in the mud or the water; in order to drive onto it we have first to place against its elevated section the logs and boards which had formed the causeway's ramp, and which had been scattered over the causeway itself. We lead the horses on to the causeway one by one. Fyodor Pavlovich unharnesses the trace horses and gives them to me to hold; I grasp them by the cold and dirty reins, while they jib agitatedly; the wind wants to tear my clothing off, the rain beats painfully into my face. Shall we go back? But Fyodor Pavlovich remains silent, and is very likely waiting for me myself to suggest returning; I, too, keep silent.

We take one causeway by storm, then another, then a third... In one spot we are stuck in the mud and almost overturn, in another the horses grow obstinate, while the ducks and gulls wheel overhead as if mocking us. From Fyodor Pavlovich's face, from his unhurried movements, from his taciturnity, I can see that this is not the first time he has had to struggle in this way, that there have been worse, and that he has already, a very long time ago, become accustomed to inescapable quagmires, water and cold rains. He has had to spend a great deal of his life doing this!

We mount an islet. Here there is a little hovel without a roof; the two wet horses pace over damp manure; at Fyodor Pavlovich's call, a bearded peasant emerges from the hut with a long switch of wood, and he undertakes to show us the road. He walks ahead in silence, measuring the depth with his stick, and probing the bottom, while we follow him. He leads us onto a long, narrow strip, which he calls the "ridge"; we must go along this ridge, and when it ends take the left, then the right, and mount another ridge, which will lead us right up to the ferry.

The air is growing darker; the ducks are there no longer, and neither are the seagulls. The bearded peasant has explained the path to us, and long since returned home. The first ridge has come to an end, and once again we paddle through the water, take the left, and then the right. But here at last is the second ridge. It leads to the very edge of the bank.

The Irtysh is wide. If Yermak had tried to swim across it at full flood, he would have drowned even without his chainmail.* The far bank is high, steep and utterly bare. A chasm is visible; within this cleft, says Fyodor Pavlovich, a road leads up the hill to the village of Pustynnoye, where I have to get to. However, our bank is sloping – an arshin above water-level; it's barren, eroded and swampy in appearance; the turbid white-crested billows lash it malevolently and instantly recoil, as if it is repulsive to them to touch this ponderous and slimy shoreline upon which, judging from the look of the place, only toads could live, or the souls of great sinners. The Irtysh doesn't splash and doesn't roar, but it sounds as if it is beating against coffins on its bottom. It's as if the place is under a curse!

We drive up to the cabin where the ferrymen live. One comes out and says it is impossible to get to the other side, the vile weather is preventing it, we shall have to wait till tomorrow.

We remain there for the night. The whole time I hear the snoring of the ferrymen and my driver, the drumming of the rain against the windows, the howling of the wind, and the angry Irtysh beating against the coffins... Early in the morning I walk to the river; the rain is still falling, and, although the wind is a little lighter, it is still nonetheless impossible to cross on the ferry. They will take me over in a small boat.

The ferrying here is maintained by a trade guild of peasant proprietors;* there is not a single exile among the ferrymen; they are all free agents with individual rights and responsibilities. They are fine, kind-hearted people. Now I have crossed the river and am clambering up the slippery hillside to come out on to the road where a horse is waiting for me; behind me they are wishing me a happy journey, good health, success in whatever I am involved in... Meanwhile, the Irtysh is still seething with anger.

12th May

5

WHAT A PUNISHMENT this flood is! At Kolyvan they will not give me post-horses; they say the water meadows along the river Ob are flooded and it is impossible to travel. They have even held the mails back and are expecting special instructions regarding them.

The station clerk advises me to travel using free, non-exile drivers, to somewhere or other called Vyoon, and from there to go to Krasny Yar; from Krasny Yar I will be conveyed twelve versts on a boat to Dubrovino, and there, at last, they will let me have post-horses. This I do... I go to Vyoon, then to Krasny Yar... They escort me to a peasant called Andrey who has a boat.

"I do have a boat, yes!" says Andrey, a fellow of about fifty, gaunt, with a little light-brown beard. "I do have a boat! Early this morning it took the Assessing Magistrate's* clerk to Dubrovino and will be back soon. Just wait and have a nice cup of tea in the meantime."

I drink some tea, then up the hill of feather mattresses and pillows... I wake up and enquire about the boat – it's not back yet. In the chamber, the women have stoked up the stove so that it will not be cold in the bedchamber, and also happen to be baking bread at the same time. The chamber is heated up, the bread is already baked, and there is still no boat.

"They sent an unreliable lad!" sighs the landlord, shaking his head. "Clumsy and slow as a woman; the wind must have scared him and he didn't set off. D'you want to 'ave some more tea, Yer Honour? It must be dull for you, surely?"

An imbecile in a kaftan torn to shreds, barefoot, drenched through from the rain, is lugging firewood and pails of water into the entrance hall. He constantly glances into the chamber at me; he shows his unkempt, dishevelled head, mutters something, moos like a calf, and back he goes. Looking at his wet face and unblinking eyes, and listening to his voice, anybody would think that they could soon start raving too.

After noonday a very tall, stout fellow comes driving up to the landlord's house; the back of his head is like a bull, and he has enormous fists, reminiscent of a European Russian pub-keeper who has run to fat. He is called Pyotr Petrovich. He lives in the neighbouring village and keeps fifty horses with his brother, conveys free, non-exiled persons, supplies troikas to the post stations, tills the land, deals in cattle, and is now travelling off to Kolyvan on some business deal.

"You're from Russia?"*

"Yes, from Russia."

"I've never been there at all. Somebody from our parts once travelled to Tomsk, now he goes round with his nose stuck in the air as if he's been right round the globe. And now shortly, so they write in the papers, they're going to lay down a railway line to us. Tell me, sir, just how can that be so? A machine works through steam – that I understand fine. But if say, it's got to pass through a village, surely it'll bust up the cabins and crush people!"

I explain to him, and he listens attentively and says: "Get along with you! Fancy that!"

I learn from this chat that this portly fellow has been more than once not only to Tomsk, but also to Irkutsk and Irbit, and that when he was already a married man he had taught himself by his own efforts to read and write. He regards the host, who has only been to Tomsk, with condescension, and listens to him unwillingly. When he is offered or served anything, he says courteously: "Kindly don't trouble yourselves."

The host and the guest sit down to drink some tea. A young peasant woman, the wife of the host's son, serves them tea on a tray, bowing low, and they take cups and drink in silence. To one side, by the stove, the samovar is boiling. I climb up the mountain of feather mattresses and cushions once again, lie down and read, then descend and write; a great deal of time passes – a very great deal – and the woman is bowing again, and the host and guest are still drinking tea.

"Ba-ba! Ma-ma!" bellows the imbecile in the entrance hall.

And still no boat! It's growing dark outside, and they are lighting a tallow candle in the chamber. Pyotr Petrovich spends ages questioning me about where I am going and what for, whether there will be a war, and how much my revolver costs, but at last he becomes sick of talking, too; he sits taciturn at the table, propping up his cheeks on his fists, engrossed in thought. The wick of the candle is burnt right down. The door opens noiselessly, the idiot enters and sits on a chest; he has bared his arms to the shoulders; they are as scraggy and scrawny as sticks. He sits and stares at the candle.

"Get out of it, get out!" says the host.

"Ba-ba!" he moos, and, stooping low, goes out into the entrance hall. "Ma-ma!"

The rain beats against the windows. The host and guest sit down to eat duck skilly; neither of them wants it, and they are only eating like this out of boredom... Then the woman lays out feather mattresses and pillows on the floor; the host and guest undress and lie down side by side.

What tedium! To keep myself amused, I transport my thoughts to my own native region, where it is spring already, and the cold rain is no longer beating on the windows, but, as if on purpose, the recollection comes into my mind of a dull, grey, useless existence; it seems as if even there the wick has burned right down, and that there, too, people are bellowing "Ma-ma! Ba-ba!" I have no inclination to return.

I spread my sheepskin coat on the floor, lie down and place the candle at my head. Pyotr Petrovich raises his head and looks at me.

"There's something I want to explain to you," he says in an undertone, so that the host will not hear. "The folk here in Siberia are a dim, untalented bunch; from Russia they bring 'em sheepskin jackets, calico cloth, crockery and nails, while they don't know how to do a thing for themselves. They can only till the soil and drive free people, and nothing else. They can't even catch fish. Dull folk, for God's sake, really dull! You live among 'em and do nothing but put on a vast amount of weight, but – as for the soul and the mind! There's nothing to do except eat! It's pitiful to watch them, sir! You know, they're fine, kind-hearted people here, they don't steal, they don't offend you, and they're not exceptional drunkards. They're not human beings, they're gold dust, but, before you can look round, they've gone and snuffed it for less than a brass farthing, with no benefit to anybody, like a fly or, say, a mosquito. You ask somebody: what does he live for?"

"A man works, can clothe himself and gets enough to eat," I say. "What else does he need?"

"He still has to understand what purpose he is living for. They must understand that in European Russia?"

"No, they don't understand."

"That's quite impossible," says Pyotr Petrovich, considering a little. "A human being is not a horse. For example, we have no justice anywhere throughout the whole of Siberia. Even if we'd had any, it would long since have frozen solid. But a man must really look for this justice. I'm a prosperous chap, powerful, have some clout with the Assessing

Magistrate, and could do a lot of damage to this here landlord right tomorrow: I could have him rotting in prison round where I live, while his kids would be wandering about the countryside... And there's no fair play against me, and no defence for him, because – we exist without any justice... Well, in the parish registers, it's only recorded that we're human beings, Pyotrs and Andreys, but in reality we come over as wolves. Or perhaps God sees and judges it all... It's no laughing matter, it's dreadful, yet the landlord lay down and did nothing but make the sign of the cross over his forehead three times, as if that was all he had to do; he makes money, hides it away, most likely, and, before you look round, he's already piled up 800 roubles odd, buys new horses all the time, and does he ever ask himself what it's all for? After all, you can't take 'em over there when you're dead! Maybe he would have asked himself, but he doesn't understand... he's not too bright."

Pyotr Petrovich carries on talking for ages. But now he has finished at last; by this time it's already growing light, and the cocks are crowing.

"Ma-ma!" moos the idiot. "Ba-ba!"

And still no boat!

13th May

6

I AM GIVEN HORSES AT DUBROVINO and continue my journey. But forty-five versts from Tomsk I am told once again that travelling is impossible, that the river Tom has overflowed the water meadows and the roads. Once more I have to go by boat. And here it is the same old story as at Krasny Yar; the boat has crossed to the other side but cannot come back, since a strong wind is blowing and heavy billows are racing along the river... We shall have to wait!

In the morning it is snowing and the ground is covered to a depth of one and a half arshins (it's 14th May!), at midday it rains, and this washes all the snow away, while in the evening, at sunset, as I am standing on the bank and watching the boat battling against the current as it approaches us, there is snow and sleet... And simultaneously there is an occurrence which does not at all tally with the snow and the cold: I distinctly hear peals of thunder. The coachmen cross themselves and say this shows it's going to get warmer.

The boat is a large one. First of all, twenty poods or so of mail are placed in it, then my baggage, all covered over with soggy bast matting; the postman, a tall, elderly man, is sitting on a package, while I sit on my trunk. A diminutive soldier covered in freckles positions himself at my feet. You could put his overcoat through a mangle, and water is pouring off his service cap down his neck.

"God bless us! Cast off!"

We row with the current, alongside bushes of rose willow. The oarsmen chat about the fact that, ten minutes or so ago, two horses have been drowned, and a boy who was sitting in the cart only just saved himself by grasping onto a rose-willow bush.

"Row, lads, row, talk later!" says the tillerman. "Put yer backs into it!" Along the river, as is customary before a storm, a gust of wind rushes past us; the bare rose willow bends down to the water and sighs, the river suddenly grows cloudy, billows begin to race chaotically...

"Turn into the bushes, lads, we'll have to wait till it's over!" says the tillerman softly.

They have already begun to swing towards the bushes, but one of the oarsmen remarks that, in the event of bad weather, we shall have to sit here in the bushes all night, and we will drown anyway, and so why not carry on? It's decided to offer it to a majority vote, and the resolution is taken to row on...

The river grows murkier, the heavy wind and rain pounds against our sides, while the shore is still far off and the bushes which we could have grabbed hold of in case of disaster are left behind... The postman, who has seen some sights in his time, remains silent and does not stir, as if frozen stiff; the oarsmen are also silent; I notice that the little soldier's neck has suddenly turned crimson. My heart becomes heavy inside me, and I can think only of one thing – that, if the boat overturns, I will cast off first my sheepskin coat, then my jacket, then...

But now the shoreline is closer and closer, the oarsmen ply more cheerfully; little by little the weight falls from one's soul, and, when there are no more than three sazhens left to the bank, I become light-hearted and merry, and the thought occurs to me:

"It's good to be a coward! Not a great deal is necessary for him all of a sudden to become very happy!"

15th May

7

I DO NOT LIKE IT WHEN AN EDUCATED and cultured exile stands at a window and gazes in silence at the roof of the neighbouring house. What does he think about while doing so? I do not like it when he talks to me about trivia, while gazing into my face with the sort of expression that seems to imply: "You're going back home – I'm not." I do not like it, because all this time I feel infinite pity for him.

The frequently employed expression, that the death penalty is utilized nowadays only in exceptional cases, is not entirely correct; all the higher measures of correction which have replaced the death penalty still continue to bear its most significant and material aspect, namely that they are for life, for eternity, and every one of these measures of correction has an objective inherited directly from the death penalty – to remove an offender from the normal human milieu for ever – and, in the view of the society in which he was born and grew up, a person committing a serious crime is considered to be dead just as much as in the times when the death penalty held sway. In our comparatively humane Russian legislation, the higher measures of correction, both penal and corrective, are almost all for life. Convict hard labour is invariably accompanied by enforced settlement for life; exile to enforced settlement is dreadful precisely because it is for life; an offender sentenced to the Prisoners' Detachments,* if society does not consent to receive him into its midst when he has served his sentence, is exiled to Siberia; deprivation of rights in almost all cases is for life, and so on. Thus, none of the higher measures of punishment yields the offender eternal rest in the grave. A prisoner might be able to reconcile his feelings to the death penalty, but on the other hand the lifelong aspect of a punishment, the consciousness that hope for anything better is impossible, that the citizen in him has died for ever and that none of his best endeavours will resurrect that citizen: all these things permit me to think that the death penalty in Europe and with us has not been repealed, but merely clothed in another form less repugnant to human sensibilities. Europe has become too accustomed to the death penalty to relinquish it without prolonged and tedious procrastinations.

I am profoundly convinced that in fifty to a hundred years' time they will regard the lifelong character of our penalties with the same perplexity and sense of embarrassment with which we now look upon the slitting of nostrils or the amputation of fingers from the left hand. And I am profoundly convinced in addition that, however sincerely and plainly we may acknowledge the obsolescence and prejudicial nature of such already disused phenomena as lifelong punishments, we are utterly unable to remedy the situation. To substitute this permanency with something more rational and more corresponding to the needs of justice, we lack at the present time the knowledge, the experience and, consequently, the courage; all attempts in this direction, irresolute and one-sided, have been able to lead us only into serious blunders and extremities – as is the fate of all undertakings not founded on knowledge and experience. However strange and sad this may be, we are not even entitled to try to resolve the fashionable question about what is most suitable for Russia, prison or exile, since we have absolutely no idea what prison is or what exile is. Just take a glance at our literature concerning prison and exile: what utter poverty! Two or three short articles, two or three names, and, for the rest, absolutely nothing, as if in Russia there was neither prison, nor exile, nor hard labour. For twenty to thirty years now our intellectual classes have been repeating the phrase that every criminal is a product of society, but how indifferent they are to this product! The cause of this lack of concern towards those under confinement and brooding in exile, incomprehensible in a Christian society and a Christian literature, lies in the extraordinary want of education of our Russian lawyers and legal experts; they have little knowledge and are as much slaves to professional prejudices as the junior pen-pushers whom they despise. They sit university examinations only in order to be able to judge a person and sentence him to prison or exile; once having entered the service and started receiving their salary, they do nothing but pass judgement and sentence, and where the offender goes after the trial, and why, and what precisely prison and Siberia consist of, they have no idea, nor have any interest in, and it does not fall within their sphere of competence: it's now the business of escort guards, and prison governors with red noses!

In the estimation of those permanent residents, officials, drivers and wagoners on the spot whom I happened to talk to, the exiles with higher education – all those former officers, officials, notaries, accountants and the specimens of gilded youth sent here for forgery, embezzlement, fraud and so forth – lead an unobtrusive and unassuming life. Exceptions are formed only by those individuals possessing the temperament of Nozdryov;* these people everywhere, and however old they are, and in whatever situation, remain themselves; they do not linger in one spot, but lead a gypsy-like nomadic life and are mobile to such a degree that they are almost imperceptible to the observer. Apart from the Nozdryovs, "unfortunate wretches" are not infrequently encountered among the intellectuals – profoundly depraved, dissolute people, frankly vile, but these have almost all been taken into account, everybody knows them and points them out. The absolutely enormous majority, I repeat, live unassuming lives.

Upon their arrival at the place of exile, the intellectuals at first wear a bewildered and dumbfounded expression; they are timid and seem to be crushed. The majority of them are financially poor, have little strength, little practical training, and possess nothing except their ability to write, which is frequently of absolutely no use to anybody. Some of them commence by selling, piece by piece, their shirts of Holland linen, their sheets, scarves and handkerchiefs, and finish up after two or three years dying in fearful penury (for instance, not long ago Kuzovlev died in Tomsk; he had played a significant role in the "Taganrog Customs House Case".* He was buried at the expense of a certain magnanimous individual, also an exile); others little by little settle down to something practical and get back on their feet; they take up trade, work as solicitors or lawyers, write in the local newspapers, or become clerks, and so forth. Their earnings rarely exceed thirty to thirty-five roubles per month.

They find life tedious. In comparison with the European Russian countryside, the Siberian landscape seems to them monotonous, barren and soundless. There is frost on Ascension Day, and watery snow on Whit Sunday.* The lodgings in the towns are awful, the streets are slushy, everything is expensive in the shops, it's not fresh and only available in meagre quantities, and many things which a European Russian is accustomed to you will not find here for love or money. The educated classes here – those involved in both intellectual and practical work – drink vodka morning, noon and night; they drink ungracefully, uncouthly and obtusely, having no idea when to stop, and without getting tipsy; after the very first two sentences a local intellectual will without fail ask you: "Shall we have a drop of vodka?" And out of boredom an exile will drink with him; at first he turns up his nose, and then, finally, of course, becomes a hardened drunkard. If we are talking of drunkenness, it is not the exiles who demoralize the local residents, but the residents the exiles.

The women here are as dreary as the Siberian landscape; they are colourless, cold, do not know how to dress, cannot sing, do not laugh, are not pretty, and, as one established resident put it in a conversation with me, "they're coarse to the touch".

When in due time Siberia brings forth its own novelists and poets, a woman will not be the hero of their novels or poems; she will not inspire or arouse anyone to lofty action, or to come to the rescue, or to "travel to the ends of the earth". If one does not count the bad pubs, family bathhouses,* and the multitude of houses of ill repute, both overt and clandestine, of which Siberian men are such great lovers, there are no amusements of any sort whatever in the towns. During the long autumn and winter evenings, an exile will sit at home or go to a permanent resident to drink vodka; they polish off a couple of bottles of vodka and half a dozen of beer between them, and then – the usual question, "Well, er, do you fancy a trip over *there*?" – that is, to the brothel. Dreariness, tedium and boredom! What is there to divert the intellect and soul? An exile will read some worthless tome such as Ribot's* *Maladies of the Will*, or on the first sunny spring day he puts on a pair of light-coloured-trousers – and that is it. Ribot is quite tedious, and besides, why read about diseases of the will if you do not have any will yourself? It's chilly in light-coloured trousers, but at least it makes a change!

8

THE SIBERIAN HIGHWAY is the longest, and, I should think, the ugliest road on earth. From Tyumen to Tomsk, thanks not to the officials, but to the natural conditions of the locality, it is still bearable; here there is a treeless plain; yesterday it rained, but by evening it had already dried out; and if towards the end of May the highway is covered with mountains of ice from melting snow, then you can drive across the open fields, selecting any roundabout path over the expanse. But from Tomsk onwards begin the taiga* and the hills; the soil does not dry out so rapidly here, one simply cannot pick out a detour, but has to travel along the highway out of sheer necessity. And it is for this reason that only after Tomsk do travellers begin to swear and contribute wholeheartedly to the complaints books. The officials conscientiously read through the complaints, and write on every one "No action taken". Why bother to write it? Chinese officials would long since have acquired a stamp.

With me from Tomsk to Irkutsk travel two lieutenants and a military doctor. One, a lieutenant of infantry, is wearing a tall, shaggy astrakhan hat, while the other, a topographer, is wearing a shoulder knot.* At each way station, dirty, wet, drowsy, worn out by the ride and the jolting, we tumble onto the divan and say with outrage: "What a foul, dreadful road!" And the station clerks and foremen tell us:

"This is nothing yet, just you wait a bit till you get to the Kozulka!"

They scare us with the Kozulka at every station starting from Tomsk, the clerks smiling enigmatically, and wayfarers coming the other way saying with malicious joy: "I've got through, now you've got to do a bit of driving!" And my imagination is so terrified that I begin to dream of this mysterious Kozulka in the form of a bird with a long beak and green eyes.

The Kozulka is the name given to the span of twenty-two versts linking the stations of Chernorechenskaya and Kozulskaya (it's between the towns of Achinsk and Krasnoyarsk). Two or three stations before the dread spot, presages are already beginning to appear. One traveller from the opposite direction says that he has overturned four times, another complains that his axle has snapped; yet another remains dismally taciturn, and, when asked whether the road was any good, responds: "Very good – Devil take it!" They all look at me with pity, as if at a corpse, because I have my own carriage.

"You'll most likely bust something and get stuck in the mud!" they say with a sigh. "You'd do better to go by relay horses!"

The closer to Kozulka, the more fearful the harbingers. In the evening, not far from the Chernorechenskaya way station, the sledge carrying my travelling companions suddenly overturns, and the lieutenants and doctor, together with their trunks, bundles, sabres and a case containing a violin, go flying into the mud. Very close to the station of Chernorechenskaya itself the driver suddenly declares to me that the shaft-pin is bent (this is the iron bolt which links the front part with the axle section; when it bends or snaps, the vehicle's underside touches the ground). At the station repairs begin. Five drivers reeking of garlic and onion to such a degree that I feel stifled and nauseous turn the filthy carriage on its side and begin to knock the crooked bolt out with a hammer. They tell me that in the vehicle, in addition, some kind of bolster has cracked, an underscrew has fallen out, three nuts have sprung off, but I do not understand a thing, and have absolutely no desire to understand... It is dark, cold, tedious, I am weary...

In the station room a tiny lamp burns wanly; there is a stench of paraffin, garlic and onions. On one divan lies the lieutenant in an astrakhan hat, asleep; on the other sits some fellow with a beard, idly pulling on his boots; he has just received an order to go somewhere to repair the telegraph; but he does not want to go – he wants to sleep. The lieutenant with the shoulder knot and the doctor are sitting at the table; they have placed their leaden heads on their hands and are dozing. The snoring of the man in the astrakhan hat is audible, and so is the tapping of the hammer in the yard outside.

They are chatting... all these station conversations everywhere along the highway centre on one and the same topic: criticism of the local authorities and abuse of the road. Most of this is reserved for the postal and telegraphic department, although along the Siberian Highway it only reigns and does not rule. To a worn-out traveller still with over 1,000 versts to travel to Irkutsk, everything recounted at the way stations seems simply dreadful. All these conversations about how some member of the Geographical Society* travelling with his wife smashed his coach up a couple of times and finally was forced to spend the night in the forest, how some lady cracked her head open from the jolting, how some exciseman had sat in the mud for sixteen hours and gave the peasants twenty-five roubles to drag him out and convey him to the station, how not a single owner of a carriage had managed to reach the station successfully – all such conversations raise an echo in the soul like the cries of a bird of ill omen.

Judging from the tales, the mails suffer worst of all. If a first-rate man could be found who would take upon himself the trouble of observing the movement of the Siberian mails from Perm, even if only as far as Irkutsk, and recorded his impressions, we would obtain a narrative which would bring tears to the readers' eyes. To begin with, all these leather packages and sacks which are bringing religion, enlightenment, trade, commerce, order and finance into Siberia remain whole days and nights at Perm without any necessity, because the slothful steamers are always late for the train. From spring right through to June, from Tyumen to Tomsk, the mails battle with overflows of monstrous dimensions from rivers, and with inextricable mud; I recall that, owing to a flood, I had to wait at one station for twenty-four hours; the mails waited with me. Over rivers and inundated water meadows the mails are carried in small boats, which do not overturn only because, most likely, the Siberian postmen's mothers are praying for them fervently. From Tomsk itself right up to Irkutsk, mail carts spend ten to twenty hours in the mud near various Kozulkas and Chernorechenskayas, which are countless. On 27th May, I was told at one way station that not long ago the bridge over the Kachka stream had collapsed under the mails, that the horses had nearly been drowned and the mails almost lost – this is one of the everyday adventures which have long since become routine for the postal service. While I was driving to Irkutsk I was not overtaken for six whole days by the mail from Moscow; this implies that it was over seven days late, and that something extraordinary had been happening to it for the entire week.

Siberian postmen are absolute martyrs. They bear a heavy cross. These are heroes whom their homeland obstinately refuses to acknowledge. They work extremely hard, battle with nature a great deal more than anybody else is forced to, at times they suffer intolerably, but they are dismissed, struck off and fined far more often than they are rewarded. Are you aware how much they earn, and have you seen a single postman in your entire life with a medal? They are perhaps a great deal more useful than those who write "No action taken", but just notice how cowed, how ground down, how timorous they are in your presence.

But now, finally, the announcement is made that the carriage is ready. We can proceed.

"Up you get!" The doctor wakes the lieutenant with the astrakhan hat. "The sooner we get over this damn Kozulka the better."

"Gentlemen, the Devil's not as black as he's painted," the man with the beard consoles us. "And anyway, if you're scared, you can always do the twenty-two versts on foot."

"Yes, if you don't get stuck in the mud!" adds the clerk.

The morning star is glimmering in the sky. It's cold; the coachmen have still not driven out of the yard, but they are already saying: "Oh,

well, it's this road again, God 'elp us!" We go at first over the open
countryside. Liquid mud, in which your wheels sink, alternates with
dry hummocks and potholes; from the log paths and planked footpaths drowning in liquid manure, logs jut out like ribs; driving over
these churns people's insides up, and snaps the axles of carriages...
But at last the countryside has come to an end, and we are on the
dreaded Kozulka. The road here is indeed awful, but I do not find
that it is any worse than, for example, that around Mariinsk* or near
Chernorechensk itself. Visualize a broad cutting along which extends
an embankment four sazhens in width constructed out of clay and
rubbish – and this is the highway. If you scrutinize this embankment
sideways on, it looks like a bank of organ pipes jutting out from the
earth, or the rows of steel pins from an open musical box. Ditches
lie along both sides. Along this bank stretch ruts half an arshin and
more in depth, they are traversed by a whole host of further ruts, and
thus the entire bank presents the appearance of a series of mountain
chains, which contain their own Kazbeks and Elbruses;* the crests
of these mountains have dried up by this time and drum against the
wheels, while at the foothills water still squelches. Nobody but a very
artful juggler could position a carriage on this bank in such a way that
it stands upright – most usually a vehicle is always in the kind of position which, until you are used to it, makes you want to cry out every
minute: "Driver, we're turning over!" Now the right-hand wheels are
sinking in a deep rut, while the left-hand ones are on the mountain
tops, now two wheels are stuck in the mud, a third is on a crest, and
the fourth is hanging loose in the air... The coach negotiates thousands of difficult situations, and meanwhile you are constantly grip-
ping your head, your side, bending low in all directions, biting your
tongue, and your trunks and boxes stage a mutiny and pile up on top
of each other and on you yourself... and just look at the driver: how
does this acrobat contrive to stay on the coach-box?

If anybody caught sight of us from sideways on, he would say we
were not travelling but going out of our minds. Wishing to distance
ourselves from the embankment, we hug the edge of the forest, trying to discover a detour; but here, too, there are ruts, hummocks, ribs
and plank roadways. After driving a short while, the coachman halts;
he grunts helplessly, with the sort of expression that seems to imply
that he wants to commit some piece of villainy, heads for the highway

− and straight into a ditch. A cracking sound rings out − bang! from the front wheels, bang! from the back − that is us crossing the ditch. Then we mount the embankment again, with more cracking. Steam is rising from the horses, the swingle trees break loose, the breech bands and shaft bows fall aside. "Come on, you blessed animal!" bellows the driver, lashing his whip with all his might. "Come on, mate! A pox on your soul!" The horses drag the carriage a dozen or so paces, then stop; however much one lashes or berates them, they simply will not go any further. There's nothing to be done − we steer for the trench once more, head down the embankment, and look for a detour yet again, then more indecision, another turn for the embankment − and so on without end.

It is heavy going, very heavy, but it grows still heavier when you consider that this hideous, pock-marked strip of land, this foul smallpox of a road, is almost the sole artery linking Europe and Siberia! And we are told that along an artery like this civilization is flowing into Siberia! Yes, that is what we are told, we are told a great deal, but if we were overheard by the drivers, postmen or these soaking, filthy countrymen who sink into the mire up to the knees beside their train of carts carrying tea to Europe, then just what opinions would they form of Europe, of its sincerity!

On this point, let us watch a wagon train. Forty or so carts carrying tea chests stretch out along the embankment itself; the wheels are half concealed in deep ruts, the scrawny, poor-quality horses stretch out their necks. Alongside the carts walk the wagoners; dragging their feet out of the mire, and assisting the horses, they have long since run out of strength... Here a section of the train has halted. What has happened? A wheel has broken on one of the carts... No, it's far better not to look!

With the intention of mocking the exhausted drivers, postmen, carters and horses, somebody has directed that piles of stone brick-bats should be piled up at the roadsides. This is to provide a reminder every minute that in a very short time the road will be still worse. It is said that in the towns and villages along the Siberian Highway live people who receive a salary for repairing the roads. If this is true, their salaries should be augmented so that they would kindly not labour at these repairs, since from their restorations the roads are becoming worse and worse all the time. According to the peasants, the repairs of roads such as the Kozulka are carried out in the following fashion: at the end of June or the beginning of July, in the very season when the swarms of midges – the scourge of life here – are at their height, folk are "driven", as they say here, from the villages, commanded to fill in the dried-up ruts and holes with brushwood, stones and brickbats, which crumble to powder in one's fingers; the renovations continue till the end of summer. Then comes the snow, covering the road with potholes and bumps which must be unique throughout the world and which jolt a person around to the point of seasickness; then comes spring and mud, then repairs again – and so on year in, year out.

Before I arrived at Tomsk I had managed to become acquainted with one Assessing Magistrate and travel two or three stations with him. I recall that, when we were sitting in some Jew's cabin eating fish soup made from perch, the village police chief entered and reported that in some spot or other the road had totally gone to ruin and that the roads contractor did not want to repair it.

"Call him here!" ordered the Magistrate.

Shortly afterwards a short, puny countryman, shaggy and with a deformed face, came in. The Magistrate leapt from his chair and hurled himself at him:

"How dare you not mend the roads, you scoundrel!" he began screaming and wailing. "It's impossible to drive over it, people break their necks, the Governor writes, the District Police Chief writes, I'm the one who's guilty in everybody's eyes, while you, you villain, a pox on your soul, damn you to hell, a curse on your ugly mug – what are you staring at? Eh? You stinking reptile! Get that road fixed by tomorrow, or else! Tomorrow I'll be driving back, and if I see the road's not mended, I'll bloody that twisted mug of yours, I'll maim you, you blackguard! Get *out*!"

The stunted little countryman blinked, broke into a sweat, pulled a still more distorted face, and darted out of the door. The Magistrate returned to the table, sat down and said with a smile:

"Yes, of course, after the ladies of Petersburg and Moscow, you can't consider the women here pleasing, but if you want to look for pretty ones, then you can find girls like that here, too…"

It would be interesting to know what the contractor managed to do before the next day. And what could he do in such a short space of time? I do not know; fortunately or unfortunately for the Siberian Highway, Assessing Magistrates do not remain long in one place; they are frequently replaced. It is recounted that one newly appointed Magistrate, on arrival at his patch, "drove" the peasants to work and ordered them to dig ditches at the sides of the road; his successor, not wishing to be outdone in originality, drove out the peasants and ordered them to fill the ditches in. A third ordered them to cover the road in his area with a layer of clay to a depth of half an arshin. A fourth, fifth, sixth, seventh – they have all striven to bring their portion of honey back to the hive.

The road remains impassable throughout the entire year: in spring it is the mire, in summer the hummocks, pits and repairs, in winter the pot-holes. That rapid travel which at one time captivated the spirit of F.F. Vigel and later of I.A. Goncharov* is now conceivable only just after the first snowfall. True, even contemporary writers do extol the rapidity of Siberian travel, but this is only because, having visited Siberia, it is very awkward not to have experienced rapid travel, even if only in one's imagination...

It is difficult to hope that the Kozulka will ever cease to snap axles and wheels. The Siberian officials have in their time really never seen a better road; even this pleases them, and the complaints books, newspaper reports and criticism from travellers in Siberia bring as little benefit to the roads as the funds allocated to their repair...

We draw up at the Kozulskaya way station when the sun is already high in the sky. My travelling companions carry on, while I stay behind to have repairs made on my carriage.

9

IF, WHILE TRAVELLING, the countryside possesses any significance at all for you, then, going from Russia to Siberia, you could have a very boring time from the Urals right up to the Yenisey. The chilly plain, the twisted birch trees, the pools, the occasional islands, snow in May and the barren, bleak banks of the tributaries of the Ob – these are all that the memory succeeds in retaining from the first 2,000 versts. That natural scenery which the indigenous peoples deify, which our fugitive exiles hold in high regard, and which will, over the course of time, serve as an inexhaustible gold mine for the Siberian poets – scenery distinctive, majestic and beautiful – begins only from the Yenisey onwards.

Let it be said without offence to the jealous admirers of the Volga that I have never in my life seen a more magnificent river than the Yenisey. A beautifully dressed, modest, melancholy beauty the Volga may be, but, at the other extreme, the Yenisey is a mighty, raging Hercules, who does not know what to do with his power and youth. On the Volga a man starts out with spirit, but finishes up with a groan which is called a song; his radiant golden hopes are replaced by an infirmity which it is the done thing to term "Russian pessimism", whereas on the Yenisey life commences with a groan and finishes with the kind of high spirits which we cannot even dream about. These, at any rate, were my thoughts as I stood on the bank of the wide Yenisey and avidly gazed at its waters, which with fearful rapidity and power surge onto the stern Arctic Ocean. There is little space between the banks of the Yenisey. The low billows strive to outstrip each other, jostle each other, form spirals, and it seems odd that this Hercules has not yet washed the banks away or drilled a hole through the bottom. On this bank lies Krasnoyarsk, the best and most beautiful of all Siberian towns, while on the other are mountains reminding me of the Caucasus, with the same smoky colour and dreaminess. I stood there and thought: "What a full, intelligent, courageous life will illumine these shores in time!" I envied Sibiryakov,* who, so I had read, had sailed on a steamship from Petersburg to the Arctic Ocean, in order to pick a way from there through to the mouth of the Yenisey; I regretted that a university has been opened in Tomsk and not in Krasnoyarsk. Many and various were the thoughts that came to me, they jostled and tangled with each other like the waters of the Yenisey, and I was overcome by a feeling of contentment.

Shortly after the Yenisey commences the celebrated taiga. Much has been spoken and written about it, and therefore one has expectations of it that it cannot live up to. At first one is really a little disappointed. Along both sides of the road stretch the usual forests of pine, larch, spruce and birch. There are no trees of five arm-girths, no crests at the sight of which one's head spins; the trees are not a whit larger than those that grow in the Moscow Sokolniki.* I had been told that the taiga was soundless and that its vegetation had no scent. This is what I had been expecting, but, the entire time I travelled through the taiga, birds were pouring out songs and insects were buzzing; pine needles warmed by the sun saturated the air with the thick fragrance of resin, the glades and edges of the forest were covered with delicate pale-blue, pink and yellow flowers, which caress not merely the sense of sight.

Apparently those who have written about the taiga have observed it not in spring but in summer, when in European Russia, too, the woods are silent and do not give out any fragrance.

The power and enchantment of the taiga lie not in titanic trees or the silence of the graveyard, but in the fact that only birds of passage know where it ends. Over the first twenty-four hours you pay no attention to it; on the second and third you are full of wonderment, and by the fourth and fifth you are experiencing the sensation that you will never manage to emerge from this green monster. Mounting a high hill covered with woodland, and gazing forwards to the east, the direction the road is going, one sees forest below, further on another hill covered with trees, beyond it another hill, just as bosky, and beyond it a third, and so on endlessly; twenty-four hours later you glance forwards from a hill and the picture is exactly the same... You know, at least, that the river Angara and the town of Irkutsk lie in front of you, but what kind of forests these are stretching to north and south on both sides of the road, and how many hundreds of versts they extend, even the drivers and peasants born in the taiga do not know. Their fancy is more audacious than ours, but even they will not take it on themselves to put a figure to the dimensions of the taiga off the tops of their heads, and the answer they give to your question is: "It hasn't got any end!" The only thing they know is that during the winter some people or other come through the taiga from the far north on reindeer sledges to buy grain, but what kind of people these are, and where they are from, not even the elderly know.

Over there along by the pines trudges a runaway exile with a knapsack and kettle on his back. How petty and insignificant, in comparison with the enormous taiga, appear his villainies, torments and he himself! He will perish here in the taiga, and there is nothing strange, nothing dreadful about this, like the death of a gnat. The population is still not dense, the taiga is mighty and invincible, and the phrase "Man is the ruler of nature" nowhere sounds so diffident and false as here. If, let us say, all the people living now along the Siberian Highway came to an agreement to destroy the taiga, and for this purpose to use axe and fire, then the old story would be repeated of the blue tit who wanted to set the sea on fire. It does occur that a forest fire swallows up five or so versts of woodland, but, in the whole vast mass of timber, sites of fires are hardly noticeable; ten years pass and, over the areas of scorched forest, young woods begin to spring up, denser and shadier than the first. During his stay on the east bank, a certain academic accidentally set fire to the forest; in an instant the entire visible mass of green was enveloped in flames. Flabbergasted by the extraordinary spectacle, he described himself as "the cause of a dreadful catastrophe". But what does some dozen versts or so signify for the vast taiga? Most probably on the site of the former fire now grows impassable forest, bears roam placidly, hazel grouse flutter, and the scholarly labours of the academic have left a far greater mark on the scenery than the dreadful catastrophe which horrified him so much. The customary human yardstick is simply not appropriate for the taiga.

And how many secrets the taiga conceals within itself! Over there a road or pathway skulks off and disappears into the gloaming of the forests. Where does it lead? To a secret distillery, to a village about whose existence neither the District Police Chief nor the Magistrate has yet heard, or perhaps to gold workings discovered by a trade association of vagabonds?* And what devil-may-care, seductive freedom wafts from this enigmatic pathway!

According to the tales of the coachmen, in the taiga live bears, wolves, elks, sable and wild goats. When there is no work at home, the countrymen living along the highway spend whole weeks in the taiga shooting game. The art of the hunter here is very simple: if the gun goes off – thank God; but if it misfires – don't ask the bear for mercy. One hunter complained to me that his gun would misfire five times in a row and only shoot properly at the sixth; going on the hunt with a treasure such as this, without a knife or a bear-spear, is a great risk. Rifles imported into the region are poor and expensive, and therefore it is no rarity to encounter along the highway smiths who know how to make guns. In general, the smiths are talented people, and this is especially noticeable in the taiga, where they certainly do not fade into the background among the mass of other talented individuals. I had out of necessity to form a short acquaintance with a certain smith whom my driver recommended to me thus: "Oh-h, he's a great craftsman! He even makes guns!" And both his tone of voice and the expression on his face reminded me of our European Russian conversations about well-known artists. My *tarantas* had broken down, and repairs were necessary, and, on the recommendation of the driver, a scrawny, pallid individual with nervy movements announced himself to me at the way station, by all the signs a very talented man and a great drunkard. Like a fine and experienced surgeon, to whom it is wearisome to treat an uninteresting malady, he cursorily and half-heartedly examined my *tarantas*, succinctly and clearly formed a diagnosis, considered a little, and, without having said a word to me, lazily set off down the road; then he glanced round and said to the driver:

"Well, what are you waiting for? Bring the carriage into the smithy, will you?"

He was assisted in repairing the carriage by four carpenters. He worked negligently and unwillingly, and it seemed that the iron assumed diverse forms without his being aware of it. He smoked frequently, delved in a pile of scrap iron with no necessity whatever, and glanced up to the heavens whenever I tried to hurry him. This is the way dramatic artists pose when they are requested to sing or recite something. From time to time, as if out of coquettishness, or wishing to impress me and the carpenters, he would raise his hammer on high, rain sparks to all sides, and with one blow resolve some very complex and abstruse problem. From an awkward weighty blow, which, it would seem, must reduce the anvil to dust and make the earth shake, the light iron plate acquired the desired form so perfectly that even a flea couldn't carp at it.* He received for his labours five and a half roubles from me; he took five for himself, and handed over the half to the four carpenters. They thanked him and dragged the *tarantas* to the station, most likely envying the kind of talent which even in the taiga knows its own worth and is just as despotic as in our large European Russian towns.

20th June

Sakhalin Island

1

Nikolayevsk-on-Amur. The steamer Baikal. *Cape Pronge and the entry to the Liman. Sakhalin a peninsula. La Pérouse, Broughton, Kruzenshtern and Nevelskoy. The Japanese explorers. Cape Dzhaore. The Tatar coast. De-Kastri.*

O N 5TH JULY 1890 I ARRIVED at the town of Nikolayevsk,* one of the most easterly points of our homeland. The Amur here is very wide, with only twenty-seven versts or so remaining to the sea; the spot is majestic and beautiful, but recollections of the past of this region, my travelling companions' tales of the savage winters and no less savage local way of life, the closeness of a penal labour colony, and the very appearance of the abandoned town with its dwindling population totally deprive one of any desire to admire the scenery.

Nikolayevsk was founded not so very long ago, in 1850, by the renowned Gennady Nevelskoy, and this is almost the only bright spot in the town's history. When, in the '50s and '60s, with no regard for the feelings of soldiers, convicts or settlers, the seeds of culture were being implanted along the Amur, the officials governing the territory had their residences and offices at Nikolayevsk; large numbers of Russian and foreign adventurists travelled here, enticed by the exceptional abundance of fish and wild animals, and apparently the town was no stranger to the humanities, since there was even one occasion when a touring scholar considered it both necessary and possible to deliver a public lecture at the club here. Now, however, almost half the houses have been deserted by their owners, are half-ruined, and their dark, frameless windows stare at you like the eye sockets of a skull. The inhabitants lead a sleepy, drunken life, and in general live in a state of semi-starvation, on what the Good Lord happens to send. They subsist by delivering fish to Sakhalin, by embezzlement of gold, by exploiting the natives, by selling *ponty*, that is, stags' antlers from which the Chinese prepare stimulant pills. On the way from Khabarovsk to Nikolayevsk, I came across quite a few smugglers; here they do not conceal their profession. One of them, showing me some gold dust and a pair of antlers, told me with pride: "My father was a smuggler too!" Exploitation of the natives, apart from the usual practice of getting them dependent on drink, making fools of them and so on, sometimes takes a novel form. For instance, the Nikolayevsk merchant* Ivanov, now dead, used to sail every summer to Sakhalin and extract a tribute from the Gilyaks* there; those who did not pay up he tortured and hanged.

There is no hotel in the town. At the public assembly rooms, I was permitted to relax after dinner in a hall with a low ceiling, where in winter, so they said, dances were held, but at my request as to where I could spend the night they simply shrugged their shoulders. There was nothing else for it – I had to spend two nights on the steamer, and when it set off back to Khabarovsk* I was as desperate as a crayfish beached on a sandbank – just where was there for me to go? My luggage was on the jetty: I walked along the bank not knowing what to do with myself. Just opposite the town, two or three versts from the shore, lay the steamship *Baikal*, on which I would enter the Tatar Strait, but I was told it would set out in roughly four or five days, no earlier, although the flag of departure was already flapping on its mast. Should I then make up my mind to go over to the *Baikal*? But it was awkward – they probably won't let you, I was told, it's still too early. A wind sprang up, and the Amur grew overcast and choppy, like the sea. I started to feel very fed up. I went into the assembly rooms, took a long time over my dinner there, and listened to them round the adjacent table talking about gold, about antlers, about a conjurer who had arrived in Nikolayevsk, about some Jap or other who took out teeth not with forceps but simply with his fingers alone. If you listen long and attentively then, my word, how remote life is here from European Russia! From the cured dry fillets of salmon which they eat here as chasers to their vodka, right through to their conversations – in everything, one senses something peculiar to the region, and non-Russian. When I was sailing on the Amur, I had the feeling that I was not in Russia, but somewhere in Patagonia, or Texas; without even mentioning the distinctive, un-Russian scenery and natural conditions, it seemed to me the entire time that the tenor of our Russian life is entirely alien to the native of the Amur, that Pushkin and Gogol are not understood here, and therefore not necessary, that our history is boring, and that we who arrive from European Russia seem like foreigners. As regards religion and politics, I noted here the most complete indifference. The priests whom I saw along the Amur eat meat and dairy produce on fast days, and, among other things, I was told tales about one of them who, dressed in a white silk kaftan, engaged in embezzling gold,* competing in this with his spiritual flock. If you want to bore a dweller on the Amur and make him yawn, strike up a conversation with him about politics, the Russian government, Russian art. And the moral code, too, is somehow peculiar to them and not Russian. The chivalrous treatment of women is elevated here almost into a cult; yet at the same time it is not considered reprehensible to hand your wife over to a friend for money; even more strikingly, on the one hand there is an absence of class prejudice – here they behave to an exile as to an equal – but, on the other hand, it's no sin to shoot Chinese vagabonds* in the forest, or even to go and secretly hunt down "hunchbacks".*

But to continue with myself. Having found no shelter, I decided towards evening to set off for the *Baikal*. But here there was a new difficulty; a considerable swell had risen, and the Gilyak boatmen would not agree to take me for any money in the world. Again I wandered along the bank, not knowing what to do with myself; besides, the sun was already going down by this time, and the waves on the Amur were growing darker. Both on my bank and on the other side, the Gilyaks' dogs were baying ferociously. "Just why did I come here?" I asked myself, and my journey appeared frivolous in the extreme. And the thought that the penal labour colony was already close, that within a few days I would be landing on the soil of Sakhalin, and did not have on me a single letter of recommendation, that they could ask me to leave and go back – this thought disturbed me unpleasantly. But then at last two Gilyaks agreed to take me for a rouble, and, in a boat knocked together from three boards, I safely reached the *Baikal*.

This ship is a seagoing steamer of medium size, a merchantman, which, after the steamships on Lake Baikal and the Amur, seemed to me to be reasonably tolerable. It plies between Nikolayevsk, Vladivostok and the Japanese ports, carrying mail, soldiers, prisoners, passengers and freight – mainly government cargo; according to the contract concluded with the Exchequer, which pays it a hefty subsidy, it has to call in at Sakhalin several times during the summer, at the Alexandrovsk Post and Southern Korsakovsk Post. The tariff is very high – there is probably not another one like it anywhere else in the world. Colonization first and foremost requires freedom and ease of movement – so high tariffs are utterly beyond comprehension. The mess rooms and cabins on the *Baikal* are cramped but clean, and are laid out entirely in the European manner; there is an upright piano. The staff is made up of Chinese, with long pigtails, and they are referred to with the English word "boys". The cook is also Chinese, but the cuisine is Russian, although all his food is bitter with spicy curry and reeks with some kind of odour like corylopsis.*

Having read a lot about the storms and ice of the Tatar Strait, I had expected to meet on the *Baikal* whalers with hoarse voices, who sprayed chewed tobacco around as they spoke; in actual fact I found highly cultured people. The ship's captain, Mr L., a native of one of the western regions of the Russian Empire, has been sailing the northern seas for more than thirty years now and has travelled them from side to side and end to end. In his time he has seen many wonders, knows a great deal, and tells interesting tales. Having spent half a lifetime wandering round Kamchatka and the Kurile Islands, he could speak, probably with more right than Othello, of "antres vast and deserts idle, rough quarries, rocks, and hills whose heads touch heaven".* I am indebted to him for much of the information which proved useful to me for these notes. He had three mates – Mr B., a nephew of the famous astronomer B.,* and two Russian ethnic Swedes, Ivan Martinich and Ivan Veniaminich – all amiable and affable people.

On 8th July, before dinner, the *Baikal* weighed anchor. With us were about 300 soldiers under the command of an officer, and a few prisoners. One prisoner was accompanied by a five-year-old girl, his daughter, who held on to his shackles as he climbed up the ship's ladder. There was, incidentally, one female convict who attracted attention to herself because she was being voluntarily accompanied to the penal colony by her husband.* Besides myself and the officer, there were several other cabin-class passengers, of both sexes, and, incidentally, even one baroness. The reader should not be surprised at such an abundance of educated people here in the wilderness. Along the Amur, and in the Primorskaya Administrative Region, the intelligentsia* forms quite a high percentage among what is, overall, a fairly small population, and the intelligentsia is relatively larger than in any province in European Russia. On the Amur there is a town where generals – both military and civilian* – alone total sixteen. Now, perhaps, there are still more of them.

The day was clear and bright. On deck it was hot, and it was stuffy in the cabins; the temperature of the water was 18°C.

Such weather was at least worthy of the Black Sea. On the right-hand shore the woods were on fire; the solid green mass was throwing up a purple flame; clouds of smoke merged into a long, black, static strip, hanging above the forest... The blaze was gigantic, but all around was peace and calm – it was nobody's business that the forest was perishing. Clearly, the green wealth belongs here to God alone.

After dinner, at about 6 o'clock, we were already at Cape Pronge. Here Asia comes to an end, and the Amur could be said to flow into the Pacific Ocean at this point if Sakhalin Island did not fall across its path. The Liman firth spreads out broadly before one's eyes, and in front a hazy strip is just visible – this is the penal labour island; to the left, losing itself in its own convolutions, the shore disappears in the mist, heading away into the unknown north; it seems as if this place is the end of the world, and there is nowhere any further on to sail to. The soul is overcome by the same feeling that Odysseus must have experienced when he sailed across an unknown sea and had a dim presentiment of meetings with extraordinary creatures. And, indeed, from the right, at the very spot where the river turns into the Liman, where a Gilyak hamlet nestles on a sandbank, some odd creatures were scudding over to us in two boats, wailing in an incomprehensible tongue and waving something. It was hard to understand what they had in their hands, but, when they had sailed a bit closer, I could make out some grey birds.

"They want to sell us some geese they've killed, that's what it is," somebody explained.

We veered to the right. Markers were set out along the whole of our route, indicating the fairway. The captain did not come down from the bridge, and the engineer did not leave the engine room;

45

the *Baikal* was moving more and more gently, as if feeling its way. Great care was needed, for it is not difficult here to run aground on a sandbank. The steamer sits twelve and a half feet deep in the water, and in some places it has to sail through a depth of fourteen feet, and there was even one moment when the keel could be heard scraping over the sand. It was precisely this shallow channel, and the particular picture which the Tatar and Sakhalin coastlines together presented, which were the main reason why, in Europe, Sakhalin was long thought of as a peninsula. In June 1787 the celebrated French navigator, Count La Pérouse, landed on the west coast of Sakhalin, above the forty-eighth line of latitude, and talked here with some natives. Judging by the account he left, he found on the coast not only the Ainos* who live there but also the Gilyaks who had come to trade with them – people with experience of the world, and well-acquainted with both the Sakhalin and Tatar Coasts. Drawing in the sand, they explained to him that the land on which they lived was an island, and that this island was separated from the mainland and from Yesso (Japan) by straits.*

Later, sailing further north along the western coast, he expected to find an outlet for the North Japanese Sea into the Sea of Okhotsk, and thus considerably shorten his way to Kamchatka; but the further up he progressed, the shallower and shallower the strait became. The depth decreased by about one fathom every mile.

He sailed north for as long as the dimensions of his craft would permit, until, reaching a depth of nine fathoms, he came to a halt. The gradual even rise of the bottom, and the fact that in the strait the current was almost imperceptible, led him to the conclusion that he was not in a strait but a bay, and that, consequently, Sakhalin was joined to the mainland by an isthmus. At De-Kastri another consultation took place between him and the Gilyaks. When, on paper, he drew for them an island separated from the mainland, one of them took the pencil from him and, drawing a line across the strait, explained that the Gilyaks sometimes had to haul their boats across this neck of land and that grass even grew on it – so La Pérouse understood. This still more firmly convinced him that Sakhalin was a peninsula.*

Nine years later the Englishman Broughton* came to the Tatar Strait. His vessel was fairly small, sitting no more than nine feet deep in the water, so that he succeeded in going a little further up than La Pérouse. Halting at a depth of two fathoms, he sent his assistant north to take soundings; on his way, the assistant came across deep places among the shoals, but they gradually grew shallower and led him now to the Sakhalin coast, now to the low-lying sandy shore on the other side, and, faced with this, he formed the picture that the two shores merged; it seemed that the bay ended here, and there was no outlet. Thus Broughton, too, came to the same conclusion as La Pérouse.

The celebrated Russian, Kruzenshtern, exploring the coasts of the island in 1805, fell into exactly the same error. He sailed to Sakhalin with his mind already made up, since he was using La Pérouse's map. He went along the east coast, and, rounding the northern capes of Sakhalin, entered the strait itself, bearing north to south, and it seemed as if he was almost on the point of solving the riddle, but the gradual reduction in depth to three and a half fathoms, the specific gravity of the water, and – most of all – his already made-up mind, compelled him, too, to acknowledge the existence of an isthmus he had not seen. But, even so, the worm of doubt still gnawed at him. "It is highly probable," he writes, "that, at one time – even, perhaps, in the not too distant past – Sakhalin was an island." On the way back, his mind was not at rest; when, in China, Broughton's travel notes came to his attention for the first time, he "grew a good deal happier".*

The error was rectified in 1849 by Nevelskoy. The authority of his predecessors, however, was still so great that when he reported his discoveries in St Petersburg, they did not believe him, considered his conduct insolent and liable to punishment, and "came to the decision" to reduce him to the ranks, and who knows where all this would have ended if it had not been for the intercession of the Sovereign himself, who found his conduct valiant, noble and patriotic.*

He was a man of tremendous energy, with a fiery temperament, cultured, self-sacrificing, humane, imbued by an idea to the marrow of his bones, dedicated to it fanatically and morally pure. One of those who knew him writes: "A more honourable man I have not chanced to meet with." On the eastern seaboard and on Sakhalin he created a brilliant career for himself over some five years or so, but he lost his daughter, who died of hunger, and he aged; his wife, too, aged, and her health failed; she was "a very young, pretty and friendly woman", who bore all deprivations heroically.*

So as to have done with the question of the isthmus and the peninsula, it is not superfluous, I think, to give a few more details. In 1710, under commission from the Chinese Emperor, missionaries from Peking drew up a map of Tatary; in compiling it, they made use of Japanese charts, and did so, apparently, because at that time only the Japanese could have known whether the La Pérouse and Tatar Straits were practicable or not. The map was sent to France, and became widely known, since it was included in d'Anville's geographical atlas.*

This map was the basis for a slight misunderstanding, to which Sakhalin owes its name. Off the western coast of Sakhalin, right opposite the mouth of the Amur, the missionaries had made on the map the inscription "Saghalien-Angahata", which in Mongolian means "Cliffs of the Black River". This name probably related to some cliff or cape at the mouth of the Amur, but in France, however, it was understood differently, and taken to stand for the island itself. From this comes the name Sakhalin, retained by Kruzenshtern for the Russian maps as well. Among the Japanese, Sakhalin was called *Karafto* or *Karaftu*,* which means "Chinese Island".

The works of the Japanese either had finished up in Europe too late, when there was no longer any need for them, or else had been subjected to some unhappy amendments. On the missionaries' map, Sakhalin had the appearance of an island, but d'Anville treated it with mistrust, and placed an isthmus between the island and the mainland. The Japanese were the first to begin exploring Sakhalin, starting in 1613, but in Europe this was accorded such little significance that when, subsequently, the Russians and the Japanese were trying to resolve the question of who Sakhalin belonged to, it was the Russians alone who talked and wrote about the "rights of first exploration".*

A new, and, if possible, thorough exploration of the Tatar and Sakhalin coasts is now long overdue. The present charts are unsatisfactory, which is obvious if only from the fact that both military and commercial vessels often run aground on sandbanks and rocks – far more frequently than is mentioned in the newspapers. Owing, in the main, to the poor charts, ships' captains are here very cautious, anxious and nervous. The captain of the *Baikal* does not trust the official chart and follows his own, which he draws up and corrects while sailing.

In order not to run aground, Mr L. had decided not to sail at night, and after sunset we dropped anchor off Cape Dzhaore. On the cape itself, on a hill, stands a little cottage, on which lives the naval officer Mr B., who places the markers along the fairway and is responsible for their supervision; behind the cottage lies the dense, impenetrable taiga. The captain sent some fresh meat over to Mr B.; I took advantage of the opportunity and went ashore in the ship's boat. Instead of a landing stage, there was a pile of large, slippery rocks, which one had to cross by jumping, and up the hill to the hut there led a row of steps made from small logs pressed into the earth almost vertically, so that, ascending, one had to keep a tight hold with one's hands. But how horrible! While I was climbing up the hill and walking to the cottage, I was surrounded by clouds, literally clouds, of mosquitoes, the air was dark with them, and there was no possibility of defending oneself. I reckon that if you were to spend the night here out in the open without previously surrounding yourself with bonfires, then you could die, or at the very least, go out of your mind.

The cottage is divided by the entrance hall into two halves: on the left live the sailors; on the right live the officer and his family. The head of the house was not at home. I found there his wife – a smartly dressed, well-educated woman – and his two daughters, little girls pricked all over by mosquitoes. In the rooms all the walls were covered with greenery from fir trees, cheesecloth was stretched over the windows, the place reeked of smoke, but in spite of everything, the mosquitoes were still there, biting the poor girls. The furnishings of the room were not luxurious, just those of the usual military post, but, in the way the room was decorated, there was a sense of something pleasant and tasteful. On the wall hung some sketches, including a woman's head, outlined and shaded in pencil. It turned out the artist was Mr B.

"Do you like living here?" I asked the lady.

"Yes, fine, the only thing is these mosquitoes."

The fresh meat did not make her any more cheerful; according to her, she and her children had long since grown accustomed to salt beef and had no liking for fresh meat.

"Though we did cook up some trout yesterday," she added.

I was accompanied back to the ship's boat by a morose sailor, who, as if he had already guessed what I felt like asking him, sighed and said: "You don't call in here of your own free will!"

The following day, early in the morning, we set off again in perfectly calm, warm weather. The Tatar coast is mountainous and abounds in sharp, conical peaks. It was lightly covered in a bluish mist; this was the smoke from distant forest fires, which here, it is said, is so dense that it becomes no less dangerous for sailors than fog. If a bird flew in a straight line from the sea across the mountains, it would surely not come across a single dwelling, or a single living soul, for a distance of 500 versts or more. The coast glinted a cheerful green colour in the sun; it could obviously get on perfectly well without mankind. At six o'clock we were in the narrowest part of the strait, between the Pogobi and Lazarev Capes, and we could see both shores very close to; at eight o'clock we passed by Nevelskoy's Cap – as they call a mountain with a knoll on the crest resembling a hat. The morning was bright with brilliant sunshine, and the pleasure I was feeling became still deeper from the proud knowledge that I was seeing these shores.

At two o'clock we entered the De-Kastri Bay. This is the place where craft sailing through the strait can shelter in a gale, and, but for its existence, navigation along Sakhalin's shores, which are uninterruptedly inhospitable, would be unthinkable.* There is even an expression "to make a bolt into De-Kastri". The bay is beautiful and constructed by nature as if to order. It consists of a circular lake, about three versts in diameter, with high banks affording protection against winds and with quite a narrow outlet to the sea. Judging from external appearances, the place is ideal, but, alas! it only appears so; seven months of the year it is covered with ice, has little protection from the east wind and is so shallow that steamers drop anchor two versts from the shore. The outlet to the sea is guarded by three islands, or, more accurately, reefs, which give the bay its distinctive beauty. One of them is called "Oyster Island"; very large, plump oysters may be found on its submerged area.

On the shore are several small houses and a church. This is the Alexandrovsk Post. The director of the post lives there, and his administrative assistant and telegraph operators. One local official who came to dine with us on board ship, a bored and boring gentleman, talked a great deal over dinner, drank a great deal and told us the old anecdote about the geese who stuffed themselves with berries used for making alcoholic cordials, got drunk, were taken for dead, plucked and thrown away, and then, after sleeping off their drink, returned home featherless. During all this, the official swore that the tale of the geese had taken place in De-Kastri, in his own backyard. There is no priest in the church, and, when needed, he travels in from Mariinsk.* Good weather here is very rare, just as it is in Nikolayevsk. I heard that, during the spring of this year, a surveying expedition had worked here, and during the whole of May there had been only three sunny days. "Would you be so good as to survey without sunlight, please gentlemen?"

In the roadstead, we came across the warships *Bobr* and *Tungus*,* and two torpedo boats. A further detail comes to mind; hardly had we dropped anchor than the sky grew black, a thunderstorm flew up, and the water took on a curious bright-green hue. The *Baikal* had before it the task of unloading 4,000 poods of government cargo, and so remained overnight in De-Kastri. The engineer and I passed the time by fishing from the deck, and some very plump, thick-headed miller's thumbs came our way, such as I had never before chanced to catch either in the Black Sea or the Sea of Azov. We also captured some plaice.

The unloading of ships here always takes a tediously long time, and is accompanied by exasperation and loss of blood. However, this is the bitter fate of all our eastern ports. At De-Kastri, the cargo is unloaded into smallish flat-bottomed barges, which can only put in to shore when the tide is rising, and so, when loaded, they often run aground; what sometimes happens, owing to this, is that, for the sake of a hundred or so bags of flour, the ship stands idle the entire stretch of time between the ebbing and flowing of the tides. At Nikolayevsk, the disorder is still greater. There, standing on the deck of the *Baikal*, I saw a steam tug, which was towing a large barge with 200 soldiers on board, lose its tug rope; the barge was carried by the current across the shipping road and was heading straight for the anchor chain of a sailing ship lying not far from us. Our hearts stood still as we waited for the barge, in just one more moment, to be ripped in two by the chain, but, fortunately, some fine people seized the tug rope just in time, and the soldiers escaped with nothing more than a fright.

2

A brief geography. Arrival on northern Sakhalin. A blaze. The land-ing stage. In a settlement. Dinner at Mr L.'s house. Acquaintances. General Kononovich. The arrival of the Governor General. Dinner and illuminations.

SAKHALIN LIES IN THE SEA OF OKHOTSK and forms a barrier against the ocean for almost 1,000 versts of the east coast of Siberia and for the entrance to the mouth of the river Amur. Its elongated form stretches from north to south, and, in the opinion of one writer, its outline is reminiscent of a sterlet.* Its position is defined geographi-cally as: from 45° 54' to 54° 53' in latitude and from 141° 40' to 144° 53' in longitude.

The northern part of the island, which is traversed by a strip of per-manently frozen soil, corresponds in position to the Ryazan Province of European Russia, and the southern part to the Crimea. The island is 900 versts in length; at its widest it extends 125 versts, and at its narrowest twenty-five versts. It is twice the size of Greece and one and a half times the size of Denmark.

The former division of the island into north, central and south is inconvenient in practice, and now it is divided only into north and south. By reason of its climatic and soil conditions, the topmost third of the island is totally unfit for settlement, and therefore does not enter into consideration; the central third is called northern Sakhalin, and the lower third southern Sakhalin; no sharply defined boundary exists between the latter pair. At the present time, in the northern sec-tion, the exiles live along the rivers Duyka and Tym; the Duyka flows into the Tatar Strait, and the Tym into the Sea of Okhotsk; on the map, both rivers converge at their upper reaches. They also live along the west coast, on a small stretch of land above and below the mouth of the Duyka. Administratively, northern Sakhalin is divided into two areas, the Alexandrovsk and Tymovsk Districts.

Having spent the night in De-Kastri, at noon the next day, 10th July, we crossed over the Tatar Strait to the mouth of the Duyka, on which stands the Alexandrovsk Post. On this occasion, too, the weather was calm and clear, such as very rarely occurs here. Over the perfectly smooth sea, whales, cruising in pairs, were sending up fountains into the air, and this beautiful and novel sight kept us entertained the whole way. But my state of mind I acknowledge was melancholy, and the nearer we drew to Sakhalin the worse it became. I was uneasy. The officer accompanying the soldiers, on finding out why I was travelling to Sakhalin, had been very surprised and had begun to assure me that I had no right whatsoever to go near the hard labour or the colony, since I was not on government service. Of course, I knew he was not correct, but all the same, I grew anxious at his words and I was afraid that on Sakhalin too, I would very likely meet exactly the same view.

When we dropped anchor at 9 o'clock, on shore large fires were blazing in five spots in the Sakhalin taiga. Through the darkness and smoke spreading over the sea, I could not see the landing stage or buildings and could make out only the dim lights of the post, two of which were red. This fearful picture, crudely cut out of the darkness, silhouettes of mountains, smoke, flames and sparks from the fires, presented a fantastical appearance. On the left side of the picture were burning monstrous bonfires, above them mountains, and from behind the mountains a crimson glow rising high into the sky from distant conflagrations; it looked as if the whole of Sakhalin were ablaze. To the right, the dark, heavy mass of Cape Jonquière juts into the sea, similar in appearance to the Crimean Ayu-Dag;* on its summit a beacon was shining brightly, while below, in the water, between us and the shore, lay three sharp-pointed reefs – the "Three Brothers". And everything was covered in smoke, as if we were in hell.

A cutter was approaching the ship, towing a barge behind it on a tug rope. It was bringing convicts to unload our steamer. The sound of bad language and Tatar voices could be heard.

"Don't let them onto the ship!" a cry rang out from on board. "Don't let them! During the night they'll strip the whole ship bare!"

"Here in Alexandrovsk, you haven't seen anything yet," the engineer told me, noticing what a distressing impression the shore had produced on me. "You just wait till you see Dooay! The coastline there's completely vertical, with dark ravines and layers of coal – it's so depressing! We used to bring two or three convicts at a time to Dooay on the *Baikal*, and I saw a lot of them in tears at the sight of the coast."

"It's not them who do hard labour here, but us," said the captain with irritation. "Now it's calm here, but you should see it in autumn

– wind, blizzards, cold weather, rain pouring over the deck – you think you've had it every minute!"

I stayed the night on board ship. Early in the morning, about 5 o'clock, I was noisily awoken. "Quickly, quickly! The cutter's going ashore for the last time! We're moving off straight away!" A minute later I was sitting in the cutter, and beside me was a young official with an angry, sleepy face. The cutter began to whistle, and we set off for the shore, towing behind us two barges of convicts. Worn out by the night's work and lack of sleep, the prisoners were sluggish and morose, and were silent the whole time. Their faces were covered with dew. There comes back to me now the recollection of several Caucasians* with sharp features, wearing fur caps pulled down to their eyebrows.

"Allow me to introduce myself," the official said to me. "Collegiate Registrar D."

This was my first Sakhalin acquaintance, a poet, author of a denunciatory poem 'Sakhalino'* which began: "Tell me then, Doctor, whether in vain..." Later on he often came to visit me and stroll with me round Alexandrovsk and its environs, telling me anecdotes, or endlessly reciting poems of his own composition. During the long winter nights, he would write tales of a liberal persuasion, but, whenever the chance presented itself, he loved to make it understood that he was a Collegiate Registrar and occupied a Class 10 post;* when an old peasant woman* came to him one day on business, and called him Mr D., he took umbrage and angrily yelled at her: "To you, I'm not Mr D., I'm Your Honour!" On the way to the shore I asked him a great many questions regarding life on Sakhalin, and about what was what there, but he took a deep, ominous breath and said: "You'll soon see!" The sun was already high in the sky. What on the previous day had been gloomy and dark, and had so daunted the imagination, was now flooded in the brilliance of early morning; the large, unsightly Cape Jonquière with the beacon, the "Three Brothers", the high, steep shores, visible miles off from both sides, the transparent mist on the mountains, and the smoke from the forest fire created, in the brilliance of sun and sea, a not unpleasing picture.

There is no harbour, and the shores are dangerous, impressive testimony of which is given by the Swedish steamship *Atlas*, which was wrecked not long before my arrival and is lying on the shore. Ships usually halt a verst from shore, rarely closer. There is a jetty, but only for cutters and barges. It's big, with a framework several sazhens in length, jutting out into the sea in the form of a letter T; the thick hardwood piles, firmly driven into the seabed, form boxes, which are filled to the top with stones; the deck is made of planks, and rails have been laid for trucks along the whole length of the jetty. On the broad tip of the T lies a pretty little cottage – the jetty office – and in the same spot stands a tall black mast. The structure is solid but does not seem very durable. During a good storm, so they say, a wave sometimes reaches the windows of the cottage, and the spray even goes flying up to the yards of the masts, at which the whole jetty shakes.

Along the shore by the jetty, evidently with nothing to do, fifty or so convicts were wandering about, some in overalls,* others in jackets or short coats of grey cloth. Upon my appearance all fifty took off their caps – very likely no such honour has ever been accorded a single other literary figure to this day. On the shore stood someone's horse, harnessed to a wide unsprung wagonette. The convicts hoisted my luggage onto the carriage, a man with a black beard, wearing a jacket over a shirt which was not tucked into his trousers, sat on the box, and we set off.

"Where does Yer Excellency wish to order me to go?" he asked, turning and raising his cap.

I asked whether there were not any quarters to let anywhere here, even if only of one room.

"To let? There certainly are, Yer Excellency, there certainly are."

I travelled the two versts from the landing stage to the Alexandrovsk Post along an excellent highway. In comparison to the roads in Siberia, this neat, even high road, with its ditches and lamps, seemed pure luxury. Alongside it a rail track had been laid. But the scenery along the way was startling in its barrenness. Up above, on the mountains and hills surrounding the Alexandrovsk Valley, through which flows the Duyka, are charred tree stumps, or, sticking out like the quills of a porcupine, the trunks of larch trees, dried out by wind and forest fires, while below, along the valley, there are tussocks and bitter grasses, remnants of the impassable swamp which was here not long ago. The recent ditch-cutting has laid bare in all its wretchedness the burnt-out marsh soil, with an inch-thick layer of poor black earth. There are no pines, no oaks, no maples – nothing but larches, pathetic, emaciated, as if they have been gnawed away, and serving here not as a decoration for woods and parks, as at home in European Russia, but as an indication of the poor marshy soil and harsh climate.

The Alexandrovsk Post – or, for short, Alexandrovsk* – presents the appearance of a small, pleasant-looking township of the Siberian type, with 3,000 or so inhabitants. It does not contain a single construction of stone; everything is made of wood – in the main, larch – the church, the houses, the pavements. Here is the residency of the Governor of the Island, the centre of Sakhalin civilization. The prison is situated close to the main street, but in external appearance it differs little from a military barracks, and because of this Alexandrovsk does not bear at all that gloomy jail-like character that I had expected.

The driver conveyed me to Alexandrovsk Slobodka, a suburb of the post, to peasant-in-exile* P. I was shown some living quarters; there was a small yard, paved in the Siberian fashion, with logs around an awning, and, in the house, five clean and spacious rooms with a kitchen, but not a stick of furniture. The landlady, a young peasant woman, fetched a table, then, about five minutes later, a stool.

"We let these rooms for twenty-two roubles with firewood, and fifteen* without," she said.

And when, an hour later, she brought in the samovar, she said with a sigh: "So you've come to this godforsaken hole!"

She had come here as a young girl with her mother, accompanying her father, who had been sentenced to hard labour and who had still not completed his sentence to that day; now she was married to a peasant-in-exile, a morose old man whom I had caught a fleeting glimpse of when I was crossing the yard; he was sick with something or other, and lay in the yard groaning under the awning.

"They must be doing the reaping now back at home in the Tambov Province," said the landlady, "and my eyes should never have seen the sight of this place at all."

And, really, there was nothing interesting to look at; through the window could be seen beds of cabbage seedlings, around them unsightly ditches, and, in the distance, gaunt, withered larch trees loomed indistinctly. Moaning and clutching his sides, the landlord came in and began complaining to me of the bad harvests, cold climate and poor soil. He had successfully served his hard labour and compulsory settlement, now owned two homes, horses and cows, and employed many workmen, while he himself did nothing, was married to a young woman, and, most importantly, had for a long time already had the right to settle back on the mainland – and he still complained.

At noon I went for a walk round the hamlet. At the edge of this hamlet stood a smart little house with a front garden and with a brass plaque on the door, while, beside the house, in the same yard, was a tiny shop. I went in to buy something to eat. The "Trading Centre" and "Trade Commissions Depot" – as this modest little shop is entitled in the printed and handwritten price lists I still have in my possession – belonged to settled exile L., a former officer in the Guards, who had been sentenced some eleven years previously by the St Petersburg Regional Court for murder. He had now served his sentence and had gone into the trading business; he also carried out various official errands, travelling both over parts of the countryside where roads had already been built, and also where there were no roads as yet; he received for this the salary of a senior overseer.* His wife was a freewoman, born of the nobility and serving as a doctor's assistant* in the prison hospital. In the shop they sold stars for epaulettes, Turkish delight, cross-cut saws and sickles, and "ladies summer hats, the very latest in fashion, the best styles, from four roubles fifty copecks to twelve roubles each". While I was chatting with the shop assistant, the owner himself entered the store, wearing a silk jacket and flowery tie. We introduced ourselves.

"Would you be so good as to dine with me?" he proposed.

I accepted, and we went into the house. It was fitted out comfortably – bentwood furniture, flowers, an American ariston,* and a rocking chair on which Mr L. rocks back and forth after dinner. Besides the lady of the house, in the dining room were four further guests, all officials. One of them, an old man with no moustache but with grey sideburns and a face like the dramatist Ibsen, turned out to be a junior doctor at the local fever hospital, and another one, also an old man, had been commended by the Field Officer of the Orenburg Cossack Force. From the very first words he spoke, this officer produced upon me the impression of being a very fine man and great patriot. He was mild, good- natured and reasonable; but when the conversation turned to politics he grew beside himself with anger, and with genuine feeling would begin talking about the might of Russia, and with contempt about the Germans and English, although he had never seen a German or Englishman in his entire life. The story was told about him that, when he had been sailing to Sakhalin, he had stopped off at Singapore to buy his wife a silk shawl, and they had offered to change his Russian money into dollars; he had then apparently taken offence, and said: "What, you think I'm going to change our Russian Christian money into some kind of heathen nigger money!" And the shawl remained unbought.

For dinner we were served soup, chicken and ice cream. There was wine as well.

"When roughly does the last snow fall here?" I asked.

"In May," replied L.

"No, it doesn't – it's in June," said the doctor resembling Ibsen.

"I know a settled exile," said L., "whose Californian wheat has given a twenty-two-fold yield."

"That's not true. This Sakhalin of yours yields nothing. It's damnable land."

"But, if you please," said one of the officials, "in '82 the wheat gave a forty-fold yield. I know this perfectly well…"

"Don't believe them," the doctor told me, "they're trying to pull the wool over your eyes."

Over dinner the following legend was related: when the Russians had occupied the island and had then begun to treat the Gilyaks badly, a Gilyak shaman had cursed Sakhalin and had prophesied that not a bit of good would ever come from it.

"And so it's turned out," sighed the doctor.

After dinner Mr L. played on the ariston. The doctor invited me to move over to his house, and so, that same evening, I set up home on the main street of the post, in one of the closest houses to the government offices. From that evening began my initiation into the secrets of Sakhalin life. The doctor told me that, not long before my arrival, during a medical inspection of cattle on the jetty, he had had a serious misunderstanding with the Governor of the Island, and in the end – so he said – the Governor had actually threatened him with his cane; the following day he was dismissed at his own request – which he had not submitted. The doctor showed me a whole pile of documents which he had written, as he put it, in defence of truth and from love of humankind. There were copies of submissions, complaints, reports and denunciations.*

"And the General isn't pleased that you've come to stay with me either," said the doctor, winking significantly.

The following day I paid a visit to the Governor of the Island, V.O. Kononovich. In spite of his being tired and very busy, he received me extremely courteously and talked to me for about an hour. He is educated, well read, and, in addition, possesses great practical experience, for before his appointment to Sakhalin he had supervised the penal settlement at Kara* for eighteen years; he speaks and writes pleasingly, and creates the impression of a man sincere and imbued with humane aspirations. I cannot forget the pleasure afforded by my conversations with him, nor how agreeably I was struck, the first time, by his constantly expressed aversion to corporal punishment. George Kennan, in his well-known book, speaks of him with great enthusiasm.

Learning that I intended to spend several months on Sakhalin, the General warned me that it was gloomy and tedious living there. "Everybody goes running off from this place," he said, "the convicts, the settled exiles and the officials. I haven't yet felt the urge to get away, but I'm already feeling fatigued from the mental labour, such a lot of which is required here, owing, in the main, to the way everything is so scattered about."

He promised me full cooperation but asked me to wait for a while, as they were preparing on the island to receive the Governor General of the Amur River Territory* and everybody was busy.

"But I'm glad you're staying with our enemy," he said, bidding me farewell. "You'll get to know our bad sides."

Until the arrival of the Governor General I lived in Alexandrovsk in the doctor's quarters. Life was not entirely commonplace. Whenever I woke up in the morning, I was reminded of where I was by the most diverse sounds. Through the open windows could be heard the rhythmical clanking of prisoners in irons passing down the street; opposite our quarters, in the army barracks, soldier instrumentalists were rehearsing their marches for the visit of the Governor General, and, as the flute was playing a part from one piece, the trombone a part from another and the bassoon a part from a third, the result was indescribable chaos; while, in our own rooms, there was the tireless whistling of canaries, and my host the doctor walking from corner to corner, leafing through law books on the move, and thinking aloud:

"If, on the basis of statute such-and-such, I submit a petition to that place, then..." etc.

Or else he, together with his son, would sit down and write out some sort of libel. If you went into the street, it was hot out there. People were actually complaining of drought, and the officers were walking about in tunics – which does not happen every summer. There is considerably more activity on the streets than in the chief towns of our European Russian districts, and this was easily explainable by the preparations for the visit of the governor of the province, but the main reason is the predominance in the local population of those of working age, who spend the greater part of their time out of doors. Besides this, grouped together in a small area there is a prison of more than a thousand men and a barracks of five hundred. They were hurriedly building a bridge across the Duyka, raising arches, cleaning, painting, sweeping, marching. Along the streets raced troikas and pairs with little bells attached – this was the horses being trained for the Governor General. Such was the haste, they were even working on their days off.

Along the street heading for the police department came a group of Gilyaks, the local aborigines, angrily barked at by the mild-tempered Sakhalin mongrels, which for some reason bark only at the Gilyaks. And here is another group – convicts in irons, some wearing caps, some without, their chains clinking, dragging a heavy barrowful of sand, while behind kids cling onto the barrow, and alongside plod guards with sweaty red faces, rifles on shoulders. After emptying the sand onto the little square in front of the General's house, the men in irons return the same way, and the ring of shackles is heard continuously. A convict wearing overalls with the ace of diamonds on them is going from yard to yard selling whortleberries. Whenever you go down the street, those sitting down stand, and everybody you meet raises his cap.

Penal convicts and settled exiles, with few exceptions, walk freely about the streets, without irons or guards, and at every step you meet them both in crowds and on their own. They are found in people's yards and houses, for they are coachmen, watchmen, cooks – both male and female – and "nannies" for the children. At first, before one gets used to it, such closeness is disturbing and creates bewilderment.

You pass some place under construction, and there are convicts with axes, saws and hammers. Well, you think, they'll threaten you and – bang! Or else you go to visit an acquaintance, and, finding him out, sit down to write him a note, while all the time behind you his convict servant stands and waits with a knife which he has just been using to peel potatoes in the kitchen. Or else, early in the morning, about four o'clock, you'll be woken up by a sort of rustling – and you will see a convict, scarcely breathing, stealing on tiptoe towards the bed. What is he doing? Why? "Clean yer boots, Yer Excellency?"

I quickly got accustomed to all this and took it for granted. Everybody takes it for granted, even the women and children. The local ladies are perfectly at ease when they let their children out for walks with male convicts on life hard-labour sentences acting as "nannies".

One correspondent wrote that, at first, he was scared of almost every bush, and on meeting a prisoner in the road or along pathways, he would feel for the revolver underneath his coat, but then he grew easier in mind, coming to the conclusion that "the penal settlement is, in general, a flock of sheep – cowardly, lazy, half-starving and ingratiating". To be able to think that Russian prisoners do not kill or rob somebody they meet out of cowardice or laziness, one must either have a very poor opinion of mankind in general or else not know mankind at all.

The Governor General of the Amur River Territory, Baron A.N. Korf,* arrived at Sakhalin on 19th July on the warship *Bobr*. On the square between the Governor of the Island's house and the church, he was met by a guard of honour, officials, and a crowd of settled exiles and convicts. They played the same music I have just mentioned. A fine-looking old man, a former hard-labour convict who had grown rich on Sakhalin, with the surname Potyomkin,* presented him with some bread and salt* on a silver dish of local manufacture. On the square stood my host the doctor, in a black tailcoat and peaked cap, holding a petition. I was seeing a Sakhalin crowd for the first time, and its sad peculiarity did not escape my notice: it consisted of men and women of working age, and there were old men and young children, but a complete absence of youths. It seemed as if the age group of thirteen to twenty did not exist at all on Sakhalin. And I could not help asking myself – doesn't this mean that the young people, on growing up, leave the island at the first opportunity?*

The day after his arrival, the Governor General proceeded to inspect the prisons and settlements. Everywhere the settled exiles, who had awaited him with great impatience, submitted petitions to him or made verbal requests. Either each spoke for himself, or else one spoke for a whole settlement, and, as the art of oratory flourishes on Sakhalin, the whole business just could not go off without speech-making; at Derbinskoye, settled exile Maslov several times in the course of his speech called the authorities "the Most All-Mercifullest Government".* Unfortunately, far from everybody addressing themselves to Baron Korf requested what was really needful; here, just as in European Russia in similar cases, the vexing dimness of the peasant was in evidence: they asked not for schools, or justice, or wages, but for various trifles – one for a government allowance, somebody else for the adoption of a child – in a word, they made submissions which could have been dealt with by the local authorities. Baron Korf treated their requests with the most complete attention and kindness; deeply moved by their distressing situation, he made promises and raised hopes of a better life.* At Arkovo, when the Deputy Prison Governor reported that "Everything was proceeding excellently* in Arkovo Settlement", the Baron pointed out to him the winter crops and the shoots of the spring corn and said: "Everything is excellent, except for the one fact that, in Arkovo, there's no grain." In Alexandrovsk Prison, as a result of his visit, the prisoners were served fresh meat and even venison; he went round all the cells, accepted petitions and ordered many convicts in irons to be unshackled.

On 22nd July, after Thanksgiving Service and a parade (it was a Church High Holiday), an overseer came racing up to announce that the Governor General wished to see me. I set off immediately. Baron Korf received me very kindly, and we talked for about half an hour. Our conversation took place in the presence of General Kononovich. Among other things, the question was put to me as to whether I had any kind of official authorization. I replied that I had not.

"Haven't you at least any authorization from some sort of learned society or newspaper?" the Baron asked.

I did have a press card in my pocket, but since I did not have in mind the idea of publishing anything on Sakhalin in the newspapers, and not wishing to mislead the people who were treating me evidently with complete confidence, I answered that I had not.

"I grant you permission to visit wherever and whomever you wish," said the Baron. "We've nothing to hide. You'll inspect everything, you'll be given a free pass to all the prisons and settlements, you'll be able to make use of the documents necessary for your work – in a word, the doors will be open to you everywhere. There is just one thing I cannot allow you: you may have no contact of any sort with the political prisoners, as I have absolutely no authority to permit this."

Dismissing me, the Baron said: "We'll talk some more tomorrow. Come along with some paper."

That same day I attended a ceremonial dinner in the Governor's quarters. There I became acquainted with almost the whole of the Sakhalin administration. At dinner, music was played and speeches were delivered. Baron Korf, in answer to a toast to his health, made a short speech, of which the following words now recur to me: "On Sakhalin, I am convinced that the 'unfortunates' live better than anywhere else in Russia, or even Europe. In this respect, much still remains before you to be done, for the path of good is never-ending." He had been to Sakhalin five years previously, and now found considerable progress, progress surpassing all expectations. His words of praise could not be reconciled in one's consciousness with such phenomena as starvation, the prostitution endemic among the exiled women and brutal corporal punishments, but the listeners had to believe him; in comparison to what had gone on five years before, the present time seemed almost like the beginning of the Golden Age.

In the evening there were illuminations. Around the street, all lit up by lampions and Bengal flares, groups of soldiers, settled exiles and convicts wandered till late evening. The prison was opened up. The river Duyka had always been wretched and muddy, with bare banks, but had now been decorated on both sides with multicoloured lanterns and Bengal flares reflected on its surface, and on this occasion it was beautiful, and even majestic, but comical as well, like a cook's daughter who has been made to try on the clothes of a society lady. In the General's garden there was music and singing. They even fired a cannon – which blew up. And yet, despite such gaiety, the streets were dismal. No songs, no accordions, not a single drunk; people roamed about like ghosts, and were as silent as ghosts. A penal colony illuminated by Bengal flares is still a penal colony, and music, when heard from a distance by a man who will never ever return to his homeland, brings on only a deadly yearning.

When I presented myself to the Governor General with some paper, he explained to me his views on the penal labour and the penal colony on Sakhalin, and suggested that I took down everything he said, which of course I did willingly. He suggested that I entitle everything I wrote "Description of the life of poor unfortunates". From our previous conversation, and from what I noted down at his dictation, I came away with the conviction that here was a generous and noble-minded man, but that he was not nearly so familiar with the "life of poor unfortunates"* as he thought he was. Here are a few lines from his account: "No one is deprived of the hope of achieving full rights; there are no lifelong punishments. A life sentence is limited to twenty years. Penal labour is not onerous. Forced labour gives the worker no personal benefit – it's in this that the onerousness lies and not in the physical strain. There are no chains, no sentries, and no shaven heads."*

The days remained fine, with clear skies and limpid air, like our autumn days in European Russia. The evenings were superb; I recall the flaming west, the dark-blue sea and the perfectly white moon rising from behind the mountains. On such evenings I liked to go for drives along the valley between the post and the village of Novo-Mikhailovka; the roadway here was smooth and even, and alongside it ran a rail track for trucks, and a telegraph wire. The further from Alexandrovsk, the narrower the valley became; the murk would deepen, and the gigantic burdocks begin to seem like tropical plants, while the dark hills loomed in on all sides. Away in the distance were fires where people were burning coal, and there would be a light from a forest fire. The moon would rise. Suddenly, a fantastical picture: trundling to meet us along the rails, on a small platform, a convict leaning on a pole, dressed all in white. I would be scared stiff.

"Isn't it time to go back?" I'd ask the driver.

The convict driver would swing the horses round, then, looking back at the mountains and fires, say: "It's miserable here, Your Excellency. It's better back home in Russia."

3

A census. Contents of the statistical cards. What I asked and how I was answered. A cabin and its tenants. The exiles' opinions of the census.

IN ORDER AS FAR AS POSSIBLE TO VISIT all the inhabited spots, and to become somewhat closer acquainted with the life of the majority of the exiles, I resorted to a device which, in my position, seemed the only way. I carried out a census. In the settlements that I visited I went round all the cabins and noted down the heads of the households, members of their families, tenants and workmen. To make my work easier, and to cut down on time, I was very obligingly offered assistants, but as my main aim in conducting the census was not its results but the impressions received during the making of it, I used somebody else's help only on rare occasions. This piece of work, carried out in three months by one person, cannot in actual fact be called a census; its results could not be said to be distinguished for their accuracy and completeness, but, in the absence of more reliable data, either in the literature on the subject, or in the Sakhalin offices, my figures will perhaps be of some use.

I used for the census small cards produced for me in the printing shop of the police department. The method of conducting the census was as follows: first of all, on the first line of each card I noted down the name of the post or settlement. On the second line I put the number of the house according to the official housing list. Then, on the third line, the status of the entrant – convict, settled exile, peasant-in-exile, free. I entered those who were free only in the cases where they took a direct part in an exile's household – for instance, forming a couple, whether legally married or not, and where in general they belonged to the exile's family or else resided in his cabin as a workman, lodger or suchlike. One's status is accorded great significance in Sakhalin usage. A penal labour convict is undoubtedly embarrassed by his status; when asked what it is, he replies: "Workman." If, before his conviction, he was a soldier, he will undoubtedly add to this: "From the soldiery, Your Excellency." Having completed his sentence, or as he himself puts it, "served out his time", he becomes a settled exile. This status is not considered inferior, as the word "settled exile" differs but little from "free settler",* not to mention the rights bound up with this title. When asked what he is, a settled exile will usually reply: "Freeman." After ten, or, under favourable circumstances stipulated in the *Statutes on Exiles*, after six years, a settled exile receives the status of "peasant-in-exile". When questioned as to his title, a peasant-in-exile answers, not without dignity, as if he cannot be considered in the same light as the rest, and is distinguished from them by something special: "I am a peasant." But without adding "in exile". I did not ask the exiles about their former calling, as there was enough information on this point in the local government offices. Except for the soldiers, they themselves, neither the urban middle classes, nor the traders, nor the clergy, would enlarge on the subject of their lost rank,* as if it were already forgotten, and they denoted their former condition by the short word – freedom. If somebody strikes up a conversation about his past, he will usually begin: "When I used to live in freedom…"

On the fourth line went the first name, patronymic and surname. As regards names I can only recall that I do not think I took down correctly a single female Tatar name. It's hard to get any sense out of a Tatar family with a lot of little girls, where the father and mother hardly understand Russian, and you have to make entries by guess-work. The Tatar names are written down incorrectly in the official records as well.

It would happen that a Russian peasant, a member of the Orthodox Church, on being asked what his name was, would reply in all serious-ness, "Karl." People such as him were vagabonds who had exchanged names on the road with some German.* Two such, I recall, were noted down by me: Karl Langer and Karl Karlov. There was a convict called Napoleon. There was a female convict named Praskovya-alias-Mariya. As regards surnames, by some strange chance there were many on Sakhalin by the names of Bogdanov and Bespalov. There were many curious surnames, e.g. Limper, Stomach, Godless, Bone-idle. The Tatar surnames, so I was told, notwithstanding the deprivation of all rights of status, still maintain on Sakhalin prefixes and particles signifying high ranks and titles. To what extent this is true I do not know, but I noted down a fair number of Khans, Sultans and Ogels. Among the vagabonds the most commonly used given name was Ivan, and surname "Don't-remember".* Here are a few of the tramps' nicknames: Mustapha Don't-remember, Vasily Countryless, Frantz Don't-remember, Ivan Don't-remember-twenty-years-old, Yakov

Without-a-nickname, Vagabond-Ivan Thirty-five-years-old,* Man-whose-title-no-one-knows.

On this line, too, I noted how the entrant was related to the head of the household – wife, son, female cohabitant, workman, tenant, son of tenant and so forth. Entering the children, I distinguished between legitimate and illegitimate, own and adopted. It is relevant to mention that you often come across foster-children on Sakhalin, and I had to write down not only the foster-children but the foster-fathers as well. Many of those living in the peasants' cabins are joint-holders or half-sharers with the landlord. In both the northern districts, there are two or even three owners per plot, and this is the situation in more than half of the households; a settled exile gets started on a plot of land, builds a house and starts up a home, and two or three years later they send him a co-owner, or else they give one plot straight off to two settled exiles. This arises from the unwillingness and inability of the local administration to look for new spots for settlement. Thus it happens that a convict who has served out his hard-labour sentence asks permission to settle in a post or settlement where there are no farm plots left, and he has to settle against his will in a household that is already set up. The number of co-holders increases especially after the announcement of imperial decrees,* when the administration is forced to find places straight away for several hundred people.

On the fifth line I marked their age. The women who were already over forty remembered theirs only with difficulty, and had to think for a bit before answering. Armenians from the Yerevan Region had no idea of their age at all. One of them answered me: "Might be thirty, but it could be fifty by now." In cases such as these, the age had to be determined approximately from their appearance and then verified from the relevant prison documents. Youths of fifteen and slightly older would usually reduce their ages. Some women would already be married, or have been engaged for ages in prostitution, yet still said they were thirteen or fourteen. The point about this is that children and juveniles in the poorest families receive a food ration from the state, which is issued only up to the age of fifteen, and here a simple calculation induces young people and their parents to tell lies.

The sixth line concerned their religion.

The seventh: where were they born? They gave me their answers to this question without the slightest difficulty, and only the vagabonds responded with some prison equivocation or "Don't remember". Spinster-Natalya-Don't-Remember, when I asked her what province she was from, replied: "A little bit from all of them." People from the same part of the country noticeably stick together, and, if they escape, it's also together. A person from Tula prefers to become co-owner of a household with somebody else from Tula, and a native of Baku with somebody from the same district. Apparently, there exist associations of compatriots. When I happened to ask about somebody who was absent, his fellow-countrymen would give the most detailed information about him.

Line eight – what year did they come to Sakhalin? Rare was the Sakhaliner who would reply straight away, without any effort.

The year of arrival on Sakhalin was a year of dreadful misfortune, and yet they either did not know or did not remember it. You would ask a convict woman what year she was brought to Sakhalin, and she would reply dully, without thinking about it: "Who knows? Must have been '83." Her husband, or the man she was living with, would cut in: "What the hell are you talking about? You came in '85!" "Yeh, could've been '85," she'd agree with a sigh. We would start to work it out and the man would turn out to be right. The men are not so slow as the women, but they too do not reply straight away, but only after thinking and talking about it for a bit.

"What year did they make you come out here?" I would ask some settled exile.

"I came in the same wave as Gladky," he would say, glancing uncertainly at his acquaintances.

Gladky was among the first wave, and this "first wave" – that is, the first visit of a ship of the Voluntary Fleet* – came to Sakhalin in 1879. I would write all this down.

Or such answers would come up as: "I spent six years doing hard labour, and this is my third year as a settled exile... Add that all up..." "So that means this is your ninth year on Sakhalin?" "Nothing like it. Before I came to Sakhalin I spent two years as well in the clearing prison." And so forth. Or there would be the reply: "I came the year Derbin was murdered." Or "Mitzul died then." For me it was especially important to receive correct answers from those who had come in the '60s and '70s; I did not want to miss a single one of them – in which, in all probability, I did not succeed. How many remained of those who had come here twenty to twenty-five years previously? A question, it might be said, with a fateful importance for the colonization of Sakhalin.*

On the ninth line I noted their major occupation and trade.

On the tenth – their literacy. Usually the question is put in the form "Do you know how to read and write?" However, the way I asked it was "Do you know how to read?", and this saved me from incorrect responses in many cases, for peasants who cannot write and can make out only the printed word say they can neither write nor read. There are also those who pretend to be ignoramuses out of modesty. "Why ask us? What reading and writing would we know?" – and only when the question was repeated would they say: "I could make out printed words at one time, but now I seem to have forgotten how to. We're a dim lot – in a word – we're plain country yokels." Those who can neither read nor write also describe themselves as having poor eyesight, or as being blind.*

The eleventh line concerned their family status – married, widower or bachelor. If married, where? – at home, or on Sakhalin? The words "married, widower, bachelor" still do not define family status on Sakhalin; here married people are very often doomed to a lonely celibate life, for their spouses live at home and will not grant them a divorce, while those who are unmarried or whose spouses have died live *en famille* and have half a dozen children per couple; because of this, for those who did not nominally lead bachelor lives but in actual fact did so, although they appeared in the official records as married, I did not consider it out of place to put down "single". Nowhere else in the whole of Russia are such unlegalized alliances so widely and openly diffused, and nowhere are they apparent in such a distinctive form as on Sakhalin.

Unlegalized – or, as it is called here, "free" – cohabitation meets with opposition neither from the administration nor from the clergy, but, on the contrary, is sanctioned and encouraged. There are settlements where you will not come across a single legalized cohabitation. "Free" couples make up households on the same basis as legalized ones, produce children for the colony, and so there is no reason to invent special rules for their registration.

Finally, line twelve: did they receive a state allowance? From the answer to this question I wanted to ascertain the proportion of the population who were not able to manage without material support from the state, or in other words, who provided for the upkeep of the colony – the colony itself, or the state? All convicts, settled exiles in the first year after completion of their penal-labour sentences, those in the almshouses,* and the children of the poorest families, compulsorily receive state allowances, whether in the form of food rations, clothing or money. Besides these officially recognized pensioners, I also noted down as living at the expense of the state those exiles who received from it a salary for various services, for example teachers, clerks, overseers and the like. But the answer I received was incomplete. Besides the usual rations, food subsidies and salaries, there is also practised on a large scale the issue of the sort of allowances that I found impossible to note on my cards, for example grants on getting married, the purchase of corn from the settled exiles at a deliberately high price and, most of all, the issue of seed, grain, cattle and suchlike on credit. Some settled exiles owe the state several hundred roubles, and will never repay them, but I reluctantly had to note them down as not receiving an allowance.

I marked each female's card lengthwise with a red pencil, finding this more convenient than having a special heading for denoting sex. I entered only those members of a family who were on hand: if I was told that the eldest son had gone to Vladivostok to look for work, and the second was a workman in the settlement of Rykovo, the first I did not enter at all, and the second I entered on a card at the place where he was living.

I went from cabin to cabin alone; sometimes I was accompanied by some convict or settled exile who had taken on the role of guide out of boredom. Occasionally, a short way behind, or at some distance there followed, like a shadow, an overseer with a revolver; he had been sent in case I needed some sort of elucidation on anything.* Whenever I put any kind of question to him, his brow would momentarily become covered with sweat, and he would reply: "I'm sorry to say I wouldn't know, Your Excellency!" Usually my companion, barefoot and capless, with my inkpot in his hands, would run ahead, noisily open the door, and manage to whisper something to the householder in the passageway – very likely, his suppositions as to my census. I would enter the cabin. On Sakhalin you come across cabins of every type, depending on who built them – a Siberian, Ukrainian or Chukhon* – but most frequently it consists of a small framework of six arshins or so, with two or three windows, without any kind of external decoration, roofed with straw, tree-bark and, on rare occasions, boards. There was not usually a yard, and round about not a single tree. One rarely comes across a shed or bathhouse in the usual Siberian style. If there are any dogs, they are sluggish, not malicious, and as I have already said, they bark only at the Gilyaks, very likely because they wear boots made of dog-skin. And for some reason these gentle and inoffensive dogs are on leashes. If there is a pig it has a halter round its neck. A cockerel is also bound by its foot.

"Why are your dog and cockerel tied up?" I would ask a householder.

"Here on Sakhalin everything's chained up," he'd crack in reply. "It's that sort of place."

In the hut there is one room, with a Russian stove. The floor is of wood, and there are a table, two or three stools, a bench and bedding either on a bedstead or made up directly onto the floor. Or else there would be no furniture at all, and only in the middle of the room would a featherbed be lying, on which, apparently, somebody had been sleeping; while on the window sill would be a bowl with leftovers of food. From the furnishings, it is not a cabin or a room, but rather a cell for solitary confinement. Where there are women and children, then, despite everything else, it is like a home and gives the appearance of normal peasant country life; but even then you will feel the lack of something important; there is no grandfather or grandmother, no old icons or furniture handed down through the family: consequently, the household lacks a past, lacks tradition. There is no special lit-up icon corner, or else it is very feeble and dim, without icon-lamps and without adornments; there are no everyday customs of behaviour; the layout has an incidental character, and it's as if the family is living, not in its own home, but in quarters, or as if they have only just arrived and still have not had time to settle in; there are no cats, no crickets are heard on winter evenings... and the main thing, it is not their home country.

The pictures of life I met with usually did not speak to me of the domesticity, cosiness and durability of the households. Most frequently I encountered in the cabin the landlord himself, a lonely, bored old bachelor who seemed to have frozen stiff with the enforced idleness and tedium; he would be wearing freeman's clothing, but from force of habit his overcoat would be slung over his shoulders in the manner of a prisoner, and, if he had not long come out of prison, then on the table would be lying a peakless cap. The stove would not be stoked, and the only crockery would be a pot and a bottle stopped with a piece of paper. He himself would speak about his life and his home derisively, with cold contempt; he would say that he had already tried everything, but nothing had come of it; he remained alone; and he had thrown up his hands at it all and given everything up in disgust. While you talked with him, a crowd of neighbours would gather and start a conversation on various topics – the administration, the climate, women... Out of boredom they were all ready to talk and listen unceasingly. It would happen that, as well as the head of the house, you would find in the cabin a whole crowd of lodgers and workmen as well; sitting on the doorstep, a penal-convict lodger, with a leather thong fastened around his hair, sewing shoes; he would reek of leather and cobbler's wax; in the passageway would be lying his children, in rags, and in the same spot, in a dark and cramped corner, his wife, who had accompanied him here voluntarily, making whortleberry dumplings on a small table; this was a family that had not long arrived from European Russia. Further on, inside the cabin itself, would be five or so men; one called himself a lodger, another a workman and another a cohabitant; one would be standing by the stove, cheeks puffed out, eyes wide open, soldering something; another, apparently a joker, had assumed an artificially silly expression, was muttering something, and the rest were laughing up their sleeves. And on the bed sat the Whore of Babylon, the mistress of the house, Lukeriya Don't-remember herself, dishevelled, emaciated and freckled; she tried to answer my questions as drolly as possible, jigging her feet up and down all the while. Her eyes were ugly and dull, and I could judge from her wasted, apathetic face how much she had experienced of prisons, convicts' halting places en route across Siberia, and illness, in her still short lifespan. This Lukeriya set the general tone of life in the cabin, and the presence of a daft, dissolute vagabond was reflected in the whole set-up of the place. Here you could not even begin to talk about the possibility of a household established in earnest. Similarly I would often find in a cabin a whole company who had been playing cards before my arrival – on their faces embarrassment, boredom and anticipation – when would I be going so that they could get down to their cards again? Or you would go into a cabin and there would not be a stick of furniture, the stove would be bare, and on the floor in a row along the walls would be sitting some Circassians,* some in caps, some with bare, short-cropped and obviously very wiry heads of hair, gazing at me unblinkingly. If I found only the female cohabitant at home, she would usually be lying in bed; she would answer my questions yawning and stretching, and as I was leaving, she would lie back down again.

The exile population regarded me as an official personage, and my census as one of those formal procedures which here are so common and usually lead to nothing. However, the circumstance that I was not a local Sakhalin official did arouse some curiosity in the exiles. They would ask me:

"What's this you're taking us all down for?"

And here arose various suppositions: some said that probably the higher authorities wanted to distribute an allowance among the exiles, others said it must be that they had really decided at last to resettle everybody on the mainland – and here the belief does persist stubbornly and strongly that sooner or later the labour colony and the settled exiles will be transferred to the mainland – while still others, feigning scepticism, said they didn't expect any good any longer, as God Himself had abandoned them – this was to arouse a retort on my part. And from the passageway or the stove, as if jeering at all these hopes and conjectures, a voice would carry, in which could be heard weariness, boredom and annoyance at the disturbance:

"Write, write, bloody write, that's all they do all the time, God 'elp us!"

I did not have to starve or generally suffer any sort of deprivation during my travels through Sakhalin. I had read that the agriculturalist Mitzul, while exploring the island, had endured extreme want and had even been forced to eat his dog. But since then circumstances have changed considerably. The present-day agriculturalist travels on excellent roads, and even in the poorest settlements there are overseers' quarters, or the so-called "posts" where it is possible to find warm accommodation, a samovar and a bed. Explorers, when they set out into the interior of the island, into the taiga, take with them American tinned foods, red wine, plates, forks, pillows and simply everything they can manage to load on the shoulders of the convicts, who substitute here for beasts of burden. It does happen even today that people feed on rotting pieces of wood with salt, and even eat each other, but this has nothing to do with the tourists or the officials.

In the following chapters I shall describe the posts and villages and on the way acquaint the reader with the various types of hard labour, and the prisons, so far as I myself managed to become acquainted with them in a short space of time. On Sakhalin the hard labour is diverse in the highest degree; it is not specialized into gold or coal, but embraces the whole field of Sakhalin life, and is scattered throughout all the inhabited places on the island. Grubbing up of woodland, building works, draining of swamps, fishing, haymaking, loading ships – all these are forms of hard labour which are of necessity so fused with the life of the colony that to detach them and talk about them as if about something existing independently on the island is only really possible in a conventional and routine glance at the subject, which first and foremost seeks out the mines and manufactories in any labour colony.

I shall begin with the Alexandrovsk Valley, and with the settlements lying on the river Duyka. This valley was the first chosen for settlement on northern Sakhalin, not because it had been explored better than the rest or because it answered the aims of colonization, but merely accidentally, for the reason that it was the closest to Dooay, where penal servitude had been first established.

4

The river Duyka. The Alexandrovsk Valley. Alexandrovsk hamlet. Vagabond Good-looking. Alexandrovsk Post. The post's past. The yurts. The Paris of Sakhalin.

WHEN THE RIVER DUYKA, or, as it is otherwise known, the Alexandrovka, was explored in 1881 by the zoologist Polyakov, it stretched at its lower reaches to a width of up to ten sazhens, there were immense piles of trees on its banks that had collapsed into the water and been washed up, in many places its low-lying areas were covered by old woodlands of silver fir, larch, alder and willow, and all around lay impassable marshy swampland. These days, this river has the look of a long, narrow pool. In width, and with its completely bare banks and feeble current, it is reminiscent of the Moscow Canal.*

One has to read the description of the Alexandrovsk Valley in Polyakov's book, then glance at it now, even if only in passing, to understand what a large amount of heavy, truly "hard" labour has already been expended on the cultivation of this spot. "From the heights of the neighbouring mountains," writes Polyakov, "the Alexandrovsk Valley appears stifling, dense and covered with woodland – an enormous coniferous forest spreads over considerable areas along the bottom of it." He describes the bogs, the impassable quagmires, the repulsive soil and the woods where "as well as enormous standing trees, the ground is not infrequently strewn with huge half-rotten trunks that have fallen through age or from a storm; between the trunks, at the roots of the trees, there frequently jut out hummocks covered with moss, while holes and ruts lie next to them." Nowadays, in place of taiga, quagmires and ruts, there stands a whole town, roads have been laid out, one sees the greenery of meadows, rye fields and vegetable gardens, and already complaints may be heard about the lack of forestry. If to this mass of toil and struggle, when they used to labour in the swamp up to the waist in water – if to this are added the frosts, the cold rains, yearning for their homeland, the insults, the birch rod – then appalling pictures arise in the imagination. Not for nothing would a certain Sakhalin official, a kindly man, every time we travelled anywhere together, recite to me Nekrasov's poem *The Railway*.*

Right by the mouth of the Duyka, a small river flows into it from the right, called the Malaya (Little) Alexandrovka, on both sides of which lies the Alexandrovsk settlement, or the hamlet, as it is called. I have mentioned it already. It forms a suburb of the post, and has already merged with it, but, since it differs from it in several aspects and exists independently of it, it should be discussed separately. It is one of the oldest settlements. Colonization began here soon after hard labour had been established in Dooay. The decision to select this of all places and not somewhere else was prompted, as Mitzul wrote, by the luxuriant water meadows, good building-wood, a navigable river and fertile land. "To all appearances," writes this fanatic, who had seen in Sakhalin the Promised Land, "it was impossible to have any doubts about the successful outcome of colonization, but of the eight men exiled to Sakhalin with this objective in 1862, only four settled on the river Duyka." But what could these four do? They worked the land with pick and spade, sowed the ground in spring, not, as it turned out, with spring but with winter grain, and finished up by beginning to make requests to be allowed back to the mainland. In 1869, on the spot where the hamlet now stands, a farm was established. Here it was intended to resolve a very important question – could the successful application of compulsory exile labour to agriculture be relied on? Over the course of three years, the labour convicts rooted up the soil, built roads and engaged in crop-farming, but on completion of their terms had no desire to remain here and applied to the Governor General with a request for transfer to the mainland, as tilling the land yielded nothing and there were no earnings to be made from it. Their request was granted. But what was called a "farm" continues to exist. In the course of time, the Duyka penal convicts became settled exiles, and from European Russia came convicts with their families who had to be settled on a plot of land; a directive was issued that Sakhalin should be considered as land fertile and suitable for an agricultural colony, and where life would not take naturally it rose little by little in an artificial manner, by enforcement, at the cost of large expenditures of money and human strength. In 1879, Dr Avgustinovich found that there were already twenty-eight houses in the hamlet.*

At the present time there are fifteen households in the hamlet. The homes here are roofed with boards, they are spacious, sometimes having several rooms, with fine outbuildings, and with vegetable gardens in the farmsteads. There is one bathhouse to every two houses.

In the Inventory of Landholdings a total of 39.75 desyatins* is shown as being under crop cultivation, and 24.5 desyatins are used for haymaking. There are twenty-three horses, and a total of forty-seven cattle, sheep and goats.

In the composition of its households, the hamlet may be considered an aristocratic settlement; there is one court counsellor, married to the daughter of a settled exile, one freeman who came to the island with his convict mother, seven peasants-in-exile, four settled exiles and only two labour convicts.

Of the twenty-two families living here, only four are unlegalized. And in its age ranges the hamlet comes near to a normal village – those of working age do not predominate so sharply as in other settlements;

here there are children, youths and men of over sixty-five and even seventy-five years of age.

The question arises – how is one to explain such a comparatively prosperous state of the hamlet, even though the local householders themselves hold the view that "you can't make a living here by raising crops"? In answer one can point to several factors which under normal conditions would be conducive to an orderly, settled and prosperous life. For instance, the large percentage of established residents who came to Sakhalin before 1880 and have succeeded in getting used to the local land and coming to feel at home on it. Also very important is the fact that nineteen men came to Sakhalin with their wives, and almost all those who settled on plots of land already had families. There are, comparatively, sufficient women, so that only nine men are "single", of whom not one lives as a bachelor. In general, the hamlet has had good fortune, and, as one of the favourable circumstances, one could also point out the high percentage of literates: twenty-six men and eleven women.

Leaving aside the Court Counsellor, who occupies the post of land surveyor on Sakhalin, why do the "free" householders and peasants-in-exile not leave for the mainland if they have the right to do so? They are kept on Sakhalin, it is said, by their success in farming, but this certainly does not apply to them all, for the hamlet's haymaking and arable land is not at the disposal of all the householders but only a few of them. Only eight have meadows and cattle, and only twelve till the land, so that in spite of everything, farming here is not on such a serious scale as to be able to provide an explanation for the exceptionally good economic position. There are no external sources of income of any sort, nobody works at a trade, and L., the former officer, alone keeps a small shop. Official data which would account for why the inhabitants of the hamlet are wealthy do not exist either, and so for a solution to the riddle one must reluctantly turn to the sole source of information in this case – ill-repute. In former times, the clandestine trade in alcohol was carried on in the hamlet on the very widest scale. The import and sale of alcohol is strictly forbidden on Sakhalin, and this created a special form of contraband. They brought in alcohol in tin boxes in the shape of sugarloaves, in samovars, and virtually carried it in their belts, but, most frequently, simply in barrels and the usual vessels, as the minor authorities had been bought off, and the higher-ups turned a blind eye. In the hamlet a bottle of bad vodka would sell for six or even ten roubles. All the prisons in northern Sakhalin obtained vodka from this very place. Even the hardened drinkers among the administration were not averse to it; I know of one such who, during a heavy drinking binge, would give away to the prisoners literally his last possessions for a bottle of spirits.

Nowadays, the talk has become a good deal more muted in the hamlet as regards alcohol. Now the rumours are of a different business – the trade in prisoners' old "rags and bones". For next to nothing they buy up overalls, shirts, sheepskin jackets, and get rid of all these rags for sale in Nikolayevsk on the mainland. Then on top of this are clandestine loan funds. In a conversation once, Baron Korf referred to the Alexandrovsk Post as the Paris of Sakhalin. In this noisy and hungry Paris, all the people who are easily carried away, or given to drink and gambling, or weak-willed, whenever they want to go on the binge or buy stolen goods, or sell their soul to the Devil, head straight for the hamlet.

In the stretch between the seashore and the post, there is one more sight worth seeing, besides the sleeper track and the hamlet which I have just described. This is the ferry across the Duyka. In the water, instead of a boat or a raft, there is a large, perfectly square box. The captain of this craft, unique of its kind, was a penal convict called Good-looking Can't-remember-my-relations. He was already seventy-one years old. He had a hunchback, his shoulder blades stuck out, one of his ribs was broken; he had a thumb missing on one hand, and all over his body were the weals he had received at some time in the past from the lash and having to run the gauntlet.* He had almost no grey hairs; his hair seemed to have faded, and he had clear, light-blue eyes which gazed out at you cheerfully and good-naturedly. He was barefoot and dressed in rags, was very lively and talkative, and loved to have a laugh. In 1855 he had deserted his military service "out of stupidity", had gone on the tramp, and had adopted the surname of "Can't-remember-my-relations". He was arrested and sent to Zabaikalye,* as he put it, to "live among the Cossacks".

"I used to think then," he told me, "that in Siberia people lived under the ground. So off I went double quick down the road away out of Tyumen* and tried to escape. I got as far as Kamyshlov, was arrested there and sentenced, Yer Excellency, to twenty years' hard labour and ninety lashes. They sent me to Kara,* where they gave me those lashes good and hard, and from there sent me here to Sakhalin, to Korsakovsk; I ran away from Korsakovsk with a mate, but only reached Dooay; there I took ill and couldn't go no further; but my mate reached Blagoveshchensk.* I'm already serving my second term, and in all I've lived here on Sakhalin for twenty-two years. And all what I done wrong was that I ran off from serving in the army."

"Why do you hide your real name now? Where's the need for that?"

"At one time I did tell an official my real name."

"And what happened?"

"Nothing at all. The official said: 'While we're making inquiries, you'll snuff it, so live with what you call yerself now. It don't make no odds to you.' That's right enough and no mistake... after all, I 'aven't got much longer to live now. But all the same, Good Lord Above, I'd like my relatives to find out where I am."

"And what do they call you?"

"My name here's Vasily Ignatiev, Your Excellency."

"And your real name?"

Good-looking thought for a bit, and then said:

"Nikita Trofimov, from the Skopinsky District, Ryazan Province."

I started to head across the river in the box. Good-looking leant continually on the bottom with his long pole, all the while straining his emaciated, bony body. It was heavy work.

"But it must be hard for you?"

"Not at all, Your Excellency. There's nobody breathing down my neck, I can take it gently."

He told me that in all his twenty-two years on Sakhalin he had never once been flogged and not once had to spend time in the punishment cell.*

"Because – they send me to saw wood – off I go and do it, they shove this here stick into my hands – I take it, they order me to stoke the stoves in the offices – I stoke 'em. You've got to obey. There's nothing to grumble to the Lord about, life's good, Glory be to thee, O Lord!"*

In summer he lived in a yurt by the ferry. In the yurt there was his ragged clothing, a round loaf of bread, a rifle and a stifling, sour smell. When asked what he needed a rifle for, he said to keep off thieves and to shoot wild snipe – and laughed. The gun was rotten and was there simply for the sake of appearances. In winter he became a wood-gatherer and lived in the office on the jetty. Once I saw him, with his trousers rolled up high, displaying his sinewy violet-coloured legs, dragging along a net with a Chinese man; in the net there was a silvery flashing of humpbacked salmon, every one as large as one of our Russian zanders.* I called across to him and he joyfully responded.

The Alexandrovsk Post was founded in 1881. One official, who had already been living on Sakhalin for fifteen years, told me that when he had arrived at the Alexandrovsk Post for the first time, he had almost drowned in a swamp. Hieromonk Irakly,* who had lived in the Alexandrovsk Post till 1886, recounted that in the beginning there had been only three houses there, and the prison had been situated in the small barracks where the musicians now live. There were tree stumps in the streets, and, in the place where a brickworks now stands, in 1882 they used to hunt sable. Father Irakly was offered the guard hut for a church, but he declined it, pointing out how cramped it was. In fine weather he would hold services on the square, while in bad weather he would only hold a shortened form of mass, either in the barracks or wherever was suitable.

"You're holding a service," he told me, "while just beside you there's the clink of shackles, a racket going on, and heat from the cooking cauldron. Here it's 'Glory to the Holy Consubstantial Trinity' – while next to you it's 'I'll batter you!'... etc."

The present growth of Alexandrovsk began with the declaration of Sakhalin's new status,* when many new official jobs were established, including one of general. A fresh spot had to be found for the new people and their offices, since at Dooay – where, up till then, the management of the penal colony had been situated – it was gloomy and cramped. In open country six versts from Dooay there already stood the hamlet, there was already a prison by the Duyka, and so, little by little, a "residency" began to develop; accommodation for the officials and their offices, a church, storehouses, shops and the like. And there also sprang up what Sakhalin could not do without, namely, a town, the Sakhalin Paris, where the urban public, which could only breathe town air and could only enjoy town pursuits, could find a society, conditions and a crust of bread answering to their needs.

The clearance of the land, the drainage of the soil and the various building works were all carried out by the convicts. Up till 1888, before the present prison was constructed, they lived in dugout yurts. These consisted of frames dug into the ground to a depth of two to two-and-a-half arshins, with sloping roofs of earth. The windows, small and narrow, were at ground level, and it was dark, especially in winter, when the yurts were covered over with snow. From the rising of the water in the soil, sometimes up to the floor, and from the constant stagnation of moisture in the earthen roofs and in the crumbling, rotting walls, the damp in the hollows was appalling. The people slept in sheepskin jackets. Both the earth all around and the water-well were continually contaminated by human excrement and all sorts of garbage, as there were absolutely no latrines or rubbish-pits. The convicts lived in the yurts with their wives and children.

At the present time Alexandrovsk occupies on the map an area of about two square versts, but since it is already merged with the hamlet, and one of its streets is approaching the settlement of Korsakovsk, so that in the very near future it will merge with it, too, its measurements are in actual fact more impressive. It contains several wide, straight streets, which, however, are not called streets, but, from old memories, "quarters". On Sakhalin they have a fashion of giving names to streets in honour of officials while they are still alive; these streets are not only entitled with surnames but even with first names and patronymics.* But, by some fortunate chance, Alexandrovsk has not as yet immortalized a single official, and the streets have preserved to this day the titles of the types of small settlements from which they originated: Brickmakers' Quarter, Clerks' Quarter, Soldiers' Quarter, Peysikovskaya. The origin of all these names is easy enough to understand, apart from Peysikovskaya. One story is that it was given this title by the convicts in honour of the ringlets of a Jew who used to trade here when the place where this street is now situated was still covered by the taiga; but, according to another version, a female settled exile called Peysikova used to live here.

There are wooden pavements along the streets, everywhere is cleanliness and order, and even in the outlying streets, where the poor are pressed close together, there are no puddles or heaps of rubbish. The heart of the post consists of its official quarter: the church, the Governor of the Island's house, his offices, a post-and-telegraph bureau, a police department with a printing works, the District Governor's house, a shop for the colonization fund,* military barracks, prison hospital, military sickbay, a mosque with a minaret which was just under construction, government houses in which the officials were lodged, and the hard-labour prison with its multiplicity of storehouses and workshops. For the most part the houses are new, built in the European style, with iron roofs, and often painted on the outside. There is no lime or good stone on Sakhalin, and so there are no stone buildings.

If one does not count the officials' and officers' quarters, and the Soldiers' Quarter where the soldiers married to free-women live – a mobile element changing every year here – then, in all, there are 298 households in Alexandrovsk. There are 1,499 inhabitants, of whom 923 are male and 576 female. If one adds to this the free population, the military and those convicts who spend the night in the prison and do not form part of any household, then a figure is arrived at of around 3,000. In comparison with the hamlet, there are very few peasants-in-exile, but, on the contrary, convicts make up a third of the entire total of householders. The *Statutes on Exiles* permit living outside prison, and consequently starting up a home, only to those convicts in the "reformee" category, but this law is constantly circumvented in view of its impracticability; in the cabins there live not only reformees but also probationers, long-term, and even life, convicts. Without even mentioning the clerks, draughtsmen and craftsmen, for whom, by the nature of their occupation, it would be inconvenient to live in the prison, there are on Sakhalin quite a large number of convicts with a family, who are husbands and fathers, whom it would be impracticable to keep in the prisons apart from their dependants; this would bring a great deal of confusion into the life of the colony. Either the families would have to be kept in the prisons as well, or they would have to be provided with lodgings and food at government expense, or they would even have to be kept back in their home region the entire time that the father of the family was serving out his hard labour.

Penal convicts under the category of "probationer" live in cabins and often, therefore, undergo less rigorous punishment than the "reformees". Here the concept of uniformity of punishment is sharply violated, but this disorder finds justification for itself in the conditions under which the life of the colony took shape; and, anyway, it is a confusion that could easily be eliminated: all that needs to be done is to transfer the remaining prisoners from the prison to live in cabins. But, in talking about convicts with families, it is impossible to reconcile oneself to another example of disorder – to the improvidence of the administration in allowing dozens of families to settle where there is no land fit for setting up a farm, or for cultivation, or for haymaking, while at the same time, in settlements in other districts provided in this respect with more favourable conditions, households are only run by bachelors, and homes do not get started up at all because of the lack of women. In southern Sakhalin, where there is a good harvest every year, there are settlements without a single woman, while, in the Sakhalin Paris, the number of free-women who have come voluntarily from European Russia with their husbands alone reaches 158.

In Alexandrovsk there is no longer any land left fit for farming. Formerly, when there was plenty of room, farm plots were issued of 100 or 200, and even 500, square sazhens, but now they are settling people on twelve sazhens, and even on nine or eight. I counted 161 households, huddling together with their buildings and vegetable gardens, on plots of farmland none of which had an area of more than twenty square sazhens. In the main, the natural conditions of the Alexandrovsk Valley are to blame for this: it is impossible to move back towards the sea, because the soil there is no good, the post is bounded at the edges by mountains, while in front it can now grow only in one direction, upriver along the Duyka, along the so-called Korsakovsk Road; here the farms are stretched out in a single row and are squashed tightly against each other.

According to information in the official Inventory of Landholdings, only thirty-six holders make use of arable land, and only nine of haymaking land. The size of the plots of arable land fluctuates between 300 sazhens and one desyatin.

Almost everybody plants potatoes. Only sixteen have horses, and thirty-eight have cows, and of these the cattle are owned by peasants-in-exile and settled exiles occupied not in crop-raising but in trade. From these few figures one has to conclude that the households in Alexandrovsk do not subsist on agriculture. What a weak power of attraction the local land possesses is clear from the fact that there are almost no householders here of long standing. Of those who settled on a plot in 1881, not a single one is left, from 1882 there remain only six, from 1883 four, from 1884 thirteen, and from 1885 sixty-eight. This means that the remaining 207 settled after 1885. Judging by the extremely small numbers of peasants-in-exile – there are only nineteen – the conclusion must be drawn that each holder sits on his plot of land just as long as is necessary to receive his full peasant's rights, that is, the right to throw up his holding and cross over to the mainland.

To this day, the means by which the population of Alexandrovsk exists remain a question that for me is still not quite resolved. Let us assume that the householders and their wives and children live, like the Irish, on nothing but potatoes, and that there are enough to last them the whole year round; but what do those 241 settled exiles and 358 penal-labour convicts of both sexes eat who live in the cabins in the roles of male and female cohabitants, tenants and workpeople? It's true that almost half the population receives a government allowance in the form of prisoners' rations and children's food subsidies.* There are wages as well. More than 100 people are occupied in the government workshops and offices. On my cards are noted quite a large number of craftsmen whom it would be impossible to do without in a town – joiners, upholsterers, jewellers, clock- and watchmakers and menders, tailors and the like. In Alexandrovsk they pay highly for articles of wood or metal, and it is not acceptable to give less than a rouble as a tip. But are prisoners' rations and small, extremely wretched earnings sufficient to carry on town life day in, day out? With the craftsmen, supply exceeds demand beyond all comparison, and the unskilled, for instance the carpenters, work for ten copecks a day to buy their bite to eat. The population here makes ends meet with difficulty, but, nevertheless, every day they drink tea, smoke Turkish tobacco,* go about in free-persons' clothing and pay for their lodgings. They buy homes from peasants-in-exile leaving for the mainland and build new ones. Around them, stalls do a roaring trade, and various kulaks who have emerged from the convict environment pile up tens of thousands of roubles.

There is a great deal here that is unclear, and I came to a full stop at the suppositions that the majority of the people settling in

Alexandrovsk are those who have come here from European Russia with money, and that illegal means are a great help to the population. Buying up prisoners' clothes and selling them in big bundles in Nikolayevsk, exploitation of the natives and newly arrived prisoners, the clandestine trade in spirits, loaning out money at very high interest rates, gambling for large sums at card games – the men engage in all these activities. And the women, both exiles and the free ones who had come voluntarily with their husbands, earn their living by depravity. When one free-woman was asked at an investigation how she came by her money, she replied: "I earned it with my body."

In all there are 332 families; of these 185 have been legalized, and the other 147 are free associations. The comparatively large numbers of exiles in families is explained not by any sort of features the households might possess which are conducive to domesticity and family life, but by chance circumstances: the thoughtlessness of the local administration in settling families on plots in Alexandrovsk, and not in a more suitable spot, and the relative ease with which, thanks to his closeness to the authorities and the prison, a local settled exile may obtain a woman.* If life has arisen and flows, not according to the usual natural order, but artificially, and if its growth depends not so much on natural and economic conditions as on the theories and arbitrary whims of private individuals, then it becomes substantially and unavoidably subject to such chance events, which, for this artificial life, end up as if they were laws.

5

The Alexandrovsk Hard-labour Prison. The common cell rooms. The fetter block. Golden Hand. The latrines. The maidan. *Convict works in Alexandrovsk. The staff. The workshops.*

I VISITED THE ALEXANDROVSK HARD-LABOUR PRISON soon after my arrival.* It consists of a large four-cornered yard, enclosed by six wooden barrack-type huts separated by a fence. The gates are always open, and a sentry walks around nearby. The yard is swept clean: no stones, rubbish, refuse or puddles of slops can be seen anywhere. This exemplary neatness creates a good impression.

The doors to all the blocks were wide open. I entered one of these doorways. There was a small corridor, with doors to right and left leading into communal cells. Above the doorways were black boards with inscriptions in white: "Barrack no. so and so. Cubic content of air thus and thus. Accommodates such and such a number of convicts." Right at the end of the corridor there was another door, which led into a small box-room, where two political prisoners, wearing unbuttoned waistcoats, in shoes but no socks, were hastily crumpling up a mattress stuffed with straw; on the window sill there was a booklet and a piece of black bread. The District Governor, who was accompanying me, explained that these two prisoners were permitted to live outside the prison, but, not wishing to stand out from the rest of the convicts, they did not avail themselves of this privilege.

"Silence! Rise!" rang out the shout of the overseer.

We entered the cell. The room was spacious in appearance, with a capacity of around 200 cubic sazhens. The windows were open, and there was a good deal of light. The walls were unpainted, splintered and dark, with oakum in between the logs; the only things that were white were the tiled Dutch stoves.* The floor was of wood, unpainted and completely bare. Right the way down the middle of the cell stretched one continuous bed-board, with a slope on both sides, so that the convicts could sleep in two rows, with the heads of one row turned up towards the heads of the other. The convicts' places are not numbered, and are in no way separated from each other, and, owing to this, it's possible to place between seventy and 170 people on the boards. There is no bedding whatsoever. Either they sleep on the hard surface, or else underneath themselves they lay torn sacks, their clothing and all sorts of rotting rubbish, extremely off-putting in appearance. On the boards lie caps, boots, bits of bread, empty milk bottles stopped up with a bit of paper or old rag, and shoe-trees; under the boards are chests, filthy sacks, bundles, tools and various bits of old clothing. Around the boards is sauntering a well-fed cat. On the walls hang clothes, pots and tools, and on the shelves are teapots, loaves, and boxes of something or other.

On Sakhalin free-persons do not take off their caps on entering the barrack rooms. This act of courtesy is obligatory only for exiles. Wearing our caps we walked around the bed-boards, and the prisoners stood, arms held along the seams of their trousers, gazing at us in silence. We gazed at them in silence, too, and it was exactly as if we had come to buy them. We went on into other cell rooms, where there was precisely the same dreadful destitution, which it is as impossible to conceal under rags as it is a fly under a magnifying glass, that same herd-like life, "nihilistic" in the fullest sense of the word, which denies personal property, solitude, comforts and sound sleep.

The prisoners living in the Alexandrovsk prison enjoy relative freedom; they do not wear irons, can leave the prison during the day and go where they like without an escort, and do not have to observe conformity of dress but wear what is suitable according to the weather and the work. Those under investigation, or who have recently been returned from an attempted escape, or who have by some chance temporarily been placed under arrest, stay under lock and key in a separate building called the "fetter block". The most widely used threat on Sakhalin is "I'll put you in the fetter block". The entrance to this fearful place is guarded by overseers, one of whom reported to us that "All was entirely satisfactory in the fetter block."

There was the clatter of a padlock, huge and clumsy, looking as if it had been bought from an antique dealer, and we entered a smallish cell room, which on this occasion housed some twenty people who had recently been brought back from attempted escapes. Their clothing was ripped, they were unwashed, wearing irons, and had on hideous boots, laced around with rags and bits of string; the hair on one side of their heads was dishevelled, while on the other, which had been shaven clean, it was already beginning to sprout again. They were all emaciated, as if they had just moulted, but they looked cheerful. There was no bedding – they slept on the bare bed-boards. In the corner stood a pot;* each could fulfil his natural requirements in no other way than in the presence of twenty witnesses. One requested to be released and promised that he really would not run away any more; another asked to have his fetters taken off and complained that he was being given too little bread.

There are cells with two or three people in each, and there are cells containing one person. In these, one comes across a lot of interesting people.

Among those in solitary confinement, one's attention was especially attracted to the notorious Sofiya Blyuvshtein, alias "Golden Hand", sentenced to three years' hard labour for attempting to escape from

Siberia. She was small and slim, already going grey, with the flabby face of an old woman. Her hands were shackled and on her plank-bed there was only a grey sheepskin jacket, serving her both as warm clothing and as bedding. She would walk from one corner of her cell to the other, and it seemed as if she were sniffing the air the whole time, like a mouse in a trap, and the expression of her face was like a mouse as well. Looking at her you would not believe that not so very long ago she was so extremely good-looking that she would bewitch her jailers, as, for example, at Smolensk, where a warder helped her escape and ran away with her himself. Like all women sent here, she lived first of all outside the prison, in "free quarters". She attempted to escape, disguising herself for the attempt as a soldier, but was arrested. While she was at large, several offences were committed in the Alexandrovsk Post; the shopkeeper Nikitin was murdered and 56,000 roubles* were stolen from the Jewish settled exile Yurkovsky. Golden Hand was suspected of all the crimes and was accused of being either the guilty party or an accomplice. The local investigating authorities have entangled her and themselves in such a thick web of all kinds of absurdities and errors that it is positively impossible to understand anything of her case at all. Be that as it may, the 56,000 still has not been found, and is serving in the meantime as the subject of the most diverse and fantastic tales.

I shall speak of the kitchens, where during my stay they prepared dinner for 900 people, of the provisions, and about how the prisoners eat, in a separate chapter. But here I shall say a few words about the latrines. As is well known, the vast majority of Russian people hold this convenience in utter contempt. In our country villages, there are absolutely no latrines at all. In monasteries, at fairs, at inns and at every type of business place where sanitary inspection still has not been established, they are revolting in the extreme. The Russian carries his contempt for the latrine with him to Siberia as well. From the history of penal servitude it may be seen that latrines everywhere in prisons have been the source of suffocating stenches and fevers, and that the prison population and administration have easily reconciled themselves to this. At Kara Prison in 1872, so Mr Vlasov writes in his article, there was no latrine at all attached to one of the barrack huts, and the criminals were led out into the square for their natural requirements, and this was not done when any single person required to go out, but when several people had gathered, and I could quote a hundred such examples. In the Alexandrovsk Prison the latrine – the usual cesspool – is located in the prison yard in a separate outhouse between the barracks. It is obvious that in building the place, they tried before all else to make it work out as cheap as possible, but all the same, compared to the past, it marks significant progress. At least it does not arouse revulsion. The building is cold and is ventilated with wooden chimneys. "Stands" have been constructed by the walls; but it is impossible to stand on them, one can only sit, and it is this that chiefly spares the latrine from filth and dampness. There is indeed a bad smell, but it is insignificant and masked by the usual chemicals, such as tar and carbolic acid. The latrine is open not only during the day but at night-time as well, and this simple measure has made pots unnecessary; the last ones remain now only in the fetter block.

By the prison there is a well, and from it may be judged the height of the soil water. In consequence of the particular structure of the local soil, the soil water, even in the graveyard, which is set on a mountain by the sea, is so high that, in dry weather, I saw graves half-filled with water. The soil round the prison and throughout the whole post is drained by ditches, but they are not deep enough, and the prison is totally unprotected against damp.

In fine warm weather, which does not often occur here, the prison is excellently ventilated; the doors and windows are opened wide, and the prisoners spend the greater part of the day outside, in the yard, or a long way off from the prison. But in winter, and in bad weather, that is, on average, almost ten months of the year, one has to make do with small casement ventilation windows and the stoves. The larch and spruce wood from which the prison and its foundations are made provides excellent natural ventilation, but is unreliable; as a consequence of the great humidity of the atmosphere of Sakhalin, and owing to the abundance of rain, and also because of the evaporation coming from inside, water accumulates in the pores of the wood, and in winter, freezes. The prison is poorly ventilated, while at the same time not a great deal of air is available for each of its inhabitants. In my journal I have noted: "Barrack no. 9. Cubic content of air 187 sazhens. Houses 65 convicts." This was in summertime, when only half of all the convicts spent the night in the prison. But here are figures from the Medical Report for 1888: "The cubic capacity of prisoner accommodation in the Alexandrovsk Prison is 970 sazhens; the number of convicts is at the very highest 1,950, at the very least 1,623, and the average over the year is 1,785; 740 are lodged for the night; to every one man there is 1.31 sazhens of air."

The number of convicts accommodated in the prison is at its lowest in the summer months, when they are dispatched out into the district on road- and fieldworks, and at its highest in autumn, when they return from the works and the ship of the Voluntary Fleet brings a new party of 400 to 500 men, who live in the Alexandrovsk Prison till they are dispersed among the rest of the prisons. This means that the smallest amount of air is available for each prisoner at precisely the time when the ventilation is at its least effective.

When the prisoner returns from the works – carried out, most of them, in bad weather – to lodge for the night in the prison, his clothes are soaking and his boots are filthy; there is nowhere to get them dry; he hangs part of his clothing by the bed-board, and, without allowing the remainder to dry off, he lays them underneath himself in place of a mattress. His coat gives off a smell of sheepskin, and his footwear reeks of leather and tar. His underwear, saturated with secretions from his skin, not dried out, not washed for ages, and jumbled up with old sacks and decaying old cast-off clothes, the cloths with which he wraps his feet, with their suffocating stench of sweat, he himself, not having had a bath for ages, covered with lice, smoking cheap tobacco, and constantly suffering from meteorism;* his bread, meat and salt-fish, which he often cures himself right here in the prison, the crumbs, the bits, the little bones, the remains of the cabbage soup in the caul-dron and the bugs which he squashes with his fingers right there on the bed-board – all these things make the air in the barracks fetid, dank and sour; it becomes so highly saturated with water vapour that, during frosts, the windows towards morning are covered from inside with a layer of ice, and it grows dark in the cabin; hydrogen sulphide, ammoniac and all sorts of other chemical combinations mix with the water vapour in the air, producing what, in the words of an overseer, "makes yer 'ead spin and yer guts turn over".

Under the system of communal cells, the maintenance of cleanli-ness in the prison is impossible, and hygiene will never emerge here from that narrow framework to which it is confined by the Sakhalin climate and the working conditions of the convict, and, whatever good intentions may inspire the administration, it will be powerless and will never be able to avoid censure. Either it must be recognized that communal cell rooms are now obsolete, and dwellings of another type substituted for them – which is already partly being done, since many convicts live not in the prisons but in cabins – or else one has to become reconciled to the filthiness as an inescapable and necessary evil, and leave the measuring of bad air in units of cubic sazhens to those who see in hygiene nothing but an empty formality.

It is, I think, hardly possible to say anything in favour of the system of communal cells. The people living in a communal cell room in a prison are not a society, a trade guild* imposing responsibilities on their members, but a gang, freeing them from all responsibilities towards the place, their neighbours and property. To order a convict not to bring in mud and manure on his boots, not to spit on the floor, and not to spread bugs, is a sheer impossibility. If there is a stench in the cell room, or if life is made impossible by pilfering, or if they sing filthy songs, then everybody is guilty – that is, nobody. I asked one convict, a former Honourable Citizen: "Why are you so untidy?" He answered me: "Because my tidiness would be useless here." And indeed, what value can personal cleanliness have for a convict, if tomorrow they are going to bring in a new party and put side by side with him a neighbour from whom insects are crawling in all directions, and who emits a suffocating odour?

The communal cell does not allow the criminal the solitude necessary to him, even if simply for prayer, reflection and that deepening of his personality which is considered necessary for him by all supporters of reformatory aims. A violent card game taking place with the permission of bribed overseers, foul language, laughter, idle chatter, the banging of doors and, in the fetter block, the clink of irons, all carrying on the whole night, make it difficult for the tired labourer to sleep, and get on his nerves, which, of course, does not fail to have a harmful effect on his nutrition and his mental health. This cattle-like, disordered life, with its coarse amusements, and with the inevitable influence of the bad on the good, acts, as has already largely been recognized, upon the morals of the criminal in the most corrupting manner. Little by little it weans him away from domesticity, that is, from the very quality which must be protected in a penal colony above all else, since on leaving the prison he will become an independent member of the colony, where, from the very first day, on the basis of law, and under the threat of punishment, he will be required to be a good householder and a fine family man.

In the communal cells it is necessary to endure and justify such ugly phenomena as slandering others and informing to the authorities, the prisoners taking the law into their own hands, and kulakism.* This last finds expression in the so-called *maidans** which have crossed over here from Siberia. A prisoner who possesses and loves money, and who has been sentenced to hard labour because of it – a kulak, a miser and swindler – leases from his fellow convicts, for a fixed sum, the right of monopoly trading in the barrack, and, if the place is busy and crowded, then the rental payment forthcoming to the prisoners could even reach several hundred roubles a year.

The *maidanshchik*, that is, the proprietor of the *maidan*, is officially designated as the "slopper-out", since he takes on himself the duty of carrying the chamber pots – if there are any – out of the cell, and of being responsible for the cleanliness of the cabin. On his place on the plank-bed there usually stands a chest about one and a half arshins in size, green or brown, while around it and beneath it are laid out pieces of sugar, small white bread rolls* about the size of a fist, cigarettes, bottles of milk and some other goods as well, wrapped up in bits of paper and grubby rags.*

Under the humble rolls and lumps of sugar is concealed an evil which spreads its influence far beyond the limits of the prison. The *maidan* is a gaming house, a little Monte Carlo, which develops in the prisoner an infectious passion for *Stoss** and other games of chance. Around the *maidan* and the cards there inevitably huddles, always willing to oblige, a cruel and implacable usury. The prison moneylenders take ten per cent a day, and even for one hour; any pawned object not redeemed during the day becomes the property of the moneylender. When they have served their labour sentences, the *maidanshchiki* and the money-lenders go out into the colony, where they do not relinquish their lucrative occupation, and so it is nothing to be wondered at that on Sakhalin there are settlers from whom it is possible to steal 56,000 roubles.

In the summer of 1890, during my stay on Sakhalin, there were reckoned to be more than 2,000 penal convicts on the books of the Alexandrovsk Prison, but only about 900 lived in the prison. Here are some figures taken at random: at the beginning of summer, on 3rd May 1890, the number of people who ate from the prison cauldron and slept the night in the prison was 1,279; at the end of summer, on 29th September, it was 675. As regards the type of convict labour carried out in Alexandrovsk itself, the chief ones to be observed here are construction and all kinds of maintenance work: the erection of new buildings, and the repair of old ones, the upkeep, in the usual municipal manner, of streets, squares and the like. The carpenter's work is considered to be the most onerous. A prisoner who was formerly a carpenter in his own home district suffers real hard labour here, and in this respect he is a great deal more unfortunate than a house-painter or roofer. The whole burden of the work is not in the construction itself, but in the fact that the convict has to drag every log to be used from the forest, and at the present time tree-felling is taking place eight versts from the post. In the summer, the men strapped to a log of half an arshin or more in width, and several sazhens in length, create a painful impression: they have an expression of martyrdom on their faces, especially if, as I often observed, they were natives of the Caucasus. It is said that, in winter, they get frostbite in their feet, and often they actually freeze to death before they have managed to drag the log to the post. The work of carpentry here presents a difficult problem for the administration as well, since on Sakhalin there are in general few people capable of systematic hard work, and a shortage of labourers is a common phenomenon, although the convicts can be numbered in thousands. General Kononovich told me that undertaking new buildings here, or having a new house built for oneself, was very difficult – there were no people available; if there were enough carpenters, there was nobody to drag the logs; if they sent people out for logs, then there were not enough carpenters. The duties of the wood-gatherers also belong here to the category of difficult labour; every day they chop up firewood, stack it, and, towards morning, when everybody else is still asleep, fuel the stoves. To judge how strenuous a certain type of labour is, and how difficult, one should take into consideration not only the amount of muscular strength expended, but also the conditions of the place and the peculiarities of the particular character of the work caused by these conditions. The heavy frosts in winter and the dampness throughout the whole year on Sakhalin place the unskilled labourer in a situation which would sometimes be scarcely bearable, a situation which, doing the same sort of work, for instance, the commonplace chopping-up of firewood, he would not experience in European Russia. The law limits convict labour to "fixed conditions", approximating it to ordinary agricultural and factory work;* it permits various alleviations to convicts in the "reformee" category, but practice, of necessity, does not always conform to this, precisely on account of local conditions and the special features of the work. Really, it is quite impossible to fix the number of hours a man has to drag a log during a snowstorm, it is impossible to free him from night work if night work is absolutely unavoidable, it is simply impossible to follow the law by freeing a reformee from convict labour on a Sunday or public holiday if, for example, he is working down a coal pit with a probationer convict, as it would then be necessary to set both of them free and bring the work to a halt. Frequently, since the labour is supervised by people who are incompetent, incapable and clumsy, more effort is expended on work than should be necessary. For instance, the loading and unloading of ships, which, in European Russia, does not demand exceptional effort from a workman, is often, at Alexandrovsk, real torture for people; a special team, particularly prepared and trained for work at sea, does not exist; every time, entirely new people are taken, and because of this, it often happens that, when the sea is rough, dreadful chaos may be observed; on the steamer they are swearing and cursing and beside themselves with rage, while below the barges are crashing against the sides of the ship, and in these barges, with twisted green faces, the men are standing up or lying down, suffering with seasickness, while around the barges float lost oars. Owing to this, the work drags on, time is wasted for nothing, and people suffer unnecessary torment. Once when a ship was being unloaded I heard the Prison Governor say: "My men haven't eaten the whole day."

A good deal of convict labour is expended on fulfilling the requirements of the prison. Work is carried on in the prison every day by cooks, bakers, shoemakers, water-carriers, charladies, cattle-hands and so on. The military and telegraph departments and the land surveyor also utilize convict labour: around fifty men are attached to the prison infirmary, in what capacity and for what purpose nobody knows, and that is not counting those who are in the service of the officials. Every official, even those in the grade of clerk-in-chancery,* might, as far as I could ascertain, take on an unlimited number of staff. The doctor with whom I was lodging, who has his son living with him, had a male cook, female cook, caretaker and housemaid. For a junior prison surgeon this is very opulent. One of the prison governors had eight regular staff: a seamstress, a cobbler, a housemaid, a butler who doubled as an errand boy, a "nanny" for his son, a washerwoman, a male cook and a charlady. The question of servants on Sakhalin is a vexing and sad one, indeed it must be so at every penal institution, and it is not a new problem. In his *Brief Description of Irregularities Existing at Hard-labour Institutions*, Vlasov wrote that when he arrived on the island in 1871 he "was struck first of all by the fact that, by the authorization of the former Governor General, convicts made up the domestic staff of the administration and military officers". According to him, women were farmed out into the service of members of the administration, not excepting unmarried overseers. In 1872, Sinelnikov, the Governor General of Eastern Siberia, forbade the placing of convicts into domestic service. But this injunction, which carries the force of law right up to the present time, is circumvented in the most unceremonious manner. A collegiate registrar requisitions half a dozen staff for himself, and, when he sets off on a picnic, he will send a dozen or so convicts on ahead with the provisions. The two Governors of the Island, Gintze and Kononovich, have wrestled with this evil but without sufficient effort; at least, I found only three directives concerning the question of domestic staff, and they were such that any person with a vested interest could freely interpret them to his own advantage. In 1885, General Gintze, as if revoking the Governor General's edict, permitted (Directive no. 95) officials to take convict women on to their staff, at a rate of two roubles a month, and this money had to be turned over to the Exchequer office. In 1888, General Kononovich repealed this order of his predecessor, stipulating: "No convicts, neither male, nor female, shall be appointed to an official's domestic staff, and no payment whatsoever shall be exacted for the labour of women. But since the government buildings and their annexes cannot remain without watchmen and without the usual services, then to each building I permit the appointment of the requisite number of males and females, who will be denoted on warrants for these purposes as watchmen, wood-gatherers, floor-washers and so forth, depending on requirements" (Directive No 276). But since the vast majority of government buildings and their annexes are nothing other than the officials' living quarters, this order was understood as permission to have a domestic staff of convicts, and unpaid for at that. In any case, in 1890, when I was on Sakhalin, all the officials, even those without the remotest connection with the prison service (for instance, the head of the postal and telegraphic office), utilized convicts on the very widest scale for the running of their homes, did not pay this staff any wages and kept them fed at state expense.

The dealing out of convicts into the service of private persons stands in complete contradiction to the views of the legislators on punishment – this is not convict labour but serfdom, since the convict is serving not the state but an individual who has no interest whatever in the aims of reformation or in the idea of uniformity of punishment; he is not a convict at hard labour but a slave, dependent on the will of the squire and his family, gratifying their whims, while getting involved in petty niggles and squabbles in the kitchen. On becoming a settled exile, he will appear in the colony as a replica of our European Russian manor-house servant – able to clean shoes and fry up cutlets, but incapable of work on the land, and so he will go hungry and be cast on the mercy of fate. And the placing of convict women in service also has its own especial inconveniences, in addition to all this. Without even mentioning the fact that in a milieu of people who are dependent on somebody else, favourites and kept women always inject a stream of something nasty and degrading in the extreme to human dignity: they are, in particular, the total ruination of discipline. One of the priests told me that there had been occasions on Sakhalin when a free-woman, or a soldier serving on a domestic staff, had had, in certain circumstances, to tidy up and clear away after a convict woman.*

What is grandly called "factory production" in Alexandrovsk has, from an external point of view, been finely and noisily established, but it does not have any serious significance at present. In the foundry workshop, which is directed by a self-taught mechanical engineer, I saw large bells, wheels for carriages and wheelbarrows, a hand mill, a little apparatus for carrying out openwork, taps, fittings for stoves and the like, but it all created the impression of being just so many toys. The objects are pretty, but there is really no market for them at all, and for local needs it would be more profitable to obtain them on the mainland or in Odessa than to run their own traction engines and keep a staff of paid workers. Of course, nobody would regret any expense whatever if the workshops were schools where the convicts learnt trades; but in actual fact it is not penal convicts who work in the foundry and metal workshops, but settled exiles, who are experienced craftsmen and who occupy the rank of junior overseer at eighteen roubles per month. Here, mere enthusiasm for producing articles is only too noticeable; wheels and hammers thunder, and traction engines whistle, merely to produce good-quality articles for sale; commercial and artistic considerations here have no relationship whatsoever to punishment, and yet on Sakhalin, as in penal settlements everywhere, every enterprise must have as its first and foremost, and as its final and most distant, goal one thing and one thing only – the reform of the criminal; and the workshops here should strive towards sending over to the mainland, before all else, not oven doors, and not taps, but useful people and well-trained craftsmen.

The steam mill, sawmill and forge are maintained in excellent condition. The people work cheerfully, very probably because they are aware of the productiveness of the labour. But here, too, the people working are, in the main, specialists who were already millers, smiths and the like in their home region, and not those who while living in their home territory did not have the ability to work, did not know anything, and now more than anybody need mills and forges where they can be trained and set on their feet.*

6

Yegor's Story

SOON AFTER HIS DISCHARGE FROM SERVICE, the doctor with whom I had been lodging went off to the mainland, and so I settled in with a certain young official, a very fine man. He had only one servant, an elderly Ukrainian woman, and now and again, once every day or so, the convict Yegor dropped in on him; this Yegor, a wood-gatherer, did not consider himself the official's servant but "out of respect" brought firewood, cleared away the slops in the kitchen and generally carried out the duties which were beyond the strength of the old lady. You would be sitting and reading, or writing something, when suddenly you would hear a sort of rustling and panting, and something weighty would be moving around underneath the table by your leg; you would glance down – and see Yegor, barefoot, gathering up bits of paper or wiping away the dust beneath the table. He was getting on for forty, and gave the impression of an awkward and lumbering person, as they say, a "clodhopper" with an ingenuous and, at first sight, rather silly face, and with a broad mouth like a turbot. He had red hair, a little thin tuft of a beard and small eyes. He would not respond immediately to questions, but would look askance and ask "Wot?" or "Whadyawant?" He would honour a person with the title "Your Excellency" but in talking to them would use the *tu* form.* He could not sit around without work for a single minute, and found it everywhere, wherever he went. He would be talking to you, but his eyes would be searching round to see if there was anything to clear up or repair. He sleeps two or three hours in twenty-four, because there is nowhere for him to sleep. On holidays and days off he usually stands at a crossroads somewhere, dressed in a jacket over a red shirt, his stomach stuck out and feet apart. He calls this "taking a stroll".

Here, in penal servitude, he had built his own cabin and made buckets, tables and unwieldy cupboards. He could make all sorts of furniture, but only "for himself", that is, for his own needs. He himself had never got into a fight and had never struck anyone; only at some time in the past had he been flayed by his father, since he had been keeping watch on the pea-bed and had let a cockerel get in.

One day the following conversation took place between us:

"What did they send you here for?" I asked.

"Whadyasay, Yer Excellency?"

"Why did they send you to Sakhalin?"

"For murder."

"Tell me how it happened, from the very beginning."

Yegor stood by the doorpost, put his hands behind his back and began:

"We'd gone to the gentleman Vladimir Mikhailich, we'd been bargaining about some firewood and us sawing it and delivering it to the depot. All well and good. We made the deal and set off home. So, we hadn't gone far from the village when the folk sent me to the office with the contract, so's I could witness to it. I was on a horse. On the way to the office Andy made me turn back; there was a big flood, you couldn't get across. 'I'll be going to the office tomorrow about the land I've rented,' he said, 'and I'll bear witness to that contract.' Fine. We went off from there together, me on horseback, my mate on foot. We got as far as Parakhin. The lads had dropped over to the boozer to have a smoke, me and Andy were left behind on the pavement by the pub. So he says: 'Yer 'aven't got a five-copeck piece, 'ave yer, mate? I wanna 'ave a drink,' he says. So I says to him:

"'You, chum,' I says, 'are the sort of man what goes to have a drink on a five-copeck bit and finishes up drinking hisself legless.' And he says: 'No I won't, I'll finish my drink and go home straight away.' We went over to the lads, we agreed among us to buy half a gallon of vodka, so we had a whip-round for it, and went into the boozer and bought it. We sat down at a table to drink it."

"Be a bit briefer," I said.

"Now wait, just don't you go buttin' in, Yer Excellency. We got this vodka down us, then him, Andy that is, went and bought half a pint of pepper brandy as well. He poured out a glass for himself and me. We drunk up our glasses together. Well then, now, all the folk went off home from the pub, an' me and 'im set off behind them as well. It really shook me up going on horseback, so I got down and sat right there at the side of the road. I sang songs and played the fool. We didn't have a bad talk. After that we got up and went."

"You just tell me about the murder," I interrupted.

"''ang on. At home I lay down and slept till morning, until they woke me up. 'Step outside, which of you walloped Andy?' They'd gone and brought Andy in, and the village constable had turned up. The constable started to cross-examine us all, but nobody confessed to the crime. But Andy was still alive, and said: 'It was you, Sergey, what hit me with a pole, and I can't remember nothing more.' Sergey wouldn't own up. We all thought it was Sergey then and began to keep watch on him to make sure he wouldn't do anything to hisself. Andy died twenty-four hours later. Sergey was put up to it by his relations, his sister and his father-in-law. 'Don't deny it, Sergey, it won't make no difference to you. Own up, but drag in anybody else around who grabbed hold of him in the fight as well – it'll go easier for you.' The very moment Andy had died, all us people gathered together before the village elder and testified against Sergey. We cross-examined Sergey, but he wouldn't confess. So we let him go and sleep the night in his own home. Several people kept watch on him there, so as he wouldn't do anything to hisself. He had a rotten old rifle there – it was dangerous.

In the morning – off he'd gone, he wasn't there, so they gathered to search for him, and they looked for him all over the village, and went running out into the fields and looked for him there. But then they came out of the police station and announced Sergey was already there. Then they started to round us up. Sergey, you see, had gone straight to the district police superintendent and the local constable, had gone down on his knees and had told them that we, Yefrem's sons, had been aiming to kill Andy for three years or so. 'We were going down the road,' he says, 'the three of us, Ivan, Yegor and me – and we agreed between ourselves to batter him. I,' he said, 'hit Andy with an old root of a tree, and Ivan and Yegor grabbed hold of him to murder him, but I got scared,' he says, 'and back I run, up behind the lads at the end.' Then they rounded us up – Ivan, Kirsha, me and Sergey, and off we went to prison in the town."

"And who exactly are Ivan and Kirsha?"

"My own flesh and blood – my brothers. The merchant Pyotr Mikhailich came into the prison and stood bail for us. And we were out on his bail till Veil Day.* We lived quite happily and with no worries. The day after Veil Day we faced trial in the town. Kirsha had witnesses, the last lad in the crowd bore him out; but me, mate, I fell right in it. At the trial I said just what I'm telling you now, as it really happened, but the court wouldn't believe it: 'Here they all talk like that and swear blind on the cross it's true, but it's all lies.' Well, they found me guilty, so off we went to jail. In jail we lived under lock and key, only I was at least chamber pot emptier, and I swept out the cells and brought in dinner. For that, they all gave me a cut of their bread each month. I got three *funty** from each man. When they'd heard the outcome they'd sent a telegram home. It all happened just before St Nikolai's Day.* My wife and brother Kirsha arrived and came to see us, and they brought something along in the way of clothing, and a few other things as well... My wife wept and wailed, but there was nothing to be done about it. When she went home, I gave her two rations of bread to take with her as a present. We cried, and I sent my respects to my children and to all good Christian folk. On the road, we were put in handcuffs. We walked along two by two. I walked along with Ivan. At Novgorod they took our papers from us, then put us in irons and shaved our heads. Then they drove us on to Moscow. In Moscow, when we halted in prison for some time, we sent a petition asking for pardon. How we travelled to Odessa* I don't remember. We had a good journey. At Odessa we were asked lots of questions in the medical unit; they took all our clothes off and examined us. Then they gathered us together and drove us on to a ship. Cossacks and soldiers led us in a row up a ladder there and planted us in the inside of the ship. We sat down on plank-beds, all of us. Everybody had his own place. There were five of us sitting on the upper bed-boards. At first we didn't understand, and they said: 'We're moving off, we're moving off!' We went on and on, and then the boat began to rock. It was so hot that people were standing around stark naked. Some folk turned pale, but it didn't affect others. Then, of course, most of them lay down. And there was a hell of a storm. People were being slung about all over the place. On and on we went, then – bang into something. We were really flung about. It had been a misty day and it had got dark. We were being flung around and were going aground, yer see, on the rocks. We thought it was a great big fish thrashing about under the bottom, turning the ship over.* They pulled the ship forwards, pulled it and pulled it, but it wouldn't come off, so they began to pull it backwards. They started to pull back from halfway up – and went clean through the bottom. So they began to stop up the hole with the sail; they plugged it and plugged it – but there was no way it was any use. The water came welling right up to the very floor where the folk were sitting, and it began to flow out under the people on to the floor. They begged: 'Don't let us die, Yer Honour!' And at first he said, 'Don't go getting into a state, don't beg, I won't let anything die!' Then the water started to come welling up under the lower bed-boards; the good Christian folk did begin to get into a state and beg; so the gentleman says: 'Well, my lads, I'll let you go, as long as you don't mutiny, but if you do – I'll shoot the lot of you.' Then he let us out. We said prayers, to stop the Lord being angry, so's we wouldn't die. We prayed on our knees. After the prayers they handed us out hard tack and sugar, and the sea began to get calmer. The next day they started taking people off on barges to the shore. There were prayers said on shore. Then they transferred us on to another boat, a Turkish one,* and brought us here to Alexandrovsk. They brought us up on to the landing stage before nightfall, but kept us there for a long time, and so we set off from the landing stage when it was already dark. The folk went along in single file, and then also night-blindness set in. One person held on to another; some could see, and those who couldn't clung tight to them. I was leading a dozen chaps behind me. They drove us into the yard in the prison and started to distribute us to our allotted barrack huts. We had supper before sleeping – what little sleep we could get – and in the morning they started to issue us with the necessaries. We rested for two days, went to the bathhouse on the third, and on the fourth they drove us out to work. First of all we dug ditches by the building where the infirmary is now. We got all the stubs and roots out, gathered up rubbish, dug and suchlike for a week or two, or perhaps something like a month. Then we brought logs from near Mikhailovka. We dragged them for about three versts and heaped them up in a pile by the bridge. Then they made us go into the vegetable garden to dig waterholes. And when haymaking came round, they started to gather the lads together; they asked who knew how to mow hay, and if anyone admitted he could, well, they wrote his name down. They dished out bread, oats and meat to our whole *artel** and made us go off with an overseer to the haymaking at the two Armudan settlements. I didn't live too bad, God gave me good health, and I did the mowing well. The overseer beat the others, but I didn't hear a single bad word. Only common folk swear and shout at each other, why wander around with a sharp tongue?... Well, it doesn't matter too much. During our free time, or when it was raining, I plaited birch-bark sandals for myself. The people would go to sleep from the work, but I'd sit and plait. I'd sell the sandals, two portions of beef a pair, and that was worth four copecks. When we'd got the haymaking over and done with and got it stacked up, we set off home. We got home, and they took us into the prison. Then they hired me out to the settled exile Sashka at Mikhailovka as a workman. At Sashka's place I did the usual peasant's work: I reaped, gathered in, threshed, dug potatoes, while Sashka took logs to the government buildings in payment for me. I ate all my own food, which I got from the government office. I worked for two months and four days, Sashka promised me money but gave me nothing. The only thing he gave me was thirty-six *funty* of potatoes. Sashka brought me to the prison and handed me back. They gave me a chopper and some rope to bring in firewood. I used to stoke up seven stoves. I lived in a yurt, carried water for one of the sloppers-out,* and swept up. I watched over his *maidan* for a Tatar-Chink.* When I came in from work, he'd entrust the *maidan* to me, and I'd do the selling, and he'd pay me fifteen copecks a day for it. In spring, when the days started drawing out, I began weaving bast sandals. They fetched ten copecks a pair. And in the summer I'd go off hunting for firewood along by the river, I'd heap it up in a big pile and sell it to the Jewish feller who runs the bathhouse. I built up a pile of sixty tree trunks as well and sold them for fifteen copecks apiece. And so I manage to make a bit of a living, as God lets me. Only I've got no time to talk to you, Yer Excellency, cos I've got to go and get some water."

"Will you become a settled exile soon?"

"In five years' time."

"Are you homesick?"

"No – there's only one thing – it's a shame about my children. They're not too bright."

"Tell me what you thought about, Yegor, when they led you on board the ship at Odessa."

"I prayed to God."

"What about?"

"That He'd send my kids some brains."

"Why didn't you bring your wife and children with you to Sakhalin?"

"Because they're quite happy enough at home."

7

The Lighthouse. Korsakovskoye. The collection of Dr Suprunenko. The Meteorological Station. The Climate of the Alexandrovsk District. Novo-Mikhailovka. Potyomkin. Former Executioner Tersky. Krasny Yar. Butakovo.

MY RAMBLES AROUND ALEXANDROVSK and its environs with the postal official, the author of 'Sakhalino', have left me with pleasant recollections. Most often we would walk to the lighthouse, which stands high above the valley, on Cape Jonquière. By day the lighthouse, if looked at from below, is a modest little cottage with a mast and lamp, but at night, however, it glows brightly in the darkness, and it seems that the penal settlement is peering at the world with its own red eye. The road to the house rises steeply, twisting round the mountain in a spiral past old larches and firs. The higher one rises, the more freely one breathes; the sea stretches out before one's eyes, and little by little thoughts arise which have nothing to do with prison, or hard labour, or the penal colony, and it is only up here that one becomes aware how wearisome and hard life is down below. Day in, day out, the hard-labourers and settled exiles undergo their punishment, while, from morning to evening, those at liberty talk only about who has been flogged, who has tried to run off, who has been recaptured and who is going to be flogged; and it's strange how you yourself become accustomed to these conversations and interests in one single week, and on waking in the morning, before all else you settle down to read the printed "General's Directives" – the local daily paper – and then you listen and talk the whole day about who has tried to escape, who has been fired on and wounded, and so on. But on the mountain, in sight of the sea and the beautiful ravines, all this comes to seem impossibly cheap and sordid, as in truth it really is.

I was told that at one time there had been benches standing on the path to the lighthouse, but they had been forced to take them away because, while out strolling, the convicts and settled exiles had written on them and had carved with their knives filthy lampoons and all sorts of obscenities. There are a lot of free lovers of this so-called "wall literature", too, but, in penal servitude, the cynicism surpasses all limits and absolutely no comparison may be made with it. Here, not only benches and the walls of backyards, but even the love letters, are revolting. It is remarkable that a man will write and carve various abominations on a bench while at the same time he is feeling lost, abandoned and profoundly unhappy. Some old man chatters about how the world has become hateful to him, how it is time for him to die, how he suffers cruelly from rheumatism, and how he has difficulty seeing, yet with what gusto he will come out, without any respite, with a stream of "cabman's language", stretched out into a long chain of every sort of choice abuse, fanciful and weird as an incantation against fever. If he can write, then it is difficult for him in a secluded spot to restrain his ardour and resist the temptation to scratch out – even if only with his fingernail – some forbidden word on a wall.

By the cottage a vicious dog strains on a chain. There is a cannon and a bell; soon, it is said, they are going to bring along and install up here a siren which will wail during mists and inflict anguish on the people living in Alexandrovsk. Standing in the lantern room of the lighthouse and gazing down at the sea and the "Three Brothers", with the waves foaming around them, your head spins and you grow terrified. The Tatar Coast can be seen indistinctly, and even the entrance to De-Kastri Bay. The lighthouse-keeper said that now and again he could see boats coming in and out of De-Kastri. The wide, broad sea down below, sparkling in the sunlight, makes a hollow roaring sound, the distant coast beckons temptingly, and everything grows sad and dull, as if you will never ever get off this Sakhalin again. A glance at the coast on the other side and it seems that, if I were a convict, I would try to escape from here, no matter what.

Beyond Alexandrovsk, upriver on the Duyka, there follows the settlement Korsakovskoye, or Korsakovsk. It was founded in 1881 and named in honour of M.S. Korsakov, a former Governor General of Eastern Siberia. It's interesting that on Sakhalin they name settlements in honour of governors of Siberia, prison governors and even doctors' assistants, but forget completely explorers such as Nevelskoy, the sailor Korsakov, Boshnyak, Polyakov and many others, whose memory is, I would suggest, worthy of more respect and attention than some Governor of Derbinskoye Prison who was murdered for his cruelty.*

There are 272 inhabitants in Korsakovsk: 153 men and 119 women. There are fifty-eight householders in total. In the make-up of its householders – of whom twenty-six have peasant-in-exile status, and only nine are convicts – in the number of its women, hayfields, cattle and suchlike, Korsakovsk differs little from the prosperous Alexandrovsk hamlet; eight householders have two houses each, and there is one bathhouse to every nine houses. Forty-five householders possess horses, and between four and nine have cattle. Many of them have two horses and three or four cows. Korsakovsk takes very nearly first place on northern Sakhalin as regards its number of established residents – forty-three householders have occupied their plots right since the establishment of the colony. Listing the inhabitants' details, I came across eight who had arrived on Sakhalin before 1870, and one of them had actually been sent in 1866. A large percentage of established residents in a colony is a very good sign.

In external appearance Korsakovsk is deceptively similar to a pretty Russian hamlet, and a remote one at that, still untouched by civilization. I went there for the first time on Sunday after dinner. It was calm, warm weather, and one could feel the atmosphere of a day off work. Men slept in the shade or drank tea; by the gates and under windows, women searched each other's heads. There were flowers in the front gardens and vegetable gardens, and geraniums in the windows. There were lots of children, all out in the street and playing at soldiers and at horses, and messing about with dogs that had had a good meal and were trying to sleep. And when a shepherd, an old vagabond, came driving home a herd of over 150 head of cattle, and the air was filled with summer sounds – lowing, the crack of a whip, the cries of women and children driving calves, the dull thud of bare feet and hoofs on the dusty, manure-covered road, and when the smell of milk arose on the air – the illusion was complete. And even the Duyka is attractive here. In places it flows through backyards, past vegetable gardens; here its banks are green and overgrown with rose willow and sedge; when I saw it, evening shadows were lying across its perfectly smooth surface: it was serene and seemed to be dozing.*

Here, too, as in the rich Alexandrovsk hamlet, we find a high percentage of established residents, women, literates, a large number of free-women, and almost exactly the same past history, with the clandestine sale of alcohol, kulakism and so forth. In former times, so it is said, favouritism also played a notable role here in the setting up of households, when the authorities lightly handed out cattle, seed and even spirit on credit, and they did so all the more lightly because, allegedly, the inhabitants of Korsakovsk were always schemers, and honoured even the most petty officials with the title "Your Excellency". But, in contrast to Alexandrovsk hamlet, the main reason for the prosperity is not the sale of spirits, or favouritism, or the closeness of the "Paris of Sakhalin", but undoubtedly successes in crop-farming. While a quarter of the householders in the hamlet have to make do without arable land, and another quarter have very little, here in Korsakovsk all the householders cultivate land and sow cereal crops; in the hamlet half the inhabitants do without cattle and still have quite sufficient to eat, while here almost all the householders find it necessary to keep cattle. It is impossible, for many reasons, to regard farming of the land on Sakhalin other than with scepticism, but it must be admitted that at Korsakovsk it has been established on a serious footing and yields comparatively good results. One simply cannot assume that every year the Korsakovians cast 2,000 poods of grain into the ground from mere obstinacy, or from a desire to gratify the authorities. I have no precise figures as regards harvests, and you cannot believe what the Korsakovians themselves say, but from several indications – for instance, the large quantity of cattle, the external conditions of life and the fact that the peasants do not go dashing to the mainland, although they have had the right to do so for ages now – it must be concluded that the harvests here do not merely provide sufficient to live on but even yield some surplus, which disposes the settled exile to establish himself permanently here.

Why the Korsakovians make a success of cereal-farming, while the inhabitants of neighbouring settlements suffer extreme want from a whole series of failures, and have already despaired of living on their own crops, is not difficult to explain. Korsakovsk is situated where the Duyka river valley is at its widest, and from the very beginning, when they first began to occupy their plots, they have had an enormous area of land at their disposal. They were able not just to take the land, but to pick and choose. At present, twenty householders have between three and six desyatins of arable land; very rarely does anyone have fewer than two desyatins. If the reader wishes to compare the plots of land here with our peasant holdings in European Russia, he must keep in mind the fact that the arable land here is not permitted to lie fallow, but, every year, is all planted to the very last inch, and therefore, as regards quantity, two desyatins here are worth three of ours. The whole secret of the Korsakovians' success lies in their use of exceptionally large areas of land. For harvest on Sakhalin, where the yield varies between two- and threefold, the land can provide sufficient grain on one condition only – when there is a lot of it – a lot of land, a lot of seed, and labour that is cheap or costs nothing whatever. In those years when cereal crops do not flourish at all, the Korsakovians are helped along by vegetables and potatoes, which also occupy a sizeable area of land here – thirty-three desyatins.

The exile colony has not been in existence long, and, with its small, mobile population, is not yet sufficiently developed for statistics; in view of the scanty material it has managed to yield up to now, one unwillingly has to form one's own conclusions solely from certain allusions and conjectures, at every suitable opportunity. If you are not afraid of being reproved for the rashness of your conclusions, and if you apply the information relating to Korsakovsk to the whole colony, then you would very probably say that, in view of the negligible Sakhalin harvest, in order to eat sufficiently and not work at a loss, each householder must possess over two desyatins of arable land, not counting hayfields and land for vegetables and potatoes. It's impossible at the present time to establish a more precise norm, but, in all probability, it would work out at four desyatins; in the meantime, however, according to the 'Report on the State of Agriculture in 1889', every holder on Sakhalin had, on average, only half a desyatin each.

In Korsakovsk there is a house which, in its dimensions, and with its red roof and comfortable garden, reminds one of a medium-size manor house. The owner of this house, the Head of the Medical Department, Dr P.I. Suprunenko, had gone away in the spring, in order to exhibit at the Prison Exhibition,* and then stayed in European Russia for good, and in the now deserted rooms I found only remnants of the luxurious zoological collection that the doctor had amassed. I do not know where the collection is now, or who is using it to study the fauna of Sakhalin, but from the few remaining specimens, elegant in the extreme, and from tales I had heard, I could judge how rich his collection must have been, and how much erudition, labour and love Dr Suprunenko must have spent in this useful work. He had begun his collection in 1881, and over a period of ten years had managed to collect almost every vertebrate found on Sakhalin, as well as much material on anthropology and ethnography. If his collection had remained on the island, it would have formed the basis for a superb museum.

Attached to the house is a meteorological station. Until very recently, it was under the authority of Dr Suprunenko; now it is run by the Inspector of Agriculture. While I was present, observations were being taken by a clerk, the convict Golovatsky, an intelligent and obliging man who provided me with meteorological tables. Conclusions may already be drawn from the observations made over nine years, and I will try to give some idea of the climate of the Alexandrovsk District. The Mayor of Vladivostok once told me that in his city, and generally speaking along the whole of the eastern seaboard, there was "no climate of any sort"; what they say about Sakhalin is that there is no climate here, just bad weather, and that this island is the most inclement spot in Russia. I do not know how far this is true: when I was there the summer was very fine, but the meteorological tables, and the short accounts of other writers, in general give a picture of extraordinarily unpleasant weather. The Alexandrovsk District has a maritime climate which is outstanding in its inconsistency, that is to say, by considerable variations in its average yearly temperature,* the number of days with precipitations and so forth; its main distinctive features are its low average yearly temperature, and the enormous number of precipitations and overcast days. I shall take for comparison the average monthly temperatures of the Alexandrovsk District and the Cherepovetsk District, Novgorod Province, where "the climate is severe, damp, changeable and unfavourable to health".*

	Alexandrovsk District	Cherepovetsk District
January	−18.9	−11.0
February	−15.1	−8.2
March	−10.1	−1.8
April	+0.1	+2.8
May	+5.9	+12.7
June	+11.0	+17.5
July	+16.3	+18.5
August	+17.0	+13.5
September	+11.4	+6.8
October	+3.7	+1.8
November	−5.5	−5.7
December	−13.8	−12.8

The average yearly temperature in the Alexandrovsk District is +0.1, that is, almost zero, while in the Cherepovetsk District it is +2.7. Winter in the Alexandrovsk District is more severe than in Archangel, the spring and summer are like those of Finland, the autumn is like it is in St Petersburg, and the average yearly temperature is similar to that of the Solovetsky Islands,* where it also equals zero. Eternal frost* may be observed in the Duyka Valley. Polyakov found it at a depth of three-quarters of an arshin on 20th June. On 14th July, underneath heaps of rubbish, and in the hollows around the mountains, he found snow, which melted only at the end of July. On 24th July 1889, snow fell on the mountains, which are not high here, and everybody dressed themselves up in coats of fur and sheepskin. The breakup of the ice on the Duyka river has been observed for nine years: the earliest was on 23rd April and the latest on 6th May. There was not once a thaw during any of these nine winters. There is frost on 181 days a year and a cold wind blows on 151 days. All this has an important practical significance. According to Chernov, in the Cherepovetsk District, where the summer is warmer and more prolonged, buckwheat, wheat and cucumber do not ripen well, and in the Alexandrovsk District, according to the evidence of the local Inspector of Agriculture, the amount of warmth sufficient for the full ripening of oats and wheat has not been observed in one single year.

What is most deserving of attention on the part of the agriculturalist and hygienist is the excessive dampness of the island. There are, on average, 189 days with precipitation in a year: 107 with snow and 82 with rain (in the Cherepovetsk District there are 81 days with rain and 82 with snow). For weeks on end the sky will be completely overcast with clouds the colour of lead, and the dismal weather which drags on day in, day out, seems to the inhabitants as if it will never end. Such weather inclines one towards depressed reflections and despondent drunkenness. Under its influence many cool and reserved people have, perhaps, become brutal, and many good-hearted people, and those weak in spirit, on not seeing the sun for weeks or even months at a time, have lost for ever their hopes for a better life. Polyakov writes that in June 1881 there wasn't one single clear day throughout the entire month, and from the reports of the Inspector of Agriculture, it may be seen that, over a period of four summers from 18th May to 1st September, the number of clear days did not, on average, exceed eight. Mists are a fairly frequent occurrence here, especially at sea, where they are a real calamity for sailors; the salty sea mists, so I was told, act in a most ruinous manner upon the coastal vegetation, on the trees and on the meadows. Further on, I shall speak about settlements where the inhabitants, owing in the main to these mists, have already given up growing cereal crops and have planted all their arable land with potatoes. Once, on a clear sunlit day, I saw a wall of perfectly white, milk-coloured mist pour in from the sea; it was as if a white curtain had been lowered from the sky to earth.

The meteorological station is provided with instruments tested in, and acquired from, the major physics laboratory in St Petersburg. It has no library. Besides the above-mentioned clerk, Golovatsky, and his wife, I noted down seven other workpeople at the station – six men, one woman. What they were doing there, I do not know.

At Korsakovsk there is a school and a chapel. There had also been a small infirmary in which were lodged together fourteen syphilitics and three lunatics; one of the latter was infected with syphilis. I heard, too, that the syphilitics used to prepare ship's cord* and lint for the surgical department. But I did not arrive in time to visit this medieval establishment, since it had been closed down in September by a young military physician, temporarily filling the post of prison doctor. If they had burned the lunatics on bonfires here by order of the prison doctors, even that would not have been surprising, since the local hospital system has fallen behind civilization by at least 200 years or so.

In one cabin, when it was already twilight, I found a man of about forty dressed in a jacket with his trousers not tucked into his high boots as is usual; he was clean-shaven and had on a grubby, unstarched shirt and something resembling a tie – he was, to all appearances, a member of the privileged classes.* He was sitting on a low, small bench eating salt beef and potatoes from an earthenware bowl. He gave his surname, which ended in -ky, and for some reason I thought I was seeing in front of me a certain former officer whose name also ended in -ky and who had been deported to penal servitude for a disciplinary offence.

"You're an ex-officer?" I enquired.

"Not at all, Your Excellency. I'm a priest."

I do not know why he had been sent to Sakhalin, and I did not ask him about it either; when a man who, not so very long ago, was called "Father" and "the Reverend Gentleman", and whose hand was kissed by everybody, is standing to attention in front of you dressed in a pitiful threadbare coat, it's not his offence you think about. In another cabin I observed the following scene. A young male convict, with dark hair and a singularly sad face, dressed in a dapper blouse, was seated at the table, his head propped on both hands, while the convict-woman householder was clearing the samovar and cups from the table. When I asked if he was married, the young man replied that his wife and daughter had come voluntarily with him to Sakhalin, but now two months had passed since she had gone back to Nikolayevsk on the mainland with the child, and she had not returned, although he had already sent her several telegrams.

"And she won't come back neither," said the landlady with a kind of malicious glee. "What's there for her to do here? Hasn't she already seen your Sakhalin, eh? Do you think it's easy here?" He remained silent, and she started up again: "And she won't come back. She's a young woman, she's free – what is there for her here? She's flown away, like a bird, and she's disappeared without a trace, that's how it is with her. It's not with her like it is with you and me. If I hadn't killed my husband, and you hadn't set a place on fire, we'd have been free as well now, but now you sit here and wait for the wind in the fields, for your missus, but you might as well really start eating your heart out now…" He was suffering, there was quite obviously lead in his soul, but she went on tormenting him and tormenting him: I came out of the cabin and her voice could still be heard.

At Korsakovsk I was accompanied round the cabins by the convict Kislyakov, quite a strange man. Very probably the court reporters still have not forgotten him. This was the same Kislyakov, a military clerk, who, at St Petersburg, killed his wife on St Nikolai's Street with a hammer and presented himself before the City Governor to announce his crime. According to his story, his wife had been beautiful, and he had loved her very much, but one day after quarrelling with her he had sworn before an icon to kill her, and from that time right up to the murder some invisible power had whispered without ceasing in his ear: "Kill, kill!" Up to the trial he had been in St Nikolai's Hospital; very probably because of this he himself considered he was a psychopath, for he more than once asked me to plead on his behalf that he should be recognized as a lunatic and shut up in a monastery.* His entire penal servitude consisted of the following: in the prison he had been entrusted with making the pegs for fastening the makeweights to portions of bread* – not hard work, one would think, yet he would hire somebody in his place, while he himself "gave lessons" – that is, did nothing. He was dressed in a lounge suit of sailcloth and had a prepossessing appearance. He was not a very bright fellow, but he was a talker and philosopher. "Where there are fleas, there you'll find kids," he'd say in a sweet, rich baritone voice every time we saw children. When people asked, while he was present, why I was drawing up the census, he would say: "They're doing it so as to send us all off to the moon. You know where the moon is?" And when, late in the evenings we would be returning on foot to Alexandrovsk, he would repeat several times right out of the blue, "Revenge is the most noble emotion."

Further up the Duyka follows the settlement of Novo-Mikhailovka, founded in 1872 and so called because Mitzul's first name was Mikhail. Many writers call it Verkhny Urochishche and to the local settled exiles it is Pashnya. There are 520 inhabitants in the settlement: 287 males and 233 females. There are 122 householders, and of these two have co-holders. In the Inventory of Landholdings, all householders are shown as having arable land, and eighty-four have neat cattle, but nonetheless the cabins, with few exceptions, are startling in their poverty, and the inhabitants declare with one voice that "you can't make a living on Sakhalin no way at all". In years gone by, so the story goes, when the poverty in Novo-Mikhailovka was really outrageous, a path led from the settlement to Dooay, a path which had been worn by the female convicts and free-women walking to the Dooay and Voyevodsk Prisons to sell themselves to the prisoners for a few brass farthings. I can affirm that the pathway has still not grown over right to this day. Those inhabitants who, like the Korsakovians, have large cultivable plots of land (from three to six and even eight desyatins), do not live in poverty, but there are few such plots, and with each passing year they become smaller and smaller, and at present, over half the householders own plots from one-eighth to one and a half desyatins in size, and this means that cereal farming yields them nothing but losses. Householders who have been here a long time, and who have learnt from experience, sow only barley, and have started to plant their arable land with potatoes.

The land here is no attraction and does not dispose a person to settle down. Of the householders who occupied plots in the first four years after the founding of the settlement, not one is left; from 1876 nine remain, from 1877 seven, two from 1878, four from 1879, and all the rest are newcomers.

At Novo-Mikhailovka there is a telegraph station, a school, a barrack hut for those receiving alms and the skeleton of an uncompleted wooden church. There is a bakehouse where bread is made for the convicts engaged on roadworks in the vicinity of Novo-Mikhailovka; they must bake it without any kind of quality control on the part of the authorities, since the bread here is revolting.

Nobody travelling through Novo-Mikhailovka should miss meeting the peasant-in-exile Potyomkin who lives there. When an important person arrives on Sakhalin, then it is Potyomkin who presents him with bread and salt; when they want to prove that the agricultural colony has succeeded, they usually point at Potyomkin. He is indicated in the Inventory of Landholdings as having twenty horses and nine head of horned stock,* but it is said that he has twice as many horses. He owns a small shop and he also has a shop in Dooay, where his son carries on business. He creates the impression of a businesslike, clever and well-off religious schismatic.* His rooms were neat, the walls were covered with wallpaper, and there was a picture: *Marienbad: sea-bathing near the Libau*. Both he and his wife were sedate, sober, and shrewd in conversation. When I drank tea at his house, he and his wife told me that it was possible to make a living on Sakhalin and that the land gave good yields, but that the whole trouble was that these days, people had got lazy, were pampered and made no effort. I asked him whether it was true what I had heard, that he had entertained one important personage with watermelons and melons from his own vegetable garden. Without batting an eyelid, he responded: "That's quite correct – melons do ripen here, as it happens."*

In Novo-Mikhailovka lives another Sakhalin celebrity, too – settled exile Tersky, the former executioner.* He coughs, clutches his chest with pallid, bony hands and complains that his stomach has been torn apart. He began to wither away from the day when, by order of the authorities, he was punished for some offence by the present Alexandrovsk executioner, Komelev. Komelev put so much strength into it that he "almost knocked my soul out". But later Komelev committed some offence – and it was a real red-letter day for Tersky. He really let himself go and in revenge ripped his colleague up so savagely that, according to his stories, the latter's body is still festering to this day. People do say that if you place two poisonous spiders in the same jar, they'll carry on biting each other till they are both dead.

Up till 1888, Novo-Mikhailovka was the last settlement along the Duyka; now there is also Krasny Yar and Butakovo. There is a road leading to these settlements from Novo-Mikhailovka. I had to ride the first half of the way – about three versts – along a road that was new, level and straight as a die, and the second half across a picturesque cutting through the taiga, from which the stumps had already been rooted up, and where the riding was easy and pleasant, as if along a pretty country road. The large specimens of trees with wood suitable for building work along the way have almost everywhere already been cut down, but even so the taiga is still imposing and beautiful. There are birches, aspens, poplars, willows, ashes, elders, black alders, meadowsweet, hawthorn and in between them grass as tall as a human being, and higher; the gigantic ferns and burdocks, the leaves of which are more than an arshin in diameter, merge with the bushes and trees into a dense, impenetrable thicket, providing shelter for bears, sable and deer. Along both sides, where the narrow valley finishes and the mountains begin, there stands a green wall of coniferous woods of silver firs, spruces and larches; above them there is once again deciduous forest, and crests of the mountains are bare or covered with scrub. I have never come across such enormous burdocks anywhere in Russia as there are here, and it is these that chiefly give the local thickets, woodland clearings and meadows their distinctive profile. I have already written that, at night, especially by moonlight, they present a fantastical aspect. In this respect the scenery is enriched by a certain magnificent plant of the family of umbellates, which, it seems, has no name in Russian; it has a straight stem which reaches as much as ten feet high, and five and a half inches thick at the base; its upper section is purple-red and it carries an umbrella of up to a foot in diameter; around this main umbrella are grouped four to six umbrellas of smaller size, giving the appearance of a candelabra. In Latin the plant is called *Angelophyllum Ursinum* (bear root).*

This is only Krasny Yar's second year in existence. It has a single wide street, but there is still no roadway, and everybody goes from cabin to cabin by way of hummocks, piles of clay and shavings, and they jump over logs, stumps and ditches in which the brown water has gone stagnant. The cabins are still not ready. One householder makes bricks, another greases the kiln, and a third drags a log across the street. There is a total of fifty-one householders. Of these, three – including the Chinaman Pen Ogi Tzoy – have abandoned the cabins they had begun and nobody now knows where they are. And the Caucasians – there are seven of them here – had already dropped work, bunched together in one cabin and huddled close together from the cold, although it was still only 2nd August. That the settlement is still young and has hardly started life is also evident from the statistics. There are ninety inhabitants, and the ratio of men to women is two to one; there are three legalized families, twenty "free associations", and there are only nine children under five years old. Three plot-holders possess horses and nine have cows. At present, all the householders receive prisoners' rations, but what they are going to live on afterwards is as yet unknown; at any rate the hopes for crop-rearing are certainly poor. Up till now they have managed to find and clear only twenty four and a half desyatins of land, which they cultivate for crops or sow with potatoes, that is to say, less than half a desyatin per household. There are no hay meadows at all. And since the valley is narrow here, and on both sides press mountains on which nothing flourishes, and since the administration will not pause to take anything whatsoever into consideration when they have to get people off their hands, and will certainly settle scores of new householders on plots here every year, the cultivable plots will remain just as they are now, that is one-eighth, one-quarter and half a desyatin, or very likely even less. I do not know who chose the spot for Krasny Yar, but it is obvious from everything that the task was entrusted to incompetent people who have never stayed in the country, and most of all, people for whom an agricultural colony was the very last subject they had ever thought about. There is not even any decent water here. When I asked where they got their drinking water from, they pointed out a ditch to me.

All the cabins here are built in identical fashion, with two windows and with poor unmatured wood, put up with the sole calculation of somehow getting one's deportation sentence over with and then leaving for the mainland. There are no quality checks on these constructions on the part of the administration, probably for the reason that there is not a single one of them who would know how to build a cabin or install a stove. There is, though, supposed to be an architect attached to the staff on Sakhalin, but during my stay he wasn't there, and even when he is, it appears, he supervises nothing but the government construction works. The place which looks most cheerful and welcoming of them all is the government house where the overseer – Ubiyonnykh by surname – lives; he is a small, frail little soldier, with an expression quite suited to his surname; in his face there really was something slain and bitterly bewildered. Perhaps this was because there lived with him in the one room a tall, plump female settled exile, his mistress, who had presented him with a numerous family. He was already earning the rate of a senior overseer, and his entire duties consisted merely in reporting to visitors that everything in the whole wide world was going satisfactorily. But he did not like Krasny Yar either, and he wanted to get off Sakhalin. He asked me whether his mistress would be allowed to go with him when he was transferred to the reserve and went off to the mainland. This question very much disturbed him.

I did not visit Butakovo.* According to the information in the Inventory of Landholdings, part of which I could verify and fill out from the priest's confession book, there are in all thirty-nine inhabitants. Only four are adult women. The total of householders is twenty-two. So far, four houses are ready, and the other householders still only have frameworks standing. There are in all four and a half desyatins of land used for planting crops and potatoes. So far, still not a single householder has cattle or fowl.

Having finished with the Duyka Valley, I shall pass on to the small river Arkay, on which stand three settlements. The Arkay Valley was chosen for settling not because it had been better explored than the rest, or because it satisfied the requirements of a colony, but it was simply selected at random, merely because it is nearer to Alexandrovsk than the other valleys.

8

The river Arkay. The Arkovo Cordon. First, Second, Third Arkovo. The Arkovo Valley. The settlements along the west coast: Mgachi, Tangi, Khoay, Trambaus, Viakhty, Vangi. The Tunnel. The Cablehouse. The Family Barrack-huts. The Dooay Prison. The Coal-mines. The Voyevodsk Prison. Those Prisoners shackled to Wheelbarrows.

THE RIVER ARKAY FALLS INTO the tatar strait, about eight to ten versts to the north of the Duyka. Not so very long ago it really was a river, and people went fishing in it for humpbacked salmon, but now, as a consequence of forest fires and unauthorized tree-felling, it has grown shallow, and towards the summer, dries up completely. However, during heavy periods of rain it overflows its banks as in spring, stormily and noisily, and then it really makes its presence felt. It has already happened more than once that the river has washed the vegetable gardens off its banks, and carried the hay and the whole of the exiles' harvest into the sea. It is impossible to guard against such a disaster, since the valley is narrow, and a person can only move away from the river by going up the mountains.*

Right by the mouth of the Arkay, where the river curves into the valley, stands the tiny Gilyak village of Arkay-vo, which has given the names to the Arkovo Cordon and the three settlements of Pervoye, Vtoroye and Tretye Arkovo. Two roads lead into the Arkovo Valley from Alexandrovsk – one, through the mountains, which was impassable when I was there, since the bridges along its way had been burnt down by forest fires – and the other, a road along the seashore; travel was possible over this latter route only when the tide was out. I set out for the Arkay for the first time at 8 a.m. on 31st July. The tide had begun to go out. It was squalling with rain. The overcast sky, the sea, on which could be seen not a single sail, and the steep clay shoreline had a forbidding air; the waves pounded dull and melancholy. Stunted, sickly trees looked down from high up on the bank; here, out in the open, each of them fights in isolation a cruel battle with the frosts and cold winds, and during the autumn and winter, through long, dreadful nights, each of them sways restlessly from side to side, bends to the ground and creaks in lamentation, and this lamentation is heard by nobody.

The Arkovo Cordon is situated near the Gilyak village. Formerly it had significance, since the soldiers who went out hunting escapees lived here, but now an overseer lives here who carries out the duties, it would appear, of Acting Governor of Settlements. Some two versts from the Cordon lies Pervoye (First) Arkovo. It has just one street, and owing to the conditions of the place, can only grow lengthways and not in width. When, in time, all three Arkovos merge, Sakhalin will have a large village consisting of one single street. Pervoye Arkovo was founded in 1883. It has 136 inhabitants – eighty-three men, fifty-three women. There are twenty-eight householders and they all live in families, except for the convict woman Pavlovskaya, a Catholic, whose cohabitant, the real landlord of the house, died not long ago; she requested me persuasively: "Get me a man appointed to run the house!" Three of them have two houses each. Vtoroye (Second) Arkovo was founded in 1884. There are ninety-two inhabitants – forty-six men and forty-six women. There are twenty-four householders, all living in families. Of these two have two houses each. Tretye (Third) Arkovo was founded at the same time as Vtoroye, and it may be seen from this how they rushed to settle the Arkovo Valley. There are forty-one inhabitants, nineteen men and twenty-two women, ten of whom are householders, with one co-owner as well. Nine live in families.

All householders in the three Arkovos are shown as having arable land, and the size of the holdings fluctuates between a half and two desyatins. One plot has an area of three desyatins. They sow wheat, barley and rye in fairly large quantities and plant potatoes. The majority have potatoes and poultry. Judging from the information compiled by the Governor of Settlements in the Inventory of Landholdings, one might reach the conclusion that, during the short time they have existed, the three Arkovos have enjoyed considerable success in farming; not without reason did one anonymous author write about the working of the land here: "This labour is rewarded with abundance owing to the conditions of the soil of the locality, which are highly favourable to agriculture, as is shown by the vigour of growth of woods and meadows." But in actual fact this is not the case. All three Arkovos belong among the poorest settlements of northern Sakhalin. There is arable land and there are cattle here, but there has not once been a harvest. Besides the unfavourable conditions common to the whole of Sakhalin, the local householders encounter a further serious enemy in the natural features of the Arkovo Valley, primarily in the soil which is so highly praised by the author I have just quoted. The topsoil here is a two-inch-thick layer of humus, and the subsoil consists of shingle which on hot days heats up so fiercely that it dries out the roots of the plants, and during a period of rain, does not let the moisture through, since it lies on the clay; because of this, the roots rot. Obviously, in such soil, the only plants that can get along without damage to themselves are ones with firm, deep-seated roots, such as, for example, burdocks, and, among cultivated plants, only root crops, swede and potatoes, for all of which into the bargain the soil has to be tilled deeper and more thoroughly than for cereals. I have already spoken of the disasters caused by the river. There are no hayfields at all; they cut hay on scraps of land in the taiga, or reap it with sickles wherever they come across it, and those who are a little more wealthy buy it in the Tymovsk District.

Tales are told of entire families who did not have a single piece of bread during the winter and lived on nothing but swede. Not long before my arrival, the settled exile Skorin had died of starvation in Vtoroye Arkovo. According to the stories of the neighbours, he ate only one *funt* of bread every three days, and he had been doing so for a very long time. "We're all expecting the same fate," the neighbours, frightened by the death, told me. I recall that, describing their everyday life to me, three women burst into tears. In one cabin, with no furniture, and with a dark, gloomy stove taking up half the room, around the female householder children were crying and baby chickens were cheeping; out she went onto the street, and out went the children and chicks after her. Gazing at them, she laughed and she cried, and apologized to me for the crying and cheeping; it was from hunger, she said, she could hardly wait for her husband to get back, he had gone into town to sell whortleberries to buy bread. She minced up some cabbage leaves and gave it to the chicks, who threw themselves on it greedily, and, finding themselves deceived, raised an even greater squawking. In another cabin, there was quartered a man hairy as a spider, with beetling eyebrows, who was a convict and who was filthy, and with him lived another man just as hairy and just as filthy; both of them had large families, and in the hut there was, as they say in Russian, "Nothing but squalor and shame". And, besides the crying and cheeping and such facts as the death of Skorin, how many indirect expressions there were of all kinds of need and hunger! In Tretye Arkovo, settled exile Petrov's cabin stands bolted because he himself "for negligence of his holding, and for slaughtering a heifer for meat without permission, has been sent to the Voyevodsk Prison, where he may now be found". Apparently the calf was slaughtered out of poverty and was sold in Alexandrovsk. The grain taken from the government on credit for sowing appears in the Inventory of Landholdings as having been sown, but the fact is, half of it has been eaten, and the settled exiles themselves do not conceal this in conversation. The cattle – such as they are – are taken from the state on credit and fed at state expense. The further you go into the forest, the more firewood you find; all the Arkovo settlers are in debt, their debts grow with every new crop-sowing and with every superfluous extra head of cattle, and, with a few, their debts have already reached an unpayable sum – two and even three hundred roubles per head.

Between Vtoroye and Tretye Arkovo lies the Arkovo Halt, where horses are changed on the journey into the Tymovsk District. It is a post station, or an inn. Judging by our European Russian yardstick, here, with the quite modest local postal service, two or three workmen under an overseer should be sufficient at the halt. But on Sakhalin they like everything on a large scale. Besides the overseer, also living at the halt there is a clerk, an errand-man, a stable hand, two bakers and two wood-gatherers, and, in addition, a further four workmen who, in reply to my question as to what they did, replied: "I carry the hay."

If a landscape painter should happen to come to Sakhalin, then I recommend the Arkovo Valley to his notice. This spot, besides the beauty of its location, is extremely rich in hues and tints, so that it is difficult to get by without the hackneyed simile of a multicoloured carpet or a kaleidoscope. Here there is dense, sappy verdure with giant burdocks glittering from the rain that has only just fallen; beside it, in an area no larger than three sazhens or so, there is the greenery of rye, then a scrap of land with barley, and then burdocks again, with a space behind it covered with oats, after that beds of potatoes, two immature sunflowers with drooping heads, then, forming a little wedge, a deep-green patch of hemp; here and there plants of the umbelliferous family similar to candelabras proudly hold up their heads, and this whole diversity of colour is strewn with pink, bright-red and crimson specks of poppies. On the road you meet peasant women who have covered themselves against the rain with big burdock leaves, like headscarves, and because of this look like green beetles. And the sides of the mountains – well, maybe they are not the mountains of the Caucasus, but they are mountains all the same.

Along the western sea coast, above the mouth of the Arkay, there are six insignificant settlements. I did not visit any of them, and I have taken the figures relating to them from the Inventory of Landholdings and the priest's confessional book. They have been established on capes jutting out into the sea, or by the mouths of small rivers, from which they have also taken their names. They started out as guard pickets, sometimes of four or five people, and then, in course of time, when these pickets turned out to be insufficient by themselves, it was decided (in 1882) to settle the largest capes between Dooay and Pogobi with trustworthy settled exiles, the majority of whom had families. The aim of establishing these settlements and the military cordons was "To allow the post, passengers and dog-sled drivers passing through from Nikolayevsk the possibility of protection and shelter on the way, and of establishing general police surveillance along the coastline, which represents the sole possible (?)* route for escaped prisoners, and equally, for the forbidden conveyance of alcohol for unrestricted sale".

There are still no roads to the coastal settlements, and communication on foot along the shore is possible only when the tide is out; in winter these settlements can be reached only by dog sled. Access is possible by boat or steam launch as well, but only in very fine weather. From south to north these settlements are laid out in the following order:

Mgachi. Inhabitants thirty-eight: twenty men, eighteen women. Householders fourteen. Thirteen have families, and only two families are unlegalized. Everybody has about twelve desyatins of arable land, but it's three years now since they stopped sowing cereals and planted all the land under potatoes. Eleven householders have occupied their plots right from the time the settlement was founded, and five of them already have peasant-in-exile status. There is good money to be made, which explains why these peasants do not rush over to the mainland. Seven men are employed in the dog-sled business, that is to say they keep the dogs by which the post and passengers are conveyed during the winter. One man engaged in hunting as a trade. As for the fishing grounds, which are mentioned in the report of the Central Prison Department for 1889, they quite simply do not exist here.

Tangi. Inhabitants nineteen: eleven men and eight women. Householders six. They have about three desyatins of arable land, but, as at Mgachi, owing to the frequent sea mists which hinder the growth of cereals, they also use it only for planting potatoes. Two householders have boats and are engaged in fishing as a trade.

Khoay is on the cape of the same name, which juts powerfully out into the sea and is visible from Alexandrovsk. Inhabitants thirty-four: nineteen men, fifteen women. Householders thirteen. Here they still have not become completely disillusioned, and continue to plant wheat and barley. Three engage in hunting.

Trambaus. Inhabitants eight: three men, five women; a fortunate settlement, where there are more women than men. Three householders.

Viakhty, on the river Viakhta, which connects a lake with the sea, and in this respect is reminiscent of the Neva. In the lake, so I was told, they catch sigs* and sturgeon.

Vangi – the most northerly settlement. Inhabitants thirteen: nine male, four female. Householders eight.

According to the descriptions of scholars and travellers, the further north one goes, the more barren and more mournful does nature become. Beginning at Trambaus, the entire northern third of the island is a plain, which is nothing else but tundra, on which the main watershed range of mountains which runs right along Sakhalin has the appearance of low, undulating peaks, taken by some writers to be alluvial deposits from the Amur.

Here and there across the marshy, reddy-brown plain extend small strips of crooked, twisted coniferous trees; the trunks of the larches are no higher than one foot [*sic*], and their crowns lie on the ground like a green pillow; the trunks of cedar shrubs spread out over the earth, between the small strips of stunted forest lie lichens and moss, and, just as on the European Russian tundras, one comes across all sorts of berries here that are coarse, bitter and strongly astringent to the taste – *mokhovki*, marsh whortleberries, *kosteniki** and cranberries. Only at the very northern tip of the plain, where the countryside again becomes hilly, does it appear as if, in a small area on the threshold of the eternally cold sea, nature wishes to smile at the farewell. On Kruzenshtern's chart relating to this area, a forest of slender larch trees is shown.

But however barren and severe natural conditions are here, according to the evidence of those well informed in this field, inhabitants of the coastal settlements still live comparatively better than, for example, the inhabitants of the three Arkovos or Alexandrovsk.

This is explained by the fact that there are few of them, and those blessings they do have at their disposal can be shared among a small number of people. Crop-rearing and harvesting are not obligatory for them; they have been left to their own resources and they choose their occupations and trades themselves. The winter road from Alexandrovsk to Nikolayevsk passes through the settlement; Gilyaks and Yakut industrialists come here to trade, and the settled exiles sell to them and exchange goods with them without using middlemen. There are no shopkeepers, runners of *maidans* or Jewish second-hand dealers here, and there are no workers in government offices who barter alcohol in exchange for luxurious fox furs and then display them to their guests with a beatific smile.

No new colonies are to be established to the south. Along the western sea coast, to the south of Alexandrovsk, there is only one inhabited spot – Dooay, a dreadful, hideous place, wretched in every respect, in which only saints or profoundly perverse people could live of their own free will. It is a military post; the population call it "the port". It was founded in 1857, but its name, Dooay, or Dui, existed earlier and related generally to that part of the coast where the Dooay mines are now located. The small and shallow river Khoynji flows through the valley in which it is situated. Two roads lead from Alexandrovsk to Dooay, one through the mountains and one along the seashore. The entire weight of Cape Jonquière presses down on the coastal sandbank, and it would have been totally impossible to travel across it if a tunnel had not been built. They dug the tunnel without consulting an engineer, and with no forethought, and as a result it has come out dark, crooked and dirty. This construction cost very dearly, but it turned out to be unnecessary, since, with the existence of a good mountain road, there was no need to go along the shore, the passage over which was restricted by factors of high and low tide. This tunnel is a wonderful expression of the Russian's tendency to waste his last resources on all sorts of caprices, buffoonery and extravagances when his most pressing needs remain unsatisfied. They dug a tunnel and the works manager went rolling over the rails in a wagon with the inscription "Alexandrovsk – The Quay", while in the meantime the convicts were living in filthy, damp yurts or dugouts because there were not enough people to build barracks.*

Immediately at the exit of the tunnel on the coast road stands a saltworks and a cable house, from which a telegraph cable descends over the sand and into the sea. In the cable house lives a convict joiner, a Pole,* and his cohabitant who, so the stories went, had given birth at the age of twelve after some prisoner had raped her at an *étape*.* The whole way to Dooay, screes can be seen on the steep, sheer coastline, on which here and there specks and strips glint blackly, an arshin to a sazhen in width; this is coal. The strata of coal here, according to specialists' accounts, are squeezed between layers of sandstone, slatey clay, clayey slate and clayey sand, which have been lifted, bent, moved or pushed down by seams of basalt, diorites and porphyry which jut out in many spots in large outcrops. It must be considered beautiful after its own fashion, but prejudice against the place is so deep-seated that you regard not only the people but even the plants with pity that they grow in this particular spot of all places. Seven versts further on, the shoreline is broken by a fissure. This is the Voyevodsk Chasm; here, quite alone, stands the dreadful Voyevodsk Prison, in which are kept the hardened criminals, including those chained to wheelbarrows.

Sentries patrol round the prison; apart from them not another living creature may be seen about, and it seems as if they are guarding some kind of rare treasure in the wilderness.

A verst further on, the coal quarries begin, then for about another verst one rises over bare, uninhabited coast and, at last, comes to another cleft, in which lies Dooay, the former capital of Sakhalin penal servitude. For the first few minutes that one drives into the street, Dooay gives the impression of a small fortress of ancient times, with its level, smooth street, like a parade ground for marches, the white spick-and-span cottages, the striped sentry box and striped posts; the only thing lacking to complete the impression is the rolling of drums. In the cottages live the head of the military command, the Governor of the Dooay Prison, the priest, officers and so forth. Across the end of the short street stands a grey wooden church, which blocks off the non-official part of the port from the onlooker; here, the cleft divides into the appearance of the Russian letter Э, sending out trenches to left and right. To the left there is a quarter which was formerly called "Zhidovskaya" (Jews' Hamlet), and to the right are all sorts of prison buildings and a quarter without a name. On both sides, but especially to the left, it is cramped, dirty and uncomfortable; there are no more clean little white cottages here; the hovels are decrepit, without yards, or greenery, or porches, and they cling chaotically to the side of the road down below, on the mountain slopes and on the mountain itself. The plots of farmland – if you can even call it farmland in Dooay – are tiny; in the Inventory of Landholdings, four households are indicated as having only four square sazhens each. It's squashed, there's not enough room to swing a cat, but all the same, the Dooay executioner Tolstykh has found a little spot in the crush and the stench and is building himself a house. Not counting the military command, the free population and the prison, there are 291 inhabitants in Dooay: 167 men and 124 women. There are forty-six householders, plus six co-holders. Most of the householders are penal convicts. What inspired the administration to settle them and their families on plots just here, in a cleft of all places, is impossible to comprehend. In the Inventory of Landholdings, only one-eighth of a desyatin of arable land is shown for the whole of Dooay, and there is no haymaking land at all. Let us assume that the men are occupied in convict labour; but what, then, do the eighty adult women do?

What is all their time spent on, the time which here, thanks to the poverty, the bad weather, the uninterrupted jingling of chains, the constant sight of uninhabited mountains and the roar of the sea, and thanks to the groaning and the weeping which can often be heard from the overseers' cabin, where punishments with the lash and birch are carried out, seems many times longer and more agonizing than in European Russia? The women spend this time in complete inactivity. In one single cabin, most often consisting of one single room, you will find a convict's family, and with it a soldier's family, two or three convict tenants or guests; in the same place there will be juveniles and two or three cradles in the corners, plus, right there, hens and dogs too, while outside in the street around the cabin there is refuse, puddles of slops, there is nothing to occupy yourself with, nothing to eat, you are fed up with talking and quarrelling, it's boring going outside – how monotonously dismal and filthy it all is, what depression and tedium! In the evening the convict husband returns from work, he is hungry and wants to sleep, but his wife starts to cry and wail: "You've ruined us, damn you! I've had it, the kids have had it!" "Oh, give over howling!" mutters the soldier on the stove. Later, everybody has gone to sleep; the children have had a good cry and have also been settled down for a long time now, but the woman is still not asleep – she thinks and listens to the roaring of the sea; now she is tormented by melancholy: she is sorry for her husband and irritated that she did not restrain herself from reproaching him. But once again the next day it is the same old story.

If one were to judge merely from Dooay alone, the agricultural colony would appear to be burdened with a surplus of women and convicts with families. Because of the lack of space in the cabins, twenty-seven families live in old buildings already long condemned for demolition, dirty and hideous in the extreme, called "married barracks". There are no rooms here, but cells with bed-boards and chamber pots, as in a prison. The inmates of these cells are distinguished by the extremely wide variety of their social composition. In one cell, with the glass knocked out of the windows, and with a stifling smell from the latrine, live: a convict and his free-status wife; a convict, his free-status wife and daughter; a convict and his settled exile wife and daughter; a convict and his free-status wife; a Polish settled exile and his female convict cohabitant – all of them, with their belongings, are lodged in one cell and sleep side by side on one continuous bed-board; in another cell there are: a convict, his free-status wife and son; a female Tatar convict and her daughter; a Tatar convict, his free-status wife and two little Tatar children in skullcaps; a convict, his free-status wife and son; a settled exile who had spent thirty-five years in hard-labour institutions but still maintained a dapper appearance, with his black moustaches, who for lack of boots would go round barefoot, but was a passionate gambler;* beside him on the bed-board his convict mistress – a creature dull, half-asleep and pitiful to look at; further on a convict, his free-status wife and three children; a convict with no wife or family; a convict, his free-status wife and two children; a settled exile; and a convict, a little old man, neatly dressed and clean-shaven. A piglet wanders round the same cell champing away; there is slimy filth on the floor, and a stench of bugs and something sour; the bugs, I was told, make life intolerable. In a third cell: a convict, his free-status wife and two children; a convict, his free-status wife and daughter; a convict, his free-status wife and seven children – one is a daughter of sixteen years old and one of fifteen; a convict, his free-status wife and son; a convict, free-status wife and son; a convict, free-status wife and four children. In a fourth cell: an army non-commissioned officer with the position of overseer, with his eighteen-year-old wife and daughter; a convict and his free-status wife; a settled exile; a convict and so on. From these barbaric lodgings and their conditions, where girls of fifteen and sixteen are forced to sleep side by side with penal-labour convicts, the reader may judge with what disrespect and contempt are surrounded here the women and children who have voluntarily followed their husbands and fathers into penal servitude, how little they are valued here and how little thought is given to the concept of an agricultural colony.

The Dooay Prison is smaller, older and many times dirtier than the one at Alexandrovsk. Here there are also common cells and continuous bed-boards, but the furnishings and fittings are poorer and the general way things are ordered is worse. The walls and floors are uniformly filthy, and from time and damp have already gone so black they would hardly get any cleaner if you washed them. According to the data in the Medical Report for 1889, every prisoner here has 1.12 cubic sazhens of air. If it reeks of slops and of the latrine here during summer, when the doors and windows are open, then I can imagine what hell it must be in winter, when in the mornings hoar frost and icicles are found inside the prison. The Prison Governor here is a former military medical orderly who saw service in the Polish regiments and who now occupies the rank of clerk-in-chancery. Besides the Dooay Prison, he also manages the Voyevodsk Prison, the mines and the Dooay Post. The compass of his duties is completely unrelated to his rank.

In the Dooay punishment cells are kept the hardened criminals, for the most part recidivists and those under investigation. To look at, they are the most commonplace people, with good-natured, rather stupid faces, which expressed only curiosity and the wish to answer me as respectfully as possible. And with the majority of them, their crimes were no more clever and no more cunning than their faces. Usually they had been sent here for five to ten years for killing somebody in a brawl, then they had tried to escape; they had been caught, run off again, and so on till they were given life sentences and placed in the category of prisoners who were non-reformable. The crimes of practically all of them were terribly dull and commonplace, at least from the point of view of superficial interest, and I purposely cited Yegor's story above so that the reader might form a judgement about the drabness and aridity of the contents of hundreds of the tales, autobiographies and anecdotes which I had occasion to hear from the prisoners and people connected with the penal settlement. However, one grey-haired old man, sixty to sixty-five years old, Terekhov by name, who was being kept in the dark punishment cell, produced on me the impression of a real villain. The day before my arrival, he had been punished with the lash, and when our conversation turned to this he showed me his buttocks, which were dark-blue-crimson from bruises. According to the prisoners' stories, this old man had murdered sixty people in his time; he was alleged to have carried on in the following fashion: he would spy out which of the newly arrived prisoners were a bit better off, and entice them into escaping with him; then, in the taiga, he would kill them and rob them, and in order to hide the traces of the crime, he would cut the corpses into pieces and throw them in the river. The last time they had tried to capture him, he had defended himself against the overseers by brandishing a large oak cudgel. Looking at his dull, tinny eyes, and his large, half-shaven skull, angular as a cobblestone, I was prepared to believe all these stories. One Ukrainian, who was also sitting in the dark punishment cell, touched me with his frankness; he requested the Prison Governor to return 195 roubles to him which had been taken from him during a search. "And where did you pick up this money?" asked the Governor. "Won it at cards," he replied, swore, and, turning to me, began to assure me that there was nothing astonishing in this, since practically the entire prison played cards, and among the prisoners, gamblers who had sums of two or three thousand roubles to lay out were not uncommon. In the punishment cells I also saw a vagabond who had cut two of his own fingers off; his wound was tied up with a dirty old piece of rag. Another vagabond had a bullet wound right through him; fortunately the bullet had passed across the external edge of the seventh rib. His wound was also bound up with a dirty piece of rag.*

It is always quiet in Dooay.* The ear soon grows accustomed to the slow, measured jangling of fetters, the thunder of the breakers on the sea and the humming of telegraph wires, and because of these sounds the impression of dead silence grows still stronger. Severity and rigorousness lie not merely on the striped posts. If somebody should unexpectedly burst into loud laughter in the street, it would sound harsh and unnatural. Right from its very foundation, life here has taken a form which can be communicated only through hopeless and implacably cruel sounds, and the ferocious cold wind which on winter nights blows into the cleft from the sea is the only thing here which sings precisely the right note. Because of this it always sounds weird when, amidst the silence, there suddenly rings out the singing of the Dooay idiot Shkandyb. He is a convict, an old man, who from the very first day of his arrival on Sakhalin refused to work, and all measures of compulsion came to nothing in the face of his unconquerable, sheer wild-animal obstinacy; they planted him in the dark punishment cell, and flogged him several times, but he would stoically endure the punishment, and after every flogging would cry out: "And I'm still not going to work in spite of all that!" They spent a lot of effort over him, and finally gave up. Now he strolls around Dooay singing.*

As I have already mentioned, the extraction of coal is carried on a verst away from the post. I visited the mine, and they led me along gloomy, damp corridors, and obligingly acquainted me with the way things were organized, but it is very difficult for me to describe all this, not being a specialist. I will refrain from technical details, and anybody who is interested in them may read the specialist work of mining engineer Mr Keppen,* who at one time directed the local pits.

At the present time, the Dooay mines fall to the exclusive use of the private company "Sakhalin", the representatives of which live in St Petersburg. According to a contract concluded in 1875 for twenty-four years, the company may utilize a strip of land on the west coast of Sakhalin of two versts along the coast and one verst into the interior of the island; they are granted free-of-charge vacant convenient places for coal depots in the Primorskaya Region on the mainland and the islands adjacent to it; the company also receives free-of-charge building material necessary for construction, and labour; the import of all objects necessary for technical and administrative work and the organization of the mines is permitted duty-free; for every pood of coal bought by the naval department, the company receives fifteen to thirty copecks; every day not less than 400 convicts are assigned to the company for use in labour; if in fact less than this number are sent out for work, then for every missing labourer the Exchequer pays the company a penalty of one rouble per day; the number of people the company requires may be supplied at night as well.

In order to fulfil the obligations it has assumed, and to protect the interests of the company, the state maintains two prisons, the Dooay and the Voyevodsk, by the mines, and a military detachment of 340 men, which every year costs it 150,000 roubles. Consequently, if, as I am told, the representatives of this company living in St Petersburg total a mere five, then safeguarding the profits of each one of them costs the Exchequer 30,000 roubles annually, without even mentioning that, due to these profits, regardless of the objectives of an agricultural colony, and as if in mockery of hygiene, more than 700 convicts, their families, soldiers and office employees have to be kept in such appalling holes as the Voyevodsk and Dooay ravines, and without even mentioning that, by handing over convicts to the service of a private company for money, the administration have sacrificed the corrective aims of punishment to the considerations of industry, that is, they are repeating the same old error which they themselves condemned.

The company, on its part, answers for all this with three important obligations: it must manage the working of the Dooay mines in a proper fashion and maintain a mining engineer at Dooay who would supervise that the extraction is carried out correctly; regularly twice a year the company must pay rent money for the coal and a fee for the convict labour; and, in working these mines, it must use convict labour exclusively in all aspects of the work connected with the undertaking. All these three obligations exist only on paper and have to all appearances already been long forgotten. The working of the pits is carried on unscrupulously, on a basis of kulakism. "No improvements in the technique of production, or research for guaranteeing it a lasting future, have been undertaken," we read in one official's report. "The work, as regards its financial organization, bears all the signs of rapacious exploitation, as the last report of the District Engineer testifies." The mining engineer who the company is obliged to have by the contract does not exist, and the mines are run by a mere foreman-miner. As regards payment, here too it is only necessary to point out in this respect what the official person just mentioned calls "rapacious exploitation". The company uses both mines and convict labour free of charge. It is obliged to pay, but for some reason it does not; the representatives of the other side, in view of such a clear infringement of the law, have been under an obligation for a long time now, but under some pretext are delaying, and, into the bargain, continue to expend 150,000 roubles a year protecting the company's profits, and both sides are behaving in such a fashion that it is difficult to say when these abnormal relationships will come to an end. The company is entrenched as deeply on Sakhalin as was Foma in the village of Stepanchikovo, and it is as inflexible as Foma.* Up till 1st January 1890, it owed the Exchequer 194,337 roubles 15 copecks; by law, one tenth of this money should go to the convicts, as remuneration for labour. How and when they settle up with the Dooay convicts, who pays them and whether the convicts receive anything, I do not know.

Every day, 350 to 450 convicts are requisitioned for work, and the remaining 350 to 400 of those living in the Dooay and Voyevodsk Prisons comprise the reserve. They could not manage without a reserve, since convicts "capable of work" are stipulated for daily use in this contract. Those nominated for work in the mines at five in the morning, on the so-called "work gang", pass into the jurisdiction of the Mines Administration, that is, a small group of private persons who comprise the "Office". Upon the discretion of this "Office" depend nomination for work and the quantity and degree of physical effort involved in each day's labour for each individual convict; by the very nature of the set-up here, it is incumbent on them to take care that the prisoners undergo uniform punishment; the prison administration here reserve for themselves merely the supervision of conduct and prevention of escapes, and have, from necessity, in all other respects washed their hands of everything.

There are two mines: the old and the new. The convicts work in the new one; here the height of the coal seam is about two arshins, and the width of the tunnels is the same; the distance from the exit to the present workings is 150 sazhens. A labourer with a small sledge weighing a pood crawls on all fours up a dank, dark tunnel; this is the hardest part of the work; then, after loading his sledge with coal, he returns. At the exit the coal is loaded in trucks and is conveyed over the rails to the storage depots. Every convict must come up with his sledge not less than thirteen times a day – this is his penal "task". In 1889–90 every convict extracted, on average, 10.8 poods a day, 4.2 poods less than the norm established by the Mines Administration. In general the productivity of the mine and of the convict labour in the mine is not very high: it fluctuates between 1,500 and 3,000 poods a day.

Settled exiles work in the Dooay mines as well, hiring themselves out voluntarily. They are placed in more difficult conditions than the convicts. In the old mine, where they work, the seam is no higher than an arshin, the work-face is 230 sazhens from the exit, and there is heavy seepage from the upper stratum of the seam, so that the work has to be done in constant damp; and they live on their own provisions in quarters which are many times worse than the prisons. But despite this, their labour is much more productive than the convicts' – by 70% and even 100%. Such are the advantages of voluntarily hired over forced labour. Hired workers are more profitable to the company than those they are obliged to have by contract, and therefore if – as is accepted here – a convict hires a settled exile or another convict in his place, then the Mines Administration will gladly put up with this irregularity. The third obligation has been coming apart at the seams for ages now. It has been the custom right since the foundation of Dooay that the poor and the simple-minded work both for themselves and for others, while simultaneously card-sharpers and moneylenders drink tea, play cards or stroll around on the landing stage with nothing to do, jingling their shackles and chatting to bought-off overseers. For these reasons dreadful sagas are constantly being enacted here. For instance, a week before my arrival, one rich prisoner, a former St Petersburg merchant sent here for arson, was birched, allegedly for reluctance to work. He was rather a stupid man, who did not have the sense to hide his money, who had paid excessive bribes and who finally grew tired of sometimes paying an overseer five roubles, sometimes the executioner three roubles, and one day, in an unhappy moment, he refused both of them point blank. The overseer complained to the Prison Governor that this here prisoner so-and-so did not want to work, the Governor ordered thirty strokes of the birch rod, and it goes without saying that the executioner put all he had into it. The merchant, when being flogged, screamed out: "I've never ever been flogged before!"* After the sentence had been carried out, he resigned himself, paid the overseer and the executioner, and, as if nothing had happened, continued to hire a settled exile in his place.

The exceptional burden of the mine work is not in the fact that the work must be done underground in dark and damp tunnels, at one moment on all fours, at another bending over; the construction and roadworks in the wind and rain require greater expenditure of physical effort from the workmen. And to anybody who is familiar with the way things are run in the Donetsk pits in the Ukraine, the Dooay mines will not seem too dreadful. The whole of the exceptional onerousness lies not in the work itself, but in the general organization and conditions, in the obtuseness and lack of conscientiousness of all types of petty officialdom, when at every step you have to suffer insolence, injustice and arbitrariness. The rich drink tea and the poor work, the overseers deceive their superiors in full view of everybody, and the inevitable clashes between the Mines and Prison Administrations inject into life a whole mass of squabbles, bits of scandal and all sorts of petty irregularities, whose weight lies above all else on the people who are under subjection – as the proverb has it: "the squires get into a fight – and their workmen get a headache". And besides, the convict, however deeply depraved or unjust he may be, loves justice above all else, and if justice does not exist among the people set over him, then from year to year he will fall into bitterness and extreme scepticism. How many grumbles there are in penal servitude because of this – morose old men, who, with earnest, vicious faces chatter never-endingly about people, about the authorities, about a better life, while the prison listens and roars with laughter, because it really does come out sounding ludicrous. Work in the Dooay mines is onerous also because, over the course of many years here, the convict without any break sees nothing but the mine, the road to the prison and the sea. His whole life seems to slip away on this narrow coastal sandbank between the clay shore and the sea.

By the Mines Office stands a barrack hut for the settled exiles working in the mines, an old barn, quite small, only with difficulty adapted for sleeping in at nights. I visited it at five in the morning, when the settled exiles had only just got up. What stench, what darkness, what a crush! Their heads were dishevelled, as if a brawl had been going on among these people all night, their faces were a yellowy-green colour, and, only half-awake, their expressions were like lunatics or people who were sick. They had clearly been sleeping in their clothes and boots, pressed tight up against each other, some on the bed-boards and some even under the boards, straight on the filthy earth floor. According to the words of the doctor who was accompanying me that morning, there was one cubic sazhen of air to three or four people. And this, by the way, was just at the time they were expecting cholera on Sakhalin, and quarantine had been stipulated for ships.

On the same morning I visited the Voyevodsk Prison. It was built in the '70s, and to form the space on which it now stands they had to tear down the mountainous shoreline over an area of 480 square sazhens. At the present time this, of all the Sakhalin prisons, is the most disgraceful; it remains wholly untouched by reform, so that it may serve as a perfect illustration of the workings of the old regimes and old prisons which at one time aroused horror and loathing in eyewitnesses. The Voyevodsk Prison consists of three main blocks and one small one, in which the punishment cells are located. Of course, it is simply not appropriate here to talk about the cubic capacity of the air or the ventilation. When I entered the prison they had just finished washing the floors, and the moist, rancid air still had not had time to thin out after the night, and lay heavily. The floors were wet and unpleasant to see. The first thing I heard was – complaints about bedbugs. Bedbugs make life impossible. Formerly they had exterminated them with chloride of lime, or let them be frozen during heavy frosts, but now even that did not help. In the quarters where the overseers lived, there was also the strong odour of the latrine and of acid, and also complaints about bugs.

In the Voyevodsk Prison are kept those convicts chained to wheel-barrows. There are in all eight of them here. They live in common cells together with the other prisoners and spend their time in complete idleness. At least, in the 'Register of distribution of convict-exiles to varieties of labour', those chained to wheelbarrows are numbered among the non-workers. Each of them is shackled in hand and foot irons; from the middle of the hand irons stretches a long chain three or four arshins long in length which is fastened to the bottom of a small wheelbarrow. The chains and the barrow hamper the prisoner, he tries to make as few movements as possible, and this undoubtedly has an effect on his musculature. The hands become so highly accustomed to every movement, even the very slightest, being accompanied by a sensation of heaviness, that even after the prisoner has been separated from the barrow and hand irons, he still feels awkwardness in his arms for a long time afterwards, and without any necessity makes strong and abrupt movements; when, for instance, he grabs hold of a cup, he slops the tea all over the place as if he is suffering from *chorea minor*. At night, whilst asleep, the prisoner keeps the barrow underneath the bed-board, and so that this should be more comfortable and easier to do, he is usually placed on the edge of the common board.

All eight men are recidivists who each have already been sentenced several times in their lives. One of them, an old man of sixty, was chained for trying to escape, or as he himself put it, "for stupidity". He was obviously suffering from consumption, and the former Prison Governor had ordered him, out of pity, to be placed a little nearer the stove. Another one, who had at one time been a guard on the railway, had been sent here for sacrilege, and on Sakhalin had been caught forging twenty-five-rouble notes. When one of the people walking round the cells with me started reproving him for robbing a church, he said: "So what? God doesn't need money." And, noticing that the prisoners were not laughing, and that the remark had created an unpleasant impression on everybody, he added, "But at least I didn't go round murdering people." A third, a former naval seaman, had been sent to Sakhalin for a disciplinary offence; he had hurled himself at an officer with fists raised. In penal servitude he had been hurling himself at people in precisely the same way: on the latest occasion he had leapt on the Prison Governor when the latter had ordered him to be punished by birching. His defence counsel at the court martial had explained this mannerism he had of throwing himself on people as a medical condition; the court sentenced him to death,* but Baron Korf commuted the sentence to hard labour for life, the lash and chaining to the wheelbarrow. The remainder were all chained for murder.

The morning was damp, overcast and cold. The sea pounded restlessly. I recall that, on the road from the old mine to the new, we stopped for a moment by an elderly Caucasian who was lying in the sand in a dead faint; two fellow countrymen were holding him by the arms, helplessly and bewilderedly glancing from side to side. The old man was pale, his hands were cold, his pulse was feeble. We discussed it and passed on, without giving him any medical assistance. When I remarked that it would not have done any harm at least to have given the old man some tincture of valerian, the doctor who was accompanying me said that the medical assistant at the Voyevodsk Prison had no medicaments of any sort whatsoever.

9

The Tym. Lieutenant Boshnyak. Polyakov. Verkhny Armudan. Nizhny Armudan. Derbinskoye. An excursion along the Tym. Uskovo. The Gypsies. An excursion in the taiga. Voskresenskoye.

THE SECOND DISTRICT OF NORTHERN SAKHALIN lies on the other side of the watershed range of mountains and is called the Tymovsk District, as the majority of its settlements lie on the river Tym, which flows into the Sea of Okhotsk. As you travel from Alexandrovsk to Novo-Mikhailovka, a range of mountains towers in the foreground, blocking out the horizon, and that section of it which can be seen from where you are is called the Pilinga. From the heights of this Pilinga a splendid panorama opens out, with one side overlooking the Dooay Valley and the sea, giving a view of a broad plain which, for a distance of over 200 versts to the north-east, is watered by the Tym and its tributaries. This plain is many times larger and more interesting than the one at Alexandrovsk. The abundance of water, the variety of building timber, the grass which grows higher than a human being, the fabulous wealth of fish and coalfields would lead one to suppose a well-fed and satisfied existence for all of a million people. And so it might have been, but the cold currents of the Sea of Okhotsk and the ice-floes which drift by the east coast of the island even in June testify with merciless clarity that when Nature created Sakhalin the last thing she had in mind was mankind and his benefit. If it were not for the mountains, the plain would be tundra, even colder and more hopeless than the area around Viakhta.

The first person to visit the river Tym and give a description of it was Lieutenant Boshnyak. He was sent here in 1852 by Nevelskoy to verify information received from the Gilyaks about deposits of coal, and then to cut across the island and to come out on the shore of the Sea of Okhotsk, where they had said there was an excellent harbour. He was given a dog sled, enough rusks to last him thirty-five days, tea and sugar, a small hand-compass, and, together with a cross of Nevelskoy's, the reassurance that "If there's rusk to satisfy your hunger, and a mug of water to quench your thirst, then, with God's aid, it's still possible to get the work done." Travelling along the Tym to the east coast and back again, he reached the west coast with difficulty, all in rags, hungry and with abscesses on his legs. The dogs refused to go any further as they were starving. Just on Easter time he holed himself up in a corner of a Gilyak hut, positively exhausted. There was no rusk, no food with which to break his fast,* his legs hurt dreadfully. The most interesting thing in Boshnyak's exploration is, of course, the personality of the explorer himself, his youth – he was twenty-one at the time – and his selfless and heroic devotion to duty. The Tym was covered with deep snow in that period, as it was March, but even so this journey gave him material for his notes which was interesting in the extreme.*

A serious and thorough exploration of the Tym, with scientific and practical objectives, was carried out in 1881 by the zoologist Polyakov.* Making his way from Alexandrovsk by means of oxen, he crossed the Pilinga with great difficulty on 24th July. There were only footpaths there, along which convicts went up and down, carrying provisions on their shoulders from the Alexandrovsk to the Tymovsk District. The height of the mountain range here is 2,000 feet. On the Admvo – the tributary of the Tym nearest to the Pilinga – stood the Vedernikovsky Camp, of which one thing only now remains – the post of camp overseer.* The tributaries of the Tym are swift, meandering, shallow and full of rapids, communication by boat is impossible, and so Polyakov had to make his way right up to the Tym itself by means of his oxen. At the settlement of Derbinskoye he and his companions got in a boat and sailed downstream.

It's fatiguing to read this account of his journey, owing to the conscientiousness with which he enumerates all the rapids and shoals he encountered on the way. Over a distance of 272 versts from Derbinskoye he had to overcome 110 obstacles – eleven rapids, eighty-nine shoals and ten spots where the fairway was dammed up by deposited trees, stumps and piled-up branches. This means that on average the river was shallow or obstructed every two versts. By Derbinskoye it was twenty to twenty-five sazhens wide, and the wider it became, the shallower it grew. Its frequent bends and convolutions, the speed of its current, and its shallows, do not permit any hope that it will ever be navigable in any meaningful sense of the word.

In Polyakov's opinion, it is suitable solely for floating rafts downstream. Only in the final 70 to 100 versts to the river mouth – that is, where colonization should be counted on least of all – does it become deeper and straighter; the current becomes less turbulent here, and there are no rapids or shallows at all; a steam-launch could get along here, or even a shallow-draught steam-tug.

When the extremely rich local fishing grounds finally fall into the hands of entrepreneurs, then in all probability substantial efforts will be made to clean up and deepen the fairway of the river; perhaps there will even be a railway along the bank to the river mouth, and without a doubt the river will repay all expenditure with interest. But this is in the distant future. At this present moment, however, with the existing resources, and when one must bear in mind only the most immediate goals, the riches of the Tym are almost totally illusory. The river yields the exile population insultingly little. The settled exiles of the Tymovsk District live in precisely the same hand-to-mouth fashion as do those in the Alexandrovsk District.

According to Polyakov's account, the valley of the river Tym is dotted with lakes, dried-up river-beds, ravines and pits; there are no even, level areas along its banks, overgrown with nourishing fodder grasses, no water meadows covered by spring floods, and only now and again does one come across meadowland covered with sedge – these are lakes overgrown with grass. On the slopes of the mountainous bank grows thick coniferous forest, and on the sloping side are birches, weeping willows, elms, aspens and whole groves of poplar. The poplars are very tall; by the bank they are undermined by the river, fall into the water and form obstructions and dams. Bird cherry, osier, sweet briar and hawthorn form some of the bushes here. The air is dark with mosquitoes. There was hoar frost on the morning of 1st August. The nearer one approaches to the sea, the poorer the vegetation becomes. The poplars disappear little by little, the weeping willows turn into bushes, and the overall picture is already dominated by the banks of sand or peat, with their marsh whortleberries, cloudberries and moss. Gradually the river broadens out to 75 to 100 sazhens, there is already tundra all around, the banks are low and marshy... A chill wind blows in from the sea.

The Tym flows out into the Nyysky Bay, or the Tro – a small waste of water which serves as the threshold to the Sea of Okhotsk, or – which is precisely the same thing – to the Pacific Ocean. The first night that Polyakov spent on the shore of this bay was clear and chilly, and a little comet with a bifurcated tail shone in the sky. Polyakov did not write what reflections filled him as he admired the comet and listened to the sounds of the night. Sleep "overcame" him. On the morning of the following day fate rewarded him with an unexpected sight: at the mouth of the bay, by its inlet, lay a dark vessel with white sides, with a deckhouse and beautiful rigging; tethered on the bow sat a live eagle.*

The shore of the bay created a dismal impression on Polyakov; he called it a typical and characteristic example of the landscape of the polar lands. The vegetation is meagre and stunted. The bay is separated from the sea by a long, narrow spit of sand which originated in sand-dunes, and beyond this spit the sullen and savage sea extends boundlessly. When at night-time the blanket falls off a little boy who has been reading Mayne Reid,* he shivers, and then he dreams of just such a sea as this. For this is – a nightmare. The surface is the colour of lead, and over it "monotonously weighs the grey sky". The stern waves pound on the deserted shoreline, on which there are no trees, they roar, and very occasionally the black dot of a whale or seal flashes in among these waves.*

To get to the Tymovsk District these days, there is no need to cross the Pilinga over steep places and bumpy, uneven roads. I have already mentioned that they travel from Alexandrovsk to the Tymovsk District now along the main road across the Arkovo Valley and change horses at the Arkovo Halt. The roads here are excellent and the horses can travel swiftly. Sixteen versts from the Arkovo Halt stands the first settlement of the Tymovsk District along the main road, with a name just like something out of an oriental fairy tale – Verkhny (Upper) Armudan. It was founded in 1884 and consists of two quarters which are set on the mountain-slope by the stream of Armudan, a tributary of the Tym. There are 178 inhabitants – 123 male and fifty-five female. There are seventy-five householders, plus twenty-eight co-owners. In comparison to the Alexandrovsk District, in the majority of Tymovsk settlements there are, as the reader will see, very many co-owners or half-sharers, few women and very few legalized families. Out of forty-two families in Upper Armudan only nine have been legalized. There are only three free-status women who have accompanied their husbands voluntarily, that is, exactly the same number as at Krasny Yar or Butakovo, which have been in existence no longer than a year. This lack of women and families in the settlements of the Tymovsk District, often startling, and not corresponding to the overall number of women and families on Sakhalin, may be explained, not by any sort of local or economic conditions, but by the fact that all the parties newly arrived on the island are sorted out at Alexandrovsk, and the local officials, in accordance with the sayings "Charity begins at home" and "Look after number one", retain the majority of the women for their own district, and, into the bargain, "the best they keep for themselves, and the ones who are not so good, they send to us", as the Tymovsk officials told me.

The cabins in Upper Armudan are thatched with straw or tree-bark, and in some the windows have not been put in or have been boarded up. The poverty is truly outrageous. Twenty men do not live at home; they have gone away to earn a livelihood. There are only sixty desyatins of cultivated land among all seventy-five householders and twenty-eight co-holders, and only 183 poods of grain had been sown, that is, less than two poods per household. But even so, crop-rearing could hardly be relied on here, however much was sown. The settlement lies high above sea level and is not protected from north winds; the snow melts here two weeks later than, for instance, in the neighbouring settlement of Malo-Tymovo. To catch fish in the summer they walk twenty to twenty-five versts to the river Tym, and hunting for fur-bearing animals has all the hallmarks of a diverting pastime and contributes so little to the settled exiles' economy that it's not even worth talking about.

I found the householders and other members of their establishments at home; they were all doing nothing, though it was not any kind of holiday or day off, and it would have seemed that, during the hot period of August, they could all have found themselves work, every one of them, young and old, in the fields, or on the Tym, where the seasonal fish were already on the move. The householders and their female co-habitants were obviously bored and were ready to sit and chat for quite a while about this, that and the other. They laughed out of boredom, and then for a bit of variety burst into tears. These people were failures, for the most part neurasthenics and whingers, "superfluous people",* who had already tried everything to earn a crust of bread, had exhausted the strength of which they had had so very little, and finally had given it all up as a bad job, because there "weren't no way at all" and you couldn't make a living "not nohow". The enforced idleness had little by little slipped into a habit, and now, like people waiting by the sea for the weather to change, they pine away, get tired, sleep reluctantly, do nothing and are most likely already incapable of doing anything at all. The only thing they really throw themselves into is games of cards. However strange it may seem, card games flourish in Upper Armudan, and the local players are celebrated all over Sakhalin. For lack of means the Armudan inhabitants play for very small stakes, but to make up for this play without respite, like in the play *Thirty Years, or the Life of a Gambler*.* With one of the most passionate and tireless card-players, the settled exile Sizov, I had the following conversation:

"Why don't they let us go over to the mainland, Your Excellency?" he asked.

"What do you want to go there for," I joked. "There's nobody to play with there, you know."

"Oh, there are real games over there."

"You play *Stoss*?" I asked, after I had been silent for a short while.

"That's quite right, Your Excellency – *Stoss*."

Later on, on leaving Upper Armudan, I asked my convict carriage-driver:

"Do they really play for stakes?"

"Yes, everybody knows they do."

"But just what stakes do they play for?"

"What do you mean, what for? Government rations, bread or things like smoked fish. They play for grub and clothes and sit round themselves cold and starving."

"But whatever do they eat?"

"What do they eat? Well – they win, they eat – they don't win, they go to bed hungry."

Lower down on the same tributary is a further settlement, slightly smaller – Nizhny (Lower) Armudan. I arrived there late in the evening and spent the night at the overseer's office, in the garret, since the overseer would not let me into the main room. "It's impossible to sleep the night there, Your Excellency, the place is crawling with bugs and cockroaches – millions and millions of them!" he said, spreading his arms helplessly. "Would you be so good as to go up to the watchtower?" To get up to the watchtower it was necessary to climb in the darkness up an outside ladder which was wet and slippery with rain. When I dropped in downstairs for some tobacco, I did indeed see "millions and millions" of insects, an amazing sight, and very probably possible only on Sakhalin. The walls and ceiling seemed to be covered with funeral crape, moving as if in a wind; from isolated spots in the crape which scurried along swiftly and raggedly one could guess what this seething, overflowing mass consisted of. A rustling and loud whispering could be heard, as if the cockroaches and bugs* were hurrying somewhere and conferring.

There are 101 inhabitants of Lower Armudan: seventy-six men, twenty-five women. Forty-seven householders plus twenty-three co-holders, legalized families four, unlegalized fifteen. There are only two free-status women. Not a single inhabitant is between the ages of fifteen and twenty. The people live in poverty. Only six homes are roofed with boards, the rest with tree-bark, and in some places, as in Upper Armudan, the windows either have not been put in at all or else have been boarded up. I did not note down a single workman; apparently even the householders themselves have nothing to do. Twenty-one have gone away to find a living. Since 1884, when the settlement was founded, only thirty-seven desyatins of arable land and vegetable gardens have been cultivated, that is, half a desyatin to each holder.

A hundred and eighty-three poods of winter and spring crops are sown. The settlement bears no resemblance whatever to an agricultural village. The inhabitants here are a disorderly rabble of Russians, Poles, Russian ethnic Finns and Georgians, hungry and ragged, who have come together not by their own will but by chance, as if after a shipwreck.

The next settlement along the main road lies on the Tym itself. It was founded in 1880 and named Derbinskoye in honour of the Prison Governor Derbin, who was murdered by a prisoner for his cruelty. He was still young, but a harsh, stern and implacable man. According to the reminiscences of people acquainted with him, he always walked round the prison and the streets with a cane which he took with him for the sole purpose of striking people. He was murdered in the bakery; he struggled, fell into the kneading trough and stained the dough with blood. His death roused general rejoicing among the prisoners, and they collected sixty roubles in small change for his murderer.

Generally speaking, the past of Derbinskoye has not been a cause for rejoicing. One part of the plain on which it now stands is narrow and was covered with a dense birch and aspen forest, while on the other side, which is more spacious, but low and marshy, and, so it would seem, unsuitable for settlement, there grew a thick spruce and larch forest. They had hardly finished cutting down the forest and clearing the ground for the cabins, prisons and storehouses, and then completed the drainage, when they had to contend with a calamity that the colonizers had not foreseen: the spring flooding of the rivulet Amga inundated the entire settlement. A new channel had to be dug for this stream, and a new direction given to it. Today Derbinskoye occupies an area of over one square verst and has the appearance of a genuine Russian village. You enter it over a splendid wooden bridge, the river is cheerful, with green banks and willows, there are broad streets, and cabins with roofs of boards, and courtyards. New prison buildings, all kinds of storehouses and granaries, and the Prison Governor's house stand in the middle of the settlement, and bring to mind not a prison but a manorial estate. The Prison Governor spends his entire time walking from granary to granary, jingling his keys exactly like a landowner of the good old days, "by day and by night guarding his substance". His wife sits by the house in the front garden, majestic as a marquise, ensuring that everything is in order. She can see, right in front of the house, the watermelons, already ripe, peeping out of the open hotbed, and the convict gardener Karatayev walking round them deferentially with an expression of slave-like zeal on his face; she can see being carried up from the river, where the prisoners fish, a choice, healthy Siberian salmon, called a "silverling", which is going to go, not to the prison, but to make cured fish fillets for the authorities. Round the front garden stroll the daughters of the Governor and his wife, the young ladies of the manor, dressed up like little angels; a milliner, a female convict sent here for arson,* sews for them. And a calm, pleasant feeling of plenty and contentment can be sensed all round; people step gently, like cats, and express themselves gently, in a pleasant tone of voice and using soft words.

There are 739 inhabitants in Derbinskoye: 442 men and 297 women, and counting the prison there are about 1,000 in all. There are 250 householders plus 58 co-holders. In external appearance, in the number of families and women, the composition by age of the inhabitants, and in general in all the statistics relating to it, this is one of the few settlements on Sakhalin which can seriously be called a settlement and not a rabble thrown together by chance. There are 121 legalized families in the settlement, fourteen "free associations", and among the lawful wives there is a significant predominance of free-status women, of whom there are 103 here; children comprise one-third of the entire population. But, in an effort to understand the economic situation of the Derbinskoye population, one still nevertheless runs up before all else against various chance circumstances, which play exactly the same leading and supporting roles here as they do in the other settlements on Sakhalin. And here natural and economic laws yield first place, so to speak, to such random factors as, for example, how great or small are the numbers of those incapable of work, those who are sick, and the quantity of thieves or former town-dwellers who take up crop-raising here only against their will; the number of people who have already been resident for a long period, the closeness of a prison, the personality of the District Governor, etc., etc. – all these are conditions which may change every five years or so, or even more frequently. Those Derbinskoye inhabitants who served out their hard labour before 1880, and settled here first of all, bore on their shoulders the settlement's difficult past, grew inured to it, and little by little grabbed the best places and plots of land, and those who came here from Russia with money and a family do not do too badly either; the 220 desyatins of land and the yearly fish-haul of 3,000 poods indicated in reports evidently specifies the economic situation of these house-holders alone; the remaining inhabitants, that is, half of Derbinskoye, are hungry, in rags, and create the impression of being unnecessary, superfluous, not living, and getting in the way of other people living. In our European Russian villages such a sharp distinction may not be observed even after a large fire.

When I arrived in Derbinskoye, and later on went round the cabins, rain was falling, and it was cold and muddy. For lack of space in his cramped quarters, the Prison Governor lodged me in a new granary, not long built, in which they had laid out bentwood furniture. They provided me with a bedstead and table and fixed a latch to the doors so that they could be locked from inside. From the evening till about two in the morning I would read or make extracts from the Inventory of Landholdings and from the Alphabetical Register. The rain drummed on the roof unceasingly, and very occasionally some belated prisoner or soldier would walk past, splashing through the mud. There was peace both in the granary and in my soul, but hardly had I put out the candle and got into bed, when rustling, whispering, knocking, splashing and deep sighs became audible... the drops falling from the ceiling onto the latticework of the bentwood chairs produced a hollow ringing sound, and after every such sound somebody would whisper in despair: "Oh, my God! Oh, my God!" Right beside the granary stood the prison. Could the prisoners possibly be crawling towards me through an underground passage? But then, a gust of wind, the rain would drum even louder, somewhere the trees would rustle – and again would come the deep, despairing sigh: "Oh, my God! Oh, my God!"

In the morning I used to go out onto the porch. The sky was grey and dismal, and it would be raining and muddy. The governor would be hastily moving from door to door with his keys. "I'll write you a sick-note all right – the sort of sick-note you'll be itching from in a week's time," he'd yell. "I'll give you sick-note!"

These words were addressed to a crowd of about twenty convicts, who, as far as could be judged from the few phrases that reached me, were asking to be allowed to go to the hospital. They were in tatters, soaked through with rain, spattered with mud and shivering; they were trying to show by acting that they were indeed ill, but on their chill

145

faces, frozen with cold, something stood out that was crooked and lying, although possibly they weren't lying at all. "Oh, my God! Oh, my God!" one of them sighed, and it seemed to me as if my nightmare were still continuing. The word "pariah" came to mind, meaning in common Russian currency the state of a human being below whom it is no longer possible to fall. During the entire period I was on Sakhalin, only in the settled exiles' barracks by the mines, and here, at Derbinskoye, were there moments when it seemed to me that I was seeing the extreme and utmost degree of human degradation, lower than which it is simply impossible to go.

In Derbinskoye there lives a convict woman, a former baroness, whom the local women call "the Working Lady". She lives a frugal working life and people say she is satisfied with her situation. One former Moscow merchant, who had traded at one time on the Tverskaya-Yamskaya,* said to me with a sigh: "The horse races are on in Moscow now!" and, turning to the settled exiles, began to describe to them what the races were like and what a vast number of people would flock every Sunday to the turnpike on the Tverskaya-Yamskaya. "Believe me, Your Excellency," he told me, agitated by his own tale, "I'd give everything, I'd give my life, just to have one glance, not at Russia, not at Moscow, but quite simply just at the Tverskaya." In Derbinskoye, by the way, live two people with the same name, Yemelyan Samokhvalov, and I recall that in the backyard of one of these Yemelyans, I saw a cock fastened by its leg. All the inhabitants of Derbinskoye, including the Yemelyan Samokhvalovs themselves, are amused by the strange and very complex combination of circumstances which finally brought two men living in different corners of Russia and with the same forenames and surnames, here, to Derbinskoye. On 27th August there arrived in Derbinskoye General Kononovich, the head of the Tymovsk District, A.M. Butakov, and one other official, a young man – all three educated and interesting people. The four of us went for a little excursion together, which from start to finish, however, was attended by such discomforts that we finished up making, not an excursion, but a poor imitation of an expedition. To begin with, it was pouring with rain and it was muddy and slippery; whatever you took hold of was wet. From the soaked back of one's head water flowed down inside one's collar, and there was a cold and soggy feeling inside one's boots. Lighting up a cigarette was a complicated and difficult problem, which we tried to solve by mutual cooperation. We got into a boat near Derbinskoye and set off down the Tym. On the way we stopped to view the fishing grounds, the watermill and the arable land cultivated by the prison. I shall describe the fisheries in their place; we unanimously acknowledged that the mill was excellent, but that the prison farmland did not look anything special and really only drew attention by its meagre dimensions; a landholder in earnest would have called it a mischievous joke. The current of the river is swift; the four oarsmen and the man at the wheel were working away in unison; thanks to the rapidity and the frequent bends in the river, the pictures before our eyes changed every minute. We were rowing along a mountain river in the taiga, but I would willingly have exchanged all its wild charm, its green banks, its steep slopes and the solitary motionless figures of fishermen for a warm room and dry footwear, all the more so as the landscape was not new to me and was monotonous, and – the main thing – was concealed in a grey rainy mist. In front, in the prow of the boat, Mr Butakov was sitting with a rifle, firing at wild ducks which we had startled by our appearance.

At present only two settlements have been founded along the Tym to the north-east of Derbinskoye: Voskresenskoye and Uskovo. To populate the entire river up to its mouth, at least thirty such settlements, at intervals of ten versts, would be needed. The administration intends to establish them at the rate of one or two a year and to connect them with a road, calculating that, in time, a highway will run between Derbinskoye and the Nyysky Bay, enlivened and protected by a whole chain of settlements. As we rowed past Voskresenskoye, the overseer was standing to attention on the bank, obviously expecting us. Mr Butakov called to him that we would spend the night at his quarters on our way back from Uskovo, and so he should get a bit more straw ready.

Soon after this there came a strong odour of rotting fish. We were approaching the Gilyak hamlet Usk-vo, which gave the name to the present Uskovo. On the bank we were met by Gilyaks, their wives, children and tailless dogs, but we observed none of that amazement that the late Polyakov had caused here with his arrival. Even the children and dogs looked at us indifferently. The Russian settlement lies two versts from the bank. There is the same picture here at Uskovo as there is at Krasny Yar. There is a broad, poorly grubbed-up street, covered with mounds and woodland grass, and, on both sides, unfinished cabins, felled trees and heaps of rubbish. All the Sakhalin settlements that are being newly built produce the identical impression of villages destroyed by an enemy or long abandoned, and only from the fresh, clear colour of the frames and shavings is it apparent that a process is going on here that is precisely the opposite of destruction. There are seventy-seven inhabitants in Uskovo: fifty-nine men and eighteen women, thirty-three householders, plus twenty superfluous people, or, in other words, co-holders. Only nine have families. When the Uskovo inhabitants and their families gathered around the overseer's office, where we were drinking tea, and when the women and children, being the most curious, came forwards, the crowd began to resemble a Gypsy encampment. Among the women, as a matter of fact, there were several swarthy Gypsies, with cunning, affectedly mournful faces, and almost all the children were Gypsies. Several convict Gypsies had been settled at Uskovo, and their bitter fate had been shared by their families, who had accompanied them voluntarily. Two or three of the Gypsy women were slightly familiar to me from a previous occasion; a week before my arrival in Uskovo, I had seen them at Rykovo walking along under the windows with bags over their shoulders, offering to tell fortunes.*

The inhabitants of Uskovo live in great poverty. There are at present only eleven desyatins of arable land and vegetable gardens under cultivation; that is almost one-fifth of a desyatin per household. They all live at the expense of the Exchequer, from which they receive prisoners' provisions, but they do not obtain these cheaply, however, since, owing to the lack of roads, they have to carry them here from Derbinskoye through the taiga on their shoulders.

We had a rest and at five in the afternoon set off on foot back to Voskresenskoye. It is not a long distance, six versts in all, but, not being used to journeying through the taiga, I began to feel fatigued after the very first verst. As before, the rain was pouring down. Immediately we left Uskovo we had to deal with a brook a sazhen in width, across which three thin, crooked logs had been thrown; everyone else got over safely, but I stumbled and collected a bootful of water. Before us lay a long straight cutting which had been cleared for the projected roadway; there was literally not a single sazhen of it which you could walk along without balancing and without stumbling. There were greasy mounds, pits full of water, bushes and rhizomes as stiff as wire, which you tripped over like a doorstep, and which were treacherously concealed under the water; but the main thing, and the most unpleasant, was the wind-fallen branches, and the piles of trees that had been felled here during the clearing of the cutting. You would overcome one pile, all in a sweat, and continue on your way through the marsh, when there would be another new pile, which you could not get past, so up you would climb again, but my companions would shout to me not to go that way, I should go to the left or right of the pile, and so on. At first I was trying simply to do one thing only – not get the other boot full of water, but I very soon gave the whole thing up as useless, and abandoned myself to the course of events. The heavy breathing could be heard of the three settled exiles who were dragging along behind carrying our things; the closeness of the air and difficulty in breathing were torture, we wanted a drink... we went along without our caps; it was easier that way.

Gasping for breath, the General sat down on a thick log. We took a seat as well. We gave a cigarette to each of the settled exiles, who did not dare sit down.

"Ouf! It's really tough going!"

"How many versts left to Voskresenskoye?"

"Still three to go."

Mr Butakov was making his way in the most sprightly fashion of all of us. In the past he had often gone long distances on foot through the taiga and tundra, and now some six versts or so were a mere trifle to him. He told me about his journey along the river Poronai to the Zaliv Terpeniya and back; the first day it's agonizing, the second day your body aches all over, but the walking is easier all the same, and on the third and subsequent days you feel as if you're on wings, as if you are not walking but being carried by some invisible power, although just as before your feet are getting entangled in *bagulnik** and sinking in the mire.

Halfway through our journey it began to get dark, and soon we were surrounded by pitch blackness; I had already lost hope that this excursion would ever come to an end, and went groping along up to my knees in water and stumbling over logs. Here and there around me and my fellow travellers motionless will-o'-the-wisps gleamed and faded; entire pools and enormous decaying trees shone with phosphorus, and my boots were bespattered with moving specks that sparkled like fireflies.

But there in the distance, thank God, a light began to glow, not phosphorescent, but a real one. Someone called to us and we replied; the overseer appeared with a lantern; taking broad strides across the puddles, in which his lantern was reflected, he led us right through Voskresenskoye,* which was hardly visible in the dark, to the overseer's office. My travelling companions had a change of dry clothing with them, and on entering the overseer's office they hastened to put them on, but I had nothing with me, although I was literally soaked right through. There was only one bed at the overseer's, and the General took it, and the rest of us, absolutely deadbeat, lay on hay on the floor.

Voskresenskoye is almost twice as large as Uskovo. There are 183 inhabitants – 175 men and eight women. There are seven "free associations" and not one single legally married couple. There are almost no children in the settlement – just one little girl. There are ninety-seven householders, plus seven co-holders.

10

Rykovskoye. The Prison. The Galkin-Vraskoy Meteorological Station. Palevo. Mikryukov. Valzy and Longari. Malo-Tymovo. Andreye-Ivanovskoye.

B Y THE UPPER REACHES OF THE TYM, in the most southerly part of the river basin, we encounter a more highly developed existence. This may or may not be relevant, but it is warmer here, nature is gentler toned, and a cold and hungry person will find more suitable natural conditions for himself than around the central or lower courses of the Tym. There is even a spot here which resembles European Russia. This similarity, so charming and moving for an exile, is especially noticeable on that section of the plain where the administrative centre of the Tymovsk District, the settlement of Rykovskoye, is situated. Here the plain is up to six versts wide; to the east it is protected a little by a low range of mountains running along the Tym, and to the west the dark-bluish spurs of the watershed mountain chain are visible. It has no hillocks or eminences, it is perfectly level, and like ordinary Russian land in appearance, with tilled fields, hay meadows, pastures and green groves. When Polyakov was here the whole surface of the valley was covered with grassy mounds, pits, gullies hollowed out by rain, small lakes and shallow little streams which flowed into the Tym; a horse with a rider would get across it at times on its knees, at times on its belly; but nowadays it has all been cleared and drained, and for a distance of fourteen versts between Derbinskoye and Rykovskoye there stretches an elegant road, astounding in its evenness and perfect straightness.

Rykovskoye, or Rykovo, was founded in 1878; the spot for it was selected and indicated with a fair degree of success by Prison Governor Non-Commissioned Officer Rykov. It is outstanding for its rapid growth, which is unusual even for a settlement on Sakhalin; in the last five years its area and population have increased fourfold. At the present time it occupies three square versts, and has 1,368 inhabitants; 831 men and 537 women; with the prison and military command included, the figure rises to over 2,000. It bears no resemblance to the Alexandrovsk Post; the latter is a small town, a little Babylon, already containing gaming houses and even family bathhouses maintained by a Jew;* Rykovo, however, is a genuine dull Russian village, with no pretensions to culture whatever. When you ride or walk along the street, which stretches for about three versts, its length and monotony quickly become tedious. Here the streets are not called *slobodki* (settlements, quarters, districts) in the Siberian fashion, as at Alexandrovsk, but are called by the ordinary Russian word for street, *ulitza*, and the majority of them have retained the names given them by the settled exiles themselves. There is a Sizovskaya Street, so called because the cabin of the female settled exile Sizovskaya stands on the corner, there is a Mountain Range Street, and a Ukrainian Street. There are a lot of Ukrainians in Rykovo, and consequently, due to this, nowhere in any other settlement will you find such splendid surnames* as here: Yellowleg, Stomach, nine with the name Godless, Bury, River, Breadroll, Greyfilly, Trough, Neverwell and the like. In the middle of the settlement is a large square, on which stands a wooden church, and round the edge are not shops and booths, as in our European Russian villages, but prison buildings, offices and the officials' living quarters. When walking across the square, one's imagination visualizes the hubbub of a jolly fair being held there, the resounding voices of the Uskovo Gypsies as they trade horses, the reek of tar, manure and smoked fish, the lowing of cows, and the shrill sounds of an accordion blending in with drunken songs; but the peaceful picture dissolves into thin air when you suddenly hear the sounds you have come to detest, the clank of chains and the hollow footfall of prisoners and guards crossing the square to the prison.

There are 335 householders in Rykovo, plus 189 "half-sharers" who run the house jointly with them and consider themselves to be holders too. There are 195 legalized families, 91 "free" families; the majority of the legal wives are free-women who have come here with their husbands. There are 155 of them. These are high figures, but one should not be comforted or carried away by them: they hold little promise of anything worth while. It may already be observed from the number of "half-sharers", those supernumerary household-ers, how large a superfluous element there is here, which possesses neither the means nor the opportunity to run a household independ-ently, and how cramped and famished it is here already. The Sakhalin administration settles people on plots in any old way, without tak-ing into consideration the circumstances, and without looking into the future, and, under such an unsophisticated method of creating new inhabited points and holdings, even those settlements located in relatively favourable conditions, such as Rykovo, all finally finish up presenting a picture of total impoverishment and reach the state of Upper Armudan. For Rykovo, given the existing amount of land fit for crop-raising, and under the conditions of local productivity, even taking into consideration other sources of income, 200 householders would be quite ample, but, in fact, including the supernumerary ele-ment, there are over 500, and every year the administration is going to send in hordes more.

The prison at Rykovo is new. It is built on the model common to all the Sakhalin prisons – wooden barrack huts containing cells, and the dirt, destitution and discomfort peculiar to these lodgings intended for the life of the herd. Of late, however, owing to several special features which it is difficult not to notice, Rykovo has come to be considered the best prison in the whole of northern Sakhalin. It seemed to be the best to me, too. Since, before all else, I had to make use of office information for my inquiries, and of the services of literate people in the vicinity of each prison, I could not help noticing first of all, throughout the entire Tymovsk District and especially in Rykovo, the fact that the local clerks were well trained and disciplined, as if they had gone through a special school; they maintained the Inventories of Landholdings and Alphabetical Registers in exemplary order. Later on, when I visited the prison, I received the same impression of order and discipline from the cooks, bakers and suchlike; even the senior overseers did not seem so overfed, so sublimely stupid and so coarse as at Alexandrovsk or Dooay.

In those parts of the prison where maintenance of cleanliness is possible, the requirements of neatness are, to all appearances, taken to an extreme. In the kitchen, for example, in the bakery, and in the living quarters themselves, the furniture, the crockery, the air and the clothing of the ancillary staff, there was the sort of cleanliness which would satisfy the most niggling sanitary inspection, and it was obvious that this tidiness is observed here constantly and does not depend on somebody or other's visits. When I visited the kitchen they were boiling up soup from fresh fish in the cauldrons – an unhealthy food item, since the prisoners fall ill with acute intestinal catarrh from the fish caught in the upper reaches of the river; but even taking this into consideration, the whole set-up seemed to suggest that here a prisoner received in full the entire quantity of dietary allowance that he was entitled to by law. It is, I think, because exiles from the privileged classes have been enlisted in the capacity of directors, managers and so forth of work within the prison, and are answerable for the quantity and quality of the prisoners' diet, that such disgraceful phenomena as putrid cabbage soup and bread mixed with clay have become impossible. From the great number of daily-allowance portions of bread which had been prepared for distribution to the prisoners, I took several at random, and weighed them, and each weighed without fail three *funty** and even a little over.

The latrine here, too, is arranged on the cesspool system, but it is maintained differently from those in other prisons. The requirements of cleanliness here are taken to a degree that is, perhaps, even inconvenient for the prisoners; it's warm inside the building, and the sour smell is completely absent. This latter is achieved by the special type of ventilation described in Professor Erisman's well-known handbook, and called, I believe, "reverse draught".* The Governor of Rykovo Prison, Mr Livin, is a talented man, with substantial experience and initiative, and everything that is good in the prison is owed chiefly to him. Unfortunately he has a strong predilection for the birch rod, which has already been marked on one occasion by an attempt on his life. A prisoner hurled himself onto him with a knife, as if onto a wild beast, and this attack had fatal consequences for the assailant. Mr Livin's constant thoughtfulness for people and, at exactly the same time, the birch rods, his rapturous delight in corporal punishment, his savagery, if you like, is a combination that is totally incompatible and inexplicable. Captain Venzel in Garshin's *Memoirs of Private Ivanov** was evidently not pure invention.

In Rykovo there is a school, a telegraph office, a hospital and the Galkin-Vraskoy Meteorological Station, which is run unofficially by a settled exile from the privileged classes, a former midshipman, a remarkably fine and hard-working man; he also fulfils the duties of churchwarden. During the four years of the station's existence, not much data has been collected, but even so the differences between the two northern districts have already been sufficiently well clarified. Whereas the Alexandrovsk District has a maritime climate, the climate of the Tymovsk District is continental, although there are not more than seventy versts between the weather stations in the two districts.

The variations in temperature and in the number of days with precipitations in the Tymovsk District are not nearly so considerable. Summers here are warmer, the winters more severe; the average annual temperature is below zero, that is to say, it is even lower than on Solovetsky Island.* The Tymovsk District is higher above sea level than the Alexandrovsk, but because it is surrounded by mountains, and lies, so to speak, in a basin, it has on average almost sixty more windless days per year, and, in particular, twenty fewer days with cold winds. A small difference may also be observed in the number of days with precipitations: there are more of them in the Tymovsk District – 116 with snow and 76 with rain; the total amount of precipitation in both districts produces a more significant difference: almost 300 mm, and the damper of the two is the Alexandrovsk District.

On 24th July 1889 there was a morning frost which nipped the ripening potato plants in the bud at Derbinskoye. On 18th August a frost destroyed the leafy tops of the potato plants throughout the whole district.

To the south of Rykovo, on the site of the former Gilyak hamlet of Palvo, on the tributary of the Tym with the same name, stands the settlement of Palevo, founded in 1886. An excellent country road leads over the level plain here from Rykovo, past groves and fields which reminded me enormously of European Russia, perhaps because I drove there in very fine weather. The distance is fourteen versts. A post and telegraph road will soon run in the direction from Rykovo to Palevo; it has been planned for a long time now and will connect northern and southern Sakhalin. This road is already under construction.

There are 396 inhabitants of Palevo: 345 men and fifty-one women. There are 183 householders, plus 137 "half-sharers", although, under local conditions, fifty householders would have been quite sufficient. It would be hard to find another settlement on Sakhalin in which there had united so many diverse circumstances unfavourable to an agricultural colony as here. The soil is composed of shingle; at one time, according to the stories of the established residents, the Tungus tribespeople had grazed their deer on the spot where Palevo now stands. Even the settled exiles discuss the fact that this region was, in remote times, the bed of the sea, and, so they say, the Gilyaks nowadays discover objects from boats in the area. There are only 108 desyatins of land under cultivation, and that includes ploughland, vegetable gardens and hay meadows; there are, however, over 300 householders. Only thirty adult women live here, one to each ten men, and, as if in mockery, as if to make the sad significance of this ratio felt even more forcefully, death called in at Palevo not so very long ago and in a short space of time had carried off three female cohabitants. Almost a third of the householders had not done any crop-rearing before their exile, since they belonged to the urban classes. Unfortunately, the list of unfavourable circumstances does not end there. For some reason also – possibly because, as the proverb puts it, it never rains but it pours – in no other settlement on Sakhalin is there such a vast number of robbers as there is here, of all places, in this long-suffering settlement of Palevo, which has been treated so badly by fate. They thieve here every night; on the day before my arrival three had been sent to the fetter block for stealing rye. Besides such people as those who steal out of need, there are also not a few so-called "nasty bastards" who harm their fellow-settlers for the pure pleasure of the thing. With no necessity at all, they slaughter cattle during the night, pull up unripened potatoes, remove frames from the windows and so on. All this entails losses and completely drains the pitiful, beggarly households, and, what is hardly less important, keeps the population in a state of constant fear.

The conditions of life speak of nothing but poverty pure and simple. The roofs of the cabins are thatched with tree-bark and straw, and there are no yards or outbuildings at all; forty-nine houses are still uncompleted and have evidently been abandoned by their owners. Seventeen owners have gone away to try to find a livelihood.

When I was going round the cabins at Palevo, I was persistently followed by an overseer, who had been appointed from the ranks of the settled exiles, a native of Pskov by birth. I recall that I asked him whether it was Wednesday or Thursday that day. He replied: "I'm sorry to say I can't remember, Your Excellency."

In a government house lives the retired Quartermaster Karp Yerofeyich Mikryukov, the oldest of the Sakhalin overseers. He arrived on Sakhalin in 1860, at the time when the island's penal settlement was only just starting up, and, of all the Sakhalin inhabitants in good health today, he alone could write the whole of the penal colony's history. He is talkative and answers questions with obvious pleasure, and at great length, as if he is senile; his memory has by now begun to deceive him, so that he can only remember distinctly the distant past; his living conditions are pretty good and have a thoroughly domestic feel to them; there are even two portraits done in oils, one of himself and the other of his late wife with a flower on her bosom. He is from the Vyatsky Province by birth, and his face is vividly reminiscent of the late writer Fet.* He conceals his real age and says he is only sixty-one, but in actual fact he is over seventy. He is married for the second time, to the daughter of a settled exile, a young woman by whom he has had six children between the ages of one and nine. The youngest is still nursing.

My conversation with Mikryukov lasted till well past midnight, and the stories he told me were all about nothing but the penal settlement and its heroes, such as, for example, Prison Governor Selivanov, who in the emotion of the moment would break locks off doors with his fist, and was finally murdered by the prisoners for his cruelty towards them.

When Mikryukov went off to his half of the house, where his wife and children were sleeping, I went outside into the street. It was a very silent, starry night. A guard was tapping, somewhere close by a stream was murmuring. I stood for a long time looking now at the sky, now at the cabins, and it seemed to me some kind of miracle that I was 10,000 versts from home, somewhere in Palevo, in this corner of the earth where they could not remember what day of the week it was, and really where they hardly needed to remember, since here it was quite decidedly precisely the same to them whether today was Wednesday or Thursday...

Still further south, along the route of the projected post road, lies the settlement of Valzy, founded in 1889. There are forty men here and not a single woman. A week before my arrival three families had been sent from Rykovo still further south, to found the settlement Longari, on one of the tributaries of the river Poronai. These two settlements, in which life has hardly just begun, I will leave to the writer who will have the opportunity of travelling to them over a good road and of observing them closely.

To conclude the survey of settlements in the Tymovsk District, there remain only two for me to mention: Malo-Tymovo (Little Tymovo) and Andreye-Ivanovskoye. They are both situated on the river Malaya Tym (Little Tym), which has its source near the Pilinga and falls into the Tym near Derbinskoye. The first and oldest settlement in the Tymovsk District was founded in 1877. In former times, when crossings were made over the Pilinga, the route to the Tym went through this settlement. It now has 190 inhabitants: 111 male and 79 female. There are sixty-seven householders and co-holders. At one time Malo-Tymovo was the main settlement and centre of the region which is now the Tymovsk District; nowadays, however, it has taken a back seat and is like a small county town that has been deprived of its status, in which all life has come to a standstill; the only thing which speaks of its former grandeur is the prison, which is fairly small, and the house where the Prison Governor lives. At the present time the post of Governor of Malo-Tymovo Prison is occupied by Mr K., a cultured and very fine young man from St Petersburg, who is obviously extremely homesick for European Russia. The enormous official living quarters, with their wide, high-ceilinged rooms, in which one's steps resound hollow and lonely, and the time, so long and so dragging, of which there is so much, with nothing to do with it, oppress him to such a degree that he feels as if he is in captivity. As if on purpose, the young man wakes up early, at four or five o'clock. He is up, has drunk his tea and has descended into the prison... and what is there to do then? Then he walks round his labyrinth, glancing every now and then at the wooden walls caulked with oakum, he walks and walks, and walks, then he has another drink of tea, and occupies some time with his botany, and then he goes walking again, and nothing can be heard except his own footsteps and the howling of the wind.

There are many established residents in Malo-Tymovo. Among them I met the Tatar Furazhiyev, who once travelled with Polyakov to the Nyysky Bay; he recalls both the expedition and Polyakov with pleasure. Also perhaps, among the old men, the settled exile Bogdanov might prove interesting as regards his lifestyle; he is a religious dissenter* who has taken up moneylending. He wouldn't let me in for ages, but, once having done so, waxed eloquent on the theme that these days all sorts of folk were wandering about, lots of them, and if you let them in, well, for all you know, they'll rob you blind, etc., etc., etc.

The settlement of Andreye-Ivanovskoye is so called because somebody or other was named Andrey Ivanovich. It was founded in 1885 on top of a swamp. It has 382 inhabitants, 277 men and 105 women. The number of householders plus co-owners is 231, although here, too, as at Palevo, fifty would have been quite sufficient. The composition of the population cannot be called successful here either. Just as we observe among the population of Palevo a surplus of the urban middle classes and *raznochintzy** who had never previously done any crop-rearing, so here, at Andreye-Ivanovskoye,* there are many non-Orthodox Christians, and non-Christians; they comprise a quarter of the entire population: there are forty-seven Catholics, the same number of Muslims and twelve Lutherans. And among the Orthodox Christians there are a good few non-Russians, for instance, Georgians. Such a motley collection gives the population the character of a mob thrown together by chance and prevents it from blending into a rural society.

11

*The projected new district. The Stone Age. Has there ever been volun-
tary colonization? The Gilyaks. Their numerical strength, appearance,
physique, diet, clothing, housing, hygienic conditions. Their character.
Attempts at their Russification. The Oroki.*

A S THE READER MAY SEE from the survey of settlements which has
just been completed, both northern districts (*okrug*) occupy an
area equal to a fairly small European Russian county (*uyezd*).* To calculate the area they cover in square versts is, at the present time, hardly
possible, since the extent of both districts to the north and south is not
limited by any defined boundaries. Between the Alexandrovsk Post and
Rykovo, the administrative centres of the two districts, the distance by
the shortest route, through the pass across the Pilinga, is sixty versts,
across the Arkovo Valley seventy-four versts. In local terms, that is not
close. Without mentioning Tangi and Vangi, even Palevo is considered
to be a distant settlement, and the founding of new settlements a little
to the south of Palevo, along the tributaries of the Poronai, has even,
in its turn, raised the question of the founding of a new district. As
an administrative unit, a district corresponds to a European Russian
county; in the Siberian understanding of the term, such a title may be
applied only to a considerable distance which you cannot travel round
in a whole month, for instance the Anadyr District,* and to a Siberian
government official working in isolation over an area of two or three
hundred versts, the splitting up of Sakhalin into small districts might
seem a luxury. But the population of Sakhalin lives under exceptional
circumstances, and the mechanism of government is much more complex here than in the Anadyr District. The subdivision of the exile
colony into small administrative districts has been brought about by
practical experience, which, besides much else of which mention still
has to be made, has shown, firstly, that the shorter the distances within
an exile colony, the easier and more convenient it is to govern, and,
secondly, the division into districts has been induced by the reinforcement of staffing, and a flood of new people, and this has undoubtedly
had a beneficial influence on the colony. With the reinforcement of the
educated staff in terms of quantity, there has resulted a considerable
increase in quality as well.*

On Sakhalin I caught a conversation about the planned new district; they talked about it as if it were the Land of Canaan, because on the map, across the whole of this district along the Poronai river, lay a road to the south, and it was conjectured that all the convicts now living in the Dooay and Voyevodsk prisons* would be transferred to the new district; that, after the resettlement, nothing but the memory would remain of these horrible places, the coal mines would be withdrawn from the "Sakhalin" Company, which had been breaking the contract for so long now, and the coal would no longer be extracted by convicts but by settled exiles on the basis of trade associations.

Before concluding with northern Sakhalin, I do not consider it superfluous to say a few words about those people who have lived here at various times and who at present live independently of the exile colony. In the Duyka Valley Polyakov found knife-shaped fragments made from obsidian, stone arrowheads, whetstones, stone axes and suchlike; these discoveries entitled him to think that in remote times in the Duyka Valley lived people who did not know of metals – people of the Stone Age. Potsherds, bones of bears and dogs, and sinker-weights from sweep-nets, found on the site of their former dwelling place, indicate that they were familiar with the craft of pottery, hunted bears, had fished with sweep-nets, and had been aided in the hunt by dogs. They had evidently obtained articles made of flint – which is not found on Sakhalin – from their neighbours, from the mainland and the nearest islands; it is very likely that during their migrations dogs played the same role as they do now, that is, they pulled sledges. And in the Tym Valley, Polyakov also found the remains of primitive constructions and crude tools. He drew the following conclusion: that "existence is possible on northern Sakhalin even for tribes at a relatively low level of intellectual development; apparently people lived here and for centuries produced the means of protecting themselves against cold, thirst and hunger; in the light of this, it is highly probable that the ancient inhabitants lived here in comparatively small communities, and were not a totally settled people."

Incidentally, when Nevelskoy sent Boshnyak to Sakhalin, he also entrusted him with the mission of verifying rumours about people who had been left on the island by Lieutenant Khvostov and who had lived, according to what the Gilyaks said, on the River Tym.* Boshnyak succeeded in running across traces of these people. In one of the settlements along the Tym the Gilyaks exchanged with him, for three arshins of nankeen cloth, four leaves torn from a Prayer Book, and explained to him that the book had belonged to a Russian who had lived there. On one of the leaves, which had formed the title page of the book, there was written in barely legible script: "We, Ivan, Danila, Pyotr, Sergey and Vasily, were set ashore in the settlement of Tomari-aniva, on the river Aniva, by Khvostov, on 17th August 1805, and we moved to the river Tym in 1810, at the time when the Japanese arrived in Tomari." Then, after inspecting the spot where the Russians had lived, Boshnyak came to the conclusion that they had lived here in three cabins and had kept vegetable gardens. The natives told him that the last of the Russians, Vasily, had died not long previously, that the Russians had been good people, had gone hunting and fishing with them, and had dressed exactly the same as them, except that they had cut their hair. Somewhere else the natives reported a further detail: two Russians had had children by native women. Nowadays the Russians left by Khvostov on northern Sakhalin have already been forgotten and nothing is known of these children.

Incidentally, Boshnyak writes in his memoirs that, while making constant inquiries as to whether there were any Russians who had been settled anywhere on the island, he learnt the following from the natives in the settlement of Tangi: around thirty-five to forty years previously, some sort of vessel had broken up off the east coast of the island; the crew had been saved, built themselves a house, and after some time, a boat as well. These unknown people crossed in the boat over the La Pérouse Strait into the Tatar Strait, and here they were again shipwrecked near the village of Mgachi, and on this occasion only one man was saved, who called himself Kemetz. Not very long after this, two Russians, Vasily and Nikita, arrived from the Amur. They teamed up with Kemetz and built themselves a house in Mgachi; they took up fur-hunting as a trade and travelled to do business with the Japanese and Manchurians. One of the Gilyaks showed Boshnyak a mirror which, he said, Kemetz had given his father as a gift; the Gilyak did not wish to sell this mirror for anything, saying that he kept it as a precious memento of his father's friend. Vasily and Nikita were very much afraid of the Russian Tsar, from which it was clear that they were fugitives or escapees. All three ended their lives on Sakhalin.

The Japanese Mamia-Rinzo* heard on Sakhalin in 1808 that Russian craft had frequently appeared on the west side of the island and that by their pillaging the Russians had finally forced the natives to slaughter some of them and drive the rest off. Mamia-Rinzo gives the names of these Russians – Kamutzi, Simena, Moma and Vasire. "In the last three," says Shrenk, "it's not difficult to recognize the Russian names Semyon, Foma and Vasily. And Kamutzi" (in his opinion) "is very similar to Kemetz."

This very short history of the eight Sakhalin Robinson Crusoes exhausts all the facts relating to voluntary colonization of northern Sakhalin. If the singular fate of Khvostov's five seamen, Kemetz and the two fugitives resembles an attempt at voluntary colonization, then this attempt must be recognized as totally insignificant and, in any case, as unsuccessful. Really it is instructive for us in the respect that all eight men, who lived on Sakhalin for a long period, till the end of their lives, took up not crop-raising but fishing and hunting as trades.

For the sake of completeness there still remains to be mentioned the indigenous local population, the Gilyaks. They live in northern Sakhalin, along the western and eastern coasts and by the rivers, mainly the Tym;* the old settlements and those of their names mentioned by the old writers have been preserved up to the present day, but even so their life cannot be called fully settled, since the Gilyaks feel no attachment to the place of their birth, or to a fixed spot in general; they often leave their yurts and go off to earn a living, wandering over northern Sakhalin with their families and dogs. But in their wanderings, even when they have to undertake long journeys to the mainland, they remain true to the island, and in language and manners a Sakhalin Gilyak differs from a Gilyak living on the mainland no less, perhaps, than a Ukrainian differs from a Muscovite. In view of this it seems to me it should not be difficult to total up the Sakhalin Gilyaks and not confuse them with those who come here from the Tatar Coast to trade. And it would do no harm to count them even if only once every five to ten years, otherwise the important question of the exile colony's influence on their numbers will still remain open for a long time and will continue to be determined arbitrarily.

According to the information collected by Boshnyak, there were 3,270 Gilyaks in all on Sakhalin in 1856. Roughly some fifteen years later, Mitzul was already writing that the number of all Gilyaks on

Sakhalin could be taken as 1,500 at most, and according to the latest information, relating to 1889, and which I have taken from the official 'Register of Numbers of Indigenes', the total number of Gilyaks in both districts is 320. If the figures are to be believed, this means that in five to ten years' time not a single Gilyak will be left on Sakhalin. I cannot judge how accurate the figures of Boshnyak and Mitzul are, but fortunately, for several reasons, the official total of 320 can have no meaning whatever. The 'Register of Indigenes' is compiled by clerks, civil servants who have had no scientific or practical training and who have not even been supplied with any kind of directions; if the information is collected by them on the spot, in the Gilyak settlements, it is done, of course, in an overbearing tone, harshly and impolitely, and with exasperation, whereas the Gilyaks' delicacy, their etiquette which does not permit of arrogant and imperious behaviour towards people, and their revulsion against every kind of census and registration, necessitate especial skill in dealing with them. Besides this, the information is gathered by the administration without any defined objectives, only as an incidental, during which the researcher does not take into consideration any ethnographic map at all, but acts as he thinks fit. Only those Gilyaks who lived to the south of the settlement of Vangi went into the register for the Alexandrovsk District, and in the Tymovsk District they were only counted near the Rykovo settlement, where they do not live, but simply happen now and again to pass through.

Undoubtedly the number of Sakhalin Gilyaks is constantly decreasing, but this can only be judged approximately, by estimation. And just how great is this decrease? What are its causes? Is it because the Gilyaks are dying out, or because they are resettling on the mainland or the northern islands? Owing to the lack of reliable statistical information,* and our talk about the ruinous influence of the Russian influx based merely on analogies, it is also perfectly possible that this influence has been totally insignificant, almost nil, since the Sakhalin Gilyaks live chiefly along the Tym and the eastern seaboard, where there are no Russians as yet.

The Gilyaks belong neither to Mongol nor Tungus stock, but to some unknown people, which was perhaps mighty at one time, and ruled the whole of Asia, but is now living out the last years of its existence on a small patch of land in the form of a none-too-numerous but still fine and cheerful race. Owing to their unusual sociability and mobility, the Gilyaks long ago managed to intermix with all the neighbouring peoples, and so to meet a pure-blooded Gilyak with no tinge of Mongol, Tungus or Aino characteristics is almost impossible. The Gilyaks have round, flat, moon-shaped faces, yellowish in colour, and unwashed, with high cheekbones, slanting eyes and a sparse, sometimes hardly noticeable beard; their hair is smooth, black and stiff, and gathered into a little pigtail on the back of the head. A Gilyak's facial expression does not betray the savage in him; it is always intelligent, gentle and naively attentive; it is either a broad, blissful smile, or else thoughtfully mournful, like a widow. When he stands in profile with his sparse little beard, pigtail and soft, feminine expression, you could draw a likeness of Kutyeikin* from him, and it becomes partly comprehensible why some travellers have attributed the Gilyaks to Caucasian stock.

I refer those who wish to become acquainted with the Gilyaks in detail to the specialist ethnographers, e.g. L.I. Shrenk.* I shall limit myself simply to those particulars which are peculiar to the natural conditions here and which may, directly or indirectly, give indications which will be useful in practice for new colonizers.

The Gilyak is of strong, thick-set build, and average, even small, in height. Tall stature would hamper him in the taiga. His bones are thick and are distinctive for the powerful development of all the appendages and protuberances to which the muscles are attached, and this leads one to assume firm, powerful muscles and a constant strenuous battle with nature. His body is lean and wiry, without a layer of fat; you do not come across obese, plump Gilyaks. Obviously all the fat is expended in warmth, of which the body of a Sakhalin inhabitant needs to produce such a great deal in order to compensate for the loss engendered by the low temperature and the excessive dampness of the air. It's clear why the Gilyak consumes such a lot of fats in his food. He eats rich seal, salmon, sturgeon and whale fat, meat and blood, all in large quantities, in a raw, dry, often frozen state, and because he eats coarse, unrefined food, the places to which his masticatory muscles are attached are singularly well developed and his teeth are heavily worn. His diet is made up exclusively of animal products, and rarely, only when he happens to have his dinner at home or if he eats out at a celebration, will he add Manchurian garlic or berries. According to

Nevelskoy's testimony, the Gilyaks consider working the soil a great sin; anybody who begins to dig the earth or who plants anything will infallibly die. But bread, which they were acquainted with by the Russians, they eat with pleasure, as a delicacy, and it is not a rarity these days in Alexandrovsk or Rykovo to meet a Gilyak carrying a round loaf under his arm.

The Gilyaks's clothing is adapted to the cold, wet and sharply changeable climate. In summertime he dresses in a shirt of blue nankeen or *daby** and in trousers of the same material and, just in case, he keeps in reserve, slung over his shoulder, a short coat or jacket of seal or dog fur; his legs are covered in high fur boots. In winter he wears fur trousers. Even the warmest clothing is cut and sewn in such a way as not to hamper his swift, deft movements in the hunt and during journeys by dog sled. Sometimes, trying to play the dandy, he will wear prisoners' overalls. Eighty-five years ago Kruzenshtern saw a Gilyak in a magnificent silken garment "embroidered with a great number of flowers"; nowadays you would not find such a beau with a lit candle at midday.

As regards the Gilyaks' yurts, here, too, the requirements of the damp, cold climate take first place. There exist summer and winter yurts. The first are built on stilts, the second present the appearance of dugouts with walls of thin logs in the form of a truncated square pyramid; on the outside the logs are strewn with earth. Boshnyak spent the night in a yurt consisting of a pit one and a half arshins in depth dug into the ground and covered with thin logs as roofing, and the entire thing had earth heaped up all round it. These yurts are made of cheap material which is always ready to hand, and so, if they have to, leaving them behind is not a matter for regret; they are warm and dry inside, and in every respect they far outstrip those wet, cold hovels made of tree bark which our convicts live in when they are working on the roads or in the fields. The summer yurts should be positively recommended to the vegetable gardeners, coal miners and fishermen, and in general to all those convicts and settled exiles who work outside the prison and away from home.

The Gilyaks never wash, so that even ethnographers find it difficult to put a name to the real colour of their faces; they do not wash their linen, and their fur clothing looks as if it has just been stripped off a dead dog. The Gilyaks themselves give off a heavy, acid smell, and you know you are near their dwellings from the repulsive, sometimes hardly bearable odour of dried fish and rotting fish offal. By each yurt usually lies a drying ground filled to the brim with split fish, which from a distance, especially when the sun is shining on them, look like filaments of coral. Around these drying grounds Kruzenshtern saw a vast number of maggots covering the ground to the depth of an inch. In winter the yurts are full of acrid smoke which comes from the open fireplace, and on top of all this the Gilyaks, their wives and even the children smoke tobacco. Nothing is known about the morbidity and mortality of the Gilyaks, but one must form the conclusion that these unhealthy hygienic arrangements must inevitably have a bad effect on their health. Possibly it is to this they owe their small stature, the puffiness of their faces, and a certain sluggishness and laziness of movement; one could also possibly ascribe to it the fact that the Gilyaks have always displayed a poor resistance in the face of epidemics. It is well known, for example, what devastation smallpox created on Sakhalin. At the northern extremities of the island, between Capes Elizaveta and Mariya, Kruzenshtern came across a settlement of twenty-seven dwellings; P.P. Glen, a participant in the famous Siberian expedition who visited here in 1860, found at that time that only traces of the settlement remained, and in other parts of the island too, according to him, he discovered only traces of the former denser population. The Gilyaks told him that over the previous ten years, that is, since 1850, the population of Sakhalin had significantly decreased due to smallpox. And those fearful smallpox epidemics which in former times laid waste to Kamchatka and the Kurile Islands would hardly have passed Sakhalin by. It should be understood that it is not the smallpox itself which is so dreadful but the low powers of resistance, and if spotted typhus or diphtheria is brought into the colony, and if it penetrates into the Gilyaks' yurts, the effect will be the same as with the smallpox. On Sakhalin I did not hear about any kind of epidemic; one may say that there have not been any here at all for the last twenty years, except, however, epidemic conjunctivitis, which may still be observed even at the present time.

General Kononovich has authorized the admission of natives to the District Infirmary and their maintenance at state expense (Directive no. 335, 1890). We have no direct observations on the morbidity of the Gilyaks, but one can form some concept of it from the presence of such pathogenic causes as the lack of cleanliness, the immoderate use of alcohol, the long-standing contact with the Chinese and the Japanese,* the constant proximity of dogs, the injuries and so on and so forth. There is no doubt that they are often sick and need medical assistance, and if circumstances allow them to make use of the authorization to receive treatment, then the local doctors will gain the opportunity of observing them more closely. It is not within medicine's power to arrest fatal extinction, but perhaps the doctors will succeed in learning the conditions under which our interference in the life of this people could bring them least harm.

Writers give varying accounts of the Gilyaks' character, but all agree on one thing – that they are not a warlike race, they do not like quarrels or fights, and they get along peacefully with their neighbours. They have always treated the arrival of new people with suspicion, with apprehension about their future, but have met them every time amiably, without the slightest protest, and the worst thing they would do would be to tell lies at people's arrival, painting Sakhalin in gloomy colours and thinking by so doing to frighten foreigners away from the island. They embraced Kruzenshtern's travelling companions, and when Shrenk fell ill this news quickly spread among the Gilyaks and aroused genuine sorrow. They tell lies only when trading or talking to a suspicious and, in their opinion, dangerous person, but, before telling a lie, they exchange glances with each other in an utterly childlike manner. Every sort of lie and bragging in the sphere of everyday life and not in the line of business is repugnant to them. I recall that in Rykovo one day two Gilyaks who had the idea I was lying to them convinced me of this. It was towards evening. The two Gilyaks – one with a small beard, the other with a chubby, womanish face – were lying on the grass in front of a settled exile's cabin. I was walking past. They called me over and started to ask me to go into the cabin and bring out their outdoor clothes, which they had left with the exile that morning; they themselves did not dare to do this. I explained that I did not have the right either to go into somebody else's cabin when the owner was not there. They were silent for a short while.

"You – politic?" (i.e. political prisoner) the Gilyak with the womanish face asked me.

"No."

"Then you – write-write man?" (i.e. clerk), he said, seeing paper in my hands.

"Yes, I write."

"And how many wages you earn?"

I was earning about 300 roubles a month, so I stated this figure. One would have to have seen what an unpleasant impression, almost one of illness, my answer produced. Both Gilyaks suddenly clutched their bellies and, bending to the earth, began to rock slightly as if they had acute stomach pains. There was an expression of despair on their faces.

"Akh, how you can speak like this?" I heard. "Why you talk so bad? Akh – like this no good! You must not!"

"Just what have I said that's bad?" I asked.

"Butakov, District Chief, big man, he only get 200, but you no chief, you little write-write man – get 300! You speak no good! Must not!"

I began to explain to them that, although the District Governor was a big man, he stayed in one place and for this reason only received 200, but, although I was only a write-write man, I had, on the other hand, come from far away, I had done over 10,000 versts, my expenses were greater than Butakov's, and so I needed more money. This reassured the Gilyaks. They exchanged glances, talked a little between themselves in Gilyak, and stopped worrying. From their faces it was clear that they already believed me.

"Truth, truth," said the Gilyak with the beard animatedly. "Good – you go now."

"Truth," the other nodded to me. "You go."

The Gilyaks conscientiously fulfil commissions they have undertaken, and there has not yet been a single case of a Gilyak abandoning mail halfway or embezzling other people's belongings. Polyakov, who often had to deal with Gilyak boatmen, wrote that they were proving to be scrupulous performers of assumed duties, in which field they were outstanding in their delivery of government goods. They are perky, intelligent, cheerful, and feel no stand-offishness or uneasiness whatever in the company of the rich and powerful. They do not recognize that anybody has power over them, and, it seems, they do not possess even the concept of "senior" and "junior". In his *History of Siberia* I. Fischer states that the celebrated Poyarkov came upon the Gilyaks, who at that time "were not subject to another's power in any way". They do have a word "Janchin" signifying superiority, but they apply this term equally both to generals and to well-off traders who have a lot of nankeen and tobacco. Gazing at a picture of His Majesty the Tsar which Nevelskoy possessed in his living quarters, they said that this must be some physically strong man who gave away a lot of tobacco and nankeen. The Governor of the Island wields enormous and even terrifying power on Sakhalin, but once, when I was travelling with him from Upper Armudan to Arkovo, we encountered a Gilyak who felt no inhibitions about shouting to us peremptorily "Stop!" and then asking us whether on our way we had come across his white dog. People say and write that the Gilyaks do not respect family seniority either. A father does not think he is superior to his son, and a son does not look up to his father but lives just as he wishes; an elderly mother has no greater power in a yurt than an adolescent girl. Boshnyak writes that he chanced more than once to see a son striking his own mother and driving her out, and nobody daring to say a word to him. The male members of the family are equal among themselves; if you entertain them with vodka, then you also have to treat the very smallest of them to it as well. But the female members are all equal in their lack of rights; be it grandmother, mother or baby girl still being nursed, they are ill treated in the same way as domestic animals, like an object which can be thrown out, sold or shoved with one's foot like a dog. However, the Gilyaks at least fondle their dogs, but their womenfolk – never. Marriage is considered a mere trifle, of less importance, for instance, than a drinking spree, and it is not surrounded by any kind of religious or superstitious ceremony. A Gilyak exchanges a spear, a boat or a dog for a girl, takes her back to his own yurt and lies with her on a bearskin – and that is all there is to it. Polygamy is allowed, but it has not become widespread, although to all appearances there are more women than men. Contempt towards women, as if for a lower creature or object, reaches such an extreme in the Gilyak that, in the field of the question of women's rights, he does not consider reprehensible even slavery in the literal and crude sense of the word. According to Shrenk's testimony, the Gilyaks often bring Aino women along with them as slaves; evidently with them a woman represents the same sort of trading object as tobacco or nankeen. The Swedish writer Strindberg, a renowned misogynist, who desired that women should be merely slaves and should serve men's whims, is in essence of one and the same mind as the Gilyaks; if he ever chanced to come to northern Sakhalin, they would spend ages embracing each other.

General Kononovich told me that he wished to Russify the Sakhalin Gilyaks. Why this should be necessary I do not know. However, the Russification had already begun long before the arrival of the General. It started when expensive coats of fox and sable fur began to turn up in the possession of some of the officials, even those earning a very small salary, while in the Gilyak yurts Russian containers of vodka appeared;* then the Gilyaks were invited to take part in capturing escapees, for which a financial reward was stipulated for every escapee killed or captured. General Kononovich has authorized the hiring of Gilyaks as overseers; in one of his directives it says that this was being done in view of the extreme need for people familiar with the locality, and for the easing of relations between the local authorities and the natives; however, he informed me orally that this innovation also had Russification as its goal. The first to be appointed to the rank of prison overseer were the Gilyaks Vaska, Ibalka, Orkun and Pavlinka (Directive no. 308, 1889); subsequently Ibalka and Orkun were dismissed "for prolonged failure to appear for the receipt of directions", and Sofronka was appointed (Directive no. 426, 1889). I saw these overseers; they had badges and revolvers. Of these, the one who was especially popular and who caught the eye most often was Gilyak Vaska, an artful, cunning and drunken man. One day, entering the colonization fund shop, I came across a whole bunch of clever people; by the doors stood Vaska; pointing to the shelves of bottles, somebody said that if you got that lot down you, you could get drunk, and Vaska smirked obsequiously and glowed all over with the joy of a sycophant.

Not long before my arrival a Gilyak overseer had killed a convict, and the local sages were now deciding how the Gilyak had shot him – from the front or the back; that is, whether to bring him to trial or not.

That proximity to a prison will not Russify, but only totally corrupt, the Gilyaks there is no need to prove. They are still far from understanding our requirements, and there is hardly any kind of possibility of making them understand that convicts are hunted, deprived of freedom, wounded and sometimes killed, not from a whim, but in the interests of justice; they see in this simply coercion, a manifestation of brutality, and they most probably consider themselves hired killers.* If Russification really is necessary, and if it is impossible to do without it, then I consider that, in the choice of means for this, not our needs, but theirs, should be taken into account above all else. The above-mentioned directive authorizing the admission of natives to the District Infirmary, the distribution of allowances of flour and groats, as happened in 1886, when for some reason the Gilyaks were suffering a famine, the directive that their belongings should not be taken away as security for the debt, and the cancellation of the same debt (Directive no. 204, 1890) – such measures as these will perhaps lead to the objective faster than the issue of badges and revolvers.

Besides the Gilyaks, there also exist in northern Sakhalin the Oroki, or Orochi, of Tungus stock. But since they are hardly heard of in the colony, and there are still no Russian settlements within the limits of the territory they occupy, I shall limit myself merely to mentioning them.

12

My departure for the south. An ebullient lady. The west-coast currents. Mauka. Krilyon. The Aniva. The Korsakovsk Post. New acquaintances. The north-east. The climate of southern Sakhalin. The Korsakovsk Prison. The fire-carts.

O N 10TH SEPTEMBER I was once more back on board the *Baikal* – already familiar to the reader – in order to voyage this time to southern Sakhalin. I was leaving with great pleasure, since I had become fed up with the north and felt as if I needed fresh impressions. The *Baikal* weighed anchor at 10 p.m. It was very dark. I stood alone on the stern, and, gazing back, bade farewell to this sombre little world protected from the sea by the Three Brothers, which now could hardly be distinguished in the night air and which in the darkness resembled three monks in black habits; in spite of the noise the steamer was making, I could hear the waves pounding against these reefs. But then at last Cape Jonquière and the Three Brothers were left far behind and disappeared in the darkness – for me, for ever; the roar of the pounding waves, in which could be heard an impotent and malicious boredom, faded away little by little… We had gone eight versts or so when lights began to glimmer on the shore; it was the dreaded Voyevodsk Prison, and a little further on the lights of Dooay appeared. But soon all this vanished as well, and there remained only the dusk, and a sinister sensation, as if after an ominous bad dream.

I then went below, and found a cheerful company. In the wardroom, besides the captain and his mates, were several passengers, too; a young Japanese man, a lady, an official of the service corps and Hieromonk Irakly, the Sakhalin missionary who was following in my footsteps to the south, so that we could both set off back to European Russia together. Our lady travelling companion, the wife of a naval officer, had fled Vladivostok, having taken fright at the cholera there, and now, somewhat reassured, was returning. She had an enviable disposition. The very slightest reason was enough for her to go off in fits of the most unaffected, bubbling and joyous laughter, till her sides ached, till she was in tears; she would begin to tell you something in her regional burring accent, and suddenly the laughter and gaiety would come gushing up like a fountain, and, looking at the lady, I would begin to laugh as well, Father Irakly would follow me, then the Jap. "Well!" the captain would say finally, with a wave of his hand, and he would also be overcome with laughter. Most probably never at any other time in the Tatar Strait, usually so angry and threatening, have people laughed so much. The next morning the priest, the lady, the Japanese man and I gathered together on the deck to make conversation. And again the laughter flowed, and the only thing lacking was for the whales to thrust their snouts out of the water and start roaring with mirth on catching sight of us.

And, as if on purpose, the weather was calm, warm and cheerful. Close at hand on the left Sakhalin shone green, or to be precise that virginal unpopulated section which the penal settlement had still not touched; to the right the Tatar coast was just about visible in the perfectly transparent air. Here the strait already bears a closer resemblance to the sea, and the water is not so turbid as off Dooay; there is more space, and it is easier to breathe. The lower third of Sakhalin corresponds to France in its geographical position, and if it were not for the cold currents, we would possess a delightful piece of countryside, and of course not only the Shkandybs and Bezbozhnys of this world would be living there now. The cold currents which come from the northern islands, where there is sometimes drifting ice even at the end of summer, bathe Sakhalin on both sides, and the eastern coast, being the most exposed to the currents and cold winds, has to suffer the most; natural conditions there are unmitigatedly harsh, and the flora is definitely polar in character. But the west coast is much more fortunate; here the influence of the cold currents is alleviated by the warm Japanese current known by the name Kuro-Sivo; beyond all doubt, the further south the warmer it is, and the southern part of the west coast is comparatively rich in flora; but all the same, alas, it is still a long way from France or Japan.*

It is interesting that at the same time as the Sakhalin colonizers have for a good thirty-five years now been sowing wheat in the arctic wastes, and laying roads to the sort of places where the only things that thrive are the lower molluscs, the warmest part of the island – that is, the southern part of the western sea coast – remains totally disregarded. Through binoculars and with the naked eye from the steamer one can see fine building-timber and coastal slopes covered with grass that is bright green in colour, and therefore must be juicy and succulent; but no dwelling is visible, nor a single living soul. However, once – it was on the second day of our voyage – the captain drew my attention to a small cluster of cabins, barns and sheds, and said: "That's Mauka." For a long time now in Mauka they have been extracting seakale, which the Chinese buy up very readily, and since the business has been established on a serious footing, and has already yielded a good livelihood to many Russians and foreigners, this spot is very popular on Sakhalin.* It's 400 versts to the south of Dooay, at a latitude of 47°, and stands out by reason of its comparatively fine climate. At one time the trade was in the hands of the Japanese; when Mitzul was here, there were more than thirty Japanese buildings at Mauka, in which forty people of both sexes lived permanently, and in spring a further 300 or so would come here from Japan and work alongside the Ainos, who then comprised the main labour-force. But now the seakale industry is owned by the Russian merchant Semyonov, whose son lives at Mauka permanently; the business is run by the Scotsman Denbigh, who is no longer young and is obviously an extremely competent man. He possesses his own house in Nagasaki, in Japan, and when I said to him, after we had become acquainted, that I would very likely be in Japan in the autumn, he amiably suggested that I stay at his house. Manzes, Koreans* and Russians work for Semyonov. Our settled exiles began to come here to earn a living only from 1886 onwards, and very probably on their own initiative, since the Prison Governors are always more interested in pickled cabbage than in fresh seakale. The first attempts were not entirely successful; the Russians were but little acquainted with the purely technical side of the business; now they have become rather more accustomed to it, and, although Denbigh is not so satisfied with them as with the Chinese Manzes, it is still seriously possible all the same to calculate that, in time, hundreds of settled exiles will earn themselves a crust of bread. Mauka comes under the jurisdiction of the Korsakovsk District. Nowadays thirty-eight people live in the exile settlement here: thirty-three male, five female. All thirty-three males maintain households. Three of them have achieved peasant-in-exile status. The women are all convicts and live as cohabitants. There are no children, and no church, and the boredom must be frightful, especially in winter, when the workers leave the seakale workings and go away. The civil authority here consists of one single overseer, and the military of a lance corporal and three privates.*

The comparison of Sakhalin to a sterlet is especially apt for its southern section, which does indeed resemble the tail of a fish. The left vane of the tail is named Cape Krilyon, the right Cape Aniva, and the semicircular bay between them the Aniva Bay. Krilyon – around which the steamer made a sharp turn to the north-east – gives the impression in sunshine of being quite an inviting place, and the red lighthouse standing alone on its crest resembles an aristocrat's country cottage. This large cape, sloping down to the sea, is green and smooth, like a beautiful water meadow. The land is covered for a long way round with velvety grass, and the only things lacking in this sentimental landscape are flocks and herds roaming in the chilly air at the edge of the woods. But they say the grass here is indifferent and the raising of farm crops is hardly possible as the Krilyon is shrouded for the greater part of the year in salty sea mists, which affect the vegetation in a ruinous fashion.*

We rounded the Krilyon and entered the Aniva Bay before midday on 12th September. The entire coast could be seen from one cape to the other, although the bay has a diameter of eighty to ninety versts.* Almost in the centre the semicircular shore forms a small hollow, which is known as the Cove, or Bukhta Lososyey, and here, on this inlet, stands the Korsakovsk Post, the administrative centre of the southern district. A pleasant occurrence was awaiting our companion, the joyous lady; in the Korsakovsk roadstead lay the Voluntary Fleet steamer *Vladivostok*, which had just sailed in from Kamchatka, and on it was her husband, the officer. How many exclamations, how much irrepressible laughter and fuss there was over this!

From the sea, the post has the respectable appearance of a small town, not Siberian, but of some other type which I will not undertake to put a name to; it was founded nearly forty years ago, when there were Japanese houses, barns and sheds scattered about here and there along the south coast, and it's very possible that the close vicinity of Japanese buildings might have had some influence on its outward appearance and given it its distinctive features. The year of Korsakovsk's foundation is considered to be 1869, but this is correct only as regards the place as a site of the exile colony; in actual fact the first Russian post on the shore of Salmon Inlet was founded in 1853–54. It lies in a gorge, which today still bears the Japanese name Hahka-Tomari, and from the sea only its main street is visible, and it appears from a distance that the roadway and two rows of houses are plunging steeply down the bank; but this is only in the perspective, in reality the rise is not so steep. The glossy new wooden buildings gleam in the sunshine, and the church shines white, with its old, simple and therefore beautiful architecture. On all the homes are poles which must be for flags, and this gives the town an unpleasant appearance, as if it is raising its hackles. Here, too, as in the northern roadsteads, the steamers halt one or even two versts from the shore, and the landing stage is only there for steam-launches and barges. A launch with officials on board came to our steamer first of all, and immediately joyous voices were heard: "Beer, boy! A glass of cognac, boy!" Then a whaleboat came sailing up; convicts requisitioned as sailors were rowing, and at the wheel sat District Governor I.I. Bely, who, when the whaleboat reached the ship's ladder, gave the commands in the military fashion, "Up oars! Rest on oars!"

After a few minutes Mr Bely and I had already become acquainted; we then came ashore together, and I dined with him. From my conversation with him I learnt, among other things, that he had only just returned on the *Vladivostok* from the coast of the Sea of Okhotsk, from the area called Tarayka, where the convicts were then laying a road.

His quarters were not large but were run in a fine aristocratic style. He loves comfort and good cooking, and this is reflected quite noticeably throughout the whole of his district; travelling subsequently round this area I found in the overseers' offices and posts not merely knives, forks and wineglasses, but even clean serviettes and guards who could cook delicious soup, and – the main thing – there was not such a hideous number of bugs and cockroaches as in the north. According to Mr Bely's account, on the roadworks at Tarayka he had lived in comfort in a large marquee-style tent, had a cook to attend on him, and read French novels in his leisure time.* By origin he is a Ukrainian, by education a former law student. He is young, not more than forty, and this, by the way, is average for a Sakhalin official. Times have changed; now a young official is more commonly found in charge of convict labour than an elderly one, and if, let us say, an artist was depicting a vagabond being punished with the lash, then in his picture the place of the former drunken captain, an old man with a crimson-blue nose, would be occupied by an educated and cultivated young man in a brand-new civil servant's official frock coat.*

We got into conversation; meanwhile evening fell and lamps were lit. I took my leave of the hospitable Mr Bely and set off to the secretary of the police department, in whose home lodgings had been prepared for me. It was dark and quiet, the sea pounded hollow and dull, and the starry night was growing overcast, as if it could see that nature was brewing up something nasty. When I had walked the entire length of the main street almost to the sea, the steamers were still lying in the roadstead, and, when I turned to the right, voices and loud laughter reached me, brightly lit windows appeared in the darkness, and it began to feel as if, on an autumn night in a small and remote town, I was making my way to the club. This was the secretary's apartments. I climbed onto the terrace up the rickety, creaking steps and entered the house. In the hall, like gods on clouds, both military and civilian officials were milling around in the sort of tobacco smoke and mist you find in pubs and damp buildings. With one of them, Mr von F., an Inspector of Agriculture, I was already acquainted – we had met previously at Alexandrovsk; as for the rest, however, we were seeing each other for the first time, although they all treated my appearance with such good humour it was as if they had been acquainted with me for ages already. They led me to the table, and I also had to drink the vodka – that is, spirit half diluted with water – and some very bad brandy, and eat tough meat which had been cooked and served up at the table by convict Khomenko, a Ukrainian with a black moustache.

Another outsider besides myself present at this soirée was the Director of the Irkutsk Magneto-Meteorological Observatory, E.V. Shtelling, who had arrived on the *Vladivostok* from Kamchatka and Okhotsk, where he had been busy requesting permission to establish meteorological centres. I also became acquainted here with Major Sh., Governor of the Korsakovsk Convict-Exile Prison, who had served previously under General Gresser in the St Petersburg Police. He was a tall, plump man, with that solid carriage, commanding of respect, which up till the present time I have chanced to observe only in urban and rural district police inspectors. Telling me of his short acquaintanceship with many well-known writers in St Petersburg, the Major would call them simply "Mike" and "Johnny", and, when inviting me to have breakfast and dinner at his place, a couple of times he quite unexpectedly used the familiar "*tu*" form to me.*

When the guests left at two o'clock and I went to bed, howling and whistling noises were resounding all around. A north-easter was beginning to blow up. The sky had not been louring since evening for nothing, then. Coming in from the yard, Khomenko reported that the steamers had departed, but in the meantime a strong gale had blown up at sea. "Well, they'll be back, most likely!" he said, and began to laugh: "Where else is there for them to ride it out?" It grew cold and damp in the room, it was probably no higher than six or seven degrees. Poor F., secretary of the police department, a young man, could not get to sleep at all from a head cold and a cough. Captain K., who lived in the same flat as him, could not sleep either; he knocked on the wall of his room and called to me:

"I receive *The Week* magazine.* Do you want to have a look at it?"

The next morning it was cold in bed, cold in the room and cold out of doors. When I went outside, a chill rain was falling, a strong wind was bending the trees, the sea was roaring, and in particularly strong gusts of wind the raindrops beat into one's face and hammered on the roofs like small gun pellets. The *Vladivostok* and *Baikal* had indeed not ridden out the storm, but had returned and were now lying in the roadstead, covered in mist. I roamed around the streets, and along the shore by the jetty; the grass was wet and water was dripping from the trees.

On the jetty by the guards' lodge lay the skeleton of a young whale, once merry, frisky and sporting over the broad expanse of the northern seas, but now the white bones of this Hercules were lying in the mud and the rain was gnawing away at them... The main street was metalled and was maintained in good condition; it had pavements, street lamps and trees, and it was swept every day by an elderly man with an identifying tattoo.* There are only government offices and official living quarters here; there is not a single house which exiles would live in. The houses are for the most part new and pleasant in appearance, and there is not that oppressive sense of government presence and bureaucracy that there is, for instance, at Dooay. In the Korsakovsk Post in general, however, if you are talking about all four of its streets, there are more old buildings than new ones, and it is not rare to find houses built twenty or thirty years ago. There are not only comparatively more old buildings, but also more established residents among the professional office staff at Korsakovsk, than in the north, and this perhaps implies that this part of the south is more conducive to a peaceful and settled life than either of the two northern districts. Here, as I noticed, there is a more paternalistic attitude, people are more conservative, and customs, even bad ones, are maintained more strongly. For instance, in comparison with the north, they resort to corporal punishment more often here and sometimes flog fifty in one session, and only in the south has there survived the disagreeable custom introduced at some time by some long-forgotten colonel – to wit, when you, a freeman, encounter a group of prisoners in the street or on the shore, you will hear from a good fifty paces away the overseer screaming: "A-tt-en-*shun*! C-a-a-ps *o-off*!" And morose people with bare heads pass by you, glancing up at you sullenly, as if, had they taken off their caps, not at fifty but at twenty or thirty paces, you would have struck them with a cane, like Mr Z. or Mr N.

I regret that I did not find the oldest Sakhalin officer, Staff Captain Shishmaryov, still alive; in length of days and length of residence here he could even have competed with Mikryukov of Palevo. He had died several months before my arrival, and I saw only the detached house in which he had lived. He had been ordered to Sakhalin right back in prehistoric times, before the penal colony had got under way, and this seemed so many ages ago that they had even made up a legend about the "Origin of Sakhalin", in which this officer's name was closely bound up with geological cataclysms; once, in far-off times, Sakhalin had not existed at all, but suddenly, as a consequence of volcanic action, a submerged rock rose above sea level, and on it sat two creatures – a sea lion and Staff Captain Shishmaryov. They say he used to go round in a knitted frock coat with epaulettes, and in official documents he would call the natives "the savage denizens of the woodlands". He took part in several expeditions, among other things sailing up the Tym with Polyakov, and from the account of this expedition it's clear that they quarrelled.

There are 163 inhabitants of the Korsakovsk Post: ninety-three men and seventy women, and including the free people, soldiers, their wives and children, and the prisoners who spend the night in the jail, the total comes to slightly over a thousand.

There are fifty-six households, of which none is of a rural farm type, but, rather, they are urban in character; from an agricultural standpoint they are completely worthless. There are three desyatins of land under cultivation, and eighteen desyatins of meadow, which the prison also utilizes. One has to see how close the farmsteads press against each other, and how they cling picturesquely to the slopes and bottom of the ravine, to understand that the person who chose this spot for the post did not bear in mind in the slightest the fact that, besides soldiers, peasant farmers would also be living here. To my question as to what business they engaged in, and how they earned a living, the householders replied, "Damn labouring," or, "Bloody buying and selling." Regarding outside earnings, as the reader will see below, an inhabitant of southern Sakhalin is far from being in such a desperate situation as a North Sakhaliner; he can find a livelihood for himself when he wishes, at least in the spring and summer months, but this little concerns the residents of Korsakovsk, since they go away to earn a living very rarely, and, like true town-dwellers, live on indefinable means – indefinable as regards their casual nature and irregularity. Some – and these are in the majority – live on money they have brought with them from European Russia, others are clerks, others sextons, others keep small shops, although by law they have no right to do so, still others barter prisoners' lumber for Japanese vodka, which they then sell, and so on and so forth. Women – even those of free status – earn their living by prostitution; even a certain woman prisoner from the privileged classes who, I was told, was a college graduate, does not form an exception. There is less hunger and cold here than in the north; the convicts, whose wives sell themselves, smoke Turkish tobacco at fifty copecks a quarter, and for this reason the prostitution seems more malignant here than in the north – though isn't it all the same really?

Forty-one prisoners live *en famille*, of which 221 couples are unlegalized. There are only ten free-status women, that is, sixteen times fewer than at Rykovo and four times fewer even than at such a hole as Dooay.

One runs across some interesting personalities among the exiles at Korsakovsk. I shall mention Pishchikov, sentenced to penal servitude for life, whose crime gave Uspensky* the material for his feature story *One for One*. This Pishchikov flayed his wife to death with a whip; she was an educated woman, and some months pregnant; the torture lasted six hours; he did it from jealousy of his wife's premarital life; during the last war she had been attracted to a captive Turk;* Pishchikov himself carried letters to this Turk, persuaded him to come to a rendezvous, and generally aided both parties. Subsequently, when the Turk had departed, the girl fell in love with Pishchikov for his kindness; Pishchikov married her and had four children by her, when suddenly a painful, jealous sensation began to gnaw at his heart.

He is a tall, lean man, handsome, with a big beard. He works as a clerk to the police department and therefore wears free-person's clothing. He is hard-working and very polite, and, judging from his expression, has retired right inside himself and withdrawn into his shell. I visited his lodgings once, but he was not at home. He occupies a small room in a cabin; it contains a neat and tidy bed, covered with a red woollen blanket, and in a frame on the wall by the bed is a portrait of some lady, most probably his wife.

Also interesting is the family Giacomini; the father, who at one time was a skipper on a ship on the Black Sea, his wife and son. All three were brought before a court martial in Nikolayev* in 1878 accused of murder, and were convicted, so they themselves maintain, falsely. The old lady and the son have already served their hard labour, but the old man, Karp Nikolayevich, is still a convict. They keep a small shop, and their rooms are very decently done out, better even than those of the rich man of Novo-Mikhailovka, Potyomkin. The elder Giacominis walked across Siberia overland, the son went by sea, and he arrived at this place three years earlier. The difference is colossal. When listening to the old man, a feeling of horror grows on you. What an overwhelming number of frightful sights he encountered, just what did he not have to suffer, when they convicted him, tormented him and then dragged him across Siberia for three years; on the way, his daughter, a young woman who was following her father and mother voluntarily to the penal settlement, died of exhaustion, and the boat which was carrying him and the old lady to Korsakovsk was shipwrecked off Mauka. The old man narrates all this, and the old lady weeps. "Well, so what?" says the old man, with a wave of his hand. "I suppose that's the way God must have wanted it."

As regards civilization, the Korsakovsk Post has noticeably lagged behind its northern counterparts. For instance, up to the present time it still has neither a telegraph office nor a meteorological station.* For the time being we can only make judgements about the climate of southern Sakhalin from fragmentary random observations of various writers who have either served here or, like me, merely come here for a short while. According to this data, if we take the average temperature, summer, autumn and spring at the Korsakovsk Post are warmer by almost two degrees than at Dooay, and winter is five degrees milder. But meanwhile, in the very same Aniva Bay, but only a little to the east of the Korsakovsk Post, at Muravyovsk, the temperatures are already considerably lower and are rather more similar to those of Dooay than of Korsakovsk. And eighty-eight versts to the north of the Korsakovsk Post, at Naibuchi, the captain of the *Vsadnik* recorded two degrees of frost on the morning of 11th May 1870 – it was snowing. As the reader may see, the south here bears little resemblance to "The South"; the winter here is just as severe as in the Olonetsk Province, and the summers are like those of Archangel.* Halfway through May, Kruzenshtern saw snow on the west shore of the Aniva. To the north of the Korsakovsk District – at Kusunnai, to be precise, where they extract the seakale – there are 149 inclement days a year, and to the south, at the Muravyovsk Post, 130. But, nonetheless, the climate of the southern district is still milder than both northern ones, and it must therefore be easier to live here. There are sometimes thaws in the middle of winter in the south, which has never once been observed around Dooay or Rykovo; the ice on the rivers breaks up earlier, and the sun emerges from behind the clouds more often.

The Korsakovsk Prison occupies what is the highest, and most probably the healthiest, spot in the post. Where the main road runs up to the prison stockade, there are some gates, very modest in appearance, and that these are not ordinary, everyday gates but the entrance to a prison is apparent only from an inscription and also from the fact that every evening there are crowds of convicts milling round them who are admitted at the wicket gate one by one and searched at the same time. The prison yard is set on an inclined plane, and so from the centre of it, despite the stockade and the surrounding buildings, you can see the pale-blue sea and the distant horizon, and therefore it seems there is a great deal of air here. When surveying the prison, the first thing one notices is the manner in which the local administration has striven to maintain a sharp segregation between the convicts and settled exiles. At Alexandrovsk the prison workshops and the living quarters of several hundred prisoners are scattered throughout the entire post, but here all the workshops and even the shed containing the fire-carts are housed within the prison yard, and living outside the prison, with very rare exceptions, is not even permitted to convicts in the category of "reformee". Here the post exists by and of itself, and the prison exists by and of itself, and it is possible to live a long time at the post and not notice that there is a prison at the end of the street.

The barrack huts here are old, it's stuffy in the cells, the latrines are much worse than in the northern prisons, the bakehouse is dingy, the punishment cells for solitary confinement are dark, unventilated and cold; I myself several times saw people confined in them shivering from the cold and damp. Here only one thing is better than in the north: the fetter block is spacious, and there are comparatively fewer people in irons. The former seamen live most tidily of all the people in the cells; they also dress more neatly and cleanly.* When I was there, only 450 people were spending the night in the prison; all the rest had been requisitioned for labour-gangs, mainly on roadworks. In all, there was a grand total of 1,205 convicts in the settlement.

The Prison Governor here loves above all else to show visitors the fire-carts. The carts are indeed splendid, and in this respect Korsakovsk has outdone many larger towns. The barrels, the fire-pumps, the axes in cases – it all had a toy-like feel to it, and gleamed as if it had been prepared for an exhibition. The alarm was sounded, and the convicts immediately came rushing out of all the workshops, without caps, without outdoor clothes – in a word, in whatever they happened to have on. In one minute flat they had harnessed themselves up and went thundering along the main street to the sea. The spectacle was effective, and Major Sh., the creator of these exemplary fire engines, was very pleased and kept asking me all the time whether I liked it. The only pity was that, together with the young men, old men harnessed themselves and ran, too; they should have been spared, even if only for the sake of their weak health.

13

Poro-an-Tomari. The Muravyovsk Post. Pervaya, Vtoraya and Tretya Pad. Solovyovka. Lyutoga. Goly Mys. Mitzulka. Listvennichnoye. Khomutovka. Bolshaya Yelan. Vladimirovka. A farm, or a firm. Lugovoye. Popovskiye Yurty. Beryozniki. Kresty. Bolshoye and Maloye Takoay. Galkino-Vraskoye. Dubki. Naibuchi. The sea.

I SHALL CONCLUDE THIS SURVEY of the inhabited spots of the Korsakovsk District with the settlements situated along the bank of the Aniva. The first, four versts south-east of the post, has a Japanese name – Poro-an-Tomari. It was founded in 1882 on the site of a tiny Aino village which had at one time been here. There are seventy-two inhabitants: fifty-three men, nineteen women. Forty-seven of these are householders, of whom thirty-eight live as bachelors. However much space there might seem to be around the settlement, there is still all the same only a quarter of a desyatin of arable land, and less than half a desyatin of hay meadow, to each householder; this implies that there is nowhere any more where such land can be found, or else it is very difficult to do so. Nevertheless, however, if Poro-an-Tomari had been in the north, 200 householders would have been living there long since, plus 150 co-holders; the southern administration is more restrained in this respect and prefers to found new settlements rather than expand old ones.

I recorded here nine elderly men between the ages of sixty-five and eighty-five. One of them, Yan Rytzeborsky, is seventy-five and has the facial features of a soldier from the time of the Ochakov campaign,* and he has aged so very much that very likely he cannot remember now whether he was guilty or not; it was somehow weird to hear that all these men were life-sentence convicts at hard labour, evil villains whom Baron Korf had ordered to be transferred to live as settled exiles simply out of consideration for their advanced ages.

A settled exile called Kostin was busy saving his soul in a dugout; he himself did not come outside, and he will not let anybody in, but spends his entire time in prayer. Everybody calls him the "Slave of the Lord", because when at liberty he had been a pilgrim;* he is a house-painter by profession but works as a shepherd at Tretya Pad (Third Chasm), probably from his love of solitude and contemplation.

Forty versts to the north there is also the Muravyovsk Post, although it exists only as a name on the map. It was founded a comparatively long time ago, in 1853, on the coast of Salmon Inlet; when rumours of war were flying about in 1854 it was withdrawn, and only re-estab-lished twelve years later on the coast of Busse Bay, or "Twelve-foot Harbour" – as the shallow lake was called which was linked to the sea by a channel, and which could be entered only by shallow-draught vessels. In Mitzul's day about 300 soldiers lived there who suffered seriously with scurvy. The aim of founding the post was to reinforce Russian authority on southern Sakhalin; after the treaty of 1875,* however, it was closed down as superfluous, and the abandoned cab-ins, so I was told, had been burnt down by escapees.*

To the settlements which lie to the west of the Korsakovsk Post leads a cheerful and pleasant road, by the very edge of the sea; to the right are steep clay slopes and screes, covered with luxurious waves of greenery, and to the left is the booming sea. On the sand, where the waves break into foam and then slide back as if exhausted, seakale thrown up by the waves lies like a brown-trimmed hemline right along the sea coast. It gives off the sickly-sweet, but not repulsive, smell of rotting seaweed, and this smell is just as characteristic of the southern sea as the wild sea-ducks which start up into the air every moment and which keep you amused all the time you are driving along the shore. Steamships and sailing boats are infrequent guests here; nothing can be seen either close up or on the horizon, and for this reason the sea seems deserted. Only very rarely does a lumbering flat-bottomed hay-barge appear, hardly moving, sometimes surmounted by a dark, unpleasant sail, or else a convict plodding along up to his knees in the water drag-ging a log behind him on a rope – these are the only pictures one sees.

The steep coast is interrupted here by a long and deep valley. The Untanai or Unta Stream flows along there, and at one time nearby stood the state-owned Untovsk Farm which the convicts called "The Laths" – it is self-evident why. At present, the prison vegetable gardens lie here, and there are only three settled exiles' cabins. This place is now called Pervaya Pad (First Chasm).

Then follows Vtoraya Pad (Second Chasm), in which there are six farm-holdings. Here the old woman called Miss* Ulyana cohabits with a prosperous old peasant-in-exile. Once, a very long time ago, she killed her baby and buried it in the ground; at the trial she said she had not killed the child but buried it alive – she thought she would stand more chance of being acquitted that way; the court sentenced her to twenty years. Telling me about this, Ulyana wept bitterly, but then she wiped her eyes and asked, "Fancy buyin' a nice little bit o' pickled cabbage?"

At Tretya Pad there are seventeen farm-holdings.

These three settlements together contain a total population of forty-six, including seventeen women. There are twenty-six householders. The people here are thoroughly solid and prosperous; they possess a lot of cattle, and some even earn their living dealing in them. The climate and soil conditions should most likely be acknowledged as the chief causes of this well-being, but I do consider, too, that if the officials from Alexandrovsk or Dooay were invited here and asked to look after things, then within one year flat, in all the three settlements, there would be not twenty-six but 300 householders, not counting co-holders, and they would all turn out to be "negligent of their abodes and insubordinate" and would all sit around without a scrap to eat. The example of these three tiny settlements is, I believe, sufficient for it finally to be taken as a rule that at the present time, when the colony is still young and not firmly established, the fewer householders the better, and the longer a street the poorer it will be.

At a distance of four versts from the post stands Solovyovka, founded in 1882. It occupies the most advantageous site of all the Sakhalin settlements; it is beside the sea, and, in addition, not far away lies the mouth of the fishing stream called the Susui. The population keep cows and sell milk. They also engage in crop-raising. There are seventy-four inhabitants, thirty-seven male, thirty-seven female. House-holders: twenty-six. They all possess arable land and hay meadows, on average one desyatin per head. The soil is good only by the sea and on the coastal slopes; further inland it is poor and used to be covered with spruces and silver firs.

There is still one further settlement on the bank of the Aniva, right out of the way, about twenty-five versts, or, if you travel there by sea, fourteen nautical miles, from the post. It is called Lyutoga, is five miles from the mouth of a river of the same name, and was founded in 1886. Communications with the post are extremely awkward – on foot along the bank, or else by launch and, for the settlers, by hay-barge. There are fifty-three inhabitants: thirty-seven men and sixteen women. Householders: thirty-three.

As regards the coast road, it passes Solovyovka, turns sharp right by the mouth of the Susui, and heads in a northerly direction. On the map the upper reaches of the Susui approach the river Naibu, which discharges into the Sea of Okhotsk, and along both these rivers, almost in a straight line from the Aniva to the east coast, there extends a long line of settlements linked by an unbroken road eighty-eight versts long. This row of settlements comprises the central core of the southern district and forms its main "facial feature", so to speak, and the road is the commencement of that same main postal highway by means of which they wish to link northern and southern Sakhalin.

I had grown either tired or lazy, and in the south I certainly did not work as hard as in the north. Often I would spend whole days on walks, outings and picnics, and no longer felt any desire to go round the cabins; so when they obligingly offered me assistance I did not turn it down. I drove to the Sea of Okhotsk and back the first time in the company of Mr Bely, who desired to show me his district, and later, when I was drawing up the census, I was accompanied on each occasion by the Inspector of Settlements, Mr Yartzev.*

The settlements of the southern district have their own special features which someone who has just arrived from the north cannot help but notice. First of all there is considerably less poverty. Unfinished or abandoned cabins, or boarded-up windows, I did not see at all, and roofing with boards is as commonplace and everyday a sight here as straw and tree-bark is in the north. The roads and bridges are worse than in the north, especially between Maloye Takoay and Siyantzy, where during serious floods and after heavy rain an impassable mire results. The inhabitants themselves look younger, healthier and more cheerful than their northern counterparts, and this, just as much as the relative prosperity of the area, may be explained by the fact that the main contingent of exiles living in the south have been short-sentence convicts, that is, people who are primarily young and less worn out by penal servitude. You meet some who are still only twenty to twenty-five, and they have already served their forced labour and now occupy holdings, and there are quite a few peasants-in-exile between thirty and forty years old.*

Another factor in the southern settlements' favour is that the local peasants-in-exile do not go rushing off to leave and cross over to the mainland; for example, in the settlement of Solovyovka which I have just described, sixteen householders out of the twenty-six have peasant status. There are very few women; there are settlements without one single female. Compared to the men, the majority of them look ill and elderly, and one has to believe the local officials and settled exiles who complain that the northern officials on absolutely every occasion send them only "goods left on the shelf" and keep the young and healthy ones for themselves. Dr Z***sky told me that once, while temporarily acting as prison doctor,* he on the spur of the moment took it into his head to examine a party of newly arrived women, and they all turned out to have female ailments.

In the south the word "co-tenant" or "half-sharer" is completely unused in everyday currency, since every plot is supposed to have only one owner, but, just as in the north, there are holders who are merely reckoned among the population of a settlement but do not have homes there. Both at the post and in the settlements there is a complete absence of Jews. On the walls of the cabins one comes across little Japanese pictures; one also often sees Japanese silver coins.

The first settlement on the Susui is Goly Mys; it has been in existence only since last year, and the cabins are not yet completed. There are twenty-four men here and not a single woman. The settlement stands on a knoll which was once called Bare Cape. The river here does not lie close to the dwellings – you have to go down the hill to it; there is no well.

The second settlement is Mitzulka, so named in honour of M.S. Mitzul.* When there was still no road, on the site of what is now Mitzulka there was a station where they maintained horses for the officials who were travelling on government business; the stable hands and workmen were allowed to build themselves homes before the expiry of their labour sentences and they settled round the station and started to run their own households. There are ten holdings here and twenty-five inhabitants: sixteen men, nine women. After 1886 the District

Governor would not permit anybody else to settle in Mitzulka, and he acted correctly in this, since the land here is indifferent and there is only enough meadowland for ten farmsteads. There are at the moment seventeen cows and thirteen horses at the settlement, without counting sheep and goats, and in the official register sixty-four chickens are recorded, but none of these figures would double if the number of households did so.

When talking about the special features of the settlements of the southern district, there is still one I have forgotten to mention – here people are frequently poisoned by aconite (*Aconitum napellus*). At Mitzulka a pig belonging to settled exile Takovoy was poisoned with aconite; he was overcome with greed, ate its liver and almost died. When I was in his cabin, he forced himself to stand, and spoke in a weak voice, but he told the story of the liver laughingly, and from his face, still swollen all over and dark-blue-purple, one could judge how dear that liver had cost him. A little before him, an elderly man, Konkov, had poisoned himself with aconite, and his house now stands empty. This house is one of the tourist sights of Mitzulka. Several years ago, L., the former Prison Governor, took some sort of climbing plant to be a grapevine and reported to General Gintze that in southern Sakhalin there were grapevines which could be successfully cultivated. General Gintze immediately sent out an order to discover whether among the prisoners there was anyone who had ever worked in a vineyard. One such turned up. It was the settled exile Rayevsky, a very tall man according to tradition. He declared himself to be an expert, they believed him, and on the very first steamer to leave sent him with a note of explanation from the Alexandrovsk to the Korsakovsk Post. There they asked him: "What have you come for?" "To cultivate the grapevines," he replied. They looked at him, read the note and simply shrugged their shoulders. The viticulturist set off to wander round the district, hat cocked on his head; since he had been commissioned by the Governor of the Island, he did not consider it necessary to report to the Inspector of Settlements. A misunderstanding occurred. At Mitzulka, his height, and the dignity with which he carried himself, seemed suspicious; they took him for a vagabond, tied him up and sent him to the post.* He was held for a long period in the prison while inquiries were made, and then he was released. Finally he settled in Mitzulka, and there he died, and thus Sakhalin has been left without any vineyards. Rayevsky's home passed to the state as payment for debts and was sold to Konkov for fifteen roubles. When he had paid the money for the house, old Konkov had winked slyly and said to the District Governor: "You just wait a bit, and I'll die, and you'll be making a lot of fuss about this house all over again." And indeed before long he poisoned himself with aconite,* and the state does have to worry over the house again.

In Mitzulka lives the Gretchen of Sakhalin, the daughter of settled exile Nikolayev, Tanya, a native of the Pskov Province. She is sixteen years old, blonde, slender and her features are delicate, soft and tender. She has already been promised in marriage to an overseer. Whenever you drove through Mitzulka, she would be sitting at the window thinking. And what a young, beautiful girl who has finished up on Sakhalin can possibly think of, and what she dreams about, God only knows.

Five versts from Mitzulka stands the new settlement of Listvennichnoye and the road here has been cut through a larch wood. It is also called Kristophorovka, because at one time the Gilyak Kristophor put out nooses for sables on the river here. The selection of this spot for a colony cannot be termed a success, since the soil is poor and unsuitable for cultivation.* There are fifteen inhabitants here. Women: nil.

A little further along, on the river Kristophorovka, several convicts had once been occupied in making various articles from wood; they were given permission to build cabins before they had completed their compulsory labour. But the location where they had settled was acknowledged to be inconvenient, and in 1886 their four cabins were transferred elsewhere, four versts or so to the north of Listvennichnoye, and these then served as the foundation of the settlement of Khomutovka. It is so called because a freeman, Khomutka by name, a peasant by status, settled here voluntarily and at one time engaged in hunting. There are thirty-eight inhabitants: twenty-five men and thirteen women. Householders: twenty-five. This is one of the most uninteresting settlements, although it, too, can boast a noteworthy feature: the settler Bronovsky lives here, and he is known throughout the south as an ardent and indefatigable thief.

Three versts further on is the settlement of Bolshaya Yelan (Large Yelan), which was founded a couple of years or so ago. "Yelans" are the name given in Siberia to river valleys in which grow elms, oaks, hawthorns, elders, ashes and birches. They are usually protected against cold winds, and, while on the neighbouring mountains and in the swamps the vegetation is startling in its poverty and differs but little from that of the polar regions, here in the yelans we find luxuriant groves and grass twice the height of a man. On summer days which are not overcast, the earth here "steams", as they put it, the humid air becomes as stifling as in a bathhouse, and the heated soil drives all the cereals to become straw, so that, for instance, in one month, rye reaches almost a sazhen in height. These yelans, which remind a Ukrainian of his native "levadas" – glens where the meadows alternate with orchards and groves – are most suitable for settlement.*

Bolshaya Yelan has forty-two inhabitants: thirty-two male, eight female. Householders: thirty. When the settled exiles were grubbing up the ground for their plots of land, they were ordered to spare the old trees where possible. And, thanks to this, the settlement does not seem new, because in the street and in the farmyards stand old broad-leaved elms, as if the settlement's forefathers had planted them.

Among all the local settled exiles, one's attention is drawn to the Babich brothers from Kiev Province; to begin with they lived in the same cabin, then they began to quarrel and asked the authorities to separate them. One of the Babiches, complaining about his own brother, once put it thus: "I fear him like a serpent."

Another five versts further on is the settlement of Vladimirovka, founded in 1881 and so named in honour of a certain major whose first name was Vladimir and who directed the compulsory labour. The settled exiles also call it Chornaya Rechka (Black Stream). Inhabitants: ninety-one – fifty-five men, thirty-six women; there are forty-six householders, of whom nineteen live as bachelors and milk their cows themselves. Of the twenty-seven families, only six are legalized. As an agricultural colony this settlement is worth both northern districts put together, but at the same time, out of the mass of women who come here with their husbands, who are free and uncorrupted by prison, that is to say, the most valuable women for a colony, only one has settled here, and not long ago she was imprisoned on suspicion of murdering her husband. The unfortunate free-women whom the northern officials torture in the "barrack rooms for families" at Dooay would be inexpressibly useful here. At Vladimirovka there are over 100 head of horned stock alone, forty horses, and good hay meadows, but the householders have no wives, and this means there are no genuine households.*

At Vladimirovka, attached to the government house where the Inspector of Settlements, Mr Y., and his wife, who is a midwife, live, there is a model farm (*ferma*), which the settled exiles and soldiers call the "firm" (*firma*). Mr Y. is interested in the natural sciences, especially botany, and he never names plants other than in Latin; when, for instance, haricot beans are served up for dinner at his house, he will say: "This is *faseolus*." He has given his nasty little black dog the name Favus.* Of all the Sakhalin officials he is the one most versed in agronomy and he applies himself to the work conscientiously and lovingly, but the harvests on his model farm are often worse than those of the settled exiles, and this arouses general bewilderment and even mockery. In my view, this random difference in harvests bears the same relation to Mr Y. as to every other official. This farm, on which there is no meteorological station, no cattle, not even to provide manure, no decent buildings, no experienced person who would occupy himself from morning till evening with the farm alone – this is not a farm, but is indeed merely a firm, that is, an idle pastime masquerading under the trademark (*firma*) of a farm. This firm cannot even be called experimental, since it occupies a mere five desyatins, and as for the quality of this land, according to one official document, land of poorer than average quality was deliberately chosen with the aim "of demonstrating to the population by example that, with a certain care and better cultivation, satisfactory results may be obtained even here".

Here at Vladimirovka a love story once took place. A certain Vukol Popov, a peasant, found his wife with his father, lashed out and killed the old man. He was sentenced to convict labour, sent to the Korsakovsk District and here detailed to work at the "firm" as coachman to Mr Y. He was a man of Herculean build, still young and good-looking, with a character that was gentle and intent – he was always silent and thinking of something. Mr Y. and his wife began to trust him from the very first, and when they went travelling away from home they knew that Vukol would neither steal the money from the chest of drawers nor drink all the spirits in the pantry. On Sakhalin he could not get married since he still had a wife in his home territory who would not give him a divorce. Such, more or less, was the hero. The heroine was convict Yelena Tyortyshnaya, the cohabitant of settled exile Koshelyov, a cantankerous, stupid and plain woman. She began to quarrel with her cohabitant, he complained, and, as punishment, the District Governor assigned her to work at the "firm". There she saw Vukol and fell in love. He also grew to love her. Cohabitant Koshelyov must have noticed this, because he began persistently to ask her to come back to him.

"Well, yes, all right then – but I know you!" she said. "Marry me and then I'll come back."

Koshelyov handed in documentary notification of his forthcoming marriage to Miss Tyortyshnaya and the authorities gave him permission for this marriage. In the meantime Vukol was declaring his love to Yelena, imploring her to live with him; she also sincerely swore her love and said to him:

"I *can* come here now and again, but I can't live here permanently; you're married; I've got a woman's duty to do, I've got to think a little bit about myself and settle down with a nice man."

When Vukol discovered that she was promised in marriage, he fell into despair and poisoned himself with aconite. Yelena was then interrogated, and she admitted: "I spent four nights with him." The story went that, a couple of weeks before his death, he gazed at Yelena washing the floor, and said:

"Ekh, women, women! I've finished up doing hard labour cos of women, and here cos of women I've got to finish it all!"

At Vladimirovka I made the acquaintance of exile Vasily Smirnov, who had been sent here for forging banknotes. He had served his compulsory labour and residence and now worked hunting sable, from which, obviously, he derived great pleasure. He told me that at one time he had been making 300 roubles a day from counterfeit notes, but was tracked down only when he had given up this line of business and taken up honest work. He discusses counterfeit notes with the tones of a specialist; in his opinion, even a silly old woman could forge the modern ones. He speaks of the past calmly, and not without irony, and he is very proud of the fact that he was once defended in court by Mr Plevako.*

Immediately following Vladimirovka there is the beginning of an enormous meadow, several hundred desyatins in area; it is semicircular in shape and about four versts in diameter. On the road where the meadow finishes stands the settlement of Lugovoye, or Luzhki, founded in 1888. Here there are sixty-nine men and only five women.

Then follows another short stretch of four versts, and we arrive at Popovskiye Yurty, a settlement founded in 1884. They wanted to call it Novo-Alexandrovka (New Alexandrovka), but this name did not stick. The Reverend Simeon Kazansky, or, more simply, Father Simon, drove to Naibuchi by dog sled to hold the service for the soldiers there at the end of the Lenten Fast, and on the way back was caught in a raging blizzard and was taken seriously ill (although other people say he was in fact returning from Alexandrovsk). Fortunately, he came across some Aino fishermen's yurts, and he took shelter in one of them and sent his driver on to Vladimirovka, where free voluntary settlers were then living; they came to fetch him and conveyed him to the Korsakovsk Post barely still alive. After this they began to call the yurts the "Priest's Yurts" – the name has also been retained by the locality. The settled exiles themselves also call their settlement Warsaw, since there are so many Catholics there. There are 111 inhabitants: ninety-five male, sixteen female. Of the forty-two householders, only ten live *en famille*.

Popovskiye Yurty stands exactly halfway along the route between the Korsakovsk Post and Naibuchi. Here the basin of the river Susui comes to an end, and after riding through a gently sloping, hardly perceptible pass over the watershed mountain range, we descend into a valley irrigated by the Naibu. The first settlement of this basin lies eight versts from the Priest's Yurts, and is called Beryozniki, because at one time there were many birches all around. This is the largest of all the southern settlements. There are 159 inhabitants: 142 men and seventeen women. Householders: 140. There are already four streets and a square, on which, it is surmised, there will in time be built a church, a telegraph office and a house for the Inspector of Settlements. It is also conjectured that, if colonization succeeds, then Beryozniki may be declared a borough (*volost*).* But this settlement is very boring to look at, and the people in it are boring, and they think, not of the future borough, but only of how to get their sentence over with and leave for the mainland more quickly. When I asked one settled exile whether he was married, he replied with boredom: "I was married, and murdered my wife." Another, who was suffering from haemoptysis (blood-spitting), found out that I was a doctor and followed me about the entire time, asking me whether he had consumption or not, and looking searchingly into my eyes. He was terrified at the thought that he would not live to get peasant-in-exile rights and would die on Sakhalin.

Five versts further on follows the settlement of Kresty, founded in 1885. Two vagabonds were murdered here once and on the site of their graves stood crosses which are no longer there; or, another variant: a coniferous wood, long since felled, once cut across the yelan in the shape of a cross. Both explanations are poetical; obviously the name of Kresty was given by the inhabitants themselves.

Kresty stands on the river Takoay, just where a tributary discharges into it; the soil is loam with a good thin coating of silt, there are good harvests every year, there is a great deal of meadowland, and fortunately the people have all turned out to be fairly decent at running their holdings; but in its first years the settlement differed but little from Upper Armudan and almost perished. The point about that is that thirty men were settled on plots here all at once; it was just at the time when they had not been sending out tools from Alexandrovsk for ages, and the settled exiles set off to this spot literally with bare hands. Out of compassion, they were given old axes from the prison, so that they could chop timber for themselves. Then for three whole years in succession, no cattle were issued to them – for the same reason as they were not sending tools from Alexandrovsk.*

There are ninety inhabitants: sixty-three men and twenty-seven women. Householders: fifty-two.

Here there is a little shop in which a retired sergeant major, formerly an overseer in the Tymovsk District, carries on business; he sells groceries, copper bracelets and sardines as well. When I dropped in at his shop, the sergeant major must have taken me for a very important official, for, with no necessity whatever, he suddenly announced to me that at one time he had been involved in something or other, but had been acquitted, and hurriedly began to show me various testimonials, and he also displayed to me, among various other items, a letter from a certain Mr Shneider, at the end of which, I recall, was the cryptic phrase: "When it starts to get warm, roast some frozen beef" – then, wishing to prove to me that he no longer owed anything to anybody, the sergeant major began to rummage around in his papers and search for some sort of receipts, but could not find them, and I came out of the shop carrying away with me the certainty of his total innocence, and a *funt* of crudely made rustic sweets, for which he had still nevertheless skinned fifty copecks off me.

The settlement following Kresty stands by a river with the Japanese name of Takoay which discharges into the Naibu. This river valley is called the Takoay Valley and it is well known because at one time voluntary free settlers lived here. The settlement Bolshoye (Large) Takoay has existed officially since 1884, but it was founded much earlier. They wanted to call it Vlasovskoye in honour of Mr Vlasov, but this name has not been maintained. Inhabitants: seventy-one – fifty-six men and fifteen women. Householders: forty-seven. Here a college-trained doctor's assistant resides permanently. A week before my arrival his wife, a young lady, had poisoned herself with aconite.

Close by the settlement, but especially along the road to Kresty, one finds firs which make excellent building wood.* In general there is a lot of greenery which into the bargain is as succulent and bright as if it has been washed. The flora of the Takoay Valley is incomparably richer than that of the north, but the northern landscape is livelier and reminded me more frequently of European Russia. True, nature there is stern and mournful, but it is stern in a Russian manner; here, however, it smiles and is sad in an Aino fashion, and arouses an indefinable feeling in a Russian soul.

In the Takoay Valley, four and a half versts from Bolshoye Takoay, Maloye (Little) Takoay stands on a small brook which flows into the Takoay.* The settlement was founded in 1885. There is a total of fifty-two inhabitants: thirty-seven male, fifteen female. Householders: thirty-five, of whom only nine live *en famille*, and there is not a single legally married couple.

Eight versts further on, at a spot which the Ainos and Japanese used to call Siyancha, and where a Japanese fishing depot once stood, the settlement of Galkino-Vraskoye, or Siyantzy, is situated. It was founded in 1884. The location – at the confluence of the Takoay and Naibu – is beautiful, but very inconvenient. In spring and autumn, and even in the summer during rainy weather, the Naibu, as capricious as all mountain streams generally are, overflows and inundates Siyantzy; the powerful current blocks the entry of the Takoay, and this, too, bursts its banks; and the same thing also happens with the smaller streams which flow into the Takoay. Then Galkino-Vraskoye takes on the appearance of Venice, and people travel around it in Aino boats; in the cabins built on low-lying ground the floors are flooded with water. The site for this settlement was chosen by a certain Mr Ivanov, who understands as little of this business as he does of the Aino and Gilyak languages, of which he is officially considered to be the interpreter; however, at that time he was Deputy Prison Governor and carried out the duties of the present-day Inspector of Settlements. The Ainos and the settled exiles warned him that the place was boggy, but he did not listen to them. Anybody who complained was flogged. In one of the floods a bull perished, and in another a horse was killed.

The confluence of the Takoay and Naibu forms a peninsula, onto which leads a high bridge. It is very pretty here – the place is perfectly idyllic. In the overseers' offices it is light and very clean; there is even a fireplace. From the terrace there is a view on to the river, and in the yard is a little garden. The watchman here is old Savelyev, a convict who, when officials spend the night in this place, performs the functions of servant and cook. Once, while he was waiting on me and a certain official at dinner, he served something in an improper manner, and the official yelled sternly at him: "You blithering idiot!" I glanced then at this meek old man and, I recall, the thought came to me that even right up to the present day the only thing a Russian intellectual had succeeded in doing with penal servitude had been to reduce it, in the most banal and vulgar manner, to serfdom.

Galkino-Vraskoye has seventy-four inhabitants: fifty male and twenty-four women. There are householders, of whom twenty-nine have peasant-in-exile status.

The last settlement along this highway is Dubki, founded in 1886, on the site of an oak wood. Over the eight versts distance between Siyantzy and Dubki, one encounters burnt-out forests with small meadows in between, on which I was told there grew *kapor** tea.

Incidentally, whenever one drives along here, they point out the stream where settled exile Malovechkin used to fish; this stream now bears his name. Dubki has forty-four inhabitants: thirty-one men and thirteen women. There are thirty households. The location is considered a good one on the theory that, where oak trees grow, the soil must be suitable for wheat. A large part of the area which is now occupied by ploughed fields and hay meadows was still fenland not long ago, but on the advice of Mr Y. the settled exiles dug a ditch a sazhen deep down to the Naibu, and now everything is fine.

Card-playing and concealing stolen goods and escapees have reached considerable heights here, perhaps because this little settlement lies at the back of beyond, and exists in its own world, so to speak. In June the local settled exile Lifanov gambled away everything he had and poisoned himself with aconite.

Only four versts remain from Dubki to the mouth of the Naibu, and it is impossible to settle over this area, since the river mouth is covered with marshes, there is sand along the sea coast and the vegetation is that characteristic of sandy maritime areas: sweet briar with very large berries and the like. The road extends to the sea, but it is also possible to journey along the river in an Aino boat.

Formerly the Naibuchi Post stood at the river mouth. It was founded in 1866. Mitzul found eighteen buildings here, both dwellings and non-residential premises, plus a chapel and a shop for provisions. One correspondent who visited Naibuchi in 1871 wrote that there were twenty soldiers there under the command of a cadet-officer; in one of the cabins he was entertained with fresh eggs and black bread by a tall and beautiful female soldier, who eulogized life here and complained only that sugar was very expensive.*

Now there are not even traces left of those cabins, and, gazing round at the wilderness, the tall, beautiful female soldier seems like some kind of myth. They are building a new house here, for overseers' offices or possibly a weather centre, and that is all. The roaring sea is cold and colourless in appearance, and the tall grey waves pound upon the sand, as if wishing to say in despair: "Oh God, why did you create us?" This is the Great, or, as it is otherwise known, the Pacific, Ocean. On this shore of the Naibuchi river the convicts can be heard rapping away with axes on the building work, while on the other, far distant, imagined shore, lies America... to the left the capes of Sakhalin are visible in the mist, and to the right are more capes... while all around there is not a single living soul, not a bird, not a fly, and it is beyond comprehension who the waves are roaring for, who listens to them at nights here, what they want, and, finally, who they would roar for when I was gone. There on the shore one is overcome not by connected, logical thoughts, but by reflections and reveries. It is a sinister sensation, and yet at the very same time you feel the desire to stand for ever looking at the monotonous movement of the waves and listening to their threatening roar.

14

Tarayka. Voluntary settlers. Their lack of success. The Ainos, the limits of their extension, numerical composition, appearance, diet, clothing, dwellings, customs. The Japanese. Kusun-Kotan. The Japanese Consulate.

IN THE LOCALITY CALLED TARAYKA, on one of the most southerly tributaries of the Poronai, which flows into the Zaliv Terpeniya, we find the settlement of Siska. The whole of Tarayka is considered administratively to be part of the southern district – only with a great deal of stretching a point, of course, since it is 400 versts from here to Korsakovsk, and the climate is abominable – worse than Dooay. The projected district which I spoke of in chapter 10 will be called the Tarayka District and it will comprise all the settlements along the Poronai, including Siska; in the meantime, however, people from the southern district are being sent here. In the official register only seven inhabitants are shown: six male, one female. I did not visit Siska, but here is an extract from somebody else's journal: "Both the settlement and the region are utterly dismal; first of all there is a lack of good water and firewood; the inhabitants make use of water from wells, and when it's raining the water is red and like water on the tundra. The bank on which the settlement is situated is composed of sand, and there is tundra all around… generally speaking, the entire area creates an oppressive and dispiriting impression."*

Now, in order to conclude with southern Sakhalin, a few words still remain to be said about those people who lived here at some time in the past and those who at present live independently of the exile colony. I shall begin with the attempts at voluntary colonization. In 1868 one of the administration offices of the Eastern Siberian region was permitted to settle up to twenty-five families on the south of Sakhalin; they had in mind in this respect free-status peasant farmers, migrants who had already settled along the Amur, but with such little success that one writer had called the organization of their settlements "lamentable", and the settlers themselves he had termed "pathetic, miserable wretches". They were Ukrainians, natives of the Chernigov Province, who previously, before their arrival on the Amur, had settled in the Tobolsk Province but also without success. The administration, proposing to them that they should migrate to Sakhalin, made them the most highly alluring promises. They promised to supply them for two years, free of charge, with flour and meal, to provide every family with agricultural implements, cattle, grain and money, all on credit, with five years to pay off the debt, and they promised to excuse them for twenty years from tax and military recruitment. Ten families from the Amur, and, in addition, eleven families from the Balagan District, Irkutsk Province, expressed a wish to resettle – 101 people in all. In August 1869 they were dispatched on the supply ship *Mandzhur* to the Muravyovsk Post, so as to be conveyed from there, via the Sea of Okhotsk, round the Aniva Cape, to Naibuchi Post, from which it was only thirty versts to the Takoay Valley, where it was proposed that they should lay the foundations of a free, voluntary colony. But autumn had already set in, there was no vessel available, and the *Mandzhur* dropped them and their belongings at the Korsakovsk Post, from which they were expected to thread their own way to the Takoay Valley over dry land. No roads existed at all at that time. Ensign Diakonov "moved off" – to use Mitzul's expression – with fifteen people to clear a narrow cutting through the forest. But he must have "moved off" very slowly, since sixteen families got tired of waiting for the cutting to be finished and set off to the Takoay Valley straight through the taiga on pack-oxen and wagons. Deep snow fell on the way, and they had to abandon some of their wagons and put runners on the others. They arrived in the valley on 20th November and immediately began to build themselves barrack huts and dugouts in which to shelter from the cold. A week before Christmas the remaining six families arrived, but there was nowhere they could be accommodated, it was too late for them to build anything for themselves, and they set off to search for shelter in Naibuchi, and from there they went to the Kusunnai Post, where they spent the winter in the soldiers' barracks; they returned to the Takoay Valley in spring.

"But it was precisely at this point that the slipshod attitude and incompetence of the bureaucracy began to have its effect," one author writes. They had promised farm implements to the value of 1,000 roubles, and four head of different sorts of livestock to every family, but when the emigrants had been sent from Nikolayevsk on the *Mandzhur* there were no millstones, no work-oxen, room could not be found on the boat for the horses and the ploughs turned out not to have any shares. In the winter ploughshares were brought on dog sleds – but only nine of them, and when subsequently the migrants applied to the authorities for the rest their request "did not attract the due attention". The oxen were sent to Kusunnai in the autumn of 1869, but they were exhausted and half-dead, no hay whatsoever had been prepared at Kusunnai, and, of the forty-one bulls, twenty died during the winter. The horses were left at Nikolayevsk on the mainland for the winter, but, since feed was dear, they were sold at auction, and new ones were bought in the Zabaikal Region with the receipts, but these horses proved to be inferior to the former ones, and the peasant-farmers rejected several of them. The grain was notable for its poor germination, and spring rye was mixed up in the sacks with winter rye, so that the plot-holders soon lost all faith in the grain and, although they had taken it from the state, they either fed their cattle with it or ate it themselves. Since there were no millstones, they did not grind the grain but simply steamed it and ate it as porridge.

After a series of failed harvests, a heavy flood occurred in 1875, which deprived the settlers once and for all of any wish to engage in farming on Sakhalin. They started migrating again. On the shores of the Aniva, about halfway between the Korsakovsk and Muravyovsk Posts, at a place known as Chibisani, a new settlement of twenty farmsteads was set up. Then they began to request permission to resettle in the Yuzhno-Ussuri (South Ussuri) District. They waited with impatience for permission to be granted as a special favour; they waited ten years and in the meantime kept themselves fed by hunting sable and catching fish. Only finally in 1886 did they leave for the Ussuri District. "They are abandoning their homes," wrote a newspaper reporter, "and travelling with practically empty pockets; they are taking a few belongings and one horse per family" (*Vladivostok*, 1886, no. 22). Nowadays, between the settlements of Bolshoye and Maloye Takoay, a short distance to one side of the road, there is the burnt-out site of a large fire; here once stood the voluntary settlement of Voskresenskoye; the cabins which had been left behind by the householders were burnt down by vagabonds. I heard that at Chibisani the cabins, the chapel, and even the house containing the school, have remained intact to this day. I did not visit it.

Only three of the free settlers have remained on the island: Khomutov, whom I have already mentioned, and two women who were born at Chibisani. Talking about Khomutov, people say that he "knocks about somewhere" and they think he lives at the Muravyovsk Post. He is rarely seen. He hunts sable and fishes for sturgeon in Busse Bay. Regarding the women, one of them, Sofiya, is married to the peasant-in-exile Baranovsky and lives at Mitzulka, while the other, Anisya, is married to settled exile Leonov and lives at Tretya Pad. Khomutov will soon die, Sofiya and Anisya will cross over to the mainland with their husbands, and thus only the bare memory will remain of the voluntary settlers.

Therefore, voluntary colonization on southern Sakhalin must be considered to have failed. Whether the blame for this is to be placed on the natural conditions which met these peasant-farmers first of all so inimically and with such severity, or whether on the other hand everything was ruined by the incompetence and slovenliness of the officials, it's hard to decide, since the experiment was short-lived, and besides, the trial was, on top of this, carried out on people obviously lacking in perseverance, who became restless in one place and who had acquired in their long wanderings through Siberia a taste for the nomadic life. It is difficult to say what the result of the experiment would be if it were repeated.* Purely as regards an exile colony, the unsuccessful trial may be instructive in two respects: first, the voluntary settlers did not take up farming for long and had spent the previous ten years before their passage to the mainland earning their living hunting and fishing; and nowadays, Khomutov, in spite of his extremely advanced age, finds it more convenient and lucrative to catch sturgeon and shoot sable than to sow wheat and plant cabbage; secondly, to keep a free-person on southern Sakhalin, when he is told in conversation day in, day out, that within a mere two days' travel from Korsakovsk lies the warm, rich South Ussuri District – especially if, in addition, he is healthy and full of life – is impossible.

The native population of southern Sakhalin, the local aborigines, when asked who they are, give the name neither of a tribe nor of a people but reply simply "aino", which means "a person". On

Shrenk's ethnographical map, the area of the Ainos' – or Ainus' – diffusion is indicated in yellow, and this colour entirely covers the Japanese island of Matsmay and the southern section of Sakhalin down to the Zaliv Terpeniya. They also live on the Kurile Islands, and because of this the Russians call them "Kurilians". The numerical strength of the Ainos living on Sakhalin has not been determined precisely, but there is no doubt, however, that the tribe is disappearing, and with uncommon rapidity at that. Dr Dobrotvorsky, who served on southern Sakhalin twenty-five years ago,* says that there was a time when there were eight large Aino villages around the Busse Bay alone, and the number of residents in one of them approached 200; around Naibu he saw the traces of many settlements. He conjectured three figures for his own period, drawn from various sources: 2,885, 2,418 and 2,050, and he considered the last to be the most authentic. According to the evidence of one writer, a contemporary of his, Aino settlements ran along both banks from the Korsakovsk Post. I, however, did not discover a single settlement near the post, and I saw a few Aino yurts only around Bolshoye Takoay and Siyantzy. In the 'Register of Numbers of Indigenes residing during 1889 in the Korsakovsk District' the number of the Ainos is put at 581 men and 569 women.

Dobrotvorsky considers the reason for the Ainos' disappearance to be the devastating wars which are supposed to have taken place at one time on Sakhalin, the negligible birth rate in consequence of the low fertility of the Aino women, and – the major factor – diseases. Syphilis and scurvy have always been observed among them; smallpox must also have occurred frequently.*

But none of these causes, which constitute the conditions for the customary chronic extinction of aboriginal tribes, yield any explanation as to why the Ainos are disappearing so fast, almost before our eyes; for in the last twenty-five to thirty years there have been neither wars nor significant epidemics, yet during this interval of time the tribe has decreased by over a half. It appears to me that it would be more accurate to assume that this swift disappearance, as if they are just melting away, is not simply because the Ainos are dying out but also because they are resettling on the neighbouring islands.

Before the Russians occupied southern Sakhalin, the Ainos found themselves almost in a state of serfdom to the Japanese, and it was all the easier to enslave them because they are gentle and meek, and – the chief point – are famished and cannot get by without rice.*

On occupying the island, the Russians freed them and preserved their freedom till very recently, protecting them from harm and injurious behaviour, and avoiding interfering in their internal affairs; in 1884 fugitive convicts slaughtered several Aino families; the story is also recounted that evidently some Aino dog-sled driver was birched for refusing to carry the post, and there have been attempts on the virtue of Aino women, but such offences and outrages are spoken of as isolated incidents and rare in the extreme. Unfortunately, the Russians did not bring rice along with their freedom; when the Japanese left, nobody caught fish any more, the earnings ceased, and the Ainos began to suffer famine. They simply could not live on fish and meat alone like the Gilyaks – they had to have rice, and it was at this point, so people say, that, despite their antipathy to the Japanese, they began to resettle on Matsmay. I have read in one newspaper article (*The Voice*, 1876, no. 16) that evidently a deputation of Ainos had gone to the Korsakovsk Post and asked to be given work, or at the very least seed for planting potatoes, and had requested to be taught how to cultivate the earth for potato growing; evidently work was refused them, and promises were made to send seed potatoes, but these promises were never fulfilled, and the Ainos, who were living in poverty, continued to migrate to Matsmay. In another report, from 1885 (*Vladivostok*, no. 28), it is also stated that the Ainos had put in some form of written applications, which had apparently not been complied with, and that they strongly desired to move from Sakhalin to Matsmay.

The Ainos are dark, like Gypsies; they have large bushy beards, moustaches and black hair; their eyes are dark, expressive and gentle. They are of medium height and powerful build, with facial features which are large and somewhat coarse, but in which, as seaman V. Rimsky-Korsakov puts it: "There is no trace of Mongol flatness, nor of the slant eyes of the Chinese." It is considered that the bearded Ainos look very similar to European Russian peasants. Indeed, when an Aino is dressed up in his robe, which looks a bit like our *chuyka*,* and does up his belt, he does take on a similarity to a merchant's coachman.*

The Aino's body is covered with dark hairs, which sometimes grow thickly, in tufts, on his chest, but he is still a long way from shagginess, even though the beard and hairiness, which are so rare among savages, have startled travellers, who on their return home have described the Ainos as hirsute. Our Cossacks, too, who last century exacted tribute paid in furs on the Kurile Islands, described them as hairy.

The Ainos live in close proximity to peoples among whom facial hair is notable for its scarcity, and it is no wonder therefore that their broad beards have caused the ethnographers great difficulty; to this very day science has still not found a real place for the Ainos in the racial system; sometimes they are ascribed to the Mongolian and sometimes to the Caucasian peoples; one Englishman* even considered that they were descendants of Jews who had been cast up on the Japanese islands in remote times. Nowadays two views seem to be the most probable: one, that the Ainos belong to their own peculiar race, which in the past inhabited all the East Asian islands; and the other view, held by our own Mr Shrenk, is that they are a palaeoasiatic folk, who were ousted long ago from the mainland of Asia on to their island outposts by the Mongol tribes, and that this people's path from Asia to the islands lay across Korea. In any case, the Aino has moved from south to north, from warmth to cold, constantly exchanging better conditions for worse. They are not warlike and cannot endure violence; it was not difficult to subjugate them, enslave them or force them out. They were forced out of Asia by the Mongols, from the islands of Nippon and Matsmay by the Japanese, on Sakhalin the Gilyaks would not let them further up than Tarayka, they encountered the Cossacks on the Kurile Islands, and thus finally found themselves in a hopeless situation. These days an Aino – usually bareheaded and barefooted, and wearing shorts cut off above the knee – who happens to meet you on the road will bow to you, gazing up at you amiably, but sadly and unhealthily, like a failure who has had a lot of bad luck, and as if he would like to apologize for the fact that, although his beard has grown long, he has still not made a career for himself.

For details of the Ainos see Shrenk, Dobrotvorsky and A. Polonsky.* The remarks about the Gilyaks' diet and clothing also apply to the Ainos, with only one addition – that the shortage of rice, the love for which the Aino has inherited from his ancestors, who at one time lived on the southern islands, is a serious hardship for them; they do not like Russian bread. Their diet differs from that of the Gilyaks in its greater variety; besides meat and fish they eat various plants, molluscs and what Italian beggars know by the general title of *frutti di mare*. They eat little but often, almost every hour; the gluttony which is peculiar to all northern savages is not observed among them. Since nursing children must pass from milk straight on to fish and whale blubber, they are weaned late. Rimsky-Korsakov saw an Aino woman suckling a three-year-old boy, who could already move around excellently by himself, and who even had a little knife in his belt, like an adult. One senses the powerful influence of the south on their clothes and on their dwellings – not the Sakhalin south, but the real south. In summer the Ainos walk around in shirts woven from grass or bast, and in earlier times, when they were not so poor, they used to wear silk robes. They wear no headgear and go around during the summer and the entire winter till snow comes in bare feet. It is smoky and stinking in their yurts, but all the same it is still much lighter, tidier and, so to speak, more "cultured" than in those of the Gilyaks. A drying ground for fish usually lies by the yurt, and this extends a dank and suffocating odour for a long way round; dogs howl and fight; here you may sometimes see a small framework cage, with a young bear sitting inside it; they will kill him and eat him in winter at the so-called "bear feast". One morning I saw an adolescent Aino girl feeding the bear by poking through on a little shovel a dried fish moistened with water. The yurts themselves are constructed of thin logs and boards; the roof, made from narrow poles, is covered with dry grass. Inside bed-boards extend along the walls, and above them are shelves of various utensils; there, besides skins, bladders of fat, nets, crockery and so forth, you will also find baskets, rugs and even a musical instrument. The head of the house usually sits on the bed-board unceasingly smoking a pipe, and if you put questions to him, he will answer reluctantly and tersely, although politely as well. In the middle of the yurt lies a hearth, on which they burn firewood; the smoke escapes through a hole in the roof. On a hook over the fire hangs a large black cauldron, in which fish soup is being boiled up, a grey, frothy liquid which I do not think any European could bring himself to eat for all the money in the world. Around the cauldron some monsters are sitting. The Ainos' wives and mothers are as unattractive as the men are sturdy and handsome. Writers have described the Aino women's appearance as hideous, and even repulsive. They are a dark-yellow, parchment-like colour, with narrow eyes and coarse features; their stiff, straight hair, which does not grow into curls, hangs down their faces in long, bristly strands, like straw on an old shed, their clothing is slovenly and hideous to look at, and besides all this they are unusually thin and wear an expression of senility. Those who are married dye their lips with something dark blue, and for this reason their faces completely lose their human form and likeness, and on the occasion that I saw them and observed the seriousness – almost sternness – with which they stirred the cauldrons with ladles and removed the scum, it seemed to me that I was watching genuine, dyed-in-the-wool witches. But the infant and adolescent girls do not create an impression of such repulsiveness.*

The Aino never washes, and lies down to sleep without undressing.

Practically everybody who has written about the Ainos has spoken of their mores in the best possible terms. There is general agreement that this race is gentle, modest, good-natured, trusting, communicative and courteous, respects property, is courageous in the hunt and, to use the expression of Dr Rollen, a travelling companion of La Pérouse, they "might even be said to be cultured and intelligent". Their customary qualities consist of unselfishness, openness and a belief in friendship and generosity. They are truthful and cannot stand deception. Kruzenshtern left them in sheer delight; he enumerates their mental qualities, then concludes: "Such genuinely rare qualities, for the possession of which they are indebted not to any elevated education, but to nature alone, have aroused in me the sensation that I consider this race the best of all others that have hitherto been known to me."*
A. Rudanovsky writes: "A more peaceable and modest population than the one we met in the southern part of Sakhalin cannot exist." Every kind of violence arouses revulsion and horror in them. A. Polonsky recounts the following lamentable episode, drawn from the archives. It happened long ago, in the last century. The Cossack Lieutenant Chorny, who had induced the Ainos on the Kurile Islands to take up Russian citizenship, suddenly had the notion of birching some of them: "The Ainos became terror-stricken at the mere sight of the preparations for the punishment, and when they began to tie the hands of two women behind their backs, in order to deal with them more conveniently, some of the Ainos fled up an inaccessible cliff, and one Aino man and twenty women and children put out to sea in kayaks. Those women who had not managed to escape were flogged, and the Cossacks took six men away with them on to their canoes, and to

prevent escape tethered their arms behind them, but so brutally that one of them died. When they threw him from a rock into the sea, bloated, and with his hands looking as if they had been scalded with boiling water, Chorny, for the edification of the Aino's colleagues, uttered the words: "That's how we do things in Russia."

And, in conclusion, a few words about the Japanese, who play such a prominent role in the history of southern Sakhalin. It is common knowledge that the southern third of Sakhalin has belonged unconditionally to Russia only since 1875; previously it was considered to be a Japanese possession. In his *Manual of Practical Navigation and Nautical Astronomy* of 1854 – a volume still used by mariners right up to the present day – Prince E. Golitzyn ascribes to Japan even northern Sakhalin and the Capes of Mariya and Elizaveta. Many, including Nevelskoy, had doubts about southern Sakhalin belonging to Japan, and evidently the Japanese themselves were not certain about it till the time when the Russians, by their weird conduct, brought it home to them that southern Sakhalin was indeed Japanese soil. The Japanese appeared on the south of Sakhalin for the first time only at the beginning of this century and no earlier than that. In 1853 Mr Busse noted down his conversation with the old Aino men who could remember the time of their independence and who said: "Sakhalin is Aino land – there is simply no Japanese land on Sakhalin." In 1806, the year of Khvostov's exploits, there was only one Japanese settlement on the shore of the Aniva, and the buildings there were all constructed from new boards, so that it was obvious that the Japanese had settled here very recently. Kruzenshtern visited the Aniva in April, during the herring run, and owing to the extraordinary multitudes of fish, whales and seals, the water looked as if it were boiling, yet the Japanese had neither bag-nets nor seine-nets, and they scooped the fish up with buckets, which implies that there was then not even a trace of the rich fishing industry which later on was to become established on such a wide footing. In all probability these first Japanese colonists were fugitive criminals, or people who had spent some time in a foreign country, and for this had been driven from their homeland.*

It was our diplomatic service which first drew attention to Sakhalin at the very beginning of this century. Ambassador Rezanov, who had been empowered to conclude a trade agreement with Japan, also had the further task of "acquiring the island of Sakhalin, which is a dependent territory neither of the Japanese nor of the Chinese". He behaved extremely tactlessly. "In consequence of the lack of tolerance from the Japanese towards the Christian faith", he forbade his crew to cross themselves and ordered that all crosses, holy images, Prayer Books and "everything which represents Christianity, or which bears the sign of the cross" should be taken away from everybody without exception. If Kruzenshtern is to be believed, Rezanov was refused even a chair at the audience, he was not allowed to bear a sword, and "in consequence of the lack of tolerance" he did not even have anything on his feet. And this was an ambassador, a Russian VIP! It would, I think, be difficult to display less dignity. Having suffered an utter fiasco, Rezanov began to feel the need to revenge himself on the Japanese. He ordered Naval Officer Khvostov to scare the Sakhalin Japanese a little, and this command was not issued in quite the usual manner, but in a somewhat roundabout way – it was in a sealed envelope, with the imperative condition that it should be opened and read only on arrival at the location.*

Thus Rezanov and Khvostov were the first to recognize that southern Sakhalin belonged to the Japanese. However, the Japanese had not occupied their new possession but simply sent the land surveyor Mamia-Rinzo to explore and find out what the island was like. In general, throughout the whole of the history of Sakhalin, the Japanese, an adroit, lively and resourceful people, have behaved in an irresolute and inert manner, which can only be explained by the fact that they were as little certain of their rights as the Russians were of theirs.

It appears that after the Japanese had become familiar with the island, the notion of a colony occurred to them, perhaps even an agricultural one, but the attempts in this direction – if there were any – could have led only to disappointment, since, according to Engineer Lopatin, the Japanese workmen either endured the winters with difficulty or else were unable to stand them at all. Only Japanese entrepreneurs came to Sakhalin, on rare occasions with their wives; they lived here in something like soldiers' bivouacs, and only a small proportion of them – a few dozen – stayed the winter; the rest returned home on junks; they did not plant anything, did not keep vegetable gardens or cattle, and brought all the necessities for life with them from Japan. The sole thing which attracted them to southern Sakhalin was the fish; it yielded them a large income, since it was caught in abundance, and the Ainos, on whom lay the whole brunt of the work, cost them next to nothing. At first the income from the fisheries reached 50,000 and later on 300,000 roubles per year, and so it is no wonder that the Japanese proprietors used to wear seven silk robes each. In the beginning, the Japanese only maintained their trading posts on the banks of the Aniva and at Mauka, and they were chiefly located in the glen of Kusun-Kotan, where the Japanese Consul now lives.* Later on they cleared a cutting through the forest from the Aniva to the Takoay Valley; their shops were to be found here close to the present-day Galkino-Vraskoye; the cutting has still not grown over today and is called Japanese Cutting. The Japanese reached as far as Tarayka, too, where they caught the seasonal fish in the Poronai and founded the settlement of Siska. Their boats even reached the Nyysky Bay; the ship with the beautiful rigging which Polyakov came across in 1881 on the Tro was Japanese.

Sakhalin interested the Japanese exclusively from an economic angle, as Tyulen Island* interested the Americans. However, after the Russians had established the Muravyovsk Post in 1853, the Japanese began to display political activity as well. The consideration that they might lose a good income and free labour made them keep careful watch on the Russians, and they tried to strengthen their influence on the island as a counterbalance to that of the Russians. But once again, very likely because of their lack of certainty about their rights, this struggle with the Russians was irresolute to the point of absurdity, and the Japanese behaved like children. They simply limited themselves to spreading slander about the Russians among the Ainos and boasting that they would cut all the Russians to bits; and the Russians had only to set up a post in some locality or other for shortly after, in precisely the same spot, but on the other side of the stream, a Japanese picket to appear as well, and, for all their desire to appear fearsome, the Japanese still proved to be peaceable, pleasant people; they sent sturgeon to the Russian soldiers and, when the latter asked them for a fishnet, they willingly complied with the request.

In 1867 a treaty was concluded by which Sakhalin would belong to both governments on the principle of common ownership; the Russians and the Japanese recognized each other's sole right to administer the island – signifying that neither the one nor the other considered the island to be theirs.* Then, by the treaty of 1875, Sakhalin finally became a part of the Russian Empire, and Japan received all our Kurile Islands as compensation.*

Next to the gorge in which the Korsakovsk Post is situated there is another glen, which has kept its name since the time when there was a Japanese village here called Kusun-Kotan. Not a single Japanese building has remained intact; there is, however, a little shop, in which a Japanese family carries on a trade in groceries and small general goods – I bought some hard Japanese pears there – but this shop is only of very recent origin. On the most prominent spot in the glen stands a white house, on which a flag sometimes flutters – a flag with a red circle on a white background. This is the Japanese consulate. One morning, when a north-easter was blowing, and it was so cold in my lodgings that I had wrapped myself up in a blanket, the Japanese Consul, Mr Kuze, and his secretary Mr Sugiama came to visit me. My first duty was to apologize that my quarters were so cold.

"Oh, no!" replied my guests, "it is extremely warm in your dwelling!"

And they strove to show, by their faces and their tone of voice, that my lodgings were not only warm but even hot, and that they were in all respects paradise on earth. They are both pure-blooded Japanese, of medium height and with the Mongolian type of face. The Consul is about forty, he does not have a beard,* his moustache is hardly noticeable and he is solidly built, while the secretary is about ten years younger, wears dark-blue spectacles and to all appearances is consumptive – a victim of the Sakhalin climate. There is also another secretary, Mr Suzuki; he is below average height, he has large moustaches, the tips of which are curled downwards in the Chinese fashion, and his eyes are narrow and slanting – from a Japanese point of view, an irresistibly handsome man. Once, talking about a certain Japanese minister, Mr Kuze came out with: "He is handsome and manly, like Suzuki." Out of doors they wear European clothes, and they speak Russian very well; when I visited the consulate, I would quite often find them reading Russian or French volumes – they have a whole cupboard full of books. They have had a European-style education and are elegantly polite, considerate and cordial. For the local officials the Japanese consulate is a nice, cosy corner where they can forget the prison, forced labour and the petty squabbles and unpleasantries of service, and consequently can relax.

The Consul serves as an intermediary between the Japanese who come here to carry on commercial enterprises and the local administration. On High Holidays he and his secretary, in full-dress uniform, walk from Kusun-Kotan Glen to the District Governor at the post and pay their respects in regard to the festival; Mr Bely reciprocates in kind; every year on 1st December he and his colleagues set off for Kusun-Kotan and there he congratulates the Consul on the Emperor of Japan's birthday. During the course of this they drink champagne. Whenever the Consul visits a warship, he is given a seven-salvo salute. It happened that, during my stay, the Orders of Anna and Stanislav Third Class* were bestowed on Mr Kuze and Mr Suzuki. Mr Bely, Major Sh. and Mr F., the secretary of the police department, solemn and in full-dress uniforms, made their way to Kusun-Kotan to confer the Orders; I, too, went with them. The Japanese were very affected both by the Orders and by the ceremonial solemnity which they love so much; champagne was served. Mr Suzuki could not conceal his delight and examined the medal from every angle with shining eyes, like a child does with a toy; I could read a conflict in his "handsome and manly" face; he wanted to rush off quickly to his own quarters and show the Order to his young wife (he had just recently married), while at the same time politeness required that he remain with the guests.*

Having concluded this survey of the inhabited spots of Sakhalin, I will now pass on to the particularities, both significant and insignificant, which go to make up the life of the colony at the present time.

15

Convict householders. Transfer to settled exile status. Selection of locations for new settlements. Setting up a household. Co-sharers. Transfer to peasant-in-exile status. Resettlement of peasants-in-exile on the mainland. Life in the settlements. Proximity of prison. Composition of population as regards place of birth and social status.

WHEN IN ADDITION TO ITS DIRECT OBJECTIVES – revenge, instilling of fear or correction – retribution has other goals laid down for it – for instance, colonization – it must of necessity constantly adapt itself to the requirements of a colony and make compromises. A prison is antagonistic to a colony, and their interests are in inverse ratio to each other. Life in the communal cells reduces a prisoner to the condition of a serf, and in the course of time, makes him degenerate; the habits of the life of the herd stifle within him the instincts of a permanently settled man and domesticated householder; his health declines, he grows old and weakens morally, and the later he leaves the prison the more reasons there are to fear that he will not turn out an active, useful member of the colony, but merely a burden to it. And this is precisely the reason why practical colonizing experience has called before all else for terms of imprisonment and enforced labour to be shortened; and in this respect our *Statutes on Exiles* have made considerable concessions. Thus, for prisoners in the category of "reformee", ten months are counted as a year, and if second- and third-category convicts – i.e. those sentenced to between four and twelve years – are detailed to work in the mines, then every year they spend at this work is considered as eighteen months.*

On their transition to "reformee" category, convicts are permitted by law to live outside the prison, build themselves homes, get married and have money. But real life has gone still further in this direction than the *Statutes*. To make the transition easier from convicthood to a more self-reliant status, in 1888 the Governor General of the Amur River (Priamur) Territory authorized the release of hard-working and well-behaved convicts before the completion of their sentences; announcing this directive (no. 302) General Kononovich promised release from work two or even three years before completion of the full term of labour. And even without legal clauses and orders, but through necessity, since it is useful for the colony, all convict women without exception live outside the prison, in their own homes and in free-persons' quarters, as do many "probationer" and even life-sentence convicts, if they have families, or they are good craftsmen, land-surveyors, dog-sled drivers and so forth. Many are permitted to live outside the prison merely "for humanity's sake" or on the reasoning that if so-and-so lives not in the prison, but in a cabin, no harm will come of it, or if life-sentence convict Z is permitted to live in free-persons' lodgings merely because he has come here with his wife and children, then not to permit the same to short-sentence convict N would be extremely unjust.

By 1st January 1890 there was a total of 5,905 convicts of both sexes in all the three districts of Sakhalin. Of these, 2,124 (36 per cent) had been sentenced to periods of up to eight years, 1,567 (26.5 per cent) from eight to twelve years, 747 (12.7 per cent) from twelve to fifteen years, 731 (12.3 per cent) from fifteen to twenty years, there were 386 (6.5 per cent) serving open-ended – that is, life – sentences and 175 (3 per cent) recidivists who had been sentenced to periods of twenty to fifty years. Short-term criminals sentenced to periods of up to twelve years make up 62.5 per cent – that is, just over half the total number. The average age of a criminal who has just received a sentence I do not know, but, judging from the age range of the exile population at the present time, it cannot be less than thirty-five years old; if to this is added an average duration of eight to ten years' convict labour, and if we take into consideration the fact that a person grows old much earlier in penal servitude than under normal conditions, then it becomes apparent that if the legal sentence is carried out to the letter, and if the *Statutes* are observed, with strict confinement to prison, labour carried out under military escort and so forth, then not only the long-term but a good half of the short-term prisoners, too, will enter the colony with their colonizing capabilities already lost.

During my visit, there were 424 convict householders of both sexes living on their own plots of land, and I recorded 908 convicts of both sexes living in the colony in the capacities of wives, male and female cohabitants, workmen, tenants and the like. In all there were 1,332 – twenty-three per cent of the total number of convicts – living outside the prison in their own cabins and in free-persons' lodgings.* As householders, the convicts in the colony hardly differ at all from the settled-exile householders. The convicts attached to households as workmen do exactly the same as our European Russian village workmen. Allocating a prisoner as a workman to a good householder, also a convict, who had been a country-dweller back home is the one aspect of penal servitude so far worked out by practical Russian experience and is without a doubt more engaging than the Australian system of working as labourers on free settlers' farms. Convict tenants only spend the night in their lodgings, but must report just as punctually for allocation to convict labour as their companions living in the prison. Artisans – for instance, joiners and shoemakers – often serve out their labour terms in their own lodgings.*

No especial disorder may be observed, because a quarter of the total number of convicts live outside the prisons; and I would readily like to submit that it is none too easy to put our system of penal servitude into order for precisely the reason that the remaining three-quarters live *inside* the prisons. We can only talk about the preferability of cabins to communal cell rooms as a probability, of course, since up till now there have been no accurate studies on this subject.

Nobody has yet proved that there are fewer cases of crime and escape among the convicts living in cabins than there are among those living in the prisons, and that the labour of the former is more productive than that of the latter, but it is highly likely that the prison statistics, which sooner or later must address this question, will make their final decision in favour of cabins. At the moment one thing is without a doubt – that the colony would be the gainer if, on his arrival on Sakhalin, every convict, with no distinction for length of sentence, was immediately set to work to build a cabin for himself and his family, and begin his colonizing activity as early as possible, while he was still relatively young and healthy; and justice would lose nothing by this, since, entering into the colony from his very first day, the offender would undergo the heaviest part of his sentence before transition to settled-exile status and not afterwards.

When his sentence comes to an end, the convict is released from labour and is transferred to the settled exiles. There are no delays that may be put on this. A new settled exile, if he has money and influence among the authorities, will remain at Alexandrovsk, or in a settlement that he likes, and he will buy or build a house there, if he has not acquired one while doing penal servitude; for such a person farming and labour are not obligatory. If, however, he belongs to the common herd who make up the majority, he will usually settle on a plot in the settlement the authorities order, and if it is cramped and there is no land fit for a farm-holding left, they will settle him in a ready-made household as a co-owner or half-sharer, or else send him to settle on a new site.*

The choice of sites for new settlements, which requires experience and some specialized knowledge, is entrusted to the local administration – that is, to the district governors, prison governors and inspectors of settlements. There are no definite statutes or directions of any kind on this subject, and the whole thing depends on such incidental circumstances as the composition of this or that bunch of civil servants: whether they have been in service for a long time already and are familiar with the exile population and the locality, as, for example, Mr Butakov in the north and Messrs Bely and Yartzev in the south, or whether they have just entered the service, and at best, are philologists, lawyers or infantry lieutenants, or at worst, are completely uneducated people who have never been in service anywhere previously, the majority of them young townspeople with no experience of life. I have already written about the official who did not believe the natives and settled exiles when they warned him that the spot he had chosen for a settlement became flooded in spring and during periods of heavy rainfall. During my stay one official travelled fifteen or twenty versts with his entourage to inspect a new site and returned home the very same day, having managed to survey the place in detail and approve it in two or three hours; he said the trip had been very nice.

The senior and more experienced officials rarely and reluctantly go off in search of new sites, since they are always occupied with other affairs, and the junior staff are inexperienced and indifferent; the administration procrastinates, the business drags on, and the result is the overcrowding of the settlements already existing. And in the end they unwillingly have to ask for assistance from the convicts and soldier-overseers, who, according to hearsay, have selected sites with success. In 1888, in view of the fact that neither in the Tymovsk nor Alexandrovsk District was there any space left for the allocating of plots of land, while the number of people needing them was growing rapidly, General Kononovich commanded in one of his directives (no. 286): "the immediate organization of parties of trustworthy convicts under the supervision of completely efficient and literate overseers who are the most experienced in this work, or even officials, and to send same in search of sites suitable for settlement". These parties roam around utterly unexplored countryside, on which the topographer has never yet set foot; they discover sites, but how high they are above sea level, what the soil and water are like, and so on, no one knows; the administration can only go by guesswork as to its suitability for settlement and cultivation for agriculture, and for this reason the final decision in favour of this or that location is made entirely at random, on the off-chance, and in so doing they ask the opinion neither of a doctor nor of a topographer – there isn't one on Sakhalin – and the land-surveyor turns up at the new site when the land has already been cleared and people are living on it.*

After our tour round the settlements, the Governor General, giving me his impressions, put it like this: "The hard labour doesn't begin in 'hard labour' but in settled exile afterwards." If weight of punishment is measured by quantity of effort and physical privation, then the settled exiles on Sakhalin often undergo more severe retribution than the convicts. A settled exile will turn up at a new site, usually swampy and covered with woodland, having with him only a carpenter's axe, a saw and a spade. He hews down the forest, grubs up the earth, digs ditches to drain the area, and all the time this preparatory work is going on he lives out in the open, on the damp earth. The charms of the Sakhalin climate, with its cloudiness, rain almost daily and low temperatures, are nowhere felt so sharply as at this labour, where, during a period of several weeks, a person will not be able to shake off for one single minute the sensation of piercing damp and feverishness. This constitutes a veritable *febris sachalinensis* (Sakhalin fever), with a headache, and rheumatic pains throughout the whole body, which derive not from infection but from climatic influences. First of all they build the settlement, and only then a road leading to it, and not vice versa, and due to this a great deal of health and strength is wasted utterly unproductively in lugging heavy objects from the post, from which there are not even any pathways leading to the new site; a settled exile, loaded down with tools, provisions and suchlike, goes through the dense taiga, now up to his knees in water, now scrabbling over mountains of trees and branches blown down in the wind, and now getting entangled in stiff *bagulnik* bushes. The 307th Article of the *Statutes on Exiles* states that those settling outside a jail should be supplied with timber for the construction of homes; here this article is taken to mean that the settled exile must cut down the timber and prepare it himself. Formerly, convicts were released to help the settled exiles, and money was issued for the hire of carpenters and the purchase of materials, but this procedure was abandoned on the grounds that, as one official told me, "Layabouts were created as a result; the convicts would be working while at the same moment the settled exiles would be playing at pitch-and-toss." These days the settlers get established through joint effort, assisting each other. The carpenter erects the framework, the stove-maker greases the stove, the sawyers prepare the boards. Anybody who has not got the strength or the skill to work, but who has got the filthy lucre, hires his colleagues. The strong and hardy take on the heaviest labour, while those lacking strength or who have lost the habit of peasant labour in prison, if they are not playing pitch-and-toss or cards, or sheltering from the cold, carry out some relatively light work. Many become exhausted, lose heart and abandon their still-unbuilt homes. The Manzes and Caucasians who do not know how to build Russian cabins usually run away in the very first year. Almost half the householders on Sakhalin have no homes, and this must be explained first and foremost – so it seems to me – by the difficulties the settler encounters on his initial attempts to set up a home. In the Tymovsk District of 1889, according to data I have drawn from the Inspector of Agriculture's report, the number of homeless householders made up fifty per cent of the total number, and in the Korsakovsk District it was forty-two per cent, while in the Alexandrovsk District, where the establishment of a household is hedged around by fewer difficulties, and where the settled exiles more often buy their homes than build them, the number is only twenty per cent. When the framework is finished, the householder is issued with glass and iron on loan. In one of his directives the Governor of the Island has said of this loan: "It is most greatly to be regretted that for this loan, like so many others, one is compelled to wait for a long period, paralysing the desire to establish one's household... In the autumn of last year, during a drive round the settled areas of the Korsakovsk Region, I frequently chanced to see houses awaiting glass, nails and iron for dampers for the stoves; today I discover these homes to be in the same deficient condition."*

It is not considered necessary to analyse a new location, even when it has already been settled. They send fifty to 100 householders to a fresh site, then add scores of new ones every year, yet still nobody will know how many people the land can comfortably suffice for, and this is the reason why, usually shortly after the place has begun to be settled, lack of space and an excess of people already begin to become apparent. The one district where this is not observed is the Korsakovsk; however, the posts and settlements of both northern districts, all of them down to the very last one, are overpopulated. Even such a conscientious and careful man as the Governor of the Tymovsk District, Mr Butakov, plants people on plots anyhow, taking no thought for the future, and in no other district is there such a large number of co-owners, or supernumerary householders, as there is in his area. It is as if the administration itself does not believe in the agricultural colony, and little by little has put its mind at rest with the thought that a settled exile will not be needing land for long – six years in all – since, when he has received peasant-in-exile's rights, he will certainly abandon the island, and under such conditions, the question of land-plots can hold merely a purely formal significance.

Of the 3,522 householders whom I noted down, 638, or eighteen per cent, are co-tenants, and if we exclude the Korsakovsk District, where they settle only one householder per plot, the percentage will be considerably higher. In the Tymovsk District, the younger the settlement, the higher the percentage of half-sharers; for instance, in Voskresenskoye, there are ninety-seven householders and seventy-seven half-sharers; this means that to find new sites, and to allot plots of land to the settled exiles, will become more and more difficult every year.*

The settled exile is placed under a binding obligation to organize his household and run it correctly. For laziness, negligence and unwillingness to establish a household, he is returned to "communal" – that is, convict – labour for a year, and is transferred from the cabin back to the prison. Article 402 of the *Statutes* permits the Governor General of the Amur River Territory "to maintain on government rations those Sakhalin settled exiles who are recognized by the local authorities as not having their own means in addition". At the present time, during the first two – and in rare cases, three – years after their release from convict labour, the majority of Sakhalin settled exiles receive clothing and food allowances from the state on the same scale as the customary prisoners' rations. The administration are impelled to give such aid to the settlers by humanitarian and practical considerations. Indeed, it is really very hard to assume that a settler could at one and the same time build himself a cabin, prepare land for cultivation and, besides this, earn his bread daily. But it is not uncommon to find in the official directives that some settled exile or other is to be taken off rations for negligence, for laziness, or because "he has not applied himself to the construction of a home".*

On the expiry of their ten years of settled exile status, the settlers are permitted to be registered as peasants-in-exile. This new status is accompanied by significant rights. A peasant-in-exile can leave Sakhalin and set up home wherever he wishes throughout the whole of Siberia, with the exception of the Provinces of Semirechensk, Akhmolinsk and Semipalatinsk;* he can – with their consent – register as a member of a peasant society,* and he can live in towns to carry on his trades or industries; he may be tried in court, and is subject to punishment on the basis of the common civilian law, and not the *Statutes on Exiles*; he may receive and send correspondence also on the common footing, without the preliminary censorship stipulated for convicts and settled exiles. But even in this new status of his, the main element of exile still, however, remains: he does not have the right to return to his home region.*

The receipt of peasant's rights after ten years is not encompassed by any special conditions. Apart from cases provided for in the footnote to Statute 375, the sole prerequisite for this is the serving of a ten-year term of settlement, regardless of whether the settled exile is a plotholder and agricultural labourer, or a craft apprentice. When our conversation turned to this subject, the Inspector of Prisons for the Amur River Territory, Mr Kamorsky, confirmed to me that the administration had no right to keep an exile in the status of settler for longer than ten years or to hedge round his receipt of peasant's rights with any sort of condition. Yet on Sakhalin I frequently encountered elderly men who had remained settled exiles for longer than ten years, but had not received peasant status. I did not manage to verify their testimonies from the itemized records, however, and so I cannot judge how correct they were. Old men can make mistakes in calculation, or simply lie, although, given the indiscipline and confusion of the clerks, and the ineptitude of the junior officials, all sorts of quirks might be expected from the Sakhalin government offices. For those settled exiles who have "conducted themselves in a thoroughly favourable manner, have engaged in useful work and have acquired a settled way of life", the ten-year term may be reduced to six. The Governor of the Island and the District Governors make the most wide-scale use of Article 377, which permits the privilege; at least, almost all the peasants I know of received this status after six years. But unfortunately the "useful work" and "settled way of life" upon which the reception of this privilege is stipulated in the *Statutes* is understood differently in each of the three districts. In the Tymovsk District, for example, they will not promote a settled exile to peasant status while he is in debt to the Exchequer and until his cabin has been roofed with boards. In Alexandrovsk a settled exile does not take up farming, he does not need tools, seed and grain, and therefore he runs up fewer debts; it is easier, consequently, for him to obtain his rights. It is a binding condition that a settled exile must be a householder, but among exiles more often than in any other walk of life you come across people who by their very nature are incapable of being householders and feel at home working as hired labourers. My question as to whether the privilege could be taken advantage of, and whether peasant's rights could, generally speaking, be gained by a settler who did not have his own household because he served as cook at an official's lodgings, or as apprentice to a shoemaker, was answered affirmatively in the Korsakovsk District, but undecidedly in both northern districts. Under such conditions, of course, one cannot even begin to talk of any sort of "norms", and if the governor of the new district requires of his settled exiles iron roofs and the ability to sing in the church choir, it would be hard to prove to him that this was arbitrary.

While I was at Siyantzy, the Inspector of Settlements ordered twenty-five settled exiles to gather by the overseers' office and announced to them that, by decree of the Governor of the Island, they had been transferred to peasant status. The decree had been signed by the General on 27th January and was announced to the settlers on 26th September. The glad tidings were received by all twenty-five settlers in silence; not one crossed himself, or gave thanks, but they all stood silently, with serious faces, as if they had all grown melancholy at the thought that on this earth everything, even suffering, has an end. When Mr Yartzev and I started to talk to them about who was going to remain on Sakhalin and who was going to leave, not one of the twenty-five expressed a desire to remain. They all said that they were longing for the mainland and would have left with pleasure that very minute, but they did not have the means to, they would have to think about it. And conversations were going on about how the money for the journey alone was not much – for did not the mainland simply adore money, too? You would have to apply to join a society, and entertain people, buy a little bit of land and build yourself a house, and, before you knew where you were, you would find you needed a good 150 roubles or so.* And where could you get hold of that? In Rykovo, despite its comparatively large dimensions, I found only thirty-nine peasants and they were all far from having any intention of putting down roots here; they were all preparing to go to the mainland. One of them, Bespalov by name, is building a big two-storey house with a balcony on his plot, like a dacha,* and everybody gazes at the building in bewilderment and cannot make out what it is for; that a well-off man with grown-up sons would perhaps remain in Rykovo for ever when he could perfectly well settle down somewhere along the Zeya* creates the impression of being a curious whim, and of crankiness. In Dubki one peasant gambler at cards, to my question as to whether he would go over to the mainland, looked haughtily at the ceiling and replied: "I shall endeavour to leave."*

The peasants are driven from Sakhalin by the sense of a lack of security, by boredom, by constant fear for their children... but the main reason is a passionate desire at least to breathe the air of freedom and to live a real life, and not that of a prisoner, before they die. And the Ussuri Area,* and the Amur, which everybody talks about as they would of the Promised Land, are so near: sail for three or four days on a steamer, and there – there is freedom, warmth, good harvests...

Those who have already migrated to the mainland and have settled there write to their Sakhalin acquaintances that on the mainland people offer them their hands to shake, and vodka costs only fifty copecks a bottle. Once, strolling along the pier at Alexandrovsk, I dropped into the shed where the launches were kept and saw there an old man, sixty or seventy years of age, and an old woman, with bundles and bags, obviously intending to be on their way. We got chatting. The old man had not long previously obtained peasant's rights, and now he and his wife were leaving for the mainland, first of all for Vladivostok, and then "where God wishes". According to them they had no money. The steamer was due to leave twenty-four hours later, but they had already trudged onto the pier, and had concealed themselves in the boat shed with their bits and pieces in wait for the steamer, as if they feared they would be turned back. They talked about the mainland with love, with reverence and with the certainty that over there, there really was a genuinely happy life. In the Alexandrovsk cemetery I saw a black cross with a depiction of the Virgin Mary and with the following inscription: "Here lie the remains of Miss Afinya Kurnikova, died 1888, 21st of May. She was eighteen years old. This cross has been put up also as a sign of remembrance of her parents' departure for the mainland 1889, 1st June."

A peasant is not released to the mainland if his behaviour is not trustworthy or he is in debt to the Exchequer. If he is cohabiting with a female exile and has children by her, the release permit is issued to him only where he provides with his property for the future benefit of his cohabitant and the children illegally begotten with her (Directive no. 92, 1889). On the mainland the peasant is registered with the rural shire he has selected to live in; the governor under whose jurisdiction the shire falls informs the governor of the island, and the latter issues a directive commanding the police department to expunge peasant so-and-so and the members of his family from the records so that formally there is one "poor unfortunate" less. Baron Korf told me that if a peasant conducts himself badly on the mainland he is exiled by administrative order to Sakhalin, this time for ever.

From what one hears, Sakhaliners live well on the mainland. I have read their letters but I did not manage to see how they lived in their new localities. However, one of them I did see, though not in the country but in a town. One day in Vladivostok,* Hieromonk Irakly – the Sakhalin missionary and priest – and I were coming out of a shop together, and some man in a white apron and gleaming high boots – he must have been a porter in a block of flats, or a janitor in a bank or government office – was overjoyed at the sight of Father Irakly, and came over to be blessed; it turned out he had been one of Father Irakly's "spiritual flock" and was a peasant-in-exile. Father Irakly recognized him and remembered his name and surname. "Well, and how are you getting on here?" he asked. "Fine, God be praised!" replied the other with animation.

Until their departure for the mainland the peasants live in the posts and settlements and maintain households under exactly the same unfavourable circumstances as the settled exiles and convicts. They still constantly continue to depend on the prison authorities and take their caps off at fifty paces if they live in the south; they are treated better and are not flogged, but all the same, they are still not peasants in any real sense, but prisoners. They live by the prison and see it each day, and a convict-exile prison and a serene agricultural existence are inconceivable next door to each other. Some writers have observed country dances at Rykovo and have heard an accordion and spirited songs there; I, however, did not hear or see anything of the kind, and I cannot visualize maidens leading rustic choral dances next to a jail. Even if, besides the jingle of chains and cries of overseers, I had happened to hear a lively song as well, I would have considered it a bad sign, for a kind and charitable person does not strike up a song outside a prison. The peasants and settled exiles and their free wives and children are ground down by the prison regime; the prison situation, like the military one, with its exceptionally strong measures and unavoidable surveillance on the part of the authorities, keeps them in constant tension and fear; the prison authorities take away from them the meadows, the best places for fishing and the best timber for prison use; escapees, prison moneylenders and thieves ill-treat them; the prison executioner strolling down the street frightens them; the overseers corrupt their wives and daughters and, most of all, the prison reminds them every minute of their past, of who they are and where they are.

The rural inhabitants here still have not formed into a society. There are still no adult non-aboriginal natives of Sakhalin, for whom the island would be their home region, there are very few established residents – the majority are newcomers; the population changes every year; some arrive, others leave; and in some settlements, as I have said already, the inhabitants create the impression not of a rural society but of a randomly assembled rabble. They call themselves brothers because they have suffered together, but they still have little in common, however, and they are alien to each other. They have different religions and speak different languages. The old men regard this motleyness with derision and ask laughingly what sort of society can there be if in one and the same village live Russians, Ukrainians, Tatars, Poles, Jews, Chukhons, Kirgizes, Georgians and Gypsies. I have already had occasion several times to mention how unevenly the non-Russian element has been allocated around the settlements.*

A motley characteristic of another type also unfavourably affects the development of each settlement: many people enter the colony who are elderly, frail, physically and mentally ill, have criminal tendencies, are incapable of labour, or have not been trained for practical work, people who, at home, lived in a town and were not involved in agriculture. On 1st January 1890, according to data which I drew from the government registers, throughout the whole of Sakhalin, in prisons and colony, there were ninety-one exiles from the nobility or gentry, and from the "urban ranks" – that is, honourable citizens, merchants, traders and foreign subjects* – there were 924, which two figures together comprise ten per cent of the total number of exiles.*

In each village there is an elder, who is elected from the householders – invariably settled exiles or peasants-in-exile – and who is ratified by the Inspector of Settlements. Usually it is staid, intelligent and literate people who finish up as elders; their duties have still not been fully defined, but they try to be like European Russian elders; they settle various small items of business, issue warrants for the hire of carts and horses, support their people when necessary and so forth, and the Rykovo elder even has his own printing press. Some receive stipends.

There is also an overseer in each settlement, most frequently a low ranker of the local military command, who is illiterate, who reports to officials passing through that everything is progressing satisfactorily, who keeps an eye on the settlers' conduct, and who makes sure they do not absent themselves without leave, and stick to their farming. He is the immediate director of the settlement, often its only judge, and his reports to the authorities are documents of no small significance in appraising how far a settled exile has succeeded in achieving the approved conduct and level of household management, and whether he has managed to settle down. Here is a specimen of an overseer's report:

*List of What Inhabitants of
Upper Armudan Settlement
Are of Bad Behayvyer*

Surname and First Name	Note on Reasons why
1. Izdugin Ananiy	Thief
2. Kiselyov Pyotr Vasilyev	Ditto
3. Glybin Ivan	Ditto
4. Galynsky Semyon	Negligent of his home and insubordinate
5. Kazankin Ivan	Ditto

16

Composition of exile population by sex. The female question. Convict women and female settled exiles. Cohabitants, male and female. Free-status females.

I N THE EXILE COLONY there are fifty-three women to every 100 men.* This ratio is correct only for the population living in cabins. There are in addition, however, the men who spend the night in the prisons, and the unmarried soldiers, for whom all those same exiled women, or women involved with the exile colony, serve – as one of the authorities here once put it – "as a necessary means for the satisfaction of natural requirements". But if this category of people is to be taken into account in the breakdown of the colony according to sex and family status, it should be done only with reservations. While living in the prisons or the barracks they regard the colony simply from the viewpoint of their needs; their visits to the colony act as a harmful external influence which lowers the birth rate, increases the incidence of disease and which is, besides, a "random" influence since it can be greater or smaller, depending on the distance of the prison or barracks from the settlement; it is precisely the role the "gold-diggers" who work in the neighbourhood on the railway play in the life of a European Russian village. If we consider all the males en masse, including the prison and barracks, then the fifty-three is reduced roughly by half and we finish up with a ratio of 100 to twenty-five.

However small are the figures fifty-three and twenty-five, they cannot be considered too low for a young exile colony, which is, besides, developing under the most unfavourable conditions. In Siberia less than ten per cent of the convicts and settled exiles are women, and if we turn our attention to the practice of deportation outside Russia, we find colonists who have already become respected farmers, who were so far from having been pampered in this respect that they would receive with delight prostitutes brought from the home country and would pay the ships' masters 100 pounds of tobacco for each. The so-called "female question" has been raised in an ugly fashion on Sakhalin, but less nastily than in the Western European exile colonies during the first period of their development.

Not only female criminals and prostitutes come to the island. Thanks to the Central Prison Department, and the Voluntary Fleet, which has managed with total success to establish rapid and convenient communication between European Russia and Sakhalin, the task of those wives and children who wish to follow their husbands and parents into exile has been considerably simplified. Not so very long ago, there was one woman who voluntarily accompanied somebody to every thirty male convicts; at the present time, however, the presence of free-status women has become a characteristic of the colony, and it is difficult by now to imagine Rykovo or Novo-Mikhailovka, for instance, without these tragic figures who "came to better their husband's life, and have lost their own". This is perhaps the sole point on which our Sakhalin does not occupy the last place in the history of exile.

I shall begin with the convict women. By 1st January 1890 female offenders in all three districts made up 11.5 per cent of the total number of convicts.* From the point of view of colonization these women have one important advantage: they enter the colony comparatively young; the majority of them are women with spirit, sentenced for offences of a romantic nature or connected with their families: "I've come cos of my 'usband", "I've come cos of me mother-in-law". These are all sacrifices to love and family despotism, rather than murderers. Even those who have come here for arson or forging banknotes are in essence suffering the penalties for love, since they were lured into the crime by their lovers.

The love element plays a fatal role in their sad existence both before and after the trial. When they are being transported into exile on the steamer, the rumour begins to circulate among them that, on Sakhalin, they will be married off against their will, and this disturbs them. There was one occasion when they requested the ship's senior officers to petition for them not to be married off by force.

Fifteen to twenty years ago, on their arrival on Sakhalin, convict women immediately entered a brothel. "In southern Sakhalin," writes Vlasov in his essay, "for lack of special quarters, the women are lodged in the bakehouse... The Governor of the Island, Depreradovich, has ordered that the female section of the prison be turned into a brothel." One could not even begin to talk of any kind of labour, since "only those guilty of an offence, or those not worthy of men's favour" ended up working in the kitchen, the rest "served needs" and drank themselves silly, and according to Vlasov the women had finally been corrupted to such a degree that in a kind of state of stupefaction they would "sell their children for a quart of spirit".

These days, when a party of women arrives at Alexandrovsk, they are first of all solemnly conducted from the landing stage to the prison. The women, bent under the weight of bundles and knapsacks, plod along the highway, listless and still not having regained their senses from seasickness, while there follows behind them, like after the clowns at a fair, a whole crowd of women, men, children and people attached to the government offices. The picture resembles the herring run in the Aniva, when behind the fish follow whole hordes of whales, seals and dolphins, wanting to regale themselves on herring full of roe. The countrymen among the settled exiles follow the crowd with honest, simple thoughts; they need a housewife. The women look to see whether there is someone in the party from their home district. And the clerks and overseers need "girls". This usually takes place before evening. The women are locked up for the night in a cell previously prepared for the purpose, and then all night conversations take place in the prison and the post about the new party, about the charms of family life, the impossibility of running a home without a woman and so on. During the very first day, before the steamer has left for Korsakovsk, the newly arrived women are allocated to their districts. The allocation is carried out by the Alexandrovsk officials, and for this reason their district receives the lion's share in respect of quantity and quality; the closer of the other two districts, the Tymovsk, receives those who are not quite so good-looking, and rather fewer of them; a painstaking selection process takes place in the north; the youngest and prettiest remain here as if sifted out in a filter, so that the good fortune of living in the south falls only to those who are approaching old age, and those "not worthy of men's favour". In making the allocation, no thought at all is given to the agricultural colony, and therefore on Sakhalin, as I have already said, the women are distributed round the districts extremely unequally, and on top of this, the worse the area, and the fewer hopes there are of successful colonization, the more women there are; in the worst district, the Alexandrovsk, there are sixty-nine women to every hundred men, in the Tymovsk, forty-seven, and in the best – the Korsakovsk – only thirty-six.*

Some of the women selected for the Alexandrovsk District are detailed to the domestic staffs of officials. After the prison, the prisoners' train-carriages, and the ship's hold, the officials' clean, bright rooms seem like an enchanted castle at first, and the lord of the castle – a good or evil genius who has boundless power over her; however, she swiftly grows accustomed to her new situation; but for ages afterwards, the prison and the ship's hold may still be heard in her speech: "I beg your pardon, I don't know, sir." "Would you be so good as to try some of this food, Your Excellency?" "Yes, just as you say, sir." Other women enter the harems of the clerks and overseers, while still others – the majority – go into the settled exiles' cabins; only those who are somewhat better off and have patronage obtain women. A convict, even one in the category of "probationer", may receive a woman, too, if he has money and enjoys influence in the sordid little prison world.

At the Korsakovsk Post the newly arrived women are also lodged in a special barrack hut. The District Governor and the Inspector of Settlements decide together which of the settled exiles and peasants deserve to obtain a woman. Preference is given to those who are already well established, domesticated and have displayed good conduct. To those few who are picked, an order is sent out that, on a certain day, at a certain hour, they should come to the post, to the prison, to obtain a woman. And so on the appointed day, all along the lengthy main road from Naibuchi to the post one here and there comes across "betrothed" and "bridegrooms" – to give them the exalted designation they are accorded here, not without irony – walking southwards. Their appearance is somehow special and distinctive: they do indeed resemble bridegrooms; one is arrayed in a red calico shirt, another in something curious resembling a planter's hat, while yet another is wearing shiny new high boots with tall heels, bought God only knows where, and in what circumstances. When they all arrive at the post, they are admitted to the women's barrack room and left there with them. In the first fifteen minutes to half an hour, the inevitable ransom is paid to embarrassment and a feeling of awkwardness; the betrothed men wander around the bed-boards, and every so often glance severely and in silence at the women, while they sit with lowered eyes. Each man chooses – without sour grimaces, without wry smiles, but perfectly seriously, treating "with humanity" plainness, old age and their prisoner-like appearance; he gazes attentively, wishing to surmise from their faces – which of them is a good housewife? At last, some woman, young or old, has "appealed" to him; he sits down beside her and strikes up a cordial conversation; she asks whether he has a samovar, and what his cabin is roofed with, boards or straw? He responds that he does have a samovar, and a horse, and a two-year-old heifer, and his cabin is roofed with boards.* Only after this domestic economic examination, when both feel that the agreement is concluded, does she make up her mind to ask the question:

"And you won't ill-treat me?"

The conversation comes to an end. The woman is registered with settled exile so-and-so, in settlement such-and-such – and the civil marriage is concluded. The settled exile sets off to his home with his cohabitant, and for a finale, so as not to fall flat on his face in the mud, but to keep up appearances, he hires a cart and horses, often with his last remaining money. At home the female cohabitant puts on the samovar, and, gazing up at the smoke, the neighbours chat enviously about how old so-and-so has gone and got himself a woman.

There is no convict labour on the island for women. True, women sometimes wash the floors in the offices, or work in the vegetable gardens, or sew sacks, but there is no constant fixed work, in the sense of hard compulsory labour, and there probably never will be. The prison has totally yielded up its convict women to the colony. When they are brought to the island, no thought is given to punishment or correction, but simply to their ability to bear children and run a farm-holding. Convict women are parcelled out to the settled exiles in the guise of workwomen, on the basis of Article 345 of the *Statutes on Exiles*, which permits unmarried female exiles "to earn a living by service to established residents in the closest settlements, until they are married". But this clause exists only as a screen against the law forbidding immorality and adultery, since a convict woman or female settled exile living with a male settled exile is not first and foremost a hired hand, but his cohabitant, and unlegalized wife, with the cognizance and consent of the administration; in the official registers and orders her life under the same roof as a male settler is recorded as "joint establishment of a household" or "combined organization of a home";* he and she together are designated a "free family". It may be said that, with the exception of a small number of women of the privileged classes, and those who come to the island with their husbands, all convict women become cohabitants. This should be taken as a rule. I was told that when one woman in Vladimirovka did not want to become a cohabitant, and declared that she had come to the penal settlement to work and nothing else, her words evidently threw everybody into bewilderment.*

Local practice has evolved its own peculiar way of regarding the female prisoner, which very probably exists in all exile colonies: she is not exactly a human being, a housewife, and not exactly a creature even lower than a domestic animal, but somewhere between the two. The settlers at Siska submitted the following application to the District Governor: "We most humbly request Your Excellency to issue us with cattle for the supply of milk at the above-mentioned place, and with members of the female sex to set up domestic households with."

The Governor of the Island, while chatting in my presence with the settlers of Uskovo, and giving them various promises, said, among other things:

"I won't let you down where women are concerned either."

"It's no good, the women being sent here from Russia in autumn, and not in spring," an official said to me. "There's nothing for a woman to do in winter, she's not a help to her man, but only an extra mouth. That's the reason good householders take them in autumn only with reluctance."

That is the way people discuss workhorses in spring when they foresee a winter of dear feedstuff. Human dignity, and the femininity and modesty of the convict woman are not taken into account in any circumstances; the implication seems to be that all this has been wrung out of her by her shame, or that she has lost it trudging around prisons and the way stations on the journey to Siberia. At any rate, when they are inflicting corporal punishment on her, they are not impeded by the consideration that it might be shaming for her. But the degradation of her character has still, however, never reached the stage where she is married off by force, or compelled to become a cohabitant. Rumours of coercion in this respect are just as much mere fairy tales as the gallows on the seashore, or the toil in subterranean caverns.*

Neither a woman's old age, nor a difference in religious beliefs, nor vagabond status, forms an obstacle to cohabitation. I came across female cohabitants of fifty years old or more, not only living with young settlers, but even with overseers who had hardly turned twenty-five. Sometimes an elderly mother and an adult daughter come to the penal colony; they both become cohabitants to settled exiles and soon begin to bear children as if in competition with each other. Catholics, Lutherans, and even Tatars and Jews, not infrequently live with Russians. In one cabin in Alexandrovsk I encountered a Russian woman in a large company of Kirgiz and Caucasian men whom she was serving at table, and I recorded her as being the cohabitant of a Tatar, or as she called him, a Chechen.* In Alexandrovsk, a Tatar called Kerbalay, who is known to everybody there, lives with the Russian woman Lopushina and has three children by her.* Vagabonds also get themselves set up on a family footing, and at Derbinskoye one of them, Vagabond Ivan Thirty-five-years-old, even declared to me with a smile that he had two cohabitants: "One here, the other one at the end of a ticket to Nikolayevsk, on the mainland." Another settled exile has already been living for ten years as if married with a woman who "doesn't remember her home district"* and he still does not know her real name or where she is from by birth.

When asked how they find life, a settler and his cohabitant will usually reply: "We live happily together." And some convict women told me that, at home in European Russia, they had endured from their husbands only insolence, beatings and reproaches over every bit of bread; here in penal servitude, however, they had seen the light for the first time. "I'm living with a good man now, God be praised, he feels for me." The male exiles do feel compassion for their cohabitants and take good care of them.

"For lack of women, the rural worker here ploughs himself, cooks for himself, and milks the cow and mends his clothes himself," Baron Korf told me, "and so, if a woman comes his way, he holds on tight to her. Look how he dresses her up. A woman enjoys honour among the exiled men."

"Which still doesn't stop her going about with bruises," put in General Kononovich, who was present at our conversation.

Squabbles and scuffles do take place, and the whole business can reach the stage of bruises, but all the same the male settler teaches his cohabitant a lesson with caution, for the force of right is on her side; he knows she is living with him without any legalization, and that she can abandon him at any time and go off to somebody else. But it is evident that the male exiles do not just have feelings of compassion for their women from circumspection alone. However easily unlegalized families on Sakhalin are set up, love in its purest and most attractive form is no stranger to them. In Dooay I saw an insane convict woman who suffered from epilepsy and who lived in the cabin of her cohabitant, also a convict; he looked after her like a conscientious nurse, and when I remarked to him that it must be a burden for him to live in the same room as this woman, he replied cheerfully: "No, not at all, Your Excellency, I do it out of humanity!" At Novo-Mikhailovka one settled exile's cohabitant has been without the use of her legs for a long time now, and day and night she lies on rags in the middle of the room, while he takes care of her, and when I began to try to persuade him that it would be less inconvenient for him if she were in hospital, he also began talking about "humanity".

Mingled in with the good and the middle-of-the-road families, one also encounters the type of "free family" to which the "problem of females in exile colonies" partly owes such a poor reputation. During the very first moment, these families alienate one with their artificiality and spurious nature and lead one to sense that here, in an atmosphere tainted by prison and captivity, the family has decayed ages ago and something different has grown up in its place. Many men and women live together because that is what is necessary, it is the "done thing" in exile; cohabitation has become the traditional order of things in the colony, and these people, feeble and weak-willed by nature, have submitted to this order of things, although nobody has forced them to. At Novo-Mikhailovka, a Ukrainian woman of fifty or so, who had come here with her son, also a convict, because of her daughter-in-law, who was found dead in a well, and who has left behind at home an elderly husband and children, is living here with a cohabitant, and she herself obviously finds this repellent and is ashamed to talk about it to an outsider. She despises her cohabitant, yet she still lives with him and sleeps with him: it is the done thing in exile. The members of such families are strangers to each other to such an extreme that however long they have lived under the same roof, even if it is five to ten years, they still do not know how old the other one is, what province they are from, what their middle name is... When asked how old her cohabitant was, a woman, gazing sluggishly and lazily at the ceiling, would usually respond: "Devil only knows!" While her cohabitant is at work, or off playing cards somewhere, his female partner lolls in bed, idle and hungry; if one or other of her neighbours comes into her cabin, she will reluctantly raise herself slightly and say yawningly that she "came cos of her husband", that she had suffered for nothing, as she was innocent: "The lads killed him, the devils, and it's me they've sent to do hard labour." The male cohabitant returns home; there is nothing to do, nothing to talk to the woman about; she would put on the samovar, but there is no sugar or tea... At the sight of his partner lazing about, feelings of tedium and uselessness overwhelm him, despite his hunger and exasperation, he heaves a sigh, and then he, too, flops straight into bed. If the women from such families earn their living by prostitution, their partners usually encourage this occupation. A male cohabitant sees a prostitute earning a crust of bread as a useful domestic animal and respects her, that is to say, he puts the samovar on for her himself and keeps quiet when she abuses him. She often changes cohabitants, choosing those who are better off, or those who have vodka, or else she merely changes out of boredom, for a bit of variety.

A female convict receives prisoner's rations, which she consumes with her male partner; sometimes these women's rations are the sole source of subsistence for a family. As a female cohabitant is formally considered to be a labourer, the male settled exile pays the state for her, as if she were a workwoman; he is obliged to convey twenty poods of goods from one district to another, or supply the post with a dozen or so logs. This formality, however, is binding only for the settled exiles involved in rural work, and is not required of the exiles who live in the posts and do nothing. On serving her sentence, a convict woman acquires settled exile status and immediately ceases to receive food and clothing allowances; thus, on Sakhalin, being transferred to settler status does not serve to alleviate one's lot; the convict women who receive rations from the government are better off than the female settled exiles, and the longer the term of hard labour the better it is for the women, and if it is a life sentence, that means that they are assured of a crust of bread for life. A female settler normally receives peasant's rights on a privileged basis, after six years.

There are at the present time more free-status women who have accompanied their husbands voluntarily than there are convict women, and there are two of them to every three of the total number of female exiles. I noted down 697 free-status women, and there were

1,041 convict women, female settled exiles and female peasants-in-exile, which means that the free-women in the colony make up forty per cent of the entire total of adult women.* Various reasons induce the women to abandon their homeland and go into exile with their criminal husbands. Some go out of love and pity; others from the firm conviction that God alone can part man and wife; still others flee their homes from shame – in the benighted rural milieu the disgrace of the husbands still falls on the wives; for instance, when the wife of somebody who has been convicted is doing her rinsing in the river, the other women will call her "Mrs Convict"; others are lured to the island, as if into a snare, by their husbands, by means of deception. Many prisoners write home while they are still in the ship's hold that it is warm on Sakhalin, there is plenty of land, bread is cheap and the authorities are kind; they write exactly the same from the prison, sometimes over a period of several years, continually dreaming up fresh enticements, and as facts have shown, their reckoning on the ignorance and gullibility of their wives is often justified.* Finally, yet others go because they are still under the strong moral influence of their husbands; they have perhaps taken part in the crime themselves, or enjoyed its fruits, and have only failed to be brought to trial by chance, through lack of evidence. The first two reasons are the most frequent: compassion and pity to the point of self-sacrifice, and an unshakeable strength of conviction. Among the wives* who have voluntarily followed their husbands, there are, besides Russian women, also Tatars, Jewesses, Gypsies, Poles and Germans.

When free-status women arrive on Sakhalin, they are not received with any especial cordiality. Here is a typical episode. On 19th October 1889, 300 free-status women, juveniles and children arrived at Alexandrovsk on board the Voluntary Fleet steamer *Vladivostok*. They had spent three or four days sailing from Vladivostok, in the cold, without hot food, and, so a doctor informed me, twenty-six of them were found to be sick with scarlet fever, smallpox and measles. The steamer arrived late in the evening. Very probably fearing bad weather, the captain required all passengers and cargo to be taken off without fail during the night. They were unloading from 12 midnight to 2 a.m. The women and children were locked up on the landing stage in the boat shed, and in a barn built for storing goods; the sick were put in a shed which had been adapted so that they could be kept in quarantine. The passengers' belongings were dumped in disorder on a barge. Towards morning the rumour went round that the barge had been torn from its moorings during the night by the heavy waves and had been carried out to sea. People began to weep and wail. One woman had lost 300 roubles together with her belongings. A report was drawn up, and the storm was blamed for everything; however, the very next day, people started to find the things which had been lost, in the prison, in the possession of the convicts.

During the first period after her arrival here, a free-woman wears a look of total stupefaction. The island, and the conditions encompassing the penal labour, stagger her. She will say with despair that, when travelling to her husband, she did not deceive herself and expected only the worst, but the reality had turned out to be more frightful than all expectations. Hardly has she finished talking to women who came here previous to her, hardly has she finished watching their everyday existence, than the conviction has already risen within her that she and her children are doomed. Although there are still over ten or fifteen years to the completion of the sentence, she already starts raving about the mainland and simply does not want to hear about the farming here, which seems to her paltry and not worth consideration. She weeps day and night, and chants lamentations for the deceased,* and prays for her forsaken relatives as if they were dead, while her husband, acknowledging his huge guilt towards her, sits sullenly, but suddenly, coming to himself, begins to beat her and abuse her for having come here.

If a free-woman has come without money, or has brought so little that there is only enough to buy a cabin, and if she and her husband are not sent anything from home, then hunger soon sets in. There is no money to be earned, nowhere to beg alms, and she and her children have to live on the one set of prisoner's rations which her convict husband receives from the prison and which is hardly sufficient for one adult.*

Day in, day out, her thoughts always work in the same direction – what to eat and what to feed the children with. From constant starvation, from mutual recriminations over every piece of bread, and from the certainty that there will never be anything better, her heart becomes hardened over the course of time, and she comes to the conclusion that on Sakhalin you will never get enough to eat with delicate feelings, and goes off to earn her five- and ten-copeck bits – as one of them put it – "with my body". The husband has also grown callous, he has no time for purity, and it all seems unimportant. Hardly have his daughters turned fourteen or fifteen years old when they are also put into circulation; the mothers sell them at home, or send them off to be cohabitants to well-off settled exiles and overseers. And all this is carried on with all the greater ease owing to the fact that a free-woman spends her time here in the most complete idleness; in the posts there is nothing to do whatever, and in the settlements, especially in the northern districts, the farming is indeed paltry.

Besides want and idleness, there is in addition a third source of all sorts of affliction for the free-woman – her husband. He can squander his rations, his wife's, and even his children's clothing, on drink, or lose them all at cards. He can lapse into a fresh crime or be shot at and wounded while trying to escape. During my stay, Byshevetz, a settled exile from the Tymovsk District, was being kept in a punishment cell at Dooay, accused of attempted murder; his wife and children were living nearby in family barracks, and their home and landholding had been abandoned. At Malo-Tymovo settled exile Kucherenko had fled, leaving a wife and children. Even if the husband is not one of those who murder or escape, the wife still has to worry every day about whether he is going to be disciplined, whether wrongful accusations are going to be brought against him, whether he will overstrain himself, grow ill or die.

The years pass, old age approaches; the husband has by now served his hard labour and term of compulsory settlement and applies for peasant's rights. The past takes its leave and gives way to oblivion, and with the departure for the mainland, a new, upright and happy life looms in the distance. But it often turns out otherwise. The wife dies of consumption and the husband leaves for the mainland old and alone; or else she is left a widow and does not know what she should do or where she should go. At Derbinskoye free-status wife Aleksandra Timofeyeva has left her Molokan* husband for the herdsman Akim, is living in a cramped, filthy hovel and has already borne the shepherd a daughter, while the husband has taken another woman to himself as a cohabitant. At Alexandrovsk, free-status women Shulikina and Fyodina have also left their husbands to become somebody else's cohabitants. Nenila Karpenko was widowed and is now living with a settled exile. Convict Altukhov "went on the tramp" and became a vagabond, and his wife, Yekaterina, a free-woman, has now entered into an unlegalized marriage.*

17

Composition of population by age. Family status of exiles. Marriages. Birth rate. Sakhalin children.

EVEN IF THE STATISTICS RELATING to the composition of the exile population in terms of age were outstanding for their perfect accuracy, and were far more complete than those I gathered, they would still nevertheless yield almost nothing. In the first place, they are dependent upon external circumstances, since they are engendered not by natural or economic conditions but by legal theories, the existing code on punishment and the will of the people who make up the prison department. With a change of outlook on the exile system in general, and on exile to Sakhalin in particular, the age groups which form the population will also change; that will happen when they start to send twice as many women to the colony, or when, with the construction of the Siberian railway, free immigration begins. Secondly, on an exile island, given the exceptional way life is ordered, these figures would not have at all the same significance as under normal conditions in the Cherepovetsk* or Moscow Districts. For instance, the minute percentage of old men on Sakhalin does not imply some kind of unfavourable circumstance such as a high mortality rate, but only that the majority of exiles succeed in serving out their punishment and leaving for the mainland before the onset of old age.

At the present time the largest age groups in the colony are those from twenty-five to thirty-five (24.3 per cent) and from thirty-five to forty-five (24.1 per cent).* Those between the ages of twenty and fifty-five, which Dr Gryaznov terms the "working age groups", form 64.6 per cent of the colony, that is, almost one and a half times as large as in Russia in general.*

Alas, the high percentage and surplus, even, of the working or productive age groups does not on Sakhalin serve at all as an index of economic prosperity; here it merely indicates a surplus of work-hands, thanks to which, even in spite of the vast number of starving, idle and unskilled, towns are built and excellent roads are laid out on Sakhalin. These constructions, which do not come cheap, and, next door to them, the insecurity and beggarly destitution of those of productive age, bring to mind a certain resemblance between the present-day colony and those times when a superfluity of labour was created just as artificially, and temples and circuses were erected, while those of productive age endured extreme and exhausting deprivation.

There is also a high proportion (24.9 per cent) of children – that is, those up to fifteen years of age. Compared with analogous Russian figures this is low,* but for an exile colony, where family life is placed under such unfavourable circumstances, it is high. The fertility of the Sakhalin women and, as the reader will see below, the low child mortality rate, will soon raise the percentage of children still higher, perhaps even up to the Russian norm. This is a good thing because, even besides all the considerations of colonization, having children around gives the convicts moral support, and, more vividly than anything else, reminds them of their native Russian village; and in addition to this, looking after the children saves the exiled women from idleness; it is also a bad thing, as those of unproductive age, who require expenditure from the colony while themselves giving nothing, make the economic difficulties more complicated; they increase the indigence, and in this respect the colony is placed in even more unfavourable conditions than the Russian countryside; once the Sakhalin children have become youths or adults, they leave for the mainland, and thus the expense the colony has borne is never recovered.

Those age ranges which are the foundation and hope of a colony which, if not already developed, is in the process of developing, form a totally insignificant percentage on Sakhalin. There are only 185 people in the whole colony between the ages of fifteen and twenty – eighty-nine male and ninety-six female, that is, around two per cent. Only twenty-seven of them are genuine children of the colony, as they were born on Sakhalin or on the journey into exile; the rest, however, are foreign to the island. But those who have been born on Sakhalin are also only waiting for the departure of their parents or husbands for the mainland, so that they can leave with them. Almost all the twenty-seven are children of well-off peasants-in-exile who have finished serving their term of punishment and are at present remaining on the island for the purpose of bringing their capital to a large round sum.

The Rachkovs of Alexandrovsk are such a family, for instance. Even Mariya Baranovskaya, daughter of a free settler and born at Chibisani – she is now eighteen years old – will not remain on Sakhalin but will travel to the mainland with her husband. Of those who were born on Sakhalin twenty years ago and who have already had their twenty-first birthday, not a single one is left on the island. There is a total of twenty-seven twenty-year-olds in the colony; thirteen were sent here to convict labour, seven came voluntarily with their husbands and seven are the sons of exiles – young people who have already learnt the way to Vladivostok and along the Amur river.*

On Sakhalin there are 860 legalized families and 782 "free" families, and these figures adequately define the domestic situation of exiles living in the colony. Generally speaking, the blessings of family life are enjoyed by almost half of the entire adult population. The women in the colony are all taken; consequently the other half, that is, about three thousand individuals who are single, is comprised entirely of men. However, this ratio, since it is conditioned by external circumstances, is subject to constant fluctuations. For instance, when, as a consequence of an amnesty from the throne,* three thousand new settlers are released all at once from prison on to landholdings, the percentage of single men in the colony rises; but when the Sakhalin settlers are given permission to work on the Ussuri section of the Siberian railway,* as happened shortly after my departure, then this percentage is reduced. Be that as it may, the development among the exiles of the family as a basis for the colony is considered to be extremely feeble, and precisely this large number of single men is pointed to as the major reason why the colony has not been a success up to the present.*

Next, we turn to the question as to why unlegalized or "free" cohabitation has become so widespread in the colony, and why, looking at the figures relating to the exiles' family situation, one gains the impression that the exiles stubbornly seem to shun legalized marriage. Really, if it were not for the free-women who voluntarily follow their husbands, there would be four times as many "free" families in the colonies as legalized ones.* Dictating for me to write in my notebook, the Governor General called such a state of affairs "outrageous" and, of course, he did not hold the exiles to blame for this. As people the majority of whom are patriarchally minded and religious, the exiles prefer legalized marriage. Unlawful partners often request the authorities' permission to have an official church wedding, but the majority of these requests have to be turned down for reasons which have nothing to do either with the local administration or with the settlers themselves. The point is that, although, with the deprivation of all rights of status, the convict's conjugal rights are frozen and he ceases to exist for his family, as if he were dead, his marital rights in exile are still nevertheless determined not by the circumstances result- ing from his subsequent life but by the will of the partner who has not been sentenced and who remains at home. It is necessary for this partner to agree to an annulment of the marriage and grant a divorce, and only then may the convicted person enter a new marriage. The partners remaining behind do not normally give this consent: some from the religious conviction that divorce is a sin, others because they consider annulment of their marriage to be unnecessary and point- less, a mere whim, especially when both partners are already nearing forty. "Getting married at his age?" a wife will reason, when she has received the letter concerning a divorce from her husband. "He should be thinking about his soul, the old dog." Still others refuse because they are scared of commencing such a highly complex, troublesome and expensive business as a divorce, or simply because they do not know where to apply with the request, or how to begin. Also fre- quently to be blamed for the fact that exiles do not enter into legalized marriages are imperfections in the itemized records, which create in each individual case a whole series of all sorts of formal details, tedi- ous and reminiscent of old-fashioned bureaucracy and red tape, and which lead merely to the convict, having squandered all his money on scribes, stamps and telegrams, finally hopelessly giving it all up as a bad job and deciding that he is simply not going to have a legalized family. Many exiles have no itemized records at all; you come across records in which the exile's family status is simply not shown, or else is indicated unclearly or incorrectly; however, apart from these records, an exile has no other documents of any sort to which he could refer in case of need.*

Information on the number of marriages which have taken place in the colony may be obtained from the registers of births, marriages

and deaths; but since here legalized marriage is a luxury not accessible to everybody, this information is far from defining the population's genuine requirements as regards legally married life; here they
get married not when they should but when they can. The average
age of those who get married here is a statistic utterly without meaning; it is impossible on the basis of this figure to draw conclusions
as to whether earlier or later marriages predominate, and to draw
any kind of inferences from this, since family life for the majority of
exiles commences long before the enactment of the church rite, and
frequently couples get married who already have children. At present
the only thing that is evident from the marriage registers is that, over
the last ten years, the greatest number of marriages were concluded
in January; almost a third of all marriages took place in this month.
The autumn increase is too small to be significant in comparison
with the January peak, so that we cannot even begin to make a comparison with our European Russian agricultural districts. Those marriages which were concluded in normal circumstances, when exiles'
free-status children married, were all, every last one of them, made
early: the grooms were from eighteen to twenty years old, and the
brides from fifteen to nineteen. But between the ages of fifteen and
twenty there are more free-status girls than men, who usually leave
the island before reaching marriageable age; and very likely owing to
this lack of young grooms, and in part due to economic considerations, many unequal marriages have taken place; young free-women,
practically children, have been married off by their parents to elderly settled exiles or peasants-in-exile. Non-commissioned officers,
Lance Corporals, military doctors' assistants, clerks and overseers
have frequently married but have "brought joy" only to fifteen- and
sixteen-year-olds.*

The weddings are enacted frugally and tediously; merry and bois-
terous weddings do sometimes take place in the Tymovsk District, and
the Ukrainians are especially raucous. At Alexandrovsk, where there
is a printing press, it is customary for the exiles to send out printed
invitation cards before a wedding. The convict typesetters have grown
bored with printing the official directives, are glad to show off their
craftsmanship, and in appearance and wording their cards differ little
from those we would see in Moscow. A bottle of spirits is issued by
the government office at every marriage.

The exiles themselves consider the birth rate in the colony excessively high, and this is the reason behind the constant sneering at women, and behind various profoundly serious observations. People say that the very climate of Sakhalin disposes women to pregnancy; elderly ladies give birth, and even those who in European Russia were barren and had already long ago given up hope of ever having children. It is as if the women are racing to populate Sakhalin, and they often bear twins. At Vladimirovka one old woman, who was going to give birth, and who already had a grown-up daughter, had heard conversations about twins, was expecting that she, too, would give birth to two, and was mortified when only one was born. "Have another look," she asked the midwife. But the birth of twins happens no more often here than in the rural districts of European Russia. Over the ten-year period up to 1st January 1890, 2,275 children of both sexes were born, and only twenty-six of them were from the so-called "fertile races".*

All this somewhat exaggerated chatter about the excessive fertility of the women, about twins, and so forth, indicates the interest with which the exile population treats the birth rate, and what an important significance it has here.

Since the numerical strength of the population is subject to fluctuations due to continuous influxes and outflows, which are, besides, random, as if at a market, the calculation of a coefficient for the general rate of childbirth in the colony over several years might be considered an unattainable luxury; it is all the harder to pin down since the statistical material collected by myself and others is very modest in extent; the total numbers of the population in previous years are unknown, and when I was acquainting myself with the material in the government offices it seemed to me it would be a labour of Hercules to bring them to light, besides which they promised the most dubious results. A coefficient may be worked out only approximately and only for the present time.

In 1889, 352 children of both sexes were born in all the four parishes; under normal conditions in Russia this number of children is born yearly in places with a population of seven thousand; and it was precisely seven thousand, plus a few hundred or so, that lived in the colony in 1889. The coefficient of childbirth here is obviously only a little higher than in Russia in general (49.8)* and in the Russian provincial districts, for instance, the Cherepovetsk District (45.4). It may be accepted that the birth rate on Sakhalin in 1889 was, relatively, as large as that in Russia in general, and if there were a difference in coefficients it was small, and very probably had no especial significance. But since, of two places with identical coefficients of general childbirth, the fertility of females will be higher in the place where there are relatively fewer of them, then obviously it may still be recognized that the fertility of women on Sakhalin is considerably higher than in Russia as a whole.

Hunger, homesickness, debauched tendencies, captivity – the entire aggregate sum of unfavourable conditions in exile does not eliminate the productive capacity of the exiles; consequently its presence does not indicate prosperity. The reasons for the heightened fertility of women and the similarly increased birth rate are, first, the idleness of the exiles living in the colony, the enforced staying at home of husbands and male cohabitants owing to the lack of seasonal work and earnings for them, and the monotony of life, under which the satisfaction of the sexual instincts is often the only possible entertainment; and secondly, the circumstance that the majority of the women here are of productive age. Besides these immediate reasons, there are also very probably other, more remote causes, which at present still cannot be observed at first hand. Perhaps one should regard a vigorous birth rate as a means nature gives populations to battle against harmful and destructive influences, and first and foremost, against such natural enemies as a small population and shortage of women. The greater the danger threatening a population, the more are born, and in this sense, the unfavourable circumstances could be said to be the cause for the high birth rate.*

Of the 2,275 births during this ten-year period, the maximum number took place during the autumn months (29.2 per cent), the minimum during the spring (20.8 per cent), and more were born in winter (26.2 per cent) than summer (23.6 per cent). The greatest number of conceptions and births has taken place up till now in the six months between August and February, and in this respect the season of short days and long nights was more favourable than the dull and rainy spring, and the summer, which is similar.

At the present time there are on Sakhalin 2,122 children in all, if one also includes the youths who had their fifteenth birthday in

1890. Of these, 644 came from European Russia with their parents, and 1,473 were born on Sakhalin or on the journey into exile; there were five children whose place of birth I do not know. There are almost three times fewer of the first category than the second; the majority of them arrived on the island at an age when children are already aware; they remember and love their home region; the second category, however, those born on Sakhalin, have never seen anything better than Sakhalin and must feel drawn towards it as their real homeland. Generally speaking, the two groups display considerable differences from each other. For instance, in the first group, only 1.7 per cent are illegitimate, whereas in the second the number is 37.2 per cent.* Those belonging to the first group are termed "free children"; the vast majority of them were born or conceived before the trial and therefore retain all their rights of status. But the children born in exile call themselves no such thing; in time they will be added to the register of poll tax payers, and will be called peasants or urban citizens, but for the present, however, their social status is defined thus: illegitimate son of a female convict in exile, daughter of a male settled exile, illegitimate daughter of a female settled exile and so on. When a certain gentlewoman, the wife of an exile, learnt that her baby had been recorded in the parish register as the son of a settled exile, she is reported to have wept bitterly.

There are almost no babies or children at all younger than four in the first group; here, the preponderance is on the side of the so-called "school ages". In the second group, among those born on Sakhalin, on the other hand, the very earliest age range predominates, and on top of this, the older the children, the fewer there are of the same age, and if we were to express the ages of the children in this group by a graph, a steep, sharp fall in the curve would be the result. In this group of children there are 203 less than one year old, forty-five from nine to ten, and only eleven from fifteen to sixteen. As I have already said, of the twenty-year-olds born on Sakhalin, not a single one remains. Thus, the lack of youths, both male and female, is made up by new arrivals, who at present yield nothing except brides and bridegrooms. The small percentage of children from the older age groups among those born on Sakhalin is explained both by infant mortality and by the fact that in previous years there were fewer women on the island, but what is most at fault here is emigration. When the adults go off to the mainland, they do not leave their children but take them with them. The parents of a child born on Sakhalin have usually already begun to serve their sentence long before he first sees the light, and by the time he has reached the age of ten the majority of them have already succeeded in obtaining peasant's rights and leaving for the mainland. The situation of a newcomer is something else altogether. When his parents arrive on Sakhalin, he is usually five, eight or ten years old; while they are serving out their hard labour and compulsory settlement, he ceases to be a child, and by the time his parents are applying for peasant's rights he has been a working man for some time already and, before leaving for the mainland altogether, has on several occasions been over to Vladivostok or Nikolayevsk to earn some wages. In either case, neither newcomers, nor people born locally, remain in the colony, and for this reason it would be more correct to call all the posts and settlements up to the present time not a colony but places of temporary settlement.

The birth of each new human being is not received cordially in the family; they do not sing lullabies over the baby's cradle, but only sinister lamentations are heard. The fathers and mothers say that there is nothing to feed the children with, that they will never learn anything worthwhile on Sakhalin, and "the best thing would be if the Merciful Lord took them as soon as possible". If a child cries, or if it is naughty, they holler at it venomously: "Shut up, why don't you snuff it!" But all the same, whatever people say, and however much they wail about it, the most useful, the most necessary and the most delightful people on Sakhalin are the children, and the exiles themselves understand this well and value them highly. Into the callous, coarse, morally dissipated Sakhalin family they inject an element of tenderness, purity, gentleness and joy. In spite of their own purity, they love their depraved mother and robber father more than anything else in the world, and if an exile who has become a stranger to kindness in a prison is moved by the affection of a dog, then what value the love of a small child must have for him! I have already said that the presence of children is a moral support to the exiles, and I would now add further to this that the children are often the sole thing that still keeps the exiled men and women attached to life and saves them from despair and terminal decline. I once had to note down two free-status women who had followed their husbands here voluntarily and were now living in the same quarters; while I was in the cabin, one of them, who was childless, spent the entire time railing at fate and jeering at herself, and calling herself an idiot and "damned" because she had come to Sakhalin, and she would clench her fists convulsively, and all this in the presence of her husband, who was also there, and who looked guiltily at me, while the other, who – as they frequently put it here – was "childed" and who had several children, remained silent, and I thought that the situation of the first woman, who had no children, must be appalling. I recall that, in one cabin, when I was noting down a Tatar boy of three years old, in a skullcap, with a broad space between his eyes, I said a few affectionate words to him, and suddenly the indifferent face of his father, a Kazan Tatar, lit up, and he nodded his head cheerfully, as if agreeing with me that his son was a very fine lad, and it seemed to me that this Tatar was happy.

The kind of influences under which the Sakhalin children are brought up, and the kind of impressions which determine their mental activity, the reader may understand from everything written above. What in the towns and villages of European Russia appears frightful is here normal. The children follow with indifferent eyes a party of convicts in irons; when the shackled convicts are dragging along a wheelbarrow, the children catch on behind and whoop with laughter. They play at soldiers and convicts. A boy goes out on to the street and shouts to his playmates: "Fa-a-all *in!* A-a-as you *we-ere!*" Or he puts his toys and a piece of bread into a bag and he says to his mother: "I'm going on the tramp." "Look out, then, or a soldier'll shoot you," his mother jokes; he goes outside and trudges along like a vagabond, and his mates, playing at soldiers, try to catch him. The Sakhalin children talk of vagabonds, birch-strokes, lashes, they know what an executioner is, and what prisoners in irons, fetter blocks and cohabitants are. Making my rounds of the cabins in Upper Armudan, I found no adults in one of the cabins; there was only a boy about ten years old at home; he was fair-haired, round-shouldered, barefooted, and his pale face was covered with large freckles and seemed as if it were made of marble.

"What's your father's middle name?"

"Dunno," he replied.

"What! How can that be! You live with your father and don't know what he's called? Shame on you!"

"'e's not my real father."

"What do you mean – not 'real'?"

"'e lives with Mum."

"Is your mother married or a widow?"

"A widow. She came because of 'er 'usband."

"What does that mean – 'came because of him'?"

"She murdered 'im."

"Do you remember your father?"

"No. I'm illigit'mate. Mum give birth to me in Kara Prison."

The Sakhalin children are pale, emaciated and sluggish; they are dressed in rags and always hungry. As the reader will see further on, they die almost exclusively from ailments of the digestive tract. The hand-to-mouth life, the diet of nothing but swedes sometimes for whole months on end, while even the better off only have salt fish, the low temperatures and the damp most often kill the child's organism slowly, exhausting it little by little, causing all its tissues to degenerate; if it were not for emigration, then within two to three generations, most probably all kinds of illnesses stemming from the profound disorder in diet would have to be dealt with in the colony. At the present time the children of the poorest settled exiles and convicts receive from the state the so-called "food subsidies".* Children from one to fifteen years old are granted one and a half roubles a month, and complete orphans, cripples, deformed children and twins three roubles. A child's right to this aid is determined by the personal judgement of the officials, each of whom interprets the word "poorest" in his own fashion; the one and a half or three roubles received is spent at the discretion of the mothers and fathers. This financial assistance, which depends so much on so many personal judgements, and which, owing to the poverty and lack of conscience of the parents, rarely reaches its destination, should have been abolished long ago. It does not reduce the penury but merely disguises it and induces the uninitiated to believe the children on Sakhalin are well provided for.

18

Exiles' occupations. Farming. Hunting. Fishing. The seasonal fish run: salmon and herring. The prison fisheries. Craft trades.

As I HAVE ALREADY SAID, the notion of adapting the labour of convict-exiles and settled exiles for agricultural work arose at the very inception of the Sakhalin exile colony. Taken in isolation, this idea is very alluring: working on the land, it would appear, contains all the elements necessary to occupy the exile, give him a taste for working the soil, and even reform him. In addition, this work is suitable for the vast majority of exiles, since our penal servitude is, for the most part, an institution composed of country people, and only one-tenth of the convicts and settled exiles do not belong to the land-working classes. And this concept has achieved success; at least, until very recently, farming was considered to be the exiles' major occupation on Sakhalin, and the island has still not yet ceased to be called "an agricultural colony".

Ploughing and sowing have been carried out on Sakhalin every year since the colony came into existence; there has been no interruption and, with the increase in population, the area of crops sown has also expanded annually. The ploughman's labour here has not only been compulsory but extremely fatiguing, and if one considers the indicators of convict labour to be compulsion and the physical strain denoted by the word "fatiguing", then in this respect it would be hard to discover more suitable employment for offenders than agricultural work on Sakhalin; up till now it has satisfied the most severe of punitive aims.

But as to whether it has been productive, and whether it has also satisfied the aims of colonization, the most diverse – and, not infrequently, the most extreme – opinions have been expressed right from the commencement of the colony until very recently. Some have considered Sakhalin a most fertile island and described it as such in their reports and dispatches, and even, so it is said, sent rapturous telegrams about the exiles at last being able to support themselves, and no longer needing to have money spent on them by the state, while others regarded agriculture on Sakhalin with scepticism and declared firmly that the growth of farm crops on Sakhalin was inconceivable. Such disagreement has derived from the fact that, in the main, the people passing judgement on Sakhalin's agriculture were those to whom the true state of affairs was unknown. The colony had been founded on a still-unexplored island; from a scientific point of view it represented a total *terra incognita* and people expressed a verdict on its natural conditions, and the possibility of agricultural development there, merely from such indicators as geographical latitude, the close proximity of Japan, the presence on the island of bamboo, cork trees and so forth. For the reporter on a casual assignment, who usually judges from first impressions, of decisive significance were the weather, the bread and butter which he was regaled with in the cabins, and whether they arrived first of all in such a dismal spot as Dooay or a place as lively in appearance as Siyantzy. The vast majority of the officials to whom the colony was entrusted had, before their entry into the service, been neither landowners nor peasants and were totally unfamiliar with farming; for their records they used on every single occasion only the data which had been collected for them by the overseers. The agronomists on the spot had little knowledge of their specialist field and did nothing, or else their reports were distinguished by flagrant bias, or, coming to the colony straight from the school bench, they limited themselves at first to the purely theoretical and formal side of affairs, and for their reports used precisely the same data which the lower ranks had gathered for the government offices.* It would seem that the most accurate information could have been obtained directly from the people who plough and sow, but this source has also proved unreliable. From fear that they might be deprived of allowances, that the issue of grain on credit might be stopped, that they might be kept on Sakhalin the whole of their lives, the exiles would usually testify that the amount of land under cultivation and the crop yields were lower than in actual fact they were. The well-off exiles who had no need of grants did not tell the truth either, but this was certainly not out of fear but from the same considerations which made Polonius agree that the cloud was at one and the same time similar both to a camel and to a weasel.* They vigilantly followed fashionable trends of thought, and if the local administration did not believe in the farming, then they did not believe in it either; if, however, the opposite tendency became fashionable in the "office", then they, too, would start avowing that, praise the Lord, one could earn a living on Sakhalin, the harvests were fine, and there was only one problem – that people today were molly-coddled, and so forth, and while saying all this, in order to oblige the authorities, they would resort to crude lies and all sorts of ruses. For instance, they would select the largest ears from the crops, and bring them to Mitzul, and he good-naturedly believed them and drew the conclusion that crop yields were excellent. Visitors were shown potatoes the size of a head, black radishes weighing eighteen *funty* and watermelons, and the visitors, gazing at these monstrosities, would believe it when they were told that the wheat on Sakhalin gave a fortyfold yield.*

During my visit, the agricultural question on Sakhalin was in a peculiar sort of phase when it was difficult to make sense of anything. The Governor General, the Governor of the Island and the district heads did not believe in the productiveness of those who cultivated the land on Sakhalin; for them there was by this time no doubt remaining that the attempt to adapt the exiles' labour to farming had met with total failure, and that to continue to insist that the colony was agricultural, come what may, meant unproductively wasting government money and subjecting people to needless sufferings. Here are the words of the Governor General, which I noted down at his dictation:

"An agricultural colony of offenders on the island is unrealizable. People should be given ways to earn money; farming, however, should only be a back-up to this."

The junior officials have expressed precisely the same view, and, in the presence of their chiefs, have fearlessly criticized the island's past. The exiles themselves, when asked how things were going, would answer nervily, hopelessly, with a bitter and ironical smirk. And yet, notwithstanding such a definite and unanimous attitude towards agriculture, the exiles still continue to plough and sow, the administration continues to hand out grain on credit to them, and the Governor of the Island, who has less faith than anybody in land cultivation on Sakhalin, issues directives in which "with a view to the adjustment of the exiles to concerning themselves with working on the land" it is confirmed that transfer to peasant-in-exile status of settlers-in-exile who are not showing much hope of success in working the plots allotted to them "can never take place". The psychology behind such contradictions is totally incomprehensible.

Up till today the amount of land under cultivation has been indicated in reports by overblown and selective figures (Directive no. 366, 1888), and nobody can say precisely how much land each holder has on average. The Inspector of Agriculture defines the amount of land per holding, on average, at 1,555 square sazhens, or around two-thirds of a desyatin, but in the particular case of the best district – that is, the Korsakovsk – it is 935 square sazhens. Apart from the fact that these figures might be false, their significance is still further diminished by the fact that the land is distributed among the plot-holders extremely unevenly: those who arrived from European Russia with money, or who have made a fortune through kulakism, each have three to five, or even eight desyatins of arable land, while there are quite a few plot-holders, especially in the Korsakovsk District, who have, in all, a few square sazhens each. To all appearances, the quantity of land increases as an absolute figure every year; the average size of a plot, however, does not grow and seems to be threatening to remain a constant size.*

Grain is sown which is obtained every year on credit from the state. In 1889, in the best district, i.e. the Korsakovsk, "out of the whole proportion of 2,060 poods of grain sown, only 165 poods were their own seeds, and of the 610 people who sowed this amount, only fifty-six had their own grain" (Directive no. 318, 1889). According to the data of the Inspector of Agriculture, the average quantity of cereal crops sown for each adult inhabitant was only three poods eighteen *funty*, and least of all was sown in the southern district. It is interesting to notice here that in the district with the more favourable climatic conditions, farming is carried on less successfully than in the northern districts and yet this still does not prevent its being, in actual fact, the best district.

In the two northern districts the total amount of warmth sufficient for the full ripening of oats and wheat has not been observed once, and in only two years has there been a sufficient amount of warmth to ripen the barley.* Spring and the beginning of summer are almost always cold; in 1889 there were frosts in July and August, and the poor autumn weather started on 24th July and continued till the end of October. One could fight the cold, and the acclimatization of cereal crops to Sakhalin would present a most worthwhile and gratifying task, were it not for the exceptionally high damp, the struggle against which will hardly ever be possible. During the period of development of the ears, flowering, ripening and particularly of full maturation, the quantity of precipitation falling on the island is disproportionately great, and for this reason the grain yielded by the fields is not fully mature, is watery, wrinkled and light in weight. Or else, owing to the abundant rain, the grain goes to ruin, rotting or sprouting in the sheaves in the fields. Harvest time here, especially of the spring crops, almost always coincides with the rainiest weather, and it sometimes occurs that the entire harvest is left in the fields because of the rain which falls continuously from August to late autumn. In the Inspector of Agriculture's report is listed a table of crop yields for the previous five years, compiled from the information which the Governor of the Island calls "idle concoctions". From this table one may conclude approximately that the average cereal yield on Sakhalin is between one- and threefold. This receives confirmation in another statistic, too: in 1889 the average quantity of cereals harvested to every adult was around eleven poods, that is, three times larger than the amount that was sown. The grain obtained from these crop yields was poor. Once, examining specimens of cereal grain supplied by the settled exiles who wished to exchange them for flour, the Governor of the Island discovered that some of it was totally unfit for sowing, while other parts were mixed up with a considerable quantity of grain that was unripened and had been nipped by frosts (Directive no. 41, 1889).

Given the occurrence of such meagre harvests, the Sakhalin landholder, in order to eat sufficiently, should have not less than four desyatins of fertile land, should value his own toil at nothing, and should pay his workers nothing either; when, in the not too distant future, the one-field system – in which no land is left lying fallow and there is no fertilization – exhausts the soil, and the exiles "realize the necessity of going over to more rational methods of cultivating the fields, and to a new system of crop rotation", then still more land and labour will be needed and crop-cultivation will be abandoned as unproductive and unprofitable.

That branch of agriculture which depends not so much on natural conditions as on the personal efforts and knowledge of the plot-holder himself, i.e. vegetable gardening, appears to yield good results on Sakhalin. It already says something for the success of vegetable garden development here that sometimes whole families live on nothing but swede for the entire duration of the winter. In July, when one lady* at Alexandrovsk complained to me that the flowers still had not come out in her little garden, I saw a sieve full of cucumbers in a cabin at Korsakovsk. It is apparent from the Inspector of Agriculture's report that the average amount for every adult from the 1889 crop in the Tymovsk District was four and one-tenth poods of cabbage, and around two poods of various root vegetables, while in the Korsakovsk District it was four poods of cabbage and four and one-eighth poods of root vegetables. In the same year there were fifty poods of potatoes to every adult in the Alexandrovsk District, sixteen poods in the Tymovsk District and thirty-four in the Korsakovsk District. Potatoes generally give good yields, and this is confirmed not only by the statistics but personal impressions as well; I did not see any corn-bins or sacks of grain, I did not see the exiles eating wheat bread, although more wheat than rye is sown here, but, on the other hand, in every cabin I saw potatoes and heard complaints about a large quantity of potatoes having rotted during the winter. With the development of town life on Sakhalin, so also, little by little, there will develop a need for a market; a spot has already been fixed at Alexandrovsk where the countrywomen sell vegetables, and it is not uncommon to meet exiles in the streets selling cucumbers and all sorts of greenery. In some places in the south, for instance Pervaya Pad (First Chasm), vegetable gardening already constitutes a substantial business.*

Crop-rearing is considered to be the exiles' main employment. Hunting and fishing are numbered among the secondary occupations which give earnings on the side. From the hunter's point of view, there is a luxuriance of vertebrate fauna on Sakhalin. Of the animals which are most valuable to a trader, sable, foxes and bears are found in particularly vast quantities here.* The sable are scattered throughout the entire island. People say that, recently, owing to the cutting down of trees and forest fires, the sable has moved away from the populated areas into the more remote forests. How true this is I do not know; in my presence at Vladimirovka, right on the edge of the settlement itself, an overseer shot with a revolver a sable which had been crossing the stream over a log, and those exile hunters I happened to get a chance to talk to usually hunted not very far from the settlements. Foxes and bears also live all over the island. Formerly the bear did not harm people or domestic animals and was considered peaceful, but since the exiles have begun to settle in the upper reaches of the river, and cut down the woods there, and block his way to the fish which comprise his staple diet, a new cause of death has begun to appear in the Sakhalin parish registers and 'Records of Accidents' – "mauled by a bear" – and by this time the bear is already being spoken of as a menacing natural phenomenon which must be battled against in earnest. One also comes across deer, muskdeer, otters, gluttons, lynxes, on rare occasions wolves,* and, even more infrequently, ermine and tigers.* Despite such a wealth of game, hunting hardly exists as a trade in the colony.

Exile-kulaks, who make a fortune for themselves here through commerce, usually earn their living through furs which they acquire from the aboriginal inhabitants for a song and in exchange for alcohol; however, this has nothing to do with hunting but with trade of a different order. Hunters from the ranks of the exiles are pretty thin on the ground here – there are very few of them. In the main, they are not tradesmen but hunters for the love of the sport, amateurs hunting with poor guns and without dogs, just for the fun of it. They sell a dead game bird for next to nothing, or swap it for drink. At Korsakovsk one settled exile, trying to sell me a swan he had killed, was asking the exorbitant price of "three roubles or a bottle of vodka". The thought must be considered that hunting will never assume the scale of an industry in the exile colony, precisely because it is hunting carried out by exiles. To earn a living by hunting one must be at liberty, courageous and healthy; the majority of the exiles, however, are neurasthenics, irresolute people of weak character; they were not hunters in their home district, and do not know how to handle a gun, and their oppressed souls are so very alien to this free-person's enterprise that a settled exile in need would rather prefer, under fear of punishment, to slaughter a calf taken from the state on credit than go out shooting wood grouse and hare. And besides, the broad development of this trade can hardly be desirable in a colony to which, in the main, those sent for correction are murderers. A former murderer cannot be permitted frequently to kill animals and to perform those bestial operations which not a single hunt can do without – for instance, slaughtering a wounded deer with a knife, biting the throat of a ptarmigan winged by a gunshot and so forth.

The major wealth of Sakhalin, and its – possibly enviable and happy – future, lies not, as people think, in fur-bearing animals but in the seasonal fish. Part, and possibly the whole, of the quantity of matter carried away by the rivers into the ocean returns yearly to the mainland in the form of seasonal fish. The *keta,* a fish of the salmon family which is the same size and has the same colour and taste as our European Russian salmon, and which inhabits the northern part of the Pacific Ocean, at a certain period of its life enters some of the rivers of North America and Siberia, and with irresistible strength, in literally uncountable numbers, tears along upstream against the current, trying to reach the very highest mountain torrents. On Sakhalin this takes place at the end of July or in the first third of August. The mass of fish observable at this time is so great, and its progress is so swift and so extraordinary, that anybody who has not seen this remarkable phenomenon for himself can have no real conception of it. One can judge the speed of the fish, and how tightly packed they are, by the surface of the river, which seems to be boiling, the water takes on a taste of fish, oars get stuck, and when they brush against a fish they send it flying into the air. The *keta* enters the mouth of the river healthy and strong, but subsequently the ceaseless struggle against the swift current, the tight crush, hunger, friction and injuries on the snags and rocks, exhaust it, it grows emaciated, its body becomes covered with bruises, its flesh grows flabby and pallid, its teeth stick out; the fish changes in appearance completely, so that the uninitiated take it for a different species and call it not a *keta* but a *zubatka.** Little by little it grows weaker; by this time it cannot resist the current, and off it goes up backwaters, or else remains behind the trees and branches that have fallen into the river, burying its snout in the bank; here it can be picked up in one's bare hands, and even the bears can draw it from the water with a paw. Finally, worn out by the sexual urge and by hunger, it perishes, and one already begins to come across large numbers of dead specimens in the middle reaches of the river, while the banks of the upper reaches are strewn with dead fish emitting a foul stench. All these torments which the fish undergoes during the period of love are called "migration to death" in Russian, because they inevitably lead to death, and not a single one of the fish ever returns to the ocean – they all die in the rivers. "Irresistible bouts of erotic attraction leading to one's demise," says Middendorf. "This is the acme of the conception of the wandering life; and we find ideals such as these in a stupid, cold, wet fish!"

No less remarkable is the herring run, which appears seasonally off the sea coasts in spring, usually in the second half of April; the herrings move in vast shoals, "in fabulous quantities" in the words of eyewitnesses. The approach of the herring is recognized each time by the following characteristic signs: a circular area of white foam occupying a broad expanse of the sea, flocks of seagulls and albatrosses, whales blowing fountains and herds of sea lions. A marvellous picture! There was such a multitude of whales following the herring into the Aniva that Kruzenshtern's ship was surrounded by them, and it had to make its way to the shore "with caution". During the herring run the sea looks as if it is boiling.*

It is not possible even approximately to determine what quantity of fish could be caught on each occasion during the herring run in the rivers of Sakhalin and off its sea coasts. A very large sum would be appropriate.

In any case, one may say without exaggeration that given a broad-based and well-run organization of the fishing industry and with the kind of markets that have already existed for so long in Japan and China, the catching of seasonal fish on Sakhalin could yield profits of millions. When the Japanese still administered the south of Sakhalin and the fishing industry had hardly begun to develop in their hands, the fish even then brought in around half a million roubles every year. According to Mitzul's calculation, the extraction of blubber on the southern section of Sakhalin required 611 cauldrons and as much as 150,000 sazhens of firewood, and the herring alone yielded 295,806 roubles a year.

With the occupation of southern Sakhalin by the Russians the fishing industry went into a phase of decline, in which it still finds itself to this day. "Where not so very long ago seethed life which gave food to the aboriginal Ainos and solid profits to the industrialists," wrote Mr L. Deyter in 1880, "now there is practically a wilderness."* The fisheries which are being conducted now in the two northern districts by our exiles are paltry, they simply cannot be called anything else. I was by the Tym river when the *keta* or Siberian salmon was already moving through the upper reaches and here and there on the green banks one would come across the solitary figures of fishermen, pulling out half-dead fish by means of hooks on long sticks. In recent years the administration, searching for ways for the settled exiles to earn some money, has begun to give them orders for salted fish. The settled exiles receive salt at a reduced rate and on credit, and the prison then buys the fish off them for a high price, in order to give them an incentive, but it is only worth mentioning this new and negligible way they have of earning money because the prison soup made from cabbage, with the addition of fish prepared by the local settlers, is distinguished, in the opinion of the prisoners, by its singularly repulsive taste and unbearable smell. The settled exiles do not know how to catch and prepare fish, and nobody teaches them; the prison has taken over the best spots for itself in the locality of the present fisheries and has given the settled exiles the rapids and shoals, where they rip their cheap self-made nets on the snags and stones. When I was in Derbinskoye, the convicts were catching fish for the prison there. The Governor of the Island, General Kononovich, ordered the settlers to be assembled and, addressing a speech to them, reproached them that, in the previous year, they had sold fish to the prison which it was impossible to eat. "The convict is your brother, and my son," he told them. "When you deceive the government, you bring harm by this action to your brother and to my son." The settlers agreed with him, but it was clear from their faces that the following year, too, brother and son would eat stinking fish. Even if the settled exiles did somehow learn how to prepare fish, this new means of earning money still would not yield the population anything, since sooner or later the sanitary inspectors should have to forbid the use as food of fish caught in the upper reaches.

I visited the prison fishery at Derbinskoye on 25th August. The rain which had persisted for ages had brought dejection over the whole of the countryside; it was difficult walking along the slippery banks. First of all we dropped into a shed where sixteen convicts under the direction of Vasilenko, a former fisherman from Taganrog,* were salting fish. One hundred and fifty barrels had already been salted – around 2,000 poods. One got the impression that, if Vasilenko had not finished up in penal servitude, nobody here would have known how to handle the fish. From the shed there was a ramp to the shore, on which six convicts were filleting the fish with very sharp knives and then throwing their entrails into the river; the water was red and cloudy. There was a heavy smell of fish and mud, mingled with fish blood. To the side, a group of exiles – all wet and barefoot, or in bast sandals – were casting a small sweep-net. While I was there they dragged it out twice, and both times it was full. The *keta* were all extremely dubious to look at. Every one of them had protruding teeth, arched backs and bodies covered with speckles. The belly of almost every fish was coloured brown or green, and watery excrement was oozing from them. A fish cast up on the bank dies very quickly if it has not already perished in the water or been killed in the net. The few specimens which had no spots on them, they called "silverlings"; they carefully laid them aside – not for the prison cooking pot, however, but "for cured fillets".*

Here people have only a shaky knowledge of the natural history of the fish which periodically enter the river, and they are still not persuaded that these should be fished for only in the lower reaches, since further up they become unfit for use. Sailing up the Amur I heard complaints from local established residents that at the river mouth they caught real *keta*, but only *zubatka* made it up as far as them, and conversations took place on the steamer about how it was time to put some order into the fishing industry, that is, to forbid it downstream.* At the same time as the prison and the settled exiles were catching emaciated, half-dead fish in the upper reaches of the Tym, the Japanese were making money from the fish in a contraband fashion, having blocked up the river with a palisade, while in the lower reaches the Gilyaks were capturing for their dogs immeasurably healthier and tastier fish than those which were being prepared in the Tymovsk District for human beings. The Japanese would load up junks and even large ships, and the beautiful craft which Polyakov encountered at the mouth of the Tym in 1881 most probably came here this summer as well.

For fishing to take on the significance of a serious industry, the colony should be moved closer to the mouth of the Tym or the Poronai. But this is not the only prerequisite. It is also necessary that free individuals should not compete with the exile population, since there is no type of business in which, where there is a clash of interests, the free would not gain the upper hand over the exiles. However, the exiles are in competition with the Japanese, who either conduct their fishing in a contraband fashion or else pay duty, and with the officials, who take possession of the best spots for the prison fisheries, and the time is already approaching when, with the construction of the Siberian railway and the development of shipping, rumours of the fabulous wealth of fish and fur-bearing animals will attract the free to the island; immigration will commence, genuine fisheries will be set up, in which the exile will take part not as a proprietor-businessman but merely as a hired hand, and then, judging from similar situations in the past, complaints will begin that the labour of the exiles is, in many respects, inferior to the labour of the free, even to that of the Manzes and Koreans; from the economic point of view, the exile population will come to be considered a burden for the island, and, with the expansion of immigration and the development of a settled and commercial way of life on the island, the state itself will find it more just and profitable to take the side of the free element and call a halt to the process of exile. And so, fish shall constitute the prosperity of Sakhalin, but not of the exile colony.*

I have already spoken of the extraction of seakale in the description of the settlement of Mauka. During the period from 1st March to 1st August, the settler earns from 150 to 200 roubles in this business; a third of his earnings go on food, and the exile fetches the other two-thirds of it home. It is a good means of earning a livelihood, but unfortunately at present it is only possible for the settled exiles of the Korsakovsk District. The workers are paid on a piecework basis, and so the size of the earnings themselves is directly dependent on skill, diligence and conscientiousness – qualities which far from all exiles possess, and that is why every last one of them does not make off for Mauka.*

Among the exiles there are a great number of carpenters, joiners, tailors and the like, but the majority of them sit around with nothing to do, or else work raising crops. One convict metal-craftsman constructs Berdan rifles,* and has already sold four of them on the mainland, another makes novel little steel chains, another moulds plaster of Paris; but all these rifles, chainlets and extremely expensive caskets depict the economic position of the colony just about as little as the fact that one settled exile in the south collects whalebone on the shore, and another gathers up trepangas.* All of this is merely incidental. Those elegant and highly priced articles of wood which were on show at the Prison Exhibition indicate only that occasionally very good craftsmen in wood land up in penal servitude; but they have nothing to do with the prison whatever, since it is not the prison which finds a market for them, and not the prison which teaches crafts to the convicts; until very recently the prison has utilized the labour of craftsmen already trained for the work. The supply of craftsmen's labour considerably exceeds demand. "There's not even anywhere to get rid of forged banknotes here," one convict told me. The carpenters work for twenty copecks a day for their crust of bread, and the tailors sew for vodka.*

If we now total up the amount of income an exile receives on average for the sale of grain to the state, hunting, fishing and so on, we arrive at the rather woeful figure of 29 roubles 21 copecks.* Meanwhile, every household owes the government, on average, 31 roubles 51 copecks. Since food subsidies, government allowances and money received through the post are also included in the total amount of income, and since the exile's income consists in the main of earnings given him by the state, which at times pays him a deliberately high rate, a good half of the income turns out to be a fiction, and the debt to the Exchequer to be in actual fact higher than is shown.

19

The exiles' diet. What the prisoners eat, and how they eat it. Their clothing. The church. School. Literacy.

WHILE HE IS LIVING ON A GOVERNMENT ALLOWANCE, the Sakhalin exile receives daily: three *funty* of bread, forty zolotniks* of meat, around fifteen zolotniks of groats and various cooked foodstuffs to the value of one copeck; on church fast days one *funt* of fish is substituted for the meat. For determining how far this allowance conforms to the true needs of the exile, the generally accepted purely academic method is profoundly unsatisfactory, consisting as it does of a comparative and, besides, purely superficial evaluation of statistics relating to the dietary allowances of various population groups abroad and in Russia. If, in the prisons of Saxony and Prussia, the convicts receive meat only three times per week, and if on each occasion the quantity does not even reach one-third of a *funt,* and if the Tambov peasant consumes four *funty* of bread a day, that does not imply that the Sakhalin exile receives a lot of meat and not much bread: it simply means that the German prison authorities are afraid of being suspected of false philanthropy, and that the diet of the Tambov countryman has an exceptionally high bread content. It is very important from a practical point of view that the evaluation of the food consumed by any group of the population should commence not with a quantitative, but a qualitative analysis, and that, at the same time, a careful study should be made of the natural conditions and circumstances of everyday life under which that group lives; without the very strictest particularization, the conclusions to the question will be one-sided and, very probably, only convincing to pure formalists.

One day, the Inspector of Agriculture, Mr von Friken, and I were returning from Krasny Yar to Alexandrovsk, I in a *tarantas*, he on horseback. It was hot, and in the taiga it was stifling. The prisoners who were working on the road between the post and Krasny Yar, without any headgear, and in shirts which were wet with sweat, most likely taking me for an official, unexpectedly stopped my horses when I drew level with them, and submitted a complaint to me that they were being issued with bread which it was simply impossible to eat. When I told them they would do better to approach the authorities, they replied:

"We've talked to Senior Overseer Davydov, and he just said to us, you're a bunch of mutineers."

The bread was indeed dreadful. When broken open it shone in the sunlight with tiny droplets of water, stuck to the fingers and had the appearance of a muddy, glutinous paste, which it was unpleasant to hold. Several portions were brought to me, and all of it was equally underbaked, made of poorly ground flour, and obviously there was an unbelievably large overplus* of bread-weight to flour used. It had been baked at Novo-Mikhailovka under the supervision of Senior Overseer Davydov.

The three *funty* of bread which are included in the food rations, in consequence of the abuse of this overplus, contain far less flour than they should do according to the 'Table'.* The convict bakers in the settlement of Novo-Mikhailovka which I have just mentioned always sold their portions of bread, while they themselves lived on the surplus which resulted from the overplus. In the Alexandrovsk Prison those who obtained their food from the prison cooking pot received fairly good bread, those living in lodgings were issued with bread that was somewhat poorer, and those working outside the post got worse still; in other words, the only bread that was any good was that which might fall under the eyes of the head of the district or the prison governor. In order to increase the overplus, the bakers and the overseers concerned with the food allowances resort to various stratagems worked out long ago by practice in Siberian camps, of which, for example, pouring boiling water over the flour is one of the most innocent; at one time, in the Tymovsk District, to increase the weight of the bread, they used to mix the flour with sifted clay. Abuses of this kind are made all the easier since the officials cannot sit in the bakehouse all day keeping watch over, or inspecting, every single portion, and complaints from those in the prison hardly ever occur.*

Regardless of whether the bread is good or bad, usually not all the rations are eaten. A prisoner consumes them calculatingly, since according to custom already long-established in our prisons and our exile, government bread serves as something like small currency. A prisoner pays with bread the person who clears out the cell, who labours in his stead, who connives at his weaknesses, he pays with bread for needle, thread and soap; to vary his meagre, extremely monotonous, and always salted diet, he saves up bread and exchanges it in the *maidan* for milk, white rolls, sugar and vodka... The majority of the natives of the Caucasus grow ill from black bread, and so try to get rid of it. And thus, if the three *funty* which the 'Table' stipulates seem fully sufficient as regards quantity, on acquaintance with the quality of the bread and the everyday conditions of the prison, this sufficiency of rations becomes illusory, and the statistics have already lost any force. Only meat which has been salted is used in the diet, and fish likewise;* it is served up boiled, as soup. Prison soup, or "skilly", is a semi-liquid gruel made from groats and potatoes boiled to a pulp, with red pieces of meat and fish floating around in it, and which a few officials commend but cannot bring themselves to eat. The soup – even that cooked for the sick – has a very salty taste. If visitors are expected in the prisons, if a puff of smoke from a steamer is visible on the horizon, if the overseers or cooks have had a row in the kitchen – all these are circumstances which have an effect on the taste of the soup, its colour and smell; the last is often repulsive, and even pepper and bay leaves do not help.

An especially bad reputation in this respect is held by soup prepared from salt fish – and it is understandable why; in the first place, this foodstuff goes off easily, and so usually they rush to use the fish which has already begun to spoil; and secondly, the sick fish caught by the settled exiles in the upper reaches of the Tym also go into the cauldron. At one time in the Korsakovsk Prison the prisoners were fed soup of salted herring; according to the Director of the Medical Department, this soup was exceptional in its tastelessness, the herring was always very rapidly boiled to tiny pieces, and the presence of small bones made swallowing difficult and caused catarrh of the gastro-intestinal tract. How often the prisoners send the soup splashing from their bowls because of the impossibility of eating it no one knows, but it does occur frequently.*

How do the prisoners eat? There are no dining rooms. At noonday the prisoners straggle along in single file, as if at a railway ticket office, to the barracks or to the outbuilding in which the kitchen is housed. Each one has some sort of vessel in his hands. By this time, the soup is usually already prepared and, boiled to a mash, is "stewing" in the closed cooking pots. The cook has a long stick with a barrel-like attachment with which he scoops up and pours out a helping to each person who comes up, and he can ladle out two pieces of meat at once, or not a single bit, depending on what he feels like. When those right at the back at last approach, the soup is by this time soup no longer, but a thick lukewarm paste on the bottom of the cauldron, which has to be diluted with water.* On receiving their helping the prisoners go off; some eat on the move, others sitting on the ground, while others eat in their own cell rooms on the bed-boards. There is no supervision to ensure that everybody has eaten without fail and does not sell or exchange his portion. Nobody enquires whether everybody has had dinner and whether anybody has fallen asleep; and if you tell those in charge of the kitchen that in penal servitude, in a milieu of ground-down and morally corrupt people, there are not a few who have to have an eye kept on them to make sure they eat, and who even have to be fed forcibly, this remark calls forth only an expression of perplexity on their faces, and the response: "I'm very sorry, I wouldn't know anything about that, Your Excellency!"

Of those who receive government rations only twenty-five to forty per cent draw food from the prison cauldrons;* the remainder have their provisions issued directly into their hands. This majority is divided into two categories: some consume the rations in their own quarters with their families or co-tenants, while the others, who have been requisitioned for labour far beyond the prison's limits, eat them where they work. Each labourer from the second category, on completion of his task, cooks up his dinner individually in a mess tin, if he is not hampered by rain, and if he does not feel drowsy after the heavy toil; he is tired, he is hungry, and frequently, so as not to have to bother over it for long, he eats the salt beef and fish still raw. If he has fallen asleep during dinner time, sold or gambled his rations away at cards, or his provisions have gone bad, or his bread has got soaked by rain, none of this concerns those overseeing the work. Sometimes some of them eat two or three days' handout in one day, and subsequently eat nothing but bread or go hungry, during which time, according to the Head of the Medical Department, while they are working on the river banks and seashores, they do not turn up their noses at mussels and fish cast up by the waters, while the taiga yields a variety of roots, sometimes poisonous. According to the testimony of mining engineer Keppen, those working in the mines would eat tallow candles.*

In the first two – and in rare instances three – years following their discharge from convict labour, the settled exiles receive an allowance from the state, and thereafter they live at their own expense and on their own responsibility. Neither in the literature on the subject, nor in the offices, are there any statistics, or any documentary information whatever, relating to the nutrition of settled exiles; but judging from personal impressions, and the fragmentary information which can be gathered on the spot, the staple food in the colony is potatoes. These and other root-crops such as turnip and swede often form a family's only food over a very long period. Fresh fish is eaten only during the fish run, while salt fish is accessible in price only to the better off.* There is just no point in mentioning meat at all. Those who possess cows prefer to sell the milk rather than drink it; the milk is not kept in earthenware vessels but in bottles – an indication that it is for sale. Generally speaking, a settled exile will very gladly sell the produce of his farm-holding, even to the detriment of his health, since, in his estimation, he needs money more than health; if you have not saved up enough money, you will not get away to the mainland, and you can eat your fill and recover your health over time, when you are free. Among the uncultivated plants used in the diet are *cheremsha* (ramson, wild garlic) and various berries such as cloudberries, whortleberries, cranberries, *mokhovki* and the like. It could be said that the exiles living out in the colony have an exclusively vegetarian diet, and this would be correct, at least for the vast majority. At any rate, this diet has an exceptionally poor fat content, and in this respect they are hardly more fortunate than those who obtain food from the prison cooking pot.*

The prisoners do seem to receive adequate clothing and footwear. The convicts, both male and female, are issued annually with a heavy cloth overcoat and a sheepskin jacket each; at the same time, however, a soldier, who does no less work on Sakhalin than a convict, receives a uniform for three, and an overcoat for two years; as regards footwear, a prisoner wears out four pairs of bast shoes and two pairs of overshoes, while a soldier gets through one pair of boot-tops and two and a half pairs of soles. But the soldier is placed in better sanitary conditions, he has bedding and a place where he can dry out in bad weather, while a convict, through sheer necessity, has to let his clothes and footwear go rotten, since, for lack of bedding, he sleeps on the overcoat, and on all sorts of worn-out old rags, which are decomposing and tainting the air with their fumes, and there is nowhere for him to dry himself off; frequently he will even sleep in wet clothing, and so therefore, until the convict is quartered in more humane conditions, the question of how satisfactory the quantity of clothing and footwear is will remain open. As regards quality, the same old story is repeated here as with the bread: those who live under the gaze of the authorities get the best clothing, while those who are in labour gangs away from the prison get the worst.*

Now to the spiritual life, to the satisfaction of needs of a higher order. The colony is called a "corrective" colony, but the kind of institutions or people who could take up the correction of offenders in a specialist fashion do not exist on Sakhalin; neither are there any directions or clauses whatever in the *Statutes on Exiles* on the subject, except a few instructions as to when an escorting officer or non-commissioned officer may use weapons against an exile, or when a priest should "exhort on the duties of truth and morality", should explain to an exile "the importance of the granted commutation of punishment" and so on; there are not even any clearly defined attitudes on this subject; but it is accepted that primacy in the field of correction belongs to the church and the school, and after that to the free element of the population who, through their authority, tact and personal example can further considerably the mellowing of the local lifestyle.

Ecclesiastically, Sakhalin forms part of the eparchy of the Bishop of Kamchatka, the Kurile Islands and Blagoveshchensk.* Bishops have visited Sakhalin repeatedly, travelling with exactly the same simplicity and enduring on the journey precisely the same discomforts and hardships as the ordinary priests. On their arrival, at church stone-laying ceremonies, the consecration of various buildings* and while doing the rounds of the prisons, they have addressed the exiles with words of comfort and hope. The nature of their guiding activities may be judged from the following extract from the directions the Right Reverend Guriya appended to one of the documents preserved in the church at Korsakovsk: "Even if faith and repentance are not to be found in every one of the exiles, they are at least present in many, which I have perceived personally; for it was nothing other than that very feeling of repentance and faith which induced them to weep so bitterly when I preached to them in 1887 and 1888. The purpose of a prison, besides punishment for wrongdoing, consists also in the stimulation of morally righteous emotions within the incarcerated, particularly so that, under a fate such as theirs, they should not fall into total despair." This outlook was also characteristic of the junior representatives of the church; the Sakhalin priests have always held themselves aloof from punishment, and have treated the exiles not as criminals but as human beings, and in this respect have shown more tact and understanding of their duty than the doctors and agronomists, who have often interfered in what was not their business.

The most prominent place in the history of the Sakhalin church up to the present day is occupied by Father Simeon Kazansky, or, as the population called him, Priest Simon, who in the '70s was the clergyman of the Aniva or Korsakovsk church. He worked in those still "prehistoric" times when there were no roads on southern Sakhalin and the Russian population, especially the military, were scattered in small groups over the whole of the south. Priest Simon spent practically the whole time in the wilderness, travelling from one group to another by dog and reindeer sledges, and in summer going by sea on a sailing boat or on foot through the taiga; he would often get frozen, be snowbound, catch diseases on the way, be tormented beyond patience by mosquitoes and bears, boats would capsize in the swift rivers, and he would frequently have to bathe in cold water; but he bore all this with singular light-heartedness, called the wilderness "his beloved desert"*
and did not complain that life was very hard for him.

In personal relationships with the officials and soldiers he conducted himself as an excellent companion, never shunned company, and had the art of slipping apt church texts into a jovial conversation. This was the way he judged the convicts: "To the Creator of the world, we are all equal" – and this in an official document.* In his time the church on Sakhalin was poorly provided for. Once, consecrating an icon-stand in the Aniva church, he expressed himself on this poverty thus: "We have not a single bell, nor books for the services; but that which is important for us is that 'The Lord is within this place'." I have already mentioned him during my description of Popovskiye Yurty. Word of him spread, by way of soldiers and exiles, across the whole of Siberia, and now, on Sakhalin, and far and wide around, Priest Simon is a legendary figure.

At the present time there are four parish churches on Sakhalin – at Alexandrovsk, Dooay, Rykovo and Korsakovsk.* On the whole, the churches are not poor, the priests each receive a salary of 1,000 roubles a year, and in each parish there is a choir whose members can sight-read from written scores and who dress in ceremonial kaftans. Services are held only on Sundays and High Holidays; on the eve of these days, the all-night vigil is celebrated, and then, at 9 a.m., mass; vespers does not take place. The local fathers do not bear any especial responsibilities called forth by the singular composition of the population, and their activities are quite as mundane as those of our rural priests, that is, they consist only of church services on Sundays and holidays, occasional ceremonies such as christenings, marriages and funerals, and school affairs. I did not hear of any personal chats with exiles, or exhortations to them.*

At Lent the convicts fast and attend the requisite church services in preparation for confession and receiving the sacrament. They are given three mornings for this. When the convicts in irons, or those living in the Voyevodsk and Dooay Prisons, fast and attend service, sentries stand around the church, and people say that this creates a dispiriting and oppressive sensation. Unskilled convict labourers usually do not go to church, since every day off is used to rest, to do their repairs or to go and collect berries; apart from all this the churches here are cramped, and it has somehow become established automatically, without anybody saying so, that only those dressed in free-persons' clothing can enter a church here, that is to say, only the so-called "general public". For instance, during my visit to Alexandrovsk, every time mass was celebrated, the front half of the church was taken up by the officials and their families; then followed a motley row of soldiers' and overseers' wives and free-women, with their children, then the overseers and soldiers, and only behind all these, against the wall, came the settled exiles, dressed in town clothing, and the convict clerks. Was it possible, if he wished, for a convict with a shaven head, with one or two aces on his back, in shackles, or attached to a wheelbarrow, to enter the church? One of the priests to whom I addressed this question replied: "I don't know."

The settled exiles receive communion, get married and baptize their children in the churches if they live nearby. The priests travel to the distant settlements themselves and then hold communion for the exiles to celebrate the end of fast periods and perform other incidental religious ceremonies. Father Irakly had "perpetual curates" at Upper Armudan and Malo-Tymovo, the convicts Voronin and Yakovenko, who read the hours* on Sunday. Whenever Father Irakly arrived in a village to hold a service, some fellow would wander round the streets bellowing at the top of his voice: "Come on, all out to pray!" Where there are no churches or chapels, the services are held in barracks or cabins.

When I was living at Alexandrovsk, the local priest, Father Yegor, dropped in on me one evening, and, after spending a little time with me, set off to the church to perform a marriage ceremony.* I went along with him. In the church the chandelier had already been lit, and the choristers were standing with blasé faces in the choir, awaiting the bridal pair. There were many women, convicts and free-people continually glancing with impatience at the door. Whispering could be heard. Then suddenly somebody at the door waved his hand and hissed agitatedly: "They're coming!" The choristers began to clear their throats. A wave of people came flooding in through the door, somebody shouted sternly, and finally the young couple entered: a convict typesetter, about twenty-five years old, in a jacket with a starched collar curled up at the corners and with a white tie, and a female convict, three or four years older, in a dark-blue dress with white lace and a flower in her hair. A cloth was spread over the carpet; the groom stepped on it first. The best men, also typesetters, wore white ties, too. Father Yegor entered from the sanctuary and spent ages leafing through a small book on the lectern. "Blessed be our God…" he proclaimed, and the wedding commenced. When the priest laid the crowns on the bride and groom's heads, and asked God to crown them with glory and honour, the faces of the women who were present carried expressions of deep emotion and joy, and it seemed to have been forgotten that the activity was taking place in a prison church, in a penal labour settlement, far, far from the home country. The priest said to the groom: "Be thou exalted, O groom, like unto Abraham..." However, when after the wedding the church had emptied, and there was a burning smell from the candles, which the churchwarden had rushed to snuff out, it all grew melancholy. We went out into the porch. Rain. By the church, in the darkness, stood a crowd, and there were two *tarantasy:* the young couple were in one, and the other was empty.

"Father, be so good as to join us!" voices rang out, and dozens of hands stretched out of the dark towards Father Yegor, as if to grab hold of him. "Please join us! Do us the honour!"

They sat Father Yegor in the *tarantas* and drove him to the quarters of the newly married couple.

On 8th September, a holiday, I was coming out of the church after mass with a certain young official, and just at this moment a body was being carried in on a bier; it was borne by four convicts in tatters and with coarse, haggard faces like our European Russian urban beggars; immediately behind followed two superfluous, redundant individuals with exactly the same appearance: a woman with two children, and the swarthy Georgian Kelbokiani, dressed in freeman's clothing (he worked as a clerk, and was entitled "Prince"), and everybody was hurrying, apparently for fear of finding the priest had left the church. From Kelbokiani we learnt that free-woman Lyalikova had died; her husband, a settled exile, had gone away to Nikolayevsk;* she had left two children, and now he, Kelbokiani, who was living in the quarters of this Lyalikova, did not know what to do with the children.

My companion and I had nothing to do, and so we went on ahead to the graveyard, without waiting for them to finish performing the funeral service. The graveyard is a verst from the church, beyond the Alexandrovsk hamlet, right by the sea, on a high, steep hill. As we were climbing the hill, the funeral procession was already beginning to catch up with us; obviously the funeral service had required two or three minutes at most. From above we could see the coffin shaking on the bier, and a young boy, who was being led along by the woman, dropping behind and tugging at her hand.

On one side there was a broad view of the post and its surroundings, and on the other, the sea, calm and shining in the sun. There are very many graves and crosses on the hilltop. We saw two side by side: these are the graves of Mitzul and Governor Selivanov, who was killed by a prisoner. The small crosses standing on the graves of convicts are all on the same model, and none has any inscription. Mitzul will be remembered for some time yet, but these people, lying under little crosses, people who committed murders, escaped, clanked along in shackles, nobody has any need to remember. Only somewhere, perhaps, in the Russian steppes, by a bonfire or in a wood, an elderly wagon-driver will, out of boredom, tell a tale about how so-and-so in his village went off on an orgy of violent highway robbery; the listener will glance at the darkness and shudder, while a nightbird shrieks – and that is all the funeral feast he will get. On a cross where an exiled doctor's assistant is buried are the words:

Passer-by! Remember thou this verse,
That to everything under the heavens there is a final hour

etc., etc. And at the end:

Farewell, old chum, until that gladsome morn!

The freshly dug grave was a quarter full of water. The convicts, puffing and panting, with sweat-covered faces, and loudly carrying on a conversation which had nothing whatsoever to do with the burial, at last carried the coffin up and placed it at the edge of the grave. It was made of unpainted boards hurriedly knocked together.

"Well?" said one.

The swiftly lowered coffin squelched into the water. Lumps of clay beat on the lid, the coffin shook, the water splashed, while the convicts, working with spades, continued talking about some business of their own, and Kelbokiani constantly glanced at us in perplexity and, spreading out his arms, protested:

"What am I going to do with the kids now? How can I take care of them! I went to the Governor, and asked him to let me have a woman, and will he? No, he won't!"

The boy Alyoshka, three or four years old, whom the woman had been leading up here by the hand, was standing and looking down into the grave. He was dressed in a woman's jacket with long sleeves which did not fit him and in faded dark-blue trousers; there were bright-blue patches on the knees.

"Alyoshka, where's your mother?" asked my companion.

"They-y've b-ur-ied her!" said Alyoshka, started to laugh, and waved his hand over the grave.*

There are five schools on Sakhalin, not counting the one at Derbinskoye, where, owing to the lack of a teacher, lessons do not take place. In 1889 and 1890, 222 children were studying in them, 144 boys and seventy-eight girls, an average of forty-four at each. I was on the island during the school holidays, there were no lessons during my visit, and so the internal life of the schools there, which must be distinctive and interesting indeed, remained an unknown quantity to me. The general view is that the Sakhalin schools are poor, furnished in a beggarly fashion, that their existence is only due to chance and not obligatory, and that their situation is extremely uncertain, since nobody knows whether they are going to continue to exist or not. They are directed by one of the officials in the offices of the governor of the island, a well-educated young man, but he is a king who reigns but does not rule, since in actual fact, the schools are run by the district governors and prison governors, upon whom depend the selection and appointment of teachers. Teaching is conducted in the schools by exiles who were not teachers in their home region, people ill-acquainted with the work and without any training. They each receive ten roubles a month for their labour; the administration finds it impossible to pay any more, and it does not appoint free-status people, as they would have to be paid not less than twenty-five roubles. To all appearances, school-teaching is considered an unimportant occupation, since overseers appointed from the ranks of the exiles themselves, who often have ill-defined responsibilities and duties, and merely run errands for the officials, receive forty and even fifty roubles each per month.* Of the male population, both adults and children, twenty-nine per cent are literate, while the figure for the females is nine per cent. And even this nine per cent relates exclusively to those of school age, so that one may say of the adult Sakhalin female that she can neither read nor write; enlightenment has not touched her; she is startling in her gross ignorance, and it appears to me that nowhere else have I seen such obtuse women, so slow on the uptake, as in this very place, amidst a criminal and enslaved population. Of the children who have come to Sakhalin from European Russia, literates comprise twenty-five per cent, while among those born on Sakhalin, however, the figure is only nine per cent.*

20

The free population. The lower ranks of the local military commands. The overseers. The educated classes.

T HE SOLDIERS ARE TERMED THE "PIONEERS" of Sakhalin, because they were living here before the penal colony was established.* Starting from the 1850s, when Sakhalin was occupied, and almost up to the '80s, the soldiers, besides their immediate duties according to the regulations, also carried out all the work which is now borne by the convicts. The island was a wilderness; there were no dwellings here, no roads, no cattle, and the soldiers had to construct barracks and homes, open cuttings through the forest and carry all the goods on their backs.

If an engineer or a scholar came to Sakhalin on a mission, several soldiers would be placed at his disposal, taking the place of horses. Mining engineer Lopatin writes: "When I formed the intention of going into the depths of the Sakhalin taiga, it was no use even thinking of travelling on horseback and transporting heavy goods on pack animals. Even on foot it was only with difficulty that I climbed over the steep mountains of Sakhalin, covered now with thick masses of fallen trees and branches, now with the local bamboo. In this fashion I had to travel more than 1,600 versts on foot."* And behind him came the soldiers, lugging his heavy baggage.

The entire – quite small – number of soldiers was spread along the western, southern and south-eastern seaboards; the spots in which they lived were called "posts". Now long since abandoned and forgotten, these posts played precisely the same role at that time as the settlements do now, and they were regarded as the pioneers of the future colony. At the Muravyovsk Post was billeted a company of fusiliers, at the Korsakovsk Post three companies of the Fourth Siberian Battalion and a section of a mining battery, while in the other posts, for instance, the Manuysk and Sortunai, there were only six soldiers at each. The six men, separated from their company by a distance of several hundred versts, under the command of an NCO, or even a civilian, lived like perfect Robinson Crusoes. Life was uncivilized, extremely monotonous and tedious. In summer, if the post was on the shore, a vessel would sail in, drop provisions for the sailors, then leave; in winter a priest came to administer the sacrament after a fast period, dressed in a fur jacket and trousers, and in appearance more like a Gilyak than a priest. Life was varied only by misfortunes; sometimes a soldier would be swept out to sea on a hay-barge, sometimes be mauled by a bear, sometimes he would be snowbound, or attacked by escapees, and sometimes scurvy would steal up on him... or else a soldier, getting fed up with sitting in a snowbound shed, or going on foot through the taiga, would begin to display "disorderly conduct, insobriety and insolence", or else get caught thieving, or embezzling munitions, or else would be brought to trial for disrespect shown to somebody or other's kept convict woman.*

Given the diversity of the work, a soldier did not have time to acquire military training and would forget everything he had been taught, the officers would be pulled down with him, and the purely military side of affairs was in a most lamentable state. Inspections were accompanied on every single occasion by confusion and expressions of displeasure on the part of the authorities.* The service was back-breaking. People who had been relieved from guard duty immediately went on to escort duty, from the escort to the guard again, or to haymaking, or to unloading state cargo; there was no rest day or night. They lived in cramped, cold, filthy accommodation which differed but little from the prisons. In the Korsakovsk Post, up until 1875, the guard was housed in the convict prison; here, too, there was a military guardhouse like a dingy dog-kennel. "Perhaps," writes Surgeon Sintzovsky, "such constrained conditions are permissible for convicts, as a measure of punishment, but a soldier on guard has no connection whatever with this, and why he should experience punishment of this sort no one knows."* They ate just as badly as the convicts, and were dressed in rags, because there were not enough garments of any kind where they were working. Whenever they pursued escapees in the taiga, the soldiers' clothing and footwear became so dishevelled that on one occasion on southern Sakhalin they were themselves taken for fugitives and fired on.

At the present time, the military guard consists of four detachments: those of Alexandrovsk, Dooay, Tymovsk and Korsakovsk. As of January 1890, the number of lower-ranking soldiers in all the detachments was 1,548. As before, the soldiers perform duties out of all proportion to their strength, intellectual abilities and the requirements of the military statutes. True, they no longer make cuttings, or put up barracks, but, just as in the past, a soldier returning from guard duty or from drill cannot count on rest: he might be detailed immediately to escort duty, or to haymaking, or to pursuing runaways. Economic necessities siphon off a significant number of soldiers, so that a constant shortage is felt in the escort, and the guard cannot be relied upon for three shifts. At the beginning of August, when I was at Dooay, sixty men of the Dooay detachment were away haymaking, and of those, half had been sent 109 versts on foot for this purpose.

The Sakhalin soldier is meek, taciturn, obedient and sober; only at the Korsakovsk Post did I see drunken soldiers who might make a row out in the streets. He rarely sings, and it is always the same thing: "Ten lasses, and only me, where there's lasses there I go... Lasses to the wood, after 'em goes I" – a jolly song, but he sings it with such boredom that, at the sound of his voice, you begin to yearn for your homeland and feel all the unattractiveness of the Sakhalin country-side. He endures all hardships submissively and is indifferent to the perils which so frequently threaten his life and health. But he is coarse, mentally underdeveloped and inarticulate, and, because he has so much to do, does not have enough time to become imbued with the sense of military duty and honour, and so is no stranger to blunders which often make him just as much of an enemy of good order as those he guards and pursues.* He displays these deficiencies of his particularly prominently when he is entrusted with responsibilities which do not correspond to his mental level, as when, for example, he becomes a prison overseer.

According to Article 27 of the *Statutes on Exiles,* on Sakhalin "the prison surveillance service is made up of senior and junior overseers, the number of whom, assuming one senior overseer to forty convicts, and one junior to twenty, shall be determined annually by the Central Prison Department". There should be three overseers, one senior and two juniors, to every forty men, that is to say, one to every thirteen. If you were to imagine to yourself that thirteen men work, eat, spend their time in the prison and so on under the constant supervision of a conscientious, skilled individual, and that above him in their turn stand the authorities in the person of the prison governor, and above the prison governor, the district governor and so on, you could rest content in the thought that everything was proceeding admirably. In actual fact, however, the supervision up till now has been the sorest spot of the Sakhalin penal labour system.

On Sakhalin at the present time there are around 150 senior over-seers, and twice as many juniors. The seniors' posts are occupied by literate NCOs and privates who have finished their service in the military contingents here, and by members of the intellectual classes, though there are very few of this last category. Lower ranks on active service comprise six per cent of the total complement of seniors, but on the other hand the positions of junior overseers are filled almost entirely by privates detailed from the local detachments. In the event of an incomplete contingent of overseers, the *Statutes* permit the appointment of lower-ranking soldiers of the local military commands to act as overseers, and so, in this manner, young Siberians who are acknowledged to be too incompetent even for escort duty are called upon to fulfil the official duties of an overseer, "temporarily" and "within the limits of extreme necessity", it is true, but this "temporarily" has already lasted whole decades, and the "bounds of extreme necessity" are constantly growing wider and wider, so that the lower ranks of the local detachments already make up seventy-three per cent of the entire staff of junior overseers, and nobody will guarantee that within two or three years the figure will not grow to 100 per cent. It should be noted in this respect that it is not the finest soldiers who are detailed to become overseers, since, in the interests of active service, the commanding officers release the less able to the prison and retain the better ones in the units.*

In the prisons there are a lot of overseers, but there is no order, and they serve only as a constant hindrance to the administration, as the Governor of the Island himself testifies. Almost every day, in his directives, he fines them, docks their pay or dismisses them altogether, one for unreliability and dereliction of duty, another for immorality, lack of conscientiousness and lack of intellectual capability, a third for the theft of government food provisions entrusted to his keeping, and a fourth for receiving stolen goods; a fifth, detailed to a barge, not only did not maintain order but actually set the example himself in pilfering walnuts on the barge; a sixth is under investigation for selling government axes and nails; a seventh has repeatedly been reprimanded for his careless surveillance of the fodder for the government cattle, and an eighth for reprehensible dealings with the convicts. From the directives we learn that one senior overseer, an army private, while on duty in the prison, created the possibility for himself of entering the women's barracks through a window, having bent the spikes back beforehand, with a view to romantic liaisons, while another, during his spell of duty, at one in the morning allowed a private, also an overseer, into the quarters where the female prisoners are kept in solitary confinement. The overseers' amorous adventures are not limited merely to the narrow sphere of the women's barracks and their solitary confinement units. In the overseers' quarters I would find adolescent girls who, in response to my question as to who they were, would reply: "I'm his cohabitant." You go into an overseer's apartment, and there he is, squat, glutted with food, fleshy, his waistcoat undone, and wearing squeaky new shoes, sitting at the table and "suppin'" tea; by the window sits a girl of about fourteen or so, her face worn and pale. He usually titles himself an NCO, or a senior overseer, and of her he says that she is the daughter of a convict, that she is fourteen and that she is his cohabitant.

While they are on duty in the prison the overseers allow the prisoners to play cards and take part themselves; they booze hard in the company of the exiles and deal in alcohol. In the orders we also encounter riotous conduct, insubordination, extremely insolent behaviour towards superiors in the presence of the convicts and, finally, beatings delivered with a stick to the head of a convict, as a consequence of which lesions were formed.

Brutal people, mentally underdeveloped, hard-drinking, who play cards with the convicts, who readily enjoy the love and alcohol of the female convicts, undisciplined and unconscientious, can only possess a negative kind of authority. The exile population do not respect them and ignore them contemptuously. They call them "knackered old geezers" to their faces, and use the "*tu*" form to them. The administration, though, does not worry in the least about raising their prestige, most likely considering that bothering themselves over it would not lead to any useful results. The officials use "*tu*" to the overseers, abuse them as they please and do not feel constrained by the presence of the convicts. One constantly hears "What are you staring at, you blithering idiot!" or "You don't understand a thing, do you, you half-wit!" How little the overseers are respected here is evident from the fact that many of them are appointed to "duties incommensurate with their official position", that is, to put it bluntly, they serve as flunkeys and errand-boys to the officials. Overseers from the privileged classes, as if ashamed of their position, try to stand out from the ranks of their colleagues in some slight way at least; one wears rather thicker braids on his shoulders, another wears a military officer's cockade, while yet another, a Collegiate Registrar, entitles himself in documents, not an overseer, but a "Controller of Works and Workmen".

Since the Sakhalin overseers have never achieved any understanding of the objectives of supervision, then over the course of time, in the natural order of things, the objectives of supervision themselves have had to be constricted little by little to their present state. Supervision as a whole has now come down to a private sitting in a cell room, ensuring that "they don't make a row" and complaining to the authorities; at convict works, armed with a revolver which, fortunately, he does not know how to fire, and a sabre which it is difficult to draw out of its rusted scabbard, he stands, gazing apathetically at the labour, smoking and feeling bored. In the prison he is a domestic servant who opens and locks doors, and on the convict work he is a superfluous individual. Although there are three overseers to every forty convicts, one senior and two juniors, one constantly sees forty or fifty men working under the supervision of only one man, or even without supervision altogether. If, of the three overseers, one is out at the convict labour, another will at precisely the same time be standing by the government shop and saluting passing officials, while the third will be moping in somebody or other's front hallway, or, with no necessity whatever, be standing at attention in the waiting room of the infirmary.*

A little must be said of the educated classes. Punishing one's fellow man in the performance of one's duty and under oath, being able to suppress disgust and horror within oneself every hour of the day, the remoteness of the places of service, the derisory salary, the boredom, the constant proximity of shaven heads, shackles, executioners, calculations over every brass farthing, petty wrangling and, most of all, the consciousness of one's total powerlessness in the struggle with the encircling evil – all of this taken together has always made service in the administration of convict labour and exile exceptionally arduous and unattractive. In the labour camps in the past served mainly people who were unscrupulous, unsqueamish, difficult to get on with, to whom it was all the same where they served, as long as they could eat, drink, sleep and play cards; respectable people, however, came here only out of necessity, and then dropped the service at the first opportunity, or else went downhill through drink, went out of their minds, killed themselves, or else little by little the environment dragged them down into its filth, like an octopus, and they, too, began to thieve, and to deal out savage floggings...

Judging from the official accounts and from newspaper reports, in the '60s and '70s the educated classes on Sakhalin were outstanding for their sheer moral worthlessness. Under the officials of the period, the prisons were turned into havens of debauchery and into gaming houses; people were corrupted, brutalized and flogged to death. The most prominent administrator in this respect was a certain Major Nikolayev, who was Director of the Dooay Post for seven years. His name is often mentioned in newspaper reports.* He was a freed serf by social status who had been handed over to the army.* As to what abilities paved the way for this brutal, uncouth man to rise to the rank of major, there is no information. When one reporter asked him whether he had ever been to the central part of the island, and what he had seen there, the Major responded: "A mountain and a valley – a valley and another mountain; everybody knows the soil's volcanic and was thrown up in eructations." On being asked what kind of thing *cheremsha* was, he replied: "In the first place, it's not a thing, it's a plant, and in the second place, it's a very useful and tasty plant; it fills yer belly full of wind, it's true, but we don't give a damn, cos we're not very often with ladies." For the wheelbarrows used for transporting coal, he substituted barrels, so that it would be easier to roll them over the tracks made of boards; in these barrels he sat convicts who had committed an offence and ordered them to be rolled along the shore. "Roll 'em vigorously for about an hour, and before you know where you are, they'll be as meek as lambs." Wishing to teach the soldiers their numbers, he resorted to playing lotto. "When a number's called out, whoever can't find it himself has to pay ten copecks; he'll pay once, pay again, and then it dawns on him that it's just not worth it. Before you know it, he'll get down really hard to those figures, and within a week he'll have learnt 'em." Crass high-flown pomposities such as these had a corrupting effect on the Dooay soldiery; they would often sell the convicts their rifles. Commencing the punishment of one convict, the Major declared that he would not remain alive, and indeed, the offender died shortly afterwards. Following this incident, Major Nikolayev was brought to trial and sentenced to convict labour.

When you ask some old man, an established settled exile, whether there have been good people on the island in his time, he will sit silent for a bit at first, as if trying to recall, and then he will reply: "There've been all sorts." Nowhere is the past so swiftly forgotten as on Sakhalin, precisely because of the extraordinarily high mobility of the exile population, which changes radically every five years here, and partly due to the absence of any decent archives in the local offices. What happened twenty to twenty-five years ago is regarded as being profound antiquity, already forgotten and lost to history. Only a few buildings and Mikryukov have survived, plus a score or so of anecdotes, and there also remain some statistics deserving no credence whatsoever, since at the time not a single government office knew how many prisoners there were on the island, how many had escaped, how many had died and so forth.

"Prehistoric" times continued on Sakhalin up till 1878, when Prince Nikolai Shakhovskoy – an excellent administrator, and an intelligent and honest man – was appointed Superintendent of Exiled Convict Labourers in the Primorskaya Region.* He left behind him the *Dossier on the Administrative System on Sakhalin Island,* a work which is in many respects exemplary and which is preserved today in the offices of the Governor of the Island. He was for the most part a purely academic worker, writing in his study. Under him, the prisoners lived just as badly as they had done before him, but there is no doubt that his observations, which he communicated to the authorities and to his subordinates, and his *Dossier,* independent and outspoken, have served as the basis for excellent new trends.

In 1879 the Voluntary Fleet began to operate, and, little by little, natives of European Russia began to take up posts on Sakhalin. In 1884 new regulations were introduced on Sakhalin, giving rise to an intensified influx – or, as they say here, "wave" – of new people.* On Sakhalin at the present time we already have three "county towns", in which reside the officials and officers with their families. Society is already so diversified, educated and cultured that, for example, at Alexandrovsk in 1888, an amateur production of *The Marriage** could be staged; when, in the same location, Alexandrovsk, on High Holidays,* by mutual consent, the officials and officers substitute for their ceremonial visits financial payments for the benefit of poor convicts or children, the number of signatures on the subscription list usually rises as high as forty. To a visitor, Sakhalin society produces a favourable impression. It is cordial, hospitable, and sustains comparison in all respects with the societies of our European Russian rural administrative districts, and the eastern sea-coast tract is considered the most vivacious and entertaining of all; at any rate, officials are transferred only reluctantly to such mainland postings as, for instance, Nikolayevsk or De-Kastri. But, just as in the Tatar Strait strong gales occur from time to time, and the sailors say that these are distant reverberations of a cyclone raging in the Sea of China or the Sea of Japan, so, too, in the life of this society the recent past and the close proximity of Siberia recur to mind every so often. What fine people finished up here after the reforms of 1884 is apparent from the directives on dismissal from official duties or on commitment for trial, or from the official statements about disorders in the service, amounting to "flagrant depravity" (Directives nos 87 and 89, 1890), or from the anecdotes and tales, even if they are only like the stories about the convict Zolotaryov, a well-off man who kept company with the officials and went on the binge and played cards with them. When this convict's wife constantly discovered him with the officials, she began to heap shame on his head for keeping the society of people who might have a bad influence on his morals. Even now one encounters officials who think nothing of swinging their arm and punching an exile – even an exile from the privileged classes – in the face, or of ordering a man who has not taken off his cap with alacrity: "Go to the Governor and tell him to give you thirty strokes of the birch." Right up to this very day, such disorders are still possible in the prisons, as, for instance, two prisoners being considered absent, whereabouts unknown, for almost a year, while at the same time they obtained food from the prison cooking pot and were even requisitioned to do convict labour (Directive no. 87, 1890). Not every prison governor knows for certain how many prisoners there are living in his jail at any given moment, how many really do draw their food from the prison cauldrons, how many have escaped and so forth. The Governor of the Island himself considers that "overall, the state of affairs in all branches of the administration in the Alexandrovsk District produces a painful impression and requires many significant improvements", and, as regards office work proper, it has been left too much to the will of the clerks, who "have held sway in a totally unsupervised fashion, judging from some forgeries which have by chance come to light" (Directive no. 314, 1888).* On the lamentable state of the investigative department here, I shall speak in its place. In the postal and telegraphic office they treat people rudely and distribute the mail to the mere hoi polloi only on the fourth or fifth day after it has arrived; the telegraph operators cannot read or write, and the principle of confidentiality of telegraphic messages is not observed. I did not receive one single telegram which had not been distorted in the most barbarous manner, and when once, by some chance, a fragment of somebody else's telegram had got into mine, and in order to re-establish the sense of both telegrams, I went to ask for the blunder to be rectified, I was told that the only way this could be done was at my own expense.

In the modern history of Sakhalin a notable role has been played by specimens of that most recent of formations, a cross between Derzhimorda* and Iago – gentlemen who in the handling of inferiors recognize nothing but fists, birches and fishwives' abuse, and who move their superiors by their education, culture and liberalism even.

But, however that may be, the "House of the Dead"* exists no longer. On Sakhalin among the educated classes directing the offices and working in them, I repeatedly met intelligent, good-natured and noble individuals, whose presence serves as sufficient guarantee that a return of the past is no longer possible. Nowadays the convicts are not rolled in barrels any more, and a convict could not be flogged to death or driven to suicide without this scandalizing society here, and without its being talked about along the Amur and throughout the whole of Siberia. Every loathsome business sooner or later comes to light in the outside world and becomes public, a proof of which is the grim Onor affair,* which, however much they tried to hush it up, aroused a lot of rumours and ended up in the newspapers thanks to the educated classes on Sakhalin themselves. Good people and good works are no longer rarities. Not so long ago in Rykovo, a female doctor's assistant died; she had served on Sakhalin for many years for the sake of an idea – that of devoting one's life to suffering people. Once, while I was at Korsakovsk, a convict was carried out to sea on a hay-raft; Prison Governor Major Sh. put out to sea in a launch, and in spite of a gale, and putting his life in jeopardy, he sailed from evening to two in the morning until he managed to track down the hay-raft in the darkness and take the convict off it.*

The reform of 1884 showed that the more numerous the administration in an exile colony, the better it is. The complexity and widespread dispersion of affairs here requires a complex machinery and the participation of many people. Business of little importance must not be allowed to divert the officials from their major duties. In spite of this, however, for lack of a secretary or of an official who would be permanently attached to him, the governor of the island is occupied for a large part of the day in drawing up directives and various documents, and this complicated and laborious red tape deprives him of almost all of the time necessary for visiting prisons and travelling round the settlements. Besides presiding over the police departments, the district governors have themselves to issue food subsidies to the women and take part in various types of committees, surveys and so forth. Prison governors and their assistants are entrusted with the investigative and police departments. Under such conditions, either the Sakhalin official has to work beyond his capacity, "work himself silly", as they say, or else, giving it all up as a bad job, he has to load an immense proportion of his work on to the convict clerks – and this is what happens most frequently. In the local offices the convict clerks are not only occupied with copying, but they even draw up documents themselves. Since not infrequently they are more experienced and more energetic than the officials, especially newcomers, it does happen that a convict or settled exile carries on his shoulders the entire office, the whole of the book-keeping, and even the investigative department. Over the course of many years, the clerk, through ignorance and lack of scrupulousness, gets all the loose ends of the office work tangled up, and since he alone can sort out this mess, he becomes indispensable and irreplaceable, and the authorities, even the most strict, are no longer able to manage without his services. Such an omnipotent clerk can be got rid of in one way only – by replacing him with one or two genuine officials.

Where the educated classes are numerous, there inevitably exists a climate of public opinion which creates a moral controlling force and makes ethical demands upon everybody which it is utterly impossible for anybody to evade with impunity, even a Major Nikolayev. There is no doubt either that, with the development of a social life, the service here will little by little lose its unattractive aspects, and the percentage of lunatics, alcoholics and suicides will be reduced.*

21

The morality of the exile population. Criminality. Investigation and trial. Punishments. The birch and the lash. The death penalty.

S OME EXILES BEAR THEIR PENALTY with fortitude, willingly acknowledge their guilt, and when you ask them why they have been sent to Sakhalin they usually reply: "They don't send you here for doing good deeds." But others are staggering in their lack of spirit and look of dejection; they whine, weep, give way to despair and swear that they are not guilty. One considers his punishment a blessing, because, to use his words, only in convict labour has he come to know God, while another tries to make off at the first opportunity, and, when they attempt to recapture him, he sweeps them aside with a large bludgeon. Together under the same roof as dyed-in-the-wool villains and sadistic monsters live offenders by accident, "unfortunates" who have been falsely convicted.* It is owing to this that the population here, when the question of its morality in general is raised, produces an extremely confused and tangled impression, so that, under the existing methods of investigation, any serious overall conclusions are hardly possible. The morality of a population is usually judged by statistics determining criminality, but in relation to an exile colony even this common and simple method proves to be unserviceable. A population of exiles, living under abnormal and exceptional circumstances, has its own, specially conditioned criminality, its own statutes, and offences which we in European Russia consider trivial are here treated as serious, while on the other hand, a large number of criminal offences are not recorded, since in the prison milieu they are considered commonplace phenomena, and almost inevitable.*

Among the exiles one observes vices and perversions characteristic in the main of individuals who are subjugated, enslaved, starved and in constant fear. Mendacity, cunning, cowardliness, lack of spirit, informing on others, thieving, every kind of secret vice – these things form the arsenal which the degraded population, or at least a vast proportion of it, puts forward against the authorities and overseers, whom they do not respect, but fear and consider their foes. To slip out of convict labour or corporal punishment, and to obtain a crust of bread, or a pinch of tea, salt or tobacco, an exile will resort to

deception, since experience has shown him that, in the fight for existence, deception is the most reliable and dependable means. Theft
here is commonplace and resembles an industry. The prisoners hurl
themselves on everything that is not nailed down, with the persistence
and greed of hungry locusts, devoting themselves mainly to eatables
and clothing. They thieve in the prison, off each other, from the settled exiles, at convict labour, during the loading of ships, and from
the virtuoso adroitness with which they carry out their pilferings one
can judge how often the robbers here must practise. On one occasion
at Dooay they stole a live ram and a vat and kneading trough; the
barge had still not pulled away from the steamer, but the stolen goods
simply could not be found. On another occasion, they robbed the
captain, they unscrewed the portholes and the compass; and another
time they clambered into the cabins of a foreign ship and made off
with the silver tableware. During unloading, entire bales and barrels
disappear.*

The exile amuses himself secretly, in thieves' fashion. To obtain
a glass of vodka which in ordinary circumstances would cost only
a five-copeck piece, he has surreptitiously to approach a dealer in
contraband goods and let him have, if not money, then his bread or
some item of his clothing. The sole mental pleasure, playing cards, is
possible only at night, by the light of candle-stumps, or in the taiga.
Any clandestine pleasure repeated frequently turns little by little into
a passion; with the excessive tendency towards imitation found among
exiles, one prisoner infects another, and ultimately such seeming trifles
as contraband vodka and card-playing lead to unbelievable irregularities. As I have already said, kulaks from the ranks of the exiles make
a fortune from the clandestine trade in vodka and alcohol; this implies
that next door to an exile with 30,000 to 50,000 roubles, one must
look out for people who systematically run through their food and
clothing. Gambling, like an epidemic, has already taken control of all
the prisons; these present the appearance of large gambling houses,
while the settlements and posts are their branch departments. The
business is established on a very wide footing, and it is even said that
the local organizers of gambling at cards – who, in random searches,
are found to have hundreds and thousands of roubles – maintain
regular business dealings with the Siberian prisons, for instance, the
one at Irkutsk, where – as the convicts put it – they carry on "real"

games. There are already several gaming houses at Alexandrovsk; in one of them, in Second Kirpichnaya Quarter, there actually occurred a scandal characteristic of dens of this sort: an overseer who gambled away all his money shot himself. Games of *Stoss* cloud the mind like a narcotic, and a convict, while gambling away all his food and clothing, will feel neither hunger nor cold, when he is being flogged feel no pain, and, however strange it may seem, even during such work as loading ship, when the side of a bargeful of coal is banging against the steamer, the waves are pounding and people are green from seasickness, a game of cards will be going on in the barge, and a conversation to do with the work is mingled with card talk. "Pu-ull *a-way*! I'll lay yer two! Ay, ay!"

At the same time the subjugated condition of the women, their poverty and abasement are conducive to the development of prostitution. When I enquired at Alexandrovsk whether there were any prostitutes there, the reply was "As many as you like!"* In view of the enormous demand, the taking up of prostitution is impeded neither by age nor by deformity, nor even by tertiary syphilis. Neither is early girlhood an obstacle. In the streets of Alexandrovsk I came across a girl of sixteen who, according to stories, had entered upon prostitution at the age of nine. This girl did have a mother, but on Sakhalin a family environment far from always saves girls from ruin. People tell of a Gypsy woman who sells her daughters and haggles over the price for it herself. One free-status woman in the Alexandrovsk hamlet keeps an "establishment" in which only her own daughters operate. At Alexandrovsk the debauchery has, overall, the character of the depravity of a city. There are even "family bathhouses" kept by a Jew, and people may already be named who earn a living by pimping.

According to government records, by 1st January 1890, recidivists – that is to say, those who have been convicted again by the regional court – comprised eight per cent of the convict labourers. Among the recidivists were those who have been sentenced three, four, five and even six times, and the number of those who, owing to further offences, had already been slaving in penal servitude for twenty to fifty years, had reached 175, i.e. three per cent of the entire total. But these are all, so to speak, "exaggerated" relapses, since the majority of those registered as recidivists have been sentenced for attempted escape. And even regarding escapees, these statistics are incorrect, since those who have been sent back from attempted flight are not always brought to trial but are controlled by being placed under house arrest. To what extent the exile population is criminally inclined, or, to put it another way, is disposed to criminal relapses, is still not known. It is true that people are tried for crimes here, but many cases lapse on account of defendants failing to appear, many case-files are sent back because of the need for further information or for questions of jurisdiction to be resolved, or else are brought to a halt because the requisite details have not been received from various Siberian offices, and ultimately, after long bureaucratic procrastination, are shelved in the archives because of the death of the accused, or his failure to return from escape; but the major reason is that it is almost impossible to rely either on the data yielded up by the investigations, which are conducted by young people who have never had an education, or on the information from the Khabarovsk Regional Court,* which tries the Sakhaliners in their absence, by documents alone.

During 1889 the number of convict labourers under investigation and on trial was 243, that is, one accused to every twenty-five convicts. There were sixty-nine settled exiles on trial and under investigation, that is, one in fifty-five, while there were only four peasants-in-exile accused of a crime, that is, one in 115. From these ratios it is obvious that, with the alleviation of one's fortune, with an exile's transition to a freer status, his chances of finishing up on trial decrease by half each time. These statistics all indicate the number on trial and under investigation, and not the incidence of crimes committed for 1889, since among the cases for this year are also shown cases commenced many years back and still not concluded. These figures might give the reader some idea of the vast number of people on Sakhalin who annually languish around on trial and under investigation, owing to the fact that cases drag out over many years, and the reader may envisage how ruinously this system must reflect on the economic conditions of the population and its mentality.*

The investigation is usually entrusted to an assistant prison governor or to the secretary of the police department. In the words of the Governor of the Island, "Processes of investigation are commenced without sufficient cause, are conducted slackly and maladroitly, and the prisoners concerned are detained on no grounds whatever." The suspect or the accused is taken into custody and placed in a punishment cell. When a settled exile was murdered at Goly Mys, four men were suspected and taken into custody;* they were placed in cold, dark punishment cells. A few days later, three were released and only one remained; he was put in irons, and the order was given to serve him hot food only every third day; then, following a complaint from an overseer, the direction was issued to give him 100 strokes of the birch, and he was kept in this way, in the dark, half-starving and in terror, until he confessed. At the same time the free-status woman Garanina was likewise being detained in the prison, suspected of murdering her husband; she, too, had been placed in a dark punishment cell and received hot food every third day. When a certain official was interrogating her in my presence, she declared that she had been ill for a long time now, and that for some reason they did not want to let a doctor see her. When the official asked the overseer appointed to the punishment cells why nobody had bothered about a doctor up till now, he replied quite literally:

"I did report it to 'is Excellency the Governor, but 'e said 'Let 'er kick the bucket!'"

This inability to distinguish detention on remand from imprisonment (and in a dark punishment cell of a convict prison at that!), the inability to distinguish the free contingent from the convicts amazed me all the more since the District Governor here is a graduate of a faculty of law, and the Prison Governor served formerly in the St Petersburg police.

Another time I visited the punishment cells with the District Governor himself, this time early in the morning. When four exiles under suspicion of murder were released from the cells, they were shivering with cold. Garanina was in stockinged feet, with no shoes, and also was shivering and squinting from the light. The District Governor ordered her to be transferred to quarters with some light. Incidentally, on this occasion I also noticed a Georgian man who was wandering like a phantom around the entrance to the punishment cells; he had been stuck here five months already, in the dark entrance hall, suspected of poisoning, and was awaiting an investigation which at that time had still not begun.

There is no assistant public prosecutor* living on Sakhalin, and there is nobody to supervise the progress of an investigation. The direction and speed of an investigation are totally dependent on various eventualities having no connection whatsoever with the case itself. In one record I read that the murder of a certain woman, Yakovleva, had been committed "with the purpose of robbery, with attempted rape beforehand, which is indicated by the bedding being disturbed on the bedstead and by the fresh scratches and indentations of nails from boot-heels on the bed on the upright board at the back of the bedstead". Reasoning such as this predetermines the destiny of an entire case; a post-mortem in such cases is not considered necessary. In 1888 a fugitive convict murdered Private Khromyaty, and the post-mortem took place only in 1889, at the request of the Public Prosecutor, when the investigation was already concluded and the dossier had been dispatched to the court.*

Article 469 of the *Statutes* gives the local administration the right, without a formal police investigation, to determine and carry out punishments for offences and misdemeanours, for which, under the common criminal law, penalties are stipulated not exceeding the forfeiting of all personal rights and property, with imprisonment. Generally speaking, on Sakhalin cases of little import are conducted by a formal police tribunal, which falls under the aegis of the police department here. Despite such a wide sphere of competence of this local court, under whose jurisdiction fall trivial cases and also a large number of cases which are considered non-serious only under the kind of circumstances found here, the population is a stranger to justice and lives without a court of law. In a place where an official has the right by law, without trial or investigation, to punish by birching and to put people in prison, and even to send them to the mines, the existence of a court there has merely a purely formal significance.*

Penalties for serious offences are determined by the Primorskaya Regional Court on the mainland, which judges cases from documents alone, without examining defendants and witnesses. The judgement of the regional court is presented on each occasion for ratification to the governor of the island, who, in the event of his disagreeing with the sentence, settles the case by his own authority; when doing so he informs the Ruling Senate* of every alteration of sentence. In the event of some offence or other seeming out of the ordinary to the administration, and the penalty stipulated for it, according to the *Statutes on Exiles,* insufficient, they apply for the defendant to be handed over to trial before a court martial.

The punishments laid down for convicts and settled exiles for offences are conspicuous for their excessive severity, and if our *Statutes on Exiles* are totally out of keeping with the spirit of the times and of the laws, this is nowhere more noticeable than in the section dealing with punishment. Penalties which humiliate and embitter a criminal, which are conducive to the coarsening of morals and mores, and long since acknowledged as injurious for the free population, have been retained for the settled exiles and convict labourers, as if a population of exiles is exposed to less of a danger of becoming hardened and embittered, and ultimately of losing all human dignity. The birch, the lash, chaining to the wheelbarrow – punishments which bring disgrace upon a convict's personal identity, and which cause pain and torment – are here employed widely.* Punishment with the lash or the birch is prescribed for every offence, be it criminal or trivial; whether it is used as a supplement, in conjunction with other penalties, or is used independently, it forms, either way, an indispensable part of the content of every sentence.

The most commonly used means of penalization is the birch rod.* As the 'Registers' show, in the Alexandrovsk District during 1889, 282 convicts and settled exiles were punished by administrative order: 265 by corporal punishment, i.e. by the birch, and seventeen by other measures. This means that in ninety-four cases out of 100 the administration resorts to the birch. Far from all of those undergoing corporal punishment are entered in the Registers; the Tymovsk District records for 1889 show only fifty-seven convicts punished by birching, and only three in the Korsakovsk District, while at precisely the same time several people in both districts are flogged every day, and sometimes a dozen or so in the Korsakovsk District. Grounds for awarding a person thirty or 100 strokes of the birch are commonly afforded by every kind of wrongdoing: failure to complete a day's convict-labour task (for instance, if a shoemaker has not finished sewing the requisite three pairs of ladies' shoes, they flog him), drunkenness, rudeness, disobedience… if twenty or thirty workmen have not finished a task, they flog all twenty or thirty. One official said to me:

"The prisoners, especially those in irons, love to hand in all kinds of absurd petitions. When I was appointed here, and went round the prison for the first time, around fifty requests were handed to me; I accepted them, but declared to the applicants that those whose petitions proved to be unworthy of attention would be flogged. Only two of them turned out to be deserving of consideration – the rest were rubbish. I ordered forty-seven men to be flogged. Following that, the next time there were twenty-five, then fewer and fewer each time, and now they don't give me requests at all any more. I've taught them a lesson."

In the south, following a denunciation from one convict, a search was made of another convict's belongings and a journal was found which contained material taken to be rough drafts for newspaper articles; he was given fifty strokes of the birch and kept in the dark punishment cell for fifteen days on bread and water. The Superintendent of Settlements, with the cognizance of the District Governor, once subjected almost the whole of Lutoga to corporal punishment. Here is how the Governor of the Island describes this: "The Governor of the Korsakovsk District has reported to me, incidentally, an extremely serious case of exceeding one's authority, which [name given] had permitted himself, and which consisted of the savage corporal punishment of several settled exiles, and in a measure far exceeding the norm established by law. This occurrence, while scandalous in itself, appears to me still more flagrant on analysis of the circumstances which provoked this punishment of both the innocent and the guilty, not excluding even a pregnant woman, without any investigation whatsoever of the affair, which consisted of a mere scuffle among settled exiles from which nothing ensued" (Directive no. 258, 1888).

A person found guilty of an offence is most commonly given thirty to 100 strokes of the birch. This depends, not on guilt, but on who has ordered the punishment, the district governor or the prison governor; the former has the right to give up to 100, the latter up to thirty. One Prison Governor always scrupulously awarded thirty, then when on one occasion he had temporarily to fulfil the duties of district governor he at once raised his usual quota to 100, as if these 100 strokes were an indispensable token of his new authority; he did not alter this token right up until the very arrival of the new District Governor, and then once again, immediately and just as scrupulously, he went back down to thirty. From over-frequent usage, punishment by birching has to a large extent become devalued on Sakhalin, since it already arouses in many people neither aversion nor fear, and, so it is said, there is already a fairly large number of prisoners who during a flogging actually do not feel any pain at all. The lash* is employed far less frequently, and only as a consequence of sentences of the regional circuit courts. From the report of the Director of the Medical Department, it may be seen that, in 1889, "in order to determine the capacity to endure corporal punishment according to the sentence of the courts", sixty-seven individuals were examined by the doctors. Of all the means of punishment on Sakhalin this is the most abominable in both its savagery and the circumstances surrounding it, and the legal experts of European Russia who sentence vagabonds and recidivists to the lash would long ago have renounced this penalty if it had been performed in their presence. However, they are protected against the disgraceful and outrageous spectacle by Article 478 of the *Statutes,* according to which the sentences of the Russian and Siberian courts are carried out at the place of exile.

The manner in which punishments are administered with the lash I witnessed at Dooay. Vagabond Prokhorov-alias-Mylnikov, a man of about thirty-five to forty, had fled from the Voyevodsk Prison, and, having constructed a small raft, set sail for the mainland. On the shore, however, they noticed in time and sent a launch in pursuit. The case on the escape was opened; they glanced into his itemized records and suddenly made a discovery: this Prokhorov-alias-Mylnikov had been sentenced by the Khabarovsk Regional Court the previous year, for the murder of a Cossack and two of his granddaughters, to ninety lashes and attachment to the wheelbarrow, but, owing to an oversight, this punishment had still not been carried out. If Prokhorov had not taken it into his head to try to escape, then perhaps the error would never have been noticed and the business would have been settled without the lashes and the barrow, but now a flogging was inescapable. On the appointed day, 13th August, in the morning, the District Governor, a surgeon and I walked unhurriedly towards the government offices; Prokhorov – who had been directed to be brought in for punishment only the previous day – was sitting on the porch with the overseers, still not knowing what lay in store for him. On seeing us, he stood up and must have guessed what was going on, for he suddenly turned quite white.

"Into the office!" commands the Governor.

We enter the office. They bring in Prokhorov. The doctor, a young Russian ethnic German, orders him to undress and listens to his heart to ascertain how many strokes this prisoner is able to endure. He resolves this question in one minute flat, and then with a businesslike air sits down to sign the certificate of examination.

"Akh, you poor chap!" he says in a sorrowful tone, with a thick German accent. "You must find it most hard wearing irons! Why don't you ask ze Herr Governor – he vill order zem to be taken off."

Prokhorov remains silent, his lips white and trembling.

"It's no use, you know," the doctor goes on and on. "It's no use anyzing any of you try to do. Zere are such suspicious people in European Russia. Akh, poor chap, poor chap!"

The certificate is ready; it is attached to the dossier of investigation on the escape. Then silence descends. The clerk writes, the doctor and the Governor write... Prokhorov still does not know for certain what he has been summoned here for – for the escape alone, or else on the old business and the escape together? He is tortured by the uncertainty.

"What did you dream of last night?" the Governor asks at last.

"I forget, Yer Excellency."

"Then just you listen," says the Governor, glancing into the itemized records. "On such and such a date of such and such a year, you were sentenced by the Khabarovsk Regional Court for the murder of a Cossack to ninety strokes of the lash. Well, then, today, you've got to have them."

And, slapping the prisoner on the brow with the palm of his hand, the Governor says in a didactic tone:

"And all for what? Because you tried to be a bit too clever. You people are always running away, you reckon things'll be better, but they end up worse."

We all go into the "Overseers' Lodge" – an old grey building of the barrack-hut type. A military doctor's assistant standing at the entrance implores in a beseeching voice, as if begging for alms:

"Your Excellency, would you care to see how we carry out our punishments here?"

In the middle of the overseers' room lies a sloping bench with openings for fastening hands and feet. The executioner Tolstykh,* a tall, stocky individual with the build of a circus strongman and acrobat, not wearing a frock coat,* and with waistcoat unfastened, nods to Prokhorov; the latter lies down without a word. Tolstykh, unhurrying, also without a word, lowers Prokhorov's trousers to the knee and begins slowly to bind his hands and feet to the bench. The Governor gazes, blasé, out of the window, the doctor paces up and down. In his hands he has some kind of medical drops.

"Could I possibly giff you a glass of vater?" he asks.

"Yes, for God's sake, Yer Excellency."

At last Prokhorov is bound. The executioner takes up a lash with three tails and, without haste, smooths it out.

"Ready – bear up!" he says, not loudly, and without swinging his arm, as if he is simply measuring his length, he delivers the first blow.

"*O-one!*" says the overseer in a voice like a church sexton.

For the first instant Prokhorov is silent, and even the expression on his face does not alter; but now a convulsion of pain runs through his body and a sound rings out – not a scream but a squeal.

"*Two!*" calls the overseer.

The executioner stands sideways on and strikes in such a way that the lash falls across the body. After every five blows, he slowly walks round to the other side and gives himself half a minute's rest. Prokhorov's hair is stuck to his brow, his neck is swollen; after five or ten blows his body, still covered by weals from previous lashings, has already turned crimson and dark blue; the skin on it splits from every blow.

"Yer Excellency!" we hear through the screeching and weeping. "Yer Excellency! Be merciful, Yer Excellency!"

And later, after twenty or thirty blows, Prokhorov seems to be intoning a ritual lament, as if drunk, or exactly as if he is delirious:

"What a poor unfortunate chap I am, ground down to the ground I am, that's what I am, I am... Just what am I being punished like this for?"

And now there is a kind of curious stretching-out of the neck, the sounds of retching... Prokhorov does not utter a single word, but simply bellows and wheezes; it seems as if, since the punishment began, a whole eternity has passed, but the overseer is calling only: "Forty-*two*! Forty-*three*!" There is a long way to go to ninety. I walk outside. All around outside it is silent, and the heart-rending sounds from the overseers' quarters seem to me to reverberate throughout the whole of Dooay. A convict wearing freeman's clothing has just walked past and glanced fleetingly at the building, and on his face, and even in his walk, is expressed horror. I enter the quarters again, then come out again, but the overseer is still counting.

Ninety at last. They rapidly untie Prokhorov's hands and feet and help him stand up. The area where he has been beaten is dark-blue-crimson from bruises and is bleeding. His teeth are chattering, his face is yellow and wet, his eyes are wandering. When he is given medicinal drops, he bites the glass convulsively... They moisten his head and lead him away to the sickbay.

"That's for the murder – there'll still be something specially for the escape," they explain to me as we are returning home.

"I love to see them getting punished," says the military doctor's assist-ant joyfully, really pleased that he has gorged himself on the repulsive spectacle. "I love it! They're such villains, such rogues... they should hang 'em!"

Not only the prisoners become hardened and embittered from the corporal punishments, but also those who carry out the punishments and are present at them. Even educated people do not form exceptions. At any rate, I did not notice that officials with a university education behaved towards flogging any differently from military doctors' assist-ants or those who have completed courses in military academies or theological seminaries. Some grow so much accustomed to lashings and birchings, and become so callous, that in the end they actually begin to find pleasure in the tearing of flesh. It was recounted to me of one Prison Governor that, when he was present at a flogging, he would whistle; another, an elderly man, would say to the prisoner with mali-cious joy: "What are you hollering for, for Christ's sake! It's nothing, it's nothing, stand up to it! Thrash him, thrash him! Lay into him!" Yet another used to order a prisoner to be fastened to the bench by the neck, so that he would be wheezing; the Prison Governor would deliver five or ten blows, go off somewhere for an hour or two, and then come back and deliver the rest.*

The court martial is composed of local military officers appointed by the governor of the island; the trial documents of the court martial, and the sentence imposed, are sent for confirmation to the governor general. In the past, those who had been convicted would lie around depressed for two or three years in punishment cells awaiting the ratification, but now their fate is decided by telegraph. The usual sen-tence of a court martial is death by hanging. The Governor General sometimes commutes the sentence, substituting for the death penalty a hundred lashes, chaining to the wheelbarrow and detention in the "probationary" category for life. If a murderer is sentenced to death, this is commuted only very rarely. "Murderers I hang," the Governor General told me.

On the eve of the execution, in the evening and throughout the night, the condemned man is taken through a "parting vigil" by a priest. This parting vigil consists of confession and a dialogue between the two of them. One priest recounted the following to me:

"At the beginning of my ministry, when I was still only twenty-five, I once had to take two prisoners in the Voyevodsk Prison through the parting vigil; they'd been sentenced to hanging for murdering a settled exile for a rouble and forty copecks. I went into their punishment cell, and, because I wasn't accustomed to this, was terrified; I ordered the sentry not to close the door behind him, and not to go away. But they said to me:

"'Don't be scared, Father. We're not going to kill you. Sit down!'

"So I ask – just where is there to sit? They point to the sleeping plank. I sat on a keg of water, then, plucking up my spirits, sat on the sleeping plank between the two criminals. I asked them what province they were from, chatted about this and that, and then began to take them through the parting vigil. Only during the confession did I look up – and being carried past the window I caught sight of the posts for the gallows and everything that goes with them.

"'What's that?' the convicts ask.

"I say to them: 'They must be building something at the Governor's quarters.'

"'No, Father, that's for hanging us with. Look, Father, d'you think it's possible to have a little bit of vodka to drink?'

"'Don't know,' I say. 'I'll go along and ask.'

"I went off to the Colonel and told him that the condemned men wanted something to drink. He gave me a bottle of vodka, and, so there should be no talk about it later, ordered the Captain of the Guard to withdraw the sentry. I got a wineglass from a guard and went to the prisoners in the punishment cell. I filled the glass.

"'No, Father,' they say, 'you get some down you first, otherwise we won't start drinking.'

"I had to drain the glass to the bottom. There was nothing to chase it with either.*

"'Well,' they say, 'that vodka has cleared our thoughts.'

"After this I carried on taking them through the vigil. I talked with them for an hour or two. Suddenly, the command:

"'Bring them out!'

"Subsequently, after they'd been hanged, because I hadn't been used to it, I was scared to go into a dark room for ages."

Fear of death and all the circumstances surrounding the organization of the execution have an oppressive and dispiriting effect on the condemned. There has not up till now been a single case of an offender going cheerfully and courageously to his execution. When convict Chernoshey, one of the murderers of shopkeeper Nikitin, was being fetched from Alexandrovsk to Dooay prior to his execution, he suffered spasms of the urinary bladder and had to keep stopping. One of his accomplices in the crime, Kinzhalov, began to chatter nonsensically. Before the execution a shroud is placed over the condemned, and the Prayer for the Dying is read. While the ceremony of execution was taking place, one of Nikitin's murderers did not manage to hear the prayer out but collapsed in a faint. To the youngest of the murderers, Pazukhin, after he had already been covered with the shroud, and had the prayer read over him, it was announced that he had been reprieved; his death sentence had been substituted by another penalty. Just how much this man must have lived through in such a short time! The all-night conversation with the priest, the solemnity of the confession, towards morning half a glass of vodka, the command "Bring them out", the shroud, the Prayer for the Dying, then joy on account of the reprieve, and right that moment, straight after the execution of his colleagues, 100 lashes, fainting away after the fifth stroke, and finally being chained to the barrow.

In the Korsakovsk District eleven men were sentenced to death for the murder of the Ainos.* All through the night before the execution, the officials and military officers did not sleep but kept going to each other's quarters and drinking tea. There was a general weariness, and nobody knew what to do with themselves. Two of the condemned poisoned themselves with aconite – a huge embarrassment for the local military command, under whose responsibility they lay. The District Governor heard the turmoil during the night, and it was reported to him that two had poisoned themselves; but even so, before the very execution itself, when everybody was gathered round the gallows, he still had to demand of the Commanding Officer of the detachment:

"Eleven men were condemned to death, yet here I see only nine. Precisely where are the remaining two?"

The Commanding Officer, instead of replying in the same official manner, began muttering nervously: "Look, hang me. Hang me…"

It was a morning in early October, dismal, cold and dark. The faces of the condemned were yellow, and their hair was standing on end from horror. An official read the sentence, trembling with agitation, and constantly stammering and hesitating over it because he could not see properly. A priest in a black chasuble gave all nine the cross to kiss and whispered to the District Governor:

"For God's sake, release me, I can't go on…"

The process was a long one: each prisoner had to have a shroud put on and be led to the scaffold. When at last all nine had been hanged, the effect was of a "whole garland" in the air, as the District Governor put it, telling me about this execution.

When the executed men were taken down, the doctors found that one of them was still alive. This chance occurrence had an especial significance: the prison – including the executioner and his assistants – which knows the secrets of all the offences committed by the inmates, was aware that this one who was still alive was not guilty of the crime for which he had been hanged.

"He was hanged on another occasion," the District Governor concluded his story. "Afterwards I couldn't sleep for a whole month."

22

Escapees on Sakhalin. Causes of escape. Composition of escapees by origin, social class and so on.

As ONE OF THE MAJOR and especially significant advantages of Sakhalin, a certain committee of 1868 pointed to its position as an island. On an island separated from the mainland by a stormy sea, it would not be difficult, it seemed, to create a large maritime prison according to the scheme: "Water, water all around, and in the middle – trouble",* and to set up a kind of Roman exile* where escape would merely be something to be dreamt about. In actual fact, however, from the very beginning of the practice of exile to Sakhalin, the island has turned out to be a *quasi insula,* an island in name only. The strait separating the island from the mainland freezes over completely during the winter months, and the water, which in summer plays the role of a prison wall, is as flat and smooth as a plain over the winter, and anyone who wishes can cross it on foot or by dog sled. And even in summer the strait is not secure; at its narrowest point, between the capes of Pogobi and Lazarev, it is no more than six or seven versts wide, and in calm, clear weather, it is not difficult, in a poor Gilyak boat, to sail as much as a hundred versts. Even where the strait is broader, the inhabitants of Sakhalin can see the coast of the mainland pretty clearly; the hazy strip of land, with its beautiful mountain peaks, day after day allures and tempts the exile, promising him freedom and his homeland. Apart from these physical conditions, the committee either did not foresee, or else did not bear in mind, escapes not to the mainland but to the interior of the island, which cause no less trouble than flight to the mainland, and therefore, Sakhalin's position as an island has far from justified the committee's hopes.

But it still nonetheless does remain an advantage. It is not easy to abscond from Sakhalin. Vagabonds, upon whom one can rely as experts in this respect, declare frankly that it is far harder to make off from Sakhalin than, for instance, from the convict-labour institutions of Kara or Nerchinsk. Even given the total lack of discipline and widest possible indulgence which took place under the old administration, the Sakhalin prisons nevertheless still remained full, and the prisoners did not flee so often as perhaps the prison governors wanted them to, since abscondments provided for them one of their most profitable means of income. The present officials acknowledge that, were it not for fear of the physical obstacles, then, with the widely scattered nature of convict labour and the deficiencies of surveillance, on the island would remain only those who like living here – that is to say, nobody.

But among the hindrances which restrain people from escaping, it is not the sea that is primarily so terrible. The impassable taiga, the mountains, the permanent damp, the mists, the lack of human beings, the bears and mosquitoes, and in winter, the dreadful frosts and snow-storms – it is these things that are the true allies of surveillance. In the Sakhalin taiga, where at every step one has to overcome mountains of timber which have fallen in the wind, and stiff *bagulnik* or bamboo which gets tangled around one's feet, where one sinks up to the waist in mires and streams, and where one constantly has to wave away the dreadful swarms of midges – under these conditions even free-persons, fully fed, can walk no more than eight versts in twenty-four hours; and a person who is worn out by prison, who lives in the taiga on pieces of rotting wood and salt, and who does not know where either north or south is, does not, generally speaking, make even three to five versts. In addition to all this, he is compelled to go, not in a straight line, but to take a route far out of his way, so as not to run into the cordon. A week or two, on rare occasions a month, is spent on the run, and then, exhausted by starvation, diarrhoea and fever, bitten all over by midges, his legs battered and swollen, wet, filthy, ragged, he perishes somewhere in the taiga, or else drags himself back forcibly, in a state of total collapse, begging God as the supreme height of good fortune to meet with a soldier or a Gilyak who will convey him back to the prison.

The cause which motivates a criminal to seek salvation in flight, and not in labour or repentance, is chiefly the consciousness of life, which has not yet gone to sleep inside him. If he is not of a philosophical turn of mind, and cannot live equally well everywhere and in all circumstances, then he cannot, and should not, *not* want to escape.

First and foremost an exile is spurred to leave Sakhalin by his passionate love for his home district. If you listen to the convicts – what happiness it is, what joy, to live in one's own place in one's own country! They talk about Sakhalin, the land here, the people, the trees and the climate, with scornful laughter, with exasperation and loathing, while in European Russia everything is wonderful and enchanting; the most daring thinking cannot acknowledge that in European Russia there might be unhappy people, since to live somewhere in the Tula or Kursk Region, to see log cabins every day, and to breathe Russian air already by itself constitutes the supreme happiness. God knows, a person might suffer poverty, sickness, blindness, dumbness and disgrace from the people around, just as long as God permits him to die at home. One old lady, a convict, who was for some time my domestic servant, went into ecstasies over my suitcases, books and quilt, purely and simply for the reason that they were not from Sakhalin but from our own part of the world; whenever the priests came to visit me, she would not approach to receive a blessing but would watch them with a smirk, because there could not be any real priests on Sakhalin. Yearning for the home country manifests itself in incessant reminiscing, sad and touching, accompanied by lamentations and bitter tears, or else takes the form of unrealizable hopes, often staggering in their absurdity, and akin to madness, or else it is demonstrated as clearly evinced and indubitable mental disturbance.*

Exiles are also driven from Sakhalin by the striving for freedom innate in man and forming, in normal circumstances, one of his most noble qualities. While an exile is young and robust, he tries to flee as far away as possible, to Siberia or to European Russia. Usually he is caught, tried and sent back to convict labour, but this is not so terrible; the slow march from *étape* to *étape,* the frequent changes of prisons, companions and escort guards, and the adventures on the way, have their own special poetry and still resemble liberty more than being inside the Voyevodsk Prison or out on convict labour. Growing frailer over the years, losing confidence in his legs, he starts making off to somewhere a bit closer, to the Amur, or even into the taiga, or up a mountain, just as long as it is a little way from the prison, so that he does not have to see the hateful walls and people, or hear the clanking of irons and the conversation of the convicts. At the Korsakovsk Post lives convict-in-exile Altukhov, an elderly man of sixty or more, who escapes in the following manner: he takes a hunk of bread, locks up his cabin, and, walking not more than half a verst from the post, he sits down on a hill and gazes at the taiga, the sea and the sky; after sitting like this for three days or so, he goes back home, draws his provisions and goes back to the hill again... In the past they used to flog him, but now they simply laugh over these "escapes" of his. Some abscond with the intention of roaming at large for a month or a week, for others a single day is sufficient. "It may only be a day – but it's mine." The yearning for freedom affects some people at certain periods only, and in this respect resembles occasional desires to go on a drinking binge or attacks of epilepsy; they say that it occurs only at a certain time of the year or month, so that trustworthy convicts, feeling the onset of an attack, forewarn the authorities of their escape on each occasion. All the escapees are normally punished indiscriminately, with either the lash or the birch, but the mere single fact, taken in isolation, that often escapes strike one from beginning to end with their illogicality and folly, that sensible, unassuming people with families flee with no clothing, no bread, no purpose and no plan, with the certainty that they will unfailingly be caught, with the risk of forfeiting their health, the trust of the authorities, their comparative freedom, and sometimes even their salaries, and the risk of freezing to death or being shot down – this illogicality alone should prompt the thought in the Sakhalin doctors, with whom lies the decision whether to punish or not, that in many cases they are dealing, not with a crime, but a sickness.

To general causes for escape one must also ascribe the fact that punishment is for life. Under our system, as is well known, convict labour is accompanied by enforced settlement in Siberia for ever. A person sentenced to convict labour is withdrawn from the normal human environment without hope of ever returning to it, and in this way dies, as it were, so far as that society in which he was born and grew up is concerned. This is why the convicts say of themselves: "Dead men don't come back from the graveyard." It is precisely this total hopelessness of the convict, and his despair, which lead him to the decision: to make off, change his fortune – it couldn't be any worse! If he does run away, then people say of him: "He's gone to change his luck." If he is caught and brought back, this is described by the phrase "His luck was out" or "Fortune wasn't going his way". Given the condition that exile is for life, escapes and vagabondage form an inevitable and indispensable evil and even serve as a sort of safety valve. If there were any possibility of depriving the exile of his hopes for escape, which he regards as the sole means of changing his luck and returning from the graveyard, then his desperation, finding no outlet, would probably manifest itself in some other fashion, and of course in a more vicious and frightful form than flight.

There is yet a further general cause of escape – this is a belief in the ease, absence of punishment and the legality, almost, of abscondment, although in reality it is difficult, penalized savagely and considered a serious criminal offence. This odd belief has been fostered among people for generations, and its origin is lost in the mists of those good old days when flight was indeed easy and escape was actually encouraged by the authorities. A factory manager or prison governor used to consider it a punishment for himself from on high if for some reason his prisoners did not abscond, and he would rejoice when they made off in whole droves. If before 1st October – the date when winter clothing was issued – thirty or forty prisoners had run away, this meant as a rule that thirty or forty sheepskin jackets would fall to the disposal of the governor. According to Yadrintzev, on reception of each new party, one factory manager would usually call out: "Whoever wants to stay, come now and get your clothes, but whoever wants to go on the run – don't bother to get them, there's no point!" Those in charge have, as it were, legalized escape by their own authority, and in their spirit has been educated the entire population of Siberia, which to this very day does not consider escape a sin. The exiles themselves tell of their escapes in no other way than with laughter, or with regret that they did not succeed, and to expect penitence or pangs of conscience from them would be in vain. Out of all those who had at some time escaped and with whom I happened to talk, only one sick old man, chained to a wheelbarrow for multiple abscondment, reproached himself bitterly because he had kept running off, but in doing so, called his escapes not a crime but "silliness": "When I was younger, I did some silly things, now I've got to suffer for 'em."

Personal grounds for escape are numerous. I would point to discontent with the prison regime, bad food in the prison, the cruelty of one or other of the superiors, idleness, incapability for labour, sickness, feebleness of will, the tendency towards imitation, love of adventure... It has frequently happened that entire parties of convicts have fled merely in order to "have a wander" round the island, and these wanderings have been accompanied by murders and every kind of abomination, inducing panic and extreme animosity among the population. I shall recount the story of an escape for the sake of revenge. Private Belov wounded the fugitive convict Klimenko during capture and escorted him to Alexandrovsk Prison. Klimenko recovered and escaped once again, this time with one single objective – to avenge himself on Belov. He walked straight into the cordon and was arrested. "Take yer mate again," his colleagues said to Belov. "It's your stroke of luck." Belov set off to bring him in. On the road escort and convict got talking. It was autumn, and it was windy and cold... they stopped to have a smoke. When the soldier raised his collar to light his pipe, Klimenko snatched his rifle from him and killed him on the spot, then, as if nothing whatever had happened, returned to the Alexandrovsk Post, where he was arrested and, shortly afterwards, hanged.

And then there is love as well. Convict Artem – his surname I do not recall – a young man of about twenty, served at Naibuchi as a watchman at a government house. He was in love with an Aino woman who lived in one of the yurts on the river Naibu, and it is said his feelings were reciprocated. He was suspected of theft one day and transferred as punishment to the Korsakovsk Prison, that is, ninety versts from the Aino woman: then he began to flee from the post to Naibuchi for rendezvous with his beloved, and kept on running off till he was wounded by a shot in the foot.

Escapes are also the subject of sharp practice. Here is one of these types of operation which combines greed for money and the most vile treachery. An old vagabond, grown grey in escape and adventure, spies out in a crowd of newcomers which ones are a bit better off (newcomers almost always have money) and tries to lure one of them into escaping with him. Persuasion is not difficult; the newcomer escapes, and somewhere in the taiga the vagabond murders him and returns to the prison. Another type of fraud, more widespread, is connected with the three roubles awarded by the government for the capture of a fugitive. Having made an arrangement beforehand with a private or a Gilyak, several convicts flee from the prison to an agreed spot, somewhere in the taiga or on the seashore, and there meet with their escort-guard: the latter leads them back to the prison as captives and receives three roubles for each; later on, of course, the share-out takes place. It is comical to look at, when a young puny Gilyak, armed with nothing but one single stick, leads in all at once six or seven broad-shouldered, imposing-looking vagabonds. On one occasion, in my presence, Private L., who is also not distinguished for his sturdy build, brought in eleven men.

Until very recently, prison statistics hardly touched on escapees. For the present, one may say that, most frequently of all, those exiles flee for whom the difference between the climates of Sakhalin and their home region is most perceptible. To this category belong first of all the natives of the Caucasus, the Crimea, Bessarabia and the Ukraine. One sees lists of escapees, or of those captured and brought back, sometimes around fifty or sixty people, on which there is not a single Russian surname, but it is all Oguls, Suleymans and Hassans. But there is not the slightest doubt either that those with life sentences and long sentences take flight more often than convicts third class,* those living in the prison more often than those outside it, and young prisoners and newcomers more frequently than established residents. Women abscond far less often than men, and this is explained partly by the difficulties with which flight is encompassed in the case of women, and partly by the fact that, in penal servitude, a woman soon acquires firm attachments. Responsibilities towards wife and children do restrain men from escaping, but it does

happen that family men also decamp. Lawful husbands flee less frequently than unlegalized husbands. When I went round the cabins,
female convicts, to my question "Where's the man you live with?" would
often reply: "Who the hell knows? *You* go and look for him!"

Alongside exiles of ordinary social status, members of the privileged
classes also make off. Leafing through the alphabetical register of the
Korsakovsk Police Department, I discovered a former member of the
nobility who had escaped, been tried for a murder committed during
the flight, and had received eighty or ninety lashes. The notorious
Lagiyev, who was sent here for the murder of the Rector of the Tbilisi
Seminary, and formerly a teacher at Korsakovsk, escaped in the early
hours of Easter Sunday 1890 together with convict Nikolsky – the son
of a priest – and also with three unknown vagabonds. Shortly after
Easter a rumour went round that three vagabonds had been seen in
"civilian" clothes making their way along the shore to the Muravyovsk
Post, but Lagiyev and Nikolsky were no longer with them; in all probability the vagabonds had incited the young Lagiyev and his companion to run off with them and had murdered them on the way, in
order to make use of their clothes and money. The son of Archpriest*
K., sent here for murder, fled to European Russia, committed a fresh
murder and was returned to Sakhalin. Once, early in the morning, I
saw him in a crowd of convicts near the mine: singularly emaciated,
round-shouldered, with dull eyes, in an old summer coat, with ripped
trousers worn over high boots, bleary with sleep, shivering from the
morning cold, he came up to the Prison Governor, who was standing
beside me, and, taking off his peaked cap and exposing his balding
head, began to request something or other.

In order to form a judgement as to the time of the year escapes are
most often committed, I have utilized the few statistics which I did manage to find and note down. In 1877, 1878, 1885, 1887, 1888 and 1889,
1,501 convicts absconded. This figure breaks down into months thus:

January	117	February	64
March	20	April	20
May	147	June	290
July	283	August	231
September	150	October	44
November	35	December	100

If one were to draw a curve of the escapes on a graph, its highest points would relate to the summer months and to those winter months when the frosts are heaviest. Obviously, the most favourable moments for carrying out escapes are when the weather is warm, when work is being carried on outside the prison, during the seasonal fish run, when the berries are ripening in the taiga, and when the set-tled exiles' potatoes are fully mature, and after these, the time when the sea is covered with ice, when Sakhalin ceases to be an island. Also conducive to the rises in the summer and winter months is the arrival of new parties on the spring and autumn voyages. Least of all abscond in March and April, because during these months the ice breaks up on the rivers, and it is impossible to obtain food either in the taiga or from settled exiles, who by the spring usually no longer have any food left themselves.

In 1889, 15.33 per cent of the average yearly complement escaped from the Alexandrovsk Prison; from the Dooay and Voyevodsk Prisons – where, besides overseers, sentries with rifles also keep guard over the prisoners – 6.4 per cent escaped in 1889, and from the prisons of the Tymovsk District, nine per cent. These figures relate only to the year under review, but if one were to take the entire available total of convicts over the whole duration of their stay on the island, the ratio of those who have run off at various times to the total complement amounts to no less than sixty per cent – that is, of every five individu-als whom you see in the prison or in the streets, three, for a certainty, will have already attempted to decamp. From talks with the exiles I gained the impression they had all gone off at some stage. It is rare for anybody, during the course of his sentence, not to arrange a holiday for himself.*

Usually an escape is planned right back in the hold of the steamer, or in a barge on the Amur, when the convicts are being conveyed to Sakhalin; on the journey, vagabonds, elderly men who have already absconded repeatedly from convict labour, acquaint the young ones with the geography of the island, with the way things are run on Sakhalin, with the means of surveillance, and with those blessings and hardships which flight from Sakhalin holds in store. If, in the transit prisons along the way, and subsequently, in the ships' holds, the vagabonds were kept separate from the newcomers, then the latter would perhaps not be in quite such a hurry to escape. Newcomers usually take flight shortly, and even immediately, after they have been handed over from the ship. In 1879, during the very first days after their arrival, sixty fled instantly, after slaughtering the soldiers on guard.

In order to escape, there is no need whatever for the preparations and precautions described in Korolenko's* excellent story 'The Flight from Sakhalin'. Escapes are strictly forbidden, and are no longer encouraged by the authorities, but the conditions of local prison life, surveillance and convict labour, and the very character of the location itself, are such that in the vast majority of cases it is impossible to prevent an escape. If today you have not managed to get away from the prison through the open gates, then tomorrow you might be able to run off from the taiga, when 200 or 300 men go out to work under the supervision of a single soldier; whoever has not decamped from the taiga will wait a month or two until he is presented to some official whose domestic staff he will join, or to a settled exile for whom he will work. Any kind of subterfuge, deception of authority, breaking out, tunnelling and so forth is necessary only for the minority who are in the fetter blocks, in the punishment cells and in the Voyevodsk Prison, and very likely, for those who work down the mines as well, since along almost the whole way from the Voyevodsk Prison to Dooay stand guards who march back and forth.

There, the outset of an escape is beset with danger, but even so, favourable opportunities come up almost every day. Disguises and all sorts of stratagems, totally unnecessary, are resorted to by seekers and lovers of adventure, such as Golden Hand, who, in order to abscond, disguised herself as a soldier.

Fugitives mostly make their way to the north, to the narrow point of the strait, between the capes of Pogobi and Lazarev, or a little bit further north: there it is deserted, it is easy to conceal oneself from the cordon and one can obtain a boat from a Gilyak, or else make a raft oneself, and cross over to the other side, and if it is winter already, two hours are sufficient to walk over on foot. The further north the point of crossing, the nearer it is to the mouth of the river Amur, which means less danger of dying from starvation and the frost; at the mouth of the Amur are many Gilyak hamlets, and not far off is the town of Nikolayevsk, then Mariinsk, Sofiisk and large Cossack villages where one can obtain employment for the winter as a labourer, and where, even among the government officials, so it is said, there are people who will give to the unfortunate shelter and a bite to eat. It often occurs that fugitives, not knowing where the north is, begin going round in circles and end up back in the place they started from.*

It not infrequently happens that escapees try to sail across the strait somewhere in the vicinity of the prison. Necessary for this is outstanding audacity, an exceptionally good opportunity and, the major thing, repeated experience beforehand, which would instil into them how difficult the journey to the north is through the taiga. The recidivist-vagabonds who flee from the Voyevodsk and Dooay Prisons set off at once to the sea, on the very first or second day after their escape. There are no considerations whatsoever in this regarding storms and perils, but simply sheer brute fear of the chase and the thirst for freedom: "Drown I may, but at least it's in freedom." They usually head down five or ten versts to the south of Dooay, to Agnevo, knock together a raft there and make haste to sail away to the misty shore, separated from them by sixty or seventy versts of cold, stormy sea. During my visit, vagabond Prokhorov-alias-Mylnikov, of whom I have spoken in the previous chapter, fled from the Voyevodsk Prison in this manner.* They sail away on hopper-barges and hay-barges as well, but every time, the sea pitilessly breaks up these barges or else casts them up on the shore. There was one occasion when convicts made off on a launch belonging to the mining department.* Occasionally, convicts get away on the very ships they are loading. In 1883 convict Frantz Kitz tried to escape on the steamship *Triumph* by burying himself in the coal-hole. When they discovered him and dragged him from the hole, he gave just one reply to all their questions: "Give me water, I haven't had anything to drink for five days."

Having somehow or other made it to the mainland, the fugitives bear west, obtaining food "in the name of Christ",* hiring themselves out, where possible, as workmen and pilfering everything that lies in temptation's way. They steal cattle, vegetables and clothing – in a word, anything that can be eaten, worn or sold. They are captured, held for ages in prisons, tried and sent back with dreadful itemized records, but many, as the reader of legal proceedings will be aware, reach as far as Moscow's Khitrov Market,* and even to their own native villages. In Palevo the baker Goryachy, a simple-minded, open and, to all appearances, good-natured man, told me how he had got to his own village, seen his wife and kids, and had once again been exiled to Sakhalin, where he was now completing his second term. It has been said, and the speculation has, incidentally, been expressed in the press, that American whalers have taken Sakhalin fugitives on board their vessels and conveyed them back to America.* This is possible, of course, but I have never heard of a single such case. American whaling vessels plying their trade in the Sea of Okhotsk rarely come near Sakhalin, and it would occur still more rarely that they would approach the island at precisely the time that there were escapees on the deserted eastern coast. According to Mr Kurbsky (*The Voice,* 1875, no. 312), in Indian Territory, on the right bank of the Mississippi, live entire parties of *vaqueros* made up of Sakhalin convicts. These *vaqueros*, if they do in actual fact exist, have made their way to America not on whaling vessels but most probably across Japan. At any rate, escapes not to European Russia, but abroad, although rare, do indeed occur, and of this there is no doubt whatever. As long ago as the 1820s our convicts were fleeing from the Okhotsk saltworks to the "Warm", i.e. the Sandwich, Islands.*

Fear of escaped convicts is enormous, and this explains why the penalties imposed for abscondment are so serious and so startling in their severity. When some notorious vagabond has decamped from the Voyevodsk Prison, or from the fetter block, the rumours of this induce dread not only in the population of Sakhalin but even among the inhabitants of the mainland; the story is narrated that, when Blokha escaped once, the rumour of this threw the inhabitants of Nikolayevsk, on the mainland, into such terror that the local Chief of Police considered it necessary to enquire by telegraph: "Blokha escaped – true?"* The chief danger that escapes pose for society consists in the fact that, firstly, they stimulate and maintain vagabondage, and secondly, they place almost every escapee in an unlawful situation, during which, in the vast majority of cases, he cannot help but commit fresh offences. The largest contingent of recidivists is made up of escapees; the most dreadful and audacious offences on Sakhalin have up till now been committed by escapees.

At the present time the chief method of preventing escape is the use of repressive measures. These measures do reduce the number of escapes, but only to a certain extent, and repression carried to an ideal of perfection would still not cut out the possibility of abscondment. There is a limit beyond which repressive measures cease to have any further effect. It is well known that a convict will continue to dash off even when a sentry is taking aim at him; he is restrained from flight neither by gales nor by the certainty that he will drown. And there is a limit beyond which the repressive measures themselves begin to form the grounds for abscondment. For example, the terrifying penalty for attempted flight, consisting of the addition of several years of convict labour to the original sentence, increases the number of those with long-term and life-term sentences and, by this very fact, also increases the number of escapes. Generally speaking, in the struggle against escape, repressive measures do not have a future, and they are strongly at odds with the ideals of Russian legislation, which sees in punishment first and foremost a means to correction. When the entire energy and ingenuity of a jailer is spent day in, day out in placing a prisoner under such intricate physical conditions that escape is made impossible, this no longer has anything to do with correction, and one can talk only of the transmutation of the prisoner into a wild beast, and the prison into a menagerie. And these measures are impracticable into the bargain; in the first place they always bear like a deadweight on the population which is not guilty of attempted escape, and secondly, confinement in a solidly constructed prison, in shackles, every kind of punishment cell including dark cells, and attachment to the wheelbarrow render a person unfit for labour.

So-called "humane measures" – every improvement in the life of a prisoner, whether it be an extra crust of bread, or hope for a better future – also significantly decrease the number of escapes. I will cite an example: in 1885 twenty-five settled exiles fled, but in 1887, after the excellent harvest of 1886, only seven did so. Settled exiles flee much more infrequently than convicts, and peasants-in-exile hardly ever. Fewest of all abscond from the Korsakovsk District, because the harvests are better there, short-term prisoners predominate, the climate is milder, it is easier to acquire peasant-in-exile's rights than in northern Sakhalin, and on conclusion of penal servitude, in order to earn a crust of bread, it is not necessary to return to the mines. The easier it is for a prisoner to make a living, the less danger there is of him decamping, and in this respect the sort of measures that may be considered extremely deserving of hope are an amelioration of the prison regime, the construction of churches, the establishment of schools and hospitals, maintenance of exiles' families, chances to earn wages and so on.

As I have already mentioned, for every fugitive captured and brought into the prison, army privates, Gilyaks and those generally employed in hunting escapees receive from the government a bounty at the rate of three roubles per head. There is no doubt that the financial reward, so tempting for a hungry person, does help matters, and increases the number of "captured, found dead and killed", but this inducement does not at all compensate for the harm which must inevitably be caused to the population of the island by the base instincts inevitably aroused in them by these three-rouble notes. Anyone compelled to hunt fugitives, as for example a soldier or a settled exile who has been robbed by them, will capture them without the three roubles, while for anybody who joins the pursuit neither in the execution of a duty nor from necessity, but from considerations of a mercenary nature, the hunt is an odious trade, and these three roubles are an indulgence of the most vile character.

According to the data I have with me, of 1,501 fugitives, 1,010 were captured or returned voluntarily; forty were found dead or killed during pursuit; 451 have disappeared without trace. Consequently, of the entire mass of absconders, Sakhalin loses one-third, despite its situation as an island. In the 'Prison Registers' from which I took these figures, those voluntarily returning, and those captured, are shown as one total, while those found dead and those killed during pursuit are not shown separately either, and so it is not known how many fall to the share of bounty hunters and what percentage of escapees perish from soldiers' bullets.*

23

Morbidity and mortality of the exile population. The way the medical service is organized. The infirmary at Alexandrovsk.

IN 1889 THE NUMBER OF CONVICTS of both sexes who were feeble and incapable of labour, in all three districts taken together, reached 632, comprising 10.6 per cent of the total. Thus, there is one convict feeble and incapable of work to every ten. And in the case of those members of the population who are capable, they do not present the impression of full health either. Among the exiled men you will not encounter any who are well nourished, plump and rosy-cheeked: even those settled exiles who do nothing are gaunt and pale. In summer 1889, of 131 convicts working on the road at Tarayka, thirty-seven were sick and the rest presented themselves to the Governor of the Island, who had come to visit them, "in the most awful state: their skin lacerated, many without shirts, bitten all over by mosquitoes, and scratched by boughs of trees, but nobody complained" (Directive no. 318, 1889).

In 1889, 11,309 applied for medical aid; in the medical report from which I have taken this figure, exiles and free-persons are not indicated separately, but the compiler of the report notes that the major contingent of patients was made up of convicts at hard labour. In view of the fact that the soldiers are treated by their own army doctors, and officials and families in their own homes, the thought must arise that this figure of 11,309 consists only of exiles and their families, that convicts form the majority of these, and that therefore each exile and each person involved in the exile system here applied for medical assistance no less than once during the year.*

Concerning the morbidity of the exile population I am able to form judgements only from the report of 1889, but unfortunately it was compiled from the data in the hospital 'Accurate Records',* which are maintained here extremely carelessly, so that I had to resort for further help to the parish registers and copy from them the causes of death over the previous ten years. In almost every instance the cause of death has been recorded by the priests from the certificates of the doctors and doctors' assistants, and there is a lot of fantasy in them,* but in essence this material is the same as that in the 'Accurate Records', no better and no worse. Plainly, both these sources were far from sufficient, and everything that the reader will find below on morbidity and mortality is not a full picture, but purely and simply feeble outlines.

Those diseases which in the report are grouped together under the two separate headings of contagious-epidemic and epidemic have up till the present day not been widespread. Thus, in 1889, measles was recorded only three times, and scarlet fever, diphtheria and croup not once. Death from these diseases, from which children are the principal sufferers, is cited in the parish registers only forty-five times over the previous ten years. Quinsy and so-called "inflammation of the throat" contribute to this figure – they possess a contagious and epidemic character, as was indicated to me on every single occasion by a series of children's deaths in a short space of time. Epidemics would usually begin in September or October, when sick children were brought into the colony on the steamers of the Voluntary Fleet; the course of an epidemic would be prolonged but mild. For instance, in 1880 in the Parish of Korsakovsk, quinsy commenced in October and finished in April of the following year, having carried off ten children in all; the diphtheria epidemic of 1888 began in the Parish of Rykovo in autumn, and continued the whole winter, then travelled to the Parishes of Alexandrovsk and Dooay and petered out there in November 1889, that is to say, it lasted a whole year; twenty children died. Smallpox is recorded once in the report, and over the last ten years eighteen people have died from it; there were two epidemics in the Alexandrovsk District, one in 1886, from December to June, and the other in the autumn of 1889. Those ferocious smallpox epidemics which once used to spread over all the islands in the Seas of Japan and Okhotsk up to and including Kamchatka, and which wiped out whole tribes such as the Ainos, now no longer occur here, or at least nothing is heard of them. Pock-marked faces are often found among the Gilyaks, but chickenpox (*varicella*) is responsible for this, and in all probability, this disease has still not died out among the natives.*

Regarding the various types of typhus, typhoid, or enteric, fever was recorded twenty-three times with a mortality rate of thirty per cent, relapsing typhus and spotted typhus three times each, with no fatal cases. In the parish registers, fifty deaths from typhuses and fevers are shown, but they are all isolated cases, scattered through the registers of all four parishes over a period of ten years. I have not found indications of a typhoid epidemic in a single newspaper report, and in all probability, there have not been any. According to the report, typhoid fever has been observed only in the two northern districts; singled out as causes are the lack of pure drinking water, the pollution of the soil near prisons and rivers, and also, the cramped conditions and overcrowding. I personally did not once come across typhoid fever on northern Sakhalin, although I went round all the cabins and visited all the infirmaries there; some doctors assured me that this form of typhus did not exist on the island at all, and it remained extremely dubious in my mind. In addition, regarding relapsing typhus and spotted typhus, all those cases which have occurred on Sakhalin up to the present day I place in the category of imported illnesses such as scarlet fever and diphtheria; one must assume that the acute infectious diseases have up till now found a soil unfavourable to their development.

"Imprecisely diagnosed feverish illnesses" are recorded seventeen times. In the report, this form of sickness is described as follows: "It has appeared principally in the winter months, come out in the form of a fever of the remitting variety, sometimes with the appearance of *roseola* (rash, eruption) and a general feeling of oppression in the areas of the brain; after a short period, between five and seven days, the fever has passed, and recovery speedily ensued." This typhoid-like sickness is very widespread here, especially in the northern districts, but not even one-hundredth of all the cases get into a report, since the sufferers usually are not treated for this illness but go through it while up and about, or else, if they do go to bed with it, it is at home lying on the stove. As I became convinced during my short stay on the island, the major role in the aetiology of this sickness is played by the chilly climate; those who fall ill are the ones working in cold, damp weather in the taiga, and who spend the night in the open air. People suffering in this way are encountered most frequently on roadworks and on the sites of new settlements. It is a genuine *febris sachalinensis*.

In 1889, twenty-seven were taken ill with croupous pneumonia, of which a third died. Evidently this illness is equally dangerous for both the exiles and the free population. In the parish registers, deaths from it are mentioned 125 times over a ten-year period, twenty-eight per cent of them in May and June, when the weather on Sakhalin is abominable and changeable, and convict labour is commenced far beyond the prison's limits, and forty-six per cent in December, January, February and March, that is, the winter.* Mainly conducive in this respect to infection by croupous pneumonia are the severe cold spells of winter, sharp changes in the weather and heavy labour in bad climatic conditions. In the report of the doctor of the district infirmary, Mr Perlin, of 24th March 1889, a copy of which I have brought with me, it says, among other things: "I have constantly been horrified by the prevalence among the convict labourers of acute inflammation of the lungs, i.e. pneumonia", and one of the causes is, in the opinion of Dr Perlin, that "the conveyance of logs from six to eight vershoks* in diameter and four sazhens in length is carried out by three workmen; assuming the weight of the log to be twenty-five to thirty-five poods, on a snowy track, in warm garments, with the accelerated activity of the respiratory and circulatory systems..." and so on.*

Dysentery, or "the bloody flux", is recorded only five times. At Dooay in 1880, and at Alexandrovsk in 1887, there were apparently epidemics of the bloody flux, and a total of eight deaths is shown in the parish registers over the ten-year period. In old newspaper articles and reports, the bloody flux is mentioned frequently; in all probability, in the old days, it was as common on the island as scurvy. Exiles, soldiers and natives suffered from it, and when this happened, the poor diet was cited as the cause.*

There has not so far been a single case of cholera on Sakhalin. I myself observed erysipelas and hospital gangrene, and obviously neither of these ailments has been eradicated in the infirmaries here. There were no cases of whooping cough in 1889. Intermittent fever is recorded 428 times, of which over half occurred in the Alexandrovsk District; in the report the reasons cited are the heat of the dwellings, without a sufficient current of fresh air, pollution of the soil near the dwellings, convict works in areas subject to seasonal flooding, and the establishment of settlements in such areas. These unhealthy conditions do all exist, but nonetheless the island does not create the impression of being a malarial region. Walking round the cabins, I did not meet anybody suffering from malaria, and I do not recall a single such settlement where they would have complained of this disease. It is very possible that many of those cases recorded were sick with this fever right back in their home territory and arrived on the island with their spleen already enlarged.

Death from "Siberian ulcer" (anthrax) is mentioned only once in the parish registers. Neither glanders nor rabies has yet been recorded on the island.

One-third of the fatal cases are caused by diseases of the respiratory organs, and phthisis (tuberculosis) in particular carries off fifteen per cent. Only Christians are recorded in the parish registers, but if we were to add to this figure the Muslims, who usually die of consumption, the resulting percentage would indeed be a momentous one. At any rate, adults on Sakhalin are susceptible to consumption to a profound extent; here it is the most common and most dangerous ailment. The greatest number die in December, when it is very cold on Sakhalin, and in March and April; fewest die in September and October. Here is a breakdown by age of deaths from tuberculosis:

From 0 to 20 years old	3%
From 20 to 25 years old	6%
From 25 to 35 years old	43%
From 35 to 45 years old	27%
From 45 to 55 years old	12%
From 55 to 65 years old	6%
From 65 to 75 years old	2%

Consequently, the age groups most susceptible to death from consumption are those between twenty-five and thirty-five, and between thirty-five and forty-five – the ages when one is in the prime of life and is able to work.* The majority of those who died of consumption were convicts (sixty-six per cent). It is precisely this predominance of those of working age and of convicts that entitles us to conclude that the considerable mortality from consumption in the exile colony depends chiefly on the unfavourable living conditions in the communal prison cells, and the burden of convict labour, which is beyond a labourer's strength and takes more out of him than the prison diet can put in. The harsh climate, all sorts of privations suffered during convict work, escape and confinement in the punishment cells, the agitated and restless life in the communal cells, inadequate fats in the diet, longing for one's home district – these are the major causes of consumption on Sakhalin.

Syphilis was recorded 246 times in 1889, with five deaths. These were all, so the report says, long-term syphilitics, with secondary and tertiary forms. The syphilitics whom I had the chance of seeing created a pitiful impression; these neglected chronic cases pointed to a total absence of medical inspection, which, given the small numbers of the exile population, could be ideal. For instance, at Rykovo I saw a Jew with syphilitic consumption; he had received no treatment for ages, was little by little falling apart, his family were impatiently awaiting his death – and all this some half a verst from a hospital! In the parish registers death from syphilis is mentioned thirteen times.*

Two hundred and seventy-one sufferers from scurvy were registered in 1889, of whom six died. In the parish registers, death from scurvy is shown nineteen times. Twenty or twenty-five years ago this ailment was encountered on the island far more frequently than in the last decade and many soldiers and prisoners perished from it. Some old newspaper correspondents who had supported the establishment of an exile colony on the island totally denied the scurvy, and yet at the same time extolled *cheremsha* as a sovereign remedy against it, and wrote that the population had laid in hundreds of poods of this remedy for the winter. The scurvy which used to rage on the Tatar Coast would hardly have spared Sakhalin, where living conditions in the posts were certainly no better. Today, the prisoners on the steamers of the Voluntary Fleet mostly bring this sickness with them. This is attested by the medical report, too. The District Governor and the prison doctor at Alexandrovsk told me that, on 2nd May 1890, 500 prisoners arrived on the *St Petersburg* and, of these, no fewer than 100 had scurvy; the doctor placed fifty-one of them in the infirmary and sickbay. One of those with scurvy, a Ukrainian from Poltava, told me he had taken sick with scurvy in the Kharkov Central Clearing Prison.* Of the general nutritional disorders apart from scurvy, I will further mention marasmus,* from which people die on Sakhalin who are still far from elderly but belong to the working age ranges. One is recorded as dying at twenty-seven, another at thirty and the rest at thirty-five, forty-three, forty-six, forty-seven, forty-eight... And this is hardly a slip of the pen from a doctor's assistant or a priest, since "senile marasmus", as the cause of death of individuals who were not old and had not even reached sixty, is mentioned in the parish registers forty-five times. The average length of a Russian exile's life is still not known, but, judging by sight, inhabitants of Sakhalin grow old and decrepit early, and for the most part, a convict or settled exile of forty already looks like an old man.

Exiles do not often attend the infirmary with nervous illnesses. For example, in 1889, neuralgia and cramps were recorded only sixteen times.* Apparently the only patients with nervous ailments* who are treated are those who come in themselves, either on foot or by some kind of transport. There have been twenty-four cases of inflammation of the brain, apoplexy and palsy, with ten deaths, epilepsy is recorded thirty-one times and disorder of the mental faculties twenty-five times.

As I have mentioned already, the mentally ill are not accommodated separately on Sakhalin; during my visit some of them were quartered in the settlement of Korsakovsk together with syphilitics, and, so I was told, one of them had actually become infected with syphilis, while others, living at liberty, laboured on an even footing with the healthy, cohabited, escaped and were tried. I personally met a fair number of lunatics in the posts and settlements. I recall that, in Dooay, one former soldier was continually rambling on about the "ethereal and celestial oceans", about his daughter Nadezhda and the Shah of Persia, and about how he had murdered the sexton of the church at Krestovozdvizhensk. In my presence once at Alexandrovsk a certain Vetryakov, who had served out a five-year term of convict labour, and who had a vacant, imbecilic expression, came up to the Superintendent of Settlements, Mr Y., and proffered his hand to him cordially. "How dare you greet me like this!" said Mr Y. in amazement. It turned out that Vetryakov had come to ask whether it was possible for him to obtain a carpenter's axe from the state. "I shall make myself a lean-to of branches, then I shall build a cabin," he said. This man, already long acknowledged to be a lunatic, was, according to the doctor's diagnosis, a paranoiac. I asked him what his father's name was. "Don't know," he replied. And yet the axe was issued to him all the same. I shall not even mention the cases of moral insanity, or the initial period of progressive paralysis* and so forth, where a fairly precise diagnosis is required. These people all work and are assumed to be healthy. Some arrive already sick, or bring the embryo of an illness with them; for instance, in the parish registers, convict Gorodov is recorded as having died from progressive paralysis; he had been sentenced for premeditated murder, which he perhaps had committed when already ill. Others, though, fall ill on the island, where every day and every hour sufficient grounds arise for a fragile individual with shattered nerves to go out of his mind.*

Gastro-intestinal ailments were recorded 1,760 times in 1889. Over the last ten years 338 have died; sixty-six per cent of this total is made up of children. The most dangerous months for children are July and especially August, in which one-third of the entire total of children's deaths occurs. Adults, too, mainly die from gastro-intestinal disorders in August, perhaps because this is the month of the seasonal fish run, and they gorge themselves. Gastric catarrh is a common malady here. Natives of the Caucasus are always complaining that "my heart aches", and after eating rye bread and the prison cabbage soup, they often suffer vomiting.

In 1889, applications to the infirmary by sufferers with women's ailments were infrequent – 105 times in all. Yet at the same time, there are hardly any healthy women in the colony. In a statement from one of the committees examining convict provisions, in which the Head of the Medical Department participated, it states, among other things: "around seventy per cent of the convict women in exile suffer from chronic female ailments". It has frequently occurred that, among a whole newly arrived party of women prisoners, not a single one has turned out to be healthy.

Conjunctivitis is the most commonly found eye ailment; its epidemic variety has still not been eradicated among the aboriginals.* About the more serious eye disorders I can say nothing, since, in the report, all eye diseases are indicated en masse by the single figure of 211. In the cabins I came across people with one eye and with wall eyes, and some who were blind; I noticed blind children as well.

In 1889, with traumatic injuries, dislocations, fractures, contusions and wounds of every type, 1,217 applied for medical assistance. These were all injuries received at convict labour, from every kind of accident, from attempted flight (gunshot wounds) and from brawls. To this group belong four cases where convict women were brought into the infirmary having been battered by their cohabitants.* Chilblains and frostbite were recorded 290 times.

Over the last ten years there have been 170 cases of unnatural death among the Orthodox Christian population. Of this number, twenty suffered the death penalty by hanging, two were hanged by person or persons unknown, and there were twenty-seven suicides; on northern Sakhalin they shot themselves (one shot himself while standing on sentry duty), while on southern Sakhalin they poisoned themselves with aconite; many were drowned, frozen to death or crushed by trees; one was torn to pieces by a bear. Besides such causes as paralysis of the heart and rupture of the heart, apoplexy, strokes affecting the entire body and so forth, a further seventeen cases of "sudden death" are recorded in the parish registers; over half of these were in the age range from twenty-two to forty, and only one was over fifty.

That is all I am able to say about the incidence of sickness in the exile colony. Despite the extremely low level of infectious disease, I still cannot but acknowledge that it is quite considerable, even if it is only on the basis of the figures just quoted. In 1889, 11,309 sufferers applied for medical aid; but since, during the summertime, the majority of the convicts live and work far away from the prison, where doctors' assistants are attached only to large groups, and since the majority of settled exiles, owing to the long distances and inclement weather, are deprived of the possibility of making their way to the infirmary, either on foot or by transport, this figure relates chiefly to that proportion of the population which lives in the posts, close to the medical centres. According to the data in the report, in 1889 there were 194 deaths, or 12.5 per 1,000. On this index of mortality one could construct a splendid illusion and presume our Sakhalin to be the healthiest spot on earth; but the following considerations must be taken into account: under normal conditions, one half of all deaths relate to children, and a little less than a quarter to old age; on Sakhalin, however, there are very few children, and practically no old people, so that, in actual fact, the coefficient of 12.5 applies only to those of working age; in addition, it is presented as lower than it is in reality, since, in calculating the figure, the population was taken as 15,000, that is, at least one and a half times larger than it in actual fact was.*

At the present time on Sakhalin there are three medical centres, one per district – at Alexandrovsk, Rykovo and Korsakovsk. The hospitals are called by the old names of district infirmaries, and the cabins or rooms in which those suffering from mild forms of sickness are placed are still called sickbays. There is supposed to be one junior physician per district, and in overall command is the head of the medical department, a fully qualified consultant doctor of medicine.* The military detachments have their own infirmaries and physicians, and it happens not infrequently that military physicians temporarily perform the duties of prison doctors; for instance, during my visit, owing to the absence of the Director of the Medical Department, who had travelled off to the Prison Exhibition, and of the prison doctor, who had handed in his resignation, the infirmary at Alexandrovsk was being run by a military physician; likewise, when I was present during the flogging at Dooay a military physician replaced the prison one. The infirmaries here follow the legal regulations for civil medical institutions and are maintained at prison expense.

I shall say a few words about the Alexandrovsk infirmary. It consists of several complexes of buildings constructed on the barrack-hut system, calculated to hold 180 beds.* As I approached the infirmary on foot, the heavy round logs of the new barracks gleamed in the sun, and the buildings gave off a smell of conifer trees. In the dispensary, everything is new, everything is shiny, there is even a bust of Botkin* moulded by a convict from a photograph. "A little bit different from him, really," said the doctor's assistant, glancing at this bust. As usual, there were enormous boxes with the Latin inscriptions *cortex* and *radix*,* a good half of which had long since gone out of use. I carried on into the barrack huts where the patients were kept. There, in the gangway between the rows of beds the floor was strewn with fir twigs.* The bedsteads were of wood. On one lay a convict from Dooay with his throat cut; the wound was about half a vershok long, dry and gaping; his breath could be heard rasping harshly. The patient complained that he had been pinned down by a cave-in on convict work, and his side had been injured; he had requested to go into the sickbay, but the doctor's assistant would not admit him, and the convict, unable to endure this offensive behaviour, had attempted suicide – he had wanted to cut his throat. There were no bandages on his neck; the wound had been left to look after itself. On the right of this patient, three or four arshins from him, was a Chinaman with gangrene, while on the left was a convict with erysipelas. In the corner was another with erysipelas… The bindings on the surgical patients were filthy; they consisted of some kind of thick ship's cord,* which had a suspect look about it, as if people had been walking all over it. The doctor's assistants and medical staff are undisciplined, do not understand questions and create an exasperating impression. The convict Sozin – he had formerly, when free, been a doctor's assistant – alone is evidently familiar with European Russian procedures, and it seemed as if, out of this whole hospital rabble, he was the one person who, by his attitude, did not disgrace the god Aesculapius.

A little later I received out-patients for treatment. The surgery is next to the dispensary and is new; it smells of fresh wood and varnish. The table at which the doctor sits is enclosed by a wooden grille, as in a bank, so that, consequently, during the reception, the patient cannot draw close, and the doctor for the most part examines him at a distance. Next to the doctor at the table sits a senior doctor's assistant, not saying a word, playing with a pencil and appearing as if he is an assistant examiner at a viva voce. Here, at the entrance door of the surgery, stands an overseer with a revolver, and some oafish individuals or other, both men and women, roam backwards and forwards. These curious arrangements embarrass patients, and I do not believe one single syphilitic or one single woman could bring themselves to speak about their ailment in the presence of this overseer with his revolver, and the louts. There were not many patients. It was all either *febris sachalinensis,* or eczema, or "my heart aches", or malingerers; the convict patients earnestly requested to be excused labour. A little boy was brought up with a boil on his neck. It had to be lanced. I requested a scalpel. The doctor's assistant and two of the uncouth characters leapt from their places and darted off somewhere, and in a little while returned and handed me a scalpel. This instrument proved to be blunt, but they told me that this could not be so, since the metalcraftsman had only recently sharpened it. Once again the assistant and the bumpkins went tearing off and after a two- or three-minute wait brought me another scalpel. I began to cut – and this also turned out to be blunt. I asked for a solution of carbolic acid; they gave it to me but not very rapidly – evidently, this liquid is not used here very often. There was no washbasin, no balls of cotton wool, no probes, no decent scissors and not even water in sufficient quantity. The average daily number of out-patients at this infirmary is eleven, the average yearly number (over five years) 2,581; the average daily number of in-patients is 138. At the infirmary there are a senior doctor and junior doctor, two doctors' assistants, a midwife (one for the two districts) and, dreadful to relate, there are sixty-eight auxiliary staff: forty-eight male, twenty female.* In 1889, 27,832 roubles 96 copecks were expended on this hospital.* According to the report for 1889, there were twenty-one forensic-medical examinations and post-mortems in all three districts taken together. Seven patients with injuries were examined, fifty-eight pregnant women, and sixty-seven were tested to determine their capacity to undergo corporal punishments imposed by the courts.

I shall here give extracts from the same report concerning hospital stock. In all three infirmaries together there were: one set of gynaecological instruments; one set of laryngoscopic instruments; two maximum thermometers – both smashed; nine thermometers "for measuring body temperature" – two smashed; and one thermometer "for measuring high temperatures"; one trochar; three Pravaz syringes* – one with the needle broken; twenty-nine tin syringes; nine pairs of scissors – two broken; thirty-four clyster pipes; one drainage pipe; one large mortar and pestle – cracked; one shaving strap; and fourteen cupping glasses.

From the 'Records of purchase and outlay of medicaments in the Medical Institutions of the Civilian Sector of Sakhalin Island' it is clear that, during the year under review, the following was expended: 36.5 poods of hydrochloric acid and 26 poods of lime chloride, 18.5 *funty* of carbolic acid, 56 *funty* of aluminum crudum, and over a pood of camphor; 1 pood 9 *funty* of camomile, 1 pood 8 *funty* of quinquina bark, and 5.5 *funty* of Cayenne pepper (how much surgical spirit was expended, the records do not say), 1 pood of oak bark, 1.5 poods of mint, 1.5 poods of arnica, 3 poods of althaea root, 3.5 poods of turpentine, 3 poods of high-grade olive oil, 1 pood 10 *funty* of inferior-grade olive oil, 1.5 poods of iodoform... In all, not counting the chloride, hydrochloric acid, surgical spirit, disinfectants and material for dressings, according to the figures in the records, 63.5 poods of medicaments were expended, and so the population of Sakhalin can brag that, in 1889, they all underwent the most enormous dosing.

From the articles of law relating to convicts' health I will cite two: (1) labour which affects the health in a harmful manner is not permitted, even at the request of the prisoners themselves (Government Recommendation, received Royal Assent 6th January 1886, Article 11); and (2) pregnant women are exempted from work until delivery, and those who have delivered are exempted for a duration of forty days. After this period labour is mitigated for those women breastfeeding their children to the degree necessary to prevent harm to the mother herself or to the baby she is feeding. An eighteen-month period is stipulated for convicted women to breastfeed their babies (Article 297, *Statutes on Exiles,* 1890 edition).

Note on the Text

The text of *From Siberia* and *Sakhalin Island* has been translated from volume 14/15 (bound as one book) of Chekhov's *Works*, from the thirty-volume *Polnoye sobraniye sochinenii i pisem* (*Complete Collection of Works and Letters*) produced in Moscow in 1978 by the Nauka (Science) publishing house. I have translated Chekhov's letters from volume four of the *Letters*, edited by M.L. Semanova, in the *Complete Collection* cited above.

Notes

p. 3, *From Siberia*: Chekhov wrote six articles which were printed in *New Times* under the general title 'From Siberia'. A further three articles were sent later. These articles were printed under the general heading 'Through Siberia' in *New Times*. Chekhov is known to have preferred the title 'From Siberia' in referring to all the articles collectively. *New Times* was one of the biggest newspapers of the time, and was owned by Aleksey Suvorin, an acquaintance of Chekhov's.

p. 3, *the coach driver*: A traveller wishing to reach a certain point in Siberia would buy a pass from the post office in European Russia for the necessary number of journeys. He would then be able, on presentation of this pass, to requisition horses from any post station in Siberia. He could either hire a sledge or carriage – the payment for which was included in the cost of the pass – or else, if he so wished, take his own carriage and simply commandeer horses (or reindeer or dogs). The exile population were meant to work as sledge- and carriage-drivers, but the free population competed with them and offered a much better service. In addition, "free" drivers would not take travellers to dingy post stations for the night, but to "friends" – for which they obviously received a cut of the takings. This is why Chekhov seems to spend most of his nights in 'From Siberia' in comfortable private homes.

p. 3, *migrants*: In the 1880s the Russian government tried to encourage voluntary resettlement in Siberia by European Russians, in order to strengthen the country's hold on its newly acquired territories. Migrants were offered incentives from the state, such as large plots of fertile land, help towards the first year's purchase of grain, tools, wood for building a cabin and so on. Vast numbers of European Russians, driven to try to start a new life by lack of land in their regions, poor-quality soil and famine, took advantage of the offer. However, it should be remembered that there was as yet no railway system into Siberia from European Russia, and, if an entire family was emigrating en masse, hiring several carriages was out of the question; therefore almost all migrants walked into Siberia. The majority of these came from the Kursk and Tambov Regions, two Central Russian provinces where the peasant's problems were particularly severe at this time. Over one-third of them carried out their trek in May and June, in the short Russian spring and summer.

Many migrants, having traipsed a vast distance, found themselves bitterly disillusioned. Through bureaucratic incompetence, either there was no land allocated to them or the local authorities had insufficient funds to provide them with the promised tools and grain. A large number very soon began to walk all the way back home again.

p. 4, *the stove*: Russian cabins generally contained large earthen stoves which occupied over a quarter of the internal floor space. Planks were suspended above the stove, being either attached to the wall or suspended from the ceiling, and during cold weather the family would sleep directly on the stove or over it on these planks.

p. 4, *cabin*: The word *izba*, which I have translated as "cabin", is usually rendered as "hut". This is grossly misleading, implying as it does that most Russian peasants and their families lived in something like a rickety garden shed or a dog kennel. Peasants' cabins were large, roomy structures sophisticatedly designed for rural living. They usually had a passage running down the centre from the front yard to the back; on the left side would be the living quarters for the family and any day-labourers hired to help in farming or around the house. These quarters would contain the stove for heating and cooking, and spinning and weaving equipment for the women. On the right of the entrance passage would be storerooms for grain, apples, agricultural implements and so forth.

p. 4, *the Kama*: The River Kama is one of the main tributaries of the Volga and one of the largest rivers of European Russia.

p. 4, *bast sandals*: Bast sandals were made from lime bark. These were typical Russian footwear of the time, and they are still worn in outlying Russian regions in summer.

p. 5, *versts*: One verst is equivalent to 1.06 kilometres.

p. 5, *brick tea*: This tea is generally made from the very worst-quality tea leaves, which are mixed with a small quantity of edible adhesive gum and pressed into blocks seven or eight inches long, four or five inches wide and an inch or so thick. When making tea, a little is crumbled into the teapot and water poured over it.

p. 6, *Ishim*: Ishim is the major administrative town of the Tobolsk District – a section of the Tobolsk Region – and is situated on both sides of the River Ishim, a tributary of the Irtysh. In the 1890s the town had a population of around 8,000.

p. 6, *nelma*: A kind of white salmon.

p. 6, *Listening to... have mothers*: Most Russian terms of abuse either relate to parts of one's mother's anatomy, or else take the form of injunctions to depart and perform intimate acts with one's own mother or the mother of the Devil.

p. 7, *dorsal tabes*: Also known by the more common modern name, loco-motor ataxia, dorsal tabes is manifested by disordered movements when walking, and is often a symptom of advanced syphilis.

p. 7, *tarantas*: A large four-wheeled carriage, consisting of a boat-shaped body without seats, with a heavy leather top, and a curtain to close the conveyance against storms. The body of the *tarantas* was moulded on to two or more short poles which united the front and rear axle-trees and served as springs to break the jolting on the road. Travellers stowed their luggage at the bottom, covered it with straw or rags, and lay on it.

p. 7, *An Egyptian dove*: A type of pigeon (*Columbia risoria* – literally "laughing dove") which, according to *Dahl's Dictionary* (St Petersburg 1880–82) sounds as if it is "overflowing with raucous laughter" – rather different from the "groans and moans" of Chekhov's doves.

p. 7, *sazhen*: One *sazhen* is equivalent to seven feet, or 2.13 metres.

p. 7, *troika*: A group of three horses attached to a small carriage or sledge.

p. 10, *The cabins... of board*: Peasant cabins were traditionally roofed with straw. A well-to-do peasant, as a status symbol, would roof his cabin with boards, and so an abundance of roofs of wooden boards rather than straw would have been a sign of a prosperous village.

p. 11, *free driver*: Exiles were meant to take up gainful employment in whatever place they were deported to, and a very obvious form of work, often subsidized by the state, was acting as coach-drivers or ferrymen to the free population. However, very soon, the free peasantry themselves realized that these could be lucrative occupations and offered their own carriages, sledges or boats for hire. A point that Chekhov makes throughout his book is that, wherever a free population and an exile population are in competition over the same type of labour, the free population invariably proves superior. Thus, with the growth of the free population in Siberia by migration, the whole point of using exile labour to develop Russia's new territories was proving a waste of time, money and effort.

p. 11, *chamber*: "Chamber" (*gornitza*) is a word that, although it had passed out of use long before in Central Russia, had remained in currency in Siberian dialect. Chekhov uses several Siberian dialect words in his travel sketches, and occasionally one occurs in *Sakhalin Island*. I have tried to render these with suitable equivalents.

p. 11, *the corner*: Russian cabins had a corner, called the "Beautiful Corner", in which hung the family icon. Below this icon usually stood a candle, which could be lit in the evenings, making the icon the focal point of the room. This corner was normally the right-hand one facing the front door, so that any visitors, on entering, could bow towards it and cross themselves.

p. 11, *St George the Victorious*: The saint who vanquished the dragon and became the patron saint of England.

p. 11, *Battenburg, Skobelyev*: Alexander Battenberg (1857–93) was a Bulgarian prince who became an Austrian general. M.D. Skobelyev (1843–82) was a Russian general who distinguished himself in the Russo-Turkish War of the late 1870s.

p. 12, *Bliny*: Small pancakes served with caviar, sour cream, herring, etc.

p. 12, *St Nikolai's Day*: This takes place on 9th May. Ascension Day 1890 was on 10th May. Chekhov wrote to his relations on 14th May 1890: "On St Nikolai's Day, 9th May, there was a frost." (In Russia 9th May would have been 21st May in the West, since Russia did not convert to the Gregorian calendar until 1917: consequently their dates were twelve days behind Western dates.)

p. 12, *townswoman... gentlewoman*: A "townswoman" was a member of the *meshchane* or "lower-middle-class townsfolk", a social class of town-dweller some notches below the wealthy "merchantry". Although the lady described in Chekhov's sketch was a townswoman, she apparently "dressed like a 'gentlewoman'" – that is, like a lady far above her station. She was therefore, by pretending to be a "lady", probably attempting to conceal the fact that she was an ordinary woman with an illegitimate baby from one of the local towns.

p. 14, *vagabonds*: The term "vagabond", as it is used in this translation, refers to convicts and exiles who had escaped from their places of settlement, who would often terrorize the other inhabitants of Siberia.

p. 14, *pood*: A pood is equivalent to 16.38 kilograms, or 36 pounds.

p. 15, *Dover's powders*: Also known as ipecacuanha, this was made from 10 per cent each of powdered ipecacuanha and opium and 80 per cent of lactose. The substance was invented by Captain Thomas Dover (1660–1742) and was used in the treatment of coughs, colds and influenza.

p. 16, *arshin*: One *arshin* is equivalent to twenty-eight inches, or 0.71 metres.

p. 17, *Yermak... chainmail*: In the sixteenth century the legendary Cossack chieftain Yermak was one of the leaders of the campaign to expand Russian territories eastward, and this involved, among other things, waging a constant battle against the local tribespeople. In 1584, pursued by Tatars, and badly wounded, he tried to reach his boat on the River Irtysh, but missed his footing, slipped into the water and was dragged down by his armour.

p. 17, *trade guild of peasant proprietors*: These guilds or associations would guarantee high standards of service, share out the labour and divide profits equally (see note to p. 36 below). The word "peasant" here implies that they are "free", i.e. non-exile, ferrymen.

p. 18, *Assessing Magistrate's*: It is difficult to find an equivalent in English of the Russian word *zasedatel*, translated here as "Assessing Magistrate". The bearer of this job description was a member of the local judiciary department, who would travel round the administrative district that the department covered, dealing with trivial cases and complaints, making sure the exiles were maintaining whatever employment they had undertaken and had not decamped, and in general ensuring the smooth running of his area. The term has also been translated as "Itinerant Prosecutor".

p. 19, *Russia*: Inhabitants of Siberia very frequently used to refer to European Russia as "Russia", almost as if it were a foreign country.

p. 23, *Prisoners' Detachments*: In the first part of the eighteenth century an unsuccessful attempt was made to divide prisoners' hard labour into work in mines, military strongpoints and factories. The mines were considered the most severe penalty, followed by the fortresses, then the factories. "Prisoners' Detachments" were used to penalize those whose offences, although not trivial, were still not considered to warrant labour in the mines in Siberia. Either the detachments were kept in prisons in European Russia, and sent out under guard to repair the roads, carry out construction works and so on, or else more serious offenders would be sent to Russian military strongpoints in Siberia to fulfil the same functions as part of the Russian state's policy of expansion. By the time Chekhov was writing, this division of labour into factory, mine and fortress work had long been abandoned as impracticable, and the "scale of penalties" had been redefined in terms of length of sentence and place where sentence was to be served. Anybody sentenced to four years' or more convict labour was sent to Siberia to serve his term; those sentenced to under four years' convict labour were placed in a "labour battalion" which was, as previously, maintained in European Russia and utilized for works useful to society. However, the whole unfairness and arbitrariness of the Russian system was demonstrated by what happened when, as Chekhov mentions here, on completion of a prisoner's sentence the peasant assembly of his village – or, if he were a townsman, the urban society or guild of which he almost compulsorily had to be a member – refused, for no reason whatever, to accept him back. In such a case the authorities would have no choice but to exile the ex-prisoner to Siberia for life. He would, of course, not be sent there as a hard-labour convict, since he had already expiated any guilt by his previous sentence; instead he would be exiled as a "permanent settler" and allotted a place to live by the authorities, possibly being given some land. But he could never ever return to his home in European Russia. The extraordinary injustice of this procedure does not need to be pointed out. Not surprisingly it bred criminals, since the ex-prisoner, now exiled for no reason, would often try illegally to flee back to Russia, would be arrested, and either would be flogged as a vagabond and sent back to Siberia, or else, if his identity was discovered, would be sent to hard labour in Siberia for breaking his conditions of exile.

p. 25, *Nozdryov*: A loudmouthed drunkard and card-sharper in the novel *Dead Souls* (1842) by Nikolai Gogol (1809–1852).

p. 25, *Taganrog Customs House Case*: In 1885, 35 individuals, including many people of very high social rank, were tried for systematic embezzlement of money and goods from the Taganrog customs house between 1878 and 1881. Of these 35, 18 were senior officials of the customs service. Several million roubles in all had gone missing. Taganrog was, incidentally, Chekhov's birthplace.

p. 25, *Whit Sunday*: In 1890, this was on 20th May.

p. 26, *family bathhouses*: A euphemism for brothels.

p. 26, *Ribot's*: Paul Ribot (1839–1916) was a French psychologist. His book *Les Maladies de la volonté* was known to Chekhov in Tomashevsky's Russian translation of 1884.

p. 26, *taiga*: A Russian term – now adopted internationally – for the dense, impassable coniferous woodlands covering most of central Siberia.

p. 27, *shoulder knot*: Senior military officers wore shoulder knots, or aiguillettes, of gold and silver thread on the right shoulder. Junior officers, army engineers, topographers and so forth wore cotton braid tipped with metal, also on the right shoulder.

p. 28, *Geographical Society*: Presumably, "Geographical Society" refers to the Imperial Russian Geographical Society founded in 1845. As the Tsarist Empire expanded to the north, east and south, this society sent out geographers, topographers, ethnographers and other experts to explore the new lands.

p. 30, *Mariinsk*: The Mariinsk to which Chekhov is referring here is a town in Tomsk Province on the north bank of the river Kiy. According to a survey conducted in 1894, it then had 7,421 inhabitants. It is not to be confused with the tiny settlement of the same name mentioned in chapter 1 of *Sakhalin Island*, which lies on the north bank of the river Amur in the Primorskaya Region and which at the time had 200 inhabitants.

p. 30, *Kazbeks and Elbruses*: Kazbek is a peak in the Caucasus 16,546 feet (5,043 m) in height. Elbrus is the tallest peak in the Caucasus, being 18,470 feet (5,629 m) high.

p. 33, *F.F. Vigel... Goncharov*: F.F. Vigel (1786–1856) was a traveller and writer who in his *Reminiscences* (Moscow, 1866) described a tour he had made through Siberia. I.A. Goncharov (1812–91) was a Russian writer, most famous for *Oblomov*. His *Frigate 'Pallada'* (1858) had been a favourite book of Chekhov's since the latter's youth. This work consisted of Goncharov's reminiscences of a round-the-world trip he had undertaken on the *Pallada* from 1852 to 1855, when he had voluntarily acted as secretary to a Russian voyage of exploration.

p. 34, *Sibiryakov*: A.M. Sibiryakov (1849–93) was a renowned explorer of maritime routes from Europe to Siberia.

p. 34, *the Moscow Sokolniki*: The Sokolniki was a large park to the north-east of Moscow.

p. 36, *trade association of vagabonds*: Almost every social or working group in Tsarist Russia formed "associations" (*arteli* in Russian) to protect their interests, even criminals marching under guard into Siberia and convicts at hard labour. The vagabonds, although they themselves were outside the law in not having identity documents – neither, of course, were they permitted to have gold in their possession (see first note to p. 43) – would have formed an "association" to protect their interests when dealing clandestinely in gold with other illegal dealers.

p. 37, *even a flea couldn't carp at it*: An obscure reference to a tale by Nikolai Leskov (1831–95) entitled *The Tale of the Cross-eyed Left-handed Smith from Tula and the Steel Flea*. The "left-handed smith" (who is known throughout the tale by the nickname "Levsha", i.e. "Leftie") undertakes, in competition with English blacksmiths, to shoe a steel flea to show the superiority of Russian exponents of the craft.

p. 41, *the town of Nikolayevsk*: Nikolayevsk was established on the River Amur in 1850 as a trading post and military strongpoint in order to reinforce Russia's eastward expansion. When the Primorskaya Region of the Russian Empire was created in 1856 (see third note to p. 59), Nikolayevsk was declared its capital. However, in 1872 the administration of Russian Far Eastern ports and rivers was moved to Vladivostok, and in 1884, with the establishment of the Amur River Territory (see third note to p. 59 and third note to p. 80), the entire administration of this area was transferred to Khabarovsk. According to the first reliable census of the area, conducted in 1897, the population of this once thriving regional capital was 4,417 (3,398 male, 1,019 female).

p. 42, *merchant*: "Merchant" means an "upper-middle-class town-dweller".

p. 42, *Gilyaks*: The Gilyaks are one of the indigenous tribes inhabiting Sakhalin and Siberia. Chekhov gives an excellent ethnographic portrayal of the Gilyaks of Sakhalin in chapter 11.

p. 42, *Khabarovsk*: Khabarovsk was set up on the right bank of the Amur in 1858 as a military post for the same reasons as Nikolayevsk was created. It became the capital of the Primorskaya Region in 1884 when the administration was transferred there from Nikolayevsk. When the Amur River Territory was formed in the same year, its Governor General established his residence at Khabarovsk. According to the 1897 census, the town's population was 14,933 (11,674 male, 3,259 female).

p. 43, *embezzling gold*: One of the forms of hard labour for convicts in Eastern Siberia was work in the gold mines, which extracted about 3,200 imperial pounds of gold per year for the Exchequer. It was, of course, an offence for convicts to keep any of this gold for themselves; similarly, private gold-prospectors had to sell any gold dust they had discovered to the accredited government agencies. However, profits from gold embezzlement were so great that almost everybody in Siberia engaged in it, and there were even thriving illegal markets in small Siberian towns trading in gold and silver at certain fixed periods every year.

p. 43, *Chinese vagabonds*: Chekhov mentions "Chinese" people on numerous occasions in his narrative. However, these are almost certainly not native Chinese, or Chinese who still had a base in China, but a group called in Russian the "Manzes". These were either Chinese who had fled from the law in their native country, or their descendants, and they were mainly settled in the East Siberian Ussuri Area and the Amur Region. Brockhaus's *Encyclopedic Dictionary* of 1896 says: "They are for the most part vagabonds, poor workmen, labourers hired by the day, criminals and other dregs from China. They are morose, have high opinions of themselves, and are uncouth and slovenly. They are Buddhists."

p. 43, *hunchbacks*: Vagabonds or escaped convicts were called "hunchbacks" because they bore large knapsacks on their backs. They were also called "kettlemen" since one of the items they invariably carried was a large kettle, either on their back or strapped around their waist.

p. 44, *corylopsis*: Corylopsis is a deciduous shrub of the genus *Hamamelidaceae* which produces fragrant primrose-yellow, cup-shaped flowers. It is native to the Eastern Himalayas, China and Japan.

p. 44, *antres vast... touch heaven*: See *Othello*, Act I, Sc. 3, ll. 140–41.

p. 44, *the famous astronomer B*: This astronomer was F.A. Bredikhin (1834–1904), Director of the Pulkovo Observatory, which was about nine miles from St Petersburg.

p. 44, *One prisoner... her husband*: On the Amur steamers, and on the *Baikal*, prisoners are quartered on the deck along with third-class passengers. Once, coming out at dawn for a stroll on the forecastle, I saw soldiers, women, children, two Chinese and prisoners in shackles fast asleep, pressed up close to each other; they were covered with dew and it was quite chilly. The escort guard was standing in the middle of the pile of bodies, holding his rifle with both hands, and he also was asleep. (CHEKHOV'S NOTE)

p. 45, *the intelligentsia*: The term "intelligentsia", or, as I have sometimes rendered it, the "educated classes", did not mean in Russian quite what it does in modern English, where it tends to imply artistic, intellectual circles. In nineteenth-century Russia the term implied the whole class of people with higher education, but especially those members of the professions – doctors, lawyers, teachers, civil servants, etc. – who had risen from the non-privileged classes to receive higher education and form a career for themselves. Up until the mid-nineteenth-century, higher education and entry into the professions had been fraught with all kinds of difficulties (although not actually made impossible) for the lower classes. But in the 1860s, there was an enormous expansion of secondary and higher education, and the universities were opened to previously excluded groups, such as women. This soon meant that, as these newly educated people rose in their professions, the old social classes (gentry, merchants, peasantry, etc.), to which all Russian citizens had compulsorily to belong, began to assume far less importance. These educated classes tended, of course, to be progressive in temperament and were highly critical of the crumbling system of Tsarist autocracy. Another term meaning roughly the same as intelligentsia was *raznochintzy* ("of various ranks"), implying the class of newly educated people who did not come from the ranks of nobility or gentry (see second note to p. 158).

p. 45, *generals... civilian*: Civilian generals were senior civil servants possessing a rank equivalent to an army general.

p. 46, *the Ainos*: An ethnographic description of the Ainos, the indigenous people of southern Sakhalin and the northern Japanese islands, is given by Chekhov in chapter 14.

p. 46, *an island... by straits*: La Pérouse writes that they called the island "Choko", but the Gilyaks must have applied the name to something else and he did not understand them. On the map drawn up by the Russian Krasheninnikov (in 1752) a river "Chukha" is shown on the western coast of Sakhalin. Does not this "Chukha" bear some resemblance to "Choko"? It's relevant to mention here that La Pérouse writes that, when drawing the island and calling it "Choko", a Gilyak also drew a small river. The word "choko" means "we". (CHEKHOV'S NOTE)

p. 46, *drawing a line... peninsula*: An observation of Nevelskoy's should be quoted in this respect: the natives usually draw a line between shores to indicate that it's possible to sail from one shore to the other in a boat, that is to say, that a strait exists between these shores. (CHEKHOV'S NOTE)

p. 46, *Broughton*: William Henry Broughton was an English sailor who visited Sakhalin in 1796 and wrote the book *A Voyage of Discovery to the North Pacific Ocean: Performed in His Majesty's Ship "Providence" and her Tender in the Years 1795–98* (London, 1804). The title of this book was given in full in the rough draft of *Sakhalin Island*, but omitted in the final version.

p. 47, *Broughton... La Pérouse... Kruzenshtern... happier*: The fact that three thoughtful and serious explorers should repeat exactly the same error as if they had come to a previous agreement speaks for itself. That they did not discover a way into the Amur was because they had at their disposal the most inadequate resources for exploration, but the most important thing was that, being people of genius, they suspected and were almost on the point of guessing that the truth was different and they must have considered the possibility. That the Sakhalin isthmus and peninsula are not myths but did indeed exist at one time has now been proven. (CHEKHOV'S NOTE)

p. 47, *Nevelskoy... and patriotic*: Details may be found in his book *Exploits of Russian Naval Officers in the Far East of Russia, 1849–55.* (CHEKHOV'S NOTE)

p. 48, *He was a man... deprivations heroically*: When Nevelskoy's wife, Yekaterina Ivanovna, travelled from European Russia to join her husband, she was ill, but rode 1,100 versts in twenty-three days, through swampy marshes, wild mountains and taiga regions, and over the glaciers of the Okhotsk Highway. Nevelskoy's most gifted associate, N.K. Boshnyak, who discovered Emperor's Harbour* when he was only twenty, "a dreamer and child" – as one of his colleagues called him – related in his memoirs: "We all crossed together on the supply ship *Baikal* to Ayan* and there transferred to the flimsy barque *Shelekhov*. When the barque began to sink, nobody could persuade Mrs Nevelskoy to make for the shore first. 'Captain and officers leave last,' she said, 'and I'll only leave the barque when not a single woman or child is left on board.' And this she did. By this time, the barque was already keeling over..." Further on, Boshnyak writes that he and his companions were often in the company of Mrs Nevelskoy, but they never heard a single complaint or reproach – on the contrary, "one could always observe in her a serene and proud consciousness of that bitter but lofty place preordained for her by Providence. Since the men went on expeditions, she usually spent the winter alone, in rooms where the temperature was as low as 5°C. When in 1852 the boats carrying provisions did not arrive from Kamchatka, everybody found themselves in a situation that was worse than desperate. There was no milk for the unweaned babies, no fresh food for the sick, and several people died of scurvy. Mrs Nevelskoy handed over her one and only cow for general disposal, and everything fresh was used for the common good. She treated the natives simply and with such consideration that it was noticed even by the uncouth savages. And she was then only nineteen years old"

(Lieutenant Boshnyak, 'Expedition within the Amur Region', *Morskoy Sbornik (Maritime Compendium)*, 1859, no. 11). Her touching treatment of the Gilyaks is mentioned also by her husband in his memoirs. "Yekaterina Ivanovna," he wrote, "would sit the Gilyaks in a circle on the floor, round a large bowl of porridge or tea, in the one room in our outhouse, which served as a hall, drawing room and dining room. Revelling in being entertained in such a way, they would very frequently pat the hostess on the shoulder and send her off, sometimes to fetch tobacco, sometimes tea." (CHEKHOV'S NOTE)

* Emperor's Harbour was renamed "Soviet Harbour" after 1917, and still bears this name today.

* Ayan was a settlement of 200 people (according to the 1897 census) who worked as whalers and traded with the indigenous tribes.

p. 48, *d'Anville's... atlas*: *Nouvel Atlas de la Chine, de la Tartaire Chinoise et de Thibet*, 1737. (CHEKHOV'S NOTE)

p. 48, *Karafto or Karaftu*: When the Japanese invaded Sakhalin in 1905 and retook its southern section, they renamed it "Karafto". In Japanese atlases it is still so named.

p. 48, *The Japanese were the first... exploration*: In 1808 the Japanese land surveyor Mamia-Rinzo, voyaging in a small boat along the western shore, was a frequent visitor to the Tatar coast, and more than once sailed from the island to the mainland and back. He was the first to prove that Sakhalin was an island. The Russian naturalist F. Shmidt praises his map very highly; he finds it "all the more remarkable because it is based evidently on his own independent surveys". (CHEKHOV'S NOTE)

p. 50, *De-Kastri Bay... unthinkable*: On the present use, and proposed future utilization of this bay, see K.A. Skalkovsky, *Russian Trade in the Pacific Ocean*, page 75. (CHEKHOV'S NOTE)

p. 51, *Mariinsk*: A small settlement on the right bank of the river Amur (see the first note to p. 30).

p. 51, *Tungus*: An Eastern Siberian people of Mongol stock. In modern-day ethnography they are called "Evenks".

p. 52, *a sterlet*: A small type of Siberian salmon.

p. 53, *Ayu-Dag*: A peak 11 miles from Yalta, about 1,800 feet high, with a conical summit surmounted by woodland.

p. 54, *Caucasians*: Inhabitants of what was then called the Caucasian

District, which stretched from the Black Sea to the Caspian Sea, and from the border of European Russia to Turkey. A large part of this area had been conquered by the Tsarist Empire in the late eighteenth and early nineteenth centuries, although the entire region finally fell to the Russians only after the Russo-Turkish War of 1877. The land is now occupied by the three independent states of Georgia, Armenia and Azerbaijan. This area is, of course, much warmer than Russia proper; therefore the Caucasians would have suffered far more than the Russians from the climate of Sakhalin.

p. 54, *Sakhalino*: A parody of 'Borodino', Lermontov's poem about the battle of the same name fought by the Russians against Napoleon in 1812, the first line of which is "Tell me then, Uncle, was it really in vain…"

p. 54, *Class 10 post*: A reference to the Table of Ranks: see the first note to p. 224.

p. 54, *woman*: There are two words in Russian for "woman". One (*baba*) could be slightly derogatory and tends to imply a woman of the peasant or urban working classes, or an uneducated woman in general, while the other (*dama*) is used for more respectable, educated women from the higher classes of society. Except where the context has made absolutely clear which meaning is implied, I have usually translated the first as "woman" and the second as "lady". Thus, for example, if in the text one reads "A certain lady told me that…", this implies that it is not one of the convict women but a lady from the administration, or perhaps an official's wife, or – a very remote possibility – a female political prisoner from the nobility, gentry or intelligentsia.

p. 55, *overalls*: What I have translated as overalls (*khalat*) should not be construed as looking like a boiler suit but was more in the nature of traditional peasant garb – a long smock made of coarse material, extending almost to the knees and secured around the waist. Caps were almost always worn at this period too, generally round and without a peak, looking like a tam-o'-shanter. The vast majority of men wore beards.

p. 56, *Alexandrovsk Post… Alexandrovsk*: Several of the settlement names in *Sakhalin Island* appear in two, three or sometimes even four forms, depending on whether their full official name is given or whether they are being referred to colloquially. For instance, the Alexandrovsk Post is referred to also as Alexandrovsk and Alexandrovka, while the Rykovsk Post is referred to as Rykovsk, Rykovo or Rykovka. Since different names would be extremely confusing to any non-Russian-speaking reader, I have usually chosen one of the shorter variants and kept to it throughout.

p. 56, *peasant-in-exile*: Chekhov does not explain the term "peasant-in-exile" until later. Convicts would serve out their hard labour and then proceed to enforced settlement. After successfully completing this settlement, the exiles would be awarded the rights of "peasant-in-exile": i.e. they would be regarded once again as free individuals who could take up what trade they wished, with the one proviso that they could not go back to European Russia (up until 1888 they had not even been allowed to leave the island).

p. 56, *twenty-two roubles... fifteen*: The rent of twenty-two roubles with firewood (or fifteen without) is for a month. Chekhov states in chapter 11 that he was earning about 300 roubles a month, and so the price was well within his range. However, when one considers that Chekhov mentions in the same chapter that Mr Butakov, the District Governor, received only 200 roubles a month, the rent would seem to be exorbitant, as Sakhalin was not exactly the tourist centre of the world.

p. 57, *overseer*: As Chekhov explains later, the overseers' (*smotriteli*) main function was to supervise the prisons, and therefore the translation "warder" might be expected. However, the overseers were also employed to supervise convict labour and ensure the smooth running of settlements for enforced exiles. Their duties sometimes had nothing to do with the prison service at all – they would be employed, for instance, as messenger boys for the administration. Therefore I have preferred the more wide-ranging term "overseer" to "warden" or "warder". As Chekhov describes later, these overseers were usually picked either from prisoners who had served their term or from the soldiery stationed on Sakhalin, or even from the local ethnic tribes. They were regarded with contempt both by the convicts and by the administration.

p. 57, *doctor's assistant*: The term "doctor's assistant" is *feldsher* (feminine *feldsheritza*) in Russian, a word which obviously derives originally from German. Generally speaking, it implied somebody who had acquired some medical training at a college and who, although not a qualified doctor, was able to make diagnoses and prescribe simple medical treatment in a doctor's absence. However, an "unqualified" doctor's assistant would be somebody with no medical training at all, who either was qualifying through on-the-job experience or else had been appointed because there was nobody else available. The vast majority of Sakhalin doctor's assistants seem, according to Chekhov, to be in the latter category.

p. 57, *ariston*: An ariston was a large mechanical musical instrument, upon which any tune could be played by means of inserting perforated cardboard or, later, tin cylinders. An early precursor of the pianola.

p. 59, *denunciations*: Here is a specimen of a denunciation sent by wire: "The duty of conscience, as set down in Article 712, Volume Three, establishes the necessity of troubling Your Excellency to hasten to the defence of justice against the impunity with which N. perpetrates his deeds of usury, forgery and torture." (CHEKHOV'S NOTE)

p. 59, *Kara*: One of the central convict-labour institutions in Eastern Siberia, consisting of a large gold mine, with a prison and penal settlement, to keep it supplied with workers. According to George Kennan, General (then Colonel) Kononovich was continually hounded while in charge of the Kara Prison by those in the Central Prison Administration in St Petersburg, who accused him of being too liberal to the prisoners. He was, in fact, recalled to St Petersburg in 1891 and was retired "on health grounds" in 1893 after facing charges of embezzlement over many years of 400,000 roubles from government funds. Soviet commentators, in trying to exaggerate the importance of Chekhov's *Sakhalin Island*, tried to suggest that the book was responsible for both the resignation of Kononovich and Galkin-Vraskoy, who retired as head of the Central Prison Administration in 1896 after seventeen years at the helm. This is extremely unlikely. Galkin-Vraskoy would have been heading for retirement age anyway, while the accusation of embezzlement levelled at Kononovich seems to have had no foundation, being an invention on the part of his professional antagonists.

p. 59, *Governor... Territory*: Each "region" of Eastern Siberia would be headed by a governor. As many as sixteen regions would make up a "territory", and the senior official of a territory would be called a governor general. The Amur River Territory, formed in 1884, comprised the area around the basin of the river Amur, and was divided into four regions, the Primorskaya Region, the Amur Region, the Zabaikal Region (or Zabaikalye, as it was usually known) and Sakhalin Island. The Governor General's administrative centre was the town of Khabarovsk in the Primorskaya Region.

Much of this area along the Amur had been annexed from China only in the 1840s and 1850s, and so there was still a very strong oriental influence there. The whole area was so removed from European Russia that its rudimentary economy was geared almost entirely to providing produce such as edible seaweed and ginseng for the Chinese and Japanese markets.

Chekhov mentions the Primorskaya Region many times in his narrative, and so a brief sketch of this area will be useful. Up until the creation of the Amur River Territory in 1884, the area had come under the jurisdiction of the East Siberian Territory, which had comprised all of Russia's newly acquired Far Eastern lands. The Primorskaya Region had then included Sakhalin Island, which was declared a self-governing administrative unit only in 1884. The Ussuri Area – along the east bank of the Ussuri river – was annexed from China in 1858 and, following this, the Primorskaya Region stretched along Russia's Far Eastern coast right from the Arctic Ocean to the border of Korea. Its area was 1,629,424 square versts, or 714,665 square miles. The Ussuri Area by itself occupied an area of 201,440 square versts, or 88,350 square miles. (The British Isles has an area of 121,600 square miles). The Primorskaya Region's administrative capital was Vladivostok. Its population in 1897, according to the official census, was 220,557 (150,826 male, 69,731 female) – 0.13 people to every square verst.

The Amur Region occupied the middle reaches of the Amur. Chekhov hardly mentions this, and so suffice it to say that it had an area of 449,500 square kilometres (inconsistently, the Brockhaus Encyclopedic Dictionary gives the area of the Primorskaya Region in square versts and that of this region in square kilometres) with a population of 62,642.

The Zabaikal Region (Zabaikalye) occupied the upper reaches of the Amur. It was considered to comprise the territory between Lake Baikal and the Chinese border (the name literally means "beyond the Baikal").

The entire Amur River Territory administered by Baron Korf (see next note), including Sakhalin Island, occupied an area of 2,570,756 square kilometres with a population of 1,031,364 – a ratio of 0.4 people per square kilometre. The vast majority of these people would have been military personnel and Cossack regiments maintaining Russia's hold on its new territories. For this reason there was a huge predominance in the number of men over the number of women.

The territory contained various gold and silver mines on the mainland. Therefore most of Russia's hard-labour convicts were deported there to dig the mines and to live in permanent exile. However, the Trans-Siberian Railway, built in the 1890s, cut straight across the territory and opened it up to the rest of the Tsarist Empire, making it far less efficacious as a place of exile and bringing to the area an inflow of free, non-convict labour.

p. 61, *Baron… Korf*: The title "Baron" is not a Russian one, and of course "Korf" is not a Russian name. Baron Korf was a member of one of the families of nobility from the Baltic States – at that time part of the Russian Empire – who, despite their relatively small numbers, played a large and conscientious role in the Tsarist civil service and, indeed, set an example to their Russian counterparts. (Kononovich's predecessor as governor of Sakhalin had been General Gintze, another Baltic nobleman).

p. 61, *the surname Potyomkin*: The mention of the name Potyomkin would immediately recall to any Russian reader one of Catherine the Great's favourites, Prince Grigory Potyomkin, who was master of the art of "false appearances". He would, for instance, erect whole sham villages full of actors playing happy and contented peasants along the routes of Catherine's royal progresses. The implication in this passage is that something similar is happening on Sakhalin for the visit of the Governor General.

p. 61, *bread and salt*: As a sign of hospitality in Russia, a distinguished visitor would be offered on arrival a loaf of bread and some salt. As a sign of acceptance of this hospitality, the visitor had to tear a piece from the loaf, dip it in the salt and eat it.

p. 61, *the young people… opportunity*: All young people born on the island, or having accompanied their parents, could leave at seventeen, since, of course, they were not considered to be criminals. However, since the aim was to turn Sakhalin into an agricultural colony, the government might have expected some of them to stay. Chekhov is suggesting that this aim has totally failed.

p. 62, *Most All-Mercifullest Government*: "Most All-Merciful" was one of the titles reserved exclusively for the Tsar. Not only is Maslov misusing it in applying it to the government, but he is using it in a ludicrously exaggerated (and ungrammatical) form.

p. 62, *Baron Korf... a better life*: And he actually raised unrealizable hopes. In one settlement, while talking about the peasants-in-exile now having the right to resettle on the mainland, he said: "And they can go home as well, to European Russia." (CHEKHOV'S NOTE)
(They were not allowed to go back home, of course.)

p. 62, *Everything... excellently*: The parrot cry "Everything was proceeding excellently..." resounds ironically throughout the book from overseers and those in charge of prisoners. It must obviously have been an official formula used when reporting to superiors. Of course, the whole book is designed to prove that precisely nothing was proceeding excellently on the island.

p. 64, *poor unfortunates*: The term *neschastnye* ("poor unfortunates"), which both Kononovich and Korf use to describe the prisoners, was the one used by the ordinary Russian people themselves. It does not translate well into English and might be better rendered by the French "*pauvres misérables*". So many people had been exiled, often for nothing more heinous than losing their identification papers, that everybody knew of individuals in one's village who had disappeared for life for the most trivial of reasons. Therefore there was a great deal of sympathy for those sent to Siberia.

However, educated people such as Kononovich and Korf would have used this description in the manner of a romantic novelist, possibly influenced by the title of Victor Hugo's *Les Misérables*, which enjoyed great popularity in Russia.

p. 64, *No one is deprived... shaven heads*: The rest of *Sakhalin Island* is spent emphasizing that, on the contrary, there *were* sentries, prisoners *were* chained up, penal labour *was* onerous and – the main element against which Chekhov fought – punishments were most definitely for life. He and the ordinary educated Russian reader of the time who was in any way conversant with the criminal law would have found it extraordinary that a senior government official such as Baron Korf was apparently not aware of this.

It should be emphasized here that Baron Korf was not a member of the country's prison administration and was visiting Sakhalin Island purely because it was one of the administrative regions of the territory of which he was Governor General.

p. 65, *free settler*: The word *poselyanin* would have implied in Chekhov's time somebody who had been encouraged by the government and given various inducements to settle voluntarily in Siberia to aid the colonization process. (See the third note to p. 3).

p. 66, *their lost rank*: When sentenced to convict labour or permanent exile (though not temporary exile) the prisoner – even if an aristocrat – was stripped of social rank and all associated privileges.

p. 66, *Karl... German*: There were a large number of Russian ethnic Germans in the Tsarist Empire, mainly descendants of Protestants or small sects who had fled in previous centuries from religious persecution in the German states. Catherine the Great gave them land along the river Volga. The Baltic provinces of the Tsarist Empire also had a large number of Germans among their inhabitants.

p. 66, *surname "Don't-remember"*: The reason for this being a common surname is that many convicts, when asked for their surname, would reply "don't remember" or "can't remember", which was then adopted as their actual surname.

p. 67, *Thirty-five-years-old*: The number forms part of the surname; in actual fact he was forty-eight years old. (CHEKHOV'S NOTE)

p. 67, *imperial decrees*: The word that I have translated as "decree" is actually *manifest* (i.e. "manifesto") in Russian. The principal meaning of this was an announcement from the throne of some momentous event to do with the Royal Family, e.g. an accession to the throne or the marriage or death of a monarch or Grand Prince. However, when signed by the Tsar himself, "manifestos" were used to announce other events of great importance, such as a declaration of war, the abolition of serfdom in 1860 or the proposal to lay a railway across Siberia, which received the royal assent in 1891.

When major royal events were announced by these decrees, often favours were granted to the populace. These included mitigation of sentences for convicts and exiles. The amnesty that Chekhov refers to from time to time as having been applied to Sakhalin is possibly the one granted in 1883 to celebrate the coronation of Tsar Alexander III. However, it should be remembered that, although Chekhov was on Sakhalin in 1890, his book was not finally published till 1894–95 and therefore he may have had in mind amnesties issued during the intervening period. For instance, when Crown Prince Nicholas, the heir to the throne, visited Siberia in May 1891 to turn the first sod of the far-eastern section of the Trans-Siberian Railway, many labour and exile sentences were reduced in commemoration of the event, and certain categories of exile were, for the first time, allowed to return to European Russia on completion of their sentences.

p. 68, *the Voluntary Fleet*: The Voluntary Fleet was set up in 1878, when a war with Turkey was looming and therefore a flotilla of speedy ships was required which would be able to combat the Turkish navy on the Black Sea and keep Russia's far-eastern coasts protected. Public subscriptions were called for, and by 1878, 300,000 roubles had been raised and three steamers purchased. At first they were used purely for military purposes, but soon began to transport a few convicts to Sakhalin and provisions to the Russian far east by sea from Odessa. By the mid-1880s, the fleet was delivering all the convicts to Sakhalin and freight to Vladivostok. There were fourteen ships in the fleet by the time Chekhov was writing *Sakhalin Island*.

In English-language history books, these ships are in fact normally referred to as the "Volunteer" Fleet. But the Russian word *dobrovolny* actually means "voluntary" or "of one's own goodwill" here, and these terms are perhaps more accurate renderings in this context, since the fleet was given its name not because anybody volunteered to work for it, but because it was established through voluntary donations from the public.

p. 69, *I spent six years... Sakhalin*: Up until 1888 no prisoner was allowed to leave the island, even on completion of his sentence. From that year on, however, on receipt of peasant's rights, ex-prisoners were permitted to migrate to the mainland and reside in Eastern Siberia.

p. 69, *their literacy... blind*: This whole passage is difficult to translate, since, whereas the English word "literate" might imply that a person was able to read but not necessarily to write, the Russian word usually translated as "literate" – *gramotny* – implies an ability to do both. Therefore, to find out whether a person could read a few words, even if he could not write, he would have to be specifically asked – as here – "Do you know how to read?"

p. 70, *almshouses*: The almshouses were for those either too old or too infirm to work any longer.

p. 70, *overseer… anything*: The overseer had of course been sent in reality to make sure that Chekhov had no contact with political prisoners, in accordance with Galkin-Vraskoy's order. The reader will notice that, when Chekhov visits a settlement to conduct his census, he is always "offered assistants" and is invariably accompanied by overseers or other officials. One wonders whether Chekhov suspected the true reason for this, and mentions his constant companions in order to imply to the Russian readership of the time that he had been kept under surveillance. As he said later, "I've got a sort of feeling as if I've seen everything but gone and missed the elephant."

p. 70, *Chukhon*: A Chukhon was a Russian ethnic Finn. Finland was at this time part of the Tsarist Empire, although the Finns as an ethnic group extended far further into Russia than the present borders of Finland.

p. 73, *Circassians*: Circassians are an ethnic group from the West Caucasian highlands.

p. 75, *the Moscow Canal*: The Moscow River divides as it flows through Moscow. A minor channel departs from it as it approaches and rejoins it on the other side of the city: this is the "Moscow Canal".

p. 75, *Nekrasov's… Railway*: Nikolai Nekrasov (1821–78) wrote poetry critical of working conditions among the peasantry and urban poor. *The Railway* is a poem about the splendid Russian railway system on which the well-to-do travelled, which was being built by forced labour by people who lived in mud hovels, went down with scurvy and other ailments, were flogged, and died in their tens of thousands.

p. 76, *Dr Avgustinovich… hamlet*: Avgustinovich, 'Some information about Sakhalin. Extracts from travel journal', *Modern Times*, 1880, no. 1. There is also his article 'Arrival on Sakhalin', *Government Messenger*, 1879, no. 276. (CHEKHOV'S NOTE)

p. 76, *desyatins*: One *desyatin* is equivalent to 2.7 acres, or 1.09 hectares.

p. 78, *all over his body… gauntlet*: The punishment of running the gauntlet, used purely in the Russian military and not on civilians, was abolished in 1863. A long, thin rod was used to inflict this punishment, and even petty offenders could be sentenced to a staggering number of strokes: the maximum permissible was 6,000! It is little wonder that Good-looking's body still bore the wounds almost forty years after he had deserted from the army.

p. 78, *Zabaikalye*: Zabaikalye – or, to give it its full name, the Zabaikal Region – is the country beyond Lake Baikal in Eastern Siberia. This name is generally taken to refer loosely to the land between the lake and the Chinese border.

p. 79, *Tyumen*: The major forwarding prison on the Siberian exile route was in the town of Tyumen, and so Good-looking means he escaped from this prison.

p. 79, *Kara*: He is referring to the penal settlement at Kara (see second note to p. 59).

p. 79, *Blagoveshchensk*: The central administrative town of the Amur Region, on the north bank of the river Amur.

p. 79, *punishment cell*: In the military and in penal servitude prisoners guilty of disciplinary offences were placed in "punishment cells". There were two types: light and dark. Both usually had a small window high up, way above the prisoner's reach, but, if a prisoner were guilty of a serious offence, a shutter would be locked across the window. Depending on the heinousness of the offence, confinement in one of these cells – usually in solitary confinement – could be accompanied by deprivation of hot food. The most severe measure was eight days in a dark cell on bare bed-boards, with hot food only every third day. A prisoner might be confined in a light cell on "ordinary" regime for up to a month, with hot food daily, while on "strict" regime he or she might be held for up to twenty-eight days, with hot food only every third day.

p. 79, *Glory... Lord*: "Glory be to thee, O Lord!" is a frequent invocation in the Russian Orthodox liturgy.

p. 80, *zanders*: A zander (also spelt "sandre") is a European species of pikeperch of the genus *Lucioperca*, highly valued as food.

p. 80, *Hieromonk Irakly*: The Russian clergy was divided into two major groups, the "white" and the "black" clergy. The "white" clergy were those who, after their initial training, opted to live in the world rather than enter a monastery; they took a full part in the life of their parish and were allowed – indeed, even expected – to marry. Those who entered monasteries (the "black" clergy) were often, after some years, sent back out into the world to teach in village schools and to become missionaries or parish priests. They were, of course, celibate. However, since the Russian Orthodox Church did not allow married priests to rise any higher than a *blagochinny* (roughly a rural dean), the higher ranks of the church hierarchy were occupied by monks or celibates and widowers from the "white" clergy.

A monk who had been sent into the world to become a parish priest was called a "hieromonk" and this is what Father Irakly was.

p. 80, *The present... new status*: The East Siberian Territory, ruled by a governor general, had been formed in 1822, with its administrative centre in Irkutsk. In 1856 there had been created the post of military governor of the Primorskaya Region, with its centre at Blagoveshchensk; this region had included Kamchatka, the coast of the Sea of Okhotsk, the area to the east of the River Amur and Sakhalin Island. The Ussuri Area had been added in 1858. The military governor of the Primorskaya Region – who was in charge of both the civil and military administration – was subordinate to the Governor General of Eastern Siberia.

The reason for Eastern Siberia still being ruled by military officers was that, of course, it had been conquered over the preceding centuries by Russian force of arms. Forts had been laid across Siberia, exactly as in the Wild West in America, and law and order had originally been maintained by the military. Up until 1884, the senior official on Sakhalin had been the head of the convict settlement, subject to the military governor of the Amur Region. In 1884 the territory administered by the Governor General of Eastern Siberia was divided into two, both headed by a governor general: the Irkutsk Territory and the Amur River Territory. The latter, with its centre at Khabarovsk, was under the control of Baron Korf, who directed both the civilian and military administrations. In 1884, Sakhalin had been placed under the direction of the governor general of the new Amur River Territory.

Up until 1875, power on Sakhalin had been held by the director of the Dooay Post, who was subordinate to superior officers in Nikolayevsk on the mainland. However, when Russia assumed sole control of the island in 1875, Sakhalin was divided into two: the North, which was still under the command of the head of the Dooay Post, and the South, which was under the command of the senior officer of the Fourth Eastern Siberian Battalion of the Line. This officer was based at Korsakovsk. In 1884, power on Sakhalin passed in its entirety to the senior military officer (General Gintze, 1884–88; General Kononovich, 1888–1893). He was in charge of the three districts Chekhov describes – the Alexandrovsk, Tymovsk and Korsakovsk – plus the police department, the heads of the local military detachments, the superintendents of settlements and governors of prisons, the inspector of agriculture, the head of the medical division, the director of the colonization fund (see the note to p. 82 below), the architects, the office administration, etc. (It should be emphasized that although the prisoners were considered to be under military discipline, and the prison service was run by people with military ranks, the prison administration was under the jurisdiction of the civilian central prison administration and ultimately the Department of Internal Affairs).

On 1st January 1891 there were around 10,000 prisoners on the island, plus 3,000 members of their families and around 1,000 officials, military personnel and others. As pointed out in the note to p. 136, convicts were dealt with under a different code from the rest of the population, being under "military discipline". This is the reason why the penal colony was headed by a military officer and why the military seemed to play such a large part on the island, escorting the prisoners to labour, guarding the prisons, providing doctors for the prisons and so forth.

p. 81, *giving names... patronymics*: If, let us say, the official is called Ivan Petrovich Kuznetsov, then one street will be called Kuznetsov Street, another Ivanov street, and a third Ivano-Petrovsky Street. (CHEKHOV'S NOTE)

p. 82, *the colonization fund*: Although Chekhov mentions the colonization fund at various points throughout his narrative, he never explains what it was. The proposal had been made in the early 1880s to open up a shop to sell goods to the population, both exile and free, at affordable prices. Any profits would go towards a fund for developing Sakhalin as a colony. However, the shop became a centre for illegal dealings, in alcohol for example. It stocked spirits for the administration which, of course, the convicts and exiles were strictly forbidden to purchase. However, they circumvented the prohibition in every conceivable manner. Profits that should have gone towards the colony went into officials' pockets. Even General Kononovich was not above suspicion: he was recalled to St Petersburg in 1891 to answer accusations that he had embezzled 400,000 roubles of government money. Although cleared, he was "retired on health grounds" in 1893.

p. 84, *children's food subsidies*: In chapter 17 Chekhov states that children's food subsidies amount to one and a half roubles per month.

p. 84, *Turkish tobacco*: Russia exported its best-quality tobacco, mainly grown in the Caucasus, and so the average working Russian was left only with *makhorka*, a cheap, extremely strong type of lower-grade tobacco. Turkey, in its turn, exported almost half its tobacco to Russia. It was of better quality than the *makhorka*, cost more, and was a "prestige" item among lower-class Russians.

p. 85, *obtain a woman*: Chekhov explains the process by which settled exiles "obtain a woman" in chapter 16.

p. 85, *I visited… arrival*: The best characterization of Russian prisons in general has been given by N.V. Muravyov in his article 'Our prisons and the prison question', *Russian Herald*, 1878, vol. IV. On the Siberian prisons which served as the prototype for those on Sakhalin, see the investigation of S.V. Maksimov, *Siberia and the Hard-Labour System*. (CHEKHOV'S NOTE)

p. 86, *Dutch stoves*: A Dutch stove – as distinct from a "Russian stove" (see first note to p. 4) – was a type of stove that became popular in the late seventeenth century after Peter the Great visited the West. It was taller and narrower than an ordinary Russian stove, although sleeping planks could still be raised above it if need be. Dutch stoves were more aesthetic than Russian stoves: they were generally decorated with tiles, either white or highly ornate. They were therefore more expensive to construct than the common Russian variant and so were found only in well-to-do peasants' cabins, landowners' houses or government buildings.

p. 87, *a pot*: What I have translated as "pot", "chamber pot" or "night pot" (*parasha*) was usually a large uncovered wooden container.

p. 88, *56,000 roubles*: The vast size of this sum may be judged by the fact that Chekhov, a famous writer, was earning 300 roubles a month and a District Governor's salary was 200 roubles a month.

p. 90, *meteorism*: An old term for the presence of gas in the stomach and its expulsion therefrom.

p. 91, *a society, a trade guild*: For an explanation of "societies" and "trade guilds" see note to p. 36 and also the first note to p. 102 below. George Kennan, in his *Siberia and the Exile System* (1893), points out that not only the free population would form associations to protect their interests, but prisoners did too. Convicts walking across Siberia to imprisonment and exile would set up an association which would make a binding agreement with the captain of the escort guard that, in return for the favour of being allowed to remove their leg-irons and manacles, the association would ensure that no prisoner escaped. This promise was always kept.

p. 92, *kulakism*: A kulak (the word's principal meaning is "fist") was a peasant who, by hard graft or corruption, had amassed a fortune. Many of these "kulaks" were renowned for their financial tight-fistedness and double-dealing. The process of obtaining money by hard bargaining and greed was termed "kulakism".

p. 92, *maidans*: A word of oriental origin still found in Turkish, Persian, Urdu and Hindi, meaning a large open space, especially a market-place. The word entered Russian via the Turkic minorities of the Tsarist Empire and, in Siberia, was used for a small open marketplace. The keeper of the maidan was called a *maidanshchik*.

p. 92, *white bread rolls*: "White bread" means, of course, not the chalky confection that we call white bread in modern times, but bread made from wheat rather than rye. In Russian, rye bread is called "black bread". Because, owing to climatic conditions, wheat is grown much less in Central Russia than rye, wheat bread was more expensive, was considered more of a delicacy and, consequently, had more prestige value. It was thought, for no reason, to be better for one's health than black bread.

p. 92, *pieces of sugar... grubby rags*: A packet of nine or ten cigarettes costs one copeck, a white roll two copecks, a bottle of milk eight to ten copecks and a piece of sugar two copecks. Transactions are carried out in ready cash, on credit or in exchange. The *maidan* also sells vodka, cards and candle-butts for games at night – this is done secretly. Cards are also hired out. (CHEKHOV'S NOTE)

p. 92, *Stoss*: A card game of chance similar to faro.

p. 94, *The law... factory work*: "Fixed conditions for construction work, given the Royal Assent, 18th April 1869", St Petersburg, 1887. According to this statute, the basis for defining various types of labour is taken to be the physical strength of the worker and the level of practice at the work. The statute defines also the number of working hours in a day, conforming to the seasons of the year and the zone of Russia. Sakhalin is placed in the central belt of Russia. The maximum number of working hours is twelve and a half in twenty four – this is in May, June and July, and the minimum is seven – in December and January. (CHEKHOV'S NOTE)

p. 94, *clerk-in-chancery*: Clerks-in-chancery were the lowest of the civil service office clerks or junior office assistants. They joined the civil service straight from college or school. They did not, when they began, even have a civil service rank. Depending on their qualifications and aptitude, they would have to work between one and ten years before being admitted to the most junior grade, rank fourteen.

p. 96, *The dealing out… convict woman*: Vlasov writes in his article: "Such a strange relationship – an officer, with a convict woman as his lover, and a soldier as his coachman – cannot but arouse astonishment and regret." It is said that this vice is permitted only in view of the impossibility of obtaining a staff of free-persons. But this is untrue. First, it is possible to limit the number of servants; the officers would find it quite possible to have only one orderly each. Secondly, the officials here on Sakhalin receive a good salary and could hire staff from among the settled exiles, peasants-in-exile and free-women, who in the majority of cases need earnings, and so would not turn them down. This thought must have occurred to the authorities as well, since there is an order in which a certain female settled exile is given permission, as she is incapable of work on the land, to "acquire the means of existence by hiring herself out to the domestic staff of officials" (Directive no. 44, 1889). (CHEKHOV'S NOTE)

p. 97, *The steam mill… their feet*: The mill and metal workshops are together in one building and get their driving force from two traction engines; the mill contains four sets of stones with a grinding capacity of 1,500 poods a day. In the sawmill the work is done by an old traction engine brought here ages ago by Prince Shakhovskoy;* it is fuelled with sawdust. In the smithy work is carried on day and night, in two shifts, and the furnaces are in constant use. A hundred and five people are employed in the workshops in all. Convicts in Alexandrovsk are also employed extracting coal, but this is hardly likely ever to meet with any success. The coal from the local mines is much inferior to that of Dooay, it looks much muddier and is mixed with shale. It does not come out cheap here, since a permanent staff of labourers works in the mines under the supervision of a specialist mining engineer. The local mines have not been called into existence from necessity, as it is not far to Dooay, and excellent coal may be obtained from there at any time. They were, though, opened for a good purpose – to give settled exiles earnings in the future. (CHEKHOV'S NOTE)

* As Chekhov explains later, Prince Shakhovskoy was one of the people from the "prehistoric" days on Sakhalin. He ran the Dooay Prison in the 1870s.

p. 98, *the tu form*: Russian, like French, has "*vous*" and "*tu*" forms. The *vous* form is used when talking to one's superiors, and strangers. The *tu* form is used to address inferiors, friends, family and God.

p. 100, *Veil Day*: This is another name for Intercession Day (i.e. the Feast of the Intercession of the Holy Virgin), 1st October. It's also known as the "Day of the Protecting Veil of the Mother of God".

p. 100, *funty*: A *funt* is a "Russian pound", or 14.45 ounces.

p. 100, *St Nikolai's Day*: There are two St Nikolai's Days in the Russian year. Here it is "Winter St Nikolai's Day", 6th December; the other – "Summer St Nikolai's Day" – is 9th May.

p. 101, *Odessa*: Odessa, on the Black Sea, was the embarkation point for prisoners travelling to Sakhalin on the ships of the Voluntary Fleet.

p. 101, *We thought… over*: This refers to the wreck of the *Kostroma* on the west coast of Sakhalin in 1886. (CHEKHOV'S NOTE)

p. 101, *another boat… one*: A steamer of the Voluntary Fleet, the *Vladivostok*. (CHEKHOV'S NOTE)

p. 102, *artel*: Trade associations – *arteli* in Russian – were co-operative associations of individuals in a trade who would work on contracts and divide up the profits. Furthermore, other groups, such as convicts on marches across Siberia, would also organize themselves into *arteli* to defend their interests against the authorities. However, sometimes, as it does here, the word *artel* simply seems to mean the group of individuals with whom one is working or living at a particular time.

p. 102, *the sloppers-out*: In British prison slang a "slopper-out" is the inmate who empties the cell's chamber pot or bucket. In the Russian prison context, however, it means the person who ran the *maidan*.

p. 102, *a Tatar-Chink*: A Chinese Manze. (CHEKHOV'S NOTE)

p. 105, *named in honour… cruelty*: Up to the present, the two men who have done most for the exile colony as regards its creation and their responsibility for it are M.S. Mitzul and M.N. Galkin-Vraskoy. A small settlement of ten dwellings, poor and not long established, was named in honour of the former, and a settlement was named in honour of the latter which already had the old and enduring name of Siyantzy, so that only in documents – and not even all of them – is it called Galkino-Vraskoye. At the same time, a settlement and large post on Sakhalin bears the name of M.S. Korsakov, not because of any particular merits or sacrifices, but merely because he was a governor general and could put the fear of God into people. (CHEKHOV'S NOTE)

p. 106, *There are 272... to be dozing*: When reading Chekhov's description of the farmers in this and other villages of Sakhalin, it may be wondered why they all seemed to live in the settlements and not in farmhouses in the middle of their land. Quite simply, this was not the Russian tradition. Farmers would live in a village and walk the short distance to their fields. Russian villages tended to be long and narrow, often consisting of a "ribbon" development along one main road. Each cabin had its own garden and farmyard, while the farmland was behind the village.

p. 108, *the Prison Exhibition*: This was the exhibition mounted in connection with the World Prison Congress held in St Petersburg in 1890. Dr Suprunenko had been designated to oversee the Sakhalin section of the exhibition.

p. 109, *average yearly temperature*: The average yearly temperature fluctuates between +1.2 and −1.2°C; the number of days with precipitations between 102 and 209; there were only 35 calm, windless days in 1881, while in 1884 the number was three times greater – 112. (CHEKHOV'S NOTE)

p. 109, *I shall take... health*: P. Gryaznov, 'Preliminary comparative study of the hygienic conditions of peasant life, and the medico-topography of the Cherepovetsk District', 1880. Gryaznov's temperatures are in Réaumur; I have converted them into centigrade. (CHEKHOV'S NOTE)

p. 109, *Solovetsky Islands*: The Solovetsky Islands are situated off the northern coast of Russia in the White Sea, which leads into the Barents Sea.

p. 109, *Eternal frost*: "Eternal frost" refers to the permanently frozen subsoil (now termed "permafrost").

p. 111, *ship's cord*: The meaning of this expression is obscure. Chekhov uses it in another medical context later in the text: see p. 320 and its fifth note for more information.

p. 111, *the privileged classes*: The privileged classes were not necessarily aristocrats or gentry but could have comprised anybody from the classes of urban merchants, priests, honourable citizens and so on. The privileges of these classes varied widely and obviously decreased the lower down the social scale a "privileged person" was. The aristocrats and gentry were allowed to own land in town and country, and, up until 1860, serfs; the urban merchantry were allowed to possess urban land and run factories; and so on. All of these "privileged" classes were exempt from certain taxes and from corporal punishment. The members of the "privileged classes" whom Chekhov mentions occasionally could possibly have been political prisoners – with whom officially, of course, Chekhov was not meant to have any contact. If prisoners from the privileged classes were exiled for "political" rather than common criminal offences, they would not be subject to hard labour or to corporal punishment; they would be allowed to wear "free-persons" clothing rather than prison overalls with aces of diamonds on the back. When Chekhov occasionally makes cryptic references to "prisoners in free-persons' clothing", he is possibly trying to hint that these were political offenders.

p. 112, *lunatic… monastery*: Monasteries, as part of their social function, provided facilities for the care of the mentally ill.

p. 112, *makeweights… bread*: Makeweights were fastened to portions of bread so that the latter would reach the stipulated weight of three *funty*.

p. 114, *horned stock*: This is the usual Russian term for cattle, sheep and goats considered together. Sheep and goats are sometimes termed "small horned stock" and cattle "large horned stock".

p. 114, *schismatic*: Following alterations in church ritual in 1660, a large number remained faithful, in spite of persecution, to the old ways. By the nineteenth century many of them had turned to commerce and industry, and enjoyed a reputation for hard work and honesty.

p. 114, *make a living… happens*: Potyomkin arrived on Sakhalin already rich. Dr Avgustinovich, who saw him three years after his arrival on Sakhalin, wrote: "The best house of all is that of the exile Potyomkin." If, over a period of three years, Potyomkin had managed to build himself a fine house, buy horses and marry his daughter off to a Sakhalin official, then agriculture has, I think, nothing whatever to do with it. (CHEKHOV'S NOTE)

p. 114, *executioner*: An executioner was not simply the person who carried out capital punishment but an individual selected by the authorities to inflict corporal punishment as well. One person was usually selected from each group of prisoners newly arrived on Sakhalin to administer punishment within that group. Some even applied for the job voluntarily, making this their "hard labour" and thinking by so doing to ingratiate themselves with the authorities and possibly have their sentences reduced. They were held in total loathing and contempt by the other prisoners.

p. 115, *imposing and... (bear root)*: The majority of writers have not found the local landscape pleasing. This is because they arrived on Sakhalin still with the impression fresh in their minds of the nature and scenery of Japan and Ceylon, or that of the Amur, and because they started from Alexandrovsk and Dooay, where the scenery is indeed wretched. The weather here is to blame in this as well. However beautiful and distinctive the Sakhalin landscape may be, if it is hidden for weeks on end in mist or rain, then it is hard to assess it at its true worth. (CHEKHOV'S NOTE)

p. 117, *Butakovo*: The settlement is so called in honour of A.M. Butakov, the Governor of the Tymovsk District. (CHEKHOV'S NOTE).
Chekhov's statement "I did not visit Butakovo" contradicts his claim that he "toured round all the settlements".

p. 117, *vegetable gardens... mountains*: About five years ago a certain important personage,* talking to the settled exiles and giving them advice, said, among other things: "Bear in mind that in Finland they sow grain on the mountain slopes." But Sakhalin is not Finland, and climatic conditions, and above all else, the state of the soil, rule out any type of cultivation whatever on the mountains here. In his report the Inspector of Agriculture advises the acquisition of sheep, which "could with advantage make use of those poor but numerous pasturelands on the mountain slopes, on which neat cattle could not find enough to eat". But this advice is meaningless in practice, since the sheep could "make use" of the pastures only during the course of the short summer, while during the long winter they will die of cold. (CHEKHOV'S NOTE).

* Chekhov mentions in chapter 2 (page 61) that Baron Korf had visited the island five years previously. It has been suggested therefore that the "certain important personage" was Baron Korf.

p. 121, *(?)*: Chekhov's own question mark.

p. 122, *sigs*: A sig is a kind of freshwater salmon.

p. 123, *mokhovki… kosteniki*: *Mokhovki* are a kind of small black-currant. *Kosteniki* (rubus saxatilis), according to the *Brockhaus-Efron Encyclopedic Dictionary* of 1898, are a distant relative of the raspberry, the berries of which, although somewhat astringent, are not unpleasant and are used in making jams and jellies. What I have translated as "whortleberries" or "marsh whortleberries" (*golubika*) are also known as bog bilberries and are found in Scotland.

p. 124, *They dug the tunnel… barracks*: It will be recalled that the report of the Central Prison Department for 1885, edited by Galkin-Vraskoy, had described the tunnel as a "remarkable construction" that would "serve as a fine basis for useful work in this distant region".

p. 124, *a Pole*: Poland at this time was part of the Tsarist Empire.

p. 124, *étape*: "Relay station" (French).

p. 127, *a passionate gambler*: He told me that during a game of *Stoss*, "electricity ran through his veins"; his hands would go numb from agitation. One of his most pleasant memories was of how once, as a youth, he had pinched a watch from the city police chief himself. He would excitedly tell tales about games of *Stoss*. I remember his phrase "Damn! Missed it!" – he'd say it with the despair of a hunter who'd just failed to hit his mark. (CHEKHOV'S NOTE)

p. 129, *His wound… rag*: I met quite a number of people who were wounded and suffering from sores, but not once did I catch a whiff of iodoform, although they get through half a pood of it every year on Sakhalin. (CHEKHOV'S NOTE)

p. 129, *Dooay*: Dooay has an exaggeratedly bad reputation among the general public. On the *Baikal* they told me of one passenger, a man already elderly and high-ranking, who, when the steamer came to a halt in the Dooay roadstead, scrutinized the shore for a long period and finally asked: "Could you tell me, please, where precisely on the shore the post is which they hang the convicts from and then throw them into the water?"

Dooay is the cradle of the Sakhalin penal settlement. The opinion exists that the thought of choosing this place for an exile colony came first of all to the convicts themselves; supposedly a certain Ivan Lapshin, who had been sentenced for patricide, and was serving his hard labour in the town of Nikolayevsk on the mainland, requested the local authorities for permission to transfer to Sakhalin and was transported here in September 1858. Settling not far from the Dooay Post, he took up vegetable gardening and crop-rearing, and, in Mr Vlasov's words, "served out his convict labour here". He could not have been brought to the island alone, since coal was already being extracted near Dooay in 1858 with the participation of convicts (see 'From the Amur and the shores of the Pacific Ocean' in the newspaper *Moscow Gazette*, 1874, no. 207). In his *Sketches in Pen and Pencil*, Vysheslavtsev writes that, in April 1859, he found around forty men at Dooay, plus two officers and one engineering officer supervising the works. "What glorious vegetable gardens," he enthuses rapturously, "surround these cosy, neat little cottages! And the vegetables ripen twice in summer."

The period of the Sakhalin penal settlement's real origin was during the '60s, when the disorders of our deportation system had reached their most extreme point of tension. Then came a time when the head of a branch of the Department of Executive Police, Collegiate Counsellor Vlasov, staggered by everything he had come across in penal settlements, declared straight out that the structure and system of our punishments were abetting the growth of serious criminal offences and were lowering civil morality. A cursory on-the-spot investigation of penal labour had led him to the conclusion that in Russia "it hardly existed" (see his *Brief Description of Irregularities Existing at Hard-labour Institutions*). The Central Prison Department, giving in its decennial report a critical survey of penal servitude, notes that, in the period under review, penal servitude had ceased to be the ultimate measure of chastisement. Yes, that was the most extreme measure of the disorder the like of which at one time had been created by ignorance, indifference and cruelty. Here are the reasons for the former irregularities:

(a) Neither the compilers of the laws on exiles, not the executors of those laws, had any clear idea of what penal servitude is, what it must consist of and why it is necessary. And actual practice, notwithstanding its long duration, had not only not created a system, but had not even produced any material for a legal definition of penal servitude.

(b) Corrective and penal aims of punishment had been sacrificed to various types of economic and financial considerations. A convict was regarded as a working force who must bring a profit to the state exchequer. If his work did not yield a profit, or showed a loss, they preferred to keep him in prison with nothing to do. Unprofitable idleness was given preference over unprofitable labour. The aims of colonization had to be taken into account too.

(c) Unfamiliarity with local conditions and therefore an absence of any definite viewpoint about the character and content of penal labour; this is evident merely from the division of the work, only recently abolished, into labour in mines, labour in factories and labour in military strongpoints.* In practice, a convict sentenced to work in the mines for life would sit in the prison with nothing to do, while somebody sentenced to four years' penal servitude in a factory would work down the mines; and in the Tobolsk Penal-Labour Prison the prisoners were occupied in moving cannon balls from one place to another, pouring sand from one container into another, etc., etc. In society, and to a certain extent in literature, a view has become established that the most difficult, most shaming, real hard labour, can only be in the mines. If, in Nekrasov's *A Russian Woman*,* the hero, instead of working down a mine, had caught fish for the prison, or cut down timber, many readers would have been left dissatisfied.

(d) The way our *Statutes on Exiles* have been left behind. To very many questions raised in daily practice, this publication provides no answer whatever, hence there is a wide field for arbitrary interpretation and unlawful actions; in the most complex cases it is often an utterly useless volume, and it must have been partly due to this that Mr Vlasov, in several administration departments of penal-servitude prisons, could not find a copy of the *Statutes* at all.

(e) The absence of unity in the administration of penal servitude.

(f) The remoteness of penal servitude from St Petersburg and the complete absence of publicity. The official reports have only recently begun to be printed, since the establishment of the Central Prison Administration.*

(g) Quite a large obstacle in eliminating the irregularities in the system of exile and penal servitude has been the frame of mind of our society. When a society has no clearly defined views on something, then its state of mind must be taken into consideration. Society is always growing indignant at the way prisons are run, yet, at the same time, every step towards bettering the prisoners' way of life meets with protests, such as, for instance, the following remark: "It's not good that a chap is gong to live better in prison or in penal servitude than at home." If a person frequently lives at home under worse conditions than he does in penal servitude, then, by the logic of such a remark, penal servitude would have to be made hell. When the prisoners were given *kvas** instead of water in their railway carriages, this was called "mollycoddling murderers and arsonists" and so on. However, as if to counterbalance such an outlook, a tendency may be observed in the best Russian writers towards the idealization of convicts, vagabonds and escapees.

In 1863 the royal assent was given to a committee whose aim was to try to discover and indicate measures for organizing convict labour on more proper foundations. The committee affirmed that it was necessary "to exile hardened offenders to a remote colony for application to compulsory labour, with the principal aim of settlement at the place of exile". And, choosing among the distant colonies, the committee settled on Sakhalin. *A priori* the committee considered that Sakhalin had the following advantages: (1) its geographical position, which safeguarded the mainland from escapes; (2) the punishment would assume the proper repressive force, since exile to Sakhalin could be considered irrevocable and permanent; (3) the large amount of space available for the activities of the offender who resolved to start a new working life; (4) from the point of view of benefit to the state, the concentration of exiles on Sakhalin represented a guarantee that the possession of our island would be fortified; (5) the coalfields could be exploited with advantage in view of the enormous need for coal. It was also supposed that the concentration of a whole contingent of exiles at hard labour on an island would reduce their maintenance costs. (CHEKHOV'S NOTE)

* When Count Speransky first presented his proposals for introducing convict labour into Siberia in 1822, the work had been broken down into labour in mines, factories and fortresses. The "fortresses" or "strongpoints" dotted all over Siberia had been built to defend and expand Russian territorial gains against indigenous tribespeople and to establish some measure of control over the tens of thousands of escaped exiles roaming through the forests. The convicts in strongpoints would have helped to further Russian expansion by clearing forests, building roads and so forth.

* In the last section of the poem *A Russian Woman* by Nekrasov (see the second note to p. 75), Princess Volkonskaya meets her husband, who is a convict, at the Nerchinsk silver mines.

* The Central Prison Administration had been established in 1879 under the control of M.N. Galkin-Vraskoy, who remained in charge until 1896.

* Kvas is a sweet, non-alcoholic drink, usually made from fermented rye bread, although it can also be made from fermented berries. A kind of kvas made from beetroot is used as the base for soups and stews.

p. 129, *he strolls... singing*: According to Doroshevich, who visited the island in 1897, Shkandyb was still strolling around and singing, and had not done a day's hard labour since arriving on Sakhalin.

p. 130, *specialist work... Keppen*: Mr Keppen, *Sakhalin Island – its Coal Seams and Developing Coal Industry*, 1875. Besides Mr Keppen, other mining engineers have also written about the coal:

I. Nosov, 'Notes Concerning Sakhalin Island and its Coal Quarries', *Mining Journal*, 1859, no. 1.

I.A. Lopatin, 'Extract from a Letter. Report on the Activities of the Siberian Branch of the Imperial Russian Geographical Society for 1868'.

I.A. Lopatin, 'Report to the Governor General of Eastern Siberia', *Mining Journal*, 1870, no. 10.

O. A. Deykhman, 'Sakhalin Island in regard to the Mining Industry', *Mining Journal*, 1871, No.3.

K. Skalkovsky, *Russian Trade in the Pacific Ocean*, 1883.

The various grades of Sakhalin coal have been described at different times by captains of vessels of the Siberian Flotilla in their reports, which have been published in *Maritime Compendium*. For the sake of completeness we might perhaps mention the following articles:

Ya. N. Butkovsky, 'Sakhalin Island', *Historical Herald*, 1882, vol. x.

Ya. N. Butkovsky, 'Sakhalin and its significance', *Maritime Compendium*, 1874, no. 4. (CHEKHOV'S NOTE)

p. 131, *Stepanchikovo... Foma*: Foma is a character from the novel *The Village of Stepanchikovo and its inhabitants* by Dostoevsky. He wheedles himself into the house of a family by flattery, hypocrisy and bullying, and, once ensconced, proceeds to take control.

p. 133, *The merchant... flogged before*: As he was a merchant he would have been exempt from corporal punishment as one of his class privileges. Therefore flogging would have been a complete humiliation for him.

p. 136, *sentenced him to death*: Although ordinary citizens were no longer subject to the death penalty in Russia, once a person had been sentenced to convict labour he was then sentenced on a different, much more severe, basis for any further offence committed during his sentence or enforced settlement. He was, in fact, treated as if he were under military discipline (this is the reason why the people in charge of the service were military officers and had such ranks as "general" and "colonel"). Therefore these further offences were judged not by a civilian judge or jury, as for an ordinary citizen, but by a commission made up of officers from the local military command. For serious offences, such as murders committed whilst under sentence, or attacks on administration officials, courts martial would be held, consisting of the most senior members of the local military and appointed by the Governor of the Island. These courts martial had the power to impose military punishments such as the death penalty, which had not been abolished for the armed forces.

p. 137, *fast*: The fast referred to is the Lenten fast of the Russian Orthodox church.

p. 137, *The Tym... extreme*: Four years later L.I. Shrenk travelled downriver along the east bank, and returned the same way. But this was also done in winter when the river was covered in snow. (CHEKHOV'S NOTE)

p. 137, *Polyakov*: He is no longer living. He died soon after his journey to Sakhalin. Judging from his hastily written outline notes, he was a gifted man with an all-round education. Here is a list of his articles:

'Journey to Sakhalin Island in 1881–82', addendum to vol. XIX of *News of the Imperial Russian Geographical Society*, 1883.

'Report on Explorations on Sakhalin Island and in the South Ussuri District', addendum to vol. XLVIII of *Observations of the Imperial Russian Academy of Sciences*, no. 6, 183–84.

'On Sakhalin', *Virgin Soil*, 1 Nov. 1886, vol. VII, no. 1. (CHEKHOV'S NOTE)

p. 138, *camp overseer*: As regards the camp, this overseer represents something like an ex-king, and he performs duties which have nothing whatsoever to do with the camp. (CHEKHOV'S NOTE)

p. 139, *at the mouth of the bay... eagle*: At the inlet a two-fathom-long pole does not reach the bottom. A vessel of large dimensions could stand in the bay. If navigation were to be developed on the Sea of Okhotsk close to Sakhalin, then craft would find a calm and totally safe mooring here in the bay. (CHEKHOV'S NOTE)

p. 139, *Mayne Reid*: Thomas Mayne Reid (1818–83), the Anglo-Irish writer, whose work consisted of adventure stories, mainly for children and generally set in America.

p. 139, *a nightmare... waves*: In the middle of June, Mining Engineer Lopatin saw ice here covering the sea; this ice remained till July. On St Peter's Day* the water froze in the tea kettle. (CHEKHOV'S NOTE)
* St Peter's Day is 29th June.

p. 141, *superfluous people*: "Superfluous people" was a term much in vogue in Russia at the time, coined originally in literary circles to describe the typical "anti-hero" of much of Russian literature of the nineteenth century: the sort of character who, like Lermontov's Pechorin, Pushkin's Onegin or Turgenev's Bazarov, feels himself to be a talented and gifted person who is not wanted by society – who is "superfluous" to it.

p. 141, *Thirty Years... Gambler*: *Thirty Years, or the Life of a Gambler* (*Trente ans ou la vie d'un joueur*) was a play by the French dramatist and novelist Victor Ducange (1783–1833). It was translated into most European languages and was extremely popular in Russia.

p. 142, *cockroaches and bugs*: Incidentally, among the inhabitants of Sakhalin, the opinion exists that the bugs and cockroaches are brought in from the forest in the moss which they use here to caulk buildings. This opinion derives from the fact that they do not even have time to finish caulking the walls before the bugs and cockroaches are already appearing in the cracks. Of course, the moss has nothing to do with it; the insects are carried in by the carpenters sleeping the night in the prison or in the settled exiles' cabins. (CHEKHOV'S NOTE)

p. 144, *a milliner... arson*: The milliner was, in fact, the prisoner who is elsewhere (page 146) described as "the Working Lady", formerly Baroness Heimbruck. She had of course been deprived of her status when sentenced.

p. 146, *Tverskaya-Yamskaya*: This was the junction of two large, fashionable boulevards in Moscow just north of the Kremlin. The Tverskaya was renamed Kalinin Prospect after the 1917 Revolution. In 1991 its former title was restored. Yamskaya Sloboda had been a small hamlet outside Moscow which had merged with it as the city expanded. The road from this hamlet joined the Tverskaya (which came right down to central Moscow) near the ring road which used to form the boundary of the ancient city of Moscow. At one time the original city had had guarded gates and turnpikes on this road to regulate entry and collect taxes from all outsiders who wished to trade inside the city. These turnpikes were by Chekhov's time no longer functioning as such, but were ceremonial arches and open gates, rather like Temple Bar in London. Just outside the north-west gate of the old city of Moscow lay the main racetracks. The major race meetings which the merchant is recalling were held on Sundays.

p. 148, *Uskovo... fortunes*: One writer who has visited Sakhalin only a couple of years after me already saw a whole herd of horses around Uskovo. (CHEKHOV'S NOTE)

p. 149, *bagulnik*: Bagulnik (Latin *Ledum palistre*) is a small, stocky shrub of the genus *Ericaceae* (i.e. the heather family). It grows in damp northern areas and bears small white or pink flowers.

p. 150, *in the distance... Voskresenskoye*: We needed three hours to walk the six versts from Uskovo to Voskresenskoye. If the reader will visualize a pedestrian laden with flour, salt beef or government goods, or somebody sick who is walking from Uskovo to the Rykovo hospital, then he will fully understand what significance the words "There's no road" have on Sakhalin. It's impossible to travel the distance either on wheels or on horseback. There have been occasions when, in an effort to travel the route on horseback, the horses have broken their legs. (CHEKHOV'S NOTE)

p. 151, *family bathhouses... Jew*: "Family bathhouses" is a euphemism for brothels. Jews in European Russia were not allowed to own land and had therefore to find other ways to earn a living. Because legal means of doing this were so circumscribed for them, some took to illegal means such as receiving stolen goods, running brothels and so on.

p. 151, *splendid surnames*: In the sixteenth and seventeenth centuries millions of Russians flooded south to the Ukraine to escape famine and disease. Over the years spent leading a nomadic life and attempting to settle down, many such individuals became known in their new area not by their real name but by their trade, the region from which they had come or distinguishing physical features. All the names Chekhov mentions here are still fairly common in the Ukraine today.

p. 153, *three funty*: *Sakhalin Island* is sometimes rather poorly organized in that references are made to individuals or circumstances which are not fully explained until later. This is an example. The reference to three *funty* of bread means nothing here; it is explained only in later chapters that the prisoners' daily allowance of bread is meant to be three *funty*, but, because of inefficiency and corruption, it is often well below this.

p. 153, *reverse draught*: In the Rykovo Prison the draught or suction is arranged in the following manner: the stoves are kept burning above the cesspit and, while this is going on, the doors are kept tightly sealed, hermetically, and so the stoves obtain the current of air necessary for burning from the cesspit, as they are attached to it by a pipe. In this way all the evil-smelling gases flow from the pit into the stove and pass into the outside air up a chimney. The building above the cesspit is heated by the stoves, and air flows from there through holes and then through a pipe into the pit; the flame of a match held near a hole is drawn perceptibly downwards. (CHEKHOV'S NOTE)

p. 154, *Captain Venzel… Ivanov*: Staff-Captain Venzel is the anti-hero of *Memoirs of Private Ivanov* by Vsevolod Garshin (1855–88). He is depicted as being cultured, kindly and gentle with his immediate acquaintances and behaving like a wild animal to the soldiers under his authority. Garshin, a close friend and supporter of Chekhov, had committed suicide.

p. 154, *Solovetsky Island*: This is the major island of the Solovetsky group (see the third note to p. 109).

p. 156, *the late writer Fet*: Afanasy Fet (1820–92) was a Russian poet who wrote about nature, love and metaphysics.

p. 158, *a religious dissenter*: Presumably Bogdanov was a schismatic or Old Ritualist. See the second note to p. 114.

p. 158, *raznochintzy*: Owing to the vast expansion of education in the mid-nineteenth century, members of the non-privileged classes could begin to enter the professions and form part of the intelligentsia for the first time in Russian society. These educated and often distinguished individuals constituted a class to whom none of the social grades seemed applicable. The term *raznochintzy* ("of various ranks") was coined unofficially to designate these people.

p. 158, *at Andreye-Ivanovskoye*: Incidentally, the former Kutaissi* noblemen, the brothers Aleksey and Teymuras Chikovani, live here. There had been a third brother, but he died of consumption. There is no furniture at all in their cabin, and the only thing lying on the floor is a feather mattress. One of them is ill. (CHEKHOV'S NOTE)

* The Kutaiss are a people from the western highlands of Georgia.

p. 159, *districts (okrug)… county (uyezd)*: Regions or provinces – the major administrative units – were divided in European Russia into smaller areas called *uyezdy* (counties) and in Siberia *okrugi* (districts). There is no difference in meaning; the terms are purely historical. Siberian districts did, however, tend to be much larger than European Russian counties. I have translated both terms by the word "district".

p. 159, *the Anadyr District*: The Anadyr District occupied the northern section of the Primorskaya Region. This district had an area of 222,000 square miles; the whole of the British Isles occupies 121,600 square miles.

p. 159, *The subdivision… as well*: See the third note to p. 80 for details on Sakhalin's change of administrative status.

p. 160, *the Dooay… prisons*: Among General Kononovich's directives is one relating to the long-desired closing-down of the Dooay and Voyevodsk Prisons.* "Having inspected the Voyevodsk Prison, I am personally convinced that neither the conditions of the locality in which it is situated, nor the importance of the offenders sustained within it – for the most part, those with long sentences or imprisoned for fresh offences – can justify the system of surveillance, or, rather, the absence of any genuine supervision, under which the prison has operated from its very inception. The state of affairs at the present time is as follows: the prison has been constructed in a narrow valley about one and a half versts to the north of Dooay, communication with the post exists only along the seashore and is interrupted twice a day by rising tides, communication through the mountains is difficult in summer and impossible in winter; the Prison Governor has his residence and offices at Dooay, and his deputy likewise; the local

military detachment, from which the guard is maintained and which sends over the requisite number as escorts for the various types of labour carried out in accordance with the contract of the 'Sakhalin' Company, is also stationed at the said post, while attached to the prison itself there is nobody, excepting a few overseers and the guard, which is changed every day, and which is left without any constant and immediate supervision on the part of the military command. Without entering into an analysis of the circumstances, the cause of which was the construction of the prison in such an unsuitable location, and the way it has been left without the possibility of any direct surveillance, I, pending the granting of permission to close down both the Dooay and likewise the Voyevodsk prisons and transfer them to other localities, must, even if only in part, redress the existing deficiencies." And so on (Directive no. 348, 1888). (CHEKHOV'S NOTE)
* By the time Doroshevich visited Sakhalin in 1897, the Voyevodsk Prison had been closed down.

p. 160, *Incidentally, when... Tym*: See Davydov, *Twofold Journey to America of the Naval Officers Khvostov and Davydov, indited by the latter, with prolegomenon by Vice-Admiral Shishkov*, 1810. In his introduction Admiral Shishkov states that "Khvostov united two opposites within his soul – the gentleness of a lamb and the passion of a lion." Davydov, on the other hand, in his words, was "more quick-tempered and fiery than Khvostov, but yielded to him in stead-fastness and fortitude". The gentleness of a lamb, however, did not hinder Khvostov in 1806 from destroying Japanese shops on southern Sakhalin on the bank of the Aniva, and in 1807, together with his friend Davydov, he looted Japanese trading posts on the Kurile Islands, and once again went marauding on southern Sakhalin. These gallant officers waged war on Japan without the knowledge of the government, and in the fullest expectation of impunity. Both ended their lives in a fashion not entirely commonplace: they were drowned in the Neva River, which they were trying to dash across as a bridge was being raised. Their exploits, which created a great deal of fuss at the time, aroused a certain interest in society towards Sakhalin, people talked about the island, and, who knows, perhaps it was precisely then that the fate was predestined of this mournful island, so terrifying to the imagination? In his introduction Shishkov expresses the opinion – which is based on nothing – that in the previous century the Russians had desired to take possession of the island and establish a colony there. (CHEKHOV'S NOTE)

p. 162, *Mamia-Rinzo*: His work is entitled *To-tats Ki Ko*. I haven't read it, of course, and in the present work I shall make use of quotations from L.I. Shrenk, author of the book *The Indigenous People of the Amur Territory*. (CHEKHOV'S NOTE)

p. 162, *Gilyaks... Tym*: The Gilyaks, in the form of a none-too-numerous tribe, live along both sides of the river Amur, on its lower reaches, starting roughly at Sofiisk, then along the Liman, along the adjacent coast of the Sea of Okhotsk, and on the northern section of Sakhalin; during the entire period over which we have information about this people, that is, 200 years, no considerable changes of any sort have taken place in the positioning of their boundaries. It is conjectured that at one time the Gilyaks' homeland was Sakhalin alone, and that only subsequently did they move from there to the neighbouring part of the mainland, crowded out by the Ainos, who had moved from Japan, having been crowded out in their turn by the Japanese. (CHEKHOV'S NOTE)

p. 163, *lack of reliable statistical information*: On Sakhalin there exists the post of interpreter of the Gilyak and Aino languages. As this interpreter does not know a single word of either Gilyak or Aino, and the majority of Gilyaks and Ainos understand Russian, this unnecessary post might serve as a good addendum to the above-mentioned overseer of the non-existent Vedernikovsky camp. If, instead of an interpreter, they would appoint to the staff an official familiar in a scientific fashion with ethnography and statistics, this would be far better. (CHEKHOV'S NOTE)

p. 164, *Kutyeikin*: Kutyeikin is a character in the extremely popular play *The Nincompoop* by Denis Fonvisin (1745–92).

p. 164, *L.I. Shrenk*: To his excellent work *The Indigenous Peoples of the Amur Territory* is appended an ethnographic map and two prints of drawings by Mr Dmitriev-Orenburgsky; Gilyaks are portrayed on one of these prints. (CHEKHOV'S NOTE)

p. 165, *daby*: Daby is a Chinese cotton material similar to coarse calico.

p. 167, *long-standing contact with the Chinese and the Japanese*: Our natives of the Amur Territory and Kamchatka contracted syphilis from the Chinese and Japanese; the Russians have precisely nothing to do with it. One Chinaman, a merchant, a great lover of opium, told me that he had one woman, his wife, living in his house in Yantai and another woman, a Gilyak by birth, living near Nikolayevsk. Given such a state of affairs it is not difficult to infect the whole of the Amur and Sakhalin. (CHEKHOV'S NOTE)

p. 170, *Gilyaks... fox and sable fur... vodka appeared*: The Governor of the Dooay Post, Major Nikolayev, told one correspondent in 1866: "In summer I have no dealings with them, but in winter I frequently buy up furs from them, and buy them at a very profitable rate; often for a bottle of vodka or a loaf of bread you can get a pair of splendid sable off them." The correspondent was staggered at the large quantity of furs which he saw at the Major's quarters (Lukashevich, 'My acquaintances at Dooay on Sakhalin', *Kronstadt Herald*, 1868, nos 47 and 49). Of this legendary major I have still to speak. (CHEKHOV'S NOTE)

p. 170, *hardly any... possibility... killers*: They have no courts, and they do not know the meaning of "justice". How hard it is for them to understand us may be seen merely from the fact that up till the present day they still do not fully understand the purpose of roads. Even where a road has already been laid, they will still journey through the taiga. One often sees them, their families and their dogs, picking their way in Indian file across a quagmire right by a roadway. (CHEKHOV'S NOTE)

p. 173, *cold currents... Japan*: Someone has proposed the project of constructing a dam in the narrowest part of the strait, which would arrest the passage of the cold current. This project can find justification for itself in natural history; it's well known that when the isthmus existed the climate of Sakhalin was outstanding in its mildness. But the implementation of this project would hardly bring any benefit. The flora of the southern part of the west coast might be enriched by a dozen or so new species, but the climate of the entire lower section of the island would scarcely change for the better. The point is that the whole of the south lies close to the Sea of Okhotsk, in which ice-floes and even ice-fields drift in the middle of summer, and the major portion of the Korsakovsk District is separated from the sea only by a quite low range of mountains, behind which there are lowlands running right down to the sea, covered with lakes and exposed to cold winds. (CHEKHOV'S NOTE)

p. 173, *seakale… Chinese… Sakhalin*: Since at this time there was no railway to connect Russia's Pacific seaboard with the hinterland of the empire, the economy of the Russian Far East was almost entirely oriented to supplying items for the eastern market, especially China and Japan. The exports of the region through Vladivostok, the main port for Siberia, consisted mainly of seakale, trepangas (a kind of edible mollusc: see the fourth note to p. 259), edible fungi, Siberian ginseng and deer horns for use in oriental medicine. For this reason the vast majority of shops and enterprises in Vladivostok and the surrounding area were owned and run by Japanese and Chinese (that is, Chinese businessmen still based in their home country, not the "Manzes" who are mentioned so often in these pages). Vladivostok's principal imports from Europe were agricultural implements, sugar, paper, silk and other cloths, and fruit, both fresh and preserved.

In 1890 Vladivostok was already the metropolis of the Russian Far East with a population of 7,300. Like most Russian Far Eastern settlements, it had been set up quite deliberately as a military outpost (indeed, its name means "Ruler of the East"). Because of this, and owing to the fact that vast numbers of settled exiles on completion of their labour sentences made their way there to earn money, the male population was nearly three times greater than the female.

p. 173, *Koreans*: The Koreans, like the Manzes, would mainly be fugitives from justice in their native land; some 20,000 of them lived in south-eastern Siberia. They had the same kind of reputation as the Manzes for vagabondage, laziness and lawlessness.

p. 174, *Semyonov… three privates*: Semyonov keeps a shop at Mauka which does not do a bad trade at all in summer; the prices for foodstuffs are high, so that the settled exiles leave half their earnings here. In the report for 1870 of the captain of the clipper *Vsadnik*, it states that the clipper, approaching the site of Mauka, had in view the setting ashore of ten soldiers there in order to prepare the spot for vegetable gardens, since it had been proposed to set up a new post in this place during the summer. I would point out in passing that this was the time when slight misunderstandings were taking place between the Russians and the Japanese on the western sea coast. I have also found a report in the *Kronstadt Herald*, 1880, no. 112: 'Sakhalin Island – some interesting information regarding Mauka Cove'. The gist of the article is that Mauka is the main base of a company which has obtained the right from the Russian government to gather seaweed for a period of ten years, and that its population consists of three Europeans, seven Russian soldiers and 700 Korean, Aino and Chinese workers.

That the seakale industry is profitable and expanding may be seen from the fact that Messrs Semyonov and Denbigh have already attracted imitators. A certain Birich, a settled exile, a former teacher who had worked as a shop manager for Denbigh, has borrowed money, built everything necessary for the industry near Kusunnai, and started inviting settled exiles to come to him. He now has about thirty people working at his plant. The work is carried on unofficially – there are not even any government overseers here. The Kusunnai Post, already long abandoned, is about 100 versts north of Mauka, at the mouth of the Kusunnai river, which was formerly considered the boundary between the Russian and Japanese possessions on Sakhalin. (CHEKHOV'S NOTE)

p. 174, *Krilyon… lighthouse… fashion*: A little to the north of Krilyon I saw the rocks on which the steamship *Kostroma* had run aground several years previously, led astray by these mists. A.V. Shcherbak, the doctor who was accompanying the convicts on the *Kostroma*, fired signal rockets while the ship was being wrecked. He told me subsequently that he had endured three long phases at the time: the first – the longest and most agonizing – was the certainty of inevitable destruction; the convicts had been overcome by panic and were wailing; the women and children had had to be sent in the ship's boat under the command of an officer in the direction where the shore was supposed to be. And the boat had soon disappeared in the mist; the second phase was where there was some hope of salvation: the sound of cannon fire reached their ears from the Krilyon lighthouse, informing them that the women and children had reached the shore safely; and the third period was of complete assurance of rescue, when suddenly through the misty air rang out the notes of a piston-cornet being played by the returning officer.

In October 1885 fugitive convicts attacked the Krilyon lighthouse, looted all the property there and murdered a sailor, throwing him over the cliffs into the abyss. (CHEKHOV'S NOTE)

p. 174, *Aniva Bay… versts*: The coast of the Aniva was first explored and described by the Russian officer N.V. Rudanovsky, a partner in Nevelskoy's Amur Expedition. The details may be found in the journal of N.V. Busse, another participant in the expedition, *Sakhalin Island and the Expedition of 1853–54* and also Nevelskoy and Rudanovsky's article 'Concerning the reminiscences of N.V. Busse' (*Herald of Europe*, 1872, vol. VIII); see also the memoirs of Nevelskoy himself. Major Busse, a highly strung and quarrelsome gentleman, writes that "Nevelskoy's behaviour towards subordinates, and the spirit of his documents and reports, is insufficiently serious", and of Rudanovsky he writes: "He is difficult as a subordinate, intolerable as a colleague and regularly makes senseless and confused remarks"; and Boshnyak, according to Busse, is "a dreamer and a child". When Nevelskoy was slowly puffing on his pipe to make it draw, this grated on his nerves. Spending the winter with Rudanovsky on the Aniva, and being senior to him in rank, the Major tiresomely required from him respect for rank and observation of all the regulations of subordination, and this was in a wilderness, living practically in each other's pockets, and when the young man was wholly immersed in serious scientific work. (CHEKHOV'S NOTE)

p. 176, *comfort... leisure time*: The time is already almost forgotten when officers and officials serving in southern Sakhalin suffered real deprivation. In 1876 they were paying four roubles for a pood of white flour, three roubles for a bottle of vodka, and "nobody practically ever sees fresh meat" (*Russian World*, 1877, no. 70), while of more ordinary people there is just nothing to say. They were literally living in destitution. The correspondent of the *Vladivostok*, no more than five years ago, reported that "nobody possessed even half a glass of vodka, while Manchurian tobacco (something like our *makhorka**) cost as much as 2 roubles 50 copecks a *funt;* the settled exiles and some overseers were smoking *Bohea* and brick tea"* (1886, no. 22). (CHEKHOV'S NOTE)

* *Makhorka* is the very cheapest type of poor-quality Russian tobacco.

* Bohea tea is very low-grade tea.

p. 176, *brand-new frock coat*: Each rank of government official had its own distinctive uniform.

p. 177, *Major Sh... to me*: Major Sh., to do him justice, treated my literary profession with the fullest respect, and the entire time I lived at Korsakovsk he tried in every way to prevent life being tedious for me. Previously, several weeks before my arrival in the south, he had taken a lot of trouble with the Englishman Howard, an adventure seeker and a literary man, too, who had been shipwrecked in the Aniva on a Japanese junk and who later on wrote some fairly considerable nonsense about the Ainos in his book *Life with Trans-Siberian Savages* *. (CHEKHOV'S NOTE)

* *Life with Trans-Siberian Savages* by B. Douglas Howard was published in London in 1893 by Longmans, Green.

p. 177, *The Week magazine*: This could well have been 'Books of the Week', a supplement to the St Petersburg newspaper *The Week*. In the May and June supplements were printed translated extracts from the book *Looking Back 2000–1887* by Edward Bellamy, an American author, in which he put forward his utopian ideas, akin to those of William Morris, of co-operative life in semi-socialistic village communes. Chekhov mentions, in a letter to Suvorin (17th December 1890), having discussed Bellamy's ideas with General Kononovich, and so it seems as if he must have obtained his knowledge of Bellamy's work from 'Books of the Week' while on Sakhalin. What point Chekhov is trying to make by mentioning this magazine is unclear. He may be attempting to hint that even here, on Sakhalin, some officials have ideas and try to keep their minds alive by reading liberal literature.

p. 178, *an identifying tattoo*: Up until the end of the eighteenth century exiles and convicts had been branded with a red-hot iron. This had then been replaced by a stamp consisting of several sharp needles forming the letters "SK" (i.e. *ssylno-katorzhny*, convict-in-exile) or "S" (*ssylny*, exile); the mark was then strewn with powder to make it ineradicable. By a law published in 1845 each convict had to have the letters "SK" tattooed on his right arm, below the elbow, every time he was apprehended. A vagabond (*brodyaga*) would have the letter "B" tattooed in the same place whenever he was caught. This was carried out by means of a small device with a trigger which depressed a series of needles into the skin. These needles, which together formed the requisite letters, had been dipped in a mixture of indigo dye and Indian ink.

This measure – like running the gauntlet, referred to in the first note to p. 78 – was abolished in 1863, not only because of the ease with which the tattoos could be eradicated, but apparently because too many people were being arrested, tattooed and then found to be innocent. Unlike the gauntlet, which was a purely military punishment, the brand and tattoo were used on both service personnel and civilians. Incidentally, since Chekhov has now mentioned two old men whom he met in penal servitude – one in chapter 4 and one here – who still bear marks of punishment received thirty to forty years previously, we can only wonder how many of the exiles on Sakhalin must have spent most of their adult lives in hard-labour institutions and exile.

p. 180, *Uspensky*: Gleb Uspensky (1840–1902) wrote about the life of the peasants and the exploited classes. He had a mental breakdown in the 1890s, and finally committed suicide.

p. 180, *captive Turk*: The "captive Turk" was presumably taken prisoner in the Russo-Turkish War of 1877. The Turks surrendered on 10th December 1877.

p. 180, *Nikolayev*: There were several towns called Nikolayev in the Tsarist Empire, but, since Giacomini was a skipper of a craft on the Black Sea, the Nikolayev mentioned here is probably that in the Ukraine, on the river Bug, 100 miles from the port of Odessa.

p. 181, *meteorological station*: During my stay on Sakhalin, M.E. Shtelling was busy petitioning for a weather centre to be established, and he was being assisted greatly in this by Military Surgeon Z***sky, an established Korsakovsk resident and a very fine man. But it seems to me that the centre should not be set up in the Korsakovsk post, which is exposed to east winds, but in some more central point of the region, for instance, in Vladimirovka Settlement. However, on southern Sakhalin, every spot has its own climate, and the most fitting thing to do would be to establish meteorological observation points simultaneously in several places: in Busse Bay, at Korsakovsk, on Krilyon and in Mauka, Vladimirovka, Naibuchi and Tarayka. This would not be easy, of course, but at the same time it should not be too difficult either. In my opinion the services of literate exiles could profitably be used for this; as experience has already shown, they soon learn how to take observations independently, and it only needs a person who would assume the work of directing them. (CHEKHOV'S NOTE)

p. 181, *Olonetsk… Archangel*: The Olonetsk Province was one of the most northerly provinces of European Russia. Archangel is a port on the northern coast of Russia bordering the Arctic Ocean.

p. 182, *Korsakovsk Prison... former seamen... cleanly*: Mr Bely has succeeded in organizing a skilful crew from their ranks for work at sea. Convict Golitzyn, small, with sideburns, is considered to be the senior seaman among them. He loves to play the philosopher. When he sits at the rudder and commands "Spars – *down*!" and "Oars – *in*!" he does this not without an overbearing sternness. Despite his respectable appearance and seniority, he was flogged two or three times during my stay for drunkenness, and, I believe, for coarse insolence. The most experienced seaman after him is considered to be convict Medvedev, an intelligent and courageous man. Once, the Japanese Consul, Mr Kuze, was returning from Tarayka with Medvedev at the rudder; besides them, there was also an overseer in the whaleboat. Towards evening the wind became fresher, and it grew dark. When they were sailing up to Naibuchi, the entrance to the river Naibu was no longer visible, and to put straight into the shore was dangerous, so Medvedev decided to spend the night at sea, in spite of the heavy gale. The overseer punched him on the ear, Mr Kuze sternly ordered him to hug the shore, but Medvedev would not obey and obstinately put further and further out to sea. They rode the storm all night; the waves flung the boat about, and every moment it seemed as if they would flood her or topple her over. The Consul told me later that it had been the most terrifying night of his life. When at dawn Medvedev drew into the mouth of the river, another whaleboat was taking in water on the sandbar. From that day on, whenever Mr Bely sends anybody out with Medvedev, he tells them every time:

"Whatever he does, please, just keep quiet and don't protest."

In the prison one's attention is attracted by two brothers, formerly Persian princes, who still to this day in letters arriving here from Persia are entitled "Your Highness". They were sent here for a murder which they committed in the Caucasus. They dress in Persian fashion in high sheepskin hats with the brim pulled down to the eyebrows and then folded back up. They are still in the "probationer" category, and therefore do not have the right to keep money on them, and one of them complained he had nothing to buy tobacco with, and smoking, it seemed to him, made his cough easier. He gums envelopes for the government offices, rather clumsily; looking over his work, I said ,"Very good." And obviously this praise gave great pleasure to the former prince.

The prison clerk is convict Geyman, a plump, handsome man with dark hair, who had formerly been an officer in the Moscow police force and had been convicted of corruption. In the prison he followed close on my heels and, whenever I turned round, he would courteously take his cap off each time.

The local executioner here bears the surname Minayev; he is a son of the merchant classes and still young. On the day I saw him, he had, according to him, birched eight people. (CHEKHOV'S NOTE)

p. 183, *Ochakov campaign*: Ochakov is now a town forty-one miles from Odessa. In 1788 it was simply a fortified Turkish outpost; the Russians took it after a six-month siege. The reference could be either to this period or to the time during the Crimean War in 1855 when Ochakov was severely bombarded by the Anglo-French fleet, which was fighting on the side of the Turks against Russia.

p. 184, *pilgrim*: The word *strannik*, which I have translated as "pilgrim", in fact relates to a member of any one of a number of sects which had existed in Russia from the eighteenth century. These sects considered that a Christian should give up absolutely everything including a fixed abode; therefore their members were eternal wanderers, hiring themselves out as day labourers in any village they came to, or begging alms "for the sake of Christ". *Strannik* has also been translated as "wanderer".

p. 184, *treaty of 1875*: Until 1875 Russia and Japan administered Sakhalin jointly. In that year, however, Russia gained sole control of the island.

p. 184, *abandoned cabins… escapees*: Formerly situated here were the Muravyovsk Mines, where the coal was extracted by soldiers from the posts who were being disciplined; that is, they had their own little penal settlement here. They were detailed to the works by the local authorities as punishment "for offences which were not really particularly heinous" (Mitzul). Whose benefit the receipts would have gone to, though, if the coal produced by the soldiers had been sold, it is impossible to say, since it all went up in flames along with the buildings.

Up till 1870 the military authorities had also founded the posts of Chibisansk, Ochekhpoksk, Manuysk, Malkovsk and many others. They have all now been abandoned and forgotten. (CHEKHOV'S NOTE)

p. 185, *Miss*: "Miss" is a word hardly used in Russian. This strange title must form part of an assumed vagabond pseudonym.

p. 186, *I drove... to... Mr Bely... Mr Yartzev*: In September, and at the beginning of October, excluding those days when a north-easter was blowing, the weather was excellent and summery. While travelling with me, Mr Bely complained to me that he was profoundly homesick for the Ukraine and that he did not desire anything so much now as to look at the cherries at the time when they were hanging from the trees. When we spent the night in the overseers' offices, he would wake up very early; you would open your eyes at dawn and he would be standing at the window reciting in a low voice: "The white light o'er the capital is breaking, the young wife soundly sleeps..."* And Mr Yartzev would also constantly recite poetry from memory. When the road began to get boring, you would ask him to recite something, and he would declaim some long poem or other, or even a couple of them. (CHEKHOV'S NOTE)

* "The white light..." is the first line of Nekrasov's poem *Masha*, written in 1853 (see the second note to p. 75).

p. 187, *The inhabitants... forty years old*: For that same reason, for instance, settled exiles between twenty and forty-five years old make up seventy per cent of the entire total of the inhabitants of the Korsakovsk Post. Formerly, when they were distributing the newly arrived prisoners round the districts, it was the custom rather than the rule to detail short-sentence convicts, as being less criminally inclined and hardened, to the south, where it was warmer. But, in determining the long- and short-term prisoners from the itemized records,* the necessary care was not always observed. For example, the former Governor of the Island, General Gintze, one day read the lists out on board the steamer which had brought them here, picked out the short-term prisoners himself, and detailed them to be sent to the south; but subsequently among these fortunate folk there turned out to be twenty vagabonds and people surnamed "Don't-remember", that is to say, the most dyed-in-the-wool and desperate of the lot. Today the above-mentioned custom has, it seems, been abandoned, since they send long-term and even life convicts to the south, while I came across short-termers in the dreadful Voyevodsk Prison. (CHEKHOV'S NOTE)

* At the place of sentence, records were made out for each prisoner containing his name, age, social class, crime, sentence, etc. A copy

of these was given to the prisoner, and another copy was sent to the Central Department of Exile Administration in Tyumen. The prisoner was meant to hand over his records to the captain of each relay of guards on the way into Siberia, but the system led to many irregularities, since, until the introduction of photographs, a triple murderer, for example, could bully a pickpocket into swapping identities and escape with a much milder punishment.

p. 187, *temporarily acting as prison doctor*: As Chekhov explains later, doctors from the local military detachment sometimes acted as prison doctors when necessary. Without exception they turned out to be more humane than the bona-fide prison doctors. For instance, it was a military doctor acting as a prison doctor who ordered the closure of the ward for the insane and syphilitic described in chapter 7, page 111.

p. 187, *M.S. Mitzul*: In the expedition of 1870 sent from St Petersburg under the leadership of Vlasov, the agriculturalist Mikhail Semyonovich Mitzul also participated; he was a man of rare moral fibre, a very hard worker, an optimist and idealist, extremely enthusiastic, and possessing, besides, the ability to communicate his enthusiasm to other people. At the time he was around thirty-five years old. He treated the mission entrusted to him with outstanding conscientiousness. Researching the soil, flora and fauna of Sakhalin, he journeyed on foot all over the present-day Alexandrovsk and Tymovsk Districts, the western sea coast and the entire southern part of the island; at the time there were no roads whatever on Sakhalin, and only here and there would someone run across wretched tracks which petered out in the taiga and the swamps, and every movement from one place to another was a veritable torture. Mitzul was struck by the idea of an agricultural colony, and this idea enthralled him. He gave himself up to it heart and soul, fell in love with Sakhalin, and, just as a mother does not see any defects in her beloved little brat, so, on the island which was to become his second homeland, he did not notice the frozen soil and the mists. He considered the island to be a blossoming corner of the earth, and he was hindered in this view neither by the meteorological data – of which there were hardly any then anyway – nor by the bitter experience of previous years, which he evidently regarded with disbelief. Surely here there were wild grapevines, bamboo, grass growing to a gigantic height and the Japanese... Subsequently in the history of the island he became a head of department and state counsellor, still carried away with enthusiasm and still working tirelessly. He died on Sakhalin of a serious nervous disorder at the age of forty-one. I even saw his grave. He left behind him the book *An Account of the Island of Sakhalin from an Agricultural Viewpoint*, 1873. This is a long ode in honour of Sakhalin's fertility. (CHEKHOV'S NOTE)

p. 188, *his height... the post*: Any strangers of strong build could easily arouse suspicion and be presumed vagabonds. Only those vagabonds who were of immense strength and stature could have hoped to survive the repeated attempts at escape from Siberia. Those of a weaker constitution would soon have perished owing to the severe conditions.

p. 189, *aconite*: One convict presented me with something like a petition, with the heading "Confidential. Something from our out-of-the-way spot. To the generous and benevolent writer Mr Ch., who has made the unworthy Island of Sakhalin joyful by his visit. Korsakovsk Post". In this petition I found a poem under the heading 'Monk's Head, or Aconite':

> Proudly buds above the stream
> In a swamp, in a ravine,
> Those little blue leaves so serene
> Famed as Aconite to medicine.
> This, the root of "Monk's Head"
> By Our Creator's hand planted
> Oft folks doth allure,
> Kills them for sure,
> And sends them all off to heaven's door.
> (CHEKHOV'S NOTE)

p. 189, *larch wood... soil... cultivation*: For those who select sites for new settlements, larch trees are a sign of poor, swampy soil. Since the clay subsoil does not let water through, it forms peat, and *bagulnik*, cranberries and moss appear, the larches themselves deteriorate and become crooked and covered with reindeer moss. It is precisely for this reason that the larches here are ugly, have small trunks and wither without reaching an advanced age. (CHEKHOV'S NOTE)

p. 190, *suitable for settlement*: Cork trees and grapevines grow here, but they are degenerate and bear as little resemblance to their ancestors as Sakhalin bamboo cane does to that of Ceylon. (CHEKHOV'S NOTE)

p. 191, *Vladimirovka... households*: In one of his orders General Kononovich attests that "in part by reason of its isolated position and the difficulty of maintaining communication, and partly in consequence of various special considerations and calculations, which before the very eyes of my predecessors were corroding and corrupting affairs everywhere that their noxious breath reached, the Korsakovsk Post has always been excluded and deprived of its fair share, and not a single one of its most crying needs has been investigated, satisfied or put forward for resolution" (Directive no. 318, 1889). (CHEKHOV'S NOTE)

p. 191, *Favus*: Favus the dog is named after the fungus *Favus griseus*, responsible for the skin disease mange.

p. 192, *Mr Plevako*: Fyodor Plevako (1843–1908) was a celebrated Moscow advocate.

p. 193, *volost*: This was the smallest administrative unit in Tsarist Russia. It was a canton of villages under the direction of one person or a small council.

p. 194, *The point about that... Alexandrovsk*: This passage seems to be written deliberately to refute the claim made in the Decennial Reports of the Central Prison Department edited by Galkin-Vraskoy that the settled exiles were supplied with "the machines, tools, apparatus and materials necessary for labour carried out on the island".

p. 195, *Close by... building wood*: On the river a verst from Bolshoye Takoay stands a mill built on the orders of General Kononovich by the Russian ethnic German convict, Lakhs; it was also he who constructed the mill on the Tym near Derbinskoye. At the Takoay mill they accept as little as one *funt* for grinding, and charge one copeck per pood. The settled exiles are well pleased, because formerly they paid fifteen copecks a pood, or else did their grinding at home on flour mills of their own manufacture, with "millstones" made from elm wood. (CHEKHOV'S NOTE)

p. 195, *small brook... Takoay*: I shall not name the minor tributaries on which stand the settlements of the Susui and Naibu basins, since they all have Aino or Japanese names which are difficult to take in, such as Ekureki or Fufkasamanay. (CHEKHOV'S NOTE)

p. 196, *kapor*: This is a plant similar to fennel or dill, used as a spice or to make herbal tea, also known as *Anetha graveolus*.

p. 197, *One correspondent… expensive*: Midshipman V. Vitgeft, 'A few words about Sakhalin Island', *Kronstadt Herald*, 1872, nos 7, 17 and 34. (CHEKHOV'S NOTE)

p. 198, *Siska… impression*: The settlement stands at a crossroads; winter wayfarers from Alexandrovsk to Korsakovsk invariably stop here. In 1869, near the present settlement, which was then Japanese, a way station for travellers was constructed. Soldiers and their wives lived here, and, later on, exiles as well. During winter, spring and the end of summer, the brisk life of the fairground would seethe here. In the winter, droves of Tunguses, Yakuts* and Amur Gilyaks would come flocking here and carry on trade with the southern natives, while in spring and at the end of summer the Japanese used to arrive for the fishing trade. The name of the way station – Tikhmenevsk Post – has been maintained right up to the present day. (CHEKHOV'S NOTE)

* The Yakuts are a people of Turkic Mongol stock living in that part of Eastern Siberia bordering the Arctic Ocean.

p. 201, *voluntary colonization… were repeated*: This experiment concerns only Sakhalin, yet D. Talberg, in his article 'Exile to Sakhalin', *Herald of Europe*, 1879, vol. V, attaches a general significance to it, and, speaking in this respect on our incapability towards colonization overall, he actually comes to the following conclusion: "Is it not time that we renounced all attempts at colonization in the East?" In their comments on Professor Talberg's article, the editorial board of *Herald of Europe* say that "We shall scarcely be able to discover another instance of such colonizing capabilities as the Russian people have displayed in their past when they took possession of the whole of the European East and Siberia", and in this respect, the esteemed editors refer to the work of the late Professor Yeshevsky, who "presents a wonderful picture of Russian colonization".

In 1869 a certain entrepreneur brought 20 Aleuts* of both sexes to southern Sakhalin from the island of Kadyak to hunt wild animals. He settled them around the Muravyovsk Post and issued them with provisions. But they did precisely nothing besides eat and drink, and, after a year, the entrepreneur removed them to one of the Kurile Islands. At about the same time, two Chinese political exiles settled at the Korsakovsk Post. Since they had expressed a wish to take up farming, the Governor General of Eastern Siberia ordered each of them to be issued with six bulls, a horse, a cow, grain for sowing and provisions for two years, but they did not receive any of these things, allegedly due to a lack of spare supplies, and finally they were sent over to the mainland. One could also, perhaps, include among the voluntary colonizers (also unsuccessful) the Nikolayevsk townsman* Semyonov, a small, somewhat skinny man of about forty, who at present is wandering all over the south of the island trying to find gold. (CHEKHOV'S NOTE)

* The Aleuts are people of various racial stock residing on the 150 islands (the Aleutian Islands) betweeen Kamchatka and Alaska.

* A townsman was a "lower-middle-class town-dweller".

p. 202, *Dr Dobrotsky... years ago*: He has left two substantial and note-worthy works: 'The southern section of Sakhalin' (an extract from an army medical report, *News of the Siberian Branch of the Imperial Russian Geographical Society*, 1870, vol. I, nos 2 and 3) and an *Aino–Russian Dictionary*. (CHEKHOV'S NOTE)

p. 202, *smallpox... frequently*: It is difficult to assume that this disease, which created such ravages on northern Sakhalin and the Kurile Islands, should have spared southern Sakhalin. A. Polonsky writes that an Aino will leave a yurt in which a death has occurred and will construct another in its place elsewhere. This custom evidently derives from the times when the Ainos would abandon their infected dwellings in terror at epidemics and would resettle in other locations. (CHEKHOV'S NOTE)

p. 203, *the Ainos... Japanese... rice*: The Ainos told Rimsky-Korsakov: "Jap-man sleep, while Aino work for him – cut wood, catch fish; if Aino not want work – Jap-man beat him." (CHEKHOV'S NOTE)

p. 203, *chuyka*: A *chuyka* was a kind of long cloth kaftan, or alternatively a long cloth coat without a collar.

p. 203, *Aino... coachman*: In Shrenk's book which I have already mentioned, there is a plate with an illustration of an Aino. See also Fr. Gelvald, *Natural History of Tribes and Peoples*, vol. II, where an Aino is depicted at full length, in a robe. (CHEKHOV'S NOTE)

p. 204, *one Englishman*: The excellent 1978 Russian edition of *Sakhalin Island* has a footnote at this point stating: "Presumably this Englishman was Howard". However, Howard merely states on page 180 of his book *Life with Trans-Siberian Savages* (London, 1893), when discussing the religious beliefs of the Ainos, that "their similarity to... the beliefs of the Hebrews... must be extremely suggestive".

p. 204, *A. Polonsky*: Polonsky's essay 'The Kurile Islands' is reprinted in the *Proceedings of the Imperial Russian Geographical Society*, 1871, vol. IV. (CHEKHOV'S NOTE)

p. 206, *Ainos' wives... repulsiveness*: Incidentally, N.V. Busse, who rarely spoke well of anybody, testifies to the character of the Aino women thus: "In the evening an Aino who was tipsy, and who was known to me as a great drunkard, came to my quarters. He had brought with him his wife, with the objective, as far as I could comprehend, of sacrificing the fidelity of the marriage bed and in this manner to entice fine gifts from me. The woman, who was quite good-looking, seemed prepared to assist her husband, but I gave the appearance of not understanding their explanations; on leaving my house, the husband and wife without ceremony obeyed the call of nature in front of my window and in full view of the sentry. In general this Aino woman did not display a great deal of feminine shame. Her breasts were almost completely uncovered. The Aino women wear the same clothes as the men, that is, some short smock-like garments, thrown open at the top, and done up round the waist with a girdle. They possess no shirts or underclothes, and therefore the least disarray in their clothing displays all their hidden charms." But even this stern writer acknowledges that "there were some quite pretty ones among the young girls, with pleasant, gentle facial features, and with passionate dark eyes". However that may be, the Aino woman has lagged far behind in physical development; she grows older and fades earlier than the men. This should perhaps be ascribed to the fact that, during the centuries-long wanderings of this race, the lion's share of the privations, heavy labour and tears has fallen to the women. (CHEKHOV'S NOTE)

p. 206, *qualities... me*: Those qualities are: "On our visit to an Aino dwelling on the shore of the Rumyanetz Bay, I noted, in the family appertaining to the dwelling, which consisted of ten people, the most happy concord, or, one might almost say, perfect equality among the co-members. We were within this dwelling place for several hours, and we could not at all descry who was the head of the household.

The eldest manifested no signs of supremacy towards the youngest. When gifts were presented to them, nobody displayed the slightest sign of displeasure at receiving less than another. They vied with each other to do us all sorts of favours." (CHEKHOV'S NOTE)

p. 207, *Japanese colonists... homeland*: Even today Japanese people who spend a long time working or studying abroad are deemed to have lost caste and sometimes find it difficult to re-establish themselves.

p. 208, *Khvostov... Japanese... location*: Khvostov plundered Japanese homes and barns along the shore of the Aniva and rewarded an Aino elder with a silver medal on a ribbon of St Vladimir.* This piracy disturbed the Japanese government profoundly and forced it to be on the alert. A little later Captain Golovin and his travelling companions were taken prisoner, as if in time of war, on the Kurile Islands. When subsequently they were released by the Governor of Matsmay, he solemnly declared to them: "You were all taken prisoner by reason of Khvostov's pillaging; but now a clarification has been dispatched to us by the authorities of Okhotsk that his plunderings were merely the deeds of a brigand. This is clear, and I therefore declare that you be repatriated." (CHEKHOV'S NOTE)

* The Order of St Vladimir was awarded for services to Russian society. It was often given to senior civil servants on retirement.

p. 209, *In the beginning... now lives*: Details in Venyukov, 'General survey of the gradual extension of Russian boundaries within Asia. Part One: Sakhalin Island', *Military Compendium*, 1872, no. 3. (CHEKHOV'S NOTE)

p. 209, *Tyulen Island*: Tyulen Island (literally "Seal Island") is a tiny island off the south-eastern tip of Sakhalin.

p. 209, *a treaty... theirs*: Probably owing to the Japanese desire that the enslavement of the Ainos should take place on a legal footing, there was included in the treaty, among other points, a speculative clause by which the Ainos, were they to enter into debt, should be able to pay it off by labour or some other service. But at the time, there was not a single Aino on Sakhalin whom the Japanese did not consider their debtor. (CHEKHOV'S NOTE)

p. 210, *the treaty... compensation*: Nevelskoy persistently identified Sakhalin as Russian territory by right of its being occupied by our Russian Tunguses in the seventeenth century, our initial account of it in 1742, and the occupation of its southern section in 1806 by the

Russians. He considered the Oroches to be Russian Tunguses, but the ethnographers do not agree with this; the initial description of Sakhalin was made not by the Russians but by the Dutch, and, as regards the occupation in 1806, the "primacy" of this occupation is refuted by facts. There is no doubt that the rights of first exploration belong to the Japanese, and the Japanese were the first to occupy southern Sakhalin. But we still went too far in our generosity; we could have given them the five or six Kurile Islands nearest to Japan "out of respect", as the peasants say, but we gave away twenty-two islands, which, if they are to be believed, now bring them in a million in income every year.* (CHEKHOV'S NOTE)

* The Kurile Islands are still a source of contention between Russia and Japan.

p. 210, *does not have a beard*: Chekhov finds it unusual that the Japanese do not have beards because almost all Russian men at the time did have them.

p. 211, *the Orders of Anna and Stanislav Third Class*: These honours were awarded for services to society.

p. 211, *The Japanese were very affected... guests*: Relationships between the local administration and the Japanese are splendid, as indeed they have to be. Besides entertaining each other with champagne on ceremonial occasions, both sides find other means, too, for maintaining these relations. I cite verbatim one of the documents received from the consul: "To the Respected Director of the Korsakovsk District. In connection with the Edict no. 741 issued by myself on 16th August this year regarding the distribution of the four barrels of salt fish and five sacks of salt dispatched by you for the nutrition of those who suffered shipwreck on the brig and the junk, in which respect I have honour to express to you, Most Gracious Sir, in name of those poor unfortunate people, highly sincere gratefulness upon your sympathy and the donations by your friendly neighbouring nation of what is for them here so important; of this I am fully convinced, that these things will always remain in their good recollection. Consul of Japanese Empire Kuze." Incidentally, this letter may give some idea of the success the young Japanese secretary has had in a short time in learning the Russian language. German officers studying Russian, and foreigners whose job is translating Russian literary works, write far worse.

This Japanese courtesy is not sugary and sickly, and is therefore appealing, and, however much a lot of it may be overdone, it is not offensive; as the saying has it – a bit of butter doesn't spoil the porridge. A certain Japanese lathe-turner in Nagasaki, from whom our naval officers bought various knick-knacks, always acclaimed everything Russian out of courtesy. He would see an officer with a bracelet charm or a purse and off he would go in delight: "What a wonderful thing! What an elegant object!" One day one of the officers brought from Sakhalin a wooden cigarette-case of crude and clumsy workmanship. "Well," he thought, "now I'll let that turner down! Let's see what he'll say now!" But when they showed the Jap the case, he did not turn a hair; he waved it in the air and uttered rapturously: "What a sturdily made object!" (CHEKHOV'S NOTE)

p. 212, *for prisoners... months*: In every administrative office on Sakhalin there is a "Table for Calculating Sentences". From this it may be seen that a person sentenced, say, to seventeen and a half years' penal servitude will in actual fact serve fifteen years and three months; and if he happens to fall under a Royal Amnesty* he will do only ten years and four months; somebody sentenced to six years will be free in five years and two months, and – under an Amnesty – three years and six months. (CHEKHOV'S NOTE)

* For information on "Royal Amnesties", see the second note to p. 67.

p. 213, *there were 424... lodgings*: I have not counted here those convicts living with officials as domestic servants. I consider that, overall, the number living outside the prison is twenty-five per cent, that is, of every four convicts the prison yields one to the colony. This percentage will rise significantly when Article 305 of the *Statutes*, which permits reformees to live outside the prison, is extended to the Korsakovsk District as well; here, at the desire of Mr Bely, all convicts without exception live in the prison. (CHEKHOV'S NOTE)

p. 213, *tenants... lodgings*: Almost all the householders at Alexandrovsk have tenants, and this gives it the aspect of a town. In one cabin I recorded seventeen people. However, crowded cabins such as these differ but little from the communal cell rooms of the prisons. (CHEKHOV'S NOTE)

p. 214, *When his sentence... new site*: Sakhalin is among the most remote parts of Siberia. Very likely in view of the exceptionally severe climate, at first only those settled exiles were compelled to set up home here who had served their penal servitude on Sakhalin itself and had in this fashion managed in advance, if not to get used, then at least to become inured to the place. Now, apparently, they want to alter this procedure. During my stay, by order of Baron Korf, a certain Yudah Gamberg, who had been sentenced to settled exile in Siberia, was sent to Sakhalin and settled at Derbinskoye; while at Dubki lives the settled exile Simon Saulat, who served his penal servitude, not on Sakhalin, but in mainland Siberia. There are, in addition, administrative exiles already here. (CHEKHOV'S NOTE)

p. 215, *The choice of sites... living on it*: In due course the selection of new sites will be put in the charge of a committee in each district made up from the ranks of the prison department, a topographer, an agronomist and a doctor, and then it will be possible to judge from the minutes of this committee why one location or another was chosen. At present, a certain amount of sound judgement may be noticed in the fact that people are settled most readily in river valleys and along byroads – either existing or planned. But plain routine may be observed in this, too, rather than some definite procedure. If they single out some river valley or other, this is not because it has been explored better than the others, or because it is the one most suitable for cultivation, but simply because it lies not far from the administrative centre. The south-western seaboard stands out by reason of its comparatively mild climate, but it is further away from Dooay or Alexandrovsk than the Arkovo Valley and the valley of the Armudan river, and so the latter are preferred. When they settle people along the route of a projected road, they do not have the inhabitants of a new settlement in mind by doing so, but those officials and dog-sled drivers who will in time travel along this road. If it were not for this modest future prospect of enlivening and protecting the highway, and giving shelter to people passing through, it would be hard to understand, for example, why the settlements are necessary which are planned to go along the main road by the Tym, from the upper reaches of the river to the Nyysky Bay. For protecting and enlivening the highway the inhabitants will very likely receive food and money allowances from the government. But if these settlements are a continuation of the present agricultural colony, and the administration relies on rye and wheat, Sakhalin will acquire several thousand more lost, destitute souls, living on God knows what. (CHEKHOV'S NOTE)

p. 217, *buy their homes... loan... condition*: It is precisely here that the settled exile would find so indescribably useful the money he must have earned during his convict term as remuneration for labour. By law, a prisoner sentenced to penal servitude in exile is allocated one-tenth of the income gained from every type of work. If, say, a day's labour on the roadworks is valued at fifty copecks, the convict must receive five copecks daily. During his period under guard, a prisoner is not permitted to spend more than half the money he has earned on his personal needs, and the amount which then remains is issued to him on release. No civil levies or legal costs may be required from this sum, and in the event of the prisoner's death it is issued to his heir. In his *Dossier on the Administrative System on Sakhalin Island* (1878) Prince Shakhovskoy, who ran the Dooay Prison in the '70s, expresses an opinion which the present administration ought to take into consideration and to accept as a guide: "Remunerating the convicts for their labour gives the prisoner at least some property, and all property attaches him to the spot; remuneration allows the prisoners, by mutual consent, to improve their diet, and keep their clothes and accommodation cleaner, and all habituation to comforts creates the greater suffering when they are removed, the more comforts there are; the complete lack of the latter and the permanently gloomy and unfriendly conditions induce in the prisoners such indifference to life, and all the more so to any type of punishment, that frequently, when the number of those chastised has reached eighty per cent of the total, one must despair of the victory of the birch over those trivial innate human requirements for the fulfilment of which he has come under the rod; remuneration of convicts, creating some self-reliance among them, eliminates the waste of clothing, aids the establishment of households, and considerably reduces state expenditure as regards establishing an attachment to the land in them when they leave and go into the settlement."

Tools are issued on credit on condition that the settled exile pays back one-fifth every year. In the Korsakovsk District a carpenter's axe costs 4 roubles, a ripsaw 13 roubles, a spade 1 rouble 80 copecks, a file 44 copecks and nails 10 copecks per *funt*. An axe for cutting down trees is issued on loan for 3 roubles 50 copecks only in those instances where the settler has not hired a carpenter's axe. (CHEKHOV'S NOTE)

p. 218, *co-tenants… half-sharers… every year*: The householder and joint-owner live in the same cabin and sleep on the same stove. Joint ownership of a plot is not impeded either by difference of religion or even by difference of sex. I remember that at Rykovo settled exile Golubyev had the Jew Lyubarsky as a half-sharer. In the same settlement the male settler Ivan Khavrievich had Mariya Vagabond as a co-owner. (CHEKHOV'S NOTE)

p. 218, *The settled exile… of a home*: I have already had occasion to speak of the poverty in which the local rural inhabitants serve their terms, despite the allowances and continual government loans. Here is a graphic depiction of this almost beggar-like life, from the pen of an official personage: "At the settlement of Lyutoga I went into the meanest hovel, which belonged to the settled exile Zerin, who was a bad tailor by trade, and who had already been trying to get established for four years. The poverty and lack of everything were staggering; apart from a rickety table and a stump of wood in place of a chair, there was not a single stick of furniture; apart from a tin kettle made from a paraffin can, there were no signs whatever of crockery or domestic utensils; instead of bedding there was a little heap of straw, on which lay a short sheepskin coat and a second shirt; there was nothing pertaining to his trade either, apart from a few needles, several grey threads, a few buttons and a copper thimble, which did duty as a pipe as well, since the tailor has bored a hole in it and inserts as far as necessary a thin mouthpiece of local cane; it turned out to contain not more than half a thimbleful of tobacco" (Directive no. 318, 1889). (CHEKHOV'S NOTE)

p. 219, *Semirechensk, Akhmolinsk and Semipalatinsk*: These were provinces in south-western Siberia, the southern parts of which imperceptibly shaded into Russia's newly acquired oriental possessions such as Tajikistan, Kirghizia and Turkestan. The Russians were still fighting intensive wars against local tribespeople in these areas, which were far from subjugated. It would have been very tempting – although dangerous – for any exile to head for these areas since, in addition to the attraction of the warmer climate, it would be much simpler than in European Russia to disappear.

p. 219, *a peasant society*: Peasants in a locality would form a society to uphold their rights, maintain prices for produce, form co-operatives to provide services, share out profits and so forth. The various urban classes (merchantry, lower urban classes, artisans, etc.) also had the right to form societies of people of their own social ranking.

p. 219, *does not have the right to return to his own region*: Up till 1888 those who received peasant's rights were forbidden to leave Sakhalin. This prohibition, which deprived the Sakhaliner of all hope of a better life, instilled people with hatred for Sakhalin and, as a repressive measure, could only have led to an increase in the number of escapes, crimes and suicides; its illusory practicality sacrificed justice itself, since the Sakhalin exiles were forbidden what was permitted to exiles to mainland Siberia. This measure was called forth by the consideration that, if the peasants left the island, then ultimately Sakhalin would merely be a place for serving out one's term of exile and not a colony. But would exile for life really make Sakhalin a second Australia? The vitality and well-being of a colony depend not on prohibitions or orders, but on the presence of conditions which guarantee a comfortable and secure life, if not for the exiles themselves then at least for their children and grandchildren. (CHEKHOV'S NOTE)

p. 220, *150 roubles or so*: In the note to p. 217, Chekhov points out that an exile would receive five copecks per day on roadworks, and so it may be seen how vast a sum 150 roubles would be.

p. 221, *a dacha*: Most city-dwellers in Russia in Chekhov's time, as nowadays, possessed a dacha, that is, a country cottage with a piece of land where they could go for weekends. These ranged from a garden shed with a bed and a tiny allotment to a large house with a considerable amount of land.

p. 221, *the Zeya*: The Zeya is a tributary of the river Amur 320 miles in length.

p. 221, *any intention of putting down roots here... leave*: I met only a single person who expressed a wish to stay on Sakhalin for good; this was an unfortunate man, a farmer from the Chernigov Province, who had come here for raping his own daughter; he felt no love for his home area, since he had left unpleasant memories of himself there, and he did not write letters to his children, now grown up, so as not to remind them of him. He will not go over to the mainland because his age will not permit it. (CHEKHOV'S NOTE)

p. 221, *the Ussuri Area*: The Ussuri Administrative Area had been annexed from China in 1858 and in Chekhov's time formed part of the Primorskaya Region. It lay on the rivers Ussuri and Sungachi and was directly opposite Sakhalin Island, being bounded to the east by the Tatar Strait; it had an area of 201,440 square versts (88,350 square miles). It was divided into the North and South Ussuri Districts. Although the climate of this area was not exceptionally good, it was far milder, especially in the south, than the rest of the Primorskaya Region or Sakhalin, so that, as Chekhov says, the prisoners regarded it as akin to the Promised Land.

p. 222, *One day in Vladivostok*: Chekhov and Father Irakly had put into Vladivostok on 16th October 1890 on their way home to European Russia by the sea route.

p. 223, *randomly assembled rabble... settlements*: 5,791 people answered my question "What province are you from?" 260 gave the Tambov Province, 230 the Samara, 201 the Chernigov Province, 201 the Kiev, 199 the Poltava Province, 198 the Voronezh, 168 the Don Region, 153 the Saratov Province, 151 the Kursk, 148 the Perm, 146 the Nizhegorodsk, 142 the Penza, 133 the Moscow, 133 the Tver, 131 the Kherson, 125 the Yekaterinoslav, 122 the Novgorod, 117 the Kharkov and 115 the Oryol Provinces; fewer than 100 come from each of the remaining provinces. The Caucasian Provinces together yield a total of 213, or 3.6 per cent. There is a higher proportion of Caucasians in the prison than in the colony, and this signifies that they serve their labour terms without success, and far from all of them leave to go into settlement; the reasons for this are frequent attempted escapes and, very probably, a high mortality rate. The Province of the Realm of Poland has yielded a total of 455, or 8 per cent, Finland and the Ost-See Provinces* 167, or 2.8 per cent. These figures can give only an approximate notion of the composition of the population by place of birth, but hardly anyone will resolve to draw the conclusion from this that the Tambov Province is the most criminal and that the Ukrainians – of whom, it is relevant to state, there are a great number on Sakhalin – are more criminally inclined than the Russians. (CHEKHOV'S NOTE)

* The Ost-See Provinces were another name for the Baltic Provinces: roughly what would nowadays be Lithuania, Latvia and Estonia.

p. 224, *honourable citizens... traders and foreign subjects*: Peter the Great, who first introduced the Table of Ranks and many of the classes into which Russian society was divided, imported a very large number of foreigners, especially Germans and Dutch, to help in his crash programme of modernization. Any foreigners staying for a prolonged period had to acquire Russian identity documents and be registered in the special social class of "foreign subjects": these individuals owed obedience to Russian law. However, by Chekhov's time, the number of foreign subjects staying for a period of any length in Russia had fallen considerably, and besides, foreign subjects guilty of serious crimes were usually deported to face trial in their own countries. Therefore the number of people in this class on Sakhalin must have been minute. The title of "Honourable Citizen" was reserved for scholars, authors, artists and so on. The "Traders" were members of the *meshchane* – people who in Peter the Great's time, although not as low in status as the working class, could not raise the money (500 roubles) to join the merchants' guild. They were usually small shopkeepers and successful artisans, and their members formed "societies" to safeguard their interests; they would try to save enough money to gain admission to the guilds of the merchantry or middle classes.

p. 224, *nobility or gentry... number of exiles*: The nobility, the gentry and the privileged classes in general do not know how to plough or how to chop wood for cabins. They should work, they should undergo the same punishment as everybody else, but they have not got the strength. They reluctantly seek light work and even frequently do nothing at all. But as if to make up for this they live in constant terror that their fate will change and they will be sent to the mines, suffer corporal punishment, be put in irons and suchlike. The majority of them are people who are already tired of life, humble and sad, and, looking at them, you cannot imagine them at all in the role of criminal offenders. But one does also come across designing sharks, impertinent and brazen individuals, thoroughly depraved, possessed by what the English call "moral insanity",* who create the impression of being somehow prison upstarts; their manner of speaking, their smiles, their walk, their fawning helpfulness – it all has an unhealthy, low, vulgar tone to it. However that may be, it is awful to be in their position. One convict, a former officer, when he was taken in the prisoners' carriage to Odessa, saw through the window "picturesque and poetic fishing grounds in which work was carried on by means of kindled tar-covered branches and torches... the verdure of the Ukraine was already beginning to gleam... Within her oak and lime woodlands, by a strip of road, violets and lilies of the valley could be distinguished... thus the scent of flowers and the scent of lost liberty are experienced together" (*Vladivostok*, 1888, no. 14). A former nobleman, a murderer, narrating to me how his friends had accompanied him out of European Russia, said: "My senses had become aroused, and I wanted only one thing – to fade away into the background, to disappear, but my acquaintances didn't understand this, and they all tried to outdo each other in showing me every kindness." Nothing acts so unpleasantly on criminals from the privileged classes, when they are being led or conveyed along the street, as the curiosity of the free, especially acquaintances. If it is desired to find out where a certain criminal is among a crowd of prisoners, and they call for him loudly by name, this causes him great pain. Unfortunately prisoners from the privileged classes who have been convicted are often jeered at in prison, in the street, and even in the press. In a certain daily paper I read about a former Commercial Counsellor,* allegedly somewhere in Siberia, going via the *étape* route; he had been invited to breakfast, and when, after breakfast, he had been escorted off further into Siberia, the hosts were missing a spoon: the Commercial Counsellor had stolen it! They wrote about a former Gentleman of the Tsar's Bedchamber that he was not bored in exile as he had oceans and oceans of champagne and as many Gypsy girls as he wanted. This kind of thing is vicious. (CHEKHOV'S NOTE)

* "Moral insanity" is in English in the original.

* Commercial Counsellor was an honorary title for the most out-standing of the urban class of "merchants", i.e. upper-middle-class townsfolk. Whereas peasant and other urban classes formed "societies" (see the second note to p. 219), the merchantry would form a "guild". A person who had been an outstanding member of this merchant's guild for twelve years could be nominated a "Commercial Counsellor".

p. 225, *fifty-three women to every 100 men*: According to the tenth census of the European Russian Provinces (1857–60) there were, on average, 104.8 women to every hundred men. (CHEKHOV'S NOTE)

p. 226, *female offenders... total number of convicts*: This figure may serve only to define the composition of the convicts according to sex; it does not yield reliable material for a comparative estimation of the morality of both sexes. Women end up in penal servitude more rarely not because they are more moral than men, but because, from the very way their life is ordered, and partly from the characteristics of their physical make-up, they are exposed to a lesser degree than men to the risk of committing serious criminal offences. They do not work in government offices, they do not go on military service, they do not go away to seasonal work, do not work in forests, in mines or at sea, and therefore are strangers to offences in contravention of official duties, or against military discipline, or offences a direct part in which requires a man's physical strength, for example, plundering the mails, highway robbery and so on; the statutes on offences against chastity, on rape, corruption and unnatural vices concern men alone. But on the other hand, they murder, torture, inflict serious injuries and conceal murders relatively more often than men; among the latter the total of murderers is 47 per cent, but among the female offenders 57 per cent. And, as for those convicted of murder by poisoning, among the women there are not only more relatively but even absolutely. In 1889 the number of female poisoners in all the three districts was shown as being almost three times greater in absolute terms than the number of male poisoners, and 23 times greater in relative terms. However that may be, women enter the colony less frequently than men, and even notwithstanding the parties of free-status women who arrive every year, there is still an overwhelming preponderance of men. Such unequal distribution of the sexes is inevitable in an exile colony, and an evening up can take place only with the discontinuation of the exile system, or when there begins a flow of immigrants to the island who will merge with the exiles, or if there appears among us our own Mrs Fry,* who will energetically propagate the idea of transporting to Sakhalin honest girls from poor families for the purpose of developing family life.

On the subject of West European and Russian exile, and on the female question in particular, see Professor I.L. Foynitzky, in his well-known book *Course of Study in Penology in Conjunction with Prison Management*. (CHEKHOV'S NOTE)

* Mrs Elizabeth Fry (1780–1845), born Elizabeth Gurney, was a renowned British prison reformer. Two volumes of her memoirs, edited by her daughter, were published in London in 1847.

p. 227, *the landing stage to the prison… thirty-six*: In one of his newspaper sketches Dr A. Shcherbak writes: "The disembarkation was completed only on the morning of the next day. The convicts selected for the Korsakovsk Post still had to be received back on board, and various receipts for delivery taken. The convicts – 50 men, 20 women – were sent without delay. In the itemized records the men's trades were not mentioned, and the women were very old. They had great difficulty getting off the ship" ('With exiled hard-labour convicts', *New Times*, no. 5381). (CHEKHOV'S NOTE)

p. 229, *samovar... horse... heifer... boards*: See the note to p. 10. His cabin being roofed with boards, and possession of a heifer and samovar, are signs that he is prosperous.

p. 229, *in the official registers... home*: For instance, the directive: "In accordance with the application of the Governor of the Alexandrovsk District, as set out in the report of 5th January, under figure 75, female convict Akulina Kuznetzova of the Alexandrovsk Prison is transferred to the Tymovsk District to establish a household jointly with settled exile Aleksey Sharapov" (1889, no. 25). (CHEKHOV'S NOTE)

p. 230, *convict women become cohabitants... bewilderment*: And besides it is difficult to see where the women would live if they refused to cohabit. No special quarters exist for them in the penal settlement. In his report for 1889, the Head of the Medical Department writes: "On their arrival on Sakhalin it is left to them to bother about getting themselves lodgings... to pay for which, some of them are not in a position to disregard any ways for raising the means." (CHEKHOV'S NOTE)

p. 230, *Rumours of coercion... caverns*: I personally treated these rumours with scepticism, but all the same, I checked them on the spot and collected all the instances which might have served as grounds for them. The story is told that three or four years ago, when General Gintze was the Governor of the Island, a certain female convict, a non-Russian, was married off against her will to a former rural police inspector. In the Korsakovsk District, female convict Yagelskaya received thirty strokes of the birch because she wanted to leave her cohabitant, settled exile Kotlyarov. In the same district, the settled exile Yarovaty complained that his woman was refusing to live with him. The direction followed: "Name unknown, flog her thoroughly." "How many?" "Seventy." They thrashed the woman, but she still stood her ground and went to live with settled exile Malovechkin, who now cannot speak too highly of her. An elderly man, settled exile

Rezvetzov, found his cohabitant with settled exile Rodin, and went off to complain. The direction followed: "Call her here!" The woman appeared. "So you, you so-and-so, don't want to live with Rezvetzov? The birch!" And Rezvetzov was commanded to punish his cohabitant with his own hands, which he proceeded to do. In the end, though, she still prevailed, and I noted her down as being the cohabitant, not of Rezvetzov, but of Rodin. These are all the instances the population can recall. If a female convict changes cohabitants too often from cantankerousness or libertinism, she is punished, but such cases are rare and arise only as a result of complaints from the male settled exiles. (CHEKHOV'S NOTE)

p. 231, *a Chechen*: Chechens are a North Caucasian people. They are Sunni Muslims.

p. 231, *Neither a... obstacle to cohabitation... by her*: At Upper Armudan I noted the Russian woman Yekaterina Petrova as cohabitant of the Tatar Tukhvatula; she has children by him; the workman in this family is a Muslim, and so are the guests. In Rykovo the settled exile Mahomed Uste-Nor lives with the Russian woman Avdotya Medvedova. In Lower Armudan the Lutheran settled exile Peretzky is living with the Jewess Leah Permut Broch, and in Bolshoye Takoay peasant-in-exile Kalevsky is living with an Aino woman. (CHEKHOV'S NOTE)

p. 231, *doesn't remember her home district*: The apparent description could well be part of the woman's surname.

p. 234, *There are... voluntarily... women*: In the first ten years from the beginning of transportation by sea, 1879 to 1889, the steamers of the Voluntary Fleet conveyed 8,430 convict men and women and 1,146 members of their families who had followed them voluntarily. (CHEKHOV'S NOTE)

p. 234, *deception... often justified*: One prisoner even boasted in a letter that he possessed foreign silver coins.* The tone of such letters is sportive and bubbling with high spirits. (CHEKHOV'S NOTE)

* Silver coins had a great prestige value in Russia. Owing to depreciation in the value of paper money, one silver rouble was worth 3.6 paper roubles.

p. 234, *Among the wives*: It occasionally happens that husbands follow their wives into exile. There are only three such husbands on Sakhalin: the ex-soldiers Andrey Naydush and Andrey Ganin at

Alexandrovsk, and peasant-farmer Zhigulin at Derbinskoye. The latter, who had come with his wife and children, is an old man, likes to play the fool, gives the impression of being a drunkard and is the laughing stock of the whole street. One old Russian ethnic German came with his wife and son Gottlieb. He cannot speak a single word of Russian. I asked him, among other things, how old he was.

"I was born in 1832," he said in German, then wrote 1890 on the table in chalk, and subtracted 1832.

One convict, a former merchant, turned up here with his steward, who, however, spent one single month at Alexandrovsk and then returned to European Russia. According to Article 264 of the *Statutes on Exiles*, Jewish husbands cannot follow their convicted wives into exile, and the latter are permitted to take only nursing babies with them, and then only with the consent of their husbands. (CHEKHOV'S NOTE)

p. 235, *lamentations for the deceased*: "Lamentations for the deceased" were not church hymns but folk incantations, chanted by the peasantry at a death, or when somebody from their village was being forcibly conscripted into the army. The night before a wedding, the bride's young female friends were supposed traditionally to intone a lament for the fact that she was leaving them for ever. These incantations differed widely from region to region, reflecting the local dialect and musical tradition.

p. 235, *a free-woman... without money... adult*: Here you are struck in the pit of your stomach by the difference in the position of this free-woman, a lawful wife, and her female convict neighbour, a cohabitant, who receives three *funty* of bread daily from the state. At Vladimirovka a certain free-status woman is under suspicion of murdering her husband; if she is sentenced to convict labour, she starts receiving rations – which means she will finish up better off than she was before the trial. (CHEKHOV'S NOTE)

p. 236, *Molokan*: Molokane (literally "Milk-Drinkers") were a radical sect, an off-shoot of the Dukhobors. The origins of the latter are shrouded in mystery, but one theory is that they were Old Ritualists (see the second note to p. 114), who were influenced by Protestants fleeing from persecution in seventeenth-century Germany. Even if this had been the case, the Molokane had by the nineteenth century become unrecognizable as Orthodox Christians and were regarded as completely heretical. The sect's members totally spurned the priesthood, ritualism, icons and splendour of the conventional Church, and they rejected worldly values, military service and any form of bloodshed. Consequently they were vegetarians and restricted their diet to vegetables, fruit and dairy produce. The Orthodox Church abstained from meat and dairy produce on fast days, but the Molokane made a point of deliberately drinking milk on these days to show their disdain for Orthodox ritual – hence their name.

p. 237, *free-status women... unlegalized marriage*: The *Statutes on Exiles* allocate space to the question of free-women, too. According to Statute 85, "Ladies who come of their own free will must not be separated from their husbands and must not be subjected to the stringencies of supervision over the entire length of the journey." In European Russia or on the Voluntary Fleet steamer, they are free from supervision, but in Siberia, however, when the party is proceeding on foot or in carts, the military escorts do not have time to make out in the crowd where the exiles and where the free-persons are. In the Zabaikal Region I saw men, women and children bathing together in the river; the escort guards were standing round in a semicircle, and would permit nobody to leave this semicircle, even children. According to Statutes 173 and 253, women who voluntarily follow their husbands "receive clothing, footwear and money for food for the whole length of the journey to the place of destination" on the scale of the prisoners' rations. But it does not say in the *Statutes* precisely how free-status women should follow their husbands across Siberia – on foot or in carts. According to Statute 406, they are, with the consent of their husbands, allowed temporary leave of absence from the place of exile to the internal provinces of the Tsarist Empire. If the husband dies in exile, or if the marriage is dissolved in consequence of a fresh crime, the wife, according to Statute 408, may return to her native district at government expense.

Describing the situation of convict-exiles' wives and children, whose only crime is that fate has made them relations of criminals, Vlasov states in his report that this is "almost the bleakest aspect of our whole system of deportation". I have already spoken of how unevenly free-status women are spread around the districts and settlements, and how little they are valued by the local administration. Let the reader remember the Dooay family barracks. The fact that free-women and their children are kept in the communal cells, as if in prison, under abominable conditions, along with prison card-sharpers and their lovers and their pigs, and are kept at Dooay – that is, the most appalling and hopeless location on the island – this fact sufficiently portrays the colonizing and agricultural policy of the local authorities. (CHEKHOV'S NOTE)

p. 237, *Cherepovetsk*: The Cherepovetsk District is in the Novgorod Region of European Russia. Its county town is Cherepovetsk – 59 degrees longitude and 47 latitude.

p. 237, *age groups... (24.1 per cent)*: Here is the table of age ranges which I compiled:

Years

From	To	Male	Female
0	5	493	473
5	10	319	314
10	15	215	234
15	20	89	96
20	25	134	136
25	35	1419	680
35	45	1405	578
45	55	724	236
55	65	318	56
65	75	90	12
75	85	17	1
85	95	–	1

Age unknown – Male 142, Female 35.
(CHEKHOV'S NOTE)

p. 237, *Those between the ages... in general*: In the Cherepovetsk District those of working age comprise 44.9 per cent of the population, in the Moscow District 45.4 per cent and in the Tambov District 42.7 per cent. See V.I. Nikolsky's book *The Tambov District. Statistics on Population and Morbidity*, 1885. (CHEKHOV'S NOTE)

p. 238, *Compared... this is low*: In the Cherepovetsk District it is 37.3

per cent and in the Tambov District around 39 per cent. (CHEKHOV'S NOTE)

p. 239, *There is a total... Amur river*: It is apparent from the table that among the age ranges of childhood the sexes are distributed almost equally, and, from 15 to 20 and from 20 to 25, there is even a certain surplus of women; but then between 25 and 35 there are more than twice as many men as there are women, and, among the elderly and very old, the preponderance may be termed overwhelming. The small number of old men and the almost complete absence of old women point to a dearth in Sakhalin families of the element of experience, and a lack of tradition. It might be relevant to state in this context that, every time I visited a prison, it appeared to me there were comparatively more old men in there than out in the colony. (CHEKHOV'S NOTE)

p. 239, *amnesty from the throne*: "Amnesties from the Throne" are explained in the second note to p. 67.

p. 239, *the Sakhalin Siberian railway*: The project to build the Trans-Siberian Railway was given the Royal Assent on 15th February 1891. The first sod of the Ussuri section – the final length – of the railway was turned by the Crown Prince, later Tsar Nicholas II, on 19th May 1891 at Vladivostok. Work did not actually begin until February 1893, and the line eventually reached its destination, Khabarovsk – a total distance of 721 versts – on 1st November 1897.

Chekhov in his book continually stresses that free persons' labour will always be better than convict labour in any field. The history of work on the Ussuri section of the railway seems to bear this out. The Siberian prison authorities were asked to form a battalion of 2,000 convicts to work on the project. By 1894 the battalion had been disbanded and the convicts sent back to their respective institutions, since their labour had proved so disastrously inept.

p. 239, *the family as a basis for the colony... present*: Although there is no evidence from anywhere to make it apparent that the cementing of an exile colony depends in the main on the development of a basis in the family, we know that the prosperity of Virginia was consolidated before they began to transport women there. (CHEKHOV'S NOTE)

p. 239, *to shun legalized marriage... ones*: If we judge merely from the bald statistics, we may draw the conclusion that the church form of marriage is the most unsuitable for Russian exiles. From the government registers – for instance, those of 1887 – we see that there were 211 convict women in the Alexandrovsk District. Of those, only 34 were within the law, while 136 were cohabiting with convicts and settlers. In the Tymovsk District in the same year, 11 out of 194 convict women were living with their lawful husbands, while 161 were cohabiting. In the Korsakovsk District not a single convict woman was living with a husband; 115 were partners in unlegalized marriages; and of 21 female settled exiles only four were married. (CHEKHOV'S NOTE)

p. 240, *It is necessary… divorce… need*: In his *The Administrative System on Sakhalin Island*, Prince Shakhovskoy writes, among other things: "Quite serious difficulties in the path of the unimpeded conclusion of marriage contracts are presented by the family records, in which the religion and family status are often not noted, and – the main thing – it is not known whether a divorce has taken place with the partner who has remained behind in European Russia; to find out about this, and, even more so, to obtain a divorce by applying through the Church Consistory Court from Sakhalin Island, is an almost impossible business."

Here is a sample of some instances of how families are set up in the colony. In Maloye Takoay, female convict Praskovya Solovyova is cohabiting with settled exile Kudrin, who cannot marry her, since he has a wife left behind in his home district. This Praskovya's seventeen-year-old free-status daughter, Natalya, is living with settled exile Gorodinsky, who will not marry her for precisely the same reason. Settled exile Ignatiev complained to me at Novo-Mikhailovka that they would not marry him to his cohabitant, because "for donkey's years" they had not been able to determine his family situation; his cohabitant implored me to intercede and said: "It's a sin to live like this, we're not young any more." I could cite several hundred such examples. (CHEKHOV'S NOTE)

p. 241, *unequal marriages have taken place… sixteen-year-olds*: Non-commissioned officers, especially overseers, are considered enviable bridegrooms; they well know their value in this respect and behave towards their fiancées and fiancées' parents with the same sort of unbridled arrogance for which N.S. Leskov so disliked "the malcontented beasts of bishops".* Over the last ten years several *mésalliances* have been made. A Collegiate Registrar has married a convict's daughter, a Court Counsellor a settled exile's daughter, a Captain a settled exile's daughter, a merchant a female peasant-in-exile, and a noblewoman has married a settled exile. These infrequent instances of cultivated and educated people marrying exiles' daughters are extremely pleasing and attractive and cannot fail to have a beneficial influence on the colony. In January 1880, in the church at Dooay, a convict was wedded to a Gilyak woman. At Rykovo I noted down eleven-year-old Grigory Sivokobylka, whose mother was a Gilyak. Generally speaking, marriages between Russians and natives are extremely rare. I was told about one overseer who was living with a Gilyak woman, who had borne a son and who wanted to be baptized so that she could then be officially married in church. Father Irakly knew of an exiled Yakut who was married to a Georgian woman; they both had only a poor understanding of Russian. As far as Muslims are concerned, they do not give up polygamy even in exile, and several of them have two wives each; for example, Jakanbetov at Alexandrovsk has two wives – Batyma and Sasena – while Abubakirov at Korsakovsk also has two – Ganosta and Verkhonisa. At Andreye-Ivanovskoye I saw an extraordinarily pretty fifteen-year-old Tatar girl whose husband had bought her from her father for 100 roubles; when her husband is not at home, she sits on the bed, and the settlers gaze admiringly at her through the door of the entrance hall.

The *Statutes on Exiles* permit exiles of both sexes to marry only after they have been in the "reformee" category for one to three years; apparently, a woman who enters the colony but is still in the "probationer" category may be only a cohabitant and not a wife. Exiled men are permitted to marry female offenders, but those of female sex, who have been deprived of all rights of status, before they are transferred to peasant-in-exile status may marry only exiles.

A free-status woman who weds an exile who is marrying for the first time in Siberia is allocated 50 roubles by the state; a settled exile who gets married for the first time in Siberia and who weds a female exile is granted 15 roubles unconditionally and the same amount on loan.

Nothing is said in the *Statutes* about the marriage of vagabonds.* What documents are used to determine their family situation and age when they marry, I do not know. That they are officially married on Sakhalin I first learnt from the following document, written in the form of an official request to "His Most High Excellency, the Head of Sakhalin Island. Certificate of Settled Exile of Tymovsk District, Rykovo Settlement, Ivan, who does not remember his family name and is thirty-five years old. That I, Don't-remember by surname, have entered legal wedlock with female settled exile Mariya Beryoznikova on 12th November last year, 1888." Two settlers had signed it because he was illiterate. (CHEKHOV'S NOTE)

* "Malcontented beasts of bishops" is a phrase from a story by Nikolai Leskov (1831–95), who, like Anthony Trollope, wrote tales with an ecclesiastical setting. The phrase was drawn by him from Peter the Great's "Church Statutes", the laws Peter drew up in his reform of the church in the early eighteenth century.

* The whole point about vagabonds is, of course, that they had no identity papers and nobody had any idea who they were or what their status was, or whether they were married already. Therefore it should have been impossible for them legally to marry.

p. 242, *Over the ten-year... races*: These figures, which I took from the parish registers of births, marriages and deaths, relate only to the population belonging to the Russian Orthodox Church. (CHEKHOV'S NOTE)

European Russians considered the southern races such as the Armenians, Georgians, etc., to be more "fertile" than them. Muslim peoples such as the Tatars were also considered to have a higher birth rate than the European races of the Tsarist Empire.

p. 242, *coefficient of childbirth... (49.8)*: According to Yanson 49.8, or practically 50, births per 1,000. (CHEKHOV'S NOTE)

p. 243, *unfavourable conditions... birth rate*: Acute catastrophes which pass rapidly, such as crop failures, war and the like, lower the birth rate, whereas chronic adversities such as high child mortality, and also, perhaps, captivity, serfdom, exile, etc., intensify it. In some families an increased birth rate may be observed in conjunction with psychological degeneration. (CHEKHOV'S NOTE)

p. 244, *the first group... the second... 37.2 per cent*: The illegitimate in the first group are children of convict women, born for the most part after the trial, in prison; in the families that have voluntarily followed their husbands, wives and parents, there are no illegitimate children at all. (CHEKHOV'S NOTE)

p. 247, *children... food subsidies*: The extent of the handout also depends on whether the official interprets only the lame, armless and hunchbacks as falling within the category of "cripples and deformed" or whether he also includes those with consumption, the feeble-minded and the blind.

How can the Sakhalin children be aided? First of all, it seems to me, the right to this assistance should not be hedged around by the requirement of a qualification such as "poorest", "cripple" and so forth. All should be aided without exception, and we should not fear deception when doing so; it is better to be deceived than to deceive oneself. The form the assistance takes is determined by local circumstances. If it were up to me, then, with the money which is now expended on "food subsidies", I would set up tearooms for all the women and children in the posts and settlements, I would issue food and clothing subsidies to all pregnant women and all those suckling children without exception, and the "food subsidies" of one and a half and three roubles a month I would retain only for girls from thirteen years old up till they were married, and I would give them this money directly into their hands.

Every year philanthropists send here from St Petersburg, for distribution to the children, sheepskin jackets, aprons and pinafores, felt boots, caps and bonnets, concertinas, spiritually edifying booklets and pens. On reception of these items, the Governor of the Island invites the local ladies to take up the distribution and handing out of the gifts. People say that the fathers sell these things for drink, or lose them at card games, that they would do better to send grain instead of concertinas, etc., etc., but these magnanimous people must not allow such remarks to disturb them. The children are usually delighted, and the mothers and fathers endlessly grateful. It would be quite appropriate if the philanthropists who interest themselves in the fate of exiles' children were to receive annually information, as detailed as possible, about the Sakhalin children, their numbers, their composition by sex and age, how many of them can read or write, how many are non-Christian and so forth. If the philanthropists were aware, for example, of how many literate children there were, they would know how many books or pencils to send, so as not to upset anybody, and how to assign the toys and clothes in the most fitting manner, taking into consideration the sex, age and nationality of the children. On Sakhalin itself everything having any connection whatever with philanthropy should be removed from the jurisdiction of the police department, who are snowed under with work as it is, and the organization of this aid should be handed over to the local people with education, among whom there are quite a large number who would be only too glad to take upon themselves this lively, energetic work. Sometimes during the winter, amateur theatricals are given at Alexandrovsk for the benefit of the children. Not long ago at the Korsakovsk Post, the professional staff collected money by subscription, bought a whole lot of different kinds of material, and their wives made up a large quantity of outer clothing and underclothes and distributed them among the children.

The children form a burden from the economic point of view, and are a "punishment from God for sins", but this does not prevent the exiles, if they have no children of their own, from taking on and adopting other people's. Those with children express the wish that their children should die, and those without children take in other people's orphans to be their own. It does happen that exiles adopt orphans and poor children with an eye to the food subsidies and all kinds of other allowances, and even reckoning on the foster-child going begging in the streets, but the majority of exiles must be guided by pure motives. Not only children become their "children", but adults, too, and even the elderly. For instance, settled exile Ivan Novikov the First, who is sixty years old, is considered the foster-son of Yevgeny Yefimov, who is forty-two. At Rykovo, Yelisey Maklakov, who is seventy, has been registered as the foster-son of Ilya Minayev.

According to the *Statutes on Exiles,* young children who follow into Siberia their parents, who have been exiled or settled there, make their way on carts; there should be one cart to every five children. What children belong in this instance to the category "young" the *Statutes* do not say. Children following after their parents receive clothing, footwear and food money for the entire duration of the journey. When his family voluntarily follows a convicted criminal into exile, the children who have already reached the age of fourteen go only at their own wish. Children who have reached the age of seventeen can leave the place of exile and return to their home region without their parents' permission. (CHEKHOV'S NOTE)

p. 249, *The agronomists on the spot... offices*: In his instructions on
the Inspector of Agriculture's report of 1890, the Governor of the
Island states: "At last we have a document which is far from complete,
perhaps, but is at least based on the data of observation, classified
by an expert, and elucidated with no desire to please somebody."
This report he calls the "first step in this direction" – this implies
that all the reports up till 1890 *were* written with the desire to please
somebody. Further on in his instructions, General Kononovich says
that the sole source of information about agriculture on Sakhalin up
until 1890 was "idle concoctions".

The official government agronomist on Sakhalin is called the
Inspector of Agriculture. It is a class VI post with a good salary.
After two years on the island, the present Inspector of Agriculture
has presented a report; this is a small, purely academic piece of
work, lacking descriptions of any personal observation made by the
writer, and his conclusions are not outstanding for their accuracy,
but on the other hand data on meteorology and fauna are set forth
concisely in the report, giving a fairly clear idea of the inhabited
section of the island. This report has been printed and will most
probably be included in the literature relating to Sakhalin. As for
those agriculturalists who served here earlier, they were all terribly
unfortunate. I have already more than once mentioned M.S. Mitzul,
who was an agronomist, then became a head of department, and
finally died of *angina pectoris* not even having managed to survive
to the age of forty-five. Another agronomist, so they say, tried to
prove that farming on Sakhalin was impossible, and was always
dispatching documents or telegrams somewhere or other, and he
also died, apparently of a profound nervous disorder; at any rate,
he is now recalled as an honest, erudite but crazy individual. The
third "head of the agricultural section", a Pole, was dismissed by
the Governor of the Island in outrageous circumstances rare in the
annals of officialdom; the order was given to issue him his travelling
expenses only when "he produces an agreement concluded with a
dog-sled driver to take him to Nikolayevsk"; the authorities evidently
feared that the agronomist, on taking his travelling expenses, would
remain on the island for good (Directive no. 349, 1888). As for the
fourth agronomist, a German who did nothing and who understood
hardly anything about agronomy, Father Irakly related to me how,

after a frost in August which had nipped the crops, he drove to Rykovo, assembled a gathering and asked grandly: "Why did you have a frost here?" The most intelligent person emerged from the crowd and answered: "We wouldn't know, if it please Your Excellency. It must be the grace of the Lord which is pleased to arrange that things happen like that." The agronomist was completely satisfied with this response, sat in his carriage and drove off home with the feeling of having done his duty. (CHEKHOV'S NOTE)

p. 249, *Polonius… weasel*: See *Hamlet* Act III, Scene 2, ll. 366–72.

p. 250, *crude lies… ruses… yield*: Writes a correspondent in the newspaper *Vladivostok*, 1886, no. 43: "The new agronomist who has arrived on Sakhalin (a Prussian subject) has marked his arrival by setting up and opening, on 1st October, the Sakhalin Agricultural Exhibition, the exhibitors at which were the settled exiles of the Alexandrovsk and Tymovsk Districts, and also the state-run vegetable gardens… The cereal grains exhibited by the settled exiles were not distinguished by anything special, if we do not take into account that among the quantity of grain supposedly brought forth on Sakhalin there had also come to be grain ordered from the famous firm of Grachov* for sowing. Settled exile Sychov of the Tymovsk District, who exhibited grain with certification from the Tymovsk authorities that he had obtained 70 poods of such wheat from the current harvest, was exposed as a fraud, that is, he had exhibited specially selected wheat." There is more about this exhibition in no. 50 of the same paper: "Everybody present was amazed in particular at the unusual specimens of vegetables, for instance, cabbage-heads weighing 22½ *funty,* black radishes weighing 13 *funty* each, potatoes of 3 *funty* and so forth. I may make so bold as to say that Central Europe could not boast of better specimens of vegetables." (CHEKHOV'S NOTE)

* Yefim Grachov (1826–77) was a renowned horticulturalist. He bred many new kinds of fruit and vegetable, for instance the Grachov musk-melon, which is apparently world renowned. He started a company to trade in seeds and plants; this firm exhibited widely in Russia and abroad, winning many gold medals, including one at the World Exhibition in Paris in 1870. After Grachov's death, the company was run by his son Vladimir, who died in 1890 when Chekhov was on Sakhalin.

p. 251, *land under cultivation... selective figures... size*: With the increase in population it is becoming harder all the time to find convenient land. River valleys covered with deciduous woodland – elm, hawthorn, elder and suchlike – where the soil is deep and fertile present rare oases amidst the tundra, fenland, mountains covered by burnt-out forest, and lowlands with coniferous forests and subsoil through which water drains badly. Even in the southern part of the island these valleys alternate with mountains and quagmires on which the scanty vegetation barely differs from the vegetation of the polar regions. Thus, the whole of the vast area between the Takoay Valley and Mauka – which are both cultivated places – is occupied by utterly hopeless swampland; perhaps they will succeed in laying roads through this swamp, but it is beyond human power to change the harsh climate. However large the area of southern Sakhalin might appear to be, up till now they have succeeded in discovering only 405 desyatins suitable for arable fields, vegetable gardens and farmsteads (Directive no. 318, 1889). However, the commission headed by Vlasov and Mitzul which was trying to resolve the suitability of Sakhalin as a penal agricultural colony found that in the central part of the island the amount of land which could be brought under cultivation "must be a great deal larger than 200,000 desyatins" and in the southern section the quantity of such land "stretches to 220,000 desyatins". (CHEKHOV'S NOTE)

p. 251, *northern districts... barley*: Details in *Report on the Agricultural Situation on Sakhalin Island in 1889, Presented to the Governor of the Island* by Mr von Friken. (CHEKHOV'S NOTE)

p. 253, *lady*: The word "lady" implies that a non-convict or non-peasant woman is being referred to.

p. 253, *That branch of agriculture... business*: For some reason the onion alone has responded poorly to cultivation. The lack of this vegetable in the exiles' regimen is made up by *cheremsha* (*Allium victoriale*) which grows wild here. This bulbous plant with a strong garlic-like smell was at one time considered by the soldiers at the posts to be a sure preventative against scurvy, and one can judge from the hundreds of poods which were laid in by military and prison gangs every winter how widespread this illness was here. People say the ramson is tasty and nutritious, but not everybody finds its odour pleasant; whenever, not just indoors, but even outside, a person came close to me who used ramsons in his diet, I would begin to feel suffocated.

Just how large the area is which is occupied by hay meadows on Sakhalin is still not known, although statistics are actually cited in the Inspector of Agriculture's report. Whatever these figures might be, the only things beyond doubt at the present time are that far from every landholder knows in spring where he is going to make hay in the summer, that there will not be enough of it, and towards the end of winter the cattle will become scrawny from lack of fodder. The best haymaking land is taken over by the ones who are most powerful – i.e. the prison and army teams; the settled exiles, on the other hand, are left either with the most distant meadows, or else with those places where the hay can be reaped with a sickle but not mown with a scythe. As a result of the subsoil, through which water can drain but poorly, the meadows here are, for the most part, marshy, and always wet, and for this reason the only things that grow on them are bitter-tasting cereal grasses and sedge, which give coarse and not very nutritious hay. The Inspector of Agriculture says that, in nutritional value, the local hay can hardly be said to be equal to half the quantity of normal hay; the exiles, too, consider the hay to be bad, and those who are well off do not give it neat to the animals but mixed with flour or potatoes. Sakhalin hay does not have at all the same pleasant fragrance as our European Russian hay. Whether those gigantic grasses which grow in the woodland valleys and along the rivers, and which people talk about so much, may be considered a good source of fodder, I will not undertake to judge. I would mention in this respect that the seeds of one of these types of grass, namely Sakhalin buckwheat, have already appeared on sale in European Russia. As to whether the cultivation of fodder grass is necessary on Sakhalin, and whether it is possible, the Inspector of Agriculture's report says not a single word.

Now to cattle-breeding. In 1889 there was one milk cow to every two and a half households in the Alexandrovsk and Korsakovsk Districts, and one to every three and a third in the Tymovsk. Almost precisely the same figures are shown for working animals, that is, horses and oxen; once again, the best of the districts, the Korsakovsk, turns out to be the most impoverished in this respect, too. However, these figures do not reflect the real state of affairs, since the Sakhalin cattle and horses are all allocated among the plot-holders extremely unequally. The whole lot of them are concentrated in the hands of nobody but the prosperous householders who have large plots of land or who are engaged in business. (CHEKHOV'S NOTE)

p. 253, *vertebrate fauna… here*: Details may be found in A.M. Nikolsky, 'Sakhalin Island and its vertebrate fauna'. (CHEKHOV'S NOTE)

p. 254, *deer… wolves*: Wolves keep far away from habitations, since they fear domestic animals. In order that such an explanation might not seem incredible, I shall cite another exactly identical example: Busse writes that an Aino, on seeing a pig for the first time in his life, was terrified; and Middendorf also states that when sheep were first reared on the Amur, the wolves would not touch them. Wild deer are scattered particularly along the western coast of the northern section of the island; here they gather on the tundra in winter, while, according to Glen, in the spring, when they go to the sea to lick salt, they can be seen in herds, in countless numbers, on the broad plains of that part of the island. In the way of birds, there are geese, various species of duck, willow grouse, capercaillie, hazel grouse, curlew and woodcock; the migrating season lasts till June. I arrived on Sakhalin in July, when there was already a deathly hush in the taiga; the island appeared lifeless, and one just had to accept the word of observers that Kamchatka nightingales,* blue tits, thrushes and siskins could be found here. There are many crows, but no magpies or starlings. Polyakov saw only one swallow on Sakhalin, and even that, in his opinion, had come to the island accidentally, having lost its way. Once I thought I saw a female quail in the grass; peering a bit more closely, I saw it was a small, beautiful creature called a *burunduk*.* This is the smallest mammal in the northern districts. According to Nikolsky, there are no domestic mice here; however, in documents dating right from the very inception of the colony, there are already mentions of "sawdust, crumbs and food spoilt by mice and rats". (CHEKHOV'S NOTE)

* The Kamchatka nightingale is a variant of the northern nightingale (*Luscinia luscinia*).

* A *burunduk* is a small, stripy animal similar to a chipmunk.

p. 254, *tigers*: The Siberian tiger is the largest cat in the world and can weigh as much as 850 British pounds. It is extremely rare and now numbers no more than 200.

p. 255, *zubatka*: A *zubatka* is a lancet-fish.

p. 256, *herring run... boiling*: One writer saw a Japanese net which "occupied a circumference of three versts in the sea and, being attached to the shore, formed a sort of sack, from which the herring were gradually scooped out". In his memoirs Busse says: "The Japanese seine-nets are numerous and of an uncommon vastness. One net encloses a stretch of about 70 sazhens from the shore. But what was my amazement when, with still about ten sazhens left to lug it ashore, the Japanese left it in the water, since these ten sazhens of net were so full of herring that, notwithstanding all the efforts of 60 workmen, they could not drag it any closer to the shore... Oarsmen, placing their paddles in the water to row, would throw up several herring with each stroke of every paddle, and they complained that they got in the way of rowing." The progress of the herring and the manner in which the Japanese fish for them are described in detail in Busse and Mitzul. (CHEKHOV'S NOTE)

p. 256, *Where not so... wilderness*: *Maritime Gazette*, 1880, no. 3. (CHEKHOV'S NOTE)

p. 257, *Taganrog*: Taganrog, a port in southern Russia on the Sea of Azov near the border with Ukraine, was Chekhov's birthplace.

p. 258, *few specimens... cured fillets*: "Cured fillets" were presumably for those higher up in the prison administration.

p. 258, *Amur... fishing industry... downstream*: It should be mentioned that on the Amur, which is very rich in fish, the fishing trade is organized very poorly, and it appears that the entrepreneurs stint on engaging specialists from European Russia. Here, for example, sturgeon are caught in large numbers, but they cannot prepare caviare in any way so that it resembles Russian caviare, even in appearance. The art of the local fish-traders has come to a full stop at cured fillets of *keta* and has progressed no further. Mr L. Deyter has written in the newspaper *Maritime Gazette,* 1880, no. 6, that evidently at one time a group of financiers had set up a fishing company on the Amur, got business going on a broad footing, and regularly treated themselves with caviare, a *funt* of which cost them personally, it is said, from 200 to 300 roubles in silver. (CHEKHOV'S NOTE)

p. 259, *For fishing to... colony*: For those exiles who are now living at the mouths of small streams and by the sea, fishing could serve as a back-up to their domestic economy and yield a certain amount of earnings, but for this it would be necessary to supply them with good nets, to settle by the sea only those who had also lived by the sea in their home region, and so on.

At present the Japanese vessels which turn up off the south of Sakhalin to fish pay duty of seven copecks in gold per pood of fish.* Duty is also payable on all products prepared from fish, for example, mineral fertilizer, herring and cod-liver oil, but the income from all these taxes does not even reach 20,000 roubles, and this is almost the only income which we obtain from the exploitation of the wealth of Sakhalin.

Besides the *keta*, its relatives the *gorbusha* (hump-backed salmon), the *kundzha* and the *chevitza** also seasonally enter the rivers of Sakhalin; permanent residents of the Sakhalin fresh waters are the trout, pike, bream, carp, gudgeon and smelt, which is called the cucumber fish as it has a strong odour of fresh cucumber. Other sea fish caught, besides herring, are cod, plaice, sturgeon and chub, which are so huge here that they swallow smelts whole. At Alexandrovsk one convict sells delicious long-tailed crayfish which are called locally "*chirims*".

Sea mammals found in vast numbers off the shores of Sakhalin are whales, sea lions, seals and sea-bears. When I was approaching Alexandrovsk on the *Baikal* I caught sight of large numbers of whales frisking through the strait in pairs. Near the coast of Sakhalin a solitary rock towers above the sea, called "Peril Rock". An eyewitness who was on the schooner *Yermak,* and who wished to explore this rock, wrote: "When we were still one and a half miles from the rock it became apparent to us that the cliff-face was entirely covered by enormous sea lions. The roarings of this vast wild herd staggered us; the creatures had reached a fabulous size, so that from a distance they seemed like continuous boulders... The sea lions were around two sazhens or more in size... besides sea lions, both the escarpments and the sea around the rock were teeming with sea-bears" (*Vladivostok,* 1886, no. 29). What dimensions the whaling and seal-catching industries could attain in our northern seas is apparent from the frightening statistic quoted by one writer: according to the calculations of the American whaling-ship owners, during the space of 14 years (up to 1861) 20 million roubles' worth of fat and baleen were taken from the Sea of Okhotsk (V. Zbyshevsky, 'Observations on the whaling industry in the Sea of Okhotsk', *Maritime Compendium*, 1863, no.

4). But despite their apparently glittering future, these industries will not enrich the exile colony, precisely because it is an exile colony. According to Brehm's* testimony, "Seal-hunting is a merciless mass slaughter, where brutality combines with total callousness. That's why they don't talk about 'hunting seals' but 'battering seals'" and "the most savage tribes behave far more humanely during this hunting than the civilized European". And when they kill sea-bears with staves the brains spurt out on all sides and the poor animals' eyes start out of their sockets. Exiles, especially those sent here for murder, must be guarded from such spectacles. (CHEKHOV'S NOTE)

* Thus they paid seven copecks' worth of gold dust rather than cash.

* Keta = *Salmo lagocephalus*. Gorbusha = *Salmo gibbus*. Kunja = *Salmo cundscha*. Chevitza (more commonly chavycha) = *Salmo orientalis*.

* The German naturalist Alfred Brehm (1829–84) travelled to Turkestan and Western Siberia, and his work *Illustriertes Thierleben* (*Illustrated Wildlife*) published in 1863–69 was translated into Russian between 1866 and 1876.

p. 259, *seakale... Mauka*: Thanks to the seakale and the comparatively mild climate I consider the south-west sea coast the sole spot on Sakhalin where an exile colony is at present possible. In 1885, at one of the conferences of the society for the study of the Amur area, an interesting communication on seakale by a present proprietor of the industry, Y.L. Semyonov, was read. This communication was printed in *Vladivostok*, 1885, nos 47 and 48. (CHEKHOV'S NOTE)

p. 259, *Berdan rifles*: Berdan rifles, invented by the American Colonel Berdan, had been adopted for general use in the Russian infantry in 1869.

p. 259, *trepangas*: A trepanga is a marine animal (*Holothuria edulis*), also called a sea slug, sea cucumber or bêche-de-mer, eaten as a delicacy by the Chinese. The word "trepanga" is originally from Malayan.

p. 259, *craftsmen... vodka*: Up till now craftsmen have found ways of earning a living only in the posts, at the residences of officials and well-off exiles. To the credit of the local educated professional classes let it be said that they pay very generously for the craftsmen's services. Such cases as the doctor who placed a shoemaker in the local sickbay under the pretence that he was ill so that he would make a pair of shoes for the doctor's son, or the official who has enlisted to his domestic staff a milliner who sews for his wife and children for nothing* – such cases are spoken of here as sad exceptions. (CHEKHOV'S NOTE)

* Although Chekhov does not name the official here, we have already been told in chapter 9 that it is the Governor of the Derbinsk Prison (see p. 144 and the accompanying note).

p. 260, *If we total… copecks*: According to the data of the Inspector of Agriculture. (CHEKHOV'S NOTE)

p. 260, *zolotniks*: One zolotnik is equivalent to 0.15 oz, or 4.27 g.

p. 261, *overplus*: The overplus is the surplus in the weight of a loaf over that of the flour used in its manufacture.

p. 261, *Table*: 'Table of dietary allowances of male and female exile convicts' compiled on the basis of the Code on Victuals and Cooked Provisions for Troops, ratified by His Imperial Majesty, 31st July 1871. (CHEKHOV'S NOTE)

p. 262, *convict bakers… overplus… occur*: The overplus is a tempter demon whose magic charms are very difficult to resist. Many have lost their conscience, and even their lives, due to it. Governor Selivanov, whom I have mentioned already, fell victim to the overplus, since he was murdered by a convict baker whom he was severely reprimanding for producing too little overplus. There really is something to cause a stir about here. Suppose that in the Alexandrovsk Prison they bake bread for 2,870 people. If only 10 zolotniks is withheld from each ration, that amounts to around 300 *funty* per day. In general, dealings in bread and grain are very profitable. Thus, for example, to embezzle 10,000 poods of flour and then conceal it gradually with flour withheld in zolotniks from the prisoners' rations, two to three years would be sufficient.

Polyakov wrote: "The bread in Malo-Tymovo was so very bad that not every dog could bring itself to eat it; it contained a mass of unground, still whole, grain, chaff and straw; one of my colleagues who was present at the inspection of the bread remarked with justice: 'Yes, it's very easy to get all your teeth stuck together with this bread, but then you could just as easily find a toothpick in it to unpick them with.'" (CHEKHOV'S NOTE)

p. 262, *meat… salted… fish likewise*: It does sometimes happen that skilly is cooked up in the prison from fresh meat; this signifies that a bear has killed a cow, or some misfortune has happened to a government bull or cow. But the prisoners often treat meat from cattle killed in such a way as carrion, and refuse to eat it. Here are some further lines from Polyakov: "The salt beef was also very bad here: it was prepared from the flesh of government oxen worn out by toil on bad and difficult roads, and not infrequently slaughtered the day before they would have died naturally, if their throats had not been cut when they were already half dead." During the periodic fish run, the prisoners are fed fresh fish, one *funt* of which is issued to every person. (CHEKHOV'S NOTE)

p. 263, *How often... frequently*: The administration knows all about this. At any rate here is the opinion of the Governor of the Island himself on this score: "In dealings on the spot in the sphere of the convicts' cooked-food allowances, there are circumstances which automatically cast a doubtful shadow over this business" (Directive no. 314, 1888). If an official says that he has lived for a whole week or a month on prisoners' diet and feels wonderful, then that means that in the prison they have prepared it for him specially.* (CHEKHOV'S NOTE)

* Chekhov may have had General Kononovich himself in mind. After carrying out a two-week visit to the Korsakovsk District, the Governor of the Island declared in his Directive no. 318 of 17th August 1889: "I found that the food was very tasty and that I could live on it and as a result of the alteration in diet suffered no after-effects to my organism, which had been wracked by illness."

p. 263, *How do the prisoners eat?... water*: How easy it is for the cooks to make a mistake in the preparation of too many or too few portions is evident from the quantities put in the cooking pots. On 3rd May 1890, at the Alexandrovsk Prison, 1,279 people drew food from the pots; in them had been placed: 13½ poods of meat, five poods of rice, one and a half poods of flour had been stirred in as thickening, there were also one pood of salt, 24 poods of potatoes, one-third of a *funt* of bay-leaves and two-thirds of a *funt* of pepper; on 29th September in the same prison, for 675 people: 17 poods of fish, three poods of groats, one pood of flour, half a pood of salt, 12½ poods of potatoes, one-sixth of a *funt* of bay leaves and one-third of a *funt* of pepper. (CHEKHOV'S NOTE)

p. 263, *Of those... cauldrons*: In the Alexandrovsk Prison on 3rd May, out of a total of 2,870, 1,279 took food from the cauldron, and on 29th September, of 2,432, only 675 did so. (CHEKHOV'S NOTE)

p. 264, *Sometimes some of them... tallow candles*: The administration and the local doctors consider the allowance received by the prisoners deficient as regards quantity, too. According to information I have drawn from a medical report, the rations contain (in grams): protein 142.9, fats 37.4 and carbohydrates 659.9 on non-fast days, and 164.3, 40.0 and 671.4 on fast days.* According to Erisman, the diet of our European Russian factory workers contains 79.3 grams of fats on a non-fast day, and 67.4 on a fast day. The more a person works, the more strenuous and prolonged the physical effort, then, according to the laws of hygiene, the more fats and carbohydrates he ought to receive. How little expectation may be placed on bread and soup in this respect, the reader may judge from all that has been said above. During the four summer months, the prisoners in the mines receive a reinforced diet consisting of four *funty* of bread, one *funt* of meat and 24 zolotniks of groats; following an application by the local administration, the same portions have also begun to be stipulated for those labourers engaged in work on the roads. On the suggestion of the Director of the Central Prison Department, the question was raised on Sakhalin in 1887 "of the possibility of altering the table of allowances in existence on Sakhalin with the objective of reducing the costs of the supply of exile convicts' provisions without detriment to the nourishment of the organism" and experiments in the supply of foodstuffs were carried out along the lines recommended by Dobroslavin. The late professor, it is apparent from his report, considered it awkward "to limit the amount of food which has already been issued for so many years to the exile convicts, without entering into the very closest study of the conditions of labour and maintenance under which these prisoners have been placed, since it is hardly possible to form a clear idea here of the quality of the meat and bread which is issued on the spot"; this notwithstanding, however, he still considered it possible to limit the annual consumption of expensive portions of meat, and he proposed three tables: two for non-fast days and one for fast days. On Sakhalin these tables were submitted for consideration to a committee appointed under the chairmanship of the director of the medical department. And the Sakhalin doctors who took part in it rose to the heights of their calling. They declared without the slightest hesitation that, in view of the conditions of work on Sakhalin, the severe climate, concentrated labour at all times of the year and in all weathers, the allowances supplied now were insufficient, and that the supply of provisions set out in Professor Dobroslavin's tables, in spite of the reduction in meat portions, would work out much more expensive than that of the existing table. Responding to the central core of the question, concerning the reduction in expense of the individual portions, they proposed their own tables, which, however, did not at all promise the kind of savings the prison department desired. "There will be no material savings," they wrote, "but to compensate for that, we may expect an improvement in the quality and quantity of prisoners' labour, a reduction in the number of sick and feeble, and the prisoners' general standard of health will rise, which will in addition reflect favourably on the colonization of Sakhalin, yielding up for this objective settled exiles in full vigour and health." This 'Dossier from the Offices of the Governor of Sakhalin', on the alteration of ration tables with the object of reducing expenses, contains twenty of the most varied reports, memoranda and statements, and deserves to be very closely studied by all those interested in prison hygiene. (CHEKHOV'S NOTE)

* Besides observing the long canonical fasts such as Lent and Christmas, a member of the Orthodox Church is meant to fast every Wednesday and Friday. On these days he abstains from meat and dairy produce.

p. 264, *salt fish… price… off*: In the shops, smoked *keta* cost 30 copecks each. (CHEKHOV'S NOTE)

p. 264, *poor fat content… pot*: As I have already mentioned, the local aboriginal inhabitants utilize a great deal of fats in their diet, and this without a doubt assists them in the struggle against the low temperature and excessive damp. I was told that, somewhere along the eastern sea coast, or on the neighbouring islands, the Russian traders are also beginning little by little to use whale blubber in their diet. (CHEKHOV'S NOTE)

p. 265, *clothing… worst*: When Captain Mashinsky was making the cutting for the telegraph along the Poronai, his convict labourers were sent short shirts which would only have fitted children. Prisoners' clothing is distinguished by its standard and clumsy cut, which hinders a working man in his movements, and that is why, during the loading of a steamship or on roadworks, you will not encounter a convict dressed in a long overcoat or smock-coat; but the discomforts caused by the cut of the clothes are easily eliminated in practice by sale or exchange. Since the most comfortable design for work, and for life in general, is the ordinary peasant cut, the majority of exiles go round in free-persons' clothing. (CHEKHOV'S NOTE)

p. 265, *Bishop of Kamchatka, the Kurile Islands and Blagoveshchensk*: Since the Kurile Islands have now passed to Japan, it would be more correct to replace this term by "Bishop of Kamchatka, Sakhalin Island and Blagoveshchensk". (CHEKHOV'S NOTE)

p. 265, *consecration... buildings*: On the consecration by Bishop Martimian of the Krilyon lighthouse, see *Vladivostok,* 1883, no. 28. (CHEKHOV'S NOTE)

p. 266, *wilderness... desert*: The wilderness, or desert, is a common image in the Russian Orthodox Church. It derives from the tradition of the Desert Fathers and implies a secluded spot for retreat from the world.

p. 266, *an official document*: His documents have a distinctive flavour to them. Requesting the authorities for a convict to assist him by carrying out the duties of a sexton, he wrote: "As for the reason why I do not have a regular sexton, this is explained by the fact that there are none to spare right now in the Church Consistory, and even if there were, with the conditions of everyday living being what they are for the clergy here, it would be impossible for a psalm-reader to exist. The past is passed. Soon, I believe, I, too, will have to remove myself from Korsakovsk into my beloved desert and say unto you: 'This thy dwelling place I leave empty.'" * (CHEKHOV'S NOTE)

* Father Simon is referring to the Spiritual Consistory formed in 1744, which was under the direction of the Holy Synod. One of its many responsibilities was the appointment of new priests, bishops and other ranks of clergy. The psalm-reader was not just a reader of psalms but a clergyman who had under his control his church's choral singing and the reading of lessons, the hours, etc; he also maintained the parish registers and church library. The "distinctive flavour" of Father Simon's documents is due to his lapsing into Old Russian – the effect would be something like that of a present-day Anglican clergyman dropping unconsciously into the language of the King James Bible.

p. 267, *parish churches... Rykovo and Korsakovsk*: Within the District of the Parish of Rykovo there is still a church at Malo-Tymovo, in which services take place only on the feast day of St Anthony the Great, the church's patron saint, and in the District of the Korsakovsk Parish there are three chapels – at Vladimirovka, Kresty and Galkino-Vraskoye. All the Sakhalin chapels and churches were built at prison expense, by convict labour, and only one, at Korsakovsk, was built on money donated by the crews of the *Vsadnik* and *Vostok* and by the servicemen living at the post. (CHEKHOV'S NOTE)

p. 267, *especial responsibilities... to them*: In his manual of criminal law, Professor Vladimirov states that the transfer of convicts to the category of "reformee" is proclaimed to them with some solemnity. He most probably has in mind Article 301 of the *Statutes on Exiles*, according to which his transfer to the aforesaid category is announced in the presence of a superior member of the prison authority, and in addition, a specially invited cleric, who shall – etc. But in practice this statute is unfeasible, since a clergyman would have to be invited every day, and besides, solemnity such as this somehow does not fit in with the working environment. Neither is the law carried out in practice concerning the release of prisoners from work on church feast-days and holidays, according to which the reformees should be released more frequently than the probationers. Such a division would require a great deal of time and trouble on every single occasion.

Really, the only thing that is unusual in the activities of the local priests is that some of them bear missionary responsibilities. During my visit Hieromonk Irakly was still on Sakhalin; he is a Buriat by birth, with no beard or moustaches; he comes from the Posol Monastery in the Zabaikal Region.* He had spent eight years on the island, and during recent years had been a priest in the Parish of Rykovo. In connection with his duties as a missionary, he would travel two or three times a year to the Nyysky Bay and along the Poronai to baptize, give Holy Communion to and marry the natives. As many as 300 Oroches were brought to the Christian faith by him. Of course, on journeys through the taiga, and especially in winter, it was impossible even to think about any kind of comforts or conveniences. At night Father Irakly would slide into a sheepskin sack; in this sack he kept both his tobacco and his watch – his travelling companions would light a bonfire and warm themselves with tea, but he would sleep in his sack all through the night. (CHEKHOV'S NOTE)

* The Zabaikal Region, as we have seen, is the land between Lake Baikal and the Chinese border. The Posol Monastery was based near the settlement of Posolsky in the Verkheudinsk District of the Zabaikal region. Its full name was the "Posol Monastery of the Transfigured Saviour". It was founded in 1681 and maintained a school for aboriginal children.

p. 268, *the hours*: In the Orthodox Church every day at the first, third, sixth and ninth hours after sunrise, a short service is held in which psalms are chanted and texts are read. These short services are called "hours". Special "hours" are held at feasts such as the end of Lent, Easter and Christmas.

p. 268, *a marriage ceremony*: In the Russian Orthodox wedding service, both bride and bridegroom have one or more "best men". A pink cloth – as Chekhov describes – is placed before the altar; whichever one of the couple steps on it first will, according to Russian belief, be the "head of the house". The priest appears from the royal gates (the wooden partitions separating the main body of the church from the area behind the altar corresponding to the sanctuary in a western church). At the end of the service, two deacons bear forward two crowns on salvers, and the priest "crowns" each member of the bridal pair as a sign that they have entered into the blessed state of matrimony. Then he intones: "Be thou exalted, O groom, like unto Abraham, and blessed like unto Isaac, and multiplied like unto Jacob." To the wife he says: "And thou, O bride, be exalted like unto Sarah, and rejoice like unto Rebekah, and be multiplied like unto Rachel."

p. 269, *Lyalikova... Nikolayevsk*: The reference to Lyalikova's husband is puzzling as settled exiles were not normally permitted to travel off the island. Possibly it is a slip of the pen for "peasant-in-exile".

p. 271, *funeral... grave*: Of the total number I noted down, 86.5 per cent were Orthodox Christians, Catholics and Lutherans together made up 9 per cent, 2.7 per cent were Muslims, and the rest were Jews and Armenio-Gregorians.* Once a year the catholic priest comes over from Vladivostok, and then the catholic exiles of the two northern districts are "made to go" to Alexandrovsk, and this occurs right at the time the roads are covered with slush and mud due to the spring thaw. The Catholics complained to me that the priest comes very rarely, the children remain unbaptized for ages, and in order that a child might not die without baptism many parents turn to the

Orthodox priest. And, indeed, I often came across Orthodox children whose parents were Catholics. When a Catholic is dying, for want of his own priest, the Russian Orthodox priest is called in, to intone "O Holy God".* At Alexandrovsk I was approached by a Lutheran who had been convicted at some time in the past of arson; he told me that the Lutherans had formed a society, and as evidence, showed me a seal on which was engraved "Seal of the Society of Lutherans on Sakhalin"; the Lutherans gather at his home to pray and to exchange ideas. The Tatars elect a mullah from their ranks, and the Jews a rabbi, but this is not official. At Alexandrovsk a mosque is being built. The mullah, Vas-Hassan-Mahmet, a handsome dark-haired man of thirty-eight, a native of the Dagestan Province, is building it at his own expense. He continually enquired of me whether, on completion of his sentence, they would allow him to go to Mecca. In the Peysikovskaya Quarter at Alexandrovsk there stands a windmill, utterly abandoned; the story goes that it was built by some Tatar and his wife. Both husband and wife cut down trees themselves, hauled logs and sawed planks without assistance from anybody else, and this labour of theirs lasted three years. On achieving peasant status, the Tatar crossed over to the mainland, but handed his mill over to the state and not to his own Tatars, since he was angry with them because they had not elected him mullah. (CHEKHOV'S NOTE)

* The Armenian Church was established in the sixth century by St Gregory: hence its name, the Armenio-Gregorian Church. It developed separately from the other Christian churches and is broadly Monophysite in tendency. It is the largest Eastern Church after Orthodoxy.

* "O Holy God" are the first words of the Orthodox service of Extreme Unction.

p. 271, *There are five schools... month*: In his report of 27th February 1890, in execution of the instructions of the Governor of the Island on the subject of trying to find trustworthy free-people or settled exiles as replacements for the convicts who perform teaching duties at the present time, the Head of the Alexandrovsk District declares that, in the district entrusted to him, neither among the free element, nor among the settled exiles, was there anybody who would have been satisfactory in a teaching appointment. "Thus," he writes, "encountering insurmountable difficulties in the recruitment of persons who by education would be suitable in any degree whatever for school work, I refrain from indicating anyone from those settled exiles or peasants-in-exile residing in the district within my charge, to whom it would be possible to entrust teaching work." Although the District Governor refrained from entrusting teaching work to exiles, they still continue to be teachers, with his cognizance and at his appointment. To avoid contradictions such as this, the simplest thing would have seemed to be to engage real teachers from European Russia or Siberia and award them the same salary as the overseers receive, but for this a radical alteration of outlook on teaching would be necessary, so that it would not be considered less important than overseers' work. (CHEKHOV'S NOTE)

p. 271, *Of the male… literate… per cent*: Judging from fragmentary data and from hints, those who are literate* serve out their sentence more satisfactorily than those who are not; there are evidently comparatively more recidivists among the latter, while the former obtain peasant's rights more easily; at Siyantzy I recorded eighteen men who could read and write, and of these thirteen, that is, almost all the adult literates, had peasant status. It is still not the custom in the prisons to teach adults literacy and writing skills, although there are days in winter when, as a result of bad weather, the prisoners sit in the prison unable to go out and mope around with nothing to do; on days such as these, they would gladly get down to learning to read and write.

Owing to the exiles' illiteracy, letters to their home region are generally written by a scribe. They depict the dismal life here, the poverty and the grief, request husbands to dissolve marriages and suchlike, but in a tone as if they were describing yesterday's booze-up, "Well, here I am at last, dropping you a little line… set me free from my marriage ties", and so on, or else they ramble on philosophizingly, so that it is difficult to follow the sense of the letter. Owing to the floridity of his style, one scribe in the Tymovsk District has been nicknamed the "College Graduate". (CHEKHOV'S NOTE)

* Regarding the meaning of "literate", see the second note to p. 69.

p. 272, *The soldiers… established*: See N.V. Busse, *Sakhalin Island and the Expedition of 1853–1854*. (CHEKHOV'S NOTE)

p. 272, *Lopatin writes… on foot*: Lopatin, 'Report to the Governor General of Eastern Siberia', *Mining Journal*, 1870, no. 10. (CHEKHOV'S NOTE)

p. 273, *sometimes a soldier... convict woman*: In the Korsakovsk Police Department, I saw the following, relating to the year 1870:

List of lower-ranking soldiers billeted at the post attached to the Putyatinsky coal mines on the river Sortunai.

Vasily Vedernikov – has taken the place of commanding officer; shoemaker, baker and cook.

Luka Pylkov – removed as commanding officer for negligence, and was arrested for drunkenness and insolence.

Khariton Mylnikov – has not been caught at anything, but is lazy.

Yevgraf Raspopov – a moron, and incapable of any type of work whatever.

Fyodor Cheglokov, Grigory Ivanov: caught stealing money, and in my presence reprimanded for riotous conduct, insobriety and insubordination.

Director of Post at Putyatinsky coal quarries on Sakhalin Island
PROVINCIAL SECRETARY F. LITKE.
(CHEKHOV'S NOTE)

p. 273, *Inspections... displeasure... authorities*: N. Sm***y recounts that, not so very long ago, in 1885, the General who had jurisdiction over the Sakhalin troops asked one soldier overseer:

"What have you got a revolver for?"

"For trimming (taming) the convicts with, Yer Excellency!"

"Fire your revolver at that stump," ordered the General.

There followed a scene of enormous confusion. The soldier could not in any way disengage his revolver from the holster, and managed it only with somebody else's help; when he had got the revolver out, he began handling it so clumsily that the order was rescinded, otherwise, instead of the stump, he could easily have put a bullet into some member of the public. *Kronstadt Herald,* 1890, no. 23.
(CHEKHOV'S NOTE)

p. 273, *Perhaps... Sintzovsky... one knows*: Sintzovsky, 'Hygienic situation of hard-labour convicts in exile', *Health,* 1875, no. 16.
(CHEKHOV'S NOTE)

p. 274, *blunders... pursues*: At the Voyevodsk Prison a convict was pointed out to me, a former escort guard who at Khabarovsk had aided some vagabonds to escape and had run off with them. In summer 1890, at the Rykovo Prison, a free-status woman was being held under suspicion of arson; her neighbour in the detention cell next door, prisoner Andreyev, complained that at night he was prevented from sleeping by the escort guards who constantly visited this woman and made a racket. The District Governor ordered the lock of her detention cell to be changed and took the key himself. The escorts, however, had another key made: the District Governor could do absolutely *nothing* with them, and the nightly orgies continued as before. (CHEKHOV'S NOTE)

p. 275, *commanding officers... units*: And this gives rise to a manifest injustice: the better soldiers who remain in the detachments only receive soldiers' rations, while the poorer ones who serve in the prison get both rations and a salary. In his *Dossier* [op. cit.] Prince Shakhovskoy lamented: "The main contingent of overseers (66 per cent) is comprised of privates of the local military commands, who receive 12 roubles 50 copecks monthly at state expense. Their illiteracy, their low level of mental development, their indulgent attitude towards possible bribery in their sphere of activities, the absence of the previous rigorous military discipline and an incomparably greater freedom of activity, lead, with few exceptions, either to an illegal arbitrariness and tyranny in handling the prisoners, or to an inappropriate humiliation before them." The present Governor of the Island, too, is of the opinion that "the experience of many years has displayed the total unreliability of supervision by men detailed from the local military commands". (CHEKHOV'S NOTE)

p. 277, *Sakhalin overseers... infirmary*: Senior overseers receive a salary of 480 roubles a year, and juniors 216 roubles. After certain periods this rate is increased by one-third, two-thirds or even doubled. Such a salary is considered a good one and is a temptation for the minor officials, for instance, the telegraph operators, who leave to become overseers at the first opportunity. There exists a fear that schoolteachers, if they are at some stage appointed to Sakhalin, and are paid the usual 20 to 25 roubles per month, will inevitably leave to become overseers.

Because of the impossibility of finding free-status people on the spot for the overseers' posts, or of taking them from the local military commands without weakening their composition, in 1888 the Governor of the Island permitted the enlistment to the post of overseer of settled exiles and peasants-in-exile who were trustworthy in conduct and already tested as to diligence. But nothing worthwhile has resulted from this measure. (CHEKHOV'S NOTE)

p. 278, *Major Nikolayev... newspaper reports*: Among others see Lukashevich, 'My acquaintances at Dooay on Sakhalin', *Kronstadt Herald*, 1868, nos 47 and 49. (CHEKHOV'S NOTE)

p. 278, *freed serf... army*: Serfs before their emancipation in 1860 had no rights whatever. Often landowners were asked to provide troops to swell Russia's armies in time of war and so handed over one or two serfs from each village they owned, or perhaps when a squire found himself in need of money, he would sell some of his serfs to the army for a certain number of years or even for life.

p. 279, *Prehistoric... Superintendent of Exiled Convict Labourers... Primorskaya Region*: Up till 1875 convict labour on Sakhalin was managed by the director of the Dooay Post, an officer whose commanders resided at Nikolayevsk on the mainland. From 1875 Sakhalin has been divided into two administrative areas, southern Sakhalin and northern Sakhalin. The two areas, which formed part of the Primorskaya Region, were placed as regards civilian affairs under the jurisdiction of a military governor, and as regards military affairs, under the commander-in-chief of the forces of the Primorskaya Region. Local control was entrusted to the governors or directors of the areas, the rank of governor of northern Sakhalin was conferred upon the superintendent of exiled convict labourers on Sakhalin and in the Primorskaya Region, whose centre of operations was to be Dooay, and the title of "Governor of the Southern District" was bestowed on the commanding officer of the Fourth East Siberian Line Battalion, who was to be based at the Korsakovsk Post. Control on the spot, both military and civilian, was focused in the form of the district governors. The administration was entirely military. (CHEKHOV'S NOTE)

p. 279, *new regulations... new people*: By these regulations, the central administration of Sakhalin is the responsibility of the Governor General of the Amur River Territory, and the local administration is the responsibility of the Governor of the Island, who is to be appointed from the ranks of military generals. The island was divided into three districts. The prisons and settlements in each district are under the personal direction of the district governors, who correspond to our European Russian district chief commissioners of police. They preside over the police departments. All the prisons, and also the settlements within their vicinities, are managed by prison governors; if the settlements are managed by a special official, he is called a superintendent of settlements; both these posts correspond to our European Russian district police superintendents. Attached to the Governor of the Island are his office director, a financial bookkeeper, a paymaster, an agricultural inspector, a land surveyor, an architect, an interpreter of the Aino and Gilyak languages, the Central Warehouse Supervisor and the Head of the Medical Department. To each of the military companies there should be a field officer, two subaltern officers and a surgeon; in addition to these, there is an adjutant of the Forces Administration Department on Sakhalin, his assistant and a military auditor.* There still remain to be mentioned the four priests and those salaried employees who are not directly connected with the prisons, for instance, the Head of the Postal and Telegraphic Office, his assistant, the telegraph operators and the keepers of the two lighthouses. (CHEKHOV'S NOTE)

* The military post of auditor was generally filled by a warrant officer and involved the duties of adjutant and secretary to a senior officer.

p. 279, *The Marriage*: A play by Gogol.

p. 279, *High Holidays*: On High Holidays, such as the Tsar's birthday and the anniversary of his coronation, senior civil servants – for instance, heads of departments – would pay ceremonial visits in full-dress uniform to other important officials. They would then "congratulate each other" upon the festival.

p. 281, *Not every prison... (Directive no. 314, 1888)*: One day spent rooting around among the office documents is enough to give way to despair at the overblown figures, incorrect totals and "idle concoctions" of various prison governors' assistants, senior overseers and clerks. I could not find the "registers" for 1886 at all. You stumble across registers which have written in pencil at the foot, in the form of an instruction: "Obviously untrue". There is a particularly large number of errors in the sections concerning the family situation of the exiles, the children and the composition of the exiles according to types of crime. The Governor of the Island told me that, once, when he required to find out how many prisoners had arrived from European Russia annually on the steamers of the Voluntary Fleet, starting from 1879, he had to turn for information to the Central Prison Department, since in the local offices the requisite figures turned out to be missing. "Despite repeated demands, no records at all were produced for 1886," the Governor complains in one of his reports. "I am placed at still more of a disadvantage in consequence of the impossibility of reconstructing exactly the desired information in the total absence of any data, which in previous years were not gathered at all. Thus, for instance, at the present time, it is very difficult to become cognizant of the total numbers here on 1st January 1887 – even of how many settled exiles and peasants-in-exile there were." (CHEKHOV'S NOTE)

p. 281, *Derzhimorda*: Derzhimorda (literally "grab his snout") is one of the loutish police constables in Gogol's play *The Government Inspector*.

p. 281, *House of the Dead*: Fyodor Dostoevsky (1821–81) was sentenced to death in 1849 for seditious activity. The sentence was commuted to life exile to Siberia; he in fact spent only eight years there before being allowed to return home. *Memoirs from the House of the Dead* (written 1861–64) was a record of his experiences in prison in Siberia.

p. 281, *Onor affair*: The "grim Onor affair" came to light only in 1893, three years after Chekhov's trip to Sakhalin. His reference to it is evidence of how he maintained his interest in the island after his journey and kept up a correspondence with officials and exiles there. An illiterate overseer at the Rykovo Prison, Vasily Khanov, had been entrusted with supervising roadworks at the remote new settlement of Onor. If any convicts returned late to the settlement from the work, Khanov reduced their rations to one-half of the norm and then one-third. When they finally dropped from exhaustion and hunger, he would shoot them in cold blood, bury them and invent diseases from which they were supposed to have died.

Incidentally, overseer Khanov had himself risen from the ranks of the convicts – he had begun a hard-labour sentence on Sakhalin in 1879. He was fifty-seven when Chekhov met him in 1890 while completing his sentence and he must have been in hard-labour institutions since 1863 at the very latest, since apparently he bore identifying tattoo marks on his arm: these tattoos had been abolished in 1863 (see the note to p. 178).

p. 281, *Good people… off it*: In the execution of their duties, the local officials often lay themselves open to serious dangers. When the Governor of the Tymovsk District, Mr Butakov, went on foot along the whole of the Poronai and back, he became ill with the bloody flux (dysentery) and almost died. The Governor of the Korsakovsk District, Mr Bely, was once sailing in a whaleboat from Korsakovsk to Mauka; on the way he was caught in a gale, and they had to put further out to sea from the shore. They were carried along by the waves and churned around for nearly 48 hours, and Mr Bely himself, his convict helmsman and a soldier who was by chance on the boat had made up their minds that their end had come. But they were cast up on the shore near the Krilyon lighthouse. When Mr Bely arrived at the lighthouse-keeper's quarters, he glanced at himself in a mirror and noticed grey hairs that had not been there before; the soldier fell asleep, and there was no way whatever he could be woken for forty hours. (CHEKHOV'S NOTE)

p. 282, *the development of a social life… reduced*: Nowadays, though, entertainments are already possible such as amateur theatricals, picnics and soirées, whereas in the past it was difficult even to get together a game of preference. Intellectual interests are now satisfied more easily, too. Newspapers and magazines are subscribed to, books are ordered, every day telegrams are received from a northern news agency;* there are grand pianos in many homes. The local poets find readers and listeners for themselves; at one time a handwritten magazine called *Flowerbud* was issued at Alexandrovsk; it ceased publication, however, after seven issues. The senior officials live in fine government quarters, roomy and warm, and keep cooks and horses, while those of lower rank hire lodgings from settled exiles and occupy whole houses, or separate rooms, with furniture and all fittings. A young official, the poet whom I mentioned earlier, has rented a room with a large number of icons, a state-bed with curtains, and even a carpet on the wall, on which is depicted a horseman shooting at a tiger.

The Governor of the Island gets 7,000 roubles per year, the head of the medical department 4,000, the inspector of agriculture 3,500, the architect 3,100 roubles and the district governors 3,500 per year each. Every three years an official receives six months' paid leave. After five years he is awarded an increment of 25 per cent of his salary. After ten years he gets a pension. Two years are counted as three. Travelling allowances are not low either. An assistant prison governor, who has no civil service rank, receives travelling expenses from Alexandrovsk to St Petersburg of 1,945 roubles 68¾ copecks, that is, a sum which would be sufficient to complete a round-the-world tour in complete comfort (Directives nos 302 and 305, 1889). Travelling allowances are issued to those retiring, and also to those taking holiday leave after completion of five to ten years since they first joined the service. The latter might not necessarily go away, since the expenses take the form of an award or gratuity. Priests are issued with travelling expenses for all the members of their family. An official who goes into retirement usually requires travelling expenses for himself to Petropavlovsk in wintertime – a distance of 13,000 versts – or to the Kholmogorsk District – 11,000 versts;* simultaneously, when submitting his application of retirement, he sends a telegram to the Central Prison Department requesting a free passage with his whole family to Odessa on a steamer of the Voluntary Fleet. It still remains to be added that, while an official serves on Sakhalin, his children are educated at state expense.

And yet the local officials are still dissatisfied with life. They are irritable, quarrel among themselves over trifles, and mope with boredom. In them and their families there is a predisposition towards consumption and nervous and mental illnesses.* While I was at Alexandrovsk, one young official, an excellent fellow, used to wander about the whole time, even during the day, with an enormous revolver. When I asked him what he was carrying this cumbersome weapon around in his pocket for, he replied in all seriousness:

"Two of the officials here intend to do me in, and they've already attacked me once."

"But just what can you do with a revolver?"

"Very simple – I'll kill 'em like dogs, I won't stand on ceremony."
(CHEKHOV'S NOTE)

* The only Russian northern news agency operating in the 1890s to which I have been able to find any reference was the Rossiyskoye Telegrafnoye Agenstvo (Russian Telegraphic Agency) based in St Petersburg.

* That is to say, about as far as they could go from Sakhalin without actually leaving the Tsarist Empire. In other words, all the officials would claim everything they possibly could on travelling expenses!

* It is startling to realize in this respect that two of Chekhov's closest contacts on Sakhalin died from precisely the causes that he mentions here. Mr Yartzev, the Inspector of Settlements in southern Sakhalin, was retired on health grounds in 1893 and died of tuberculosis in St Petersburg in 1895 at the age of thirty-eight, while Mr Bely, the Governor of the Korsakovsk District, also left Sakhalin in 1893 and died in a St Petersburg psychiatric hospital in 1903 at the age of forty-eight. It will be recalled from chapter 13 (see the note to p. 186) that Mr Bely was desperately homesick for his native Ukraine and that to while away the time both he and Mr Yartzev would declaim long chunks of poetry.

The fate of some other prominent individuals who appear in Chekhov's narratives may also be mentioned. The Governor of the Malo-Tymovo Prison, Mr K. (whose full name Chekhov never gives – it was in fact Klimov), was another to die in St Petersburg of tuberculosis: in his case in 1897, aged thirty-three. It will be recalled that in chapter 10 (page 157) Chekhov describes him as a "cultured and very fine young man from St Petersburg, who is obviously extremely homesick for European Russia". Mr Butakov, Governor of the Tymovsk District, died in 1895 at the age of thirty-nine. I have been unable to find the cause.

Dr A.V. Shcherbak, the Voluntary Fleet doctor whom Chekhov met on Sakhalin and whose articles he refers to frequently, died in 1894 at the age of forty-six. Governor General Baron Korf died in 1893 at the age of sixty-two. The officials who encountered Chekhov on his trip to Sakhalin must have wondered whether the writer had brought with him a deadly curse that affected anybody with whom he had dealings.

Incidentally, the reader may well have noticed that although throughout the book there are very many references to the Governors of the Korsakovsk and Tymovsk Districts, Messrs Bely and Butakov, the name of the Governor of the Alexandrovsk District is never given and, indeed, Chekhov hardly ever mentions him. This is presumably because the Governor of the Island had his residency in this district and therefore whenever Chekhov was there he would have talked to General Kononovich rather than the local head. The unfortunate gentleman who missed out on being immortalized by Chekhov was named Sergey Nikolayevich Taskin; he was born in 1863, and apart from this I can unearth no further details whatever about him.

p. 283, *unfortunates… falsely convicted*: Mr Kamorsky, the Prison Inspector for the Governor General of the area, told me: "If, out of 100 convict labourers, 15 to 20 decent ones ultimately emerge, we are obliged for this not so much to the corrective measures we utilize as to the Russian courts, which dispatch into hard labour such a large number of the good and trustworthy element of society." (CHEKHOV'S NOTE)

p. 283, *morality… inevitable*: The natural and unconquerable striving towards the highest good, that is, liberty, is here regarded as a criminal tendency, and escape is punished by convict labour and the lash as a grave criminal offence; a settled exile who from the purest of motives, "for the sake of Christ", that is, out of pure charity and sympathy, gives a fugitive shelter for the night is punished for it by convict labour. If a settled exile is indolent or leads his life in a state of intoxication, the Governor of the Island can send him to the mines for one year. On Sakhalin, even debts are considered a criminal offence. As punishment for debts, settled exiles are not transferred to peasant status. The resolution of the police authority on returning a settled exile to convict labour for a one-year period for slothfulness, negligence in setting up a home and premeditated evasion of payment of debts owed by him to the state, has been ratified by the Governor of the Island, with the addition that this settled exile should beforehand be handed over to labour for the "Sakhalin" Company to work off his debts (Directive no. 45, 1890). In short, convict labour and the lash are often imposed on an exile for misdemeanours which, in ordinary circumstances, would have earned reprimand, arrest or imprisonment. But on the other hand, thefts and burglary, which are committed so often in the prisons and settlements, rarely give rise to a court examination, and if a judgement were to be formed from the official statistics, one could arrive at the utterly false conclusion that exiles actually treat other people's property with more respect than the free population do. (CHEKHOV'S NOTE)

p. 284, *loading of ships… barrels disappear*: The convicts throw sacks of flour into the water and later retrieve them from the bottom, most probably by night. The first mate on one ship told me: "You don't have time to look round before they've cleaned the whole place out. For instance, when they're unloading barrels of salt fish, each of them tries to stuff his pockets, his shirt and his trousers full with fish. And they really get it hot for doing it as well! You find yourself grabbing hold of fish by the tail, the snout…" (CHEKHOV'S NOTE)

p. 285, *prostitutes… many… like!*: The police department, however, gave me a list on which there were only thirty prostitutes, who were given a clean bill of health every week by the doctor. (CHEKHOV'S NOTE)

p. 286, *the Khabarovsk Regional Court*: The Central Circuit Court for the whole of the Primorskaya Region was based at Khabarovsk, the region's capital. Therefore Chekhov refers to both the "Khabarovsk" and the "Primorskaya" Regional Courts; they mean precisely the same thing.

p. 286, *During 1889… mentality*: In 1889, 171 convicts were on trial and under investigation for escape. The case of the attempted escape of a certain Kolosovsky was opened in June 1887 and lapsed owing to the failure of witnesses to appear for cross-examination. A case of breaking out of prison and escape was commenced in September 1883 and sent for judgement before the Primorskaya Regional Court by the Public Prosecutor in July 1889. The case of Lesnikov was begun in March 1885 and concluded in February 1889 and so forth. The greatest number of cases in 1889 – 70 per cent – related to attempted escapes; next came murder and general complicity in murder – 14 per cent. If it were possible to discount the escapes, then a half of all the cases would concern murder. Murder is one of the most frequent offences on Sakhalin, most likely because half the exile population is made up of convicted murderers. The killers here commit murder with singular light-heartedness. When I was at Rykovo, in the government vegetable gardens there, one convict walloped another across the neck with a knife so as not to have to work, as he explained, since those under investigation lay around in the punishment cells and did nothing. At Goly Mys the young joiner Plaksin killed his friend for a few silver coins. In 1885 fugitive convicts fell upon an Aino village and, apparently merely for thrills, set about torturing the men and women, raped the latter – and in conclusion hanged the children on the cross-beams. The majority of murders are staggering in their senselessness and savagery. Murder cases drag out a fearfully long time. For instance one case was opened in September 1881 and concluded only in April 1888; another case was begun in 1882 and finished in August 1889. Even the case of the Aino families that I have just referred to is not yet concluded. "The case of the murder of the Aino families was resolved by a court martial, and eleven of the accused exiled convict labourers were executed; the judgement of the court martial in relation to the remaining five accused is still unknown to the police department. Representations have been made to the Governor of Sakhalin Island in reports of 13th June and 23rd October 1889." Cases of "altering one's name and surname" drag out an especially long time. Thus, one case began in March 1880 and is continuing to this day, since information has still not been received from the administration of the Yakutsk Province. Another case was begun in 1881, and another in 1882. Eight convicts are on trial and under investigation "for forgery and sale of forged banknotes". It is said that forged banknotes are manufactured on Sakhalin itself. Convicts unloading foreign steamers here buy tobacco and vodka from the barmen and usually pay with forged notes. The Jew off whom 56,000 roubles was stolen was exiled for the forgery of banknotes; he has already served his sentence and strolls around Alexandrovsk in a hat and overcoat, and wears a gold chain. He is always talking with the officials and overseers in an undertone, half-whispering, and, incidentally, it was owing to the denunciation of this odious individual that a peasant-in-exile with a large family, also a Jew, was arrested and put in irons; at one time he had been sentenced to convict labour for life "for mutiny" by a court martial, but on the journey across Siberia, by means of a forgery, the length of his punishment was shortened in his itemized records to four years. In the 'Register of those under investigation and on trial during the past year of 1889', there is recorded, among other cases, one of "theft from the armoury of the Korsakovsk military detachment"; the accused has been on trial since 1884, but "there is no information in the files of the former Governor of southern Sakhalin regarding the time when the investigation commenced and finished, and when the preliminary examination took place is unknown" and in 1889, on the instruction of the Governor of the Island, this case was transferred to the regional court. What this seems to mean in actual fact is that the accused will be tried a second time. (CHEKHOV'S NOTE)

p. 287, *taken into custody*: According to the *Statutes on Exiles*, in order for an exile to be taken into custody, the authorities are not fettered by the regulations set out in the laws on legal procedure. An exile may be detained in any circumstances as soon as he is under any suspicion (Article 484). (CHEKHOV'S NOTE)

p. 287, *assistant public prosecutor*: The public prosecutor for any region would be based at the central administrative town, while each district within that region should have had a resident assistant public prosecutor to oversee investigations within the area under his jurisdiction. The presence of an assistant public prosecutor would have injected some objectivity into investigations which the Sakhalin system obviously lacked.

p. 288, *dossier... court*: In the past it would sometimes happen that trial dossiers mysteriously disappeared or that cases terminated suddenly "for enigmatic reasons" (see *Vladivostok,* 1885, no. 43). It is worth mentioning that once, even a dossier on a case which had been decided by a court martial was stolen. In his account Mr Vlasov mentions the life-sentence convict Ayzik Shapira. This Jew lived in Dooay and dealt in vodka there. In 1870 he was charged with the corruption of a five-year-old girl, but in spite of the presence of the girl herself and the existence of evidence, the case was hushed up. The investigation into this case was conducted by an officer of the military contingent of the post, who had pawned his rifle to this very same Shapira and was financially dependent on him; when the case dossier was removed from the officer, the papers incriminating Shapira were found to be missing. Shapira enjoyed great esteem in Dooay. When once the Director of the Post asked where Shapira was, he was told: "They've all gone off to have a cup of tea." (CHEKHOV'S NOTE)

p. 288, *local administration... significance*: One rainy night in the settlement of Andreye-Ivanovskoye, a pig was stolen off S. Suspicion fell on Z, whose trousers were soiled with pig excrement. A search was made of his property, but no pig was found; nonetheless, however, the Rural Society* passed a sentence that the pig belonging to the landlord of his living quarters, A, should be confiscated, since he might have been guilty of receiving stolen goods. The District Governor confirmed this sentence, although he considered it unjust: "If we don't uphold Rural-Society sentences," he told me, "Sakhalin will be left without a court altogether." (CHEKHOV'S NOTE)

* Each village or area would have a society of peasants to look after its members' interests and to decide disputes between them. See the second note to p. 219.

p. 288, *the Ruling Senate*: The Senate had been set up by Peter the Great to administer the country. It could take some low-level governmental decisions, but all real executive power rested with the Tsar. One of the Senate's many functions was to adjudicate on appeals against sentences from law courts. When the censors refused Chekhov permission to publish Chapters 20 and 21 of *Sakhalin Island*, he contemplated appealing to the Senate.

p. 289, *punishments… employed widely*: The ace of diamonds on his back, the shaving of half the head and the use of fetters, which served in the past to prevent escape and as the most convenient method of distinguishing an exile, have lost their former significance and are preserved chiefly as a punishment by humiliation. The ace, a rectangular patch up to three and a half inches long on all sides, should, according to the *Statutes*, be a different colour from the clothing itself; until very recently it was yellow, but since this is also the colour of the Amur and Zabaikalye Cossacks,* Baron Korf has ordered that the aces should be made from black cloth. But on Sakhalin the aces have lost all meaning, since people have long since got used to them and do not notice them any more. The same may be said of shaven heads. On Sakhalin heads are shaved very rarely – only those who have been brought back from an escape, who are under investigation, or who are chained to wheelbarrows are shaven, and in the Korsakovsk District there is no shaving carried out at all. According to the 'Statutes on those held in custody' the irons must be between five and five and a half *funty* in weight. During my stay, only one female, Golden Hand (see p. 87–88), was in fetters; she wore handcuffs. The wearing of shackles is obligatory for probationary convicts, but the *Statutes* permit them to be removed if necessary for the performance of convict labour, and since irons are a hindrance to every kind of work, the vast majority of convicts are freed from them. Far from all life-sentence convicts, even, are in irons, although according to the *Statutes* they should be kept in manacles and leg irons. However light the irons are, they still to a certain extent hinder movement. People get used to these as well, although far from everybody does. I would occasionally see prisoners no longer young who, in the presence of outsiders, would conceal their irons underneath the flaps of their smock-coats; I have a photograph on which is portrayed a crowd of Dooay and Voyevodsk convict labourers on a work gang, and the majority of those in irons are trying to stand in such a way that the irons do not show on the photo. Obviously, as a punishment of disgrace, chains in many instances achieve their purpose, but the feelings of humiliation which they arouse in an offender have hardly any connection with genuine shame at his offence. (CHEKHOV'S NOTE)

* As the Tsarist Empire expanded east and, in the 1840s and 1850s, annexed disputed border territories from Mongolia and China, detachments of Cossacks were sent to settle permanently in the Amur and Zabaikalye areas and assist the military in consolidating Russian territorial gains.

p. 289, *the birch rod*: The "birch rod" or "rod" used in corporal punishment was in fact a bundle of five or six long canes bound together.

p. 290, *The lash*: The lash consisted of a short wooden handgrip and a long central thong dividing towards its tip in up to three separate lashes.

p. 292, *Tolstykh*: He was sent to convict labour for cutting his wife's head off. (CHEKHOV'S NOTE)

p. 292, *frock coat*: The officials would have been wearing frock coats as part of their civil-service uniform.

p. 294, *Not only the prisoners... the rest*: Yadrintzev tells of one Demidov, who, in order to uncover all the details of a certain crime, ordered the executioner to torture the murderer's wife, who was a free-status woman who had accompanied her husband to Siberia voluntarily, and consequently was not legally subject to corporal punishment; then he tortured the murderer's eleven-year-old daughter; the little girl was suspended in the air, and the executioner birched her from head to foot; the child was even given several strokes with the lash, and when she asked for something to drink she was given dried salted fish. She would have been given even more lashes had not the executioner himself refused to continue the beating. "And yet, nevertheless," says Yadrintzev, "Demidov's cruelty is a natural consequence of the education he must have received, managing a large number of exiles over a lengthy period" ('The situation of the exiles in Siberia', *Herald of Europe*, 1875, vols XI and XII). In his account, Vlasov tells of Lieutenant Yevfonov, whose weakness "on the one hand led to the barracks in which the convicts lived being turned into a dive of a pub, with card games, and into a whole den of crimes of various types, while on the other his impetuous cruelty provoked bitterness on the part of the convicts. One offender, wishing to save himself from an excessive number of birch-strokes, murdered an overseer before the punishment."

The present Governor of the Island, General Kononovich, always opposes corporal punishment. When the sentences of the police department and the Khabarovsk Court are presented to him for ratification, he usually writes: "Ratified by me, apart from the corporal punishment." Unfortunately, because he is too busy, he visits the prisons very rarely and does not know how often, even within two or three hundred paces of his quarters, people are birched on the island, and he judges how many have been punished merely from the registers. Once, when I was sitting in the drawing room of his quarters, he said to me, in the presence of some officials and a visiting mining engineer:

"Here on Sakhalin, we resort to corporal punishment extremely rarely, indeed, hardly ever." (CHEKHOV'S NOTE)

p. 295, *nothing to chase it with either*: Russians, when drinking vodka, bite into something, preferably piquant, immediately after downing a glass, to ward off drunkenness. The priest is rather reluctant to drink, since, strictly speaking, this was not permitted to clergymen.

p. 296, *the murder of the Ainos*: See the second note to p. 286.

p. 297, *Water... trouble*: This quotation seems to have come from the convicts on Sakhalin themselves. Various visitors to Sakhalin heard this expression used, and one visitor, when asking whether the convicts had any songs, met with the reply: "What kind of songs would we 'ave 'ere, Guv? There's only one – 'Sakhalin's an island, water all around, in the middle – trouble'". (It rhymes in Russian, of course.)

p. 297, *Roman exile*: The Romans had a form of exile called *deportatio in insulam*, i.e. transportation to an island. The main islands utilized for this were Sardinia, Crete, Cyprus and Rhodes.

p. 300, *mental disturbance*: Among the officials and sailors of our town of Vladivostok, nostalgia* may not infrequently be observed; I myself saw two insane officials there – a legal specialist and a bandmaster. If these cases are not infrequent in the milieu of those who are at liberty and living in comparatively healthy surroundings, then it is evident of itself that, on Sakhalin, they must be very frequent. (CHEKHOV'S NOTE)

* Nostalgia is here used in its original sense of a mental illness.

p. 303, *convicts third class*: Exiles of the third class were those serving between four and seven years. Convicts serving less than four years would not usually have been sent to Sakhalin or Eastern Siberia. They were normally sentenced to "labour battalions" and utilized on construction works, in repairing the roads, or in working in prison factories in European Russia or Western Siberia.

p. 304, *Archpriest*: An archpriest was the senior priest in charge of all the clergy in a large church. Priests and their families were considered members of the privileged classes (see the second note to p. 111).

p. 305, *In 1889... holiday for himself*: I recall that once, when I was approaching a steamer on a launch, a barge was casting off from the side, full to overflowing with escapees; some were glum, some roaring with laughter; one of them had no feet left at all – he had lost them with frostbite. They were being returned to Nikolayevsk. Gazing at this barge swarming with people, I could imagine how many convicts there must still be roaming over the mainland and round the island! (CHEKHOV'S NOTE)

p. 306, *Korolenko's*: V.G. Korolenko (1853–1921) was a Russian author who in 1881 was sentenced to three years' exile in Siberia and subsequently wrote many short stories about Siberia and the exile system, e.g. 'The Flight from Sakhalin'.

p. 307, *Fugitives... they started from*: Once some escapees stole a compass at Dooay to find the north and avoid the cordon at Cape Pogobi, but the compass led them straight into the cordon. I was told that, of late, so as not to have to go along the guarded western sea coast, the convicts had begun to try out another route, namely, to the east, to the Nyysky Bay, from there north along the shore of the Sea of Okhotsk, towards capes Mariya and Elizaveta, and then to the south, in order to sail across the strait opposite Cape Pronge. This, they told me, was the path taken by, among others, the notorious Bogdanov, who had absconded not long before my arrival. But this is hardly likely. It is true that a Gilyak track runs along the whole length of the Tym, and one regularly comes across yurts, but the round journey from the Nyysky Bay is long and hard; one must recall how many deprivations Polyakov had to endure, descending from the Nyysky Bay to the south, in order to appreciate all the risk of travelling from this bay to the north.

How dreadful conditions are for escapees I have already mentioned. Fugitives, especially recidivists, little by little grow used to the taiga and the tundra, and there is nothing marvellous in the fact that some actually sleep while on the move. I was told that the ones who could get furthest of all on the run were the Chinese vagabonds, the *hunhuzy** from the Primorskaya Region, since they are supposed to be able to live for months at a time on nothing but roots and herbs. (CHEKHOV'S NOTE)

* *Hunhuzy* was the name that the Chinese vagabonds gave themselves. They would be on the run from Chinese justice, but many of them would very soon also break the law in Russia and would become fugitives or escapees there as well. These *hunhuzy* were notorious for forming robber gangs that would lay waste to whole villages and spread terror through south-eastern Siberia.

p. 307, *It not infrequently happens… this manner*: On 29th June 1886, from the naval vessel *Tungus*, a little over 20 miles from Dooay, they noticed a black dot on the surface of the sea. When they had drawn somewhat closer, they caught sight of the following: on four strung-together logs, drifting somewhere or other, were two men sitting on protuberances in the bark of the trees; around them on the raft were a bucket of fresh water, a loaf and a half of bread, an axe, a pood or so of flour, a little rice, two stearin candles, a piece of soap and two bricks of tea. When they were taken on board and asked who they were, it turned out that they were convicts from the Dooay Prison who had fled on 17th June (meaning they had already been on the run for twelve days) and that they were sailing "away, over there, to Russia". About two hours later a heavy gale blew up, and the steamer could not put in to Sakhalin. One wonders what would have happened to the escapees in such weather if they had not been taken on board the ship. (See *Vladivostok*, 1886, no. 31.) (CHEKHOV'S NOTE)

p. 307, *They sail away… mining department*: In June 1887 the steamship *Thyra* was being loaded with coal in the Dooay sea-road. As usual the coal was being conveyed to the boat on barges which were being drawn on a hawser by a steam-launch. Towards evening the wind began to freshen, and a heavy gale blew up. The *Thyra* could not remain at anchor and put into De-Kastri. They dragged a barge to the shore near Dooay, then the launch sailed off to the Alexandrovsk Post and took shelter in a small river there. That night, when the weather had abated somewhat, the launch's crew, which was made up of convicts, showed the overseer a fake telegram from Dooay in which the order was given to put out to sea in the launch immediately, to save the people on board the barge, which had allegedly been swept out to sea by the gale. Not suspecting a deception, the overseer allowed the launch to leave the wharf. But instead of heading south, towards Dooay, the launch set off to the north. On board were seven men and three women. Towards morning the weather changed for the worse; off Cape Khoay the engine became flooded; nine were drowned and washed up on the shore, and only one was saved, on a plank – the former helmsman on the launch. This sole survivor, Kuznetsov by surname, is now a servant in the mining engineer's quarters at the mines at the Alexandrovsk Post. He would serve me tea. He was a robust, dark-skinned, quite handsome man of about forty, obviously proud and untamed; he reminded me of Tom Ayrton in *The Children of Captain Grant*.* (CHEKHOV'S NOTE)

* *The Children of Captain Grant* – a novel by Jules Verne (1825–1902). I cannot resist commenting on Chekhov's vast knowledge of "light" literature: in *Sakhalin Island*, along with the learned references to over 110 books and pamphlets dealing with geography, ethnography, coal-mining, etc., Chekhov has also mentioned adventure stories by Jules Verne and Thomas Mayne Reid (see the second note to p. 139) and the French play *Thirty Years in the Life of a Gambler* (see the second note to p. 141). He also displays a wide-ranging knowledge of children's literature in the selection of books he sent to Sakhalin after his return to St Petersburg. One wonders where he found the time to read this kind of literature among all his other commitments – and just why did he read it? To relax between his medical and his literary work? Was he thinking possibly of writing an adventure novel at some stage? (He wrote several excellent children's stories and some years previously had produced a rather wooden detective novel entitled *The Hunting Party*). One can only say that it is impossible to think of Tolstoy or Dostoevsky settling down to read children's adventure stories – or, if they did so surreptitiously, they would certainly not have admitted it openly in one of their works!

p. 307, *in the name of Christ*: Pilgrims (see the first note to p. 184) or beggars would request "alms in the name of Christ" or "for the sake of Christ".

p. 307, *Khitrov Market*: Khitrov Market was a large open market in Moscow, the area around which, like London's East End in the nineteenth century, was a haven for all kinds of criminals, escaped convicts and vagabonds.

p. 308, *American whalers... America*: "American whaling men have taken fugitives from Botany Bay," writes Nerchinsky Starozhil. "They will take fugitives from Sakhalin in the future."* (CHEKHOV'S NOTE)

* The byline of the correspondent, "Nerchinsky Starozhil", literally means "Long-standing resident of Nerchinsk".

p. 308, *escapes... abroad... Islands*: 'Exiled hard-labour convicts in Okhotsk', *Russian Antiquity*, vol. XXII. And here is one interesting case among many others. In 1885 reports appeared in the Japanese newspapers that nine foreigners of some description had been shipwrecked off Sapporo. The authorities sent officials to Sapporo to render them assistance. As best they could, the foreigners explained to the envoys that they were Germans, their schooner had been wrecked and they had saved themselves in a small boat. Then they were taken from Sapporo to Hokodate. Here they were spoken to in English and Russian, but they understood neither language and only replied "Zherman, Zherman." It was ascertained only with difficulty who was the ship's captain, and when an atlas was placed before this captain, and he was asked to point out where the wreck had taken place, he spent ages running his finger over the map and could not find Sapporo. Their replies were generally unclear. At that time a Russian cruiser lay in Hokodate. The Governor General dispatched a request to the captain asking him to send a German interpreter. The captain sent a senior officer. Suspecting that they were Sakhalin convicts, those same fugitives who not long before had attacked the Krilyon lighthouse, the senior officer resorted to cunning; he lined them up in military file and commanded in Russian: "By the left – a-bout *turn!*" One of the foreigners failed to maintain his role and immediately carried out the command, and thus it was revealed to what nation these wily Odysseuses belonged. See *Vladivostok*, 1885, nos 33 and 38. (CHEKHOV'S NOTE)

p. 308, *Bloka escaped – true?*: This Blokha is widely known for his escapes, and also because he has butchered many Gilyak families. Of late, he has been kept in the fetter block in manacles and leg irons. When the Governor General was touring the fetter block with the Governor of the Island, the latter ordered the manacles to be taken off Blokha, and, this having been done, obtained from him his word of honour that he would run off no longer. It is interesting that this Blokha has a reputation for being an "honest man". Whenever he is being flogged, he screams: "I did it, Yer Excellency, I did it! I really deserve this!" It is extremely likely he will keep his word. A reputation for honesty pleases convicts.* (CHEKHOV'S NOTE)

* According to one of the Sakhalin officials, A.S. Feldman, reminiscing many years later, Chekhov possessed a remarkable gift for gaining the prisoners' confidence. According to Feldman (*Literaturnoye Nasledstvo*, vol. LXVIII, page 596) Chekhov even managed to win over Blokha: "Blokha was morose, unsociable, cruel and sly, but even he changed out of all recognition when talking to Chekhov, and in the sound of his voice we heard tones which we had not even assumed this human wild beast possessed."

p. 310, *those voluntarily returning... bullets*: The *Statutes on Exiles* differentiate on the degree of punishability between escape and absence without leave, escapes within Siberia and escapes beyond Siberia, and also between first, second, third, fourth and subsequent escapes. It is considered "absence without leave", and not escape, if a convict is captured earlier than three days, or if he voluntarily returns earlier than seven days from the time he commenced his flight. For a settled exile these periods are increased, in the first case to seven days, in the second to fourteen. Escape beyond Siberia is considered a more heinous offence, and is penalized more seriously, than escape within Siberia; this distinction is founded, no doubt, on the consideration that, for flight to European Russia, a far greater exertion of ill will is required than for a flight to some Siberian region. The most lenient punishment laid down for a convict for escape is forty lashes and the prolongation of his term of convict labour by four years, and the most severe is 100 lashes, convict labour for life, attachment to the wheelbarrow for three years and detention in the category of "probationer" for twenty years. See Articles 445 and 446, *Statutes on Exiles,* 1890 edition. (CHEKHOV'S NOTE)

p. 311, *In 1889... during the year*: In the Korsakovsk District in 1874, the ratio of those who had been ill to the overall total was 227.2:100. See Dr Sintzovsky, 'Hygienic situation of hard-labour convicts', *Health*, 1875, no. 16. (CHEKHOV'S NOTE)

p. 311, *Accurate Records*: 'Accurate Records' were specifically for recording doctors' diagnoses, recommended treatments and dosages.

Therefore one would expect a translation such as "medical records" or "clinical records". However, I have kept the Russian term *Pravdivye knigi* in translation, although it means nothing in English, in order to preserve the irony. As Chekhov explains, the records are inaccurate and slipshod and contain a great deal of fantasy.

p. 311, *cause of death... fantasy in them*: Among other things, I came across such diagnoses as excessive feeding from the breast, insufficient development for life, mental disease of the heart, internal exhaustion, curious pneumonia [corruption of "croupous pneumonia"] and "small box". (CHEKHOV'S NOTE)

p. 312, *chickenpox among the natives*: Concerning the epidemics of this disease, which gripped the whole of Sakhalin in 1868, and on the vaccination of the aboriginal tribespeople in 1858, see Vasilyev, 'A Journey to Sakhalin Island', *Archive of Forensic Medicine*, 1870, no. 2. To combat the itching caused by varicella, the Gilyaks use melted seal fat, with which they smear their entire body. Since the Gilyaks never wash, their attacks of chickenpox were accompanied by the sort of itching which never occurred among Russians; abscesses would form from the scratching. In 1858, though, there was an epidemic of smallpox on the island, and it was extremely virulent; one old Gilyak told Dr Vasilyev that two had died out of every three. (CHEKHOV'S NOTE)

p. 313, *croupous pneumonia... winter*: In July, August and September 1889, there was not a single case. Over the last ten years there has been only one death from croupous pneumonia in October; this month may be considered the healthiest on Sakhalin. (CHEKHOV'S NOTE)

p. 314, *vershoks*: One vershok is equivalent to 1.75 inches, or 4.4 centimetres.

p. 314, *the report... and so on*: By the way, in this report I found the following: "Convicts are subjected to savage punishments with the birch, so that directly from the chastisement they are brought unconscious to the infirmary." (CHEKHOV'S NOTE)

p. 314, *Dysentery... the cause*: Dr Vasilyev often encountered Gilyaks on Sakhalin suffering from dysentery. (CHEKHOV'S NOTE)

p. 315, *between twenty-five and thirty-five, and between thirty-five and forty-five... work*: I would remind the reader that the ratio of these age groups to the total population is 24.3 per cent and 24.1 per cent. (CHEKHOV'S NOTE)

p. 315, *Syphilis... thirteen times*: Syphilis is found most often at the Alexandrovsk Post. This accumulation of cases here is explained in the report by the considerable quantity of newly arrived prisoners and their families, troops, craftsmen and the entire mass of fresh inhabitants, by the arrival of vessels in the Alexandrovsk and Dooay sea-roads, and by the summer seasonal industries. In the report the measures taken against syphilis are also indicated: (1) examination of the convicts on the 1st and 15th of each month; (2) the examination of contingents newly arrived on the island; (3) weekly examination of women of dubious morality; (4) observation of those formerly suffering from syphilis. But regardless of all these examinations and observations, "a considerable percentage of syphilitics slip through the net of registration". Dr Vasilyev, who was commissioned to go to Sakhalin in 1869 to distribute medical supplies to the aboriginals, met no Gilyaks suffering from syphilis. The Ainos call syphilis "the Japanese disease". The Japanese who come to work in the fishing industry must present to the consul a medical certificate stating that they are free of syphilis. (CHEKHOV'S NOTE)

p. 316, *scurvy... Central... Prison*: The prolonged stay in Central Prisons and holds of steamers is conducive to scurvy, and it has often occurred that, soon after their arrival on the island, prisoners have fallen ill in whole crowds. One newspaper correspondent writes: "The last consignment of convicts from the *Kostroma* arrived in good health; now they have all gone down with scurvy" (*Vladivostok*, 1885, no. 30). (CHEKHOV'S NOTE)

Kharkov is a large city in the Ukraine. The prisoner to whom Chekhov is referring, since he is a Ukrainian, would presumably have committed his crime in his native region. After sentence he would have been kept for some time in the Kharkov Prison, while administrative arrangements were made to send him to Sakhalin; he would then have been dispatched to the Moscow Central Clearing Prison, where he would have joined the rest of the convicts bound for the island from different parts of the empire. With all these other prisoners he would have been transferred back down to Odessa in the Ukraine to embark on the Voluntary Fleet steamer for exile. In other words, this Ukrainian had taken sick with scurvy right at the very beginning of his journey into exile months before and it had not been detected in any medical examination.

p. 316, *marasmus*: Marasmus is progressive wasting, especially associated with old age. Wherever Chekhov has used an archaic term (e.g. "bloody flux" for dysentery or "phthisis" for TB), I have translated it into the equivalent nineteenth-century English term in order to preserve the flavour of the original.

p. 316, *nervous illnesses... times*: A convict with migraine or sciatica is readily suspected of malingering and is not admitted to the infirmary; once I saw a whole crowd of convicts requesting the Prison Governor to be allowed to visit the infirmary, and he refused the lot of them, not wishing to sort out who was sick from who was fit. (CHEKHOV'S NOTE)

p. 316, *nervous ailments*: The phrase "nervous ailments" in nineteenth-century medical terminology did not imply mental illness, as it frequently does now, but meant ailments of the nervous system, which is why Chekhov includes here neuralgia, cramp, palsy, etc.

p. 317, *progressive paralysis*: The progressive paralysis which Chekhov presumably had in mind was an ailment suffered by syphilitics which ultimately manifests in psychiatric disorder, but which is often imperceptible in its initial stages. The nervous system progressively suffers damage, leading to loss of brain cells.

p. 317, *sufficient grounds... out of his mind*: For instance, the gnawings of conscience, yearning for one's home area, constantly degraded self-respect, loneliness and all kinds of petty convict labour unpleasantness. (CHEKHOV'S NOTE)

p. 318, *Conjunctivitis... aboriginals*: Dr Vasilyev: "A great influence on the origin of illness among the Gilyaks is the constant contemplation of the snowy wilderness... I know from personal experience that, within a few days, from constant contemplation of the snowy wilderness it is possible for blennorhoea of the mucous membrane of the eye to occur." The convicts are very much disposed to infection by night blindness. Sometimes it "falls on" whole groups, as they say, so that the convicts grope their way along holding on to each other. (CHEKHOV'S NOTE)

p. 318, *convict women... cohabitants*: The compiler of the report comments on these instances with the following remark: "The distribution of female convicts to male convicts for cohabitation bears the character of compulsion for the former." Some convicts, in order not to be dispatched to convict labour, mutilate themselves;

for instance, they cut off fingers on their right hand. The malingerers are especially ingenious in this respect; they apply red-hot five-copeck pieces to their body, purposely get their feet frostbitten, use some kind of Caucasian powder which, when sprinkled in a small wound or even a scratch, creates a filthy sore with a festering head; one sprinkled snuff into his urethra, and so on. Those who like to simulate illness the most are the Manzes, who have been sent here from the Primorskaya Region. (CHEKHOV'S NOTE)

p. 319, *194… 12.5… 15,000… larger than it in actual fact was*: Actually the coefficient of 12.5 should be closer to 12.9, working from the figures of 194 and 15,000. The figure in the official report Chekhov was working from may have been generously rounded down to give a more favourable impression.

p. 319, *consultant doctor of medicine*: A Consultant Doctor of Medicine would have written a research dissertation and acquired a higher medical degree.

p. 320, *the Alexandrovsk infirmary… 180 beds*: The infirmary occupies an area of 8,574 square sazhens and consists of eleven buildings laid out on three sites: (1) the administrative block, containing the dispensary, surgical room and doctor's surgery, four barrack huts, a kitchen with a female unit attached and a chapel; this, strictly speaking, is what is called the infirmary; then there are (2) two blocks for syphilitics, male and female, a kitchen and an overseers' room; (3) two blocks occupied by the epidemics unit. (CHEKHOV'S NOTE)

p. 320, *Botkin*: Who is also the head of the medical department.*
(CHEKHOV'S NOTE)

* Sergey Botkin (1832–89) was a renowned surgeon and physiologist, Professor of the Military Medical Academy.

p. 320, *Latin inscriptions cortex and radix*: The words "*cortex* and *radix*" are in Latin script in the original. The meaning is of course "remedies made from bark and roots" – i.e. herbal medicines.

p. 320, *the floor… fir twigs*: Fir twigs would have been used to purify the air and to keep out mosquitoes.

p. 320, *The bindings… ship's cord*: The reference to "ship's cord" is obscure. The term used in Russian is actually "sea hawser" (*morskoy kanat*), but an intact hawser would seem rather too weighty to tie round an arm or leg as a binding; therefore I have translated it as "cord". Possibly the cord was being used for ligatures or tourniquets:

in modern times deep wounds are packed with lint or gauze in long thin ribbons which little by little are removed as the edges of the wound begin to heal and knit. Maybe the twine was being used for this filling of wounds in the absence of other material. The reference may also be to thicker rope which would have been unpicked and the oakum used to pack the wound, since this material is extremely absorbent and was at one time widely used for binding wounds in military hospitals and on ships. Presumably, being ship's rope, the cord, to render it waterproof, would have been dipped in tar or creosote; both of these are strong antiseptics and were used to cauterize and disinfect wounds in the army and navy up until the middle of the nineteenth century. Possibly what Chekhov is suggesting is that the prison hospital was so archaic and so poorly provided for that it was still using materials which had become obsolete elsewhere forty or fifty years previously.

p. 321, *the Alexandrovsk infirmary... twenty female*: This depiction of the infirmary at Alexandrovsk was presumably written as a rebuttal of the Central Prison Department report for 1885, which said: "The infirmaries are supplied with all requisite surgical medicaments, and medical aids are procured by the central prison administration from the best St Petersburg drug manufacturers and delivered annually by the ships of the Voluntary Fleet."

p. 321, *In 1889... on this hospital*: Outer clothing and underlinen cost 1,795 roubles 26 copecks; food subsidies 12,832 roubles 94 copecks; medicaments, surgical instruments and apparatus 2,309 roubles 60 copecks; commissariat and office expenses and so forth 2,500 roubles 16 copecks; and medical staff 8,300 roubles. Buildings are repaired at prison expense; auxiliary staff are unpaid. Now I would like to make a comparison. The district hospital in the town of Serpukhov, Moscow Province, which is *sumptuously* laid out and totally satisfies the modern demands of science, where the average daily number of in-patients in 1893 was 43 and out-patients 36.2 (13,278 per year), where the doctors perform serious operations almost every day, deal with epidemics, maintain a complex system of registration and maintenance of clinical notes and so on – this, the best hospital in the district, cost the local council 12,803 roubles 17 copecks in 1893, including, for insurance and repair of buildings, 1,298 roubles. (See 'Review by the Serpukhov Council of Sanitary and Medical

Organizations for 1892 and 1893'.) Medicine on Sakhalin works out as very expensive, yet meanwhile the infirmary is disinfected "by fumigation with chlorine", there is no ventilation, and the soup which was prepared in front of me for the patients at Alexandrovsk tasted extremely salty, since it had been boiled up from salt beef. Until very recently, allegedly "due to non-delivery of the requisite number of items of crockery and because of the lack of order in the kitchen", the patients were fed from the communal prison cooking pot (Directive of the Governor of the Island no. 66, 1890). (CHEKHOV'S NOTE)

p. 322, *Pravaz syringes*: A Pravaz syringe was a syringe designed by the French doctor Charles Gabriel Pravaz (1791–1833) to treat subcutaneous infection.

Extra Material

on

Anton Chekhov's

Sakhalin Island

Anton Chekhov's Life

Anton Pavlovich Chekhov was born in Taganrog, on the Sea *Birth and Background* of Azov in southern Russia, on 29th January 1860. He was the third child of Pavel Yegorovich Chekhov and his wife Yevgenia Yakovlevna. He had four brothers – Alexander (born in 1855), Nikolai (1858), Ivan (1861) and Mikhail (1865) – and one sister, Maria, who was born in 1863. Anton's father, the owner of a small shop, was a devout Christian who administered brutal floggings to his children almost on a daily basis. Anton remembered these with bitterness throughout his life, and possibly as a result was always sceptical of organized religion. The shop – a grocery and general-supplies store which sold such goods as lamp oil, tea, coffee, seeds, flour and sugar – was kept by the children during their father's absence. The father also required his children to go with him to church at least once a day. He set up a liturgical choir which practised in his shop, and demanded that his children – whether they had school work to do or not, or whether they had been in the shop all day – should join the rehearsals to provide the higher voice parts.

Chekhov described his home town as filthy and tedious, and *Education and Childhood* the people as drunk, idle, lazy and illiterate. At first, Pavel tried to provide his children with an education by enrolling the two he considered the brightest, Nikolai and Anton, in one of the schools for the descendants of the Greek merchants who had once settled in Taganrog. These provided a more "classical" education than their Russian equivalents, and their standard of teaching was held in high regard. However, the experience was not a successful one, since most of the other pupils spoke Greek among themselves, of which the Chekhovs did not know a single word. Eventually, in 1868, Anton was enrolled in one of the town's Russian high schools. The courses at the Russian school included Church Slavonic, Latin and Greek, and if the entire curriculum was successfully completed, entry to a university was guaranteed. Unfortunately, as the shop was making less and less money, the school fees were often unpaid and lessons were missed. The teaching was generally mediocre, but the religious education teacher, Father Pokrovsky, encouraged his pupils to read the Russian classics and such foreign authors as Shakespeare, Swift and Goethe. Pavel also paid for private French and music lessons for his children.

Every summer the family would travel through the steppe by cart some fifty miles to an estate where their paternal grandfather was chief steward. The impressions gathered on these journeys, and the people encountered, made a profound impression on the young Anton, and later provided material for one of his greatest stories, *The Steppe*.

At the age of thirteen, Anton went to the theatre for the first time, to see Offenbach's operetta *La Belle Hélène* at the Taganrog theatre. He was enchanted by the spectacle, and went as often as time and money allowed, seeing not only the Russian classics, but also foreign pieces such as *Hamlet* in Russian translation. In his early teens, he even created his own theatrical company with his school friends to act out the Russian classics.

Adversity   In 1875 Anton was severely ill with peritonitis. The highschool doctor tended him with great care, and he resolved to join the medical profession one day. That same year, his brothers Alexander and Nikolai, fed up with the beatings they received at home, decided to move to Moscow to work and study, ignoring their father's admonitions and threats. Anton now bore the entire brunt of Pavel's brutality. To complicate things further, the family shop ran into severe financial difficulties, and was eventually declared bankrupt. The children were withdrawn from school, and Pavel fled to Moscow, leaving his wife and family to face the creditors. In the end, everybody abandoned the old residence, with the exception of Anton, who remained behind with the new owner.

Although he was now free of his father's bullying and the hardship of having to go to church and work in the shop, Anton had to find other employment in order to pay his rent and bills, and to resume his school studies. Accordingly, at the age of fifteen, he took up tutoring, continuing voraciously to read books of Russian and foreign literature, philosophy and science, in the town library.

In 1877, during a summer holiday, he undertook the seven-hundred-mile journey to Moscow to see his family, and found them all living in one room and sleeping on a single mattress on the floor. His father was not at all abashed by his failures: he continued to be dogmatically religious and to beat the younger children regularly. On his return to Taganrog, Anton attempted to earn a little additional income by sending sketches and anecdotes to several of Moscow's humorous magazines, but they were all turned down.

The young Chekhov unabatedly pursued his studies, and in June 1879 he passed the Taganrog High School exams with distinction, and in the autumn he moved to Moscow to study medicine. The family still lived in one room, and Alexander and Nikolai were well on the way to becoming alcoholics. Anton, instead of finding his own lodgings, decided to support not only himself, but his entire family, and try to re-educate them. After a hard day spent in lectures, tutorials and in the laboratories, he would write more sketches for humorous and satirical magazines, and an increasing number of these were now accepted: by the early 1880s, over a hundred had been printed. Anton used a series of pseudonyms (the most usual being "Antosha Chekhonte") for these productions, which he later called "rubbish". He also visited the Moscow theatres and concert halls on numerous occasions, and in 1880 sent the renowned Maly Theatre a play he had recently written. Only a rough draft of the piece – which was rejected by the Maly and published for the first time in 1920, under the title *Platonov* – has survived. Unless Chekhov had polished and pruned his lost final version considerably, the play would have lasted around seven hours. Despite its poor construction and verbosity, *Platonov* already shows some of the themes and characters present in Chekhov's mature works, such as rural boredom and weak-willed, supine intellectuals dreaming of a better future while not doing anything to bring it about.

As well as humorous sketches and stories, Chekhov wrote brief résumés of legal court proceedings and gossip from the artistic world for various Moscow journals. With the money made from these pieces he moved his family into a larger flat, and regularly invited friends to visit and talk and drink till late at night.

Studies in Moscow and Early Publications

451

In 1882, encouraged by his success with the Moscow papers, he started contributing to the journals of the capital St Petersburg, since payment there was better than in Moscow. He was eventually commissioned to contribute a regular column to the best-selling journal *Oskolki* ("Splinters"), providing a highly coloured picture of Moscow life with its court cases and Bohemian atmosphere. He was now making over 150 roubles a month from his writing – about three times as much as his student stipend – although he managed to save very little because of the needs of his family. In 1884 Chekhov published, at his own expense, a booklet of six of his short stories, entitled *Tales of Melpomene*, which sold quite poorly.

Start of Medical Career and First Signs of Illness

There was compensation for this relative literary failure: in June of that year Anton passed all his final exams in medicine and became a medical practitioner. That summer, he began to receive patients at a village outside Moscow, and even stepped in for the director of a local hospital when the latter went on his summer vacation. He was soon receiving thirty to forty patients a day, and was struck by the peasants' ill health, filth and drunkenness. He planned a major treatise entitled *A History of Medicine in Russia* but, after reading and annotating over a hundred works on the subject, he gave the subject up and returned to Moscow to set up his own medical practice.

First Signs of Tuberculosis

Suddenly, in December 1884, when he was approaching the achievement of all his ambitions, Chekhov developed a dry cough and began to spit blood. He tried to pretend that these were not early symptoms of tuberculosis but, as a doctor, he must have had an inkling of the truth. He made no attempt to cut down his commitments in the light of his illness, but kept up the same punishing schedule of activity. By this time, Chekhov had published over three hundred items, including some of his first recognized mature works, such as 'The Daughter of Albion' and 'The Death of an Official'. Most of the stories were already, in a very understated way, depicting life's "losers" – such as the idle gentry, shopkeepers striving unsuccessfully to make a living and ignorant peasants. Now that his income had increased, Chekhov rented a summer house a few miles outside Moscow. However, although he intended to use his holiday exclusively for writing, he was inundated all day with locals who had heard he was a doctor and required medical attention.

Chekhov made a crucial step in his literary career, when in *Trip to St Petersburg and* December 1885 he visited the imperial capital St Petersburg *Meeting with Suvorin* for the first time, as a guest of the editor of the renowned *St Petersburg Journal*. His stories were beginning to gain him a reputation, and he was introduced at numerous soirées to famous members of the St Petersburg literary world. He was agreeably surprised to find they knew his work and valued it highly. Here for the first time he met Alexei Suvorin, the press mogul and editor of the most influential daily of the period, *Novoye Vremya* (*New Times*). Suvorin asked Chekhov to contribute stories regularly to his paper at a far higher rate of pay than he had been receiving from other journals. Now Chekhov, while busy treating numerous patients in Moscow and helping to stem the constant typhus epidemics that broke out in the city, also began to churn out for Suvorin such embryonic masterpieces as 'The Requiem' and 'Grief' – although all were still published pseudonymously. Distinguished writers advised him to start publishing under his own name and, although his current collection *Motley Stories* had already gone to press under the Chekhonte pseudonym, Anton resolved from now on to shed his anonymity. The collection received tepid reviews, but Chekhov now had sufficient income to rent a whole house on Sadova-Kudrinskaya Street (now maintained as a museum of this early period of Chekhov's life), in an elegant district of Moscow.

Chekhov's reputation as a writer was further enhanced when *Literary Recognition* Suvorin published a collection of sixteen of Chekhov's short stories in 1887 – under the title *In the Twilight* – to great critical acclaim. However, Chekhov's health was deteriorating and his blood-spitting was growing worse by the day. Anton appears more and more by now to have come to regard life as a parade of "the vanity of human wishes". He channelled some of this ennui and his previous life experiences into a slightly melodramatic and overlong play, *Ivanov*, in which the eponymous hero – a typical "superfluous man" who indulges in pointless speculation while his estate goes to ruin and his capital dwindles – ends up shooting himself. *Ivanov* was premiered in November 1887 by the respected Korsh Private Theatre under Chekhov's real name – a sign of Anton's growing confidence as a writer – although it received very mixed reviews.

However, in the spring of 1888, Chekhov's story 'The Steppe' – an impressionistic, poetical recounting of the experiences of

453

a young boy travelling through the steppe on a cart – was published in *The Northern Messenger*, again under his real name, enabling him to reach another milestone in his literary career, and prompting reviewers for the first time to talk of his genius. Although Chekhov began to travel to the Crimea for vacations, in the hope that the warm climate might aid his health, the symptoms of tuberculosis simply reappeared whenever he returned to Moscow. In October of the same year, Chekhov was awarded the prestigious Pushkin Prize for Literature for *In the Twilight*. He was now recognized as a major Russian writer, and began to state his belief to reporters that a writer's job is not to peddle any political or philosophical point of view, but to depict human life with its associated problems as objectively as possible.

Death of his Brother

A few months later, in January 1889, a revised version of *Ivanov* was staged at the Alexandrinsky Theatre in St Petersburg, arguably the most important drama theatre in Russia at the time. The new production was a huge success and received excellent reviews. However, around that time it also emerged that Anton's alcoholic brother, Nikolai, was suffering from advanced tuberculosis. When Nikolai died in June of that year, at the age of thirty, Anton must have seen this as a harbinger of his own early demise.

Chekhov was now working on a new play, *The Wood Demon*, in which, for the first time, psychological nuance replaced stage action, and the effect on the audience was achieved by atmosphere rather than by drama or the portrayal of events. However, precisely for these reasons, it was rejected by the Alexandrinsky Theatre in October of that year. Undeterred, Chekhov decided to revise it, and a new version of *The Wood Demon* was put on in Moscow in December 1889. Lambasted by the critics, it was swiftly withdrawn from the scene, to make its appearance again many years later, thoroughly rewritten, as *Uncle Vanya*.

Journey to Sakhalin Island

It was around this time that Anton Chekhov began contemplating his journey to the prison island of Sakhalin. At the end of 1889, unexpectedly, and for no apparent reason, the twenty-nine year-old author announced his intention to leave European Russia, and to travel across Siberia to Sakhalin, the large island separating Siberia and the Pacific Ocean, following which he would write a full-scale examination of the penal colony maintained there by the Tsarist authorities.

Explanations put forward by commentators both then and since include a search by the author for fresh material for his works, a desire to escape from the constant carping of his liberally minded colleagues on his lack of a political line; desire to escape from an unhappy love affair; and disappointment at the recent failure of *The Wood Demon*. A further explanation may well be that, as early as 1884, he had been spitting blood, and recently, just before his journey, several friends and relations had died of tuberculosis. Chekhov, as a doctor, must have been aware that he too was in the early stages of the disease, and that his lifespan would be considerably curtailed. Possibly he wished to distance himself for several months from everything he had known, and give himself time to think over his illness and mortality by immersing himself in a totally alien world. Chekhov hurled himself into a study of the geography, history, nature and ethnography of the island, as background material to his study of the penal settlement. The Trans-Siberian Railway had not yet been constructed, and the journey across Siberia, begun in April 1890, required two and a half months of travel in sledges and carriages on abominable roads in freezing temperatures and appalling weather. This certainly hastened the progress of his tuberculosis and almost certainly deprived him of a few extra years of life. He spent three months in frantic work on the island, conducting his census of the prison population, rummaging in archives, collecting material and organizing book collections for the children of exiles, before leaving in October 1890 and returning to Moscow, via Hong Kong, Ceylon and Odessa, in December of that year.

The completion of his report on his trip to Sakhalin was *Travels in Europe* to be hindered for almost five years by his phenomenally busy life, as he attempted, as before, to continue his medical practice and write at the same time. In early 1891 Chekhov, in the company of Suvorin, travelled for the first time to western Europe, visiting Vienna, Venice, Bologna, Florence, Rome, Naples and, finally, Monaco and Paris.

Trying to cut down on the expenses he was paying out for *Move to Melikhovo* his family in Moscow, he bought a small estate at Melikhovo, a few miles outside Moscow, and the entire family moved there. His father did some gardening, his mother cooked, while Anton planted hundreds of fruit trees, shrubs and flowers. Chekhov's concerns for nature have a surprisingly modern ecological ring: he once said that if he had not been a writer he woud have become a gardener.

Although his brothers had their own lives in Moscow and only spent holidays at Melikhovo, Anton's sister Maria – who never married – lived there permanently, acting as his confidante and as his housekeeper when he had his friends and famous literary figures to stay, as he often did in large parties. Chekhov also continued to write, but was distracted, as before, by the scores of locals who came every day to receive medical treatment from him. There was no such thing as free medical assistance in those days and, if anybody seemed unable to pay, Chekhov often treated them for nothing. In 1892, there was a severe local outbreak of cholera, and Chekhov was placed in charge of relief operations. He supervised the building of emergency isolation wards in all the surrounding villages and travelled round the entire area directing the medical operations.

Ill Health   Chekhov's health was deteriorating more and more rapidly, and his relentless activity certainly did not help. He began to experience almost constant pain and, although still hosting gatherings, he gave the appearance of withdrawing increasingly into himself and growing easily tired. By the mid-1890s, his sleep was disturbed on most nights by bouts of violent coughing. Besides continuing his medical activities, looking after his estate and writing, Chekhov undertook to supervise – often with large subsidies from his own pocket – the building of schools in the local villages, where there had been none before.

Controversy around   By late 1895, Chekhov was thinking of writing for the thea-
The Seagull   tre again. The result was *The Seagull*, which was premiered at the Alexandrinsky Theatre in October 1896. Unfortunately, the acting was so bad that the premiere was met by jeering and laughter, and received vicious reviews. Chekhov himself commented that the director did not understand the play, the actors didn't know their lines and nobody could grasp the understated style. He fled from the theatre and roamed the streets of St Petersburg until two in the morning, resolving never to write for the theatre again. Despite this initial fiasco, subsequent performances went from strength to strength, with the actors called out on stage after every performance.

Olga Knipper   By this time, it seems that Chekhov had accepted the fact that he had a mortal illness. In 1897, he returned to Italy to see whether the warmer climate would not afford his condition some respite, but as soon as he came back to Russia the coughing and blood-spitting resumed as violently as before. It was around this time that the two founders of the Moscow Arts Theatre, Vladimir Nemirovich-Danchenko and Konstantin Stanislavsky, asked Chekhov whether they could stage *The Seagull*. Their aims were to replace the stylized and unnatural devices of the classical theatre with more natural events and dialogue, and Chekhov's play seemed ideal for this purpose. He gave his permission, and in September 1898 went to Moscow to attend the preliminary rehearsals. It was there that he first met the twenty-eight-year-old actress Olga Knipper, who was going to take the leading role of Arkadina. But the Russian winter was making him cough blood violently, and so he decided to follow the local doctors' advice and travel south to the Crimea, in order to spend the winter in a warmer climate. Accordingly, he rented a villa with a large garden in Yalta.

When his father died in October of the same year, Chekhov *Move to the Crimea* decided to put Melikhovo up for sale and move his mother and Maria to the Crimea. They temporarily stayed in a large villa near the Tatar village of Kuchukoy, but Chekhov had in the meantime bought a plot of land at Autka, some twenty minutes by carriage from Yalta, and he drew up a project to have a house built there. Construction began in December.

Also in December 1898, the first performance of *The Seagull* at the Moscow Arts Theatre took place. It was a resounding success, and there were now all-night queues for tickets. Despite his extremely poor health, Chekhov was still busy raising money for relief of the severe famine then scourging the Russian heartlands, overseeing the building of his new house and aiding the local branch of the Red Cross. In addition to this, local people and aspiring writers would turn up in droves at his villa in Yalta to receive medical treatment or advice on their manuscripts.

In early January 1899, Chekhov signed an agreement with *Collected Works Project* the publisher Adolf Marx to supervise the publication of a multi-volume edition of his collected works in return for a flat fee of 75,000 roubles and no royalties. This proved to be an error of judgement from a financial point of view, because by the time Chekhov had put some money towards building his new house, ensured all the members of his family were provided for and made various other donations, the advance had almost disappeared.

Chekhov finally moved to Autka – where he was to spend the last few years of his life – in June 1899, and immediately began to plant vegetables, flowers and fruit trees. During a short period spent in Moscow to facilitate his work for Adolf Marx, he re-established contact with the Moscow Arts Theatre and Olga Knipper. Chekhov invited the actress to Yalta on several occasions and, although her visits were brief and at first she stayed in a hotel, it was obvious that she and Chekhov were becoming very close. Apart from occasional short visits to Moscow, which cost him a great expenditure of energy and were extremely harmful to his medical condition, Chekhov now had to spend all of his time in the south. He forced himself to continue writing short stories and plays, but felt increasingly lonely and isolated and, aware that he had only a short time left to live, became even more withdrawn. It was around this time that he worked again at his early play *The Wood Demon*, reducing the dramatis personae to only nine characters, radically altering the most significant scenes and renaming it *Uncle Vanya*. This was premiered in October 1899, and it was another gigantic success. In July of the following year, Olga Knipper took time off from her busy schedule of rehearsals and performances in Moscow to visit Chekhov in Yalta. There was no longer any attempt at pretence: she stayed in his house and, although he was by now extremely ill, they became romantically involved, exchanging love letters almost every day.

By now Chekhov had drafted another new play, *Three Sisters*, and he travelled to Moscow to supervise the first few rehearsals. Olga came to his hotel every day bringing food and flowers. However, Anton felt that the play needed revision, so he returned to Yalta to work on a comprehensive rewrite. *Three Sisters* opened on 31st January 1901 and – though at first well-received, especially by the critics – it gradually grew in the public's estimation, becoming another great success.

But Chekhov was feeling lonely in Yalta without Olga, and in May of that year proposed to her by letter. Olga accepted, and Chekhov immediately set off for Moscow, despite his doctors' advice to the contrary. He arranged a dinner for his friends and relatives and, while they were waiting there, he and Olga got married secretly in a small church in the outskirts of Moscow. As the participants at the dinner received a telegram with the news, the couple had already left for their honeymoon. Olga and Anton sailed down the Volga, up the Kama River and along the Belaya River to the village of Aksyonovo, where they checked into a sanatorium. At this establishment Chekhov drank four large bottles of fermented mare's milk every day, put on weight, and his condition seemed to improve somewhat. However, on their return to Yalta, Chekhov's health deteriorated again. He made his will, leaving his house in Yalta to Maria, all income from his dramatic works to Olga and large sums to his mother and his surviving brothers, to the municipality of Taganrog and to the peasant body of Melikhovo.

After a while, Olga returned to her busy schedule of rehears- *Difficult Relationship* als and performances in Moscow, and the couple continued their relationship at a distance, as they had done before their marriage, with long and frequent love letters. Chekhov managed to visit her in Moscow occasionally, but by now he was so ill that he had to return to Yalta immediately, often remaining confined to bed for long periods. Olga was tortured as to whether she should give up her acting career and nurse Anton for the time left to him. Almost unable to write, Anton now embarked laboriously on his last dramatic masterpiece, *The Cherry Orchard*. Around that time, in the spring of 1902, Olga visited Anton in Yalta after suffering a spontaneous miscarriage during a Moscow Art Theatre tour, leaving her husband with the unpleasant suspicion that she might have been unfaithful to him. In the following months, Anton nursed his wife devotedly, travelling to Moscow whenever he could to be near her. Olga's flat was on the third floor, and there was no lift. It took Anton half an hour to get up the stairs, so he practically never went out.

When *The Cherry Orchard* was finally completed in *Final Play* October 1903, Chekhov once again travelled to Moscow to attend rehearsals, despite the advice of his doctors that it would be tantamount to suicide. The play was premiered on 17th January 1904, Chekhov's forty-fourth birthday, and at the end of the performance the author was dragged on stage. There was no chair for him, and he was forced to stand listening to the interminable speeches trying not to cough and pretending to look interested. Although the performance was a success, press reviews, as usual, were mixed, and Chekhov thought that Nemirovich-Danchenko and Stanislavsky had misunderstood the play.

459

Death   Chekhov returned to Yalta knowing he would not live long enough to write another work. His health deteriorated even further, and the doctors put him on morphine, advising him to go to a sanatorium in Germany. Accordingly, in June 1904, he and Olga set off for Badenweiler, a spa in the Black Forest. The German specialists examined him and reported that they could do nothing. Soon oxygen had to be administered to him, and he became feverish and delirious. At 12.30 a.m. on 15th July 1904, he regained his mental clarity sufficiently to tell Olga to summon a doctor urgently. On the doctor's arrival, Chekhov told him, "*Ich sterbe*" ("I'm dying"). The doctor gave him a strong stimulant, and was on the point of sending for other medicines when Chekhov, knowing it was all pointless, simply asked for a bottle of champagne to be sent to the room. He poured everybody a glass, drank his off, commenting that he hadn't had champagne for ages, lay down, and died in the early hours of the morning.

Funeral   The coffin was transported back to Moscow in a filthy green carriage marked "FOR OYSTERS", and although it was met at the station by bands and a large ceremonial gathering, it turned out that this was for an eminent Russian general who had just been killed in action in Manchuria. Only a handful of people had assembled to greet Chekhov's coffin. However, as word got round Moscow that his body was being transported to the graveyard at the Novodevichy Monastery, people poured out of their homes and workplaces, forming a vast crowd both inside and outside the cemetery and causing a large amount of damage to buildings, pathways and other graves in the process. The entire tragicomic episode of Chekhov's death, transportation back to Moscow and burial could almost have featured in one of his own short stories. Chekhov was buried next to his father Pavel. His mother outlived him by fifteen years, and his sister Maria died in 1957 at the age of ninety-four. Olga Knipper survived two more years, dying in 1959 at the age of eighty-nine.

Anton Chekhov's Works

Early Writings   When Chekhov studied medicine in Moscow from 1879 to 1884, he financed his studies by writing reports of law-court proceedings for the newspapers and contributing, under a whole series of pseudonyms, hundreds of jokes, comic sketches and short stories to the numerous Russian humorous magazines and more serious journals of the time. From 1885, when he began to practise as a doctor, he concentrated far more on serious literary works, and between then and the end of his life he produced over 200 short stories, plus a score or so of dramatic pieces, ranging from monologues through one-act to full-length plays. In 1884 he also wrote his only novel, *The Hunting Party*, which was a rather wooden attempt at a detective novel.

A number of his stories between the mid-Eighties and his journey to Sakhalin were vitiated by his attempt to propagate the Tolstoyan moral principles he had espoused at the time. But even before his journey to the prison island he was realizing that laying down the law to his readers, and trying to dictate how they should read his stories, was not his job: it should be the goal of an artist to describe persons and events non-judgementally, and let the reader draw his or her own conclusions. This is attested by his letter to Suvorin in April 1890: "You reproach me for 'objectivity', calling it indifference to good and evil, and absence of ideals and ideas and so forth. You wish me, when depicting horse thieves, to state: stealing horses is bad. But, surely, people have known that for ages already, without me telling them so? Let them be judged by jurymen – my business is to show them as they really are. When I write, I rely totally on the reader, supposing that he himself will supply the subjective factors absent in the story." After Chekhov's return from Sakhalin, this objectivity dominated everything he wrote. *Invention of a New, "Objective" Style of Writing*

A further feature of Chekhov's storytelling, which developed throughout his career, is that he does not so much describe events taking place, but rather depicts the way that characters react to those – frequently quite insignificant – events, and the way people's lives are often transformed for better or worse by them. His dramatic works from that time also showed a development from fully displayed events and action – sometimes, in the early plays, quite melodramatic – to, in the major plays written in the last decade or so of his life, depicting the effects on people's lives of off-stage events, and the way the characters react to those events.

His style in all his later writing – especially from 1890 onwards – is lucid and economical, and there is a total absence of purple passages. The works of his final years display an increasing awareness of the need for conservation of the natural world in the face of the creeping industrialization of Russia. The breakdown of the old social order in the face of the new rising entrepreneurial class is also depicted non-judgementally; in Chekhov's last play, *The Cherry Orchard*, an old estate belonging to a long-established family of gentry is sold to a businessman, and the final scenes of the play give way to the offstage sounds of wood-chopping, as the old cherry orchard – one of the major beauties of the estate – is cut down by its new owner to be sold for timber.

Major Short Stories   It is generally accepted that Chekhov's mature story-writing may be said to date from the mid-1880s, when he began to contribute to the "thick journals". Descriptions of a small representative selection of some of the major short stories – giving an idea of Chekhov's predominant themes – can be found below.

On the Road   In 'On the Road' (1886), set in a seedy wayside inn on Christmas Eve, a man, apparently from the privileged classes, and his eight-year-old daughter are attempting to sleep in the "travellers' lounge", having been forced to take refuge from a violent storm. The little girl wakes up, and tells him how unhappy she is and that he is a wicked man. A noblewoman, also sheltering from the storm, enters and comforts the girl. The man and the woman both tell each other of the unhappiness of their lives: he is a widowed nobleman who has squandered all his money and is now on his way to a tedious job in the middle of nowhere; she is from a wealthy family, but her father and her brothers are wastrels, and she is the only one who takes care of the estate. They both part in the morning, on Christmas Day, profoundly unhappy, and without succeeding in establishing that deep inner contact with another human being which both of them obviously crave.

Enemies   Chekhov's 1887 tale 'Enemies' touches on similar themes of misery and incomprehension: a country doctor's six-year-old son has just died of diphtheria, leaving him and his wife devastated; at precisely this moment, a local landowner comes to his house to call him out to attend to his wife who is apparently dangerously ill. Though sympathetic to the doctor's state, he is understandably full of anxiety for his wife, and insists that the doctor come. After an uncomfortable carriage journey, they arrive at the landowner's mansion to discover that the wife was never ill at all, but was simply getting rid of her husband so that she could run off with her lover. The landowner is now in a state of anger and despair, and the doctor unreasonably blames him for having dragged him out under false pretences. When the man offers him his fee, the doctor throws it in his face and storms out. The landowner also furiously drives off somewhere to assuage his anger. Neither man can even begin to penetrate the other's mental states because of their own problems. The doctor remains full of contempt and cynicism for the human race for the rest of his life.

In 1888, Chekhov's first indubitably great narrative, the novella-length 'The Steppe', was published to rapturous reviews. There is almost no plot: in blazing midsummer, a nine-year-old boy sets out on a long wagon ride, lasting several days, from his home in a small provincial town through the steppe, to stay with relatives and attend high school in a large city. The entire story consists of his impressions of the journey – of his travelling companions, the people they meet en route, the inns at which they stay, the scenery and wildlife. He finally reaches his destination, bids farewell to his travelling companions, and the story ends with him full of tears of regret at his lost home life, and foreboding at what the future in this strange new world holds for him. *The Steppe*

Another major short story by Chekhov, 'The Name-Day Party' (also translated as 'The Party'), was published in the same year as 'The Steppe'. The title refers to the fact that Russians celebrate not only their birthdays, but the day of the saint after whom they are named. It is the name day of a selfish lawyer and magistrate; his young wife, who is seven-months pregnant, has spent all day organizing a banquet in his honour and entertaining guests. Utterly exhausted, she occasionally asks him to help her, but he does very little. Finally, when all the guests have gone home, she, in extreme agony, gives birth prematurely to a still-born baby. She slips in and out of consciousness, believes she too is dying, and, despite his behaviour, she feels sorry for her husband, who will be lost without her. However, when she regains consciousness he seems to blame her for the loss of the child, and not his own selfishness leading to her utter exhaustion at such a time. *The Name-Day Party*

'A Dreary Story' (also known as 'A Tedious Story') is one of Chekhov's longer stories, originally published in 1889. In a tour de force, the twenty-nine-year-old Chekhov penetrates *A Dreary Story* into the mind of a famous sixty-two-year-old professor – his interior monologue constituting the entire tale. The professor is a world expert in his subject, fêted throughout Russia, yet has a terminal disease which means he will be dead in a few months. He has told nobody, not even his family. This professor muses over his life, and how his body is falling apart, and he wonders what the point of it all was. He would gladly give all his fame for just a few more years of warm, vibrant life. Chekhov wrote this story the year before he travelled to Sakhalin, when he was beginning to display the first symptoms of the tuberculosis which was to kill him at the age of forty-four. Therefore these musings of the old professor may be an indication of Chekhov's own state of mind at the time.

The Duel   In Chekhov's 1891 story 'The Duel', a bored young civil servant has lost interest in everything in life, including his lover. When the latter's husband dies, she expects him to marry her, but he decides to borrow money and leave the town permanently instead. However, the acquaintance from whom he tries to borrow the money refuses to advance him the sum for such purposes. After a heated exchange, the civil servant challenges the acquaintance to a duel – a challenge which is taken up by a friend of the person who has refused to lend the money, disgusted at the civil servant's selfish behaviour. Both miss their shot, and the civil servant, realizing how near he has been to death, regains interest in life, marries his mistress, and all are reconciled.

Ward no. 6   'In Ward no. 6' (1892), a well-meaning but apathetic and weak rural hospital director has a ward for the mentally disturbed as one of his responsibilities. He knows that the thuggish peasant warden regularly beats the lunatics up, but makes all kinds of excuses not to get involved. He ends up being incarcerated in his own mental ward by the ruse of an ambitious rival, and is promptly beaten by the same warden who used to call him "Your Honour", and dies soon afterwards. This is perhaps Chekhov's most transparent attack on the supine intelligentsia of his own time, whom he saw as lacking determination in the fight against social evils.

Three Years   In 1895, Chekhov published his famous story 'Three Years', in which Laptev, a young Muscovite, is nursing his seriously ill sister in a small provincial town, and feels restricted and bored. He falls in love with the daughter of her doctor and, perhaps from loneliness and the need for companionship, proposes marriage. Although she is not in love with him, she accepts, after a good deal of hesitation, because she is afraid this might be her only offer in this dull town. For the first three years this marriage – forged through a sense of isolation on one side and fear of spinsterhood on the other – is passionless and somewhat unhappy. However, after this period, they manage to achieve an equable and fulfilling relationship based on companionship.

In the 'The House with a Mansard' (1896), a talented but lazy young artist visits a rich landowning friend in the country. *The House with a Mansard* They go to visit the wealthy family at the title's "house with a mansard", which consists of a mother and two unmarried daughters. The artist falls in love with the younger daughter, but her tyrannical older sister sends both her and her mother abroad. The story ends some years later with the artist still wistfully wondering what has become of the younger sister.

In 'Peasants' (1897), Nikolai, who has lived and worked *Peasants* in Moscow since adolescence, and now works as a highly respected waiter at a prestigious Moscow hotel, is taken very ill and can no longer work, so he decides to return to the country village of his childhood, taking with him his wife and young daughter, who were both born in Moscow. He has warm recollections of the village, but finds that memory has deceived him. The place is filthy and squalid, and the local inhabitants all seem to be permanently blind drunk. Since anybody with any intelligence – like Nikolai himself – is sent to the city as young as possible to work and send money back to the family, the level of ignorance and stupidity is appalling. Nikolai dies, and the story ends with his wife and daughter having to become tramps and beg for a living.

In 1898, Chekhov published 'The Man in a Case', in which *The Man in a Case* the narrator, a schoolmaster, recounts the life of a recently deceased colleague of his, Byelikov, who taught classical Greek. A figure of ridicule for his pupils and colleagues, Byelikov is described as being terrified of the modern world, walking around, even in the warmest weather, in high boots, a heavy overcoat, dark spectacles and a hat with a large brim concealing his face. The blinds are always drawn on all the windows in his house, and these are permanently shut. He threatens to report to the headmaster a young colleague who engages in the appallingly immoral and progressive activity of going for bicycle rides in the countryside. The young man pushes him, Byelikov falls down, and although not hurt, takes to his bed and dies, apparently of humiliation and oversensitivity.

The Lady with the Lapdog

'The Lady with the Lapdog' (1899) tells the story of a bored and cynical forty-year-old senior bank official who, trapped in a tedious marriage in Moscow, takes a holiday by himself in Yalta. There he meets the thirty-year-old Anna, who is also unhappily married. They have an affair, then go back to their respective homes. In love for possibly the first time in his life, he travels to the provincial town where she lives, and tracks her down. They meet in a theatre, and before her husband returns to his seat, she promises to visit him in Moscow. The story ends with them both realizing that their problems are only just beginning.

Sakhalin Island

As well as being a prolific writer of short fiction, Chekhov also wrote countless articles as a journalist, and the volume-length *Sakhalin Island* ranks as one of the most notable examples of his investigative non-fiction. As mentioned above, Chekhov's decision to travel to Sakhalin Island in easternmost Siberia for three months in 1890 was motivated by several factors, one of them being to write a comprehensive study of the penal colonies on the island. Although he had the permission of the authorities to carry out his research, his ambition was to probe beyond the Tsarist propaganda on the subject issued by the Central Prison Department, following the lead of the American journalist George Kennan who had visited Russia in 1885–86 and written a series of articles for an American magazine condemning the Siberian exile system.

This system was extremely complex, involving as it did various categories of banishment, such as exile to convict labour, and exile to live and work in a Siberian settlement, which, although not entailing imprisonment, still consisted of loss of legal rights as with a convict. A further category was exile to a settlement with full free-person's rights, but with no right ever to return to European Russia.

Sakhalin, since it was an island, and as far away from central Russia as one could go without leaving the country, was used at the time exclusively as a destination for long-term hard-labour convicts, who – apart from those on life terms – would serve out their sentences, then proceed to live in a local village to serve for several years with the status of a felon who was rehabilitating himself by learning to live a productive life in the community. Finally, when this period of "probation" was over, he or she would have their free-person's rights restored to them and could leave for the mainland – but were still not allowed back to central Russia; they had to remain in Siberia for life. The authorities hoped by this policy to turn Sakhalin into a thriving colony on the lines of Australia, and numerous dishonest reports appeared in the European Russian press, planted by the government, claiming that this aim was being achieved. Chekhov toured round the entire island, visiting all the prisons and most of the settlements, and generally spending up to nineteen hours a day gathering material and writing up his findings. Chekhov returned from Sakhalin at the end of 1890, but it took him three years to write up and start publishing the material he had collected. The first chapter was published in the journal *Russian Thought* (*Russkaya Mysl*) in late 1893, and subsequent material appeared regularly in this magazine until July 1894, with no objection from the censor, until finally, the chapters from number twenty onwards were banned from publication. Chekhov took the decision to "publish and be damned" – accordingly the whole thing appeared in book form, including the banned chapters, in May 1895.

The first chapters contain a detailed, rather dry exposition of the geography and early exploration of the island. Then Chekhov gives an in depth portrayal of all the prisons and most of the inhabited spots there, and finishes off with a harrowing analysis of the colony itself – the various kinds of labour, the way the exiles lived, and an examination of whether the aim of colonizing the island for the Russian Empire by sending the country's worst criminals there was in fact being achieved.

The book caused enormous interest and discussion in the press, and over the next decade a number of substantial ameliorations were brought about in the criminals' lives. But, although Chekhov's work was a contributory factor to this, these improvements may well have happened anyway, with the liberalization of the country's intellectual climate, and the weakening of the autocratic Tsarist system of government.

However, Chekhov's work made sufficient impression for the noted author and critic A. Bogdanovich to write in a review of a second edition of the work in 1902: "If Mr Chekhov had never written anything other than this book, his name would be for ever inscribed in the history of Russian literature, and would never be forgotten in the history of Russian exile."

Major Plays   Chekhov first made his name in the theatre with a series of one-act farces, most notably *The Bear* and *Swan Song* (both 1888). However, his first attempts at full-length plays, *Platonov* (1880), *Ivanov* (1887), and *The Wood Demon* (1889) were not entirely successful. The four plays which are now considered to be Chekhov's masterpieces, and outstanding works of world theatre, are *The Seagull* (1896), *Uncle Vanya* (1899), *Three Sisters* (1901) and *The Cherry Orchard* (1904).

The Seagull   The central character in *The Seagull* is an unsuccessful playwright, Trevlev, who is in love with the actress Nina. However, she falls in love with the far more successful writer Trigorin. Out of spite and as an anti-idealist gesture, Trevlev shoots a seagull and places it in front of her. Nina becomes Trigorin's mistress, and subsequently marries him. Unfortunately their baby dies, Nina's career collapses, and Trigorin leaves her. However, on Trevlev renewing his overtures to Nina, she tells him that she still loves Trigorin. The play ends with news being brought in that Trevlev has committed suicide offstage.

Uncle Vanya   The second of Chekhov's four dramatic masterpieces, *Uncle Vanya*, a comprehensive reworking of the previously unsuccessful *Wood Demon*, centres on Vanya, who has for many years tirelessly managed the estate of a professor in Moscow. However, the professor finally retires back to his estate with his bored and idle young wife, with whom Vanya falls in love. Vanya now realizes that the professor is a thoroughly selfish and mediocre man and becomes jealous and embittered at his own fate, believing he has sacrificed his own brilliant future. When the professor tells him that he is going to sell the estate, Vanya, incensed, fires a pistol at him at point-blank range and misses – which only serves to compound his sense of failure and frustration. The professor and his wife agree not to sell up for the time being and leave to live elsewhere. Vanya sinks back into his boring loveless *Three Sisters* life, probably for ever.

In *Three Sisters*, Olga, Masha and Irina live a boring provincial life in their brother's rural country house remote from Moscow and Petersburg. All three remember their happy childhood in Moscow and dream of one day returning. A military unit arrives nearby, and Irina and Masha start up relationships with officers, which might offer a way out of their tedious lives. However, Irina's fiancé is killed in a duel, Masha's relationship ends when the regiment moves on, and Olga, a schoolteacher, is promoted to the post of head-mistress at her school, thus forcing her to give up any hope of leaving the area. They all relapse into what they perceive to be their meaningless lives.

The Cherry Orchard

The Cherry Orchard, Chekhov's final masterpiece for the theatre, is a lament for the passing of old traditional Russia and the encroachment of the modern world. The Ranevsky family estate, with its wonderful and famous cherry orchard, is no longer a viable concern. Various suggestions are made to stave off financial disaster, all of which involve cutting down the ancient orchard. Finally, the estate is auctioned off, and in the final scene, the orchard is chopped down offstage. The old landowning family move out, and in a final tragicomic scene, they forget to take an ancient manservant with them, accidentally locking him in the house and leaving him feeling abandoned.

Select Bibliography

Standard Edition:

The most authoritative Russian edition of Sakhalin Island can be found in volume 14/15, edited by V.I. Kuleshov, of Chekhov's Полное собрание сочинении и писем (*Polnoye sobraniye sochinenii i pisem*; *Complete Works and Letters*) produced in Moscow in 1978 by the Nauka publishing company.

Biographies:

Hingley, Ronald, *A New Life of Anton Chekhov* (Oxford: Oxford University Press, 1976)

Pritchett, V.S., *Chekhov: A Spirit Set Free* (London: Hodder & Stoughton, 1988)

Rayfield, Donald, *Anton Chekhov* (London: HarperCollins, 1997)

Simmons, Ernest, *Chekhov: A Biography* (London: Jonathan Cape, 1963)

Troyat, Henri, *Chekhov*, tr. Michael Henry Heim (New York: Dutton, 1986)

Additional Recommended Background Material:
Helman, Lillian, ed., *Selected Letters of Anton Chekhov* (1984)
Magarshack, David, *Chekhov the Dramatist*, 2nd ed. (London: Eyre Methuen,1980)
Malcolm, Janet, *Reading Chekhov: A Critical Journey* (London: Granta, 2001)
Pennington, Michael, *Are You There, Crocodile?: Inventing Anton Chekhov* (London: Oberon, 2003)

Appendices

A Selection of Chekhov's Letters

1. To: M.N. Galkin-Vraskoy*

20th January 1890,
Malaya Italyanskaya Street, no. 18
St Petersburg
(c/o A.S. Suvorin)

Your Excellency, gracious sir Mikhail Nikolayevich,
With the intention of departing in spring this year with literary and scientific objectives to eastern Siberia, and having the desire, among other locations, to visit Sakhalin Island – both its central and its southern sections – I make so bold as most humbly to request Your Excellency to render me all possible assistance in achieving the aims stated.

With sincere respect and devotion I have the honour to be Your Excellency's most humble servant,

Anton Chekhov

* Mikhail N. Galkin-Vraskoy (1834–1916) had been head of the Central Prison Department since its formation in 1879.

2. To: M.V. Kiselyova*

26th January 1890,
St Petersburg

Respected Mariya Vladimirovna,
They've brought me the "Index" of articles in *Maritime Compendium** from 1862 to 1868; they've asked me to return it tomorrow morning. At the present moment I'm making extracts from articles on Sakhalin, swearing like a blackguard, and feeling myself to be in dreadfully low spirits...

* *Mariya V. Kiselyova (1859–1921) was a writer and editor.*
* *The* Maritime Compendium *was a monthly journal which had been published in St Petersburg since 1848.*

3. To: Mikhail Chekhov*

28th January 1890,
St Petersburg

...Almost everything has been arranged with Galkin-Vraskoy. The route is: the river Kama, Perm, Tyumen, Tomsk, Irkutsk, the river Amur, Sakhalin, Japan, China, Colombo, Port Said, Constantinople and Odessa. I shall visit Manila as well. I'm leaving Moscow at the beginning of April...

* *Mikhail P. Chekhov (1865–1936) was Chekhov's youngest brother.*

4. To: M.V. Kiselyova

28th January 1890,
St Petersburg

...Is my future spouse,* from whom I am fleeing to Sakhalin, still happy with my Indian gift? If not, I shall send her an additional something, a Japanese idol, or something of that sort...

* *This is an arch reference to the Kiselyovs' little daughter, Sasha.*

5. To: A.S. Suvorin*

17th February 1890,
Moscow

...After your departure, I have become utterly bored. The sun is shining like hell, there's the scent of spring in the air, and I am annoyed that I am not yet on my way to Sakhalin. It would be a fine thing now to be sitting on the deck of a river steamer, or galloping across the steppe in a *tarantas*...

* *Aleksey S. Suvorin (1834–1912) was a media magnate in Russia, who supplied Chekhov with research material on Sakhalin.*

6. To: A.S. Suvorin

19th–21st February 1890,
Moscow

Thanks for your trouble. Kruzenshtern's Atlas I need either now or on my return from Sakhalin.* Now would be better. You write that the map it contains is poor; I've bought a good one at Ilyin's for 65 copecks.

Day in, day out I read and write, read and write... the more I read, the more strong becomes my conviction that over the next two months I will not succeed in doing a quarter of what I had intended, while I won't be able to hang around more than a couple of months on Sakhalin: those damn steamers won't wait! The toil is varied, but tedious; you've got to be a geologist, meteorologist and ethnographer, however, I'm not accustomed to this, and I find it boring. I'll carry on reading about Sakhalin till March, while I still have some money, then I'll sit down to write some stories.

* *Rear Admiral I.F. Kruzenshtern made a round-the-world voyage between 1803 and 1806, and drew up charts en route.*

7. To: A.P. Chekhov*

25th February 1890,
Moscow

...It is essential for me to have as detailed an acquaintance as possible with what has been written in the newspapers about Sakhalin, for I find it interesting not merely from the point of view of the information contained. The data speaks for itself, of course, but what is needed in addition is a historical interpretation of the facts which comprise the kernel of the data. The articles have been written either by people who've never been to Sakhalin and understand nothing of the matter in question, or else people who have a vested interest, who have made a lot of money in connection with the question of Sakhalin, and have maintained their innocence. The sheer nerve of the former, and the subterfuges of the latter – both of them obscuring and impeding factors – must be more valuable for the researcher than any data, the majority of which are random and incorrect; these factors typify extremely well the relationship of our society in general to this subject, and to the business of imprisonment in particular.

At any rate, spare the public library from your visits. What you have done already is enough. The rest will be copied out by my sister, whom I've engaged on a paid basis, and who will begin her visits to Rumyantzev's Library the third week of Lent…

* *Alexander P. Chekhov (1855–1913) was Chekhov's eldest brother.*

8. *To: A.S. Suvorin*

28th February 1890,
Moscow

I've received both the books and Kruzenshtern's Atlas… Tell your library that I shall be obliged to them to my dying day. Tomorrow I'll return to you, via the shop:

[1] the index to *Russian Antiquity*; [2] Vysheslavtsev; [3] *Herald of Europe*, 1872, VIII; and [4] three volumes of the *Maritime Compendium*, 1858, XII, 1859, II, and 1859, X… I've already sent the second volume of Kruzenshtern to you, and I shall dispatch the atlas just as soon as what I need has been copied out.

I shall keep pestering you about books right up until I leave. I'm even appending a list of magazines I need to this letter. Please be assured, Your Excellency, that I am already being sufficiently chastised for the botheration I'm causing you; from reading the books you've sent, cockroaches are starting to swarm round my brain. The damn work is so laborious and tedious that I reckon I might snuff it from boredom before making it to Sakhalin…

There are delicious fish on Sakhalin, but no hot drinks…

Yours,

A. Chekhov

PS Our geologists, ichthyologists, zoologists and so forth, are dreadfully ill-educated people. They write so clumsily that not only is it tiresome to read, but occasionally you even have to rework phrases to make sense of them. But the importance and seriousness of the material more than make up for this.

9. To: A.S. Suvorin

4th March 1890,
Moscow

...I've already begun to write about Sakhalin. I've completed five or so pages on the "history of exploration". It hasn't come out too badly, and does appear to be expert and authoritative. I've begun to describe the geography, too, with temperatures and capes – not too bad either. I'm quoting foreign authors slavishly, but it's coming out in my work in so detailed a fashion and in such a tone that it seems I myself speak every language superbly. It's an utter fraud...

10. To: N.M. Lintvaryova*

5th March 1890,
Moscow

...This summer I won't be visiting you, since in April I'm departing, due to requirements of my own, to Sakhalin Island, from where I'll be returning in December. I'm travelling there across Siberia (11,000 versts), and coming back by sea. It appears that Misha has written to you that allegedly somebody or other has ordered me there on official business, but this is rubbish.

I'm ordering myself out there on my own business, and at my own personal expense. There are a large number of bears and fugitives on Sakhalin, so in the event of Messieurs les wild animals making a dinner out of me, or some vagabond cutting me up, I beg you to remember me kindly.

Of course, if I have the time and manage to write what I want about Sakhalin, I'll send the book off to you as soon as it comes out; it'll be tedious, specialized, and will consist of nothing but figures, but permit me to count on your indulgence: reading it, you'll suppress your yawns...

*Natalya Lintvaryova (1863–1943) was a friend of Chekhov's.

11. *To: A.S. Suvorin*

9th March 1890,
Moscow

On the score of Sakhalin we are both mistaken, but you are very likely more in error than I am. I am departing totally convinced that my trip will yield a valuable contribution neither to literature nor to science: I do not have sufficient knowledge, time or pretension for this. I have neither plans like Humboldt,* nor even like Kennan.* I wish to get something written, even if only 100 or 200 pages, and thus to repay a little the science of medicine, towards which, as you know, I have been a swine. Possibly I will not succeed in writing anything, but even so the journey is not losing its spice for me: by reading, gazing round in all directions, and keeping my ears open, I shall find out and learn a great deal. I still haven't set off, but thanks to those books which I've read from necessity up to now, I've discovered much of the kind of stuff that everybody ought to know on pain of forty lashes and which I was so ignorant as not to have known earlier. In addition I dare say that the journey will involve six months' unremitting physical and mental labour, and this is essential for me, since I'm a Ukrainian* and have been growing indolent for some time now. I have to take myself in hand. Even assuming my excursion is an utter triviality, a piece of obstinacy and caprice, yet just you consider and then tell me what I'm losing by going. Time? Money? Will I undergo hardships? My time costs nothing. I never have any money anyway, and as far as hardships go, I'll be travelling in horse-drawn carriages and carts 25 to 30 days, no longer, and the entire remaining time I'll be sitting on the deck of a steamer or in a room and will bombard you unremittingly with letters. Even assuming that the journey will yield me precisely nothing – nonetheless, however, might there not occur, during the entire journey, two or three of the kind of days which I'll recall my whole life with delight or bitterness? And so on and so forth. And there you have it, my good sir. None of this is convincing, but then, you, too, have been writing quite as unconvincingly. For instance, you write that no one needs Sakhalin, and that it possesses no interest for anybody. Does this really seem to be true? Sakhalin may be uninteresting and unnecessary only for a society which does not exile thousands of people there and does not expend millions on it. After Australia in the past, and Cayenne,* Sakhalin is the sole spot where colonization by offenders may be studied; it's a subject of interest to the whole of Europe – and we don't need it? No longer than 25 or 30 years ago our very own Russians,* while exploring Sakhalin, achieved astonishing feats, for which a human being might be idolized, but we don't need all this, we don't even know who these people were, but only sit gazing at four walls and complaining that God has created mankind so imperfectly. Sakhalin is a place of unbearable sufferings, which only a human being, whether free or subjugated, is capable of causing and undergoing. Those who have worked close to this island, and on it, have tried to resolve problems involving fearful responsibility, and are trying to resolve them now. I regret that I'm not a sentimentalist, otherwise I would say that we should go to places such as Sakhalin on pilgrimages of worship, as the Turks go to Mecca, while sailors and those who study imprisonment should regard Sakhalin in particular as the army authorities regard Sevastopol. From the books which I have read and am reading now, it's clear that we have allowed millions of people to rot in prisons, to rot for no purpose, without any consideration and in a barbarous manner; we have driven people tens of thousands of versts through the cold in shackles, infected them with syphilis, perverted them, multiplied the number of criminals, and put all the blame on to red-nosed prison overseers. Nowadays the whole of educated Europe knows that it's not the overseers who are guilty, but all of us, but none of this has anything to do with us, it's just not interesting. The much-extolled '60s did nothing for the sick and imprisoned, transgressing thereby the major precept of Christian civilization. Nowadays at least something is being done for the sick, but for those in prison – nothing. The study of confinement in prison is of no interest whatever to our lawyers and legal experts. No, I do assure you, Sakhalin is both necessary and of interest, and the only thing to be sorry about is that it's I who am going, and not somebody else more versed in the subject and more capable of arousing the interest of society. I personally am going out there for the most trivial of reasons.

Regarding my letter about Pleshcheyev, I have written to you that I had aroused indignation among my young friends due to my idleness, and to justify myself I have written to you that, despite my idleness, I've still got more done than my friends, who do precisely nothing. I've at least read the *Maritime Compendium* right through, and been to see Galkin-Vraskoy, while they've done nothing. That's the sum total of what I have to say, I reckon…

[*This letter is in reply to Suvorin's mystified note to Chekhov regarding his proposed journey. Suvorin had claimed in this note that "no one needs Sakhalin, and it possesses no interest for anybody".*]

* *Alexander Humboldt (1769–1859) was a German scholar who had explored parts of Siberia and Asiatic Russia, and left records of the experience.*

* *George Kennan (1845–1924) had in 1886 visited the prisons of Siberia and written articles on them.*

* *Chekhov's claim that he is a Ukrainian is a joke.*

* *Cayenne was the main town of French Guyana, to which serious offenders were deported from France.*

* *Chekhov has in mind the expeditions of Nevelskoy, Busse, Boshnyak and others, which he refers to extensively in* Sakhalin Island.

12. *To: I.L. Leontyev**

16th March 1890,
Moscow

...My route will be: Nizhny Novgorod, Perm, Tyumen, Tomsk, Irkutsk, Sretensk, along the Amur to Nikolayevsk, two months on Sakhalin, Nagasaki, Shanghai, Hankow, Manila, Singapore, Madras, Colombo (in Ceylon), Aden, Port Said, Constantinople, Odessa, Moscow, St Petersburg, Church Street...*

* *Ivan L. Leontyev (1856–1911) was a writer and dramatist.*
* *Church Street was where Chekhov was living at the time.*

13. *To: M.I. Tchaikovsky**

16th March 1890,
Moscow

I sit at home, never going out, and reading about how much Sakhalin coal cost per ton in 1863, and how much Shanghai coal cost, I read about amplitudes, NE, NW, SE and other winds which will blow upon me, when I shall observe my own seasickness off the coasts of Sakhalin. I read about soil, subsoil, sandy-loam clay and clayey sandy loam. Nonetheless, I still haven't gone out of my mind and actually sent off a short story yesterday to *New Times*, and soon I shall be sending my play

The Wood Demon to the *Northern Herald* – the latter very reluctantly, since I don't like seeing my own plays in print.

Modest I. Tchaikovsky (1850–1916) was a writer and critic.

14. *To: N.A. Leykin**

31st March 1890,
Moscow

…Soon I shall be setting off en route. I am awaiting the breaking of the ice on the Kama. We shall see each other again in December, and in the meantime I entreat you to think well of me, a humble sinner. I will be living on Sakhalin not less than two months. You can imagine the boredom I shall experience in the evenings.

Nikolai A. Leykin (1856–1911) was a writer and editor.

15. *To: A.S. Suvorin*

1st April 1890,
Moscow

…You reprove me for "objectivity", calling it indifference to good and evil, and absence of ideals and ideas and so forth. You wish me, when depicting horse-thieves, to state: stealing horses is bad. But surely people have known this for ages already without me telling them so? Let them be judged by jurymen – my business is to show them as they really are.

When I write, I rely totally on the reader, supposing that he himself will supply the subjective factors absent in the story.

16. *To: V.M. Lavrov**

10th April 1890,
Moscow

Vukol Mikhailovich! In the March issue of *Russian Thought*, on page 147 of the literary section, I came across the following phrase: "Only yesterday, even the high priests of unprincipled writing such as Messrs Yasinsky and Chekhov, whose names", etc., etc. Literary reviews normally remain unanswered, but in the given case we may speak not about a critical review, but about libel pure and simple. I might even have let libel go unanswered, but in a couple of days I'm leaving European Russia, possibly never to return again, and I am unable to refrain from responding.

An unprincipled writer, or – what amounts to one and the same thing – a blackguard, I have never been.

It's true that my entire literary activity has consisted of an uninterrupted series of blunders, sometimes quite crude and blatant, but this is explained by the limitations of my gifts, and not in the slightest by whether I am a good or bad human being. I've never blackmailed anybody, never written lampoons or denunciations, never fawned, told lies or written offensively about anybody – in short I've written a great number of short stories and leading articles which I would gladly have thrown out because of their worthlessness, but there is not a single line for which I ought now to feel ashamed...

*Vukol Lavrov (1852–1912) was the editor of the liberal literary journal Russian Thought.

17. To: A.S. Suvorin

15th April 1890,
Moscow

...I'm setting off on 18th April... I don't really want to go, and would gladly have stayed, but it's best to get the trip over and done with this year, rather than put it off to next year. I've piled up enough money now, but even so, I would like to ask you for 1,000 roubles, plus the 100 I paid back to Yezhov, for any unforeseen eventuality...

18. To: A.S. Suvorin

15th April 1890,
Moscow

Well, and so, my dear friend, I'm off on Wednesday, or, at the very latest, Thursday. It would be nice not to be going. I received the money, thanks very much; although 1,500 roubles is a lot,* I've got nowhere to put them, and I would have had sufficient money to buy things in Japan, since I've saved enough.

I've got the sort of feeling as if I'm setting off to war, although I can't see any perils before me, except toothache, which I will inevitably suffer from en route.

Since – talking about documentation – I'm armed with nothing else but a passport, and that's all, there might possibly be some unpleasant clashes with the powers that be, but this will be a transient misfortune. If they won't show me anything, then I'll simply write in my book that they didn't show it to me – *basta*, and I won't allow myself to get agitated about it. In case I'm drowned or something of that sort, please bear in mind that everything I possess and may possess in the future belongs to my sister; she will pay off my debts.

I will unfailingly wire communications to you; I shall write even more frequently. The address for telegrams will be: Tomsk, Editorial Office, *Siberian Herald*, Chekhov. Letters written up to 25th July I will definitely receive; if written any later, they will not find me on Sakhalin…

I've bought myself a sheepskin jacket, and army officer's waterproof leather coat, big boots and a large knife for cutting up sausages and hunting tigers. I'm armed from head to toe.

* *In response to Chekhov's request for Suvorin to advance him 1,000 roubles (see letter 17 above) Suvorin had, in fact, sent 1,500.*

19. *To: A.S. Suvorin*

18th April 1890,
Moscow

I've been held up in Moscow for one more day. Thanks for the telegram. Yes, write to me only on Sakhalin, since letters won't catch up with me in Siberia…

Don't use the word "Sakhalin" in your telegrams. It sounds in the ears of the administration as unpleasantly as the Peter-Paul Fortress.*

The river Ob is still iced over, and therefore I shall have to go from Tyumen to Tomsk by horse-drawn vehicles. It's an infernally boring and overcast region. Moreover, it's impossible to wait till the ice breaks up, since navigation only commences from 10th May.

Thanks for the press card. You'll receive my next letter from the Volga, which they say is very beautiful. I'm going purposely to Yaroslavl and not Nizhny Novgorod to take in more of the Volga.

My writings for the newspaper might not commence before Tomsk, since up to there it's already been well travelled, and is now hackneyed, exhausted as a subject, and lacks interest...

The Peter-Paul Fortress is one of the major landmarks of St Petersburg. It had a reputation as Russia's most fearsome place of confinement for political prisoners.

20. To: M.P. Chekhova*

29th April 1890,
Yekaterinburg

The Kama is the most extraordinarily boring of rivers. To appreciate its beauties you'd have to be a local aborigine, to sit immobile on a barge by a barrel of petroleum or a sack of roach, and do nothing but swill bad vodka all day. The banks are barren, the trees are bare, the earth is brown, there are long strips of snow, and there's such a wind that the devil himself couldn't blow so sharply or adversely. When a chill wind is blowing and there are ripples on the water – which after high water has the colour of coffee dregs – you begin to feel cold, bored and uneasy... The towns on the Kama are all grey; it seems as if their inhabitants are employed in producing clouds, tedium, wet fences and mud for the streets – and that's their sole occupation...

In Russia all the towns are identical. Yekaterinburg is exactly the same as Perm or Tula. It's also similar to Suma, and to Gadyach as well...

The local people instil something like horror into an outsider. They have prominent cheekbones, large foreheads, and are broad-shouldered, with tiny eyes and utterly enormous fists. They are born in the local iron foundries, and it's not a midwife who's present at their birth, but a mechanic...

Mariya P. Chekhova was Chekhov's sister.

Many of the following letters describe localities or incidents in language which is almost word for word the same as in the travel sketches 'From Siberia'. Therefore only extracts have been translated which do not appear in the sketches or which throw extra light on them.

21. *To: M.P. Chekhova*

4th–17th May 1890,
Krasny Yar to Tomsk
Tomsk,
16th May

At five or six o'clock we drink tea in the cabin. Tea on a journey is a real boon. Now I know its value and drink it with frenzy. It's warming, disperses sleep, and a great deal of bread is eaten with it – for, in the absence of any other foodstuffs, bread has to be eaten in large quantities; that's why the peasants consume so much bread and grain products. You drink tea and chat to the local peasant women, who here are intelligent, love their children, are compassionate, hard-working, and are more free than in European Russia; their husbands don't abuse them or beat them, since they are quite as tall, strong and intelligent as their lords and masters; they act as sledge- and carriage-drivers... There is no diphtheria. Smallpox reigns, but, strangely enough, it's not so infectious as in other places; two or three fall ill and die – and that's the end of the epidemic. There are no hospitals or doctors. They are treated by doctors' assistants. Blood-letting and cupping glasses are utilized on a terrific and grandiose scale. En route I carried out an examination of a Jew who was sick with cancer of the liver. The Jew was worn out and could hardly breathe, yet this didn't stop the doctor's assistant from attaching a dozen cupping glasses to him. A word about the Jews wouldn't be out of place. Here they till the soil, act as cabmen and coach-drivers, maintain ferry boats, trade, and have the title "peasant" because both *de jure* and *de facto* they really are peasants.* They enjoy universal respect, and, according to the Assessing Magistrate, are often elected to the post of village elder. I noticed one Jew, tall and thin, who puckered his brows with distaste and spat whenever the Assessing Magistrate told scabrous anecdotes – a most pure soul; his wife cooked delicious fish soup. The wife of the Jew who is suffering from cancer entertained me with pike roe and the most delicious white bread. Exploitation is simply unheard of. A word about the Poles would not be out of place either. They were exiled here from Poland in 1864.* They are fine people, hospitable and extremely sensitive to others. Some have a very prosperous lifestyle, others are poor and serve as clerks at the way stations. The former returned to their homeland after the amnesty, but soon returned to Siberia – here life is more prosperous – while the latter dream of their homeland, although they are already elderly and sick... Perhaps I shall write to you of the Tatars* as well? Do permit me! They are not very numerous here. They're fine people. In the Kazan Province even the clergymen speak highly of them, and in Siberia they are "better than the Russians", as the Assessing Magistrate said to me in the presence of some Russians, who bore this out in silence. Heavens above, how rich Russia is in fine people. If it were not for the cold, which deprives Siberia of its summer, and if it were not for the government officials, who corrupt the peasants and exiles, Siberia would be a part of the world which is prosperous and fortunate to the very highest degree.

There's nothing to have for dinner. Clever people, when travelling to Tomsk, normally take along with them half a pood of snacks. I, however, have turned out to be a fool, and so for two weeks have eaten nothing but milk and eggs, which they cook in the following fashion – the yolk hard-boiled and the white soft. I got sick and tired of this diet in a couple of days. I've only had a dinner twice over the entire route, if you don't count the fish soup, which I ate even though I'd had enough to eat after drinking tea. I've had no vodka; Siberian vodka's repulsive, and besides I went off it while travelling to Yekaterinburg. However, one should drink vodka. It activates your brain, which grows sluggish and obtuse from the journey, and therefore one grows stupid and flabby...

From strain, from the especial botheration with suitcases and so forth, and perhaps from the farewell booze-ups in Moscow, I suffered in the mornings from coughing up blood, which induced in me a feeling somewhat akin to depression, and aroused melancholy thoughts; but this blood-spitting ceased towards the end of the journey; now I don't even have a cough; it's a long time since I coughed as little as I do now, after a two-week spell in the fresh air...

* Jews were allowed to own land and join the ranks of the peasantry in the borderlands of the Empire, including Siberia: they were not given this privilege in Central Russia.
* In 1864 there was a general uprising against Russian rule in Poland, which at that time was part of the Tsarist Empire. This revolt was put down with great brutality, and hundreds of thousands of Poles were deported to Siberian exile.

* *"Tatars" was a very vague term used collectively for various races of Mongolian and Turkic stock. The significance of the phrase "even the clergymen speak highly of them" is that they were all Muslims and the average Russian Orthodox Christian would therefore be expected to regard them with some circumspection.*

22. To: M.P. Chekhova

20th May 1890,
Tomsk

...From lack of anything to do, I've got down to my impressions of the journey, and I'm sending them to *New Times*; you'll be able to read them after 10th June, roughly. I'm writing a little about everything: a bit of this, that and the other. I'm writing not for renown, but in connection with cash, in consideration of the advance I took...

In two and a half days' time I'll be in Krasnoyarsk, and in seven and a half to eight days in Irkutsk. It's 1,500 versts to Irkutsk.

23. To: A.S. Suvorin

20th May 1890,
Tomsk

...At Tyumen they told me that the first steamer to Tomsk would leave on 18th May. I had to go galloping along in horse-drawn vehicles. The first three days all my sinews and joints ached, but then I got used to it and felt no pains at all. The only thing was that, from lack of sleep and the constant struggle with my baggage, from the bucking around and lack of food, I suffered from blood-spitting, which ruined my disposition, but apart from that was of no consequence.

When I left, I promised to send you travel sketches beginning from Tomsk onwards, since the route between Tyumen and Tomsk has been portrayed for ages already and been exploited a thousand times. But in your telegram you have expressed a desire to have my Siberian impressions as soon as possible, and even, My Liege, have had the cruelty to reproach me with a poor memory, in that I have allegedly forgotten about you. It has been quite definitely impossible to write en route; I've been keeping a short diary in pencil and am able to offer you now only what has been noted in this diary. So as not to write at great length, and not to get in a muddle, I've divided all the impressions I've jotted down into chapters. I'm sending you six of them. They're written personally for you. I've written for you alone, and therefore have not been scared to be too subjective in my sketches, nor am I afraid that there are more Chekhovian feelings and thoughts in them than material about Siberia. If you find any lines of interest and worth printing, then entrust them to a beneficent publicity, with my name at the bottom, and print them, too, in separate chapters, dishing them out bit by bit with a tablespoon. You might give them the general title 'From Siberia' and then 'From Zabaikalye', then 'From the Amur', etc.

You'll be getting the next section from Irkutsk, where I'm setting off to tomorrow, and on the road to which I will be spending no less than ten days – the road's bad...

I've been as hungry as a dog on this journey. I've stuffed my belly full of bread, so as not to dream of turbot, asparagus and things like that. I've even been dreaming of buckwheat porridge. For whole hours at a time I've dreamt of these things...

Post to Sakhalin goes both by sea and through Siberia, so if people do write to me I'll receive their correspondence frequently. Don't lose my address: Sakhalin Isl., Alexandrovsk Post...

[*The local Assistant Police Chief visits Chekhov, with whom he wishes to discuss a play that he has written. He goes home to fetch this play, then...*]

Hold it! The policeman's come back... And then – he's suggested to me that we go and inspect the brothels of Tomsk.

I've just come back from the brothels. Repulsive. It's 2 a.m...

24. *To: M.P. Chekhova*

25th May 1890,
Mariinsk*

Spring is beginning; the fields are turning green, the trees are bursting into leaf, and cuckoos and even nightingales are in song. It was a lovely morning today, but at 10 o'clock a cold wind blew up and it started to rain.

I've left my poor suitcase in Tomsk, in enforced exile as punishment for its unwieldiness, and in its stead bought a piece of rubbish for 16 roubles (!)* which they servilely laid in the bottom of my vehicle. You can now go bragging everywhere that we have a carriage. In Tomsk I bought a carriage for 130 roubles, with a folding top and so forth, but of course no springs, for Siberia simply doesn't recognize the existence of springs. There are no seats, but the bottom is large and flat, you can stretch out at full length. Now the travelling's very comfortable. I'm afraid neither of winds nor the rain. I'm only waiting for the axle to snap, since the road is abominable...

*As pointed out in the first note to p. 30, the Mariinsk from which Chekhov sent this letter should not be confused with the settlement of the same name on the north bank of the river Amur.
*16 roubles was an exorbitant sum to pay for a suitcase.

25. To: A.P. Chekhov

5th June 1890,
Irkutsk

My European brother!
Of course it's unpleasant living in Siberia; but it's better to be in Siberia, and to feel oneself to be a noble human being, than to live in Petersburg, and have a reputation as a drunk and a rogue. I'm not speaking of present company...
Siberia is an extensive and chilly land. I go on and on without seeing an end to it. I've seen little that's interesting and novel, but on the other hand I've felt and experienced a great deal. I've battled with flooded rivers, with cold, with mud you simply can't get out of and with hunger and desire for sleep. I've had the kind of sensations you wouldn't undergo for millions of roubles in Moscow. You ought to come to Siberia! Ask the Public Prosecutor to exile you here.
Of all the Siberian cities, Irkutsk is the best. Tomsk isn't worth a brass farthing, and none of the district administrative towns are any better than Krepka, where you had the carelessness to be born.* The most annoying thing of all is that there's nothing to eat in these petty little towns – and, since they are on the route across Siberia, My God how you feel it! You approach a town hoping to get a whole mountain down

you, and when you arrive – crash! There are no sausages, no cheese, no meat, not even any herrings, but the same old fresh eggs and milk in the villages.

Generally speaking, I'm satisfied with my journey, and don't regret coming. It's hard going, but then the relaxation is wonderful. I delight in taking a rest.

From Irkutsk I'm moving on to Lake Baikal, which I'll cross by steamer; from Baikal it's a thousand versts to the river Amur, and then it's on a steamship to the Pacific Ocean…

I arrived here yesterday, and the first thing I did was to set off to the bathhouse, then lay down to sleep. God, how I slept. It's only now that I really understand what sleep means.

* *Krepka is a hamlet 75 miles from Taganrog, Chekhov's birthplace.*

26. *To: A.N. Pleshcheyev*

5th June 1890,
Irkutsk

Well then, what can I write to you about? Everything is so broad and so long that I don't know what to begin with and what to choose. Everything I have lived through in connection with Siberia I would divide into three epochs: (1) From Tyumen to Tomsk, 1,500 versts of bloody terrifying cold both day and night, sheepskin jackets, felt boots, cold rains, winds, a desperate battle to the death with flooded rivers; the rivers had overflowed water meadows and roads, and I was constantly exchanging my carriage for boats and sailing like a Venetian in a gondola; the boats, waiting for them on the shore, sailing, etc. – this all took up so much time that the two days before I got to Tomsk, despite all my efforts, I managed to do only 70 versts instead of 400–500; there were in addition some really scary, unpleasant moments as well, especially when a wind would spring up suddenly and begin to buffet the boat. (2) From Tomsk to Krasnoyarsk – 500 versts, inextricable mud; my vehicle and I stuck in the mud like flies in thick jam; how many times I smashed up my carriage (it's my own), how many versts I went on foot, how many smuts there were on my face and clothing! I wasn't travelling, but having a mud bath. And, to make up for it, how I swore! My brain wasn't thinking, but simply coming out with swear words. I was worn down to the point of total exhaustion and was extremely glad when we got to the Krasnoyarsk post station. (3) From Krasnoyarsk to Irkutsk it's been 1,566 versts,* heat, smoke from forest fires, and dust; dust in your mouth, up your nose and in your pockets; you take a look at yourself in the mirror, and it's as if you've been putting on greasepaint. When, on my arrival in Irkutsk, I went to clean myself up in the bathhouse, the soap suds that flowed down from my head weren't white, but an ashy-grey and reddy-brown sort of colour, as if I'd been scrubbing down a horse...

The road is totally safe. All this stuff about robberies, attacks and villains is all nonsense and fairy tales. My revolver is utterly unnecessary, and night-time in the forest is quite as safe as daytime on the Nevsky Prospect.* For a pedestrian, though, it's another matter.

*Chekhov has made a mistake. A glance at any map will show that the distance between Krasnoyarsk and Irkutsk that he gives as 1,566 versts is far shorter than the distance from Tyumen to Tomsk, which he states above is 1,500. We can only conclude that in the letter above there has been a slip of the pen. (Thanks are due to the editor of the first edition (1993) for pointing out this error of Chekhov's.)
* The Nevsky Prospect is the main thoroughfare of St Petersburg.

27. To: M.P. Chekhova

13th June 1890,
Post Station "Listvenichnaya"
(on the shores of Lake Baikal)

The steamer doesn't leave before Friday, 15th June, so till Friday we have to sit on the shore staring at the water and waiting... the point is that, on the 20th, a boat leaves from Sretensk to sail along the river Amur, and, if we don't manage to make that, we'll have to wait for the next one, which leaves on the 30th. My Godfathers, when will I finally get to Sakhalin?

We travelled to Lake Baikal along the shore of the Angara river, which has its source in the Baikal, and discharges into the river Yenisey. Have a good look at a map. The banks are picturesque. Mountain after mountain, and on those mountains one solid mass of woodland. The weather is marvellous, serene, sunny, warm; I travelled along feeling for some reason extraordinarily healthy; I had such a sense of well-being that

I find it impossible to describe. This was most likely a reaction after the sitting about in Irkutsk, and because the shore of the Angara is similar to Switzerland. It's somehow novel and distinctive. We drove along the bank, reached the river mouth, and turned left, and there right in front of us was the shore of Lake Baikal, which in Siberia they call the Sea of Baikal. It's like a mirror. The other shore, of course, is not visible – it's 90 versts off. The banks are high, steep, rocky, and covered with woodland; to right and left headlands can be seen jutting out into the water like the Ayu-Dag.* It's like the Crimea. The post station "Listvenichnaya" lies right by the water's edge and is startlingly similar to Yalta. The only thing is there are no buildings on the mountains, since they're too steep and it's impossible to construct anything on them.

We've hired lodgings in a little barn... Near the windows, two or three arshins from the foundations, the Baikal commences. We pay a rouble a day. The mountains, forests and mirror-like surface of the Baikal – everything is poisoned by the consideration that we've got to sit here till Friday. What are we going to do with ourselves here? Moreover, we still don't know what we'll have to eat. The local population live on nothing but *cheremsha*. There is neither meat nor fish; we were given no milk, but merely promised it. We were fleeced 16 copecks for a little white roll. I bought some buckwheat grain and a piece of cured pork, and had some porridge boiled up; it didn't taste very nice, but what can you do, you've got to eat. We searched through the village all evening, to see whether anybody would sell us a chicken, but didn't find one... but, to make up for it, there is vodka!...

A scrubby little steamship turned up at midnight; we went to look at it and ask whether they might not have something to eat. They told us that tomorrow we could get dinner, but now it was night-time, the kitchen hadn't been stoked up, and so forth. We thanked them for "tomorrow" – at least there was still hope! But alas! In came the captain and said that at 4 a.m. the bloody little ship would be off to Kultuk. Thanks a lot! In the bar, which was so tiny there wasn't enough room to turn round, we got a bottle of bitter beer down us (35 copecks it cost) and saw a bead of amber on a plate – it was salmon roe... We came back home – and slept. Sleeping has become repugnant to me. Every day you lay your sheepskin coat on the floor with the woollen side up, place a crumpled-up coat and pillow at its head, and go to sleep on these mounds in your trousers and waistcoat. Civilization, where art thou?

Congratulate me – I sold my carriage at Irkutsk. How much profit I made I won't say otherwise Mum'll fall down in a dead faint and won't sleep for five nights...*

* Ayu-Dag is a peak 16 versts from Yalta, 1,903 feet (580 metres) high.
* Chekhov made a huge loss, of course, on selling his carriage.

28. To: A.N. Pleshcheyev

20th June 1890,
steamship Yermak,
on the Amur river

Hello! I send you greetings, my dear friend, from a first-class cabin on board the steamer Yermak. I'm sailing up the Amur. My journey by horse-drawn vehicles is over and done with; my big boots have been locked away out of sight, my ugly mug has had a good wash, I've changed my linen, and the Moscow con man has been transformed into a lord of the manor. The steamer judders, it's difficult writing; the shores of the Amur are beautiful, but too wild; I personally have grown fed up with the absence of people. I am still under the influence of Zabaikalye, over which I travelled. It's a magnificent area. Generally speaking, from the Baikal onwards begins Siberian poetry, while up to the Baikal it was mere prose...

29. To: N.A. Leykin

20th June 1890,
Amur river,
off the village of Gorbitza

...Baikal is marvellous, and it's no wonder the Siberians don't call it a lake, but a sea. The water is extraordinarily translucent, so you can see through it as if through air; it has a delicate turquoise hue, very agreeable to look at. The banks are mountainous and covered with woodland; all around there is an impenetrable mass of game and wildfowl – so thick you can't see a chink of light through them. There's an abundance of bears, sables, wild goats, and every old kind of game you can think of, who occupy their time by living in the taiga and making meals of each other. I spent two days living on the shores of Lake Baikal.

Whilst I was sailing, conditions were hot and placid.

Zabaikalye is splendid. It's a combination of Switzerland, the Don country and Finland.

I drove on horse-drawn vehicles over 4,000 versts. The journey was thoroughly successful. I stayed fit the whole time and only lost a penknife from my luggage. God grant everybody to travel in this fashion. The road is totally safe, and all these tales of escapees, nocturnal attacks, and so on, are nothing more than fairy tales, legends of the distant past. A revolver is a completely superfluous item. Now, I'm sitting in a first-class cabin and feel as if I'm in Europe. I've got the kind of feeling as if I've passed an examination.

30. *To: M.P. Chekhova*

21st June 1890,
steamship *Yermak,*
Amur river,
near Pokrovskaya
21st, 6 p.m.,
not far from Pokrovskaya Village

We've gone and hit the rocks, been holed, and are now undergoing repairs. We've run aground and are pumping water. On the left is the Russian shore, and on the right the Chinese. If I were to return home now, I'd be entitled to crow that "I didn't visit China, but saw it from three sazhens away." We'll spend the night in Pokrovskaya, and we're arranging an excursion.

If I were a millionaire, I'd have my own steamer on the Amur without fail. It's a fine and curious part of the world... On the Chinese shore there's a guard post, a tiny little hut, while on the bank are piled up sacks of flour, and Chinamen in rags carry them on litters into the hut. And then, beyond the post, there's dense, endless forest...

31. *To: M.P. Chekhova*

23rd–26th June 1890,
between Pokrovskaya and Blagoveshchensk

I wrote to you that we'd run aground. At Ust-Strelka, where the Stilka river merges with the Argun (have a look at a map) the steamer, which sits two and a half feet deep in the water, hit the rocks, was holed in several places, and, after taking a hold full of water, settled on the bottom. They've begun to pump out the water and attach patches; a naked sailor has climbed down into the hold, and is standing up to his neck in water, feeling for the holes with his heels; each one is being closed over from inside with cloth smeared with tallow, then they lay on top of it a board, on which they place a prop, which, like a column, rests against the ceiling – and that's the repair job. They were pumping out from five in the evening till night-time, but the water still hadn't decreased; they had to put the work off till morning. In the morning they found several fresh holes and started patching up and pumping all over again. The sailors pump, while we, the public, stroll along the decks, gossip, eat, drink and sleep; the captain and his mates do the same as the public, and are not in any hurry. On the right is the Chinese shore, on the left Pokrovskaya Village inhabited by Amur Cossacks; if you want you can go and sit down in Russia, or make a journey into China – there's no prohibition. The heat during the daytime is unbearable, so you have to put on a silk shirt...

25th June

We've set sail again. I've already travelled 1,000 versts along the Amur and have seen the most sumptuous of landscapes; your head reels with delight... And what heat!

What warm nights! It's misty in the mornings, but warm...

I constantly inspect the shores through binoculars and catch sight of an infernally vast amount, a bottomless pit, of ducks, geese, loons, herons and all kinds of other rascals with long noses. It would be well worthwhile hiring a country cottage out here!...

The villages are exactly the same as along the river Don; there are differences in the construction of the buildings, but they are not significant. The inhabitants don't have regular jobs, and eat meat even during Holy Week; the young women smoke cigarettes, and the older ladies pipes – it's quite accepted here...

On the steamer the air is incandescent with talk. Here people are not afraid to speak out loud. There's nobody to arrest you, and nowhere to be exiled to, so you can play the liberal as much as you like... If some misunderstanding happens at Ust-Kara, where convicts carry out forced labour (among these prisoners are many sentenced for political offences, who do not have to work), then the whole of the Amur is up in arms. Denunciations are not acceptable. A fugitive political prisoner may travel on a steamer right to the ocean with no fear that the captain will betray him. This is explained in part by the total indifference towards everything done in European Russia. Each individual says: "What's it got to do with me?"

32. To: I.P. Chekhov*

31st August 1890,
Sakhalin

Request Malyshev* dispatch to Governor of Sakhalin Island General Kononovich curriculum European Russian district council schools, list of textbooks on teaching methods. Expound detailed as poss. composition school councils. Order Suvorin send COD requisite textbooks (150) for senior pupils, for juniors 300. Leaving September. Healthy. Chekhov.

* *Ivan P. Chekhov (1861–1922) was Chekhov's brother. He was a schoolteacher, hence the textbook-related letter.*
* *Malyshev was a senior Moscow school inspector whom the Chekhov family had known since the 1870s.*

33. To: A.S. Suvorin

11th September 1890,
steamer *Baikal*,
Tatar Strait

Greetings! I'm sailing through the Tatar Strait from northern to southern Sakhalin...

I spent exactly two months on northern Sakhalin. I was received extremely affably by the local administration, though Galkin hadn't written a single word about me. Neither Galkin, nor Baroness Musquash,* nor any of the other geniuses I was stupid enough to apply to for assistance, have rendered me the slightest help; I've had to act on my own responsibility.

The Sakhalin General, Kononovich, is a cultured, educated and decent man. We were soon getting on very well, and everything went swimmingly. I shall bring back some documents from which you will be able to see that from the very outset I was placed in the most favourable of conditions. I saw everything; the question is now, therefore, not what I saw, but how I saw it.

I don't know what will come out finally, but I've done quite a lot. There's enough for three dissertations. I've been getting up at five every morning, going to bed late, and every day has been spent under heavy strain from the thought that there is still a great deal I haven't done, and now that I'm finished with convict labour, I've got a sort of feeling as if I've seen everything but gone and missed the elephant.*

A word in passing – I had sufficient patience to make a census of the entire Sakhalin population. I toured round all the settlements, went into all the cabins and talked to every single person; taking the census, I utilized a card system, and I've already noted down around 10,000 labour convicts and enforced settlers. In other words, there isn't a single convict or settled exile on Sakhalin who hasn't had a chat with me. The census of the children has been especially successful, and I'm placing quite a few hopes on it…

I have attended a flogging with the lash, after which I dreamt for three or four nights of the executioner and the repulsive bench upon which the floggings are carried out.

I'd write you some more, but there's a lady sitting in the cabin tirelessly laughing at the top of her voice and chattering away;* I simply haven't got the strength to write; she's been roaring with laughter and blathering since yesterday evening…

* *"Baroness Musquash": Baroness Ikskul von Hildeband was a well-known Russian society figure.*
* *"I've seen everything and missed the elephant" is a quotation from the verse 'The Inquisitive Man' by Krylov. A visitor to a museum is so engrossed by the insects in the cases that he fails to notice the stuffed elephant. This expression is now semi-proverbial in Russian.*
* *This is Chekhov's true view of the woman whom in chapter 12 of* Sakhalin Island *he describes as "ebullient and having an enviable disposition".*

34. *To: Ye. Ya. Chekhova*

6th October 1890,
Korsakovsk Post

Dear Mum, hello! I'm writing you this letter almost on the eve of my departure for European Russia... It's been three months, you know, since I've seen anybody apart from convicts or those who can talk about nothing but hard labour, the lash and convicts. A dismal life. I want to get as quickly as possible to Japan, and from there to India.

I'm well, if you don't take into consideration flashing lights in one eye, which now occurs frequently with me, and after which I have a severe headache every time. There were lights in my eyes both yesterday and today, so I'm writing this letter with a headache and with a feeling of heaviness throughout my entire body. My haemorrhoids are also making themselves felt. Whilst living in the south of Sakhalin, I drove a few times from the Korsakovsk Post to Nai-buchi... The waves cast up a boat with six American whalers which had been shipwrecked off the coasts of Sakhalin; they are now living at the post, and having a high old time roaming round the streets; they're waiting for the *Petersburg* and will leave together with me.

35. *To: A.S. Suvorin*

9th December 1890,
Moscow

...Hurray! Well, here I am at last sitting once again at home at my own table, praying to my own discoloured household gods and writing to you. I now have a kind of pleasant feeling, as if I've never been away from home at all. I'm healthy and happy to the marrow of my bones... Whilst I was living on Sakhalin, I experienced merely a certain bitter taste deep inside me, as if from rancid butter, but now, in retrospect, Sakhalin appears to me to be utter hell. I worked intensely for two months, with no mercy on my stomach, and during the third month grew thoroughly worn out due to the sour taste, boredom and the thought that cholera was on the way to Sakhalin from Vladivostok, and that I might therefore run the risk of spending the winter in the labour colony. But thank Heavens, the cholera died out, and on 13th October the steamer was transporting me away from Sakhalin... We bypassed Japan, as there's cholera there...

[In Hong Kong] they have superb roads, horse-drawn trains, a railway up the mountainside, museums and botanical gardens; wherever one looks one sees that the English take the utmost care and consideration for those who work for them; there is even a club for sailors; I travelled on a rickshaw – that's to say, on human beings – bought all kinds of old rubbish off the Chinese and got thoroughly irritated when I heard my Russian travelling companions vilifying the English for exploiting the natives. Yes, the English exploit the Chinese, sepoys and Hindus, I thought; but to make up for it they give them roads, water pipes, museums and Christianity; you exploit them as well, but just what have you given them?

En route to Singapore two corpses were cast into the sea.* When you see a dead human being wrapped in tarpaulin falling head over heels into the sea, and you remember that it's a good few versts to the bottom, a terrified feeling creeps over you and for some reason you begin to feel you're going to die yourself, and will be thrown into the sea... Singapore I have no very clear memory of, since, touring round it, for some reason I grew melancholy and almost burst into tears. But then came Ceylon. This place is paradise. Here, in heaven, I travelled over 100 versts by railway, and gorged myself up to my throat with palm forests and bronze-skinned women...

God's world is good. The only thing that is not good is us. How little justice and humility there is in us, what little understanding we have of the word patriotism! A drunk, dissipated debauchee of a husband loves his wife and children, but what sense or use is there in this love? According to the newspapers, we love our motherland, yet how is this love expressed? Instead of learning, we have insolence and self-importance beyond all measure, instead of labour we have indolence and swinishness, we have no justice, our conception of honour goes no further than honour for a uniform, a uniform which routinely serves to adorn our benches for the accused in court. We need to work hard, and all the rest can go to the devil. The main thing is to render justice, "and all the rest shall be added unto us"... *

How glad I am that I managed everything without Galkin-Vraskoy! He didn't write one single line about me, and I turned up on Sakhalin a total stranger...

* *This material was later used in Chekhov's short story 'Gusev'.*
* *See Matthew 6:33.*

The First Chapter of *Sakhalin Island* in Russian

I

Г. Николаевск-на-Амуре. Пароход Байкал. Мыс Пронге и вход в Лиман. Сахалин полуостров. Лаперуз, Браутон, Крузенштерн и Невельской. Японские исследователи. Мыс Джаоре. Татарский берег. Де-Кастри.

5 июля 1890 г. я прибыл на пароходе в г. Николаевск, один из самых восточных пунктов нашего отечества. Амур здесь очень широк, до моря осталось только 27 верст; место величественное и красивое, но воспоминания о прошлом этого края, рассказы спутников о лютой зиме и о не менее лютых местных нравах, близость каторги и самый вид заброшенного, вымирающего города совершенно отнимают охоту любоваться пейзажем.

Николаевск был основан не так давно, в 1850 г., известным Геннадием Невельским, и это едва ли не единственное светлое место в истории города. В пятидесятые и шестидесятые годы, когда по Амуру, не щадя солдат, арестантов и переселенцев, насаждали культуру, в Николаевске имели свое пребывание чиновники, управлявшие краем, наезжало сюда много всяких русских и иностранных авантюристов, селились поселенцы, прельщаемые необычайным изобилием рыбы и зверя, и, по-видимому, город не был чужд человеческих интересов, так как был даже случай, что один заезжий ученый нашел нужным и возможным прочесть здесь в клубе публичную лекцию. Теперь же почти половина домов покинута своими хозяевами, полуразрушена, и темные окна без рам глядят на вас, как глазные впадины черепа. Обыватели ведут сонную, пьяную жизнь и вообще живут впроголодь, чем бог послал. Пробавляются поставками рыбы на Сахалин, золотым хищничеством, эксплуатацией инородцев, продажей понтов, то есть оленьих рогов, из которых китайцы приготовляют возбудительные пилюли. На пути от Хабаровки до Николаевска мне приходилось встречать немало контрабандистов; здесь они не скрывают своей профессии. Один из них, показывавший мне золотой песок и пару понтов, сказал мне с гордостью: "И мой отец был контрабандист!" Эксплуатация инородцев, кроме обычного спаивания, одурачения и т.п., выражается иногда в оригинальной форме. Так, николаевский купец Иванов, ныне покойный, каждое лето ездил на Сахалин и брал там с гиляков дань, а неисправных плательщиков истязал и вешал.

Гостиницы в городе нет. В общественном собрании мне позволили отдохнуть после обеда в зале с низким потолком – тут зимою, говорят, даются балы; на вопрос же мой, где я могу переночевать, только пожали плечами. Делать нечего, пришлось две ночи провести на пароходе; когда же он ушел назад в Хабаровку, я очутился как рак на мели: камо пойду? Багаж мой на пристани; я хожу по берегу и не знаю, что с собой делать. Как раз против города, в двух-трех верстах от берега, стоит пароход Байкал, на котором я пойду в Татарский пролив, но говорят, что он отойдет дня через четыре или пять, не раньше, хотя на его мачте уже развевается отходный флаг. Разве взять и поехать на Байкал? Но неловко: пожалуй, не пустят; скажут: "рано". Подул ветер, Амур нахмурился и заволновался, как море. Становится тоскливо. Иду в собрание, долго обедаю там и слушаю, как за соседним столом говорят о золоте, о понтах, о фокуснике, приезжавшем в Николаевск, о каком-то японце, дергающем зубы не щипцами, а просто пальцами. Если внимательно и долго прислушиваться, то, боже мой, как далека здешняя жизнь от России! Начиная с балыка из кеты, которым закусывают здесь водку, и кончая разговорами, во всем чувствуется что-то свое собственное, не русское. Пока я плыл по Амуру, у меня было такое чувство, как будто я не в России, а где-то в Патагонии или Техасе; не говоря уже об оригинальной, не русской природе, мне все время казалось, что склад нашей русской жизни совершенно чужд коренным амурцам, что Пушкин и Гоголь тут непонятны и потому не нужны, наша история скучна, и мы, приезжие из России, кажемся иностранцами. В отношении религиозном и политическом я замечал здесь полнейшее равнодушие. Священники, которых я видел на Амуре, едят в пост скоромное, и, между прочим, про одного из них, в белом шелковом кафтане, мне рассказывали, что он занимается золотым хищничеством, соперничая со своими духовными чадами. Если хотите заставить амурца скучать и зевать, то заговорите с ним о политике, о русском правительстве, о русском искусстве. И нравственность здесь какая-то особенная, не наша. Рыцарское обращение с женщиной возводится почти в культ и в то же время не считается предосудительным уступить за деньги приятелю свою жену; или вот еще лучше: с одной стороны, отсутствие сословных предрассудков – здесь и с ссыльным держат себя, как с ровней, а с другой – не грех подстрелить в лесу китайца-бродягу, как собаку, или даже поохотиться тайком на горбачиков.

Но буду продолжать о себе. Не найдя приюта, я под вечер решился отправиться на Байкал. Но тут новая беда: развело порядочную зыбь, и лодочники-гиляки не соглашаются везти ни за какие деньги. Опять я хожу по берегу и не знаю, что с собой делать. Между тем уже заходит солнце, и волны на Амуре темнеют. На этом и на том берегу неистово воют гиляцкие собаки. "И зачем я сюда поехал?" спрашиваю я себя, и мое путешествие представляется мне крайне легкомысленным. И мысль, что каторга уже близка, что через несколько дней я высажусь на сахалинскую почву, не имея с собой ни одного рекомендательного письма, что меня могут попросить уехать обратно – эта мысль неприятно волнует меня. Но вот наконец два гиляка соглашаются везти меня за рубль, и на лодке, сбитой из трех досок, я благополучно достигаю Байкала.

Это пароход морского типа средней величины, купец, показавшийся мне после байкальских и амурских пароходов довольно сносным. Он совершает рейсы между Николаевском, Владивостоком и японскими портами, возит почту, солдат, арестантов, пассажиров и грузы, главным образом казенные; по контракту, заключенному с казной, которая платит ему солидную субсидию, он обязан несколько раз в течение лета заходить на Сахалин: в Александровский пост и в южный Корсаковский. Тариф очень высокий, какого, вероятно, нет нигде в свете. Колонизация, которая прежде всего требует свободы и легкости передвижения, и высокие тарифы: это уж совсем непонятно. Кают-компания и каюты на Байкале тесны, но чисты и обставлены вполне по-европейски; есть пианино. Прислуга тут – китайцы с длинными косами, их называют по-английски – бой. Повар тоже китаец, но кухня у него русская, хотя все кушанья бывают горьки от пряного кери и пахнут какими-то духами, вроде корилопсиса.

Начитавшись о бурях и льдах Татарского пролива, я ожидал встретить на Байкале китобоев с хриплыми голосами, брызгающих при разговоре табачною жвачкой, в действительности же нашел людей вполне интеллигентных. Командир парохода г. Л., уроженец западного края, плавает в северных морях уже более 30 лет и прошел их вдоль и поперек. На своем веку он видел много чудес, много знает и рассказывает интересно. Покружив полжизни около Камчатки и Курильских островов, он, пожалуй, с большим правом, чем Отелло, мог бы говорить о "бесплоднейших пустынях, страшных безднах, утесах неприступных". Я обязан ему многими сведениями, пригодившимися мне для этих записок. У него три помощника: г. Б., племянник известного астронома Б., и два шведа – Иван Мартыныч и Иван Вениаминыч, добрые и приветливые люди.

8 июля, перед обедом, Байкал снялся с якоря. С нами шли сотни три солдат под командой офицера и несколько арестантов. Одного арестанта сопровождала пятилетняя девочка, его дочь, которая, когда он поднимался по трапу, держалась за его кандалы. Была, между прочим, одна каторжная, обращавшая на себя внимание тем, что за нею добровольно следовал на каторгу ее муж. Кроме меня и офицера, было еще несколько классных пассажиров обоего пола и, между прочим, даже одна баронесса. Читатель пусть не удивляется такому изобилию интеллигентных людей здесь, в пустыне. По Амуру и в Приморской области интеллигенция при небольшом вообще населении составляет немалый процент, и ее здесь относительно больше, чем в любой русской губернии. На Амуре есть город, где одних лишь генералов, военных и штатских, насчитывают 16. Теперь их там, быть может, еще больше.

День был тихий и ясный. На палубе жарко, в каютах душно; в воде +18°. Такую погоду хоть Черному морю впору. На правом берегу горел лес; сплошная зеленая масса выбрасывала из себя багровое пламя; клубы дыма слились в длинную, черную, неподвижную полосу, которая висит над лесом... Пожар громадный, но кругом тишина и спокойствие, никому нет дела до того, что гибнут леса. Очевидно, зеленое богатство принадлежит здесь одному только богу.

После обеда, часов в шесть, мы уже были у мыса Пронге. Тут кончается Азия, и можно было бы сказать, что в этом месте Амур впадает в Великий океан, если бы поперек не стоял о. Сахалин. Перед глазами широко расстилается Лиман, впереди чуть видна туманная полоса – это каторжный остров; налево, теряясь в собственных извилинах, исчезает во мгле берег, уходящий в неведомый север. Кажется, что тут конец света и что дальше уже некуда плыть. Душой овладевает чувство, какое, вероятно, испытывал Одиссей, когда плавал по незнакомому морю и смутно предчувствовал встречи с необыкновенными существами. И в самом деле, справа, при самом повороте в Лиман, где на отмели приютилась гиляцкая деревушка, на двух лодках несутся к нам какие-то странные существа, вопят на непонятном языке и чем-то машут. Трудно понять, что у них в руках, но когда они подплывают поближе, я различаю серых птиц.

"Это они хотят продать нам битых гусей," объясняет кто-то.

Поворачиваем направо. На всем нашем пути поставлены знаки, показывающие фарватер. Командир не сходит с мостика, и механик не выходит из машины; Байкал начинает идти все тише и тише и идет точно ощупью. Осторожность нужна большая, так как здесь нетрудно сесть на мель. Пароход сидит 12½, местами же ему приходится идти 14 фут., и был даже момент, когда нам послышалось, как он прополз килем по песку. Вот этот-то мелкий фарватер и особенная картина, какую дают вместе Татарский и Сахалинский берега, послужили главною причиной тому, что Сахалин долго считали в Европе полуостровом. В 1787 г., в июне, известный французский мореплаватель, граф Лаперуз, высадился на западном берегу Сахалина, выше 48°, и говорил тут с туземцами. Судя по описанию, которое он оставил, на берегу застал он не одних только живших здесь айно, но и приехавших к ним торговать гиляков, людей бывалых, хорошо знакомых и с Сахалином и с Татарским берегом. Чертя на песке, они объяснили ему, что земля, на которой они живут, есть остров и что остров этот отделяется от материка и Иессо (Японии) проливами. Затем, плывя дальше на север вдоль западного берега, он рассчитывал, что найдет выход из Северо-Японского моря в Охотское и тем значительно сократит свой путь в Камчатку; но чем выше подвигался он, тем пролив становился все мельче и мельче. Глубина уменьшалась через каждую милю на одну сажень. Плыл он к северу до тех пор, пока ему позволяли размеры его корабля, и, дойдя до глубины 9 сажен, остановился. Постепенно равномерное повышение дна и то, что в проливе течение было почти незаметно, привели его к убеждению, что он находится не в проливе, а в заливе и что, стало быть, Сахалин соединен с материком перешейком. В де-Кастри у него еще раз происходило совещание с гиляками. Когда он начертил им на бумаге остров, отделенный от материка, то один из них взял у него карандаш и, проведя через пролив черту, пояснил, что через этот перешеек гилякам приходится иногда перетаскивать свои лодки и что на нем даже растет трава – так понял Лаперуз. Это еще крепче убедило его, что Сахалин – полуостров.

Девятью годами позже его в Татарском проливе был англичанин В. Браутон (Broughton). Судно у него было небольшое, сидевшее в воде не глубже 9 фут., так что ему удалось пройти несколько выше Лаперуза. Остановившись на глубине двух сажен, он послал к северу для промера своего помощника; этот на пути своем встречал среди мелей глубины, но они постепенно уменьшались и приводили его то к сахалинскому берегу, то к низменным песчаным берегам другой стороны, и при этом получалась такая картина, как будто оба берега сливались; казалось, залив оканчивался здесь и никакого прохода не было. Таким образом, и Браутон должен был заключить то же самое, что Лаперуз.

Наш знаменитый Крузенштерн, исследовавший берега острова в 1805 г., впал в ту же ошибку. Плыл он к Сахалину уже с предвзятою мыслью, так как пользовался картою Лаперуза. Он прошел вдоль восточного берега, и, обогнув северные мысы Сахалина, вступил в самый пролив, держась направления с севера на юг, и, казалось, был уже совсем близок к разрешению загадки, но постепенное уменьшение глубины до 3 $\frac{1}{2}$ сажен, удельный вес воды, а главное, предвзятая мысль заставили и его признать существование перешейка, которого он не видел. Но его все-таки точил червь сомнения. "Весьма вероятно," пишет он, "что Сахалин был некогда, а может быть, еще в недавние времена, островом." Возвращался он назад, по-видимому, с неспокойною душой: когда в Китае впервые попались ему на глаза записки Браутона, то он "обрадовался немало".

Ошибка была исправлена в 1849 году Невельским. Авторитет

его предшественников, однако, был еще так велик, что когда он донес о своих открытиях в Петербург, то ему не поверили, сочли его поступок дерзким и подлежащим наказанию и "заключили" его разжаловать, и неизвестно, к чему бы это повело, если бы не заступничество самого государя, который нашел его поступок молодецким, благородным и патриотическим. Это был энергический, горячего темперамента человек, образованный, самоотверженный, гуманный, до мозга костей проникнутый идеей и преданный ей фанатически, чистый нравственно. Один из знавших его пишет: "Более честного человека мне не случалось встречать." На восточном побережье и на Сахалине он сделал себе блестящую карьеру в какие-нибудь пять лет, но потерял дочь, которая умерла от голода, состарился, состарилась и потеряла здоровье его жена, "молоденькая, хорошенькая и приветливая женщина", переносившая все лишения геройски.

Чтобы покончить с вопросом о перешейке и полуострове, считаю не лишним сообщить еще некоторые подробности. В 1710 г. пекинскими миссионерами, по поручению китайского императора, была начертана карта Татарии; при составлении ее миссионеры пользовались японскими картами, и это очевидно, так как в то время о проходимости Лаперузова и Татарского проливов могло быть известно только японцам. Она была прислана во Францию и стала известною, потому что вошла в атлас географа д'Анвилля. Эта карта послужила поводом к небольшому недоразумению, которому Сахалин обязан своим названием. У западного берега Сахалина, как раз против устья Амура, на карте есть надпись, сделанная миссионерами: "Saghalien-angahata", что по-монгольски значит "скалы черной реки". Это название относилось, вероятно, к какому-либо утесу или мысу у устья Амура, во Франции же поняли иначе и отнесли к самому острову. Отсюда и название Сахалин, удержанное Крузенштерном и для русских карт. У японцев Сахалин называли Карафто или Карафту, что значит китайский остров.

Работы японцев попадали в Европу или слишком поздно, когда в них уже не нуждались, или же подвергались неудачным поправкам. На карте миссионеров Сахалин имел вид острова, но д'Анвилль отнесся к ней с недоверием и положил между островом и материком перешеек. Японцы первые стали исследовать Сахалин, начиная с 1613 г., но в Европе придавали этому так мало значения, что когда впоследствии русские и японцы решали вопрос о том, кому принадлежит Сахалин, то о праве первого исследования говорили и писали только одни русские.

Давно уже на очереди новое, возможно тщательное исследование берегов Татарии и Сахалина. Теперешние карты неудовлетворительны, что видно хотя бы из того, что суда, военные и коммерческие, часто садятся на мель и на камни, гораздо чаще, чем об этом пишут в газетах. Благодаря, главным образом, плохим картам командиры судов здесь очень осторожны, мнительны и нервны. Командир Байкала не доверяет официальной карте и смотрит в свою собственную, которую сам чертит и исправляет во время плавания.

Чтобы не сесть на мель, г. Л. не решился плыть ночью, и мы после захода солнца бросили якорь у мыса Джаоре. На самом мысу, на горе, стоит одиноко избушка, в которой живет морской офицер г. Б., ставящий знаки на фарватере и имеющий надзор за ними, а за избушкой непроходимая дремучая тайга. Командир послал г. Б. свежего мяса; я воспользовался этим случаем и поплыл на шлюпке к берегу. Вместо пристани куча больших скользких камней, по которым пришлось прыгать, а на гору к избе ведет ряд ступеней из бревнышек, врытых в землю почти отвесно, так что, поднимаясь, надо крепко держаться руками. Но какой ужас! Пока я взбирался на гору и подходил к избе, меня окружали тучи комаров, буквально тучи, было темно от них, лицо и руки мои жгло, и не было возможности защищаться. Я думаю, что если здесь остаться ночевать под открытым небом, не окружив себя кострами, то можно погибнуть или, по меньшей мере, сойти с ума.

Изба разделяется сенями на две половины: налево живут матросы, направо – офицер с семьей. Хозяина дома не было. Я застал изящно одетую, интеллигентную даму, его жену, и двух дочерей, маленьких девочек, искусанных комарами. В комнатах все стены покрыты еловою зеленью, окна затянуты марлей, пахнет дымом, но комары, несмотря ни на что, все-таки есть и жалят бедных девочек. В комнате обстановка не богатая, лагерная, но в убранстве чувствуется что-то милое, вкусное. На стене висят этюды и, между прочим, женская головка, набросанная карандашом. Оказывается, что г. Б. – художник.

"Хорошо ли вам тут живется?" спрашиваю я даму.

"Хорошо, да вот только комары."

Свежему мясу она не обрадовалась; по ее словам, она и дети давно уже привыкли к солонине и свежего мяса не любят.

"Впрочем, вчера варили форелей," добавила она.

Провожал меня до шлюпки угрюмый матрос, который, как будто догадавшись, о чем мне хочется спросить его, вздохнул и сказал:

"По доброй воле сюда не заедешь!"

На другой день рано утром пошли дальше при совершенно тихой и теплой погоде. Татарский берег горист и изобилует пиками, то есть острыми, коническими вершинами. Он слегка подернут синеватою мглой: это дым от далеких лесных пожаров, который здесь, как говорят, бывает иногда так густ, что становится опасен для моряков не меньше, чем туман. Если бы птица полетела напрямик с моря через горы, то, наверное, не встретила бы ни одного жилья, ни одной живой души на расстоянии пятисот верст и больше... Берег весело зеленеет на солнце и, по-видимому, прекрасно обходится без человека. В шесть часов были в самом узком месте пролива, между мысами Погоби и Лазарева, и очень близко видели оба берега, в восемь проходили мимо Шапки Невельского – так называется гора с бугром на вершине, похожим на шапку. Утро было яркое, блестящее, и наслаждение, которое я испытывал, усиливалось еще от гордого сознания, что я вижу эти берега.

Во втором часу вошли в бухту де-Кастри. Это единственное место, где могут во время бури укрываться суда, плавающие по проливу, и не будь ее, судоходство у сахалинских берегов, которые сплошь негостеприимны, было бы немыслимо. Даже есть такое выражение: "удирать в де-Кастри". Бухта прекрасная и устроена природой точно по заказу. Это круглый пруд, версты три в диаметре, с высокими берегами, защищающими от ветров, с нешироким выходом в море. Если судить по наружному виду, то бухта идеальная, но, увы! – это только кажется так; семь месяцев в году она бывает покрыта льдом, мало защищена от восточного ветра и так мелка, что пароходы бросают якорь в двух верстах от берега. Выход в море сторожат три острова, или, вернее, рифа, придающие бухте своеобразную красоту; один из них назван Устричным: очень крупные и жирные устрицы водятся на его подводной части.

На берегу несколько домиков и церковь. Это Александровский пост. Тут живут начальник поста, его делопроизводитель и телеграфисты. Один местный чиновник, приезжавший к нам на пароход обедать, скучный и скучающий господин, много говорил за обедом, много пил и рассказал нам старый анекдот про гусей, которые, наевшись ягод из-под наливки и опьяневши, были приняты за мертвых, ощипаны и выброшены вон и потом, проспавшись, голые вернулись домой; при этом чиновник побожился, что история с гусями происходила в де-Кастри в его собственном дворе. Священника при церкви нет, и он, когда нужно, приезжает из Мариинска. Хорошая погода бывает здесь очень редко, так же как в Николаевске. Говорят, что весною этого года здесь работала промерная экспедиция и во весь май было только три солнечных дня. Извольте работать без солнца!

На рейде мы застали военные суда Бобр и Тунгус и две миноноски. Вспоминается и еще одна подробность: едва мы бросили якорь, как потемнело небо, собралась гроза и вода приняла необыкновенный, ярко-зеленый цвет. Байкалу предстояло выгрузить четыре тысячи пудов казенного груза, и потому остались в де-Кастри ночевать. Чтобы скоротать время, я и механик удили с палубы рыбу, и нам попадались очень крупные, толстоголовые бычки, каких мне не приходилось ловить ни в Черном, ни в Азовском море. Попадалась и камбала.

Выгружают здесь пароходы всегда томительно долго, с раздражением и порчей крови. Впрочем, это горькая участь всех наших восточных портов. В де-Кастри выгружают на небольшие баржи-шаланды, которые могут приставать к берегу только во время прилива и потому нагруженные часто садятся на мель; случается, что благодаря этому пароход простаивает из-за какой-нибудь сотни мешков муки весь промежуток времени между отливом и приливом. В Николаевске беспорядков еще больше. Там, стоя на палубе Байкала, я видел, как буксирный пароход, тащивший большую баржу с двумя сотнями солдат, утерял свой буксирный канат; баржу понесло течением по рейду, и она пошла прямо на якорную цепь парусного судна, стоявшего недалеко от нас. Мы с замиранием сердца ждали, что вот еще один момент и баржа будет перерезана цепью, но, к счастью, добрые люди вовремя перехватили канат, и солдаты отделались одним только испугом.

Acknowledgements

The Publisher wishes to thank William Chamberlain, Christian Müller and Brian Reeve for their editorial work. This book is dedicated to Delano Minette.